More Than A Few Good Men

by
Robert J. Driver, Jr.
Lieutenant Colonel U.S.M.C. (Ret.)

MARINER
PUBLISHING

Buena Vista, VA

1 3 5 7 9 10 8 6 4 2

Library of Congress Control Number: 2009937912
More Than A Few Good Men
Robert J. Driver, Jr.
Includes Bibliographical References

p. cm.

1. United States Military—Marine Corps 2. Marine Corps—Vietnam War
3. Marine Corps—Korean War

I. Driver, Robert J., Jr. 1933— II. Title.

ISBN 13: 978-0-9841128-3-8 (hardcover : alk. paper)

ISBN 10: 0-9841128-3-9

Mariner Publishing
A division of
Mariner Media, Inc.
131 West 21st ST.
Buena Vista, VA 24416
Tel: 540-264-0021
www.marinermedia.com

Printed in the United States of America

Dedication

This book is dedicated to those brave young Marines and Navy Corpsmen who came home from Vietnam in body bags; to those who came home missing limbs and or their sanity from the hell of combat we experienced; and to those of us who endured it and somehow returned to normal lives; they were all more than a few good men. Lest we forget.

Foreword

"It's a funny thing, but, as the years go by, I think you appreciate more and more what a great thing it was to be a United States Marine...People will tell me what a shame it was I had to go back into the service a second time, but I'm kinda glad I did. Besides, I am a U.S. Marine and I'll be one till I die."

—Ted Williams

FINAL INSPECTION

"The Marine stood and faced God,
Which must always come to pass.
He hoped his shoes were shining,
    Just as brightly as his brass.

Step forward now, Marine,
How shall I deal with you?
Have you always turned
    the other cheek?
To my Church have you
    been true?

The Marine squared
His shoulders and said,

No Lord, I guess I ain't,
Because those of us who carry guns,
    Cain't always be a Saint.

I've had to work most Sundays,
And at times my talk was tough.
And sometimes I've been violent,
Because the world is awfully rough.

But I never took a penny,
That wasn't mine to keep.
Though I worked a lot of overtime,

When the bills got just too steep.
And I never passed a cry for help,
Though at times I shook with fear,
And sometimes, God, `forgive me,
I've wept unmanly tears.

I know I don't deserve a place,
Among the people here,
They never wanted me around,
Except to calm their fears.

If you've a place for me here, Lord,
It needn't be so grand,
I never expected or had too much,
But if you don't, I'll understand.

There was a silence all around the throne,
Where to saints had often trod.
As the Marine waited quietly,
For the judgment of God.

'Step forward now, you Marine,
You've borne your burdens well.
Walk peacefully on Heaven's streets,
You've done your time in Hell.'

—Author Unknown

Table of Contents

Introduction ix

1. My Beginning 1

2. Boot Camp, February-April 1953
   Parris Island, South Carolina 13

3. 2nd Service Regiment, May 1953-January 1955
   Camp Lejeune, North Carolina 21

4. Education and Training, 1955-1959
   Guilford College, Summer Training, and OCS 47

5. Hawaii, 1960-1963
   Platoon Commander, Executive Officer and Commanding Officer,
   Company C, 1st Battalion, 4th Marines 75

6. 2nd Infantry Training Regiment, 1963-1964
   Camp Pendleton, California 107

7. Transplacement Battalion, December 1964-February 1965
   Commanding Officer, Company I, 3rd Battalion, 1st Marines 109

8. En Route to Okinawa, March 1965 113

9. Okinawa, April-May 1965
   Commanding Officer, Company A, 1st Battalion, 9th Marines 115

10. Da Nang TAOR, June-September 1965
    Commanding Officer, Company A, 1st Battalion 9th Marines
    Operations Blastout, County Fair, and Golden Fleece 145

11. H&S Company, September-December 1965
    Commanding Officer, Company E, 2nd Battalion, 9th Marines 187

12. Excerpts from Captain William A Coti, December 1965
    CO, E/2/9, After Action Report on Operation Harvest Moon 205

13. Da Nang TAOR, January-March 1966
    Commanding Officer, Company E, 2nd Battalion,
    9th Marines, Operations Rough Rider and Double Eagle II 221

14. Da Nang TAOR, March 1966
    Operation Kings   267

15. The War Continues, April-June 1966
    Echo Company, 2nd Battalion, 9th Marines   315

16. HQMC, 1966-1969   361

17. Okinawa, 1969   365

18. An Hoa, September 1969-January 1970
    S-3, 2nd Battalion, 5th Marines   367

19. Da Nang, February-June 1970
    Officer in Charge, Da Nang Barrier, S-2, 1st Marine Division   431

20. Operation Pickens Forest, July-September 1970
    S-3 2nd Battalion, 7th Marines   457

21. Marine Corps Career After the War, 1970-1979
    Quantico, Command & Staff College, and
    Marine Corps Recruiting Station, New Orleans   475

Epilogue   489

Awards   499

Contributors   507

Glossary   521

Bibliography   537

Introduction

This book started out to be the memories of my life and Marine Corps career written for my children and grandchildren. I recall that in September 1953, I was a 19 year-old Private First Class having to take leave to Staunton, Virginia to see my grandfather, who was on his deathbed. As I sat there holding his hand, it suddenly dawned on me that I had never talked with him about his youth and his life growing up in the Shenandoah Valley of Virginia. I foolishly tried to ask him the questions I had neglected to ask as he lay dying, and he was unable to answer. For some reason I never forgot that moment, and later I determined that I would write something about my life for my descendants.

My wonderful wife, Edna, saved my letters to her from Parris Island in 1953 up through my last tour in Vietnam, which ended in 1970. There were hundreds of them, neatly tied with ribbons, in shoeboxes in our attic for 30 years before I finally got them down and started reading them. They read almost like a diary. I wrote her details on every event that happened to me, Marines we knew, my companies in 1965-66, and my battalions in 1969-70.

Having written numerous books on Civil War Confederate soldiers, I noted that nothing had been written on the brave young Marines and Corpsmen with whom I went into battle. The command chronologies of the units I served in are now declassified, so I was able to obtain copies of them, along with unit diaries, rosters, etc., from Headquarters, Marine Corps. The published accounts of the Marine Corps in Vietnam were helpful as an overview but rarely covered small unit actions. Some individual reminiscences have been published, but nothing directly on what we accomplished.

For almost 30 years, I avoided going to the Wall in Washington, D. C. because I knew I would shed tears when I saw all of the names I knew etched in stone. Someone told me about the "2/9 Network" of Marines who had served in the "Hell in a Helmet" battalion in Vietnam. Through contacts with the men I had served through the network, I was persuaded to attend my first reunion of the battalion. I was amazed! I met Marines from general to private who had served in the battalion and many who had been in my company. We went to the Wall as a group and found our friends and compatriots. We all shed tears for them. I have continued to do so over the years. Each year, we lay a wreath for them at the Wall. In 2007 and 2008, I had the privilege of laying it. That night in 2008, we looked at names of the Marines who had died on the night of 24-25 March 1966. I was joined by my Company Executive Officer, Gerry Hornick; Artillery Forward Observer, Dave Garner; Platoon Commander, John Kasparian, Machine Gunners Steve Clemons and Gabe Coronado; and others who had served in the company later. It was a simple scene with Dave leading us in prayer. Thanks to Dick Sasser, a Fire Team Leader who provided the wreath, we will continue this act of remembrance as long as we can.

I sent out over 100 questionnaires to the Marines I had served with, and got about a 20% response. Following up with telephone calls, I persuaded a number to send me the information I requested plus photographs. I learned from talking with my fellow Marines that many are still suffering from posttraumatic stress disorder in various ways. Many have divorced, turned to alcohol, and are still trying to put their lives together. Perhaps this book will help them understand what we all went through. Many felt rejected by people in their communities with they returned home and never spoke of the war again until I contacted them. Perhaps this is one of the answers; direct contact with their comrades who were in the foxholes with them.

I initially planned to just write about my tours in 1965-66 and 1969-70, but decided to expand this book to include what happened to the Marines and Corpsmen in Echo Company, 2nd Battalion, 9th Marines, through July 1966. By then, most of the men I served with were casualties or had rotated back to the States. The accounts of the action after I left are some of the most compelling I have ever read or heard.

The 9th Marines moved to northern I Corps soon after most of the men I knew left the company. The information on what happened to those who went north is contained in their individual sketches at the end of the book.

Chapter One

My Beginning

'Marines are born, not made,' or so the saying goes. I don't necessarily fit into that category. My Driver ancestors immigrated to this county from Germany, probably to escape religious persecution. Ludwig Trieber, my ancestor, was born in Darmstadt, Hesse about 1730. He came to this county, from Rothenstein, Wurttemberg, via Rotterdam, Holland, and landed in Philadelphia in 1749. He farmed near York, Pennsylvania, before migrating up the Shenandoah Valley. Then Lewis Driver, anglicized from Trieber or Triever, a Dunker, so named for their practice of immersion, was a member of the sect of German-American Baptists who opposed military service and the taking of oaths. They settled in Rockingham and Augusta counties, Virginia.

My mother's family, the Swopes (Swoope, Swoap), also came to America from Germany and moved into Augusta and Rockbridge counties. Great-grandfather, Henry Swope, purchased land about three miles from Brownsburg in 1843. His father, George Swope, Jr., was born in Pennsylvania in 1776, died in Rockbridge County in 1853. The Henry Swope house, which stood until 2007, has now been torn down. Both great-grandfathers and their sons were farmers, millers, threshers, carpenters, and stock raisers.

Both families acquired large farms and built homes to accommodate their families. The Drivers tended to intermarry with others Dunkers, but by the time of the Civil War some had intermarried into the Scots-Irish and English families in the Valley. The same held true for the Swopes. Some of the Drivers served in Confederate military units. Others served as teamsters and in other non-combatant rolls. My great-grandfather, Thomas Driver, a farmer living in Augusta County when the war started, was exempt from military service because of a dislocated hip. His family became members of the Lutheran church. My other great-grandfather, Henry Swope, was too young to serve. His family also became Lutherans.

My grandfather, Minor Solomon Driver, was well-educated, and became a lumber inspector for both the Chesapeake & Ohio and Norfolk & Western railroads. He lived in Staunton, Virginia. His wife, Lena Wells, was apparently an Episcopalian, as they became members of that church. They are both buried in the Pleasant Hill Lutheran Church cemetery in Augusta County, beside the graves of his father and mother. My father, Robert Jett Driver, was the only son and first born in this family. He was named after Robert Jett, an Episcopal Bishop of Virginia. Dad graduated from Shenandoah College. He and my mother are also buried in that cemetery.

1

Grandfather, William Henry Swope, who probably attended the field schools in the area, was a successful farmer, sawmill operator, and thresher near Brownsburg in Rockbridge County. His older brother was conscripted into Confederate service and died in a Union prisoner of war camp at Camp Chase, Ohio. Grandfather Swope did well in all his business ventures, but during the great depression in the 1930s, he loaned money that was never repaid, signed notes for his friends and neighbors, and had to borrow money from the local bank, which foreclosed on his property. He was married twice and raised a large family. My mother, Emily Mae Swope, was a product of his second marriage. She was the only family member to receive an education after high school, graduating from Kings Daughters Hospital Nursing School in Staunton.

My father was the plant manager for the Texaco Oil Company in Staunton when they were married. I was their first-born child. He was later promoted to plant manager in Roanoke, Virginia and later Rocky Mount, North Carolina. My brother, William Minor Driver, was born there. In 1940, we moved to Greensboro, North Carolina, where my dad took over as plant manager.

We lived in the downstairs of a new four-unit apartment house. It was a great location for me, as there were plenty of youngsters my age to play with. Marbles, playing war with lead soldiers, and spinning tops are some of the things I remember from my earlier years. There were two vacant lots next to where I lived. One became our sports field and, during WWII, the other was for foxholes, trench lines and our war games. One end of that lot became the Victory garden for some of our neighbors. With plenty of children of all ages in the neighborhood, we played football and baseball nearly everyday after school and on the weekends until dark. We had a peach basket on a telephone pole for basketball, but football and baseball were our favorites.

We didn't have organized sports, but we played pick up games at school athletic fields or in the parks in Greensboro. I remember getting a football uniform for Christmas one year. We played tackle football even without helmets and pads, but when I had both, I started playing with the older and larger boys. The first time I made a tackle leading with my head, I got knocked out. I didn't realize that the thin plastic-like helmet with wool padding was no protection. Later, playing on the school teams with better equipment, I got knocked out again making a tackle on a larger boy. In one pickup football game, I remember tackling Eddie McDonald and breaking his leg. Fortunately, he and his parents forgave me. I received a kick in the mouth which drove my two front teeth back in another game. There were no face masks used then. We played tackle without any equipment.

Baseball in the summer consisted of pickup games between neighborhood teams. Because of World War II, we had no coaches or umpires. We used the school fields, parks, and vacant lots, using boards for bases, and furnished our own equipment. When we broke a bat, we nailed it back together and taped it. When the covers came off the baseballs, we taped them and used them until they fell apart. Gloves were patched and re-laced until they were completely worn out. I managed to hurt my arm by pitching batting practice the day before I pitched a game, and my arm never fully recovered. With a coach, I certainly would not have been allowed to do that, but I didn't know any better.

On Saturday mornings my brother and I got our 25 cent allowance for the week, and off we went with our friends to the theater. They showed double feature westerns with news, cartoons, and a serial, like the "Green Hornet," between the feature films. Movies cost nine cents, and we would stop at a five and dime store across from the theater and buy a huge bag of popcorn for five cents. After the movie, we usually went to an ice cream parlor and got a five cent cone. Sometimes we would stop in the newsstand and buy a comic book or go to the sporting goods store and buy a model airplane kit. I did chores for other people for extra money. I mowed grass, raked leaves, shoveled snow, or ran errands for the elderly.

My brother and I attended St. Andrews Episcopal Church in Greensboro, and I can still remember my mother tying our offering in the end of a handkerchief so I wouldn't lose it on the way to Sunday school.

I was a fairly good student and attended Central Elementary and Junior High School. I still remember all my teachers' names. In Junior High School, I was a member of the Safety Patrol. We wore white belts with badges and stopped traffic and made sure the way was clear before students crossed the streets. I was the announcer on the intercom on national holidays and other events, reading the traditional quotations.

When World War II started, I remember listening to President Roosevelt on the radio. We followed the war closely, as several young men from our neighborhood, as well as two of my uncles and one of my aunts, were in the service. Playing cowboys and Indians was our great pastime besides sports, until the war started and then we played "Army." Most of our toy weapons were our Red Rider BB guns and homemade rifles, pistols, etc., built of wood by the older boys. As the war went on, we acquired tents, helmet liners, cartridge belts, and cast off caps from all the services. When school was out, we would erect our tents next to our house and all the neighborhood boys would camp in them at night. In the winter, we would dig foxholes in the lower lot and, having acquired an old iron stove, would bake potatoes, etc.

The school sponsored scrap drives and I remember the first aluminum drive when the area around the flagpole in front of the school was piled high with old pots and pans. There were scrap metal drives all the time. Between my home and the school was a house that had been recently repaired, and I received permission to gather up the old pipe and other pieces of iron and take them to school. With my brother's help, we would gather up as much as we could carry each morning and haul it to the school. We also crawled under every house in our neighborhood and gathered up the scrap metal we found. One year I was in line to be the Colonel in the Junior Marines for all the scrap metal I had brought in. However, on the last day, Tommy Fesperman, whose father was a baker, brought in a big oven and he won. I was second and was a Major in the Junior Marines. We also saved tinfoil, paper, string, tin cans, grease, and other items for the war effort.

My brother and I saved some of our allowances and bought Saving Stamps. We had books, and each time we had an extra dime we would buy a ten cent savings stamp at the post office and paste them in our books.

On Sunday afternoons, my family would often ride out to the Greensboro airport to see the planes landing and taking off. My brother and I especially wanted to see the military aircraft. We witnessed several crashes, both private planes.

During the war, I was sent several times to visit my grandparents, aunts, uncles, and cousins in Staunton and Rockbridge County. One year I was put on a bus with a piece of paper pinned to my shirt telling where I was going; the bus driver and the passengers made sure I got there safely. While I enjoyed these visits, I missed my friends and being able to play baseball. I had little to do at my grandparents' house in Staunton, but I was allowed to go to the movies, work jigsaw puzzles, and my aunt and uncle who lived there would take me to the park. When I visited my grandparents in Rockbridge, my grandfather would have all of the farm or threshing hands eat lunch at his table, and I would sit beside him and he always buttered my corn on the cob. As I grew older, I went with the threshers. My job was tying off the sacks of wheat when they were full and changing the chutes. When I stayed with my aunts and uncles, I helped with the chores, as they were all farmers. Everyone raised huge gardens and I helped weed them and gather the eggs, feed the chickens, carry milk buckets, crank the cream separator, butter churn, and the homemade ice cream maker, shuck the corn, slop the hogs, carry wood, and many other chores. On Friday nights, we would go to the local store where one of my aunts, Elizabeth Wade, would trade eggs and butter for groceries. My uncle, Bud Wade, who was a barber, would drive us to the store in his Ford coupe, and we children would ride on the fenders or hang on to the sides down the dusty dirt roads. The children would play "kick the can" and or "fox and hounds" until the adults were ready to go home. We usually had a dime to spend and would buy a Pepsi Cola and a candy bar. On Saturdays, my uncle would cut hair and then drive his school bus to Lexington in the evening, taking anyone who needed a ride. With gas rationing, many people took advantage of this, and he made a little money too. I occasionally got to go to town and see a movie. In those days, the bus driver owned the bus.

When I visited my uncle Earnest Swope, his son, Earnest, Jr., showed me how to plow a field with a team of horses. He got a great kick out of me trying to keep the plow in the ground and control the animals at the same time.

When the weather was especially hot, we would drive to Rockbridge Baths to picnic and swim in the Maury River. I was a bit of a daredevil, and one Sunday afternoon I waded across on the large rocks, being just able to keep my nose above water. My Uncle Bud was swimming in the area called the 'blue hole' and he said he would take me back across. I got on his shoulders, but when we got in deep water I panicked and grabbed him around the neck. He had to fight me off. As I was going down for the third time, a minister, who was picnicking on the bank, jumped in, swam out, and rescued me. He gave me artificial respiration and I soon came around, coughing up water. When I got back to Greensboro, I went to the YMCA and took swimming lessons.

Christmas visits were always fun. The wheat had been thrashed and the barnyards along the way had huge straw stacks in them. The fields were filled with shocks of corn. The Shenandoah Valley was a large wheat growing area until after World War II. None of my relatives in Rockbridge had central heating; they had large wood stoves and/or fireplaces, as well as kitchen stoves. My grandparents still heated with a central fireplace, and I remember coming down in the morning and backing up to the fire, sneaking and eating raw dough from the bread that was rising on the hearth. When I went to bed at night an iron that had been heated on the stove was wrapped in a towel and placed to keep my feet warm. We always slept under a pile of quilts and blankets. My grandfather was an avid hunter, and he kept a pack of hound dogs that slept on or under his wraparound porch. They would start barking and howling when anyone came and would knock you down trying to be friendly. I was taken on my first "snipe hunt" with my father, grandfather, uncles, and cousins. They left me in the woods holding a sack to catch the snipe when they drove it to me. It was a cold, dark night, but I don't remember being afraid in the woods alone. After an hour or so, they came and got me. Riding my bicycle on gravel roads proved to be no fun. I had gravel in my arms from bicycle spills into my 20s.

Towards the end of World War II, I sold newspapers at the Greensboro Overseas Replacement Depot. Mr. Stein would load a bunch of us in his station wagon after school and take us to the camp, where we would sell the papers in front of the mess halls. German prisoners of war worked in the mess halls, and they would sneak us ice cream or a piece of cake occasionally. Some of them spoke English and were generally very friendly.

I remember when President Roosevelt died. I, along with thousands of others, lined the railroad tracks as the train slowly pulled through Greensboro, heading to Washington, D.C. Everyone placed their right hand across their chest in a final salute.

When VE and VJ days happened, Greensboro went wild. People were celebrating on Main Street, and it was packed with the military in uniform as well as civilians. Everyone was screaming and shouting; thankful that the war was over. During a visit to my grandparents in Staunton that summer, I got to see General Patch in a parade down the main street.

As I got older, I started helping other boys with their paper routes, and my reward at the end of the route was a chocolate nut sundae at the local drugstore. I later took over a paper route until we moved to Charlottesville.

When the war in Europe ended, there was an effort to help the millions of refugees. Greensboro had a lot of large tobacco warehouses, and these were filled with donations of clothing to be sent there. I remember helping to sort the clothing and recall that some of the items being sent were better than what I had on.

In 1946, my parents rented a new house in the Glenwood section of Greensboro. My brother and I didn't like it much, since we had so many friends in the Blandwood Avenue area where we lived. I was able to continue going to Central Junior High School, but he had to transfer to Peck School, which was just across the road from our house. Actually, there were large athletic fields immediately across the street, and they were lighted at night, so we could play sports all the time. I had to take the trolley to and from school, or ride my bicycle, but I continued to play football and baseball on the Junior High School teams.

In March 1949, my dad took a job as the manager of the Texaco plant in Charlottesville, Virginia. This move bothered my brother and me more than just moving to another part of town. We quickly made friends, although I detested being the 'new boy' in Lane High School. While I liked the school, I didn't like what they did to me academically. In Greensboro I was taking 9th grade math. At Lane I was placed in a Algebra class, with only two months left in the school year. Naturally, I failed the course. How they thought I could learn 7 months of Algebra in 2 months, was beyond me. I complained to my mother, but she didn't do anything about it. Near the end of the school year I was given a placement test to see where my talents and interests lay. I was told that everything indicated I should be a policeman, fireman, etc., and nothing about attending college. The next year, I was placed in the Diversified Education class. I took typing, bookkeeping, and business courses as well as the normal English, science and history classes.

I played on the baseball team for two years, although I cut the back of my hand open in the spring of 1950, and missed a lot of that season. Being left handed, there was always a need for a southpaw pitcher. I played on the Junior Varsity football team that year, and did quite well as an end. My problem was I only weighed about 145 pounds. I was tall and skinny.

When we arrived in Charlottesville I got a job delivering the Richmond Times-Dispatch each morning seven days a week. This got me up and out early each morning, rain or shine, as it was the only way I could earn spending money at the time. Later my friend, Ted Wood, got me a job in a grocery store and I was able to give up the paper route. Meanwhile, my father had opened a gas station across from the high school and I helped him as much as I could, and still play sports.

Like all teenage boys, I had discovered girls, and much of my spending money was spent on buying clothes, taking a girl to the movies, dances, and/or parties. Fortunately, some of my friends had cars or access to the family car, so I could double date with them. On special occasions, I was able to use our family car.

I attended the First Baptist Church in Charlottesville and made a lot of lifelong friends there. Our group called ourselves 'The Dukes,' after 'the Amboy Dukes' from a movie. We sang in the choir, attended church camp together, and even had a summer league baseball team. 'Skeeter' McCauley, 'Abe' Hawkins, Eddie T. Moore, Ted Wood, 'Sonny' Coleman, 'Buddy' Johnson, 'Hugo' Douglas, Benton Barr, and others were members of our group.

I still remember when the Charlottesville Marine Corps Reserve unit was called up at the beginning of the Korean War. They paraded down Main Street to the railroad depot, where they left for active duty. Some were seniors in Lane High School. Others were high school graduates, and about half the company were students at the University of Virginia. Some of these young men were killed and wounded later on in Korea. I was impressed with the quality of these young Marines marching off to war.

In March 1951, we moved to Elkin, North Carolina, where my dad took a job as the Texaco plant manager. I was once again the 'new boy' in school. One of the problems was that we lived about five miles from Elkin. My brother and I could ride to school with my father when he went to work, but getting home in the evening was sometimes a problem. School was out before my dad could give us a ride home. Fortunately, Elkin had a great YMCA, so we could go there and play sports until he arrived. I played on the Elkin High School baseball team and pitched fairly well. They called me the 'Wild Lefthander,' and 'Lefty' became my nickname.

I had no problem adapting to the new school, and by playing baseball I met most of the boys in the junior and senior classes. Not really knowing any girls that well, I went stag to the Junior-Senior prom that year.

That summer was really a downer. I lived too far from town to have a part-time job, and there were no boys of my brother's or my ages living around us. We usually hitchhiked into Elkin and played tennis and went to the YMCA for a swim. I generally did not date anyone that summer, as I had no transportation.

I was glad when school started my senior year, and I played on the football team. Surprisingly, I was elected Co-Captain. We had a fairly good team, and I enjoyed the season immensely. I played both offensive and defensive end. Our archrival was Jonesboro, which was located just across the Yadkin River from Elkin. We beat them handily, and I sacked or hurried their quarterback, "Dizzy" Gillam, numerous times. I kept the defensive line fired up with my chatter and encouragement. I was an excellent receiver on the short pass routes, which our two quarterbacks were able to throw better than long ones down the field. For our Homecoming game and dance, I was able to bring down Cornelia Ann 'Neal' Jarman, my girlfriend from Charlottesville. She stayed with one of my female classmates, and my parents let me use the car.

One big relief was that we moved into town. The house wasn't as nice, but it was within walking distance of school for my brother and me, and also close to downtown and the YMCA. During the basketball season, I acted as the team scorekeeper so I got a ride to all the away games.

When the second semester started, I was still enrolled in Diversified Education classes so I was able to work in the afternoons. I was hired by the *Elkin Tribune*, the local newspaper, as a sports and advertising writer. This paper was published twice a week, and they agreed to let me leave in the afternoons to play baseball. I worked for a very brilliant and talented gentleman, Allen Browning. He did almost everything for the newspaper and he took me under his wing. My first efforts were the coverage of the local basketball games and tournament, which were always played in the local YMCA. He was very patient with me, and I soon caught on to exactly what he wanted for my sports columns. He was very understanding about my desire to play baseball, and I pitched fairly well that year.

Before graduation, a number of the members of the football team had talked to our head coach, Bob Yarborough, about playing in college. He had graduated from Guilford College, near Greensboro, and had played on their football team. Our first problem was being accepted to the college. None of us were outstanding students, and I was taking only the business courses. However, we all applied and all five of us got accepted.

His letters of recommendation must have been something else! Guilford was a small, Quaker-oriented college that gave athletes only partial scholarships. I would have to work my way through, but I was used to working all the time.

Bob Driver
High School Graduation

Following graduation, I started working full time at the *Tribune* and covered the local semi-pro team, sponsored by Chatham Mills of Elkin. Mr. Browning also had me writing advertising copy and visiting the local merchants to sell them the advertisement. I was successful in this, plus it gave me a chance to get out of the office during the day. Later, he had me start learning to operate a linotype machine, which I didn't really care to learn. One of the linotype operators, a former Marine, cautioned me that they would probably make me an operator if they got the chance. This made my decision to go to college much easier. I gave them my two weeks notice before football practice started at Guilford. I had saved about $500.00 over the summer, and paid my entrance fees, and hoped to get a scholarship and a part time job at the school.

In August of 1952, the four of us—Billy Francis, J.B. Gentry, Bill Barnette and myself—rode down to Guilford to try out for the football team. Eldon Parks, our fifth class member, had decided to forgo football tryouts. We stayed in the dormitories, which were hot all the time. There was no air conditioning. I think we were all discouraged when we saw the size of the players. Bill Barnette decided discretion was the better part of valor and didn't try out, but he stayed with us anyway. We started with two workouts a day, and the heat really took a toll on us. I took a pounding during the two-on-one blocking and tackling drills. I did better in the scrimmages, but I would get mowed down by the much larger linemen when they ran an end around play. I only weighed 155 pounds, not enough for a college end. J. B. Gentry quit the last day of practice before school started and went home. A few days later, I decided I was tired of being a blocking and tackling dummy and quit too. Coach Maynard, a tough old Navy veteran, understood, and gave me a part time job working in his office for 25 cents an hour! There was little to do but answer the telephone and take messages, so it was a good place to study in the afternoons. I also got a part time job reporting on Guilford sports for the Greensboro papers. I would call in the highlights after the game and they would write up the article. No byline for me!

While I loved history, I was intrigued by psychology, so I chose it as my major and history as my minor. My faculty advisor recommended I take German, which was a big mistake on my part. I passed the other freshman courses but failed German.

I worked at Mr. Hollowell's grocery/lunch room at noon and in the evenings, and this paid for my meals with a little left over. With the purchase of books, supplies, and fees, my $500 had rapidly evaporated. When the semester ended, I was at a loss as to how I could continue in college. I had decent grades, except for German.

I worked over the Christmas holidays delivering mail in Winston-Salem, where my parents were then living. It paid good money, and the regular carriers let me work as many hours as they could, but I did not have enough money to enroll for the second semester. I still owed the college about $500.00. The Marine Corps was offering a two-year enlistment program. I had always thought highly of them, and the veterans I talked to told me that if you're going to fight, go with the Marines. The Marines were better trained and disciplined than the Army. I didn't consider the Navy or the Air Force because they wanted you to enlist for four years. I wanted to do my time and return to college. One Marine veteran told me all the Corps would offer me was "A pack, a rifle, and a hard time." I got all three.

I went to the Greensboro post office and talked to the Marine recruiter. He scheduled me to take the physical and mental exams in Raleigh. I took the bus to Raleigh and stayed overnight in the YMCA with enlistees for the other services. The next morning we took our physical and mental exams, which I passed. While standing outside an interview room on the top floor, I watched as buses loaded with draftees arrived and they poured into the downstairs area. They were herded around like sheep, and I was glad I wasn't one of them.

My Beginning

On 7 February 1953, I returned to Raleigh for a screening physical and transportation to Parris Island, South Carolina. There, I met two other Marine enlistees I went through boot camp with, Cassidy and Tarleton—both dropped out of Duke University to enlist. Cassidy was from Pittsburgh, Pennsylvania. Tarelton was from Kentucky. Cassidy was the younger of the two and had played high school sports. Tarleton was older and looked (and was) out of shape for the coming ordeal.

Chapter Two

Boot Camp,
February-April 1953
Parris Island, South Carolina

We changed buses in Yamesee, South Carolina and arrived at Parris Island about 2200 that night. We were ushered into the receiving barracks, were issued a blanket, and told to sack out. There were already a number of new recruits there and more continued to come in during the night so no one got any sleep. Early the next morning, we were herded into the mess hall for breakfast by troop handlers, who didn't give us a bad time. During the next few days, we took another physical, had a dental exam, got our heads shaved, and drew a few pair of utilities and 'boondockers' (which are brogan type shoes), shaving gear, etc. Almost two days were spent taking mental tests, which I did well on. We also mailed home all our civilian clothes.

After morning chow, we were turned over to the D.I.s, who I still remember well! We were on the yellow footprints for the first time. They chewed on us a little there then herded us, with our full sea bags, to our training battalion and our Quonset huts. Our Platoon was divided into squads. There were 75 or so of us in the beginning. Each squad was assigned to one of the huts. We drew linens, blankets, and other equipment that day, harassed all the way. Everything was thrown at us and the D.I.s were on our case every moment. We stood at rigid attention at every turn.

The huts were left over from WWII and had concrete decks, double metal bunks, metal wall lockers, and wooden footlockers. There were oil stoves in the huts, but they were never lit while I was there.

That night, they put the fear of God in us. About a half dozen D.I.s at a time would descend on each hut. They had us stand at attention in front of our bunks with nothing but our skivvies on. They had a plan. They picked out the biggest men in each hut, harassed them, and then knocked them asshole over teakettle across the bunks. The D.I.s were cursing and shouting about us being maggots and lesser forms of life, come to screw up their beloved Corps and they were not going to let that happen! The sounds of recruits falling, bunks being turned over, and loud cursing and shouting were enough to terrorize anyone. By the time they got to me, I was standing at rigid attention and didn't move a muscle! I think they knew they had made their point and didn't knock over any more of us. For the first time in my life I was glad I was only six feet tall, and not any taller!

We were only issued one blanket, a mattress cover, pillow case, and two sheets. We nearly froze that first night from sleeping in our underwear. Later, we learned to crawl under our mattress cover, put on our sweat suits, and put our field jackets over us after the D.I.s left for the evening.

The next morning, we were greeted about 0300 with the noise of large metal GI cans being turned over, and recruits who did not jump up immediately were turned over from their bunks. We had five minutes to make a head call, shave, and fall back outside. Needless to say, no one had time to do more than take a leak and dry shave. After chow, we were marched to the armory to draw our rifles and 782 gear. We arrived there about 0400. We had nothing on but our underwear and utilities, and the armory was located in the middle of the old airfield in a hanger with nothing around for hundreds of yards. The wind was whistling off of the Atlantic at a good clip, and we stood there at attention shaking like hound dogs shitting peach seeds and our teeth chattering. We all pissed ourselves. I was as cold as I have ever been in my life. At about 0500, the armory finally opened and we drew our M-1's, 782 gear, and field jackets. We weren't allowed to put the field jackets on until we returned to our huts.

We were drilled incessantly. Every move was closely watched and supervised by the D.I.s until we learned to stand at attention, make facing movements, and march and double time in a military manner all with a D.I. shouting in our ears, thumping those who made the same mistake twice or who failed to react promptly. Push-ups were their favorite punishment for mistakes. Each morning we had physical training, which included squat jumps, sit-ups, pull-ups, push-ups, squat thrusts, and running. Running with our rifles with fixed bayonets over our heads was another form of punishment.

Our senior D.I. was Sgt. Shelton; a red faced, red haired Alabamian, and a wounded veteran of Korea. He was borderline sadistic, especially after a hard night of drinking. His favorite punishment was duck walking us everywhere we went. On Saturdays and Sundays, we had to do it with our full locker boxes on our shoulders.

The junior D.I. was Cpl. Lopes, another Korean Veteran from California. He was always very military in his approach and never abused us. We looked forward to when he had the platoon by himself.

During the third week, our mental test results came back and we lost six or eight men who had difficulty reading, writing, and/or doing math to what was called the 'slow learners platoon.' They would attend school part of each day until they were able to handle the curriculum taught by the regular instructors. The ones that were successful would be assigned to another platoon and resume training. There was no 'motivation platoon.' That was the D.I.s job.

Much of our classroom instruction was on the M-1 rifle. We learned the names of every part, and how to field strip it blindfolded. We had a rifle inspection at least once a day, and if they found a speck of dust or rust, you were in big trouble. I, and all the rest of my platoon, spent at least one night sleeping on a disassembled M-1! From day one we had to remember our serial number and our rifle number. You would be doing push-ups and sit-ups forever if you forgot either of them! For years I remembered my rifle number, but now I can only recall my serial number.

The D.I.s gave me a hard time because I was the only Reservist in the platoon, having only signed up for two years. When they found they could not convince me to sign up for three or four years and become a 'Regular,' they let it drop and it was never mentioned again.

We had to field day our hut every Saturday. This meant that we hauled everything out, scrubbed the floors and walls on our hands and knees using toothbrushes, and then cleaned everything and put it back in place. Saturday afternoons were supposed to be free time with a chance to write home. Our D.I.s preferred to march us to the sand pit, where we were made to double time while holding our rifles on the back of our hands and our bayonets in our mouths. Needless to say, everyone's rifle and bayonet ended up in the sand since we repeated this exercise until everyone was completely exhausted. We spent the rest of the afternoon cleaning our weapons and gear with little time left to write home.

We also washed our clothes on the weekend. We scrubbed them with some harsh lye soap and our scrub brushes, which were part of our "bucket issue," a tin bucket that also served as a stool at times. Washing clothes on a concrete wash rack in the winter is no fun. The water was always cold, and we got wet and cold from the ordeal. Our hands were raw from the effort, but our clothes were clean. We had a "clothes line watch" to make sure they weren't stolen by members of others platoons while they dried.

Our Platoon 65 was in Company O, 4th Training Battalion at Parris Island. Our platoon members were a mixture of young men from upstate New York, Pennsylvania, Indiana, the Carolinas, Georgia, and Florida. I tended to get along well with everyone.

I wrote my future bride, Edna Mae Guyer, who was a senior in Elkin High School.

23 February, Parris Island:

"This Marine Corps is really rough. I knew it would be hard, but I expected nothing like this. They keep us on the go 16 hours a day. I like it all right here, except for these stupid Yankees. They're always throwing off on the South, especially North Carolina. The other Carolina boy [Madison] and I really have a hard time. They shoot more bull than any group of boys I have ever seen. Thank goodness for Washington's Birthday! We didn't have to drill today, no classes either. I didn't get homesick until yesterday. We were waiting to go to church and I went walking along the shore, listening to the choir in the church. We go to church in shifts. I really got it bad then. According to our tentative schedule we are to receive our furloughs on April 25th. We may leave either earlier or later depending on how rushed they are."

The longer we stayed there, the more we bonded as a unit. Sectional differences were forgotten, and it was our platoon against all the others. Parris Island was rapidly filling up with new recruits. Whole platoons were arriving from New York, Boston, Philadelphia, and other large cities. New companies and battalions were added to handle the influx of future Marines.

We were becoming very proficient in drill and the manual of arms. We marched leaning over backwards in an almost goosestep fashion, digging our heels into the asphalt. Our 'boondockers' required new heels every two weeks. Only a few recruits were being issued boots at this time. You could hear any platoon coming with the rhythmic 'clomp, clomp, clomp' as they strutted down the roads to the classroom and the mess hall, with the D.I.s chanting "your left—right—left."

We passed our inspections with flying colors, and some of the petty harassment by the D.I.s stopped. The Platoon moved to the rifle range in mid-March. I am left-handed, and during the week of snapping in, the marksmanship instructors wanted me to learn to shoot right-handed. I convinced them that I had shot a rifle for a long time and I would be successful shooting left-handed. Our platoon pulled butts, or the targets, during some of our snapping in week.

I wrote, *"We are out at the rifle range now for 3 weeks. It is much prettier out here than where we were before. We're going to our first movie tonight. About time, I'd say!"*

The next week we started firing and we improved our scores every day. I fired expert on qualification day and heard nothing more about shooting right-handed! We fired from the off hand position from the 200 yard line, sitting and kneeling from the 300 yard line, and prone from the 500 yard line. I got in a groove at the 500 and had 9 of 10 bull's eyes. We also learned to fire the .45 caliber pistol.

Our third week at the rifle range was spent on mess duty. We were up and in the mess hall by 0300, since chow was served early for the shooters who had to be on the firing line at first light. I worked on one of the serving lines and rather enjoyed it. It was a chance to chat briefly with the recruits from the other platoons. We were very well fed, as we could eat as much as we liked, and the cooks were good to us compared to the D.I.s! We frequently raided the ice cream lockers when the cooks weren't looking! Ice cream sandwiches were passed out to everyone in our platoon.

I had an old Marine Corps trick played on me the first day of mess duty. The Mess Sergeant sent me to the supply hut for '20 yards of skirmish line.' Needless to say, the Supply Sergeant got a great kick out of my request, and handed me 20 yards of twine. The Mess Sergeant roared with laughter, when I returned with the twine, and told me what 20 yards of skirmish line really was. He gave me easy assignments after that.

Upon our return to main side, our D.I.s were changed. SSgt. R.G. Widdowson became our senior D.I., and Sgt. G.L. Sanchez and PFC A.K. Brown, recently out of boot camp and D.I. school himself, were the junior D.I.s. Widdowson had recently returned from Korea and was a professional Marine. There was no more petty harassment with him in charge. He was all business, and we could tell he was there to help us become better Marines. Sgt. Sanchez, also just back from Korea, tried to be tough, but it was not in his nature. He still commanded the respect of all of us. PFC Brown was from Maine, and we could hardly understand his commands. He had that nasal twang from that area, but we made the best of it. We hated it when he marched the platoon anywhere.

We were issued our dress uniforms when we returned from the rifle range. We received two sets of greens that were heavy woolen things for winter-wear, two sets of khakis, two sets of gabardines, and a raincoat with a liner that doubled as an overcoat. Our dress shoes were brown, but we were required to use black polish on them. We spent a great deal of time shining these shoes.

One Saturday, the D.I.s decided to have a boxing 'smoker' between the platoons. Our luck was to be matched up with a platoon that had a bunch of Golden Glove fighters from West Virginia! We didn't win a single match! John Ebersole, a big guy from Harrisburg, Pa., had just had his front teeth pulled. Being 'gung ho,' he volunteered to fight in the heavy weight bout. He got beaten to a bloody pulp!

During our last few weeks of training, we picked up a few men from other platoons who had been set back for medical and other reasons.

My worst tour of guard duty was one night during a tropical storm or hurricane. The wind was howling, the rain came down in sheets, and there

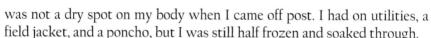

was not a dry spot on my body when I came off post. I had on utilities, a field jacket, and a poncho, but I was still half frozen and soaked through.

About 10 days before we graduated, some twenty of us were promoted to Private First Class.

16 April, Parris Island:

"We've gotten our stripes sewed on now. We can't wear them until next week, though. Everyday we are having inspections, almost every time we turn around. Our final inspection is next Thursday and we're dreading that one. Everything has to be perfect. We're going to Savannah, Georgia tomorrow for a parade. First time off the island in 9 weeks! They will be pretty strict on us, so we won't have much fun, but it'll break the monotony. I've got to go on guard duty now so I'll have to close."

Our platoon was graduated as the Battalion Honor Platoon. There were 65 of us in Platoon 65. We excelled in the final inspection and graduated from boot camp. I had added 10 pounds of muscle to my frame and was in the best physical condition of my life. We had all volunteered to go to Korea, and some eventually did go there, but not until after further training.

We boarded busses for home. We stopped in Beaufort to change and saw our first Coca-Cola machine in three months! We lined up to get our first soda. I bought two. I inhaled the first and savored the taste of the second one.

I enjoyed my 10 day leave by chasing the girls and hanging out with my old friends from high school and Guilford College. The break ended too soon and I headed back to Parris Island.

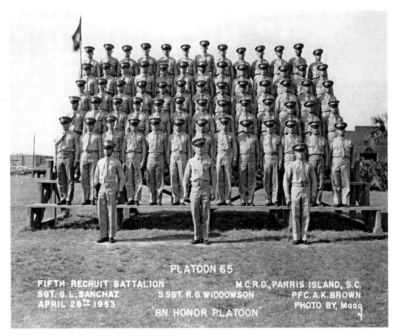

Platoon 65, BN Honor Program
Fifth Recruit Battalion, MCRD (Marine Corps Recruit Depot)
Parris Island

Top Row, L-R: Ellington, Driver, Eversole
Bottom Row, L-R: Reilly, Rieger

Chapter Three

2nd Service Regiment,
May 1953-January 1955
Camp Lejeune, North Carolina

May 19, Camp Lejeune:

"When I got back to Parris Island there was nothing for us to do, but they kept us busy having 500 of us pick up paper on a field about the size of a ball park. I came to Camp Lejeune Thursday by bus and naturally they put us right to work. I'm a company clerk now. It's easy work but I don't like sitting around all day. I've put in for a journalism school but I don't know if I will get it. Harry James is giving a concert tonight and a bunch of us are going to it. I've got to clean my rifle for tomorrow's parade. The Commanding General is leaving. There's going to be 15,000 men in it."

When I arrived at Camp Lejeune, I was assigned to the 2nd Service Battalion. Because I was a Reservist with less than two years to serve, I was not sent to a school I was qualified for; instead, I was given an MOS to become a laundry machine operator! That lasted until the red headed Corporal with his drooping mustache asked all those who could type to raise their hand. I was assigned as a Clerk/Typist and my MOS was changed accordingly.

Technical Sergeant Huber was my 1st Sergeant. He was a no-nonsense veteran of two wars who I grew to respect greatly. He worked all of the clerks hard but explained our duties in detail, which I quickly grasped. I made out guard duty rosters, NCO duty rosters, typed ID cards, liberty cards, leave papers, allotments, discharges, DD 214s, made all Service Record Book entries, and correspondence. We were almost a casualty company, as we had been assigned a large number of men with only a few weeks or months remaining on their enlistments, and I had to work nights processing all their paper work. I was also given the additional duty as the company mail clerk, which got me out from behind the desk every morning and afternoon for a few minutes.

We lived in modern two story brick barracks, shaped like an H, with open squad bays on the two wings and the heads and office spaces in between. The only cooling during the summer months was large fans. In the winter the barracks were pleasant, but not during the warm months. The sergeants blocked off their end of our squad bay with wall lockers and slept on single bunks. Rifle racks and GI cans were down the center aisle. With the high humidity you had to clean and oil your rifle daily.

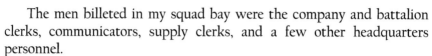

The men billeted in my squad bay were the company and battalion clerks, communicators, supply clerks, and a few other headquarters personnel.

The battalion headquarters was a brick office building near our barracks, and I had to go there twice a day to pick up the mail. We had a small PX nearby with a barbershop, post office, etc. The mess hall was close by also. Reveille went at 0530, followed by a company formation for roll call. We then returned inside to clean up and fall out for chow formation at 0630. We were marched to the mess hall by the Duty NCO but were allowed to straggle back. We had a similar formation at noon and evening to march to the mess hall. Since I had to pick up and distribute the mail, I was allowed to go to early or late chow at noon. We had to draw our liberty card from the Duty NCO to go off the base. One of the 1st Sergeant's punishments that did not go on a man's record was to pull his liberty card for a certain period of time.

I wrote my bride-to-be upon her graduation from high school,

"I wish I could be there but I'm going home for the first time this weekend. [My family had moved back to Staunton, Va.]. I haven't seen my parents, grandparents or my brother since I joined. I know how excited you are by now, as I know I was. After it was over there was a let down for me. I don't really know why but it made me feel as if something had been lifted from me. No matter how hard you try, you'll never be together again. So take a good look at the class of '53, it was a good one, I know. I've got guard duty tonight so I must close for now."

I didn't know it at the time but it was my last tour of guard duty. I didn't come off post until 0700 the next morning, and I went to late chow. When I reported to the company office, Tech Sergeant Huber wanted to know where I had been. I explained I had just gotten off guard duty and went to late chow and came to work as soon as I could. He told me, "You make up the guard roster for my signature, and I don't want to see your name on it again." I said "Yes sir," and obeyed his order.

15 June, Camp Lejeune:

"You were right, your letter was waiting for me. The other mail clerk had stuck it under my pillow for me. The guy who sleeps under me woke up and told me it was there. I left [Elkin] at 1300 Sunday and was here on the base at 2200. I came back a different way, through Sanford and Dunn and it's a little shorter. [I thumbed all the way. Servicemen in uniform had no trouble catching rides, as many of the men who picked us up had served

in WWII, and hadn't forgotten how much they appreciated a lift when they were in service. I rode in cars with large families who squeezed over to make room for me. Truck drivers would also stop and pick you up. Servicemen with cars would always pick you up, regardless of what uniform you were wearing.] I'm spending the night in the company office and am acting in the place of a Corporal [Duty NCO]. He cut his foot and somehow I had to take his place."

7 July, Camp Lejeune:

"I just got back from Staunton. Had a good time while I was home although it rained right much. Got back just in time for a big parade today. The heat was terrible and guys were fainting all over the place. Jon Smith [a friend from Wilson, New York, who was in my platoon in boot camp] lost his arm up to the shoulder Friday night. We were headed north when he sideswiped a logging truck tearing his arm off. It was horrible. [I was sitting in the back seat directly behind him, and it happened so quickly he didn't realize he had lost his arm until he pulled over and said 'Oh my God! My arm!'] There were six of us in his car and the guy sitting beside him slipped over and drove him to the Naval Hospital. We tied off his arm with his necktie, picked him and his arm up, and loaded them into the back seat with a close friend within a matter of seconds. The rest of us waited until the highway patrolman came and gave our statements. It happened in a bad curve on a 'short cut' road, and I believe the truck driver was over the centerline. [I've never driven with my arm out the window since. Jon was one of the nicest guys I had ever met and an excellent Marine.] I called the hospital tonight and he's doing o.k. I'm going to see him tomorrow."

26 July, Camp Lejeune:

"I'm sorry I didn't make it this weekend but Uncle Sam comes first. They stopped everyone from leaving the base at 0630 Friday morning and only a few are getting off the base today. A big draft for Korea came in (2500 Marines and 200 Navy Corpsmen). [The Korean War was coming to a close and the Marine Corps was sending in additional troops before the truce was signed.] We have been working ever since. This is the first time since the Korean War started that troops left directly from here. They are sending 8 trainloads, 3 leaving today (right now) and 5 leaving tomorrow. The 3rd Marine Division is on its way to Korea from California and the 3rd Marine Air Wing from Jacksonville, Florida, is also on its way. 3 Army Divisions (rumor) are also going. Another draft is expected tomorrow. Although it's Sunday everyone is still working."

I volunteered to go, but Master Sergeant Harold E. Bird, the new 1st Sergeant, said I could not be spared. I had to do all the paper work to send those leaving our company. Master Sergeant Bird was a wounded veteran of two wars who had recently married a Navy nurse. He was as gruff as they come with most everyone, but he had a heart of gold. He often invited me to his quarters for dinner, which I enjoyed, but I felt rather out of place. He took care of all of the Marines under him and gave us long weekends whenever he could. Thursday evenings were always field days, but the clerks got by with cleaning the offices, which didn't take very long.

Captain Charles J. Papa was our Company Commander. He had been seriously wounded in Korea and was just out of the hospital. He was short with dark complexion, and looked weak and pale. He was very professional and was the type of leader I would like to follow into combat. I found him easy to work for, but I always made sure I had my ducks in a row before briefing him. 1st Lt. William M. Cryan, also just back from Korea, was the Company Executive Officer until he was replaced by 2nd Lt. Wayne F. Burt. All became career Marines.

8 August, Camp Lejeune:

"I just got back. I caught a ride from Greensboro right to the base only a few feet from my barracks. I'm going to bed early tonight as I've already seen the stack of work piled up on my desk for tomorrow."

17 August, Camp Lejeune:

"I started back from Elkin about 1600. Had fairly good luck. I got rides to Winston-Salem, then Greensboro, then Sanford, and then Lillington, and then one to the base. Got in about midnight. Bad news today, no more long weekends for anyone!"

20 August, Camp Lejeune:

"I finally got an afternoon off to go to the [Onslow] beach. It was cloudy, the water was rough, and the wind kept blowing sand in our faces, yet it was worth it to get away from the office. We got another clerk in today and another gets out of school Saturday we may get (rumor)."

24 August, Camp Lejeune:

"We only had 41 men to join our company today, to be discharged. Got back about 2330. Had a ride from Siler City to Camp Lejeune. Rode in a new Oldsmobile, too. I guess you're wondering why I was so sleepy. Well, it's like this. I sit in this office and work eight hours a day, five days a week, not counting working nights. All I do is eat and sleep except for an occasional movie at night. Plus riding 275 miles each way, I'm simply worn out."

26 August, Camp Lejeune:

"James Caufield and I went canoeing this afternoon. It wasn't much fun, though. I did get a little tan. He's a tall, nice looking guy from West Virginia."

30 August, Camp Lejeune:

"Back in shackles. The weekends go too fast for me. I had a headache all day but it is gone now. The work is piling up and I can't make a dent in it. Lost another clerk today. That makes three in four days."

I continued visiting Elkin most weekends. I stayed with Bill Barnette and his mother. She treated me like another son. Bill got drafted into the Army that summer and was sent to Ft. Jackson, S.C., and later to Korea. He had bought an old T Model Ford coupe, which he let me drive, and told me to take it to Camp Lejeune while he was in training.

9 September, Camp Lejeune:

"Believe it or not that little ole' car made it back. It took 5 hours and 45 minutes. It didn't use any water or oil and not too much gas. I got an hour's sleep before going to work. I really felt great all day. Went to bed at 1900 last night and I felt like a million this morning." [What I didn't tell her was that the lights went out near Goldsboro and I had to drive along slowly, but there was no oncoming traffic at 0300 in the morning! It was a starlit night, but I almost fell asleep several times. The other problem was the accelerator pedal broke, and I had my foot on a steel rod most the way. It wore a hole in my dress shoes, so I had to purchase a new pair the next day.]

21 September, Camp Lejeune:

"I'm putting in a little overtime tonight. For some reason I don't feel too bad with only one hour's sleep. I got back about 0500 this morning but I had to wait in Jacksonville a while for a bus. I don't like to ride busses. They're making us wear khakis to work now and there goes my laundry bill. We have a new Colonel and he's plenty tough. Before I have been able to do most of my own laundry. It is still hot down here. I'm sitting here with no shirt on and still sweating. The 1st Sergeant has gone to the rifle range for two weeks. The SNCO acting in his place 'just ain't got it.'"

22 September, Camp Lejeune:

"I just got through talking my way out of standing the Division Parade tomorrow. It's not that I mind marching, but if I don't work, it will still put me behind. We have 27 men being discharged next month."

5 October, Camp Lejeune:

"Just got back from chow. We had hamburger, corn, potatoes, cabbage, salad and cake. Just fair. [They served us 'B' rations left over from WWII at least one meal a day during my two years at Camp Lejeune. The meat was so greasy it was difficult to eat. The Marine Corps never throws anything away!] I've got to work late tonight as we are discharging 22 men tomorrow. Our company is getting smaller every day. The more that go the better I like it!"

8 October, Camp Lejeune:

"I worked until 2330 last night. I've worked 55 hours in 4 days. I haven't been to a movie, the P.X, or anywhere else this whole week."

That weekend I took Eddie Benz from New York to the Duke-Georgia Tech football game in Durham. Danny Park, who I graduated from high school with, was a team manager and he got us passes and we carried the chains on one side of the field. I wrote that "the game was the best I had ever seen." Sonny Jurgureson was the Duke quarterback at the time.

20 October, Camp Lejeune:

"Sid, the guy with all the records, went home and brought them back. Everyone in the squad bay is thanking him! Eddie Benz is on the battalion football team and is getting ready for practice. He's wearing the most 'holy' tee shirt I have ever seen! I kind of wish I were going out for the team."

There is a long break in my letters to Edna. She may have been dating someone else so I stopped writing her. However, we were soon back together.

1 February 1954, Camp Lejeune:

"I'm not very mad! We got left [in Greensboro] by my so-called buddy and had to thumb back. It was really cold! I still haven't been to bed and it's after seven now. I'm really sleepy! Caufield has been asleep since chow, clothes and all."

15 February, Camp Lejeune:

"I am really sleepy. We got back about 0400. I drove to Clinton and then Regan drove on in. I'm standing by in the Company Office until 1300 and then I'm going to the dentist."

24 February, Camp Lejeune:

"Here it is 1800 and I'm just getting off from work. That's the Marine Corps for you! It's pouring rain so I don't really mind, as I'm not going anywhere tonight. I left Greensboro about 2130 and got here at 0200. I got some sleep for a change! The whole 2nd Marine Division is going to sea in April. Leaving the 18th and coming back the 1st of May. Sounds like real fun! We'll 'hit the beach' just like they do in the movies!"

During this period, I had been promoted to Corporal. I now had a little more rank to go with all the responsibility and authority I had been given.

2 March, Camp Lejeune:

"We really had a time getting back. It poured rain all the way. In Clinton the water was so high that the engine flooded out and we sat there for a half-hour waiting for someone to push us out. We didn't get here until 0600. I am standing Duty NCO tonight. Corporal Frank Cappella and I went to school yesterday afternoon and we have to go again tomorrow. It's on our work. [Cappella was seriously wounded in Korea as an infantryman. His MOS was changed and he was assigned to our company as the unit diary clerk. Frank was from Washington, D.C.] I went to the dentist Monday and had two teeth filled, but it didn't hurt. Two more this Monday and I will be finished with the dentist. John Madden said he sent you a 'smile.' He had 5 front teeth pulled! We call him 'Andy Gump.' Captain Papa told me that I might not have to go to sea in April. Sounds good but it would be a lot of fun."

8 March, Camp Lejeune:

"Back in the saddle again! Got a ride with Bill Beck from Greensboro. He attended Guilford College when I was there and played on the football team. He went through boot camp with J.B. Gentry [high school classmate]. One of my buddies from boot camp is going to Korea in April. He just got married a month ago, but he isn't bitter. He feels that it will test his marriage. That's one way of looking at it I guess. I've got to wash clothes!"

11 March, Camp Lejeune:

"I'm dropping you a quick line before going to see Tex Beneke at the Camp Theater. Frank Cappella and I are going along with a bunch of others. I sprained my knee playing tennis yesterday and it is giving me a fit. The doctor told me to stay off of it as much as possible and no running. We are going to get 96-hour passes before long, I think. All it lacks is the approval of the Secretary of the Navy. That will really make it nice. Got to get dressed now and hobble to the show. Frank is hollering at me!"

22 March, Camp Lejeune:

"It was cold last night and this morning thumbing back. No one was up when I got in so I slept for a few minutes. One of the guys just walked up and handed me three new tee shirts. He thanked me for keeping him off guard duty as much as possible. I told him I didn't play favorites, and thanked him for them."

23 March, Camp Lejeune:

"It has rained here all day. I wonder what it is saving for the weekend? Just got back from a good meal of steak, mashed potatoes, corn, ice cream, and pie. Good chow for a change!"

24 March, Camp Lejeune:

"I'm standing Duty NCO tonight. Baseball practice starts tomorrow. Frank Cappella and I are going out for the team. Jerry is too, after he gets back from emergency leave. [Onnie E. 'Jerry' or 'Rip' Lane was an all-state running back for the Winnsboro, S.C. high school team and attended the University of South Carolina before enlisting. 'Rip' played in the same backfield with King Dixon, who became an All American and a Marine officer after graduation.] We went out and threw some this afternoon."

4 April, Camp Lejeune:

"I got a ride back with six guys from my company. Good luck for a change. I didn't get any sleep but at least I didn't have to stand out in the cold all night thumbing. One of the guys had to sit up beside me in the back seat. He curled up against me and slept most of the way. He was real small so it wasn't uncomfortable."

6 April, Camp Lejeune:

"I'm going on maneuvers the 15th or 16th, or so it looks. I won't be back until the 1st of May. Cappella was going but they changed it to me. That's the way the ball bounces!"

11 April, Camp Lejeune:

"I'm back in the saddle again, just like Gene Autry. This place gets a little more 'chicken' every day. Now we have to check out to go to the bathroom! I still don't know if I'm going to sea or not. My name wasn't read out this morning on the embarkation roster—but it changes every day. After I left you last night I walked up the road towards the exit and I met some men from Camp Lejeune and got a ride back with them."

13 April, Camp Lejeune:

"Just back from playing tennis—won a couple, then got mad and lost out. I can't play when I get mad. The racket was busted and every time I hit the ball it would lob into the net. Ten 'boots' just reported in from Parris Island. More work for me tomorrow!"

14 April, Camp Lejeune:

"I got the afternoon off today and played tennis. I won three matches—mainly because I didn't get mad—not once! Regan made Corporal today—I was glad to see him get it. I'm still not sure if I'm going on those damn maneuvers or not. The rear echelon has to work day and night, including weekends. Cappella and Regan are staying behind. Caufield and Lane are going."

15 April, Camp Lejeune:

"I found out today that I'm not going on maneuvers after all. Played some more tennis yesterday with Dick Swink. He got married about a month ago. He went home to Cheraw, South Carolina, last night to see his wife. Said he couldn't stay away if he had too! He went to Georgia Tech before he came in the Marines. I beat him two sets, 6-3 and 6-0. I'm improving. Tony Pastor and his band were here tonight. Dick, Jerry, Caufield and I went. It was really a good show. The vocalist sang 'Write Me One Sweet Letter' and I thought about yours. Jerry and Caufield are rolling their packs for the maneuver. They're teasing me about writing you."

19 April, Camp Lejeune:

"I got back about 0330. Caught a ride in a new Ford convertible to Sanford and drove all the way. It was really a nice running car. Then I caught a ride all the way to the base, but in Clinton the battery went dead and we had to drive the rest of the way with no lights! The moon was bright enough that we didn't need them. Frank fell asleep in the sun yesterday and he looks like a boiled lobster! I don't see how he will sleep tonight!"

20 April, Camp Lejeune:

"I'm standing Duty NCO tonight. I just got back from playing tennis. It's really getting warm down here. It's nice now but this summer—Phew! My brother is playing on his high school baseball team. He made an A+, 4 A's and a B+ on his last report card. I wish I took after him in that respect! A guy from Michigan wanted your address but I told him no soap! He gets out in July and is going to Michigan State on a football scholarship. He's nice looking, too. I may have competition but I don't want to invite it!"

I was disappointed that Edna and her family were moving to Michigan this summer.

21 April, Camp Lejeune:

"Just got back from the Camp Theater. Count Bassie and his band put on a show. It was fairly good. Cappella and two others from our company really had a ball last night or this morning, they weren't sure which. They got high off of beer in Wilmington and took their girls to Carolina Beach and went swimming in the nude! They said 'a good time was had by all.' I can imagine! They've been trying to work me hard. We got 18 new men in yesterday and sent 17 on leave. Mucho work! I played tennis a while this afternoon but I quit from lack of competition. Honest!"

22 April, Camp Lejeune:

"I had forgotten about the dance being this weekend. I've borrowed some dress blues so I should really be sharp! We had steak for chow tonight and I had three big ones! It was really good! I'm about to bust, though!"

26 April, Camp Lejeune:

"I had really good luck last night. Got a ride from the campus [Women's College of the University of North Carolina in Greensboro] to Siler City. Then I got a ride right to the front door of the barracks. Arrived at 0430 and the lights were on. Then I remembered

we lost an hour due to day light savings time. Cappella's whole body is one red blister! He went to Carolina Beach and got roasted. Regan's the same way. Silly boys! I played tennis this evening but I should have stayed in bed. I lost 8-6. Too tired to do much good."

27 April, Camp Lejeune:

"I played more tennis today—finally got back to my winning ways."

29 April, Camp Lejeune:

"Well, the troops came back today, every one of them. Lane, Caufield, and all the rest, and they were the dirtiest, scroungiest looking bunch you have ever seen. They were filthy, their clothes were filthy, and their filth was filthy. I was kind of glad to see them, though. None of them had shaved or taken a bath in a week. If anyone ever looked like the Marines you seen in movies, they were it! The men from Puerto Rico came in with them— by the truck, jeep, am-track, and tank load. All of them had beards and hadn't had a hair cut in nearly two months. Moran says he is going to Greensboro tonight. I hope he isn't that stupid. There will be many, many drunks tonight. When 26,000 Marines are turned loose—they had better stand by in Jacksonville! Naturally, it had to rain tonight. Jerry was glad it waited until they got out of the field. We got wet anyway at the outdoor movie. I'm standing Duty NCO tonight, like always. I am quitting after tonight, if possible."

30 April, Camp Lejeune:

"Today was pay day and no day to be working in the office. Everything always happens at once. My address starting Monday will be H&S Co., 2nd Service Battalion." [The battalion had been reorganized and more men were assigned to our company.]

3 May, Camp Lejeune:

"I got back this morning about 0600. I'm so sleepy! Jerry has been asleep all evening. "Big Ed" Morrison [one of the Company armorers and from New York City] and I played tennis today. I won, of course. We went swimming afterwards—nice pool, and the water was fine. Ed is really the Burt Lancaster type—handsome and rugged. He is really a nice guy too. I went swimming with my watch on tonight and the watchband broke."

4 May, Camp Lejeune:

"Trying to squeeze this in before going to hear Louie Armstrong. Jerry is going with me. Jerry said he would come up this weekend if you weren't going home. [To date her roommate.] We are both a little low financially. We have $15.00 between us. He and

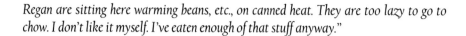

Regan are sitting here warming beans, etc., on canned heat. They are too lazy to go to chow. I don't like it myself. I've eaten enough of that stuff anyway."

5 May, Camp Lejeune:

"Ed Morrison and I just got back from playing tennis. I won 6-3, 2-6 and 6-2. Improving, huh! Louie Armstrong was really good last night. They were an hour and 50 minutes late getting here, though. They had a big fat colored woman singing and she was a panic! She weighed at least 300 pounds and the way she bounced around I thought the stage would cave in! We are moving to a barracks down the street in the morning. They're never satisfied as to where we should stay."

10 May, Camp Lejeune:

"I really had a hell of a time last night. Caught a ride from Greensboro to Liberty and then an Army MP picked me up. He just laughed when I told him I had lost my cap. He took me to Sanford. I caught a ride to Lejeune with one of those guys who knows a short cut so we ended up out in the boondocks about 15 miles off the main highway. He finally found his way back to the right road about 0630. I got back to the base in time to go to work. I stood in Sanford for about an hour before I caught a ride and I don't think I thawed out until I took a hot shower tonight. I am so sleepy and tired all I'm going to do after I finish this letter is hit the sack! No movie or tennis for me. Too cold anyway!"

11 May, Camp Lejeune:

"Just got back from seeing 'Miami Story' with Barry Sullivan, a fairly good gangster movie. Jerry, Caufield, Gene Woodall from Charlotte, N. C. and Bill Shiver from Brunswick, Ga., went with me. [Woodall was the Company Supply NCO and Shiver, who had attended Georgia Tech, was a new Clerk.] I really caught up on my sleep last night. I'm going to bed shortly and get some more of that good stuff. I played some tennis today. The weekend layoff didn't help my game any. I still won, though. I'm going to get out of this company office. I'm starting to hate myself, and everyone here, so it is time to move on for me. I may not get as many weekends off at Battalion, but at least I won't be working for a bunch of idiots."

12 May, Camp Lejeune:

"Well it finally happened today. I got mad at this screwed up first sergeant of ours [not MSgt. Bird] and went to see the personnel chief at battalion headquarters and told him I would not work there any longer. He told me to come up to battalion and work for him, so I'm at the battalion and satisfied. The work is harder but I don't have to work for an idiot!

Cappella is making sergeant Friday and is trying to transfer too. He can't take it either. We have a big inspection on the 22nd and another on the 25th. Just got through washing clothes. Frank and I washed together, as usual. Right now it's pouring rain. I've shaved, showered and brushed my teeth so there is nothing to do until lights out but write to you. Five o'clock comes too early for me!"

17 May, Camp Lejeune:

"I reached here this morning after three rides. One ride was from the Women's College to Sanford with the Army. I caught another ride almost to the base with the Navy, and finally one with a Marine to the base. The Marine was from Buena Vista, Virginia and knows my uncle [Otis Flint] real well. It's 1900 now and I just finished working. I'm really beat. Seems like they want everything done on Mondays. It seems to be my wit is at its best on Monday mornings after not having any sleep. I kept the other clerks dying with my wisecracks today! I don't get it!"

18 May, Camp Lejeune:

"I had a fairly easy day for a change. I spent most of the morning standing in line to get paid. Right now everyone is getting ready to go on liberty. Much money will be spent tonight! Cappella is off to Wilmington. He'll be back about morning, maybe. The usual payday poker games are going on across bunks all over the place. I never gamble with my few dollars." [I had an allotment to Guilford College to pay them off, sent my brother money each month, and had a savings bond deducted.]

19 May, Camp Lejeune:

"This is one of those nights with absolutely nothing to do. It's pouring down rain outside and the barracks are practically empty. Charlie Whitmire [from near Asheville, N.C.], the originator of 'you don't know do you,' is sitting here worrying me. He is really a character. Everyone dies laughing when he's around. Played tennis yesterday. I wasn't too hot but finally won 8-6. It was quite a set. Freddie 'Popsicle' (easier than Pospychala) and I played. [He was one of the clerks.] Everyone here is squaring away gear for the inspections. I've just finished myself. I marked all of my clothing, and cleaned my rifle and bayonet."

24 May, Camp Lejeune:

"I made it back in four hours and fifteen minutes! I couldn't have done much better if I were driving myself. After the ride I caught up town I caught a ride to Siler City. I got out and immediately caught a ride to Sanford with some paratroopers, and then I caught one with two Marines all the way to the base. They were from Pennsylvania

but had been to Greensboro for the weekend. Right now I am very dirty from washing windows, scrubbing, waxing and polishing floors, etc. I am also very much squared away for the inspection. I'm going to take a good hot shower, shave and sleep. They'll have to drag me out in the morning!"

Edna's parents had moved to Flint, Michigan to work in the car industry and she went there for the summer. I spent most of my weekends with my high school friends from Elkin at Carolina and Myrtle beaches.

3 June, Camp Lejeune:

"Frank and I are sitting here bitching at each other. We wouldn't be happy otherwise. He went to Carolina Beach last night and had a good time, but no swimming in the nude! We had fried chicken twice today. I don't know what the Marine Corps is coming too! It's really getting hot down here now. Electric fans are going everywhere. These khakis melt in this heat."

7 June, Camp Lejeune:

"I just came in from lying out in the sun reading 'Shiloh,' a Civil War novel. Jerry was out there with me reading 'Tarawa.' He's gung ho for that stuff, too. Frank and I washed clothes tonight and what a time I've had keeping them hanging on the line. I took the afternoon off and went to Onslow beach after lunch. It was real nice out there. Windy but cool! There were four ships out there loading Marines for maneuvers in Puerto Rico. I hear that one company from the 8th Marines is going to Honduras to train their equivalent of our Marines. It's rumored that the whole Division may go but I doubt it. I spent most of the morning having my rifle inspected and drawing gear. Then I stood in line to get paid. I only drew $14.00. I guess that will be enough money for one weekend at the beach."

8 June, Camp Lejeune:

"I just got in from playing a little touch football. It really got hot out there. We had a big time anyway. I'm back working in the company office again as MSgt. Bird has taken over the company again. It's a mess but I've got 8 months to square it away. I've got to work tonight so I have to close."

13 June, Camp Lejeune:

"Saturday evening. I just got back from the beach. We stayed out there about four hours and really had a time. Three carloads of us went out—seventeen in all. Played *touch football and my team won. I threw the winning and only touchdown pass. Not much doing out there although the beach was crowded. I broke down and drank a beer—Jerry drank about half of one and Regan finished it. I smoked another cigar yesterday. You had better get down here quick and square me away! We are going to Carolina Beach tonight if nothing happens. 'Treetop' Smith, Jerry, Regan, Joe Galante, and Sam Scifo, plus myself. 'Treetop' is the one who caught the touchdown pass—a North Carolina to Michigan pass that is!"*

14 June, Camp Lejeune:

"A bunch of the guys are doing the Indian wrestle here—got to have something to do, although today was payday. I'm going to Staunton this weekend even if I have to walk. I'm about to crack up in this place. The gang is going to muster at Carolina Beach tonight but not this lad—every Marine who can make it will be there. Edward Martin is going to Korea on the July draft. Elkin has quite a representation over there. Tomorrow I've got to wash clothes for sure. I've run out of everything but socks."

15 June, Camp Lejeune:

"Just came back from chow and it is getting ready to storm outside. We need some relief from this heat. I was working so hard today I almost missed chow twice. Someone had to remind me both times. We are really busy. Frank wasn't much good today, too much weekend! He has quit drinking, though. It really felt strange loafing around the barracks all weekend. I read and played ping-pong with Jerry and Regan. Ed Morrison just came in and wants me to go to the drive-in with him. Guess I'll have to make it since 'Sands of Iwo Jima' with John Wayne is playing. I can't pass up a gung-ho movie!"

17 June, Camp Lejeune:

"Am I getting the kidding! Some guy came in drunk last night and crawled in the rack with me. When the lights came on this morning we were both sleeping away. No one noticed us for nearly 10 minutes and then they woke us up. I laughed myself silly. He staggered around, got dressed, and said he was in the wrong barracks. To top it all off, Jerry was sleeping in my bunk and I had to wake him up so I could go to bed. What a time!"

21 June, Camp Lejeune:

"I went to Lexington [Virginia] this weekend to see my brother. He has really grown—he's nearly as tall as I am but skinnier. His voice is changing and he is quite a character. He really goes after the girls too—not like his brother! I left here Friday about two and got there about 0100 Saturday morning. Then we had to talk the rest of

the morning, so you can guess how much sleep I got. We went with one of my cousins to Staunton to get his new Oldsmobile – a two toned green one with dark top and light body. It was a holiday coupe and really a beauty. I drove it around Saturday night and Sunday. Sunday we went on a family picnic in the mountains [Goshen Pass] and had a good time. We had the usual ball game and went swimming. That mountain water was really cold! My uncle knew a guy stationed at Cherry Point and got me a ride back as far as Kinston. I drove from Roxboro to Kinston—a new 1954 Chevrolet. I was here by 0400 and got a whole hour's sleep."

22 June, Camp Lejeune:

"I've been out throwing baseball with one of the guys I work with. I'm soaking wet from it but it really feels good."

23 June, Camp Lejeune:

"We went to the beach today. It was too hot to stay long. It was worth it though. Glad we came back early as we had a rainstorm about an hour after we arrived."

24 June, Camp Lejeune:

"I'm out in the sun trying to write. The breeze is blowing the paper so this may end up a mess. I've got to work tonight as the fiscal year ends on 30 June. Three entries must go into each man's record book. That adds up to 1500 entries in 500 record books—nice job, huh? I have to stand an inspection this Saturday. I have to lay out all my clothes and equipment on the bunk [Junk on the bunk inspection.] I don't have to march in the parade, thank goodness! The last one I stood the inspecting officer congratulated me for having the best display, so I might as well do the same this time."

28 June, Camp Lejeune:

"I went to Winnsboro with Jerry [Lane] Saturday morning. We didn't get there until 2030 so we just went out and messed around all night. His girl had gone to Myrtle Beach and he was really pissed. He started to get drunk but I talked him out of that. Sunday we went swimming at the local pool. Not a very big or nice one—no room to swim. There was quite a crowd of people there, though. We started back about 1800 and were back at midnight. We took his car back and had car trouble. Overheated. The temperature was 103 Saturday and Sunday. I drank more ice water than there is in Lake Michigan! Winnsboro is a mill town like Elkin but entirely different. Negroes! I've never seen so many anywhere! There is a liquor store on every corner and the town is very dirty compared to Elkin. The town itself is larger than Elkin but our high school is larger and much better in every

respect. I'm really catching it from the characters around here. I guess you've heard Tony Bennett's latest 'Please Driver.' well they holler at me 'Please Driver, once more around the park again!' They seem to get a kick out of harassing me about it."

The next day I continued, "I've been playing ping-pong and not very good either. I don't play enough to be good. I'm going to work tonight and try to have everything squared away before the weekend. We are getting off from Friday evening until Tuesday morning. I heard from my Aunt [Mary Payne, a retired Navy nurse] in Washington, D.C. today. She wants me to come up. The Boston Red Sox are playing a double header there Monday—so you know where I'll be. I've got to see Ted Williams play, as he is my idol! My uncle is a Staff Sergeant in the Air Force and really a nice guy. He flies around the country taking movies of maneuvers. What a job! Cappella is hollering at me to get to work so I had better close."

29 June, Camp Lejeune:

"It is really hot here. Up in the 100s at least. Everyone is sweating through their uniforms and mine is a mess. I've been out playing football for the past hour and a half. The sun was really boiling. We always pick the worst time to do anything. Today was payday and nearly everyone took off tonight for town. I wanted to go to the drive-in but we have to work tonight. I'm getting tired of this. No overtime! I guess I'll close for now as it is almost time for MSgt. Bird to come in and back to the salt mines!"

30 June, Camp Lejeune:

"I'm really tired. I worked from 0730 this morning until 2130 tonight, stopping only to eat, and I am really shot."

1 July, Camp Lejeune:

"Today has really been hot—what a way to start a new month! We had a Division parade today—20,000 men. General Lewis B. 'Chesty' Puller took over as Division commander. He is really 'gung-ho' and quite a hero. He has more medals than the law allows. I really felt sorry for the men parading. I was wet just sitting here typing. I finished those damn record books today. Am I glad of that! Frank and I are getting ready to go to Washington. I had all my trousers cleaned and I washed my khaki shirts and ironed them myself. Oh boy what a job I did!"

General Puller's arrival brought many needed changes in the way things were done in the 2nd Marine Division. Ties were not required when on base in the summer months. Utilities could be worn to the outdoor movies instead of khakis. Morning roll call formations were ended. Section heads would report to the 1st Sergeant any men that were missing. NCOs could carry their liberty cards at all times. We could wear utilities to work in the offices. The Staff NCO clubs were opened for beer at lunchtime, and many other small but important things that the troops appreciated.

General "Chesty" Puller

2 July, Camp Lejeune:

"Tuesday night. This is really a sleepy bunch around here; everyone is racked out for the night. Big weekend! From what I've heard many girls lost their virginity over the holiday! I got back from Elkin about 0100 and got almost three hours sleep for a change. I had good luck thumbing except from Winston-Salem to Greensboro."

7 July, Camp Lejeune:

"I am really tired after that long weekend in Washington. My brother Billy came up and we had a fairly good time. I got there about midnight Friday and didn't see the sun until 1100 Saturday when Billy came in and woke me up. We went down town and saw a couple of movies that afternoon. On Sunday we had a family picnic and went swimming. We took in the double header on Monday and really enjoyed it. Ted Williams hit 2 bases loaded home runs, 2 doubles and walked 5 times. The trip up and back was a killer. There were six of us and five trying to sleep. The heat was awful going up but it was nice coming back. I got in at 0530 this morning so no sleep! Everyone is sleeping off the weekend so I had better join them!"

8 July, Camp Lejeune:

"I didn't have time to write last night so how does 0515 strike you? I went to the beach yesterday and stayed about two hours. It was cloudy and windy so I didn't get much sun. When I got back from the movie tonight MSgt. Bird came in and wanted me to work so I did, getting the promotion cards set up for the promotion tests."

9 July, Camp Lejeune:

"It's really getting hot down here—temperatures in the 90s. I've got to work again tonight so I'll close."

10 July, Camp Lejeune:

"Just came in from lying out in the boiling sun. It was really hot but I didn't have anything else to do. Jerry, Regan, and I lay out there talking and listening to the radio until almost dark. The pay clerk is on leave so I'm trying to do his work and mine. I'm getting way behind in both. I'm not working nights doing someone else's work either. I sound real tough, don't I? You betcha! One of my buddies was passing out cigars today. His wife had a girl yesterday morning. The whole barracks was smoking 'stogies' today! We are sending another group on maneuvers this month and they're packing tonight."

10 July, Camp Lejeune:

"Friday night. It's another lonely night. Everyone is taking off for the weekend but me. I've got to work tonight and tomorrow. I'm going to Carolina Beach tomorrow afternoon or Sunday. A rifle range detail just came in. They've been out firing for two weeks. They were really glad to be back. Jerry was over the hill for two days but only got a warning. He was really lucky!"

11 July, Camp Lejeune:

"Sunday. Believe it or not I stayed here for once. I had to work all day yesterday and still have work to do to today, so I have really kept busy. It poured rain all day yesterday and is cloudy and cool today –which is good! Got some typing to do so I'll close for now."

14 July, Camp Lejeune:

"I went to the beach today and had quite a time. The ocean was really rough but we fought it anyway. Wasn't so hot for a change. We're going to Special Services to see some combat films tonight. They should be good. 'Please Driver' by Tony Bennett is playing now and I'm catching it, as usual."

19 July, Camp Lejeune:

"Back in the 'boondocks' again. Got back about two this morning from Elkin. I really enjoyed the trip despite the ride. My high school friends brought me to Winston-Salem Sunday afternoon and we went swimming at Crystal Lake. I had a sore throat so I didn't take to the water. It was real sticky as it was getting ready to rain and I really wanted to go."

21 July, Camp Lejeune:

"I just got back from the beach. It was real nice out there today. It rained this morning and cooled things off quite a bit. We went out at one o'clock and about two it cleared off and was real nice. I am really tan now! I have one of the best even if I do say so! We met some Women Marines Reservists from Charlotte, New Jersey and West Virginia. They're here for two weeks summer training. It's started to rain again. Good, because it was getting hot again. Fine sleeping tonight!"

22 July, Camp Lejeune:

"We went to a movie tonight and then to the Camp Cafeteria for some ice cream. They had some good records on the jukebox and we almost spent the night listening to them. I may go to Pennsylvania with [Wayne 'Sug'] McCardle. He's been asking me and I've never been up there so I should go while I have the chance."

24 July, Camp Lejeune:

"I didn't go the Pennsylvania after all. I thought it over and decided it wasn't worth it. I still remember that trip to Washington. It is just too hot to be cramped up in a car for

6-8 hours. Not too many went home this weekend. We are planning a big trip to the beach tomorrow afternoon."

26 July, Camp Lejeune:

"I've been over playing ping-pong. I'm getting worse instead of better. It is a good way to work off excess energy, though. We're having real tropical weather down here. It clouds up and rains everyday, which really helps to cool things off. I have to work again tonight. I'll certainly be glad when we get caught up. I've been hoping for this for a year now."

28 July, Camp Lejeune:

"We were out at the beach all afternoon. We played tag football most of the time. Our team lost 24-12. It's good exercise. I heard from Johnny Ebersole today. We went through boot camp together and he was in this battalion awhile before going to Korea. He likes it about like [Bill] Barnette likes it. Not a damn bit! He got married before he went and his wife is expecting in November. He won't get to see his baby until it's eight months old, and is he bitter! He made Corporal in June and says it really helps over there. He and I have always been the best of friends. I nicknamed him 'Toothless One' in boot camp and it stuck with him! He hates for anyone but me to call him that though! 'Treetop' Smith from Jackson, Michigan gets out tomorrow. He was out at the beach playing football with us this afternoon. He left me his writing table."

29 July, Camp Lejeune:

"I didn't have to work tonight but the way the work is piling up I should have. I saw 'Retreat Hell' last night. I had seen it before but I enjoyed it more this time. I'm getting more 'gung-ho' every day. I am strictly 'Semper Fi.'"

30 July, Camp Lejeune:

"Here comes another weekend with nothing to do. We do have an inspection tomorrow morning. Jerry is here complaining about walking guard duty. I don't blame him, as I never liked it either. I've been playing ping-pong all evening but I'm not improving much. I have a five day basket leave coming so hurry up and come down so I can take it."

Basket leaves were given to personnel who had worked overtime and weekends or done something exceptional, as a reward. The leave papers were torn up and thrown in the trash basket if he returned on time. Hence the term 'basket leave.'

2 August, Camp Lejeune:

"One more weekend down the drain. All I accomplished was getting a better suntan. Today was payday and everyone is either playing poker or heading for Jacksonville. Me? I've got to work tonight. Frank and I have about 60 reports to do. It is really hot down here now, but for some reason it doesn't bother everyone so much. We're just getting use to it, I guess."

During the summer, I had a long talk with Captain Papa about applying for Officer Candidate School. I had qualifying scores. He recommended that I go back to college and apply after graduation. He said my chances for promotion would be much better. I took his advice.

4 August, Camp Lejeune:

"I just got back from the beach. It was really hot out there today. We had three carloads to go out and did we have a time! We all indulged in a little beer. I would like to go out for the Battalion football team but with some of the giants I see running around here, I doubt if I will. They play for blood in Marine Corps football. Jerry and Regan are going out. Regan was a first string guard last year."

5 August, Camp Lejeune:

"Today has really been a scorcher. The temperature is over 103 degrees and not a breeze is stirring. Four of us took off to the beach right after work and finally cooled off a bit. The water was real rough so we didn't stay in long. We're getting ready to go to the drive-in now. The barracks is a real sweatbox. We are going to have a General's inspection next Saturday and I really hate it. Guys will be passing out right and left. I don't think I will have to fall out for it. Frank is on leave so that almost makes it a sure thing. His sister is getting married."

10 August, Camp Lejeune:

"Waiting on a buddy to come back from chow before heading for the beach for a nice swim to cool off. We've got a little boy here now taking a month's on the job training in the Marine Reserve. He's so small and young looking we nicknamed him 'Son.' He's from Kentucky and is coming on active duty after he finishes high school next June. My brother looks 21 beside him. We're working every night this week getting ready for the General's inspection. My last one will be in December thank goodness!"

11 August, Camp Lejeune:

"What a gay time I'm going to have this weekend. I'm standing Duty NCO Saturday. I've got a lot of work to do in the office anyway, so I'll spend most of my time working. I'm going to the beach Sunday and relax. It rained last night and things cooled off considerably. They are putting larger electric fans in the squad bays and they really feel good! Frank is lying here listening to the radio and making wisecracks at everyone walking by. We are the two of the wisest I know. He turned 22 today. What is he going to do? Hit the rack!"

12 August, Camp Lejeune:

"One of the guys was asleep just now and someone gave him a hot foot! He really woke up fast. It burned his foot! Jerry is sitting here eating potato chips and messing up my rack. I've had to give him the word on that! Got to go to work now so I'd better close."

14 August, Camp Lejeune:

"The inspection went off very well and if I do say so our company looked the best. We've spent yesterday afternoon and night and this afternoon at the beach. I had a good time and didn't drink any beer this time."

17 August, Camp Lejeune:

"Today has been a long, hot one. I've been out playing tennis with Freddy Pospychala 'Popsicle.' He's a 'Yankee' but a nice guy. Bill Plant, one of the Battalion Mail Orderlies, just came in off leave. He took 20 days leave but only stayed 8. He couldn't stand it at home. No good movie on tonight so I'll indulge in a few games of cards and then catch up on my sleep."

19 August, Camp Lejeune:

"Today I took over as 1st Sergeant of the Company as Master Sergeant Bird went on leave. I also accrued his headaches and problems. For 10 days I won't be able to go anywhere or do anything but work, eat, and sleep. We have 491 enlisted Marines, 38 officers and 16 Navy Corpsmen to control. One thing for sure it will be a fast 10 days. I went to the beach yesterday and baked in the sun a while. It is really hot here, 101 degrees Monday and 98 degrees Tuesday."

22 August, Camp Lejeune:

"Sunday. I just got back from the beach. Frank Cappella, Andy Persha, Gene Stowers, and I went out. It was really nice out there. It rained last night and cooled everything off. Jerry and Regan went to White Lake yesterday with everyone in their outfit. They aren't back yet, but a couple of guys have come in and said they're all drunk or getting that way. They will really feel good tomorrow! The 1st Sergeant's job is for the birds. If I don't go crazy this week then I'm safe for the rest of my life. Everyone a rank higher and up is chewing me out all day long and you can't say too much back to them. You may be writing to me in the brig before long for striking an officer or some sergeant. Eight more days of this!"

Edna came back for her sophomore year at the Women's College and we resumed dating.

20 September, Camp Lejeune:

"This is a very tired and sleepy Marine tonight. I got back about 0430 this morning. It rained here this morning and cooled everything off. That's why I'm not out playing football. Ha! They are out there playing now. I may not have to go on maneuvers after all. At least that is the latest 'scoop.' They're starting a big card game on the rack next to mine so I'll really get a lot of sleep tonight. Jerry won $70 over the weekend."

28 September, Camp Lejeune:

"We ['Sug' McCardle and Jerry Lane] made it back by 0430 which is very good time considering the drivers and the speed. We are having a big inspection tomorrow but I'm not standing it, thank goodness! Everyone else is busy getting ready."

11 October, Camp Lejeune:

"We got back about 0500 this morning. I'm so doggone sleepy I can hardly hold my head up. 'Sug' has already curled. We picked up Plant and Moran at the bus station so we made out on the gas deal. I drove from Guilford to Raleigh, Jerry to Kinston and 'Sug' to the base. Frank has been really kidding me about getting out early. He's singing 'Reenlistment Blues' to me."

I applied for an early release from active duty to return to Guilford College in time to enroll for the second semester in January. It was approved by HQMC.

16 November, Camp Lejeune:

"The troops landed Tuesday morning and are due in Friday evening. The Air Wing has really put on a show for us. They've zoomed over all day long. We can hear the firing down towards the beach. 'Sug' got back from Pennsylvania o. k. but was caught for speeding near Tarboro and it cost him $30.00. He said he enjoyed it but 12 hours driving each way was not fun."

8 December, Camp Lejeune:

"We had a rough time coming back but came through all right. It really poured rain. It sleeted here Monday and the weather is still cold. Most of the sleet has melted but there is ice everywhere. I went to the PX tonight and bought two pair of all wool socks ($2.50) for $1.75 a pair, also a tiepin and cuff links. I'm going to need some good civilian gear when I get out. I bought Mrs. Barnette a GE toaster. A nice one."

15 December, Camp Lejeune:

"We were paid today and 'Sug' is in a big poker game. So far he is about even. Last night I had to work getting the Christmas leave papers ready. We are about caught up on them. Now we've got to start on the New Years leave papers."

During this period the 2nd Service Battalion was reorganized as the 2nd Service Regiment, thus becoming much larger.

I did go home to Beavertown, Pennsylvania with McCardle. His father owned a bar and inn in the heart of the town. I enjoyed the trip and his family treated me great. It was the two 12 hour rides that I didn't enjoy.

4 January 1955, Camp Lejeune:

"Well, the first time and only time I've been over the hill was yesterday morning. I didn't get in until 0915 and was I pissed. Everything went wrong. I forgot my bag and had to go back to Guilford College and get it. Then I decided to come back down 421 rather than 70. Then I passed up short rides to Sanford, and ended up taking one there anyway. I stood there for 2 hours before catching one to Fayetteville. I nearly froze. Some clown picked me up and said he was going to Fayetteville and then let me out five miles from town. Anyway, I got to Jacksonville about 0800 and called MSgt. Bird. Then I had to wait an hour on a bus going to the base. The MPs boarded the bus at the main gate and wrote us up for being late. Bird had a frown on his face when I reported and he pretended to chew me out. Everyone in the office broke in to laughter, including he and I! He tore the MP report up when it came in. Mad! I reckon! I've never had such a twenty-four hours in my

life when everything went wrong. I only slept 12 hours last night, as I was so beat. I signed my release papers today. Only 14 more days!"

5 January, Camp Lejeune:

"I had a letter from Johnny Ebersole today. He is still in Korea and is the father of a four-month old daughter he has never seen. He was married two weeks before he got his orders overseas."

11 January, Camp Lejeune:

"We had a good trip back. 'Sug' stayed awake most of the way and we talked a lot. I've sold most of my clothes but I'm saving my emblems for you and Sue [Mrs. Barnette, who treated me like a son.] I saw in the Elkin Tribune that J. B. Gentry had been to Machine Gun School in Korea. He'll be coming home soon. J.B. is a Corporal now. I've spent the whole day checking out and goofing off. The first day since joining I've done so and it really feels strange. I had my chest x-ray and preliminary physical. Tomorrow, I get the rest of my physical and a dental check up. It's harder to get out than get in."

Among the clothing I sold was an 'Ike Jacket,' which the Marines had at that time. They were no longer being issued, but the orders read that they could still be worn on leave and liberty, and were extremely popular with the troops. I had purchased mine for $5.00 in 1953, wore it for almost two years, and sold it for the same amount in 1955. It may have been passed down for a few more years before they were disallowed. They were extremely comfortable compared to the heavy green blouses that we were issued.

On my last night at Camp Lejeune, all of the guys in the barracks went to the Enlisted Club, which I never frequented, and gave me a send off to civilian life. I believe I had two or three beers, more than I had ever drunk.

Chapter Four

Education and Training,
1955-1959
Guilford College, Summer Training, and OCS

The following morning, I said my good byes to the officers and Staff NCOs. In a way I hated leaving MSgt. Bird, as I considered him a father figure. He was what a man and a Marine should be. Someone took me to the bus station and I caught a bus to Greensboro. When I arrived there, I had not arranged for anyone to pick me up. I put my sea bag on my shoulder and my small suitcase in the other hand and hitchhiked to Guilford College. A rainstorm came up and I got soaked to the skin waiting to catch a ride. I made up my mind, then and there, that one of the first things I was going to buy was a car!

I found out from the students I knew where I had been assigned a room and met my roommates. They were a couple of nice guys from Eastern North Carolina. Vann Cuttrell, one of my new roomies, was a quarterback on the football team. Bill Wallace was my other roommate that semester. I spent most of the evening unpacking and getting some of my civilian clothes back from my friends from Elkin.

The next day, I enrolled to finish my freshman year in college and signed up for the G.I. Bill. It paid $110.00 a month. That would cover my tuition and books, but left me nothing to live on. I arranged with Mr. Hollowell, who owned a grocery store/diner, to work part time for him at lunchtime and evenings again, and he would furnish my meals. I also took some part time jobs after classes to give myself some spending money. With my mustering out pay and what I had saved in the Marine Corps, I was able to make ends meet.

I managed to make passing grades in all my classes that semester. I had no trouble getting back into the swing of college life.

I enrolled in summer school and took my required Math courses and a couple of electives, in the two sessions that were offered, plus I worked part time. Edna had gone back to Michigan for the summer, and helped her father build a new house.

Stanley Rose, a Marine veteran from Mt. Airy, was attending summer school, and we roomed together. He had graduated from Gardner-Webb Junior College and came to Guilford to get his Bachelor's degree. He served in Golf Company, 2nd Battalion, 5th Marines in Korea. After talking it over, we decided to join the Marine Reserve unit in Greensboro, as we both needed the extra money.

17 June 1955, Guilford College:

"Math is giving me a hard time, as I expected. Bob Allred [a former Army paratrooper] has been helping me but I haven't learned much. We're on geometric progressions now. The only test we are going to have is the final on June 28th. Pray for me!"

22 June, Guilford College:

"We had a special math class tonight at 1830 for those who haven't quite caught up. This meant me! Everyone is coming in from Ham's [a beer joint that also served food on the edge of Greensboro, and a popular hangout for Guilford students]. Allred is really drunk. He'll keep us up all night with his war stories!"

1 July, Guilford College:

"Just finished three hours of studying for tomorrows final. I reviewed all my homework and reworked some of the problems I missed. Today has been another hot one. I wanted to go to the lake but studied instead. Sure hope I pass after all of this effort. They are trying to get me to write for the Winston-Salem Journal and get that scholarship of $100.00. I was supposed to get it before, but never did. They want me to write for the Greensboro Record, too." [They wanted me to cover the Guilford football, basketball, and baseball games and call them in before their deadlines. I had done this my freshman year to earn a little extra money]

6 July, Guilford College:

"I passed Math with a C. This semester is mostly Trig and I'm really in the dark. It's too hot to study or concentrate on anything."

13 July, Guilford College:

"I've got a test in Educational Psychology tomorrow and one Friday and Saturday in Math. I've really got plenty to do. School isn't out until the 30th of July. I'm going to try and get a job here for the rest of the summer."

18 July, Guilford College:

"Today is really a scorcher. It was hot at 0730 when I got up. We're going to the lake after lunch. I went swimming yesterday evening and the water was almost hot. We're on Calculus now. I failed the Trig part but we're going to have review classes and take another test. Only 13 of 38 passed the first one."

20 July, Guilford College:

"*I have a test in Educational Psychology tomorrow and one in Calculus on Saturday. I understand Calculus better than I did Trig, so I should pass the test. Stanley Rose and I went down to the Marine Reserve last night and signed up. We get paid $4.00 a meeting every Wednesday night. During the school year, it's every other Sunday afternoon for 4 hours at $8.00. Not bad, huh!*" [They also told us we would be eligible for promotion to Sergeant in 6 months].

1 August, Guilford College:

"*I've finished my exams! Stanley Rose and I moved into Bill Atkins' [Army veteran from Mt. Airy, and a student at Guilford] house. We have the whole upstairs. I have a job at the Vick Chemical Co. here in Greensboro for the rest of the summer. I'm working from 1630 until 0100. Pay is $1.19 an hour. I'm an assistant mechanic. I have to have a car to get back and forth to work and Stanley and I are going to look for one in Greensboro tomorrow.*"

7 August, Guilford College:

"*I bought a 1946 Plymouth yesterday. It's light blue and in fairly good shape. It has new seat covers and upholstery on the sides. It cost me $240.00.*

8 August, Guilford College:

"*I started to work last night. It's not too bad. I watch a machine that puts cellophane on boxes of cough drops and adjust it and fix it when something messes up. The hours are bad but the pay is certainly good enough.*"

12 August, Guilford College:

"*I'm working at the Jefferson Standard Country Club on the weekends as I told you. I worked Friday from 1400 until 2300 and Saturday and Sunday from 1100 to 2300. The car seems to be o.k. I like it better every time I drive it. Stan went home to Mt. Airy. I think I told you he is getting married on September 3rd.*"

I continued working both jobs the rest of the summer until school started. I was able to pay off my car loan and was debt free when classes started.

One of my roommates that year was Jim Shelton from Winston-Salem. He had attended Davidson College before transferring to Guilford. He was a member of the Marine Corps Platoon Leaders Program and he joined our Reserve unit. Jim became a pilot and rose to the rank of Colonel in the Marine Corps. Both Stanley Rose and I made Sergeant in the Reserves during the winter.

My sophomore year went quickly and I passed all my courses, plus worked part time. During the second semester, Eldon Parks, one of my high school classmates from Elkin, and I bought out the school soda shop, which was located in an old WWII temporary building on campus. We were only open at lunch time and from 1900 to 2100 at night. We usually alternated nights, Monday through Friday, and were only open at lunch time on Saturdays. We didn't make much money, but it was a good business experience.

I again enrolled in summer school with the mission to get my foreign language courses out of the way. I took a part time job at the Sears Mail Order plant in Greensboro. Edna went home to Michigan for the summer.

5 June 1956, Guilford College:

"I started to work yesterday and it's not a bad job. We sort packages into mailbags. I was tired after lifting a couple hundred of those mailbags, though. Stanley Rose and I work together so we can talk, etc., while we work. Eldon graduated yesterday and he is really happy. His mother and father were down."

10 June, Guilford College:

"I've been very busy the last two days. I registered for summer school Wednesday morning, worked in the afternoon and attended Reserve meeting that night. Last night Ira [Nance] and I moved from one dorm to another. Ira made 5 trips in the afternoon and we made 6 apiece last night. We are very tired! There are about 150 here in summer school but only about 50 living on campus. I've already been assigned a term paper in PE 25. Back in the saddle again! Stanley is retaking the Math courses in summer school. We are both working hard at Sears. I like it o.k. I may work there next fall, too. They want me to."

11 June, Guilford College:

"We went to Ham's last night and had a few beers. Bill Beck was there. He's got 70 days to do before he gets out. He's going to get in our Reserve unit if he comes back to Guilford. He may get a scholarship to North Carolina to play football. Summer school is o.k. but hot and even dull at times. I'm going to be working until 2000 the next two weeks, taking the place of a guy who has gone to Reserve camp."

15 June, Guilford College:

"I had so much Spanish to translate I didn't have time to write you last night."

18 June, Guilford College:

"I just got back from the Dairy [diner]. I had to go out there and get something to eat, as Hollowell's was closed when I got off from work at 2020. I translated part of my Spanish homework before I went, but I got too hungry to study anymore. We really worked hard today. Monday is always the hardest anyway. We had so many packages that the boss and his assistant had to help us for two hours. Joe Ed [Satterfield, from Winston-Salem, a football player at Guilford, who later joined the Marine Reserves] was over here today but I missed him."

25 June, Guilford College:

"Corporal Nick Laney in our unit shot 242 out of a possible 250 to win the trophy for the individual high shooter among the Reserves at summer camp [Parris Island]. The Colonel who presented it to him said he would probably win the Reserve shooting title for the country, which is quite a feat. He's a real nice guy, too."

26 June, Guilford College:

"I just finished my Spanish translations for tomorrow. It took me exactly one hour and a half. I made $51.50 for my first two weeks at work but I spent or owed it all anyway."

28 June, Guilford College:

"I heard from Billy [my brother] today. He's working hard [9 ½ hours a day with the Virginia Highway Department survey crew], but likes it fine. I just finished translating a few pages of Spanish. Well, I tried anyway. I'll be glad when I get the foreign (and I do mean foreign) language out of the way. My check is due tomorrow [G.I. Bill $110 a month] and I get paid at Sears Thursday, but I owe it all."

2 July, Guilford College:

"I just got back from the Dairy. I had to go out there and eat since I didn't get off from work until almost 2000. I've still got 4 pages of Spanish to translate. I made a C on the last Spanish quiz."

4 July, Guilford College:

"Today has been the hottest day of the year here. We had a thunderstorm a while ago and it's cooled off now. The biggest tree on campus was knocked over on three cars and a power line a while ago. The lights went out all over the campus except here. They only went dim. I had a wisdom tooth pulled this afternoon and the juice has worn off and am I going to spend a miserable 4th! The dentist said the lower one was coming in toward the molar and both would have to come out. He said he might have to cut through the bone to get to it. He added that I could plan on being in bed for 3 or 4 days when he is ready to do the job. I'm going to wait until I get back from summer camp. We are having our final in Spanish on Thursday. Summer school will be halfway over!"

6 July, Guilford College:

"I went down to the Reserve unit today and drew some new uniforms for some of my old ones. It won't be long before I go to Parris Island again. Thrill! Thrill! Thrill! I've started on my term paper for Physical Education, 'Health Education in the Secondary Schools.' Much work to be done!"

8 July, Guilford College:

"This is one hell of a way to spend Saturday night—I've been working on my term paper for the last three hours and I'm only about halfway through."

10 July, Guilford College:

"I'm working on my Spanish for tomorrow. We are going to have a test Thursday. We have one coming up in PE about next Tuesday. Well, I'll have to close and get on the Espanola!"

11 July, Guilford College:

"I just finished studying for my Spanish test. It's 0100 now. I had to go to the Reserve meeting tonight. We are going to have a field problem this coming Sunday. I'm glad, now I will have something to do."

12 July, Guilford College:

"I just finished my term paper and am I glad. We are having a test in class next Tuesday, though. Today has been quite an uneventful one for me; class, eat, work, eat, *shower and shave, and term paper finished! I did fair on the Spanish test this morning. We are having another on Saturday and the Comprehensive on the 21st (Saturday a week)."*

15 July, Guilford College:

"We had a lot of fun on the field problem today. We practiced stream crossing, etc. We had a softball game. The meal was an 85 cent tray of barbecue, hot rolls, ice tea, milk, and apple pie. Very good! Stanley was there."

18 July, Guilford College:

"I got my check from the Reserves today—$53.00, so I made a car payment. I only owe $170.00 more. I'll be glad when I finally get it paid off. I get my G.I. Bill check Friday, but I owe all that to the school. My next one will be for the insurance on my car, $70.00, and another car payment." [I also had paid the dentist for pulling my wisdom teeth]

24 July, Guilford College:

"I didn't get a chance to write you last night as I didn't get off from work until 2000 and then I had to study until midnight for a Spanish test. I passed the Spanish Comprehensive test."

I finished up summer school on July 30th and passed all my courses. I had about a week break before I was off to summer camp with the Reserves. Because of summer school, I was unable to go to Parris Island with my unit in July so I was sent with a group of men in the same situation to train with another Reserve unit at Camp Lejeune.

6 August, 3rd Special Infantry Co., Reserve Training Regiment, Camp Lejeune:

"Well, I'm down at hot, humid Camp Lejeune again. We have been messing around doing nothing all day. We start firing the rifle range tomorrow. We joined an outfit from New London, Connecticut today. They are all screwed up. Stanley Rose and I are bunking together. He and I are having a lot of fun getting these 'boots' squared away. I went over to see Jerry Lane, but he had gone home for the weekend to see his wife. Only a handful of the old guys I knew were still there. Stanley and I took a couple of them to the base drive-in last night."

13 August, Camp Lejeune:

"Today has been a bitch. We have been out in the field all day in 100 degrees heat. We had about 20 of the Yankees fall out and 2 of our boys. Stanley and I are going to the 'slop-chute' just as soon as we finish cleaning our rifles. I fired 219 out of 250, which is the same as I fired at Parris Island in 1953, so I haven't lost my shooting eye. These Yankees are all right but our boys are showing them up. Their officers and Staff NCOs are always complimenting our men."

19 August, Guilford College:

"Well I finally got back from summer camp last night. I was neither sorry nor glad to leave as I had enjoyed it and wasn't looking forward to going back to work at Sears. We got to Greensboro about 2130 last night. They were having a back to school jamboree in the Sears Parking Lot across from the bus station and the streets were filled. The J.C.s were having a big convention at Guilford when we got there. I went down with one of the guys still around and drank all the free beer I wanted. Ira, Sonny Gainey, and I have moved into a couple of rooms near the college. It is fairly nice and only $15.00 a month. The people are real old and emigrants from Germany. I didn't get a chance to write you last week as we had two night problems and didn't get in until late. They really kept us busy. Stanley and I went to Carolina Beach Saturday night and spent the night down there. We had a fairly good time. We sure drank enough beer. I never did get to see Jerry [Lane]. I called him Thursday night but he had already gone home on a 96 -hour pass. I got my grades—2 B's and a C. How does that strike you!!"

20 August, Guilford College:

"I'm about ready to go back to Camp Lejeune after working today. I worked from 1300 until 2000 and it really wore me out. Stanley came in with a nice cold. I had one when I was down there. I forgot to sign up for my GI Bill when school was out so now I'll have to wait until I get that to pay my insurance on my car. However, it is due Thursday so I'm going to the bank tomorrow and try to borrow it. Ira is going to lend me enough to make my car payment. I really fouled up!"

22 August, Guilford College:

"I just got back from the Reserve meeting. There weren't too many there tonight. Vacation time, I guess. They had two letters from you to me."

23 August, Guilford College:

"I think I've finally gotten my insurance on my car settled. It cost me $70.00 but that's better than the $86.00 I paid last year. The old German couple we live with have been jabbering away all night. I wake up to them in the morning too. It's enough to drive one crazy. They read out of the Greensboro paper to each other in German and correct the one reading."

27 August, Guilford College:

"I worked from 0900 until 2000 today. I'm pooped! I'm going to spend the night at Bob Beck's tomorrow night. He's from Durham and works at Sears. [He was also a student at Guilford College.] He and his roommate live in an apartment in Greensboro and his roommate is gone for a week."

30 August, Guilford College:

"I've been working 9 hours a day and had a Reserve meeting last night. I had new plugs and points put in the car and the motor tuned up. It runs a lot better. I ordered new seat covers for the front seat. Beck has been cooking, etc., around here. He'll make a good wife someday if he keeps this up!"

4 September, Guilford College:

"I went to see my brother over the weekend. He is all ready for school. He was studying logarithms while I was there. We went up to VMI and looked around Saturday and watched the football practice. I went to Charlottesville Sunday and saw my parents. They are doing o.k. and both are working. I saw all the old gang I went around with. Benton Barr got married in June and his bride is expecting already. He got his wings from the Air Force and got married the next day. [He was later killed in a plane crash.] 'Skeeter' McCauley gave his girl a ring Saturday night. He and she were on clouds. He graduated from North Carolina State and has a scholarship to Duke University for physical therapy this fall. Abe Hawkins just got out of the Army and is going to William & Mary. Monday we went up and watched the University of Virginia practice. They looked big in the line but their backs didn't show too much. I got back about 2430 last night. Worked hard today and am I pooped!"

5 September, Guilford College:

"I just got back from drill. I had to teach a class on military courtesy and discipline. I did o.k., I guess. They issued us the new gabardines tonight. Nice! They look a lot better in the summer than the khakis."

7 September, Guilford College:

"I spent the night at Beck's last night. We stayed up and listened to 'Tubby' Thompson, his roommate, tell us about his 'experiences' at Eastern Carolina College."

8 September, Guilford College:

"The football players have started coming in at Guilford. Most of them will be here by tomorrow as they're going to issue equipment then. Ira will have his hands full. He's going to be the equipment manager this year."

10 September, Guilford College:

"Yesterday I went over to the gym to help Ira give out the equipment to the football team. From what I saw we should have a much better team. We've got some big ones, for a change. One just got out of the Marines and weighs 240. Bobby Holloway [Elkin High School and just out of the Navy] is down and is going out for the team."

Edna returned to the Woman's College for her senior year while I started my junior year at Guilford. Bill Barnette, just out of the Army, and I decided to live off campus that year. We found a place between the college and Greensboro with a very nice older couple. I continued to work part time at the Sears Mail Order plant.

When the Marine Officer Procurement Officer, Major Redmond, visited Guilford that year, I signed up for the Platoon Leaders Program, leading to a commission after graduation.

That spring, I decided to try out for the baseball team. The first day of practice we exercised, and then Coach Stewart Maynard seated us on the benches to talk to us. It was a cold, windy March day and he got long-winded. I was freezing by the time he got through. The first event for the pitchers was fielding bunts off the mound. The field was used for all sports and was full of holes and divots. When my turn came to field a bunt, I ran off the mound to my right and bent down to catch the ball, stepped in a hole and twisted my knee. It popped and I fell to the ground in pain. I could not straighten my knee or stand on that leg. They carried me to the dressing room and then to the local doctor who looked after Guilford students. The doctor x-rayed me and said I had chipped the bone in my knee and had to have an operation on it. He referred me to an orthopedic surgeon at Duke University. I hobbled around on crutches until I could get an appointment with the surgeon. He scheduled my surgery for my spring break.

Edna drove me down that day and returned 3 days later to pick me up. 'Skeeter' McCauley, my friend from Charlottesville, now a student at Duke, had surgery on both his knees the same day.

Bob Beck let me stay in his apartment near the Woman's College campus so that Edna could check on me. He and his roommates were gone on spring break. I was bed ridden for several more days. By the time spring break was over, I was back on campus on crutches.

In the meantime, I had traded my old Plymouth in for a 1950 Dodge sedan. It was a box of a car, but it proved to be a very reliable one.

I worked diligently to get my knee in shape and was walking and jogging by the time school was out. I received orders to Quantico for 12 weeks training, so I didn't enroll in summer school that year.

20 June 1957, Foxtrot Company, 2nd Training Battalion, Marine Corps Schools, Quantico, Virginia:

"Well, it is about like Parris Island all over again except it is hot as hell here and it was cold there. There are 1,300 PLCs [Platoon Leaders Class] here for just the Junior Course. There is 7-800 here for the Senior Course, plus a large group from the Naval Academy. The Marine Corps messed me up again. I ended up catching a bus up here. [I was supposed to go by train]. I still haven't gotten my baggage. I had to borrow everything—even a toothbrush! I came up from Richmond with Milton Barbour from Lexington, N.C. He is a senior at the University of North Carolina. John Daley's son, John Daley, Jr. is here from Yale. We have guys here from all over the U.S."

22 June, Camp Barrett, Quantico:

"It has really been hot up here but I'm getting use to it. I failed my physical because of the operation on my knee. The regulations say you can't have had an operation on a joint within 6 months. Mine was 4 months ago. I have a wavier in to the Battalion Commander for the 2-month period. If he doesn't pass on it then I'm going to the Commandant, Sec. of the Navy, or the President if I have to. I hope to know more Monday or Tuesday. My Platoon Sergeant said he recommended me and thought I had a good chance of getting the wavier. We got off at noon today. I had to get some nametags sewn on and Mary [my Aunt] and Barbara [my cousin] did it for me. I was supposed to be back at 2200 tonight but I don't think they will check so I'm staying over in Washington until tomorrow

evening. We are going on a picnic tomorrow. We have 2 married men in our platoon and they say they will not miss their wives. They are both here until September 7th, too." [I was going to complete the Senior Course after the Junior Course in one summer, rather than the two separately.]

24 June, Camp Barrett, Quantico:

"I still haven't heard any word on my wavier and probably won't until the last of the week. They won't let me do any of the real physical work until I hear from higher up. I was the Candidate Platoon Sergeant, the highest rank for any candidate, for all of last week. We had an inspection Saturday morning and our platoon was the best and we are first in the chow line this week. Our Company placed first too. I have a nice cold, as does everyone here, from the change in climate. King Dixon, who plays first-string halfback at the University of South Carolina, is in our platoon. He's a real nice guy and knows 'Rip' Lane. There are two guys from University of North Carolina, one from Western Carolina and one from Pfeiffer."

25 June, Camp Barrett, Quantico:

"The movie 'D.I.' starts in Washington tomorrow and we are required to see it this weekend. We just got a new guy in our platoon. He's 6' 5 ½" and weights 215 pounds. He's a football player from the University of Minnesota. We sat outdoors for a lecture today and it rained on us for the second straight day. I still have my nice cold from this change in climate."

My appeal for a wavier was disapproved, but the Battalion Commander assured me I would be accepted in the next Officer Candidate Class after I graduated. With that assurance I chose not to appeal higher and returned home. I returned to Greensboro in time to go to summer camp with my Reserve unit.

21 July, Marine Barracks, Philadelphia:

"Stan and I went to hear Stan Donahoe on the 'Steel Pier,' last night. We are only one block away. We also went to Atlantic Beach, which is very nice."

22 July, Marine Barracks, Philadelphia:

"Well, we're here and it's as hot a hell.100 degrees with no relief in sight. The train ride was o.k. but I was unable to sleep. I dozed once all night long. The train caught fire between the cars and that got everyone up and raising hell. We saw the Phillies-Reds

double header yesterday. Burned up but they were fairly well played games. We took a tour of the base today. There are only 200 Marines stationed here, all the rest are Navy. Ships are docked only a few hundred yards from the barracks. They even have battleships, carriers and submarines here. We have brig guard Thursday and base guard Friday. We fire the pistol range tomorrow morning."

25 July, Marine Barracks, Philadelphia:

"Philadelphia is a big disappointment. Dirty and stinking. We went on a moonlight cruise the other night. It was all servicemen and USO girls. I've been holding down an office job the whole time because MSgt. Gross [the senior regular enlisted man on the Instructor and Inspection staff in Greensboro] thinks there is something the matter with it [administration]. I spent all day at different Marine activities getting our payroll in order. I met a Tech Sergeant I knew at Camp Lejeune and he asked about MSgt. Bird. He has been stationed here 3 years. The training here has been good as well as interesting. We are guarding the brig as well as the gates. They have 10,000 civilian employees coming and going everyday. The chow has been excellent. I'll draw $30.00 pay tomorrow and $50.00 next week, so I should save some."

29 July, Marine Barracks, Philadelphia:

"We have been practicing the new Marine Corps drill today. Stanley [Rose] and I are going to Atlantic Beach tonight or tomorrow morning."

31 July, Marine Barracks, Philadelphia:

"Stan and I had a good time at the beach [Atlantic City], but boy it cost us! We were glad to get back. We had an inspection this morning and guard duty at the brig after that. I was warden. Big deal! We are going out in the field for an overnight problem tomorrow. We'll be back Wednesday afternoon or night."

Our company fired the rifle range the last two days of training and we took another train ride back to Greensboro. I continued to work part time at the Sears Mail Order Plant during the next year.

Edna was back in college, finishing up her senior year. I enrolled for my junior year at Guilford College. Bill Barnette and I continued to live off campus. I stayed busy studying and dating Edna on the weekends. Our Reserve training was changed to just one full weekend a month, for which we continued to receive 4 days pay.

I decided to give baseball another try that spring and made the team. I made my first start against Yale, which was making a southern tour. I didn't pitch that badly but had a couple of errors behind me and we lost. I enjoyed playing baseball again, but my chronic sore arm never allowed me to throw freely.

The Quaker, 1956 Guilford College Baseball Team
Bob Driver, back row far left

Edna graduated from the Women's College with a degree in Mathematics and took a job as a computer programmer with Western Electric in Winston-Salem. We went to Flint, Michigan and were married on 7 September 1957. During our honeymoon, we visited the Gettysburg National Military Park. It was foggy on the day we were there so we spent it driving around looking at the monuments.

We visited my parents and other relatives in Virginia before returning to Greensboro. We found a furnished apartment near Guilford College within easy commuting distance to her work in Winston-Salem and I entered my senior year at Guilford.

By the end of my junior year, I had been promoted to Staff Sergeant. I decided that instead of going to summer camp I wanted to receive some Marine Corps schooling that would enhance my efforts to attend Officer Candidate School. I chose Drill Instructor's School at Parris Island. Big mistake! I chose it because it was 5 weeks long and the SNCO Infantry Training School at Camp Lejeune was only 4!

I reported to Parris Island in the dog days of July when they flew flags because it was too hot for the recruits to train. Our starched uniforms and the shoe polish off of our dress shoes melted in the heat. We wore the old sun helmets you only see in the movies. My face peeled many, many times, despite the sunscreen provided by the Navy corpsmen. We changed uniforms 2 or 3 times a day. When we drilled in the afternoons, the red flag would be waving, meaning it was 95 degrees or higher, but we drilled anyway. The asphalt melted under our feet and stuck to the bottom of our shoes. Platoons of recruits lay in the shade across the drill field watching us.

The training would have been fine except for General Randolph McCall Pate's 13 Man Squad Drill. Pate had seen the British execute it and thought it would be great for our Marine Corps. When he became Commandant, he had the Marine Corps adopt the drill. Who in the Corps has ever seen a 13-man squad fall out for drill! Someone was always absent for some reason, if 13 men were actually assigned to a squad. In the Fleet Marine Force, you were lucky to turn out 10 men! The drill required 13 men to take different steps and half steps in a turning movement. Each man had to know how many steps and half steps to take in his position. When a man was absent someone else had to close ranks and fill in his position. Few could do it correctly. It became a nightmare! The D.I. School instructors were the best of the best, and they didn't say one word against the drill, but every student sure did! It drove us crazy trying to memorize the different steps each of the 13 men had to take to complete a turn and then teach it to recruits! Needless to say, I was glad to graduate and return to civilian life. I will never forget MSgt. T.B. Wiggins, the Chief Drill Instructor, and his classroom 'Ya hear! Ya know! Ya got that!' in his Georgia accent, as he stressed a point to you. The first thing the new Commandant did when Pate stepped down was to abolish the 13-man drill!

Driver at Drill Instructor School, July 1958

Drill Instructor School, MCRD Parris Island, July 25, 1958

I kept applying for Officer's Candidate School, but the Marines were cutting back on their officer strength and were relying heavily on the Naval Academy, NROTC students, and the PLC Program for officers.

Robert J. Driver
Guilford College Graduation

With graduation approaching, I started interviewing for a job. I went to work for Lee Manufacturing Company in Greensboro as a management trainee. I really didn't see any future in working for them, so when the chance came I quit and went to work for the North Carolina State Employment Service as an interviewer. Stanley Rose had gone to work there and liked it. The job was fine, but I did not relish the thought of sitting behind a desk as a career. I kept applying for OCS, and Major Redmond would call and tell me the class was cancelled or it was for aviators only. Finally, in the summer of 1959, I was accepted for the class in September.

Summer camp with the Reserves that year consisted of amphibious warfare training at the Naval Base in Little Creek, Virginia.

26 July, Little Creek, Virginia:

"We got here about 1530. We got everything squared away by 2000 and went to the [Virginia] beach. It's about like Myrtle Beach except it is more expensive."

28 July, Little Creek, Virginia:

"This old boy is plenty pooped. We had dry net training today. Twice down and once up the nets. Then we crossed barbed wire obstacles 3 times. This afternoon we went aboard ship and made 2 landings on one of the beaches. It is really hot here but only 2 men fell out. A company from Buffalo, New York had 11 men fall out. It poured rain tonight so it is a little cooler. We are going to make more landings tomorrow and Wednesday."

3 August, Little Creek, Virginia:

"Stanley Rose and I went to the beach for a while today, not much to do as it was storming. We had our parade yesterday and everyone said we looked real sharp. It was in the 90's and the field was soaked with dew so we ruined a uniform and our dress shoes. I had to wear the shoes on liberty anyway. Stanley Rose, [SSgt. Willie] Nesbit, and I went to the beach yesterday, drank a few beers and messed around. Dick Parker [a Guilford College student from New Jersey who had joined the Marine Corps Reserve] saw Bill Gilliam and his wife from Guilford. He teaches school here. We have really had some good training here. We went out in rubber boats Friday and that was a lot of fun. They have really kept us busy. We're up at 0430 and finish up about 1630 in the afternoon. By the time we clean our rifles and equipment and eat chow, it is time for lights out."

4 August, Little Creek, Virginia:

"We are going to be out until midnight tomorrow so this will be my last letter. We're going to make a night landing from rubber boats so it should be fun. We're going to make an assault from helicopters in the morning. We went out in the water and made a landing from amphibious tractors this morning. We are going to leave here Saturday morning at 0800 and should get back to Greensboro by 1300 or 1400."

I was in fairly good shape for Quantico when I returned from summer camp, but I continued doing physical training and running each day after work and on the weekends. I wanted to be in top physical condition when I reported for OCS. I reported to the 25th Officer Candidate Course, Quantico, Virginia on 14 September 1959 and was assigned to 3rd Platoon, A Company, Training and Testing Regiment.

15 September, OCS, Quantico:

"I arrived safe and sound. I can sure tell I'm back in the Corps! I've already gotten my hair cut (head shaved) and we take our physicals tomorrow. We are down beyond the Air Station in the brick barracks on the Air Station side of the railroad tracks."

16 September, OCS, Quantico:

"I don't have much time to write, as this is boot camp all over again. We took our physicals today. My eyesight is 20/30 in one eye and 20/40 in the other. Guess I'll be wearing glasses soon. The weather is cold here at night and in the morning—and I didn't bring any of my sweaters! We'll draw uniforms tomorrow, thank goodness! There are three other ex-enlisted Marines here [in my platoon] but only one is married. Only seven out of 46 in my platoon are married. I like my instructors so far."

19 September, OCS, Quantico:

"Well, the first week is over and I'm glad to see it pass. We have area liberty tonight. We have a club with TV, beer and all but I am not in the mood. You have to wear civilian clothes, too. I've been working all afternoon trying to square all my gear away—washed 2 belts, cartridge belt, web sling, packs and several other pieces. Shined my boots three times each since they are new [The Marine Corps was still issuing raw hide boots, but required you to shine them]. I dyed my dress shoes 3 times as they are new [the Marine Corps was still issuing brown shoes and required them to be dyed black]. I starched and ironed 2 sets of utilities and 2 caps and feel like I've just warmed up. The pressure is on the individual here to keep squared away. Last night after chow we had a field day for 2 ½ hours, and then I had to shine boots, clean my rifle and web gear, shower, etc. in less than an hour. They made us go to bed so we shined shoes by moonlight and cleaned our rifles and bayonets also. I got back up at 0430 and took a shower and shaved. Reveille went at 0530. We had to clean the barracks, eat chow, make our bunk, dress, etc. and fall out at 0645—plus roll call. Enough of this! I'm tired but I think I can make it o. k."

21 September, OCS, Quantico:

"Writing in a rush as usual. I've got to have my knee x-rayed Wednesday. I think it is o k., though. We started our rough physical work today. They start giving out 'chits' [evaluations] tomorrow so we are on the run. I'm fairly squared away. We are sweeping, swabbing and dusting, etc. before lights out. I've been getting up half an hour before reveille and shaving, etc. I'm going to keep doing so, too. My electric razor comes in handy. I spent yesterday trying to get myself in shape or rather my gear. I'm keeping most of my gear in the car and suitcase and get it out as I need it."

23 September, OCS, Quantico:

"I'm writing during field day so I must hurry. I have duty Saturday until 1700. I have Candidate Company First Sergeant, which is the top billet, and I can't get out of it. We have an inspection, too. I'll make reservations at the Hostess House. You can catch a cab from the train station to it." [My wife was attending training at the Western Electric Labs in Summit, N.J. and came back and forth on the weekends].

28 September, OCS, Quantico:

"We made a 5 mile hike yesterday. I made it o.k. but the heat was terrible. One man fell out with heat stroke. We started getting chits yesterday. I've been getting them but I had fewer discrepancies than most. The football game is at 1000 Saturday morning."

Testing and Training (T&T) Regiment had a football team that competed with the other organizations on the base. The 1st Platoon in our company was our 'football platoon,' as most of its members played on the team. Our attendance was mandatory and we marched to and from the stadium in uniform.

5 October, OCS, Quantico:

"We just finished another fine hot day. We had bayonet fighting, ran the obstacle course and 4 laps so I am kind of tired. I got back fairly early yesterday and cleaned all my gear and shined my boots, but no inspection. We have another hike tomorrow and it will probably be hot again."

6 October, OCS, Quantico:

"We just got in after another nice hike. I'm really pooped! It was in the 90's again today. We beat B Company back by 14 minutes, by running, and they had 13 men fall out and we didn't lose a man. I've got Corporal of the Guard Thursday night and Squad Leader Thursday also, so I shouldn't have any duty on the weekend. We have a test Thursday on Marine Corps History. I should do well on it."

12 October, OCS, Quantico:

"The hike today wasn't too bad. No one fell out of our platoon and they put us in the lead coming back and we had a lot of spirit all the way. The Major seemed to enjoy us. I heard from Bill [my brother] and he wants to come into the Marines. I talked with an officer here about it (a VMI graduate) and he gave me some information to send him. [Bill failed the eye exam and spent 2 years in the Army Engineering Corps at Ft. Benning, Ga.] We had to wear greens to chow tonight so [Ralph] McLean [a graduate of Yale], [Charlie] Kellenbarger, Wolf and Grace and myself went into town to eat. We also put in and picked up our laundry. We had a nice time, telling jokes, etc. We fall out at 0715 in the morning, so everyone is busy squaring away."

13 October, OCS, Quantico:

"Another day gone. We ran the Reaction Course this morning. Teams of ten men were given a problem and 15 minutes to do them. My team completed 3 of 4, which was the best of all. We had a good group of men. We drilled and had classes on creeping and crawling and then did it. Our utilities really looked good when we were through! I found out yesterday I was the only man in the company to make 100 on the Marine Corps History test. Outstanding! I've got to study for the test Thursday on weapons. I hope to keep up my average—95.5. It is probably the best in the class."

14 October, OCS, Quantico:

"We had an easy day today due to the rain. I studied for tomorrow's test and saw a film on the BAR. It has turned cold here, too. I had Tousignant [a graduate of the University of North Carolina and fellow married Officer Candidate] check on an apartment where we looked Sunday. He's been living out there since August 20, and likes it o.k. He has a furnished apartment for $87.50 a month but pays electric, gas, and heating bills. He says the furniture is fairly nice. They have plenty of closet space and a real nice kitchen."

15 October, OCS, Quantico:

"I'm down at the OC Club having a cool beer. Not a very good place to write letters but if I had stayed in the squad bay I'd be pushing a mop or broom. We ran 2 ½ miles today and I was kind of beat. After chow I got a haircut and had my officer uniforms fitted. That sounds good, doesn't it? I didn't do too well on the test today. I think I made an 82, which pulled my average down to 91. That is still almost the highest in the class. Charlie Kellenbarger came down here with me. He's married and from Iowa. He went to a small college in Missouri. It has been real cold here the last few days. It seems winter is here to stay. We have another hike Monday and a night problem that night, so I'll be beat the rest of the week. We have three more hikes next week also."

17 October, OCS, Quantico:

"Another week almost gone. Next week will separate the men from the boys. The first cut is next week. We've got a field day in a few minutes and an inspection in greens tomorrow. I need you here, as we're starting classes on map reading with formulas and coordinates."

20 October, OCS, Quantico:

"Well, we have really been at it the last 2 days. Had an 8-mile 'run' last night. Got back about midnight. Made a 10-mile 'run' this afternoon in 1½ hours. I had to carry a damn BAR (16 lbs.), and it really beat me to death. We didn't stop the whole time. I was the first man carrying a BAR to finish. The D.I.s couldn't believe it! I went down to the Hostess House and made reservations for this weekend. I ate a good steak, got my laundry done, and came right back. I'm so beat this letter probably won't make sense."

26 October, OCS, Quantico:

"I went on the first of our little 'bird walks' [long hikes] for the week. Wasn't too bad as the weather was cool. I won't get to write you again before Saturday with the training schedule we are on. I've got guard duty from 0400 until reveille in the morning. We have a three- hour hike scheduled. I'll be worn out tomorrow night!

2 November, OCS, Quantico:

"I made it back at 2100 tonight. [I had gone to Greensboro for the weekend] I studied some more coming back. I've already shined my boots and gotten my uniform ready for tomorrow."

3 November, OCS, Quantico:

"Another day gone and am I glad! I failed the Map Reading Test. 50% of the class did, so they may curve it. Sure hope so! That ruins my 90-point average. We had our usual nice little 'bird walk' today and will have one tomorrow and Wednesday. We will have nothing more in the field after that. We have a clothing inspection Saturday."

4 November, OCS, Quantico:

"Another day gone and am I glad! We spent the day in the field and will do the same tomorrow. I've got to carry a BAR, too. I didn't feel bad today when we were told 50% of all the Candidates failed the Map Reading Test. 24 of 39 in our platoon failed. They're going to curve it so I'll pass all right. We have another General Subjects test next week. I went into town tonight to do laundry and eat. Got back about 2100 and cleaned my rifle, etc. It is after 2200 now."

5 November, OCS, Quantico:

"Another nice hike today and day in the field. I carried the BAR again today. We are already getting squared away for Saturday's inspection. I washed and dried my web gear tonight and sewed nametags on my socks and gloves. The new Commandant of Marine Corps Schools, Quantico, is going to inspect us tomorrow. General [Edward W.] Snedeker is his name. We are going to have a field day in the morning and put on a demonstration for him. On Friday, a big newspaperman from New York is going to be here. We will put on a demonstration for him, also. On Monday, the Commandant of the British Marine Corps will be here—we'll do the same for him."

7 November, OCS, Quantico:

"We finally got this week over with! I could sleep for a week! I've had 15 hours sleep in 4 days. The trip to Marine Barracks, 8th & I, was well worth it. The troops up there are the sharpest I have ever seen. We got back about 2130, ate chow, had a field day of our squad bay, worked on our gear until 0100, up again at 0430 and worked on our gear. The inspection was a flop. It rained so we laid out our gear on our racks, which are too small for all of it, so we got chewed out for not having it squared away. We are getting ready to go to see the Quantico football game. Next week shouldn't be too bad although we will be out in the field 4 days. We have only one night problem, though. We have a clothing inspection next Saturday. We get off a half-day on November 10th [Marine Corps Birthday] and all day the 11th off. The hikes are getting longer and the pack in getting bigger!"

8 November, OCS, Quantico:

"I didn't get to finish the letter Saturday before the ball game. Quantico won 15-3. It was a thriller. Bill [my brother] didn't get here until the third quarter, as he took the bus. He looks good and is making better grades than last year. He made a 10.00 on thermodynamics. We went into Quantico and ate supper, and I got my laundry done. Kellenbarger went with us. We drove out to the Basic School and saw Danny Carr [a Guilford graduate who had completed the PLC Program and was commissioned a 2nd Lt. He was also in the Greensboro Reserve unit] and a boy Bill knew from VMI. I've got to quit and study as we have another Map Reading test tomorrow. We had our General Subjects test Thursday and I made a 92 on it."

9 November, OCS, Quantico:

"I've made up my pack for tomorrow's hike, polished my boots, got all my gear squared away, and pressed a uniform for tomorrow. I have still got to clean my rifle and bayonet. The fudge you brought is really good. You got quite a few compliments on it."

10 November, OCS, Quantico:

"We had a ceremony with the cake cutting, etc. and then went to the chow hall and had T-bone steaks and all the trimmings. I came back to the barracks and read a little and then slept until 1700. We had free beer and chow at the OC Club tonight. They were really going strong when I left. I'm going to study all day tomorrow for Friday's test. Sunday I am going to do the same for Tuesday's test on Drill & Ceremonies. Then I will have to study Tuesday and Thursday nights for Friday's test. We are already calling next week 'Hell Week.' We have two tests, two night problems and a long hike—plus the usual training. I have guard duty from 2400 until 0200 the night before the last test, but I'm going to trade with a guy who has it this Sunday morning. His wife is coming down and he wants to stay with her."

11 November, OCS, Quantico:

"The hike wasn't too bad today, although it was 11 miles. It took up the whole morning, so that helped. We learned how to load pack animals all afternoon so that was easy. They brought the horses over from the base stables. Kellenbarger, McLean, [Dick] Hoehn [Dartmouth graduate] and I went into town tonight and ate chow and had a couple of beers. We got back just in time for a cleanup detail. Your fudge is still going strong. I'm trying to ration it out for the rest of the week."

13 November, OCS, Quantico:

"I spent the day resting and studying. I didn't get up until 0800. I ate 3 eggs, 3 pieces of French toast, 2 pieces of toast cover with hash ['Shit on a Shingle' in Marine Corps parlance], cake, milk, and juice. I came back and studied until 1500, took a shower and went to chow again. I went into town tonight to get my washing done, then came back and cleaned my rifle, etc. We have a night problem tomorrow so I won't get a chance to write. Friday night I'll be getting ready for Saturday's inspection. Another football game here this weekend so we won't get liberty until late. Guess I'll do my laundry, eat supper, take in a movie, and retire early. I'll be studying all day Sunday for Tuesday's test on Drill. I'll review that Monday night. On Tuesday, we will be out all night and come in Wednesday morning, another long hike. I plan to study Wednesday night for Friday's test, as we are out in the field Thursday night also. On Friday night, we'll be preparing for Saturday's inspection. After the inspection, I will see you again and this ordeal will be almost over. On Monday before Thanksgiving, we have a Physical Evaluation Test, Tuesday a Comprehensive Exam and then have a 17 mile hike and a night problem and come in Wednesday at noon. After that it is all over but the shouting!"

16 November, OCS, Quantico:

"Just finished our inspection and we were 'excellent' in the words of the Colonel. We're sure glad it is over with. We're getting ready to fall out for drill. It's raining here but we're going to the football game anyway. It doesn't rain in the Marine Corps! Should be a nice mess. Ft. Campbell is undefeated, too."

17 November, OCS, Quantico:

"Quantico won 29-7 yesterday. It was a real good game. King Dixon played well, as usual. Ft. Campbell was undefeated and had only given up 14 yards rushing in 7 games. Quantico had 224 yards in the 1st half. I spent another lazy day studying and squaring away. Our Drill test covers drill, ceremonies, interior guard, etc. There are 65 questions. I made 86 on the General Subjects exam. We had to get up at 0700 this morning. Our dear Sergeant Instructor had the duty and he's bucking for OCS."

18 November, OCS, Quantico:

"Real good news—we have our inspection Friday afternoon and we get liberty afterwards! Other good news—I checked on my pay and they have been paying me as a PFC instead of as SSgt. I'll have quite a bundle coming Friday!" [SSgt. Marler, the senior D.I., drove me to disbursing that Friday and he was really upset when he found out I was making more money than he was!]"

19 November, OCS, Quantico:

"Well I passed another one! I made 94 on the Drill test. I only have one more to go. We had a 'Dog & Pony Show' for some visitors from Headquarters, Marine Corps, today. We ran 5 miles—20 laps around the drill field in formation. Both my legs were knotted up when we finished. Other platoons drilled, ran the obstacle course, etc. It really turned cold here today. It was raining this morning. Then it got real windy and cold. Tomorrow night we spend in the field in foxholes. We'll freeze our you-know-what's off! We come in at 0600 Thursday morning. I saw [SSgt. Willard] Poss today. He was drilling the Regimental Drill Team. He said he had heard I was doing real well and knew I would make it. [Poss, a Georgian, had served in the 2nd Service Regiment at Camp Lejeune with me. When he made Corporal, he volunteered for Drill Instructor's School at Parris Island. I last saw him there when I went though D.I. School, when I drilled his platoon!] Kellenbarger and I are down at the base library studying? We came down and had a steak for supper."

29 November, OCS, Quantico:

"It was a long ride back [from Greensboro] but I made it before dark. I haven't cleaned my rifle yet. They are going to keep us busy the rest of the week but it suits me as the time goes faster. It isn't long until Thursday!"

30 November, OCS, Quantico:

"Another day gone and we are closer to graduation! I took the Map Reading test tonight and passed it! We started turning in our gear today. We practiced our parade 2 hours, ran the obstacle course and had drill—easy day. Bring me two silver dollars when you come. We have to give them to the sergeants when they give us our first salutes after we graduate."

We graduated as scheduled and Edna pinned my Second Lieutenant bars on me. We shook hands with everyone in our platoon, as some of them were going to Flight School at Pensacola, Florida and not to the Basic School at Camp Barrett. We were bussed out the Basic School and reported in. I was assigned to the 3rd Platoon, Company B, The Basic School, Marine Corps Schools, Quantico, Va.

OCS, December 5, 1959

8 December, Basic School:

"Well, I'm getting ready to spend my first night at the 'Conrad-Hilton' as they call it. It is really nice, though. We didn't do much this morning. We had 2 lectures and bought our swords. I had to pay $18.00 down (1/3). I like my Staff Platoon Commander, Captain [L.N.] Angelo—talks like Boston. We had liberty from 1130. I went out to Melrose Gardens and talked to the manager. He said he would have our apartment cleaned up and painted.

I opened a bank account ($20) and wrote a check for $15 to VEPCO to get the electricity turned on. I don't know what we are going to do for money. I've got to finish paying for my sword and buy the belt, etc. for it. I have to order whites, dress blues, gabardines, and a topcoat, plus white shoes, white cover, etc. It's a total of $650, so we are told. Also, we may have to buy another green blouse. Brother! We have got to pay the rest of our rent on the apartment, plus next month's. Car insurance is due also and I've got to have it by the 7th as that is when it runs out, and my decal, too. We'll have to economize!"

9 December, Basic School:

"We are getting ready for an inspection of the barracks tomorrow morning. I went into town tonight and washed clothes. It was real cold out. I was glad to get back to the barracks although we don't have any heat in our room. We drew textbooks today— about 30 of them. I put them in the car, as I'll be keeping them at home. We drew all of our other gear except rifles. Tomorrow we have photos made. I filled out the form for your dependents ID card—however, you won't get it until you can come out here and have your picture made, etc. I'll draw $401.00 a month ($200 on the 15th & $201 on the 30th) clear each month after taxes and Social Security. The honeymoon is over here—we start training tomorrow and it will be mostly physical. Boot camp over again! I saw Danny Carr today. He looks real good but is tired of this place. His class finishes in April. I've been trying to get my gear squared away so I won't have so much to do when we come back after the first of the year."

14 December, Basic School:

"I called about the apartment today; they promised again that it would be cleaned up. I'm going out one evening and check. I've gotten a wall locker in the married men's locker room and am in the process of moving my gear down there. I'm tired of these inspections! All we did today was drill for an hour and an hour of physical training. We are supposed to have a hike and run the obstacle course sometime this week."

15 December, Basic School:

"Pay Day! I drew $280. I put $80 in the checking account. We had the same schedule as yesterday. Passed room inspection in the morning. We had a class at 1500 and then liberty. I'm going into town and get my name tag sewn on my field jacket and buy some map reading gear. I'm planning on going to the basketball games tonight. Atlantic Christian plays Catholic University at 1830 and Quantico plays Mt. Saint Mary's at 2000. Should be a couple of good games. Quantico is undefeated."

Edna left her job at Western Electric and moved to Quantico to be with me. I didn't have any leave on the books and we were supposed to stay in the area until classes resumed in January. Unofficially, we were told we could leave the area as long as we didn't get caught! Edna and I took the train to Detroit, Michigan to visit her parents.

The training at the Basic School was excellent and prepared us well to be platoon commanders. Most of the training was infantry orientated, as the Marine Corps stuck with its tradition of 'everyman is a rifleman.'

The married officers car-pooled from Melrose Gardens each day. This helped cut down on our gas expenses.

We snapped in for the rifle range in the worst weather imaginable. The ground was covered with a sheet of ice and snow and the wind made it seem like the arctic. We wore as many layers of clothing as possible, but we didn't get much out of it. The week we fired the rifle range was milder and the snow and ice was gone. We had rain and some gale force winds, but I managed to fire expert with both the rifle and pistol. Our staff platoon commanders were senior captains. Some we learned to respect, and others we disliked. Captains Angelo and Snell were tough on us but also easy to talk to, so they were the two favorites. We graduated from the Basic School in July 1960 and I finished in the top 1/3 of my class.

Basic School, Quantico
L-R: Driver & Richard Huckaby
June 1960

The class before us advised the married officers who wanted to go to the 1st Marine Brigade in Hawaii to put 'Hawaii will extend' on the forms we filled out for preference of duty station. We were all Reserve officers at that time with three years obligated service, so by extending, we would serve 3 full years in Hawaii. I applied for a regular commission and received it in Hawaii.

Chapter Five

Hawaii,
1960-1963
Platoon Commander, Executive Officer and Commanding Officer, Company C, 1st Battalion, 4th Marines

Edna was pregnant with our first child, but we decided to drive across country and see the sights as we went. I traded in my old Plymouth for a new Volkswagen 'bug,' as we didn't think the Plymouth would make it that many miles. We were told gas was expensive in Hawaii, and the 'bug' was very economical on it.

We visited with my relatives in Virginia, and I gave my aunt, Elizabeth Wade, my old Dodge sedan. She had always been good to my brother and I, and he had lived with her and her husband, H.B. 'Bud' Wade, while in high school.

We visited Edna's parents in Michigan before heading to California. We took a scenic tour across the western states, stopping at Yellow Stone National Park among others, before reaching California. When we arrived in San Francisco, I had to turn my car in 5 days before we sailed to Hawaii to insure it would go on the ship we were going aboard. During our stay in San Francisco, we stayed in the Marine hotel there. Having shipped our winter clothing to Hawaii, we nearly froze in the 60-degree temperatures of the port city. We still managed to see most of the sights in San Francisco.

When we boarded the U.S.S. *General Mitchell*, we found several other Marine couples headed to Honolulu also. Don and Rickey Brooks were en-route to the Marine Corps Air Station at Kanehoe Bay, and Jack and Barbara Maxwell were going to the Marine Barracks at Pearl Harbor. We became good friends, and that has lasted over the years. I am no seaman, and the rolling of the ship did not agree with me. I spent considerable time eating crackers and trying to keep my food down. Edna played bridge with the other wives and laughed at me.

Upon our arrival at Pearl Harbor, we were greeted by our hosts, Bob and Jan Hamilton. Bob was a platoon commander in Company D, 1st Battalion, 4th Marines; the unit I was initially assigned to. We became great friends with the Hamiltons.

When I reported into the battalion, it was commanded by Lieutenant Colonel P.H. McArdle, a handsome, highly decorated veteran of two wars. He was tough but fair, which is all any officer could ask for. I was with Company D for three days and then transferred to Company C. I was assigned as a rifle platoon commander, relieving Joe Fiorientino, who played on the battalion football team. I was fortunate to have Sergeant Beard as my platoon sergeant. He was a career Marine who had a knack for handling troops. We got along famously and he led the platoon when I became the duty 'student' for the company.

My first Company Commander was Captain Broderick, a Mustang (former enlisted Marine who had been commissioned) who had arrived in Hawaii just before me. He was a big, balding, red-faced man who seemed to have trouble with his new authority and responsibility. He wasn't able to cope with his duties or make the proper decisions. He was soon relieved and became the Battalion Legal Officer. 1st Lieutenant Jim Caswell was the Company Executive Officer, and an excellent one. A graduate of the Naval Academy, he had been with the company for about two years and was the glue that kept us together during Captain Broderick's short reign. He was a smart, soft-spoken man with a ready smile on all occasions. He later received a serious leg wound in Vietnam.

I didn't get to spend very long working with my platoon before I was sent to the Brigade NBC School for two weeks training, after which I became the company NBC officer. A few weeks later, I was sent to the Brigade Aerial Terrain Appreciation School for more training. I had an excellent group of young Marines in my platoon who adapted easily to the rigorous training schedule. Sergeant Beard finished his 3-year tour in Hawaii and Sergeant Paul E. Robitaille became my Platoon Sergeant. He and I worked well together and got along famously. He was a tireless leader who got the best out of everyone. Some of my sergeant squad leaders were not the best, and I had to find other billets in the company that they could fill so that my deserving Corporals could be the leaders. Our reputation for squaring away problem Marines caused the company commanders to assign them to my platoon. Sometimes it is hard to make a 'silk purse our of a sow's ear,' but we did out best.

1st Lieutenant Don Alford became my second Company Commander. He was a big man with a loud voice, and the most profane officer I ever met. However, he was an excellent officer who knew his tactics and how to handle Marines.

By the time I was able to be with my platoon more, we were involved in changing weapons. We turned in our old faithful M-1s and BARs for the M-14 rifle. Weapons platoon turned in their .30 caliber machine guns for the new M-60. We spent a week at the rifle range firing and testing these new weapons. They were lighter, but I didn't find the M-14 as accurate at 500 yards as the M-1. A selector was on the M-14s that replaced the BARs, allowing it to fire on full automatic.

One of our missions was to field test the weapons. Our battalion flew down to Hilo on the 'big island' from where we were, then trucked up to the Army Training area. We also ran a battalion tactical test while we were there.

5 October 1960, Pohokaloa:

"We have started getting ready for our Battalion Field Exercise and our company has the toughest problems because they fouled up before. I think we will do all right. Half of my platoon has the flu as well as half the company. The weather is really changeable. It has warmed up some today although it is windy. Hope it holds for the problem."

12 October, Pohokaloa:

"We have been going night and day so I haven't had a chance to write. The training area is on the side of a mountain 6,000 feet high and is covered with lava beds and dust! The dust is really bad and the high winds really blow it around. It's like a desert except for some vegetation and a few trees. The lava is very sharp and jagged and the dust is about ankle high—so this has got 'Wagon Train' beat all to hell. I've been switched around twice now and I'm getting tired of it. Jim Maurer is no longer playing football [battalion team] so he has taken over one of the test platoons and Jim Baier has the other one since he isn't going to school for the time being. That leaves me with the short timers, and the sick, lame and lazy. The camp is bearable and that's about all. I'm not spending much money—just on Pepsi's and beer. Chow costs me $1.10 a day. We are going to be out tonight until 0300, tomorrow night until 0600 and Friday night until midnight. I may be a little tired by then. It's cold at night but shouldn't be too bad. The winds usually die down. Jack Maxwell is here [as an umpire or evaluator] and is out every night so I haven't seen much of him. He leaves Friday or Saturday. The flight down was real good. I rode in the cockpit part of the way and got to see some of the islands we will be on later. The ride up here (35 miles) is mostly up hill and it took two hours over terrible roads. However, I'll be glad to go back down anytime! Our training runs through Friday so I don't know when we will be back. I'll try to let you know in advance. Did the manager lower the rent? [We were living off the base until quarters on base became available and were having water/sewage problems.] I sure hope so as we can sure use the money. We fired the new weapons yesterday. I really like the machine gun and so does everyone else. The M-14 is o.k. but a lot of people still like the M-1 better. General [R.G.] Weede [Brigade Commander], Colonel's [J.W.] Antonelli [Regimental Commander] and [William G.] Thrash came out and watched us fire and fired themselves."

We completed our training on the island of Hawaii and returned to Kaneohe Bay. Training continued on the island of Oahu. Sometimes we were able to use the Army firing ranges at Schofield Barracks on the other side of the island. We hiked out to the old Bellows Air Force Base and ran tactical problems in the sand and underbrush. Most of that base was a recreation area used by all the services. The Kaneohe Marine Corps Air Station had almost no area for infantry to train in.

On 7 January 1961, my son and namesake, Robert Jett Driver, III, was born at Tripler Army Hospital. I took Edna to the hospital and the doctor said it would probably be the next day before my child would arrive. Jack and Barbara Maxwell invited me to stay with them at the nearby Naval Base, so I spent the night on their couch. I drove to the hospital early the next morning. Edna and child were doing fine, but he had been born about 2 hours after I left and no one had bothered to notify me!

Our battalion was selected to be the aggressors for Operation Green Light, to be held at Camp Pendleton and 29 Palms in California. We would be defending the beaches against the landing force of the entire 1st Marine Division. Because we were going to be gone for at least a month, Edna flew home to Michigan to present her parents with their first grandson.

The battalion boarded a troop ship in Pearl Harbor and sailed for California in the middle of March 1961. When we were one day from landing at San Diego, our orders were changed. The ship turned around and we headed back to Pearl Harbor. The "Laos Crisis" had occurred, and more Marines were wanted in the South Pacific.

5 April 1961, U.S.S. Navarro:

"As you probably know, we aren't allowed to say where we are or where we are going or anything else, but you'll either hear over the radio or read it in the newspaper long before I can write and tell you. Just don't worry about me or where we are going. This is what we're in here for [the Marine Corps] and this is how it will be so long as there isn't peace in the world. We have been at sea for two weeks and this is the first time we have been able to send mail. We will be able to send it regularly soon. We should receive our first mail tomorrow, also [Pearl Harbor]. Needless to say, I got seasick the second day out and was feeling woozy until a few days ago. I'm getting use to it now. I've been doing a lot of reading and playing cards but little or no bridge. Dominos is an interesting game for a long voyage. I've stayed away from the all night poker games. During the trip, I've gotten rid of two poor squad leaders and now have three good ones. I had one man promoted to Lance Corporal yesterday. We have free laundry service and our meals have been fairly good. Everyone is anxious to get ashore—no matter where it is! Everyone has grown tired of each other. Jim Caswell has grown a mustache but he is going to shave it off tomorrow. At night we have been getting together with Lt. Hugh Jenkins and Lt. Jim Champlin (the Combat Cargo Officer stationed on the ship) and singing hillbilly and

western songs. Jim plays the guitar, Jenkins the fiddle and the rest of us join in and we really have a time! We had a man in our company have his appendix taken out last week aboard ship. It ruptured while they were operating but it was successful. He was in bad shape for a few days and they had to airdrop medicine to the ship, which helped to break the monotony."

The officers and staff NCOs were allowed ashore in Hawaii. Most of the officers headed for the Naval Officers Club for a steak dinner and drinks.

9 April, U.S.S. Navarro:

"I finally got mail today. I had three letters from you. I'm glad you got home o.k. We finally got the word we could go ashore [Okinawa] but we are still sworn to secrecy as to our location."

Again, only the officers and staff NCOs were allowed ashore. Most of use headed for the Kadena Air Force PX and Officers Club and another good dinner and drinks. We remained off shore for three days before heading back towards Pearl Harbor.

10 April, U.S.S. Navarro:

"Well, we are leaving here in a day or two but we can't disclose where we are or where will be going. We haven't had any mail lately—but we should get some tomorrow. You won't be hearing from me for a few days, then you'll get one or two letters and then it will be a few more days and then you will be hearing from me regularly. Don't worry about me as things have calmed down some over here."

11 April, U.S.S. Navarro:

"We are still aboard ship and will be leaving tomorrow. I'm really tired of this shipboard life. I never feel clean or seem to breathe without smelling oil or fumes. Check our important papers and see if my immunization record is there. I got 5 shots the other day. I just finished paying the company. It amounted to almost $7,000 dollars! This doesn't count the officers, or the amount that comes out of allotments, etc."

17 April, U.S.S. Navarro:

"We have arrived at our destination but are still unable to tell anyone where we are. We are still aboard ship and cannot go ashore. We didn't get our mail today either.

The Navy has liberty but we don't. We were able to watch TV tonight. Saw 'Rawhide.' Everyone is reading 'Hawaii.' Guess I'll start on it soon. I'm beginning to be a good dominos player. The ship is out of stamps so you might send me a few. We've run out of about everything. Everyone is about to go nuts sitting around on this ship. They have treated us real well but we are bored to death."

19 April, U.S.S. Navarro:

"I can finally tell you that we have been to Okinawa. It is unclassified as of 0700 this morning. Richard Huckaby and Richard Heath were both gone when I tried to call them. Both were at sea. I ran into Mark Loveless, Rudy Gentry, and several others I knew from OCS and Basic School. Don and Jim ran into Jimmy Lemons from Greensboro the last night ashore and he tried to call me at the ship but couldn't get me. [Lemons had been in the Greensboro Reserve unit.] We should be in Long Beach on the 28th, off load on the 29th, and move to Camp Pendleton on the 30th."

20 April, U.S.S. Navarro:

"Well, after 11 more days at sea we're pulling into Pearl Harbor Saturday morning. I haven't felt good the entire trip. I've been seasick the whole time. Today the sea calmed down and I felt better. I have been assigned temporarily as Company Executive Officer, as Jim Caswell took over A Company last week. He is really happy. [Jim] Maurer and [Harry] Ling are still TAD but should rejoin us soon so I'll be back with the 2nd Platoon. I may get the job permanently after the Camp Pendleton problem. Harry is going to be the S-2 of the Battalion and Jim will be Legal Officer when Captain Broderick leaves. We are getting a new Lieutenant at Pearl Harbor, just out of Basic School, and some more men. Larry Cassidy has taken over as S-4. I am still the Mess Officer and it's a real job with officers coming and going. We are going to be at Pearl Harbor only 24 hours. I may have the duty for a few hours while we are there. None of the officers from 3/12, etc., have stood any duty and I've had it 5 times, so I'm trying to get out of it. I'd like to go to Ft. DeRussy and get some sun, a good meal, and some drinks. I need them all! We had a Battalion Field Day yesterday and Charlie Company came in a close 3rd. 17 to 19 points to Bravo and 21 for Delta."

21 April, U.S.S. Navarro:

"We got in port today and I got about 10 letters from you and really enjoyed reading them. Jack Maxwell came down to the ship and picked me up and we went to his house, and then went swimming at Kahieei Beach near the Honolulu Airport. Don and Rickey [Brooks] came over about 4 and we drank beer and ate supper. We had roast beef, corn on the cob, and some of Rickey's blueberry pie. The meal was outstanding. Don and Jack brought me back to the ship in time to stand the duty."

27 April, U.S.S. Navarro:

"*Tomorrow is our last day at sea. We are scheduled to pull into Long Beach at 0900. I am going to Camp Pendleton with the first group of vehicles and find out where everything is located pertaining to Charlie Company. 'Cheerful Charlie' will have to unload the ship and maintain a guard over the gear on the docks until it all gets moved. We are joining 28 enlisted men and one officer when we get there. I now have 38 men in my platoon—the most I have ever had. We have been aboard ship 38 days Saturday. Everyone is bored stiff. We have had too much chow, sleeping, and reading, and not enough exercise. There are 1,500 men on board counting the crew.*"

28 April, U.S.S. Navarro:

"*We're due in Long Beach in the morning and morale has shot up 100%. The news from Laos looks bad again. I don't think we will be making a trip there anytime soon or if we do go we will probably fly. I am really looking forward to living on land again. This having one person over you, one person under you, and one beside you when you go to bed in getting old!* "

30 April, Camp Pendleton:

"*We got here about noon yesterday. This camp (Las Pulgas) is 13 miles from anywhere—main side and Oceanside are the closest civilization. There is bus service into Oceanside, but that is all. Most of the hills (more like mountains) are real steep and have little or no vegetation. It is real nice during the day but cold as heck at night. I had to get up and put my long johns on and put my sleeping bag over me last night. I ran into Larry Dill at Long Beach. He's a motor transport officer now. He said [Don] Stoner, Pope and [Joe] Nardo were still here. Nardo is going to flight school soon. Sergeants Robitaille [now my Platoon Sergeant], [Ferrell R.] White [Platoon Guide], Barber [Squad Leader] and Jewewski [Squad Leader] tried to buy Jim Maurer and I all the beer we could drink last night. Jim is the XO now. He'll be taking over as Legal Officer after the problem is over but we have a new Communications Officer, so Jim Baier will be coming back to the company, or so it looks like. I'll have Weapons Platoon after the problem.*"

1 May, Camp Pendleton:

"*We took a nice long hike this afternoon. I've got two blisters on my toes to show for it. We are going to have a tank demonstration tomorrow. Should be interesting. I fell down a bank on the hike today and tore the knee out of my trousers and skinned my knee. I was only 10 feet from the road! We don't have any movies out here, so there is nothing to do at night but listen to the radio, read, write letters, and drink beer. I haven't done much of the latter.*"

2 May, Camp Pendleton:

"We ran squad tactics, hiked 10 miles and watched a tank demonstration today. We'll be working with the tanks Thursday. I took two pictures of the platoon on a tank. Real gung ho! I paid the troops yesterday and two men from my platoon went to Tijuana, Mexico and got rolled. They came in about 0900 this morning."

3 May, Camp Pendleton:

"I had another short day and long night. We spent the morning on the infiltration course and this afternoon on a live fire squad problem course. I was safety officer all day. We hiked back. I'm getting back into shape now and I really enjoyed the hike. We are going to working with tanks tomorrow all day. Should be a lot of fun—and work. I saw SSgt. Beard yesterday. He is stationed here now and just made E-6. One of the men in my platoon, Lance Corporal Nickels, left for home tonight to be married Saturday. He is a real fine young man and was one of three we recommended to attend the Naval Academy. Battalion dropped the ball on this, as usual. I told him to make sure he was doing the right thing and really loved the girl. We gave him six days off without taking leave. He is going to bring his wife to Hawaii, as he has a year left on his tour over there. She had a job lined up in Hawaii with the same company she works for now. Don and Jim are still commuting to L.A. [their wives were there]. They had to go to 29 Palms today to look over the area we are going to use up there in the problem."

4 May, Camp Pendleton:

"Today started out to be an enjoyable one. We worked with tanks all day and really enjoyed it, and did plenty of running, etc. My cold, which I contracted aboard ship, has gotten worse and I can hardly talk and can't breathe through my nose. When we came in from the field, I found my wallet had been stolen from my wall locker. It had $52.00 in it. Anyway, Joe Fiorientino [now in D Co.] had one of his men clean up the hut, and two men from Charlie Company came up to fix up a rack and wall locker for our new lieutenant and he was in here with the door closed. I contacted the Delta Company 1st Sergeant and he checked into it and found the man with my wallet and $127.00. Some of my important papers were in the wallet. The man would not confess. While we were investigating, we found his old wallet with my ID card and Kaneohe O Club card and—in a secret compartment—his Social Security card! We called CID and they locked him up and said they would probably break him in an hour. I hope I will get my money back. I'll get my ID card back tomorrow. I hope he will confess and tell the CID where he hid my papers. They are almost as valuable as the money. I just hope it gets cleared up before we leave here."

7 May, Camp Pendleton:

"We had Happy Hour Friday afternoon at the club at main side and only a few officers showed up. The Colonel didn't like it at all. Saturday morning, Ray Wood, an aviator attached to us, and I went to Los Angeles. He has an uncle up there and we stayed with him. We went to see Hollywood and it's a real loser. There is really nothing there. We went to a strip show and hit a few bars. His uncle is a former concert piano player, and he played quite a few numbers for us. He lives in a big mansion and has a special room (more like a gym) where he holds concerts. It was really beautiful and he plays well for 73. His wife was real nice to us. We didn't go to the baseball game, as it's too hard to get to the ballpark and back from where we were. I took Ray with us to the field Friday and we threw hand grenades and fired rifle grenades. He had never done this before, as he came in through the Naval Aviation Cadet Program. He is from Jacksonville, Florida and went to Jacksonville University. Our new officer, Bob Handrahan, came in Friday. He seems like a real nice guy. He was a staff sergeant before OCS. He's married and has a four-year-old son. I am going to bed now and try to get rid of this cold. All they have given me is APCs. I am really hoarse now. On top of that, I have an abscessed wisdom tooth!"

9 May, Camp Pendleton:

"We had another long day in the field. We have a night attack tonight. My cold is a little better today. I'm taking some new pills and nose drops. One of my new sergeants is 41 years old! He came in 2 days after Pearl Harbor and got out in 1945. He came back in, in 1952. He's been stationed at Quantico for four years."

10 May, Camp Pendleton:

"The man who stole my wallet confessed today. He destroyed all my papers by tearing them into shreds and throwing them into a dumpster. I still don't know when I'll get my money back. We went out and fired all of our weapons today. It was really hot and windy. I have a good tan on my face and arms but my nose peeled, as usual. I was safety officer again. Tomorrow we are going to combat town. We don't have any of these facilities in Hawaii. I have to teach a class to the company tomorrow so I had better close and get busy."

11 May, Camp Pendleton:

"We had quite a day today. We used combat town and after the problem nine of the buildings burned down. Jim Maurer was running the show and will catch hell about it more than likely. He told Colonel McArdle about it and he wasn't too happy! My laundry cost over $5.00 this time and it is the last I'm going to send it out. Bob Handrahan and I *washed clothes last night and it cost us a quarter each. I ironed my utilities tonight. Driver's home laundry! Jim Maurer is now in the hut, and he, Handrahan, John Clements, and I are arguing about whether Jim will get a court martial! Quite a bit of speculation!"*

12 May, Camp Pendleton:

"Another long day in the field and a hike back. I led the hike back. We had live firing all day today. We have an inspection tomorrow by Don Alford. The big problem starts next Friday and runs through June 3rd—so don't expect any mail—as I won't even have a chance to take a shower! We have seen quite a few snakes but no rattlers yet! I've got to close for now and get my gear ready for the inspection."

13 May, Camp Pendleton:

"It looks like Joe Fiorientino will be transferred back to our company. Jim Maurer thinks he can straighten him out. I don't like it but he'll be going to the 3rd Battalion when we get back—I hope! [The Marine Corps had increased its manpower and had activated the 3rd Battalion, 4th Marine Regiment.] We had an inspection today and my 2nd Platoon was the best—as usual. We gave them liberty at noon. Today was payday also. There was a big cheer when early liberty was announced. Everyone has taken off for the weekend but us [Ray Wood and I]. We still may go to the bullfights if we get a chance. Guess we will drink beer tonight."

14 May, Camp Pendleton:

"I didn't go to Mexico after all. I slept in late and no one else wanted to go. Jim Maurer told me I will get Weapons Platoon even if Fiorientino does come back to Charlie Company, and Joe will get 2nd Platoon, even if he is senior to me. I can hardly wait until 14 June when I make 1st Lieutenant. The money will be nice, too."

15 May, Camp Pendleton:

"Another day gone. I spent it riding around in a jeep and walking over the terrain we're going to defend on the problem. My platoon is going to defend the beach. General [David M.] Shoup [Commandant of the Marine Corps] is going to watch the landing. We are going to have a new regime when we get back. Colonel McArdle is going to be the CO of Service Battalion. Major Pearce [XO] is rotating back to the states in August. Major [John R.] Keith [S-3] is going to 3rd Battalion as XO. Captains [Bob] Yackel [S-1], Fortmeyer [Air Liaison Officer], Colia [S-4], Lt's Ollice [Asst. S-3], Gardner [S-2], and Captain Willcox [Asst. S-3], all leave at the end of the week. Don Alford is going to be the S-3 as of 6 July. Jim Maurer will have the company until we get a new captain. He will then

be the Legal Officer. Captain Broderick leaves in July (we hope). John Clements moves to Asst. S-3, George Griggs [Company B] moves to S-2. We are getting a new Warrant Officer [Art Bodree] as S-1. On 1 July Lt.'s Lou Burton, [Hugh] Jenkins, [Bill] Allen, West and Fiorientino all go to the 3rd Battalion. Jim Baier is going to A Company to be the XO. I'll be XO of C Company for a while again. We are getting Lt. Col. [John R. Stevens] as CO, 2 Majors, 3 Captains, a 1st Lt. and 4 2nd Lt.'s. Enough changes?"

16 May, Camp Pendleton:

"Tomorrow we start digging positions down near the beach. We'll have 3 days to complete them. Major Keith is coming down tomorrow to look them over. We had our pictures made today for TV in Hawaii. The whole battalion was seated on a hillside. I had to give a class on map reading today. I didn't get into it very deep. We made another trip to the beach and played volleyball. Tomorrow I have the duty so I won't have to go to the field tomorrow night. Everything is tied up with security now as the Division had started dropping recon people and landing them from submarines. We captured two this morning. Should be an interesting night!"

17 May, Camp Pendleton:

"Standing the duty. All the other officers have gone to a special Happy Hour at Camp Del Mar. We spent a busy day on the beach digging positions and putting up barbed wire. We rode out but had to walk back—about 5 miles so I'm kind of tired. Colonel McArdle was down on the beach today—also 22 jeep loads of officers and NCOs who are going to be umpires for the problem. Colonel McArdle had me change a few positions but seemed pleased with the progress we had made. We saw a deer and a bobcat near the beach today. Rabbits, squirrels, and other animals are all over the place. The newspapers out here are full of pictures and stories about the landing. 42,000 men are involved, plus 71 ships and 300 planes."

18 May, Camp Pendleton:

"We spent another long day on the beach. We're always having visitors, etc. My platoon is really doing a good job. Everyone is working real hard and enjoying it. They really want to foul up the 1st Division. I've got to close and get my aggressor uniform ready to go. This is my last letter for a while."

23 May, Camp Pendleton:

"The problem was called at noon today to get ready to move to 29 Palms. You should have seen us when we came in today! I had a five-day growth of beard and was filthy from head to toe. The only thing I changed was my socks. I really enjoyed the problem except for the lack of sleep. General Shoup came after all. I got a lot of good comments from everyone on the defensive positions on the beach. I'm still half a sleep."

Following the defense of one of the landing beaches, my platoon fell back under Highway 101 to a large ridgeline overlooking the access from the beach. We dug in there for the night. I had to spread my platoon out in three positions acting as a full company. I stayed with the squad nearest the access route. I had a two man listening post out in front of our position and had my men on 50% alert. A company from the 1st Marine Division attacked us about 0230 the next morning. The listening post had fallen asleep and failed to give us early warning, but our line fired on them when they assaulted. The umpires stopped the firing before they got very close because of the danger of injury from the blank rounds. During the cease-fire, I pulled my platoon off the hill and fell back to another position. I didn't want to be captured by any of the 1st Division, as most of their platoon leaders were my classmates in OCS and or Basic School.

24 May, Camp Pendleton:

"We made a helicopter assault yesterday, and they were waiting for us. Jim Maurer, Sgt. Robitaille, Cpl. Cunningham, and 5 men stole a truck and got away. I got away with 4 men and spent the night trying to get back into our lines. I finally got back at 0830 this morning. I spent 4 hours sitting in one position with one of my men [PFC Granahan] behind a small bush with the enemy all around us—we didn't get caught but we sure froze! We were nearly caught a half dozen times. We ran a mile or so several times to evade their security. I was so tired I couldn't even talk. We had several people hurt. LCpl. Reynolds has a dislocated kneecap. LCpl. Snyder, Sgt. Stuckus, PFCs Tittle and Hoeppner, all had knee injuries. PFC McKeehan has a broken rib and Sgt. Nuimatea has a bad foot. This was from my platoon alone! LCpl. Moye lost a finger – left index, luckily he is right handed. He was one of the men recommended for the Naval Academy. One man turned a mechanical mule over and is given a 50-50 chance to live. A man in Bravo Company was hit in the mouth with a rifle grenade and lost all his front teeth. This was all on our side and they had 6 times as many men as we did. I know of one broken leg and one broken ankle in Delta Company. The hills are really steep and it is easy to get hurt. Most of the injuries were due to carelessness on someone's part."

3 June, Camp Pendleton:

"We are finally out of the field after 12 days and am I glad! That week in the desert was really bad. It was 120 degrees one day. The nights were real cold and usually windy.

Everyone was in rags and looked like bums – the rocks and dirt tore up our boots and trousers like they were paper. We didn't shave or bathe the entire time! Wow! We stunk like a herd of goats! We were really bad! [In leading my platoon across the desert, I came across a deadly coral snake. I stopped and turned to warn the men, and when I turned back around it was gone. Thank goodness!] Colonel McArdle and Don Alford were really pleased with our performance. Guess who we kicked off our hill? Don Stoner—it could not have pleased me more if it had been a General! He was huffing and puffing and we made his troops look bad. He is going to Okinawa in January. Some of the other officers I ran into were Joe Staley (our neighbor in Melrose Gardens), Wayne Smith, Driskell, Conners, Kelly, Pitney, Jesdale, Rivers, Holbrook, Jennings, Tom Miller (V. P. I.) and several more. [All these officers had been in my OCS or Basic School classes.] Jim Maurer is going to the 3rd Battalion so I am going to be the CO on the trip back to Hawaii, and I won't get any leave until then. Colonel McArdle won't grant leave past the 28th of June anyway because of the change of command ceremony. We rode back from 29 Palms in the latest plane the Marine Corps has—the GVI—they can carry 110 combat loaded troops or several vehicles. They're pressurized and have jet assisted take off and are turboprops."

4 June, Camp Pendleton:

"I've spent a quiet Sunday doing nothing much. Slept until 1000, ate chow, read the paper, read a pocketbook, washed and ironed 2 covers, got my uniform ready for tomorrow's trip, and straightened up a bit. I went to town [Oceanside] last night and had a few drinks. Woody [Ray Wood], Jim Moore, our new Communications Officer, and another new Lt., John Mitka, all went. We got back about 0100."

5 June, Camp Pendleton:

"I have spent the day signing leave papers as 30% of the company is going on leave for 13 days. When they get back 10% of the company can go on 30 days leave. We are deliberately staying here to give the 30% a break so they can go back to Hawaii on the ship. Most of the married personnel are going back to Hawaii next Wednesday. Lt. Handrahan and I are left to take the company back. I did get my clothes washed today and had two good meals. Tonight we had fried chicken, corn on the cob (I ate 3 ears), mashed potatoes, peas, dressing, salad, apple pie, lime sherbet, and milk or coffee. Last night, we had some of the best steaks I have ever eaten and I ate two of them! We also had eggs, French fries and a lot more. The company gave Don [Alford] a 23 jewel Lord Elgin today. They also gave Jim Maurer a nice camera. My platoon really worked hard on the problem. Naturally, I think I have the best platoon in the Marine Corps—bar none! I have really enjoyed working with them and it has been an experience I will never forget. I saw in the Navy Times that Nick Laney was selected for Staff Sergeant [Greensboro Reserve unit]. I only wish Stanley [Rose] would make it." [He did.]

6 June, Camp Pendleton:

"Spent another dull day here with nothing to do. The advance party leaves tomorrow for Kaneohe Bay. I've got to sit here until the 17th before we go to San Diego to go aboard ship. We sail the 19th and arrive in Honolulu on the 28th."

8 June, Camp Pendleton:

"Spent another boring day signing leave papers and trying to get the company administration squared away. Everyone always wants to go at the same time."

10 June, Camp Pendleton:

"I went to the Camp Pendleton Rodeo yesterday. They had several movie and TV stars there. Glenn Ford made a short talk and he was stationed here during WWII as a Marine. They estimated 100,000 people would attend and it was packed. The rodeo itself was free and only refreshments, rides, etc., cost anything."

11 June, Camp Pendleton:

"I went to the bullfights yesterday and it was quite an experience. We got off the bus at the border and walked across. We were immediately surrounded by taxi drivers, pimps, etc., and they offered us every kind of woman we wanted and any sex act. This, plus pictures, movies, shows, and this went on all over town in every shop and store we went in. We got there early so we walked to the bullfight and really got a view of how the Mexicans live. There is a lot of poverty and slums but it is side by side with nice looking houses. The bullfights got off to a bloody start but the third match was really good. The toreador killed the bull with the first thrust of his sword. There were six matches in all but the crowd made the fight. If it was a good kill the women (Americans of course) would throw their shoes into the arena and the college boys would throw their wine sacks. Everyone would stand up, wave their handkerchiefs and shout 'O lay!' It was quite an experience. We got back about 2130 last night after waiting for 2 hours to catch the bus. They don't allow passengers to stand up on the buses here so once the seats were filled everyone had to wait. What a mob! 1stSgt. Orth's mother passed away today. He is going on emergency leave tomorrow. Sgt. Robitaille didn't get to go back early. We are flying 115 more men back."

13 June, Camp Pendleton:

"I had another busy day today. Spent most of it working on administrative matters for the company and last minute reports, etc. Our company is going to the Los Angles

Dodgers-Chicago Cubs game in LA tomorrow. Bob Handrahan, Tom Solak [Company B] and John Mitka are going too. We have to wear our uniforms but we get in free and the Marine Corps furnishes the transportation. We had three men promoted to Lance Corporal today. Wortham from my 2nd Platoon made it and I was glad to see it. [He was the only black Marine in my platoon and a good man.] I saw in the Navy Times that Dick Hoehn had extended to make the trip to Okinawa with his battalion. Captain Snell [Basic School] was transferred to the Military Advisory Group in Vietnam. Guess he will see Bao and Ming over there. [They were Vietnamese Marine Officers who had attended the Basic School in my class.] I did get some clothes washed today. Washed my field jacket, underwear, and socks. I bought some 1st Lieutenant bars today. The S-1 Chief said my promotion would be sent to Kaneohe Bay and then over here, and I might not get it tomorrow." [I didn't get it until we returned to Hawaii].

15 June, Camp Pendleton:

"Another busy day today. We had a man locked up in Compton, California for being drunk and disorderly. I sent Bob Handrahan up there to bring him back. The man (colored) got married and was in jail an hour and a half later. His wife wouldn't have anything to do with him after that! He pleaded not guilty today or he could have gotten out of jail. We collected the bail money from the troops and Bob went after him. He is trying to keep from going back to Hawaii. I took checks to the hospital yesterday and talked to Moye, who lost his finger. He was in good spirits and his hand looked good but has been slow to heal and he's having trouble getting the use of it back. He uses a whirlpool daily and also exercises it to stretch the skin. He may have to have skin grafts. I enjoyed the ballgame. The Dodgers won 7-0 and Don Drysdale, the pitcher, also hit a home run. The game was in the LA Coliseum, which is a beautiful stadium, but was not built for baseball. They had 30,000 Boy & Cub Scouts there so you can imagine the noise. I am about through packing, and my locker box and pack are already gone. I'm going to wash clothes tomorrow and hope they will last until we get back."

16 June, Camp Pendleton:

"I got my money and my wallet back today. Bob Hamilton just got back off leave and guess what! His wife is pregnant again. Heard that Ed Williams' (Bravo Company) wife had a baby girl. He went back early. Don Alford is back now and he really had a time in Las Vegas and Laguna Beach. He and Woody are flying back. All our troops are back but one, and he isn't due until tomorrow morning. I just hope we get everyone aboard and back o. k."

18 June, U.S.S. Cavalier:

"I'm back aboard ship again and unhappy about it. The ship is due to be scrapped when it comes back from the Far East. Tom Solak, Dick Grace, Bob Handrahan and I are in one compartment together. Our bus broke down bringing us here from Camp Pendleton. San Diego is a nice town and from what I have seen and I would not mind being stationed here. Bob Handrahan and I went on liberty last night and hit all the Officer's Clubs, and they are nice. We are going out to eat in one tonight."

22 June, Kaneohe Bay:

"Your husband is back in Hawaii and sure misses you! We got in about 1000 this morning after a fair trip. It was hot, etc., but I didn't get sick at all! [Lt.] Lou Spevetz and Gunnery Sergeant Hoagland met us at the docks with our new company commander, Captain Bob Miller. He just reported in yesterday from Barstow, California. He seems real nice but rather quiet. Don Brooks came over to the company officer about 1130 with our car, and we three (the CO, Don & I) ate lunch together. I took Don back to work about 1300. This afternoon I went up to battalion and got my promotion—2 weeks late! I lost about $40.00 according to Disbursing. I went to the housing office and we are 6th on the list! The lady said it would be a week or two weeks before we were assigned. I picked up Don after work and checked into the BOQ. Then we went to his house for supper. Their house [they had purchased one off base] is really nice. It really feels good to be back. I am going to remain the XO. We are getting 25 new men tomorrow but we're losing 50 old ones to 3rd Battalion next week."

29 June, Kaneohe Bay:

"I have really been busy. This XO's job is no pushover. I'll be working Saturday morning this week! We have an administrative inspection on the 17th of next month. We have a Brigade inspection the 4th and the IG inspection the 14th of August. We also have the change of command ceremony Wednesday. Captain Miller is letting me run things until he gets his feet on the ground."

30 June, Kaneohe Bay:

"Bob Hamilton and I went to Ft. DeRussy last night and ate supper and had a few drinks. He is number one on the housing list and should move in Friday; however, Dean Van Lines is on strike, so he won't be able to get his furniture moved in but he has a lot of gear in his room here. I went over to Pearl Harbor and had lunch with Jack Maxwell. He really likes his job as Exchange Officer. Jack made reservations for the Brooks and us for the opening of the new Officers Club at Pearl Harbor on the 15th. $15.00 a couple, but *it includes the meal and drinks. Vic Damone is going to be there. It's formal so I'll have to wear my whites. [I had to cancel our reservations as Edna and Jett didn't get back in time.] The Brooks are having a party Sunday afternoon and I'm invited to eat dinner with the Handrahans, so Sunday is going to be a busy day."*

3 July, Kaneohe Bay:

"I went to the Brooks, and they were having an Aloha Party for Bob Shackleford and his wife. The Maxwells, Allens, and Major Reid and his wife were there. I had another busy day today but seemed to get a lot done. Don Brooks called about 1600 and said 'Captain Brooks wants to speak to Lt. Driver.' We went to the club with some of his friends and he invited Bob Finn and myself home with him for supper. We played bridge and had a real nice time. I ordered a lot of the photographs taken during our maneuvers. They are really good. I ordered 2 of my platoon taken after the 29 Palms part of the problem. Gunnery Sergeant Dick, who is doing the work, is going to try and get me a negative so I can get a large one made of them. General Weede's son's picture was in the 'Windward Marine' and he had a big write up."

5 July, Kaneohe Bay:

"The change of command ceremony came off real well. Charlie Company looked great and I took some movies. The reception afterwards went off well, too. I talked with Colonel Stevens and his wife and they asked where you were. Also Colonel and Mrs. McArdle, Colonel and Mrs. Antonelli, General and Mrs. Weede. I met Mrs. Miller, and she is real nice. The Caswells invited us over for bridge one night after you get back. Bob Hamilton and I went to Ft. DeRussy yesterday and met his brother-in-law, who is over here on vacation. We got a bit of sun, too. We have really been working our butts off in the company. Everything seems to happen at once. Captain Miller and I are getting along real well. We see eye to eye on most things. We are going to be inspected to death between now and the 15th of August. We go to Pohokola the 11th of September for two weeks."

8 July, Kaneohe Bay:

"Last night after writing you I went to Happy Hour with Ray Wood. I talked with Colonel Stevens and Major Pearce. I came back and changed clothes and went to steak night. We had tenderloin steak, with all the trimmings and a bottle of wine for $1.95! Can't beat that!"

A strange thing happened about this time. Lt. Colonel John F. Stevens, who had been the regimental executive officer, was assigned as the battalion commander. He came in like a whirlwind and with a complete dislike for most of the officers in the battalion. I never understood why, except we had always done better than 2/4 on every evaluation. He was a 'staff study' man. I was called into Lt. Colonel Stevens' office one day and was told I was now the Battalion Motor Transport Officer. I was stunned! I knew nothing about motor transport, and was not mechanically inclined. He offered no explanation, and with his usual sarcastic smile, dismissed me.

We had just been issued the Mighty Mites, the new answer to the long reliable jeep, and the mechanical mules, which were both pieces of junk. The Marines Corps bought them because they were lightweight and helicopter transportable. There was no usage data on spare parts, so the Marine Corps supply system had stocked only a minimum amount.

The motor transport section of the battalion had one Staff Sergeant, the Motor Transport Chief, who was a good man but an alcoholic. When he was sober, he could fix anything but he was not a good troop leader. On Monday mornings, he could hardly function. I had a long heart-to-heart conversation with him about his problem, and he did better. The mechanics were all school trained, but not all of them were up to date on the new vehicles. I sent as many as I could to Brigade schools to learn about the two lemons. The drivers were all school trained. The drivers for the rifle companies were all detailed men, but licensed.

With the sand and grit of the Oahu training areas, the first thing to cause problems were the wheel bearings. I don't know where they were tested, but the front-end wheel bearings wore out quickly, and we had difficulty getting the replacement parts. The mechanical mules could not be driven on the highways on Oahu, so they had to be trucked to and from training areas. They proved difficult to operate in the sandy areas we trained in. They had mechanical issues also. Our dead line list grew dramatically. Fortunately, the Brigade had allowed us to keep a half dozen of the old jeeps as back up, and they kept us going.

Lt. Colonel Stevens assigned me a 'staff study' to determine the amount of transportation it would require to mount-out the battalion. I spent a lot of time with the S-4 and the motor transport officers at higher levels, and determined the number of trucks, trailers, jeeps, etc. it would take and presented them to the Colonel. He questioned me closely on my figures, but I didn't hesitate to use the sources of my information. He added some additional requirements, such as 30 days supplies of ammo, food, water, etc. In a few days, I reported back to him with the new figures. He again scrutinized my work closely and tried to find some flaws in it, but he could not. Before I left his office, I made the point that there was not enough motor transport on the island of Oahu to meet these requirements. I believe that was my last staff study, but others suffered on!

In September, the battalion went to Pohokola on the big island for training. I was still the Motor Transport Officer and we loaded and unloaded our vehicles from a Navy LST. Once we reached the Army training area and set up our motor pool in tents, I was detailed as an umpire.

Jett Driver receiving his 4th Marines Baby Cup from Mrs. Col. Antonelli
L-R: Antonelli, Jett, Edna & Bob Driver

17 September 1961, Pohokola:

"I've really been kept on the go being an umpire everyday but today, so I am a little tired. I wanted to go on a tour of the island today but we had a 1000 meeting, so I couldn't go. Six Marines turned over a truck last night and one suffered a broken collarbone, and I have to investigate that. I haven't been to the Motor Pool but once since I have been here. All of the officers are going to Hilo for a luau tonight. It costs $6.00 without drinks. The bus leaves in 15 minutes so I have to hurry."

Later that fall, the Battalion made a landing on the island of Maui. When Motor Transport got ashore, we found all the mechanical mules with flat tires and some of the Mighty Mites. Large hedges grew near the shoreline on the island and they were covered with large thorns. These thorns and branches had been broken off by wind and our vehicles and punctured their tires. We used every patch we had and could purchase from the local gas stations and stores on the island. My men patched over 1,000 tires, and often they were flat again in half a mile. We even had patches flown in by helicopter from Oahu, but it was an impossible task. The tires were just too thin to operate in this environment. We made all kinds of reports on these problems, but I don't know how many of our recommendations were ever carried out.

I continued my duties as Motor Transport Officer until January 1962. The Battalion had a New Year's party and Edna and I attended. During the party, I was told by the Adjutant or XO, that I was going to the Philippines as Liaison Officer for 3rd Battalion, 4th Marines. This new Battalion was going to be the aggressor force against the landing of the 3rd Marine Division there in March. I had just moved into quarters and was becoming part of my new son's life again, and this fell like a bombshell on me! Stevens did not speak to me; he just gave me one of his knowing sneers. He didn't have the balls to tell me! Many of the officers in the battalion were single, and would have jumped at the chance to go. I had spent more time away from Kaneohe Bay than all of the other officers. At least I would be out from under his command!

I reported to the 3rd Battalion on the appointed date and met with the S-3 Major Hittinger, XO Major Keith, and the CO, Lt. Colonel Reese. Other than Major Keith, the welcome was a hostile one, as if I was an invader from another planet. The rivalry between the battalions was that intense. The S-3 explained that I would be sent over to work with the Tactical Exercise Control Party of the 3rd Marine Division, who would be running the exercise, and if 3rd Battalion needed any information they would contact me. I never received one message or request in the 3 months I was on Okinawa and in the Philippines!

11 January 1962, Okinawa:

"The flight over was real good, although it took 10 hours to get here. The service was excellent and the food o.k. I sat beside an Air Force Major and we had a vacant seat between us so we played gin rummy and talked. We stopped at Wake Island to refuel and flew over Iwo Jima on the way. The TEC headquarters is very disorganized, but we go to work tomorrow. We are staying at Camp Hague, which is one of the older camps; all Quonset huts. Our rooms aren't much but will do. My house girl charges $5.00 every two weeks and she does all the washing, ironing, etc. She barely speaks English. They all eat a lot of fish so they smell like them. Ugh!"

15 January, IX MEF, CTF-79, 3rd Marine Division:

"I am sitting here at work with nothing to do. We haven't done a thing all morning and it doesn't look like we will. I can see that this is going to be a long and lonesome 4

months. *Everyone has been real nice over here. We are working with majors and colonels but they don't pull their rank and let their hair down quite a bit. We went to the Kadena Air Force Base Club for drinks and dinner last night. Drinks were 15 cents and I had a porterhouse steak (1 ½ lbs) for $2.50. The only trouble with the clubs is the slot machines. Everything is so cheap it's tempting to spend your money in them. I ran into Captain Young who just came over from the Brigade. He's in Disbursing. I met Captain Burt who was a 2nd Lt. and XO of the company I was in at Camp Lejeune. He remembered me and said he had wondered if I had come back in. I told him about MSgt. Bird [he had died of cancer] and it was the first he had heard of it."*

16 January, CTF-79, Okinawa:

"Spent another day doing little or nothing. I was a dreary one too, poured rain and was cold. We went to chow at Kadena again last night. I had a filet. It was really good."

17 January, CTF-79, Okinawa:

"Just got back from a tour around the island. It was interesting but there wasn't much to see. I took pictures of fishing villages, temples, scenery, children, and a cave. Five of us went to the Ft. Buckner Club for supper last night. It was real nice and they had a good floorshow. I saw Lt. Tribble [OCS and Basic School] there. He just got over here in December. He said Dave Fanning [OCS and Basic School] was almost out of flight school."

18 January, CTF-79, Okinawa:

"I just got back from chow and wanted to drop you a line before going back to work. We didn't do anything until about 1600 and then were called on to do something and we have to work tonight."

19 January, 9th MEF, TF 79 (TEC), Okinawa:

"I bought a camouflaged rain hat today similar to Bob Hamilton's and some name tags. Four of us went to Kadena last night and played bingo. Prizes run from $20.00 to a Volkswagen and a mink stole."

20 January, TEC, Okinawa:

"We went to Naha shopping today in the Thieves Market. We bought camouflaged utility caps. The real experience was going through the different shops and seeing the food they had for sale. The smells were something, too. Each shop had its own specialty—food, grain, clothes, etc."

22 January, TEC, Okinawa:

"They finally put us to work today. I'm the Assistant S-2 in the TEC. Nothing difficult yet."

23 January, TEC, Okinawa:

"I met Captain Dunwell from 3/12. He's a friend of Don Brooks. It has really been cold. I'm sleeping in a sleeping bag. We have a stove in the hall but it doesn't do any good in the rooms."

26 January, TEC, Okinawa:

"Col. Reese, Major Hittenger, and Harry Ling got in yesterday. They had 5 days in Japan. Lucky stiffs! The Colonel and Major are going to the Philippines tomorrow. We went to Kadena and played bingo last night and Major Hittenger won half a jackpot $12.50. Two people won the VW. I got the two Windward Marines and saw that some of my old troopers in Charlie Company got promoted, and one from Motor Transport. We finally got down to some real work today as more people came in from Hawaii."

29 January, TEC, Okinawa:

"I ran into Captain Comer today. He's going to South Vietnam in a few days. He told me of all the changes in the 1st Battalion. Bob Hamilton is going to be the CO of Alpha Company. Captain Macy is going to be the S-4. Captain Comer is the Assistant S-3 when he gets back. Three new lieutenants have reported in, including one who is real senior. I'm really glad Bob Hamilton is getting a company. He deserves it! I am going to teach two classes in the Umpire School at Camp Hansen, February 15th and 19th."

30 January, TEC, Okinawa:

"I found out today I will be released to 3/4 as soon as the problem is over. This means I have to take everything with me to the Philippines which I didn't want to do."

31 January, TEC, Okinawa:

"I talked with Captain Burt for quite a while at the club. He remembers Staff Sergeant Poss and was glad he got commissioned."

2 February, TEC, Okinawa:

"I talked with Major Hittinger today and he was the Officer Selection Officer in North Carolina from 1953-1956. He knows Major Redmond."

3 February, TEC, Okinawa:

"Spent the day shopping in Koza and at the Ft. Buckner PX. Colonel Reese has gone to Japan to check on our liberty up there so I hope he comes back with good news."

4 February, TEC, Okinawa:

"I saw Don Stoner last night. His battalion just got over here. Most of the officers are from my Basic Class and extended to come."

5 February, TEC, Okinawa:

"I guess Bob Hamilton and Gene Dixon are real happy in their new jobs. [Dixon took over the 106 Platoon.] Maybe I'll get 81's when John Clements leaves in May. It is a little discouraging to go to the Army, Navy and Air Force clubs and see them with their dependents. They have nice housing, commissaries, etc. and the Marines have nothing in comparison. The natives call Marines 'the animals' over here. The Marines are ready to go and the rest aren't—that's the difference."

6 February, TEC, Okinawa:

"I would like to send my greens home by WO [Killer] Cain, if possible. [Cain was a former enlisted Marine pilot, and one of the last of a dying breed from WWII and our next-door neighbor at Kaneohe Bay.] I'll be going to the Philippines on the 5th of March, but don't say anything about it to anyone."

9 February, TEC, Okinawa:

"Colonel Reese called Major Hittenger today and said the battalion would have liberty in Japan from 11-16 April. The battalion should have sailed from Pearl Harbor today."

10 February, TEC, Okinawa:

"I ran into Doug Wood at the Kadena club last night. He is a Navy Lt. (j.g.) now and is aboard the cruiser U.S.S. Los Angles. We talked for a long time about everyone we knew at Guilford and in Greensboro. [His twin brother David, served in the Marine Corps Reserve unit in Greensboro.] His ship in on its way to Hawaii and the mainland."

13 February, TEC, Okinawa:

"Just finished playing hand ball with Glenn Whitmer. He's a pilot, TAD [Temporary Additional Duty] from the Air Wing in Japan. He was an enlisted man before, too. We got beat but neither of us has played very much. Everyone is going to the Philippines by Friday, except me, so I will be on my own."

Edna wrote that our son Jett was now walking on his own, something I really wanted to see.

15 February, TEC, Okinawa:

"I saw Captain Dunwell on his way back from South Vietnam today. He is supposed to fly to Hawaii today. I taught the class in Umpire School today at Camp Hansen. It went fairly well, but I have done a lot better. I ran into Danny Carr, Mark Loveless and Kenneth Payne. Danny got over here last August and is an XO of a rifle company in the 9th Marines. Mark leaves here next month. He's the CO of a Motor Transport Company. Ken just got here. He was stationed at Camp Lejeune. He graduated from Catawba College and is from Danville, Va. Ken was in the 'football platoon' is OCS. He's a good friend of Pat Carlisle."

16 February, TEC, Okinawa:

"Colonel Reese, Major Hittinger, Harry Ling, Captain Heiser and a clerk left for the Philippines today."

18 February, TEC, Okinawa:

"I went to Kadena for a jazz session and chow. The music was really good. I had my usual steak for supper!

19 February, TEC, Okinawa:

"I had a class in Umpire School at Camp Hansen so I spent the day up there. I ran into Barney Glaser, who is going to be an umpire for the exercise. He got married before coming over here. I saw Mark Loveless and Danny Carr, too."

21 February, TEC, Okinawa:

"I've had intestinal flu the past four days, but it seems to be letting up. It really kept me running! We played some tennis and handball today. We played doubles in tennis and won. It keeps me in shape and helps pass the time away."

26 February, TEC, Okinawa:

"A ship came in today and we've got three new officers in our hut. One is a tennis player and has challenged me. Glen Whitmer just got back from Japan and we're going to Camp Kinser to play basketball tonight. I'll be sore tomorrow!"

28 February, TEC, Okinawa:

"WO Wyrakowski just moved into our hut today. He came from Hawaii and works in Disbursing."

1 March, TEC, Okinawa:

"Glen Whitmer and I are going to the Kadena PX tomorrow after we get off. In a way I hope someone else gets XO of Bravo Company, 1st Battalion and I get 81's when John Clements leaves. Tom Solak is about ready and I saw where Larry Cassidy is going to Regiment, so maybe they can wait! I was glad to learn of Lt. Col. Stevens pass over and his pending retirement. I'm sure everyone in the battalion is overjoyed!"

3 March, TEC, Okinawa:

"The party was at one of our Captain's girlfriend's house. She works at the embassy here. The Colonel and some of the higher ups attended along with some embassy people, some schoolteachers, etc. It was just a cocktail party and everyone went to the Kadena club for chow. I saw Danny Carr last night at Kadena. He's on the baseball team and isn't going on the problem. [He pitched for Guilford College.] Glen and I played tennis tonight after chow and I won as usual."

7 March, TEC, Mindoro:

"I'm down at hot, dusty Mindoro now and it is just that—hot and dusty. It looks a lot like California but it doesn't get cool at night. We flew down Tuesday morning in GVIs, the latest planes the Marine Corps has. I saw Major Keith yesterday and we talked for a while. The battalion hardly got off the ship at Subic Bay, so they are glad to get down here. I'm sleeping in a tent with 6 other officers. We have lights, beer, and a two-mile ride for a shower, but it's not too bad. I went to 3rd Battalion and picked up some old mail. I had a letter from Ray Wood. He's a pilot for United Air Lines now. I saw Joe Fiorentino while I was there. Colonel Reese, Major Hittinger and Harry Ling are all up north. When I went back down this morning I saw Jim Catlett. He's ready to go back to Hawaii, too! I ran into Robin Cobble last night, who I knew in Basic School. He's with the 7th Communications Battalion and is out here from California for the problem. The Filipino people are real friendly. Most of them speak English well, as it is taught in the schools. They wave and yell as you go by. I took some pictures of the women who want to do our laundry and also of a big water buffalo and its calf. The calf walked right up to me and was perfectly tame. The natives ride them around. The area we are in is covered with cane fields, just like Hawaii. They use tractors here, but you still see some plowing with water buffalos. A Marine pilot was killed here yesterday in a crash."

9 March, TEC, Mindoro:

"Writing from the Mindoro dust bowl! It is really bad and getting worse. Glen Whitmer and I are going to Manila tomorrow for 3 days. We signed up for a tour and are staying in an air-conditioned hotel in down town Manila. We went into the town of San Jose last night. They have set up some bars, etc., and are bringing in entertainers from Manila. We talked with the owner of the only hotel last night for about an hour. He was a guerilla leader on the island against the Japanese in WWII. He is 62 now and says he is forgetting a lot. I took some pictures of a beautiful church in San Jose but am saving most of my film for Manila. We went down to the river and went swimming this afternoon. Took some beer and really had a ball."

13 March, TEC, Mindoro:

"I had a real nice trip to Manila. We left Saturday morning about 0800 and flew into Sangley Point. We stayed there until about 1300 getting our laundry done, PX call, chow, etc. We caught a bus over to Manila and stayed in the Maubuhay Hotel, which is o.k., but nothing to brag about. Glen Whitmer and I stayed together. We ate our meals at the Sea Front Restaurant, which is an American Government operated club for military and civilians. We went to several nightclubs but they were too expensive.

On Sunday, we took a tour of the city, which was real interesting. We visited the walled city built by the Spanish in the 18th century, Ft. Santiago, that was the last stronghold of the Japanese; Ft. McKinley National Cemetery, which looked a lot like the Punchbowl in Hawaii; and the President's 'white house,' which was used by General McArthur when he was head of the Armed Forces here. The house is really beautiful with huge chandeliers and many nice paintings. We also visited a marketplace, several of the old churches, St. Thomas University, the International Airport, 'Beverly Hills' of Manila, where all the rich live, and a Chinese cemetery, where we witnessed an actual funeral.

It was really something to behold. Hundreds of people were wearing black mourning bands, carrying signs, or playing musical instruments. The widow was hysterical and trying to kill herself in the car and her family had to pin here down to the seat. She was passing out and screaming that she wanted to join her husband, etc. The cemetery was full of beautiful tombs that cost thousands of dollars.

On Monday, we went to Pahsajan Falls, about 2 ½ hours from Manila, and one of the biggest tourist attractions in the Philippines. It was really beautiful—an area covered with coconut palms by a large river. They take you up to the falls in native boats, which they have to lift over some of the rapids. The trip is through a huge gorge with cliffs from 100 to 300 feet up on either side covered with jungle. There are 2 falls, separated by about a mile. The trip down we ran the rapids! Tuesday morning we went back to Sangley Point, picked up our laundry, got a hair cut, ate chow and left about 1430 for San Jose. The flight took about an hour and we caught a helicopter ride back to base camp. The only thing I wanted to do and didn't was to visit Corrigedor. Last night Glen, Dean Coursen, and I ran down to the shower point, about a mile and a half away, but we made it without stopping.

A small tornado just blew through our tent covering me with dirt! What a place!"

15 March, TEC, Mindoro:

"Glen and I ran down to the shower point again tonight. Colonel Reese and Major Hittinger were down today. He said his wife had written that you were helping their son with math. Dan Burger and I are going to fly to the North Camp tomorrow."

18 March, TEC, Mindoro:

"It's a real hot Sunday here, must be 100 degrees out side. We had a small shower yesterday and it cooled things off and settled the dust. Glen Whitmer and quite a few officers moved up north yesterday so things are rather quiet around here. I went up north Friday and saw Harry Ling, Hugh Jenkins, Lou Burton, Bill Rowley, and Ken Lydic. Ken told me about you being mad because I had to come out here early and was doing nothing. I understand that Colonel Andreski from FMFPAC is going to take over the 4th Marines

and Major Keith is going to be his XO. This is just rumor. General Condon, Commanding General of the 1st Marine Air Wing, has been down here quite a bit. He is here today so everyone is running around like a chicken with its head cut off."

19 March, TEC, Mindoro:

"The temperature hit 112 degrees here yesterday and I would say it was at least that today. I went into San Jose last night. I saw Jim Catlett, Joe Fiorientino and Hugh Jenkins. They think they may get to fly back to Hawaii. I have been busy today. I went on a helicopter recon this morning for about 2 hours. It was a real experience. Just the two of us and we flew over some of the most beautiful country in the world. We saw rice paddies and fishing villages along the coast and rugged mountains and jungle inland. There are a lot of ranches here too, and huge rivers that are almost dry now, but you can see the large areas they cover during the rainy season."

20 March, TEC, Mindoro:

"I had the duty yesterday, which kept me tied up all day. It has really been hot here. I had a heat rash around my waist, but I treated it and it went away in a few hours. We were required to go to a fiesta is a small town here Monday night. It was a real loser. The girls that were supposed to dance didn't show up until after 2200 and we had been sitting there since 2000. The beer and the soft drinks they were selling were hot and they charged us two prices for them. We have the afternoon off so I hope to go swimming. It is about the only thing to do around here!"

23 March, TEC, Mindoro:

"I just got back from Cubi Point (Subic Bay) on a trip to get a check cashed and to see some umpires about the problem. I flew up with Nelson Hendricks from the 3rd Battalion. The base is o.k., but I would not want to be stationed there. I did get a fair meal; the steak wasn't good, too tough, but I did get to sleep in a bed for a change! Major Hittinger wasn't much help when I talked with him Thursday. He said only a few officers whose wives were expecting or had had children while they were away, plus a few of the battalion, would fly back! I've been out here since the 10th of January and others will get to fly back and I may not! Task Force 79 on Okinawa has to endorse my orders before I go back to the 3rd Battalion, so I may end up flying to Okinawa and meeting them in Japan. There is a chance that they will let a few go on leave in Japan and then fly back, space-available. The battalion is breaking camp and is going to the hills today. I'll be glad when Monday gets here and we are busy with the problem."

25 March, TEC, Mindoro:

"Tomorrow the problem starts and everything and everyone seems to be busy doing something. I am sure tired of this organization? There is not much organization to it and that is the trouble. Nothing more on coming home except everyone will fly from Subic Bay if they get to go. So far Majors Keith and Hittinger, Captain Heiser, Lt. Byrgoyne, and 1 NCO from each company will go."

27 March, TEC, Mindoro:

"The problem seems to be going well and the VIPs seem pleased. TEC has been one big dog & pony show for the last two days, with hundreds of reporters, observers and brass getting briefed and being shown demonstrations. I took Ray Steinburg of 'Newsweek' around today. We flew up to the 3rd Battalions CP, flew up in the mountains to visit one of the companies and stopped at the Division CP. He works out of Tokyo and gave me his phone number and told me to look him up. One man from the Division died of heat stroke today. The weather has been real hot and there have been quite a few cases of heat stroke and heat exhaustion."

29 March, TEC, Mindoro:

"They decided to run the problem through the 31st so it will be the 2nd of April before we go aboard ship. I've been keeping fairly busy but not nearly as busy as I'd like to be. The time passes too slowly! The Navy had a death aboard a ship. There have been three reported cases of snake bites that I know of this month."

I flew to Okinawa and had my orders endorsed, picked up my gear, and caught a flight to Subic Bay. I boarded the ship, which the battalion was on, at Subic Bay. I was then given leave and allowed to fly back to Hawaii space-available. I caught a flight from Subic Bay to Clark Air Force Base, and then another hop back to Hawaii.

Following a brief leave, I was reassigned back to Charlie Company, 1st Battalion, 4th Marines as the XO. Captain O.K. Steele, who had been recently promoted, was the new CO. Steele was a tall, athletic officer who had served as a platoon commander in the Brigade reconnaissance company, and as General Weede's aide. A Stanford graduate, he was the ideal Marine company commander; smart, tactically sound, and a leader by example. I truly enjoyed working for him. He was demanding but fair in dealing with the officers and men of the company. He led the hikes to Bellows and other training areas with his long strides, and the troops struggled to keep up. As the XO, I and the company Gunnery Sergeant were in the rear, keeping the column closed up and moving. We both had our hands full, as we double-timed to keep up with his rapid pace. I believe I learned more about being a company commander from him than any of the others I had served under. The company excelled in every way under his leadership. However, his tour was almost up and he was transferred to the battalion headquarters as the Assistant S-3, and I took command of the company in August 1962.

Change of Command
Company C, 1st Bn., 4th Marines
Lt. Driver taking command from Cpt. Steele

    I spent the next four months as the company commander, and I saw it as the best possible billet I had ever held. The company continued to excel under my leadership, passing the Brigade and IG inspections. The only thing the IG noted was that we had too much oil on the machine guns! I was fortunate to have three excellent lieutenants in the company: Bob Handrahan, Dave Brown, and Chuck Shelton.

    Captain Dan Quick reported aboard, and I was reassigned to the battalion staff as the Adjutant. Colonel Alfred I. Thomas, who won the Silver Star on Iwo Jima, had command of the battalion. A veteran of two wars, he was as tough as nails and an excellent leader who also led by example. I found him easy to work for. He demanded the best from everyone and he got it.

My new billet called for a Top Secret Clearance, as I had the additional duty of Classified Control Officer. I attended the Naval Registered Publications School at Pearl Harbor to learn my new duties in this area.

The battalion was sent to Pohokola on two training exercises while I was the Adjutant. In addition to other regular live fire training, we ran Battalion Tactical Tests on both occasions and came out far ahead of the other battalions. In addition to my duties as Adjutant, I acted as the S-1 on both problems and graded out 100%. Major Macy, now on the regimental staff and serving as an umpire, reduced our score to 93% because he felt it was too high compared to the other battalions, and we could not be perfect! I told Colonel Thomas but he just shrugged it off, as he was happy about beating the other two battalions.

Under Colonel Thomas, there were no more truck rides down to Hilo. We hiked all the way on both occasions. Most of the battalion could trek the 35 miles, but it was all downhill, which was hard on your legs and especially on your toes. When we finished both hikes, I threw away a pair of boots and wore shower shoes for a week until the blisters on my toes healed enough to wear shoes and socks again. All of the officers and men in the battalion were in similar shape.

During our time on Oahu, Colonel Thomas marched the battalion from the Kahuka training area on the northern part of the island all the way around through Honolulu and around the southern part and back to Kaneohe Bay. I believe only about 100 officers and men completed the hike of 50 miles. I was one of them. We halted several times to eat, drink water, and take salt tablets. On our last stop near Bellows Beach, I made the mistake of eating a can of 'C' ration peaches. When we completed the trek at our headquarters at Kaneohe, I was on my last legs and was so weak I could hardly walk. I made it to a head and threw up the peaches. I lost about 10 pounds and was totally dehydrated. WO Art Bodree, the S-1, put me in my car and drove me home. I spent the weekend drinking a lot of water but when Monday morning rolled around, I couldn't hold my pants up! My uniform looked like it was about to fall off of me! The whole battalion was in bad condition, with many men down with blisters and other aches and pains.

1st Battalion, 4th Marines on the march from Kahuka, 1962
Lt. Col. A.I. Thomas, front right; Lt. Driver, 3rd on right

When the battalion was in garrison, we often played touch football or volleyball at lunchtime. Colonel Thomas often joined us. On one occasion, Art Bodree threw me a touchdown pass on the first offensive play we ran. Colonel Thomas was on the opposing team, and from then on that day he covered me one-on-one like a wet blanket. I could not get off the line of scrimmage against him! He played college football and was still quite an athlete.

Chapter Six

2nd Infantry Training Regiment,
1963-1964
Camp Pendleton, California

I finished my three years in the 1st Marine Brigade, and my family sailed back to San Francisco in September 1963. We flew to Michigan and visited my wife's family during my leave. I learned that a Cadillac dealer had some cars to be delivered to the Los Angeles area. My next duty station was Marine Corps Base, Camp Pendleton, so we drove a Cadillac convertible cross-country and got paid for it. This worked out great as I had to pick up our car at the Long Beach Naval Base. Charlie Kellenbarger and his family were stationed in the area, so he took me to Long Beach to pick up my vehicle.

When I reported to Camp Pendleton, I requested to be assigned to the 2nd Infantry Training Regiment. Colonel Don P. Wykcoff commanded the regiment, and Major Spencer was the Adjutant/Personnel Officer. He took one look at my service record and wanted me to be his assistant. I had no objection, but I believed I should spend some time as the XO of one of the training companies, and he agreed. I spent two months that winter as an XO, and found that my main duties were to act as a safety officer during live fire exercises and observe the training exercises. In addition, I paid the company every two weeks and had other administrative duties. The troop handlers, Corporals, and Sergeants were responsible for the leadership and training of the new Marines. They maintained discipline and set an example for the new men. Most of the enlisted instructors were detailed from the 1st Marine Division. They were Sergeants and Staff Sergeants who had to pass through a board of officers and senior enlisted men to determine if they were knowledgeable and qualified to teach some of the 70 courses each new Marine received. During 1964, 102 companies of new Marines, totaling 20,000 men, received their infantry training at the 2nd ITR. In addition, we gave special training to visiting units of the other Armed Forces, including the civil engineering corps, naval beach groups, aviation units, ships detachments, landing parties (Navy and Marine), and Marine Reserve units. In the summer, we also assisted with the Devil Pup program.

Following my two months as a company XO, I became the Assistant Adjutant/Personnel Officer and Legal Officer for the regiment. I attended the Naval Justice School for several weeks. Major Spencer was a career administrator in the Marine Corps, and we got along well. Our clerks worked long hours to prepare the orders and service record books of all these new Marines when they joined and departed the regiment. My desk would be piled high each morning when I came to work and again after lunch each day. We often worked late in the evenings. As Legal Officer, I assigned the officers of the regiment to court-martials and investigations. This brought me in to contact with all of them.

Family housing was scarce at Camp Pendleton, so we lived off base in San Clemente, a beautiful, but expensive, beach city only a few miles north of the base. Most of the married officers lived off the base and in that area.

I bought an old Chevrolet convertible from a Marine going overseas for $300.00. This gave Edna our VW to shop, run errands, doctor's appointments, etc. One day, Dave Cartwright and I had just started up Highway 101 towards San Clemente when the top blew off! Fortunately, I was able to pull over and put the old top in the back seat. That weekend I bought a case of beer and had a 'put the top back on' party! Dave Cartwright, Frank Powell, Jack Maxwell, Jim Blake, Don Bullard, and perhaps others showed up and we tacked a new top back on the old convertible! The wives and children joined us for a cookout and a trip down to the beach, and a good time was had by all!

Most of the officers worked out at lunchtime, and I began playing a lot of handball. I loved the game, but re-injured my knee making a sharp cut. I ended up having to have surgery on the same knee I had hurt playing baseball. The Naval surgeon said that the inside of my kneecap was rubbing against the bone, causing my knee to swell. He smoothed off the bone and said I should be fine, but no more hand ball! My lunchtimes were now spent rehabilitating my knee.

On 6 October 1964, my daughter Diana Renee was born at the Laguna Beach Hospital. This time I was present and was able to watch the delivery!

Around this time, I learned I had been selected for Captain. This was great news, but I also knew it meant I would be receiving orders soon. A month later, I received orders to the 1st Marine Division, 3rd Battalion, 1st Marines, which would be deploying to Okinawa in 1965. Things were heating up in Southeast Asia, and I believed it would only be a matter of time before the Marines were sent in. Major Spencer gave me permission to attend the two-week Counter Insurgency School before I was transferred. I believe that this school helped me become aware of what Marines would be facing in Vietnam. Most of the instructors had been to Vietnam as observers or advisors, and they gave us excellent presentations and training on mines and booby traps. We walked trails at Camp Pendleton that closely resembled what we would face over there.

Chapter Seven

Transplacement Battalion,
1963-1964
Commanding Officer, Company I,
3rd Battalion, lst Marines

I reported in to 3rd Battalion, lst Marines in December 1964, and was assigned to command Company I, or India Company. 3/1 was a transplacement battalion, which was the Corps method of replacing infantry battalions assigned to the 3rd Marine Division on Okinawa. Most of the Marines assigned to the battalion were on leave over the holidays, but I wanted to get an early start with those on hand.

My XO was lst Lt. Bronson C. Jacoway, Jr., who had been with the company for a year. 2nd Lt. Richard G. McHenry led the lst Platoon. Staff Sergeant Jimmy A. Morton was his platoon sergeant. He was a former Drill Instructor and an All-Marine football player. 2nd Lt. James D. Jones, Jr., was the 2nd Platoon commander. Staff Sgt. Elwood McMichael was his Platoon Sergeant. 2nd Lt. William E. Zelm was the 3rd Platoon Leader. Staff Sergeant Emery F. Elswick was his Platoon Sergeant. 2nd Lt. Peter Lequeur, who had been with the company for some time, was the Weapons Platoon Commander. Staff Sergeant G.L. Winters was initially his Platoon Sergeant, until he proved unsatisfactory. First Sergeant J.Q. Smith was my top enlisted Marine. He had spent most of his career in Marine Aviation but had chosen to be a First Sergeant rather than a Master Gunnery Sergeant. Gunnery Sergeant H.F. Hiles was the company gunny.

A First Lieutenant was commanding the company when I took over. He assured me that all of the company property was there, as the records showed. I made the mistake of signing for the gear without making a property inventory of my own. When I visited the Company Supply NCO, he reluctantly told me that everything had been turned in on paper when the old members of the battalion departed. Their checkout sheets confirmed that, but the company was actually missing over 100 field jackets and 100 sleeping bags. These were the most prized items that Marines wanted to keep when they were discharged or transferred. I could have had a big investigation as to how this was allowed to happen, but most of the signers on the checkout slips were long gone. I talked with the Battalion Supply Officer, lst Lt. J. N. Rodgers, and he informed me that he could write off 10% of the missing items, but I would have to come up with the rest! I had a meeting with my officers and staff NCOs and explained to them the problem. They all had contacts throughout the 1st Marine Division, Marine Corps Base and San Diego. We didn't have much in the way of trade material with other units, but Sergeant Ferrell R. White, my new Supply NCO, who had been in my platoon in Hawaii informed me that we had a lot of cases of C rations. We all made contacts all up and down the West coast and, surprisingly, we were able to trade C rations for sleeping bags and field jackets! 1st Sergeant Smith had numerous contacts in the Air Wing units at El Toro and Santa Ana, and came up with some 50 of the needed items. I contacted my friends at ITR and in the other infantry battalions and was able to trade the C rations for more of them, and in some cases they were just given to me. I would have done the same for them! By the time the men reported back from leave, we were able to fully equip them.

I spent hours going over the Service Record Books of all 200 of my enlisted Marines and the Officer Qualification Jackets of my Lieutenants. Most of the junior enlisted men were fresh out of the Infantry Training Regiments at Camp Pendleton or Camp Lejeune. I was impressed with the fact that almost all were high school graduates and had done well in boot camp and in the follow on training. The Staff NCOs and NCOs were a mixed bag. Some had served in infantry battalions recently while others came from other units, and I had a number of members of the Marine Corps Rifle & Pistol Teams. They had spent most of their careers shooting; therefore they were not in good physical condition or up to date on their duties and responsibilities in an infantry company. This became a real problem, but I had five good, hard charging Lieutenants, and this helped immensely.

The troops reported back from leave on 2 January 1965, and we immediately began training. I held an all hands meeting of my company the first day. I explained who I was, what we were going to do, and how we were going to do it. I told them that their training was going to be hard and as realistic as we could make it. They should take the training seriously, as it might save their life someday. I explained that I would tolerate no racial bias in my company. I considered each man a 'green fighting machine' and skin color, religion, or anything else didn't matter to me. Promotions would come as rapidly as I could make them to the most deserving. Every man should try to not only know his job, but also the next step up, automatic rifleman, fire team leader, squad leader, platoon sergeant, etc. Promotion boards made up of myself, the 1st Sgt., the Gunnery Sgt., the Platoon leaders, and Platoon sergeants would make the recommendations for promotion. I told them that I felt that we would be in Vietnam during our tour in the Far East, and if I were a betting man, I would bet on it. I was right!

I believe the company took me at my word, as our Lock-On training commenced with enthusiasm. We started with the basics, hand and arm signals, fire team tactics, squad tactics, platoon tactics, company tactics, each day and each week we progressed through the training schedule. We ran day and night training exercises, including live fire exercises. For the company, the live fire problem, company in the assault on a fortified position, was the culmination of our training. The importance of teamwork, trust and confidence in each other, and use of supporting arms, grew as we covered the San Mateo and Case Springs training areas of Camp Pendleton. We had physical training daily and climaxed our training with a 20-mile hike. The Battalion Field Exercise was the final training test for the battalion.

I can only recall one incident in which any of my young Marines got into trouble. One night I got a call at home from the San Clemente Police Department. They had arrested 3 of my men who were underage trying to buy beer. The Police Sergeant said he understood that they were going overseas in a few weeks and he would release them into my custody if I would come down and sign for them. I dressed and went down to the Police Station, signed them out, and drove them back to the barracks on the base. It was a quiet drive. I dropped them off and never said anything to anyone about it.

The troops were given a 96 hour pass just before we sailed. Lt. Zelm got married to his college sweetheart at the San Mateo Chapel with all of the officers present.

We were bussed to the San Diego Naval Base on March 14th and went aboard the *U.S.S. Breckinridge.*

L-R: Lts. McHenry, Jacoway, Jones, Laqueur & Cpt. Driver
March 1965

Chapter Eight

En Route to Okinawa,
March 1965

19 March, Honolulu:

"The Colonel stuck to his word on not letting us off the ship Saturday night [in San Diego]. A few had their wives down to see us off but not many, although there was a crowd on the docks. I think we at least deserved a band, but didn't have one. I'm rooming with Captain Welsh and Lt. Daigle. We get along fine. We had a quiet and uneventful trip to Pearl Harbor. There is little for any of us to do but read, eat and watch the movies. The meals are excellent, even better than on the U.S.S. Mann coming back from Hawaii. I played shuffleboard today and am keeping myself in good shape to offset the chow. Others seem to be gaining weight. We're planning on spending the day at Ft. DeRussy and get some sun and a good meal and a few drinks before we leave.

PFC Granahan, who was in my platoon in Hawaii and spent the night with me on a side of the hill during 'Operation Green Light,' is now a Sergeant and on his way back to the 1st Marine Brigade. Bob Wolfenden is aboard this ship also. He's taking some artillery Marines to Okinawa."

20 March, At sea:

"We're on our way to Japan now and I've just recovered from my usual case of seasickness. I finally got a shot and some new medicine last night and I've been o.k. today. The weather has been kind of rough so this is the main reason for my seasickness.

We docked at Pearl Harbor and were met with the usual Navy band, signs, etc. It really looked good. I went to Ft. DeRussey and spent the day there. I called Ron Davia and he and his family are fine. Called the [Charles & Pat] Kellenbargers, and they came over about 2200 and we sat in the bar and talked til 0130 and then they took me back to the ship.

Charlie came on Operation 'Silverlance' to Camp Pendleton but didn't even land. They were aboard ship for 30 days and now the entire 1st Marine Brigade is gone except for part of his squadron.

Hawaii hasn't changed much except for more new hotels. It's starting to look like Miami Beach. We had beautiful weather the first day out and I've gotten a good tan, then we hit rough weather and you know me! We got into Yokohama on Monday and the PX is closed on that day. The Captain of the ship is trying to get them to open it for us. George Welsh and I went to the Naval Officers Club for dinner and a massage. That's the first time I've had anyone walk on my back! We ate a good Chinese meal of sweet and sour pork, wontons, rice with chicken, and chicken with bamboo.

All of my company got back on board on time. A sergeant from Captain Marada's company took off with a Japanese girl. We didn't have any problems in Hawaii, either. Lt.s Jacoway, Laqueur, and Zelm had a ball last night and really did the town. They're suffering now!

Captain Shubert came aboard yesterday, and it looks as if we'll be going to Vietnam this summer. We're supposed to go to the rifle range right away and will train on the island for a while, then go to Mt. Fuji in Japan, and then to Da Nang.

2/4 and 3/4 are at Camp Hansen now. 1/4 is at Camp Schwab. Guess I'll get to see them in a couple of weeks when we move up there to fire the rifle range. It appears that the 4th Marines and the whole Brigade may stay but this is still rumor."

Thursday, At sea:

"We are still at sea and only halfway there. I spent the morning playing cribbage with George Welsh. After lunch, I went up and got some sun but it was too windy to stay long."

Friday, At sea:

"Washed clothes today! Exciting, huh! All we had to do was turn them in and pick them up two hours later."

Saturday, At sea:

"I've been playing bridge all morning and didn't do too badly. Made one misplay but played most of my hands well. My partner and I had 2100 points in two games. George Welsh won the ship's bridge tournament this afternoon."

Sunday. At sea:

"It really got rough yesterday. It was all I could do to keep my chow down. I've never seen it as rough; it was all I could do to stay in my bunk."

Tuesday. At sea:

"We left for Okinawa this morning and get to Okinawa on Thursday, April 1st."

Chapter Nine

Okinawa,
April-May 1965
Commanding Officer, Company A,
1st Battalion, 9th Marines

2 April, Camp Hansen:

"Finally on Okinawa! Got to bed at midnight last night and it's about 1000 now, so I have been rather busy. The old 1/9 and the Division Band met us at the dock. They were rather glad to see us! Saw Bill Gray and Jim Stivers and talked for quite a while. The BOQ is nice. Things are a lot better than 1962 when I was here, although construction is still in progress everywhere you look. I feel like an executive with the office I have. Pine paneling and nice furniture (for the Marine Corps). The barracks are better, too. I've seen half the people I know in the Marine Corps—Captains Mills, Dick Pyne, Bob Donahue, Mike Eddy, Jim Champlin, and many others. Major Turner, who was the I&I in Greensboro, N.C., is the Regimental S-3.

My nasan [housekeeper] is about 40 years old, 4 feet tall, and has gold teeth and is double ugly. Major Brooks, who lives next door, says she is the best. I believe it, as she did 5 shirts, 2 sets of utilities, 1 cover, 1 set of khakis, skivvies, socks, towels, etc. as well as shining 4 pair of boots and shoes, plus cleaning the room, making the bed, etc."

4 April, Camp Hansen:

"Well Saturday and Sunday really have no significance over here other than church services on Sunday. I worked until 1500 today. We're still drawing gear but we've got our packs made up and ready to go. Things appear to be getting worse in Vietnam. This island is full of rumors.

The Officers' Mess is really nice and the food is excellent. The bar is a popular place, naturally."

5 April, Camp Hansen:

"Colonel [Frank E.] Garretson, the Regimental Commander, spoke to the battalion today. He's a good speaker and impressed everyone. As it stands now, we'll fire the rifle range, do some field training and then move to the Northern Training Area for counter guerilla training for a week or ten days. Everything changes from day to day. It's really the 'Division in motion.'

Worked until 2000 tonight. We've sure got a lot to do and a short time to do it in. We're having a Battalion Cocktail Hour tomorrow night, coat and tie. We have Duty Company also so I'll go back to work after it is over."

6 April, Camp Hansen:

"Just got home from a Regimental Reception with free booze! Talked with Major Turner for a while. He left Greensboro and spent three years at the Naval Academy, then three years at FMF Atlantic in Norfolk.

We're having a briefing by General [William R.] Collins tomorrow. He's the Commanding General of the 3rd Marine Division. We are also getting our pictures made for the cruise book. Don't know when I going to get my work done!"

7 April, Camp Hansen:

"In addition to having our pictures made and listening to Gen. Collins, the Colonel inspected the company. We had a promotion board tonight and got two men promoted to Corporal and four to Lance Corporal. One of the new Lance Corporals is [D.K.] Pemberton, from Flint, Michigan.

I'm going on a recon of training areas tomorrow and plan to stop by Camp Schwab and see 1/4. I saw Sergeant Major McPhail, who was in 1/4 in Hawaii.

Lt. Daigle fell and has a compound fracture of both wrists [repelling off a cliff at Raid School]. He'll probably be hospitalized for 6 months. He was Captain Welsh's Executive Officer.

My nasan ruined my two short sleeve dress shirts. She tore the collar on one and the new one turned yellow when she washed it. I'm buying some new ones."

8 April, Camp Hansen:

"Had a party at the club tonight. There was a band and about 25 hostesses. Even the Colonel came. The music was good and the bachelors enjoyed the girls. Jacoway and Laqueur were doing all the latest dances from the states and it was a lot of fun. Toured most of the ranges today, since we'll be going to field after the rifle range. Got an inspection and a hike tomorrow. Our Company has Riot Control so none of us can drink."

9 April, Camp Hansen:

"I just played volleyball for 3 hours. It poured rain all morning so the hike was called off.

Went down with George Welsh to see Lt. Daigle today. He seems to be doing o.k. considering he has steel rods through the bones of his hands and weights to keep them elevated. He says the worst thing is not being able to scratch! He may be going back to the states soon. His wife called him today. She's due next month and has trouble and is in bed for 6 weeks. It will be their fourth child.

We went to the Kadena Officers Club for a few drinks. Met Dave Howe there. I also met Mick Harris, an Australian Captain who works for Major Turner. He's quite a character. He's hard to understand with all the 'bloody's' he uses.

I just heard we had two more battalions of Marines land in South Vietnam. Heard a company commander got shot during the landing. We're almost the only ones left on the island. 3/4 left yesterday. 2/4 had a mount out today. I don't know if they are leaving or not."

10 April, Camp Hansen:

"Getting ready to get on the trucks [to go to the Northern Training Area] so I'm taking a minute to write."

11 April, Jungle Warfare School:

"Had my usual busy day today. I climbed the second highest mountain on Okinawa today. It was similar to climbing the mountains in Hawaii. Going up there again in 15 minutes so this has to be fast. It did stop raining today for the first time since we have been here.

I haven't shaved since I've been here so I'm getting quite a growth. I had my second bath tonight. Sure was nice. The 1st Sergeant sees that the mail, etc., gets up here each day."

12 April, Jungle Warfare School:

"Another busy day today and hot, too! Getting 4-5 hours sleep doesn't help either. Last night there was a rat in the tent. He woke me up gnawing on a box and I threw a boot at him twice. It was 0300. What next?

Just got word we're going to raid training when we get back to Camp Hansen starting May 7 for 21 days. The schedule will be even rougher than this one. I'm sure it will be good training, though. It involves quite a few hours of swimming and operating in rubber boats off of submarines.

I have trouble knowing what day it is up here. It's supposed to rain tomorrow so we should be miserable again."

13 April, Jungle Warfare School:

"I'm sitting here in the tent with the radioman and it's pouring down rain, as usual. It started at 1100 and hasn't let up and it's 1600 now. Haven't been very busy, only a few hours this morning. Lt. Jacoway is out in the field with one of the platoons. Captain Welsh and I are about the only ones around. Had another man injured today. He got a piece of bamboo in his eye. He's the third with an eye injury up here. My beard has started to itch a little and I'm thinking about shaving it off but I guess I can last two more days."

15 April, Camp Hansen:

"Got up at 0500 this morning for nothing. It poured rain and it was so windy we couldn't shoot. Just out there long enough to get soaked and have to clean the weapons."

16 April, Camp Hansen:

"I fired 226 with the M-14 rifle on the range today. Now I'm praying for rain tomorrow! Lt. McHenry is going TAD to the rifle and pistol range for 3 months. Captain [C.E.] Taylor [S-2] is going to Vietnam for 30 days. I ran into Dave Fanning this morning at 0515! He had just gotten back from Da Nang. They've just changed the working hours from 0730 to 1900. Should make the time pass even faster. Guess they're putting us on a near combat training period."

17 April, Camp Hansen:

"Fired real well with the rifle today. Not so hot with the pistol, as usual. Heard today that 3/4 landed at Da Nang. Saw them leave last week but didn't know for sure where they were going."

18 April, Camp Hansen:

"I fired 222 (expert) with the rifle and 321 (sharpshooter) with the pistol. Zelm tied me with the rifle but all the other officers fired lower. It was really windy and we had 18 non-qualifiers.

All the officers went to Kadena and proceeded to get high. Got back about midnight. No hangover, though. Saw Dan Quick and he asked about you. I'm Camp Duty Officer tomorrow so I'll have a dull day. I played 7 games of ping pong today and beat the best player in the company."

19 April, Camp Hansen:

"Spent most of the day in the field. We have 10 Vietnamese officers and enlisted men attached to our company. They all understand English fairly well but don't speak it too well. Lt. Kee, who has been to Basic School, speaks very well and acts as interpreter. He's quite a character.

Lt. Gregory with Vietnamese Marine Officers, May 1965, Okinawa

I'm going to the Northern Training Area tomorrow on a recon by helicopter. Should be an interesting trip. Captain Welsh's company has been up there a week now. It's been raining almost every day so I imagine they are miserable."

20 April, Camp Hansen:

"Ran into Kent Shockey and Tom Rodhouse last night, also Mike Eddy. Kent is the Regimental Adjutant, Rodhouse the Supply Officer and Eddy the Assistant S-3 of 9th Marines. I've been doing some reading today, mostly reviewing for the guerrilla warfare school."

21 April, Camp Hansen:

"Today was total frustration. Didn't get to make the trip to NTA because the helicopters weren't available, couldn't take the company to the field because of working parties. Can't go the field again tomorrow because of working parties but may get to NTA if the choppers are flying."

22 April, Camp Hansen:

"*Spent the day in the field today. Had the Vietnamese with us shooting rifle grenades and throwing hand grenades. The Vietnamese are good with weapons, but seem a little lazy. They hiked back with us and looked a little bushed. Might have been my pace? Ha!*"

23 April, Camp Hansen:

"*Rode to NTA in a helicopter with Colonel Keith and Major Turner. We finished up the promotion board tonight. Sure glad that is over. Lost a filling a few minutes ago, the same one I lost before. Something else to do tomorrow!*"

25 April, Camp Hansen:

"*Had a busy day today. We're still getting ready to go to the NTA. Played basketball for a while tonight and I'm pooped. The humidity is really high over here. Worst than Hawaii, even. Went to Happy Hour at the club tonight. What a riot! Everyone got plastered but me. I behaved myself, believe it or not! My lieutenants are the worst hell raisers around. Jacoway is the leader, naturally.*

Got to close and get packed. I haven't done a thing yet! I'm taking George Welsh's camera and radio up there for him."

6 April, NTA:

"*Up at NTA now and it is really a wilderness or jungle, as you like it. The Base Camp where Lt. Jacoway, the Gunny, and I are staying is o.k. Finally got a shower and brushed my teeth tonight. Even had a beer! The training here is good and the troops are really enjoying it. It's rugged, though.*

Sergeant [R.H.] Neeld, my Chief Clerk, started counting the days the day we went aboard ship and brings it up every day. I told him I'm not interested until we run out of months. More Marines are getting killed and wounded in Vietnam. We seldom hear their names, so don't know if we know any of them."

27 April, NTA:

"*We're having a nice rainy day today. It's poured most of the day and foggy the rest of the time with 100% humidity. Luckily we were in the classroom most of the day so we weren't too wet.*"

28 April, NTA:

"Well, I thought the wind would blow us away last night. The tent pegs came out twice and I got soaked. The troops in the field were a lot worse off, though. We had one man break an arm, one stick a piece of bamboo through his hand and another injured his eye. The sun just came out and everyone is busy hanging everything out to dry. Looks like a big outdoor laundry!"

29 April, NTA:

"Well, just as I predicted it has poured rain again today. It started last night and has poured off and on all day. It's been windy and when I came in a while ago the wind had blown the side of the tent over and my sleeping bag got wet. I just put on dry socks and boots before going back out in it. Not much use, really, but it feels good now.

I'm getting a good growth of beard now. Some of the men in B Company have really got long ones.

Lt. Jacoway and two platoons are up on Iye-dake Mountain now and I know they're miserable slipping and sliding through the mud. 2/4 is supposed to land in Vietnam this week. 1/4 will probably land also. Heard on the news that a battalion had landed in Santa Domingo. The Marines are busy everywhere, it seems."

1 May, NTA:

"All the troops are in the field and I'm sitting here in Base Camp directing the exercise. Not much to do really. I was too busy yesterday to write. It was midnight before the platoon leaders got to bed.

The rain stopped yesterday and today has been nice. Hope the next 3 days will be the same. The Major who runs the school here and works for Colonel Keith is going with him to Da Nang for a few days tomorrow.

Had a man break a leg today. He fell off a cliff. I've had two other men require stitches. Looks like we'll be shorthanded for raid training next week. We'll probably have some men hurt there also. Delta Company did."

Waterman Ship at NTA
Okinawa, May 1965

3 May, Camp Hansen:

"Just got through work in preparation for raid school. I'm rather beat after that 3-hour ride back from NTA. The only consolation is that I will be busy for the next 21 days. I understand it is mostly physical training and they try to make it as rough as possible. Everyone is a student and is treated alike. What did I make Captain for? The 1st Sergeant wants to go to raid school, even at his age. He'll be the first 1st Sergeant to ever go through it." [He made it through the school. Gunnery Sergeant Hiles stayed in the rear, as he realized he could not make it.]

4 May, Camp Hansen:

"I spent a busy day with piles of paper work and getting ready for raid school. Went down there today and met Captain [Thomas W.] Rich, who runs the school. After seeing and hearing about it I think it's even rougher than I imagined. I'll be busy for 21 days and exhausted!

We have arrived at [Amphibious] Raid School and tomorrow the fun begins. I'm sitting in the chow tent with the troops (the only tent with lights) and everyone is writing letters and reading the Stars & Stripes. The lights are dim so this may be a bit blurred. It's raining as usual but tomorrow it is supposed to stop. Hope! Hope! We're going to Subic Bay in the Philippines to operate off of submarines from the 14th till the 20th. We're flying there and back. It should be a real experience!"

6 May, Raid School:

"I passed the PT Test with flying colors. I was really pooped, though. Passed everything in the swim test but the 50-meter underwater swim. I got a cramp in my leg and came to the surface. It was a rainy miserable afternoon for the swim test but it was hot and the sun was out for the 3 mile run this morning. We had 49% to pass the PT Test. Delta Company only had 40%.

We're all sitting around writing letters but you could have heard a pin drop while the news was on. 1/4, 2/4 and 3/3 were the battalions that landed in South Vietnam. It won't be long before we'll be going down there!"

8 May, Raid School:

"Guess you noticed two letters dated Thursday. That shows how little days and dates mean out here. I asked someone what day it was last night and he said 'Thursday' so I wrote it without question. Later there was a big debate over what day it was. Humorous, huh!

I swam more today than I have in the last 15 years. It must have been 3 miles. We had 2 hours in the morning, 3 hours in the afternoon and an hour tonight. Tomorrow we start with rubber boats. At least we're not in the water! The news just said we were to have 4 inches of rain during the next 18 hours. It's pouring now and has been on and off all day."

9 May, Raid School:

"Spent the day at the beach, so to speak. We worked with rubber boats all day and are going out again tonight. The weather was real good but it looks like rain again tonight. Just got back from our night work with the boats. Wasn't too cold and miserable after all."

10 May, Raid School:

"Another miserable day. It poured rain all day and is still coming down. We worked with the rubber boats again today and will again tonight. Also had the 'Bear Pit' today. They have a pit 12 feet deep and filled with a foot or two of mud and eight men get in, four on a side, and try to throw each other out. I didn't get thrown out but it was a miserable experience. The Colonel [Ludwig] came out and watched the 1st Platoon go through. He didn't seem too impressed. Everyone got filthy but luckily no one got hurt. Got to close and go get wet, rain or ocean who cares!"

11 May, Raid School:

"Just finished chow and I'm sitting out in front of the tent writing and listening to the radio.

After pouring rain all night and all morning it finally quit. The sun came out about 1630 and everyone is trying to dry out their gear. We're getting double rations out here but everyone says I'm thinner in the face. We had ice cream tonight for the first time and needless to say it was all eaten. Morale really went up with the sun coming out and the ice cream.

I missed Colonel Keith this afternoon. He just got back from Vietnam and came out to see how the school was going. I was at the demolition range when he came. We don't have air transportation so the trip to Subic Bay has been called off. We're got more night work with the rubber boats tonight. No rest for the weary!"

12 May, Raid School:

"Spent another day in rubber boats and running the knife and bayonet courses. We've got more boat work tonight. We have our regular PT and 500 yard swim tomorrow. I saw Colonel Keith today. He had some interesting news on what's going on 'Down South.'

'Down South' refers to South Vietnam. Heard that three more battalions of Marines will land in South Vietnam within the next 3 weeks. I guess they mean us! Just got back from rubber boat training and we had our usual rain!"

13 May, Raid School:

"Well, we're back in the same grind again. They increased the amount of PT we're doing each morning. I'll survive though. Two more weeks to go! Colonel Keith was out today and asked about you and Jett.

I'm writing by flashlight so don't know if you can read this or not. It's pouring rain as usual and just got back from night rubber boat work.

Heard today that the [1st Marine] Brigade from Hawaii is here to stay and the dependents there will be sent home."

14 May, Raid School:

"Our day of rest has been a leisurely one. We had PT this morning and the 500 yard swim test this afternoon, but in between I got a hot shower, a meal, made a PX run for a haircut, and accomplished a lot of paper work. The swim test turned out to be easy. Getting in shape, I guess.

We're all sitting around reading and writing letters in front of the tent. I can't believe we don't have training tonight! We had the usual rain this morning but since then the sun had been out and it has been beautiful. The Colonel and Major [J.L.] O'Toole [S-3] were out this afternoon. Major O'Toole made the swim with us. Neither had much to say. I had a long talk with Major [Harold A.] Hatch [XO of the battalion] today and I'm getting a new Gunnery Sergeant. Anything will be an improvement!"

15 May, Raid School:

"Just got through PT for the second time today. I just had a nice hot shower. No night work tonight! We're all taking it easy and I'll be in bed by 2000. Everyone goes to bed early here! We start repelling tomorrow and tomorrow night. It should be a lot of fun, ha! It will be a lot of hard work, I'm sure. Today we had classes on tying knots, but I'm not too good at it. I'm left handed you know! Lt. Daigle is being air evacuated soon. He's the Lt. who broke both wrists.

We're all sitting around in front of the tent writing letters and listening to the radio. More Marines killed and wounded on patrol in Vietnam. Saw a Life magazine article on Marine helicopters in Vietnam, showing the death of a pilot and the wounding of the gunner, quite a tragic scene. The troops just caught a frog and have a string around its leg and are 'walking the frog.'

We're in between rainstorms, as it has poured here most of the day and just quit a few minutes ago. The weatherman says more rain tomorrow. Lt. Laqueur made 1st Lt. He's out here taking pictures of us. Lt. Jacoway took one of me doing pull ups this afternoon. I know that was pretty!

The troops aren't satisfied with the PT they do, they're down swimming and working on pull-ups, climbing ropes, etc. It must be nice to be that young and energetic! Someone just found a dud shell alongside the road and we had to call EOD [Explosive Ordinance Disposal]. It looks like a WWII relic. This beach was used for a landing, I understand."

16 May, Raid School:

"Spent the day climbing up and down cliffs. I'm not too good at it as I'm a little leery of hanging 100 feet in space. I hurt my elbow the first try but did o.k. after that.

It's been raining most of the day and more is predicted. The sun was out for a while today but not for long! Tonight we repel some more, until 2200. Tomorrow's schedule is almost the same except for repelling out of helicopters, which should be fun.

We are going to put on a demonstration for General [Lewis W.] Walt on the 25th. He's to be the new Commanding General of the 3rd Marine Division. We've also scheduled a beer party for the 28th, when we graduate. Got to get ready for night repelling so I'll close for now."

17 May, Raid School:

"Another rainy day. It's poured on and off all day and the prediction is for more. We repelled off cliffs and out of helicopters today. Lt. Jacoway was put over a cliff on a stretcher during a demonstration today. He was a little nervous to say the least!

Good news! They just cancelled training for tonight! Cheers went up in every tent. It's going to be down to 60 degrees tonight and it's pouring rain, so it's a good idea."

19 May, Raid School:

"Another rainy day. Training has been called off tonight again. The weather report says 12 more hours of rain! Lt. Laqueur hasn't had a letter from his girlfriend in about a week. Everyone had been riding him and he's getting a little upset about it. Can't blame him!"

A/1/9 Raid School, May 1965

20 May, Raid School:

"Spent a busy day in the rubber boats today. Amphibious tractors towed us out about a mile and we rowed in. Tonight we do the same thing. I found a sea snake today when we landed. It caused quite a bit of excitement, to say the least. We had had a lecture on snakes yesterday.

Last night's cliff assault went a lot better. No one fell. It even seemed easier the second time. Tomorrow is our administration day and I get to get a haircut, etc. I've got a lot of laundry to be done also even though we have laundry service out here. It's rather irregular due to the weather."

21 May, Raid School:

"Another day of pouring down rain. We were out in the boats this afternoon. Amphibious tractors were towing us. It was a lot of fun. Tonight we have the same thing. Last night we had a landing. It went real well. The instructors had nothing but compliments for us.

Saw Colonel Keith at chow today. He said he was coming out to watch us tonight. Captain [Joe] Marada's Company [C] had 2 men drown in a stream crossing exercise today. The instructors and 8 of my men went up to find the bodies. Haven't heard who they are. It's a tragic thing but the training is necessary to prepare us for Vietnam.

126

It poured rain today but I managed to get a haircut, PX call, hot shower, and dry, clean clothes before getting wet again. My nasan was happy to see me but not all the dirty clothes and boots I brought her to do. I'm getting spoiled with her shining my boots!

My men just came back after finding the two bodies. One of the instructors found one of the bodies and pulled it out.

The new 2/9 arrived today. We are no longer the 'boots' on the island. They start training in the Northern Training Area and Raid School next week."

22 May, Raid School:

"Had the 1,000 yard swim today. Only had one man out of 100 to fail it. A storm came up and the 3rd Platoon didn't get to make it. They're going to do it tomorrow. We had a 6-mile paddle in rubber boats scheduled for tonight but it was cancelled too. It rained as hard as I've ever seen it rain anywhere for about 3 hours. It turned cold and everyone curled up in their sleeping bags and slept. Now everyone is lying about reading their mail and writing their sweethearts and or wives. I've got the radio on and 2 candles going to see by.

Heard on the radio just now that a new record for rainfall during May on Okinawa has been set. It's still coming down and we've had over an inch today.

5 more days of school! The training is excellent but I'm getting a little tired of it. I'm a company commander without a job most of the time as the instructors handle most of the training. We just got back two Marines from Vietnamese language school and sent 2 more. They'll be a big help down south.

The 1st Sergeant just showed me some slides of myself in the 'Bear Pit.' My baldhead easily identifies me. Another Marine has a picture of me when I fell while repelling. Blackmail!"

23 May, Raid School:

"Didn't have a chance to write last night. We finished the afternoon schedule late and started the evening schedule early. We had a night cliff assault and 5 men fell down about 50 feet. Lt. Jones was one of them, but luckily he wasn't hurt. One Marine has a chipped or cracked knee cap. Everyone followed instructions about falling and this was the main reason no one was hurt. I banged my knee a little but it is o.k. today. We spent this morning on the cliffs again and had swimming and boating in the afternoon. It turned out to be a nice day after all. We're going on the cliffs again tonight.

The Colonel was out again yesterday. Major Hatch, Captains [James D.] Shubert [Asst. S-3], De Martino [CO, H&S Co.] and ["B." Louis] Avera [S-4] are going to Vietnam soon as the advance party. He also said we would be getting the new jungle boots and lightweight uniforms before going. [Didn't happen!] The heat down there now is about 100 degrees and the humidity is about that high. Lt. Laqueur finally got a letter last night and was he happy! Captain Rich, who runs the school here, is from Conway, S.C. He went to the Naval Academy and has orders in July to HQMC. He's a real fine officer. We think alike about a lot of things."

24 May, Raid School:

"The sun finally came out today and we had a beautiful day for a change. Colonels Keith and Ludwig were both here today for the rehearsal for General Walt's visit tomorrow. Neither had much to say.

We have the 6-mile paddle tonight. It should be boring for me as a passenger. The 3rd Platoon had a nice day for the 1,000-yard swim. All but one man in the company made it and he had a bad arm.

Just got in from the 6-mile paddle. We did it in 2 ½ hours. That's as good as any company has done in the school. I paddled part of the way. We have a raid tomorrow and then the dog & pony show for the General."

25 May, Raid School:

"Glad today is over! Had a raid this morning and the General's visit in the afternoon. The raid came off fairly well. The General's visit came off real well. He was real pleased with everything he saw. He complimented everyman he observed. He was really interested in our training as he participated in two raids during WW II. Colonels Keith and Ludwig were pleased also.

We've got a typhoon warning now and the school may end tomorrow. I hope it is in a way but I would like to culminate the training with a good raid."

Major General Lewis W. Walt (2nd from L), observes a demonstration of rappelling from a helicopter while touring Raid School.
L-R: Driver, Walt, Cpt. Rich, Col. Quilici & Col. Keith

26 May, Camp Hansen:

"Raid school is over! We had to leave the area due to the typhoon. Got back about 1400 today. It's going to be nice to sleep between two sheets tonight!

Ran into Harry Ling today. He's in the new 2/9, also Captain Russ Lloyd from ITR and Lynn Osborne and Cliff Rushing from Kaneohe. Harry said Jim Baier is down at [MCAS] Futema [Okinawa] as an Air Observer. He crashed the other day and he and the pilot walked away without a scratch. The plane was a total loss.

The bar in the Officer's Mess was closed tonight so Laqueur, Jones, Zelm and I bought a case of beer and sat around here and drank it tonight and shot the breeze. The typhoon is supposed to hit tomorrow although it may be veering away from the island. Sure hope so!

We did real well in Raid School. Zelm made the highest grade ever on the final exam. He only missed 2 questions. I missed 8. The company had 71% to complete the final PT test, which was 3% better than Delta Company. We beat them in everything."

27 May, Camp Hansen:

"Had a busy day today with all the paper work piled up after three weeks. We have a promotion board tonight so that is taken up, too! Tomorrow we're going to have a company party at a beach recreation area near here. It will be a good time to relax for a change. I've invited Colonels Ludwig and Keith. Heard today that the 7th Marines left the states on the 24th. Guess Don Brooks is on his way!"

On this same date, Corporal Edward F. Dresch was presented with the Navy-Marine Corps Medal for heroism. "While on liberty at Newport Beach, California, he observed a woman lying face down in the turbulent waters off shore, swam to her side and succeeded in bringing her to safety. Shortly before reaching dry land, he heard a man yelling for help, approximately 50 yards out, who appeared to be on the verge of drowning. Cpl. Dresch again entered the water, swam out to the almost exhausted victim and managed to bring him ashore." Dresch was an excellent Marine.

Dresch Award: Cpl. Edward F. Dresch is presented the Navy-Marine Corps Medal by Lt. Col. Verle E. Ludwig, CO 1/9

29 May, Camp Hansen:

"I have been busy as usual. Yesterday was rather hectic. We're changing our training schedule around to make a raid from a destroyer on Monday night. This has thrown everything out of kilter as all the training has to be changed. I'll be working all day today and tomorrow too. Lt. McHenry came back from TAD today. He's settled down a bit now.

The company beer party yesterday a big success. The Colonel [Ludwig] and the instructors from the raid school came down. We had an officers and staff NCO against the troops volleyball and softball games. We won the volleyball but lost the softball. Too many beers! Only two or three men got out of hand and they were no real problem."

30 May, Camp Hansen:

"Spent a frustrating day. We were supposed to fire on 2 ranges along with Delta Company. The ammunition didn't show up until 1145 so we sat and waited from 0730 on. Tomorrow we are going aboard the destroyer. It should be interesting. We will be the first Marines to operate off of it."

2 June, Camp Hansen:

"Riding out another typhoon. It's pouring rain, over 5 inches already, but the winds haven't been bad at all. We were aboard ship, the U.S.S. Diachenko [APA—123], when we got the word on the typhoon. We had to paddle in and move back to Camp Hansen. We spent all day yesterday and last night using the rubber boats off the ship. It was real good training but we didn't get to make the raid again. Maybe Colonel Keith will let us graduate anyway, this time!

Major Hatch and the others just got back from Vietnam and briefed us as to what we would be doing. Won't be long now!"

3 June, Camp Hansen:

"The typhoon blew over without a lot of damage. Had a lot of rain, though. We have Riot Control Company tonight. Going to the field overnight tomorrow night so no letter."

5 June, Camp Hansen:

"It poured rain the last two days, as usual, so naturally we were quite miserable in the field. Lt.s Jacoway and Zelm, 1st Sgt. Smith, and SSgt. Morton left for Vietnam this morning, so you can see we're getting short here. We'll be leaving in about a week.

We had a party at the club Thursday night. Lt. Laqueur was celebrating his promotion and we celebrated to send Jacoway and Zelm on their way. You might as well go ahead and watch the TV shows on Vietnam. At least you will have some idea of what is going on down there and what it is like. They're glorified a little but generally tell the truth.

It's officer's fitness report time so I've got a lot of work to do on the Lt's. I chewed McHenry a new one this morning. I've never been so mad at him before. He failed to take his platoon out and fire a range because it was raining, just took it upon himself to cancel it. I made him take them out this afternoon."

6 June, Camp Hansen:

"Just got back from the PX and stocking up for 'down south.' George Welsh and Brooks West went along. We had lunch together and a few drinks. I worked on fitness reports today. I hate doing them but want to get them out of the way before we leave.

7 June, Camp Hansen:

"Sent 2 platoons down to load the ship today. Lt.s Laqueur and Jones went with them, so McHenry is the only one left around. My room is empty now except for the gear going in my Val Pac suitcase.

Started taking malaria pills today. One big pink one and 3 little white ones. They are supposed to give you diarrhea but they haven't bothered me yet. I'll take the same dosage once a week."

8 June, Camp Hansen:

"We're making final preparations to leave now. We start loading tomorrow. Tomorrow night may be my last letter for a while but don't worry as we're going by ship and it takes a while and of course, no mail goes off until we get there. I'll be thinking about you and the babies and will mail one long letter just before we get off."

9 June, Camp Hansen:

"We go aboard ship tomorrow so this will be my last letter for a while. I love and miss you darling and I'll be thinking of you and the little ones every spare moment

L-R: Driver, GySgt. Hiles, 1st Sgt. Smith, Lt. Jones, Lt. Laqueur
A/1/9 Okinawa, 1965

ALPHA COMPANY

HQ

CAPTAIN R. J. DRIVER JR.
Company C O

1stLT B. C. JACOWAY JR.
Company X O

1stSGT J. Q. SMITH
Company 1stSgt

GYSGT E. G. GUNDERSON
Company GySgt

SGT R. H. NEELD
Company Admin Chief

CPL J. L. SCHIMKOLA JR.
Company Admin NCO

LCPL L. W. COSSETTE
Co. Admin Man

PFC J. R. MOXON
Company Messgr

SGT F. R. WHITE
Co. Supply NCO

LCPL E. P. PRATHER
Company Driver

LCPL R. C. HEMPEL
Company Radioman

Alpha Company HQ

1st PLATOON

1stLT P. LAQUEUR
Platoon Commander

SSGT J. A. MORTON
Platoon Sgt

SGT M. TINO
Plt Guide

LCPL T. J. NICKLAUS
Plt Radioman

SGT R. E. DYER
1st Sqd Ldr

CPL J. P. BOONSTRA
1st Fireteam Ldr

PFC I. J. HILLER
Auto Rifle

PFC J. W. MAHLER
Rifleman

PFC G. A. FINLEY JR.
Rifleman

LCPL C. J. ANDERSON
2nd Firetm Ldr

PFC M. SOTO JR.
Auto Rifle

PFC D. R. PETERSON
Rifleman

PFC K. D. MAJORS
Rifleman

LCPL E. W. LACEY
3rd Firetm Ldr

PFC R. M. LARUE
Auto Rifle

PFC G. V. HEATH
Rifleman

LCPL J. H. MULNEAUX
Grenadier

CPL R. O. KING
2nd Sqd Ldr

CPL G. W. NETEMEYER
1st Firetm Ldr

Alpha Company, 1st Platoon

Alpha Company, 1st Platoon

Alpha Company, 2nd Platoon

Alpha Company, 2nd Platoon

3rd PLATOON

1stLT W. E. ZELM
Platoon Commander

SSGT E. F. ELSWICK
Platoon Sgt

SGT J. W. LUTZ
Plt Guide

LCPL W. G. SMALLWOOD, JR.
Plt Radioman

SGT J. R. MARTINEZ
1st Sqd Ldr

CPL J. R. SASSER
1st Firetm Ldr

LCPL J. S. MALIN
Auto Rifle

PFC R. T. JOHNSTON
Rifleman

LCPL R. E. BENTLEY
Rifleman

LCPL M. R. OLSON
2nd Firetm Ldr

PFC T. S. PIASCYK
Auto Rifle

PFC R. E. WILSON
Rifleman

LCPL G. L. LESTER
3rd Firetm Ldr

PFC D. C. COKLEY
Auto Rifle

PFC R. W. VERUSIO
Rifleman

PFC M. R. BEAL
Rifleman

LCPL J. L. LEWIS
Grenadier

SGT V. G. WHITE
2nd Sqd Ldr

CPL R. M. CARRO
1st Firetm Ldr

Alpha Company, 3rd Platoon

Alpha Company, 3rd Platoon

WPNS. PLATOON

Alpha Company, Weapons Platoon

Alpha Company, Weapons Platoon

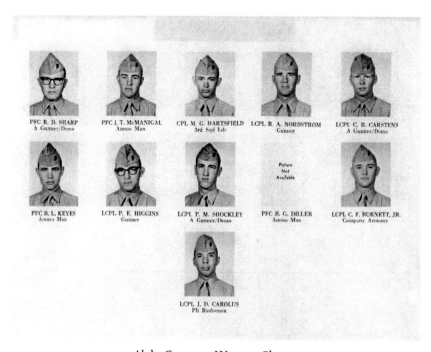

Alpha Company, Weapons Platoon

Alpha Company, 1st Section, 81's Platoon

Chapter Ten

Da Nang TAOR,
June-September 1965
Commanding Officer, Company A,
1st Battalion, 9th Marines
Operations Blastout, County Fair, and Golden Fleece
"The troops were magnificent!"

The battalion embarked aboard the *U.S.S. Okanogan* [APA 220] on 10-11 June 1965. The *U.S.S. Matthews* accompanied us, carrying some of our equipment. The trip to Vietnam proved uneventful. We continued our physical fitness training each morning and weapons and tactical reviews in the afternoon. On June 15th, we test fired our M-14s, 45s, M-60s, 3.5s and M-79s at floating targets. Classes included recognition of VC grenades and landmines. Correct radio procedures were reviewed. Upon our arrival near Da Nang we were briefed on the situation in that area. Our mission was to relieve the 3rd Battalion, 9th Marines' sector in the defense of the Da Nang airfield. The rules of engagement were stressed; we could only fire upon someone shooting at us. Ammunition was issued, but none could be loaded into the chamber. In other words, we had to load our weapons before firing. One day's "C" rations were issued to each man. Eight Navy corpsmen were assigned to each rifle company. A detail from each company was to remain aboard the ship to assist in the off loading.

The first thing we noticed when we arrived off the coast was the heat and humidity. The temperatures ranged from 100 to 130 degrees, so we were told! On the morning of June 16th we climbed down the cargo nets into the Landing Craft Mediums and headed for shore. Much to our surprise a welcoming committee greeted us on the beach. It consisted of Vietnamese army officials with a color guard and young girls throwing flowers. Trucks hauled us to the airfield, where the officers and men of 3/9 were waiting. They had finished their thirteen - month tour of duty and headed for the ship to return to Okinawa. I met several members of my old company in Hawaii there. SSgt. Robitaille and Sgt. Welch came to visit me. Lt.s Jacoway and Zelm, 1st Sgt. Smith, and SSgt. Morton joined us and briefed the company on their experiences while operating with the ARNV.

We spent our first night ashore in an old overgrown area on the airbase. There was a shell of a concrete building in the center which was used as the company CP. There were a few trees which provided a little shade for the troops in their pup tents, as the temperatures approached 100 degrees. The area was infested with centipedes and rats, one of which nipped me on the finger during the first night there.

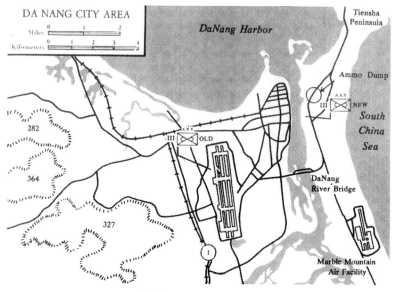

Da Nang City Area Map

My company was assigned to defend the inland side (west and north) of the airfield perimeter. The company's tactical area of responsibility ran from the main road heading westward, around the northern end of the defenses, and tied in with Company C on our right flank. It was flat and covered with rice paddies. Nothing had been done by 3/9 to improve the defenses, as they consisted of old metal watch towers, some dozen in number, and a couple of old concrete bunkers left over from the French regime. The towers were about 30 feet off the ground and made of steel with metal steps leading up to the tower. There was a rectangular metal box with a hole in the floor for access. Some were even leaning over. They were built to hold a much smaller Vietnamese, not a lanky Marine with flak jacket, helmet, weapon, etc.

The bunkers were too small for our Marines. I squeezed into one and was almost overcome with the smell of urine. They dated from the French era also. We filled sand bags and built our own defensive positions. We cleared fields of fire by cutting and burning brush in front of the wire where we could safely operate, staying well clear of the minefields. Two platoons, reinforced by attached machine guns and rocket launchers, manned the perimeter each night.

The towers had triple concertina and an unmarked minefield in front of them. Since the towers were built, the Vietnamese Army and Air Force personnel had been allowed to build huts for their families right up to the wire on the western side. The view of the Marines in the towers overlooked a sea of huts and humanity and nothing else. The northern end did provide some open rice paddies to observe any enemy movement in that area. There was about 20 yards of land between the barbed wire and the road that ran around the base, which was unpaved. The increased vehicular traffic around the base sent up columns of dust, which often obscured the vision of my Marines. We were so crowded that the company CP was established toward the south end of the airfield, in an open area next to the runway.

18 June, Da Nang Air Base:

"The heat and dust here are terrible. I don't have a thermometer but it's between 90-110 degrees every day. It's about 90 degrees at night and I sleep in my skivvy drawers. The soil is loose sand and every vehicle going by covers the area with dust. The unit here before us made no effort to improve living conditions and it's a pig sty. Our company doesn't have showers yet but we're working on getting them. I have been out two days on recons and will be making a helicopter recon tomorrow. I got interrupted at chow for a recon of the line with Col. Ludwig. The Colonel was well pleased with our defensive positions. He went along with all the changes I wanted to make. This must be the busiest airport in the world during the day. It's unbelievable the number of planes & helicopters taking off and landing. The noise here keeps you from getting any sleep. Artillery fires all night and the planes & vehicles fill in the gaps. Mosquitoes aren't too bad, but it's the dry season. I must drink a gallon of water a day. You really sweat and the salt tablets are a must.

Lt. Laqueur took out the first patrol from the Battalion today. The corpsmen had their hands full treating the people. The people live in complete poverty that's almost unbelievable. The health and sanitation of the Vietnamese is appalling also. I can't begin to describe it. Lt.s Jones and McHenry are taking patrols out tomorrow, Zelm Sunday. Two more (patrols) Monday, plus we're manning positions 24 hours a day & building them too."

Because of the heat and dust, we had to relieve the men in the towers every 2 hours, and this kept most of the company on the move during the day. The troops had to wear gloves to keep from burning their hands climbing the steel ladders during most of the day. There was only room for them to stand up in the metal boxes they were in. The towers were manned from dawn to dusk, and this area was covered by two man patrols between positions after dark.

Company B killed one of their own men. The man disobeyed orders by coming out of his hole and didn't answer the challenge. Five Marines also drowned in a tank when they got into deep water. Some of them reportedly could not swim.

My Marines reported flare sightings and sounds of gunfire from the areas they could observe. Back at the company CP we erected tents, sand bagged them for protection, and dug a defensive trench line facing across the airstrip. We obtained a large mess tent and some Seabees (the U.S. Navy construction force), seeing our plight, built us some mess benches and heads. 1stSgt. Smith borrowed a generator from the Air Force, which gave us electricity and powered a reefer so the cooks assigned from battalion could serve us hot meals. We tried to show a movie before evening chow, but the films broke so many times, the bulbs burned out, or something else happened that we never saw one to its completion. This didn't last long, as the battalion communications officer showed up one day and commandeered the generator for their use. That ended our hot meals and anything cold to drink. Water was a big problem, as it had to be carried in 5-gallon cans. We later received a water buffalo (water tank on wheels), and this ended that problem. Aluminum wash pans were purchased from the Vietnamese, and these served to wash and shave in and to wash our clothes in. I wrote my wife, "*You will be proud of me washing my own clothes. It's a real chore but it beats sending it out as they get lost.*"

1st Sgt. Smith obtained an aluminum wing tank from the Air Force and, with the help of the Seabees, we converted it into a shower. We were wearing green sateen utilities, which were much too heavy for the heat and humidity we had to endure. The sleeves of the jackets would not roll up except into a large, uncomfortable ball that restricted arm movement and any airflow. Most of my men resorted to cutting the sleeves off for more comfort. The name tags, required on Okinawa, had to be removed. Our attached Corpsmen administered our anti-malaria pills (one large and three small ones) weekly, and two salt tablets to each man every morning. The "Docs," as they were affectionately called, also inspected the men's feet for emersion foot and other problems. They, along with the officers and NCOs, made sure the men dried their feet and changed their socks as often as possible.

The maps we used dated from 1950, and many villages had disappeared and many new ones existed; of course none of them were on the maps.

General Walt flew over one Marine position and noticed the men filling sandbags wearing white under shirts. He didn't want to see any one outside with white tee shirts on, so the men had to labor in their utility jackets. Green under shirts had not been issued. The rules of engagement continued to change. The men were allowed to chamber a round, but they had to keep the safety locked on their weapons.

General Walt spoke to the battalion on June 17th. I don't believe many of my company were able to attend his talk because of guard duty.

That same day, we were assigned an artillery forward observer team from 1/12, another FO team from the battalion's 81 mm mortar platoon, a forward air control team, a radio relay team, and a section of 106 recoilless rifles. We were also assigned a few of the Vietnamese Popular Forces (older men from the area) to be used when operating off the base.

On 18 June, we learned with sorrow that PFC Leroy A. Bourgeois of Houston, Texas, serving in Company B, was killed in action while on patrol outside the base. He was the first casualty in the battalion. I made a helicopter recon with the colonel that day and recorded, *"the terrain is quite pretty to look at but real rugged. Rice paddies everywhere and numerous large and small streams."*

The next day, the Battalion CP moved to Hoi Cam ARVN Training Camp, 2 ½ miles southwest of the airfield at the base of Hill 327. The same day my company and Company D began local patrols outside the base. These patrols gave us valuable training operating in the rice paddies, information on the terrain, and kept the men sharp and in shape for what was to come. Lt. Zelm took our patrol out and we lost radio contact with them, but nothing happened.

The jungle utilities worn by the departed 3/9 were finally laundered and reissued to us. They were a big improvement; lighter, with sleeves that rolled up, and large pockets on the trousers and jackets. They were easier to wash and didn't require any pressing. You would sweat and get them wet and your body heat would dry them out when you stopped.

24 June, Da Nang Air Base:

"The jets rev their engines and take off right beside us. You can't hold a conversation for 30 seconds without being interrupted by them. A Vietnamese Air Force plane crashed here today. The pilot was saved but badly burned. Two Air Force men on the ground were injured while saving him."

25 June, Da Nang Air Base:

"We went out and fired some ARVN ranges today and while waiting, they accidentally shot one of their own men in the stomach. One of our corpsmen treated him. Heard three little girls were killed by artillery fire last night. It's a cruel war. The VC shot a village

chief last night in the same village. The country is overrun with children. All shapes, sizes, and infected with different diseases. Like kids everywhere and they are all cute."

27 June, Da Nang Air Base:

"Made a recon with the Colonel yesterday. Spent the whole morning riding and walking around the area. The countryside is beautiful down by the river. Everything is real green and the rice paddies are symmetrical. We are still working on our positions and sending out patrols. So far no casualties."

We continued patrolling the area south of the airfield with negative results. During a patrol of the pipeline to Red Beach the next day, a squad received sniper fire from the vicinity of Fung Hoa, ½ mile south of the airbase. They did not return fire because of the civilians in the area.

28 June, Da Nang Air Base:

"Companies B & D and a company from 2/3 are conducting a sweep today and the helicopters started taking off at dawn and are still going strong. We're listening to the radio traffic between the companies."

29 June, Da Nang Air Base:

"B & D companies captured 14 VC suspects. Two of them were the ones who blew up a jeep & killed 2 Marines last week. They had no casualties. We now have a monkey as a mascot. He is still wild and messes everywhere, but the troops like him. We sent a 40-man detail swimming this afternoon. It's really hot and they should enjoy it. I was nominated to be General Walt's aide, but since I'm a company commander he wouldn't take me. I'm glad, as I didn't want the job anyway."

We were fortunate to join SSgt. J.G. Mains, who transferred to us from Company B. Mains, a former Drill Instructor, had just been promoted to his new rank. He replaced SSgt. Winters, who was transferred to I Corps Security. SSgt. Winters was totally incompetent to lead troops, was physically weak, and could not keep up in the field. He came to us off of embassy duty, and I wondered how someone so inept could have ever passed the physical fitness test and how he got promoted to his present rank.

Live fire training continued at a near by ARVN training facility. Learning the rifle companies were to receive 60 mm mortars, SSgt. Morton acquired a new one and ammunition from the nearby Special Forces Camp. We retrained one of the 3.5 rocket teams as mortar men, and we were the first company to conduct live fire training with them. I had acquired a .45 caliber sub machine gun from Special Forces and fired it for the first time.

On 30 June, one of my patrols searched the area north of the airfield and returned with negative results. That morning at 10 o'clock, we witnessed the crash of a B 57 Canberra bomber from the 8th Bomber Squadron, U.S. Air Force.

"As it was taking off, the front end gave way and it went sliding down the runway past us, came to a halt, and burst into flames. The pilot was calm enough to release his bombs and napalm before he stopped skidding, and this probably saved his and the copilot's life. They jumped out and a Marine from C Co. helped pull one free just as the plane burst into flames. The napalm made a big fire in the middle of the runway but caused no damage. The bombs went rolling down the runway but didn't go off. Ammunition and one bomb not released went off and, needless to say, we stayed in the trenches for a while."

The plane missed C Company's positions but went through some of the wire into the minefield. The fireworks didn't end for the company with nightfall.

"Last night was like a bad dream. About 0130 mortar fire started coming in on the end of the airstrip. I awoke and across the runway planes were on fire all over the area. You could hear and see firing on that side of the field, also. We jumped in our trenches and took up defensive positions. Two air policemen came running across the runway toward us and we halted them and let them come into our lines. They were scared to death and had thrown their weapons away. They lay in the bottom of our trenches and shook with fear. We didn't fire a round and no one was hurt. C Co. was the one that got hit, and they had three men wounded, one seriously. The VC got through the fence [by tunneling under it] and dynamited the planes. They killed an air policeman by throwing a grenade into his jeep. C Co. believed they killed 5-7 VC. There were blood trails in the area. One dead VC was found this morning and one wounded was found later in the day and he confessed that they were a special mission assault team from North Vietnam. B Co. made a sweep of the area where the mortar fire came from and caught 2 suspects. The found the mortar positions we were fired on from. The rounds landed about 50-75 yards from us, and the next tent to mine has a nice hole in it. I was in my skivvies with a sub machine gun. Quite a sight! It happened too fast to really get scared."

1st Sgt. Smith, Gunnery Sgt. Gunderson, and SSgt. Lutz helped to calm down our young Marines. 1st Sgt. Smith, noting a mortar round has severed a bulk fuel line in front of our position, took some men and stopped the leak.

The VC failed to arm most of the mortar rounds aimed at our position, and the dozen or so rounds made a neat line beside the runway, ending about 50 yards from our position. We had to evacuate the area until an EOD team removed them the next day. If the VC forward observer had added 50 yards and fired for effect, they would have hit right on us. They had a clear view of our position from south of the field.

The VC had pinned down C Company in their positions using small arms, automatic, and 57 recoilless rifle fire. They blew the wing off of one of the C-130s, parked wing tip to wing tip, across the field from us. It started burning.

The Air Force claimed, "The Communist force, numbering almost a hundred men, virtually ran over a South Vietnamese Army unit guarding the base. This time no mortars or rockets were used. The Communists ran wildly among the parked aircraft, firing and throwing satchel charges. Six planes were destroyed, and three were damaged. The attack took less than 30 minutes and the Communists didn't lose a single man, killed or wounded. By the time counter fire began to be leveled at the attackers, they had already disappeared into the night." [For another account of the overall action that night see Philip Caputo's A RUMOR OF WAR, pages 175-180.]

We witnessed the whole action, and nothing could be further from the truth. The first C-130 burned and set fire to the wing tip of the next one, and so on during the night, we witnessed this debacle on the part of the Air Force. Their loss was 2 C-130s burned and one damaged. Two of the C-130s could have been saved if the Air Force had acted promptly to move them. Parking planes wing tip to wing tip was a dumb mistake, compounded by inadequate security and no attempt to save the aircraft.

The captured VC turned out to be a North Vietnamese soldier. He told his interrogators that his unit had trained in the mountains near Da Nang for 30 days for this mission. The wounded NVA said that the attack on the airbase was conducted by a sabotage company, to which his assault team was attached. They were supported in the attack by four 81 mm mortars and 57 mm recoilless rifles. Part of their mission was to destroy the helicopters parked at the southeast end of the airfield. For some reason, they were not attacked. He was one of 14 men assigned to slip into the base and blow up planes under the cover of the mortar barrage. He was wounded in the shoulder by machine gun fire before he got into the base itself.

Lt. Philip Caputo wrote, "I expected to find the base in shambles, but it was very large and most of it had escaped serious damage. Still, the attack had had more than a minor effect. Two big transports lay at the south end of the field, both totally destroyed, bits of their wings and engines scattered

Planes destroyed by VC on Da Nang Airbase

about. Two fighter planes nearby looked like broken toys and a third was just a pile of ashes and twisted metal. A truck was towing another damaged plane to the side of the runway. Stopping to look at the wreckage, we saw the holes the VC sapper teams had blown or cut in the chain link fence along the perimeter road. They had come through the sector my platoon had manned back in March and April."

The immediate reaction by the Marine command was the installation of more telephone lines, more permanent positions, and walking posts were discontinued. I now manned the lines with 2 reinforced platoons, while the CP group and the remaining platoon acted as a reaction force. The Vietnamese government responded by moving all huts, etc., 300 yards back from the perimeter of the airfield. The Air Force reacted by building revetments for their aircraft. The Marine helicopters were moved to a new field near Marble Mountain.

We joined three new men by transfer from Company F, 2nd Battalion, 9th Marines that day: Cpl. J.E. Collins, and LCpl.s H.A.L. Clugston and Carl F. Metras.

On the evening of 2 July, I marched the CP group and the reserve platoon to a civilian complex of gray buildings about half mile away. I never understood this order, as it placed us too far from the airfield to react, and put us in a cul-de-sac that was indefensible, surrounded by buildings built right up to the barbed wire fences. We spent the night on the porches of the complex. During the night, about 0055, an Air Force Policeman had an accidental discharge of his weapon, putting the whole perimeter on alert for the rest the evening.

Things quieted down around the perimeter and we had no more nighttime incidents. With our heavy commitments, I tried to let the men sleep during the day. It was too hot and noisy for me, but the troops managed to get a little rest. My 1stSgt. was able to get some sheets and mattresses from one of the Navy ships, so we were sleeping on one sheet atop the mattress on a wooden cot with a mosquito net over it.

We welcomed back a number of men who had been left on Okinawa to send on the gear and supplies left by the battalion. SSgt. F.V. Kruck, Sgt.s R.E. Dyer and E. Velasques, Jr., Cpl. Edward F. Dresch, and PFCs J.A. Abbott, B.G. Diller, G.A. Letendre, J.W. Richardson, and F.E. Temple, reported on 5 July. We also joined LCpl. R.F. Crogan and PFC C.R. Laberdee for duty.

On the 4th of July, my company acted as part of the honor guard for a visit by General [Victor H.] Krulak. Twice during the day, I showed him around my part of the perimeter. He was very pleased with our efforts. I saw a U-2 spy plane land that day. This was the first one I had ever seen.

On 7 July, LCpl. J.R. Moxon was struck by a line strung across the road on Highway No. 1 while driving one of our vehicles. The area was searched, but no enemy was found.

The next day, my company was hit hard for Military Police duty. Cpl. s L.F. Albritre and E.G. Hansen, LCpl.s B.E. Bentley, R.M. Howell, J.W. Laird, M.V. Lane, H.W. Ruben, R.L. Saffell, P.M. Shockley, and D.G. Smith were sent to augment I Corps. Most of these men were serving as squad or fire team leaders.

8 July, Da Nang Air Base:

"Another quiet night and another scorcher of a day. Lt. Zelm took out a patrol last night but had no contact. This was the first nighttime patrol for us. Lt. Laqueur has one tonight. The temperature must be 110 at least. I consume canteen after canteen of water and numerous Cokes but never seem quite satisfied. One of our men was sniped at early this morning but luckily he was not hit."

9 July, Da Nang Air Base:

"Had some activity last night. A squad size patrol of ours was fired on. No one was hit. We had snipers firing at us until about midnight. After that, things calmed down quite a bit. We are getting beer today for the first time. The troops are really happy. We get two cans a day and have a four or five day supply. Now all we have to do is get enough ice to get it cold enough to drink! The water in our homemade showers was hot last night when I took a shower. Think it's hot there, huh!"

The next day, I told my wife and my brother about acquiring the .45 caliber grease gun.

"Lt. Laqueur and 2 SSgt.s have gotten carbines and SSgt. Morton a shotgun. They're good for patrols, etc., but mine is heavy. The ammunition weighs more than the weapon. We've been having dust storms and it makes it miserable. It gets into and on everything."

The battalion suffered its first large group of casualties on 12 July. Company B was conducting a sweep south of the Song Cau Do River, when they were engaged by an estimated VC company. They lost three killed and seven wounded during the day, most caused by mines and booby traps. Company B killed 22 VC and captured 2. 2/9 had 11 men wounded last night including 2 Lt.s.

15 July, Da Nang Air Base:

"Just came off the lines, took a shower, shaved, and got a letter from you! Had a quiet night, but it was too hot to sleep until 2 a.m. I can't sleep now, as I have a 9:30 meeting with the Colonel. Lt. Zelm got his regular commission and his promotion to First Lieutenant yesterday. He was really happy over both. He bought a case of beer for us, but we can't drink but 2-3 before going out to our positions. I can't drink much anyway."

The same day we lost one of our clerks, LCpl. Moxon, to Service Battalion. Three days later, GySgt. E.G. Gunderson was medically evacuated to Clark Air Force Base hospital in the Philippines. He had a reoccurrence of an old case of jock itch. I believe he didn't want to serve in a rifle company in the field and aggravated his condition by constantly scratching it. He was a team shooter in the Corps, and later did good service training snipers.

16 July, Da Nang Air Base:

"[Secretary of Defense Robert J.] McNamara is coming and we're working almost around the clock to impress him with our positions. General [Frederick J.] Karch and the Colonel were around yesterday. They were pleased with our positions for a change. McNamara is going to inspect tomorrow, so everything has to be perfect. I just finished washing clothes. It was quite a chore with three days piled up. This afternoon we're firing our weapons on one of the local ARVN ranges. We are scheduled to be relieved by Bravo Company on the 20th and I'll get to sleep with my clothes off for a change, especially the boots. The last two nights have been quiet. Hope they stay that way for the time McNamara is here."

19 July, Da Nang Air Base:

"McNamara came in today and we had to rush around like a bunch of chickens with our heads cut off for nothing. He didn't even come by our positions and half the company sat out there in the hot sun and baked. Had another quiet night, just hope it continues.

Lack of ice is a big problem here. It's expensive and hard to come by. Cokes are easy to get but beer is non-existent now other than the local stuff which tastes o.k. but is made with bad water. We've gotten five new men in from the states in the last few days. The start of a replacement system, I guess."

20 July, Da Nang Air Base:

"They're going to split up the company. Lt. Zelm and his platoon are being transferred to 2/9 on the 23rd along with Lt. Jacoway and some more people from the Weapons Platoon. I lose another platoon in September and the last one in November. The

1stSgt. will get transferred in October, and I'm going to 2/9 on 17 December if I'm still the Company Commander. I get a platoon from 3/3 and a new XO, etc. Quite a scramble and everyone is discouraged by it, but know we'll have to make the best of it. Captain Harris of the Australian Army is the XO of B Company now. I think I've mentioned him to you before. He's a real nice guy."

Lieutenant McHenry was transferred to Company D that day. With his departure SSgt. Morton took command of Weapons Platoon.

21 July, Da Nang Air Base:

"The Colonel called me and said he wanted to see me. He informed me I would be transferred to 2/9 on 3 September instead of Brooks West. I pretended to be disappointed over it, but inside I was very happy. There has been a lot going on I haven't told you about, but it boils down to I don't think he's too hot of a leader and he doesn't really know what's going on in the battalion. He has indicated that we should keep information from the troops, which I consider completely wrong. I think they should be as well informed as possible. All of the company commanders tried to pin him down on tactics, etc., aboard ship. He talked in vague generalities and wouldn't really commit himself on anything, which led us to believe he didn't know anything about tactics; or at least he left that doubt in our minds. He's content for the battalion to sit on the airstrip forever and morale is starting to drop. Our company has been on the line 34 days without relief, and B & D Co.s have been getting plenty of rest and are going on operations. Since our battalion was involved in the defense of the airstrip when the VC saboteurs hit, he was apparently chewed out by the General or Generals' and has passed the buck on to the company commanders although we had nothing to do with the area they came through. Needless to say, I'm happy to go and 2/9 has a real strong CO and I know Captains Ling, Rushing, Osborne, Dean, Lloyd, and others over there. Don't worry about this; I've always been loyal to him and will continue to be. He indicated I would get a good fitness report.

The last two nights have been quiet. Tonight, B Co. is going to relieve us and we have three nights off. Not the days, with patrols and working parties, etc."

22 July, Da Nang Air Base:

"It sure felt good to sleep on a cot for a change without my boots on! Two more nights to go if nothing happens. We're in an alert status on 1 hour notice to move anywhere in the Division area. It was 129 degrees here yesterday. It was almost too hot to move. The water in the water cans burned your hands when you washed. The troops had movies last night."

25 July, Da Nang Air Base:

"Had a busy three days and no chance to write. We have been transferring people and joining people and it's a real mess. I transferred Lt. Zelm and his platoon to 2/9 and was supposed to receive a platoon from 3/3. Instead, I got all their brig rats and bums. The Colonel went to Regiment & Division today but no final outcome. I'm hoping to send the whole mob back. 1st. Lt. [J.J. "Jack"] Carroll is my new XO, and I believe he will be a good one. He has spent 3 months as an advisor down here with the Vietnamese Marines and has been with 3/3 down at Chu Lai. I got Lt. Patrick Gilstrap also. No comment."

Needless to say, nothing was ever done about the transfers. Every man from 3/3 had had office hours, a court-martial, or both. They came from all five companies, some with MOS's I didn't even rate. To top it off, we were shorted 10 men.

During this period, Captain Clyde D. Dean, CO of E/2/9, was riding on top of an Ontos during an operation south of Da Nang when it hit a land mine, killing the driver and blowing Dean about ten yards into a rice paddy. Dean was unhurt.

27 July, Da Nang Air Base:

"We are back on the line now. One of our sentries shot himself in the little finger with a .45. He's o.k. The 1st Sgt., Lt. Laqueur, and SSgt. Morton went with me and toured Da Nang. Not too much to see and it was stinking and filthy. It was a scorcher that day."

The troops got liberty in Da Nang that afternoon for a few hours. When the trucks were ready to leave Da Nang, Sgt. Xavier Rodriquez, who had too much to drink, and was moping over the fact that his brother was fighting down near Chu Lai without him and refused to get on the truck. Sgt. Lutz ordered he and LCpl. Ray Avila aboard, but they still refused and the truck departed. Avila told Sgt. Lutz he was staying with Rodriquez, and they started walking back to the airfield. Both were unarmed. Just before dark, another truck driver stopped and picked them up. "Are you guys crazy, don't you know you could get killed out here?" asked the trucker. They acknowledged that they could be, and rode with him back to camp.

When they returned to the company area, Lt. Zelm called them into his tent. "He was really mad," Avila recalled. "He was swearing at us and asking me questions. He asked me if I had heard Sgt. Lutz's order. I replied, 'Yes, sir.' He yelled at me several times asking me why I didn't comply. He wanted to know why I didn't leave Rodriquez and get on the truck. There was a pause, and then I said, 'Sir, Marines don't leave Marines behind.'

There was silence for a moment and then he yelled, 'Get the fuck out of here,' and that was the end of it."

We continued with the defense of the airfield with 2 platoons. I had Lt. Gilstrap's platoon start over with fire team and squad tactics, to try and mold them into a cohesive unit. It had started raining in the evenings, and the men got soaked in their fighting holes. The company started receiving a regular supply of beer and soda but ice continued to be a problem. The staff NCOs were out during the day trying to scrounge some so the troops could have something cold to drink. The chow improved but bread was in short supply. We had ice cream one time since arriving in Vietnam, and that was during General Krulack's visit.

28 July, Da Nang Air Base:

"Just heard over the news the confirmation that they had bombed two SAM missile sites near Hanoi. We had heard about it last night from the Air Force. I had said when the plane was shot down that we would bomb them within a week and it came true. We've gotten the new helmet liners and are wearing them in lieu of the old steel pot and liner. We also have the new jungle utilities but not the boots as yet. They're due next month."

30 July, Da Nang Air Base:

"We've had two quiet nights in a row. C Company had some action last night and found some blood in the area where they had fired on the VC. Tonight is our last night on the line. We become Division reflex company on one hour alert. Could prove interesting."

On 1 August, a cow strayed into the minefield south of us and had its leg blown off. One of C Company shot it to end its misery. We learned that 2/9 was conducting a two-company sweep, and we were their reserve company. They had 3 wounded yesterday. D Company lost four wounded on their sweep, including Lt. McHenry's Platoon Sergeant. They killed 15 VC and captured several.

2 August, Da Nang Air Base:

"Sitting here watching the war go on. Artillery started firing about 0530, then 44 helicopters took off with troops and Phantom jets took off to fly close air support missions. The helicopters are still going strong. Last evening we sat here and watched the Phantoms make air strikes about 2 miles away. Just like the demonstrations at Basic School! Lt.

Zelm's platoon has been fired on every night since going to E-2-9. One man we transferred has been wounded, but not seriously."

LCpl. Metras was one of those transferred. "Our platoon became 1st Platoon, Echo Company, 2nd Battalion, 9th Marines. We did a lot of sweeps south of the Air Base, including the Cam Ne villages. We burned them down a few times. We were stationed in one of them. Every night about 5 o'clock a sniper would shoot at us across the rice paddies. One evening we brought an Ontos to our line and aimed it at the hut the sniper fired at us from. At 5 o'clock that evening, all of the platoon were sitting on their fox holes when the sniper fired. The Ontos fired and there was no more hut. The sniper never fired at us again."

Also on August 2nd, LCpl. D.J. Maloney of the 2nd Platoon was wounded while sitting on top of a bunker. The wound was superficial and he returned to duty. The area the shots came from was searched the next day but nothing was found. *"Delta Company is conducting a sweep today and we may be involved,"* I noted. *"Lt. Jacoway called from E-2-9 and said we were supposed to furnish some people down there."*

During August, the battalion was assigned to Operation Blast Out I, conducted in the Cam Ne and Cau Do villages south of Da Nang. My 2nd Platoon was assigned to guard the Division Class V dump, near Red Beach. At 0350 on 5 August, they were attacked by fire from the nearby Esso Tank Farm. They returned fire with their machine guns and the enemy fire ceased.

Officer-SNCO Volleyball Game, August 1965, Da Nang
L-R: SSgt. Kruk (back), Sgt. Evans (face only), Cpt. Driver,
GySgt. Morton, Lt. Gilstrap, Lt. Jones (face only) & Sgt. Neeld

6 August, Da Nang Air Base:

"Lt. Laqueur's platoon had a grenade thrown at them last night, luckily no one was hurt. They're guarding an ammo dump. We had a rainstorm the other day that almost blew the tent down. It took six of us to hold it up! We had a flood but all our gear is on pallets so no problems. The Vietnamese who is the company laundryman baked the officers & the staff NCOs a huge cake each. It's real good. Both read 'Vietnam USA 2-8-65 USMC Da Nang.'"

On 8 August, there was a fire in the tent occupied by the 1st Squad, 3rd Platoon. They were getting ready to go on patrol and two men were getting grenades out of a bag and one accidentally pulled the pin on an illumination grenade. They heard the pop of the fuse and one ran out shouting 'Grenade.' The bag burned and the resulting fire blew up a white phosphorus and a fragmentation grenade lying beside the bag. The tent and contents were destroyed and the 14 men lost everything they owned. We lost 8 M-14 rifles, a .45 caliber pistol, and an M-79 grenade launcher.

8 August, Da Nang Air Base:

"We are busy getting clothing, weapons, etc. for the squad. We're still sitting around the airstrip conducting patrols, etc. It's really getting boring. Starting to have disciplinary problems. Today is the hottest in a long time. Must be 120-125 degrees now. No rain in about a week. Yesterday we had another bad dust storm.

Lt. Jones's platoon went down across the river today to reinforce B Company. They will be back in 2 days. Four NCOs went on a sweep with an ARVN company yesterday and they captured 9 VC. They got a first hand view of the torture methods used to get information out of the VC. They beat them, cut the insides of their legs with knives and nearly drowned them before they talked. They had to dig them out of the ground [spider holes], when they captured them."

Jones and his men returned tired but happy. They were not fired on, but got to see what was going on across the river. B Company captured 9 VC suspects and one confessed to have been in one the mortar attack on the airfield and on the Tank Battalion CP the other night when 21 Marines were wounded. He confessed and implicated others as VC in addition to those captured. He also told where the mortars were hidden.

13 August, Da Nang Air Base:

"I sent Jones' & Gilstrap's platoons to make a sweep with an ARVN company. Sent two sergeants also. They usually enjoyed seeing a little action.

About the news on D Company's sweep [The national news coverage had picked up on the story of Company B burning huts with cigarette lighters]. It went all the way to the president and he backed us up all the way. Perhaps one or two individuals did get carried away but the whole area is VC and we had four men wounded during the operation. I think I told you about B Company killing a 65-year-old women firing a Thompson submachine gun at them and a 10-year-old girl firing a rifle. Whether they were forced to do it or what but it doesn't matter – they shoot at you and we have no choice but to shoot back – to kill. Innocent victims have been killed since wars first began and this one is no different. Sometimes the civilians are warned to leave the area and don't – so they get killed and wounded. If the VC make them stay there isn't much we can do about it. As Sherman said 'War is hell.' The newspapers and TV probably didn't mention that D Company was under fire from the houses burned, for the entire day. Luckily the VC were bad shots. Newsmen should report facts but should find reasons behind events and stop trying to sell stories for sensationalism. This is what the public wants, good or bad, but it isn't fair to the men doing the job over here. Many reporters, etc. are no longer welcome here."

I added to my brother, *"It's a difficult war as it is—not knowing just who the enemy is and they never opposing us in strength—just sniper fire, a burst of machine gun fire, booby traps, and mines. You never see him for very long. You shoot one and he is pulled down in a tunnel or trench and the area is a maze of them. All you find is a pool of blood, vomit, scalp or whatever. Tunnels sometimes begin and end in houses and who can say which house sniper fire comes from? It's still hot as hell here but we're living fairly good. Ice is the big problem. We're getting beer and soft drinks now on a regular basis. We still haven't gotten jungle boots. The rainy season starts next month so we'll need them for sure then."*

I continued to my wife, *"We now have a horse. They've named it 'Shame on you.' It's very old and with no teeth but the troops ride him and enjoy taking care of him. We also have 3 or 4 puppies. I don't know what we will do with them when we move. The horse is only the size of a large pony."*

15 August, Da Nang Air Base:

"We are packed and ready to move south of the river. 2 platoons are guarding an ammo dump and 1 is guarding a bridge. 2/9 is going to clear out Cam Ne (1) and (2) this time for good. We're going to stay there this time.

3/9 landed yesterday and one company has moved in beside us. C Company has moved south of the river to support 2/9's operation. Saw Lt. Zelm and his platoon today. He's fine. His company will be on the operation."

Lt. Zelm"s near miss bullet hole in helmet

16 August, Da Nang Air Base:

"What a night last night was! You've probably read about the 'probe' of the airbase here. We were right in the middle of it. I think most of the [3/9] Marines were shooting at shadows but they fired all night long and were only 50-75 yards away from us. We were in and out of the trenches all night long.

You may have seen me on TV—Huntley-Brinkley. John Rich of NBC news took some film of 3/9 landing and taking over our positions around the airstrip and I was helping to push a [mechanical] mule across a stream bed when I noticed the cameraman taking pictures. I had a cover on but no shirt. I also helped him film some of the scenes and some of my men were in it.

We had a terrible dust storm yesterday. It almost blew us away. Everything was completely covered with it. All my washing going for nothing!"

The new 3rd Battalion, 9th Marines took over the defense of the airbase. My company was relieved on August 16, and we were glad to go. We moved to an area south of Red Beach near Marble Mountain. The 1st Platoon was assigned to the defense of the Phong Le Bac Bridge over the Song Cau Do River. They were to assist the 787th Regional Force Company of the ARVN, who directed the traffic flow across the bridge and inspected the vehicles and people entering and leaving the Da Nang area. That night, the VC mortared the 3rd Tank Battalion CP from the vicinity of Cam Ne (5), about 2,000 yards from the bridge. The ARVN fired 20-25 rounds from their 60 mm mortars and fired their machine guns into the village. The 1st Platoon received sniper fire and returned it. No one at the bridge was hurt.

As soon as it got dark, Gunnery Sgt. Hiles with the CP group started saying, "They're coming! They're coming!" Nothing would quiet him down until the senior corpsman sedated him for the night. Hiles, a veteran of World War II and Korea, should have retired, but he reenlisted to finish 30 years service. He was an excellent instructor on weapons and was good with the troops. However, the men referred to him as 'The Night Watchman,' until he was transferred to battalion. I made SSgt. Morton, the senior SNCO, the company Gunnery Sergeant. He did an outstanding job in that billet.

On 17 August, VC in boats were seen crossing the river. The ARVN at the bridge opened fire while the Marines boarded a LVT and rushed to the site. The VC beached their boat on the north bank and fled. These may have been part of the force that tried to penetrate the airbase perimeter the next night without success. One man from H&S Company of our battalion was wounded.

19 August, Marble Mountain:

"We're slowly moving all our gear to the Battalion CP site. Hope to finish up tomorrow. The platoons are still gone and it's hard to move all our gear with 12 men and 1 truck.

Heard SSgt. [Emory] Elswick and another man [PFC Mikel R. Beal] who used to be in this company were wounded yesterday with 2/9 on an operation."

20 August, Marble Mountain:

"The Chu Lai battle has really turned into something. There are hundreds of casualties on our side and they run over a thousand for the VC. Capt. Bruce D. Webb, who you may remember from Hawaii, got killed. Lt. Carroll was his XO before coming here."

Lt. J.J. Carroll, X.O.

21 August, Marble Mountain:

"Went out and visited Bravo Company today. George Welsh is doing fine. The area is real sandy and the only way you can travel is by tank, Ontos, or LVT. They're staying in abandoned houses and holes during the day & just in the holes at night. They're fired on every night but haven't had but few casualties. We'll be relieving them there soon."

23 August, Marble Mountain:

"We had a real scorcher today. Must have been 120 degrees and not much of a breeze stirring. You should have seen me washing clothes with a washboard this morning! I've got housewives' knees! Made a helicopter recon of the area and the terrain is beautiful but tricky. All the rice is about to ripen and it's waist to shoulder high and dark green."

By this time, most of my Marines and I were not wearing any underwear. Each man was carrying 3-5 canteens of water. Many of the men carried towels wrapped around their necks to absorb the sweat and to wipe their faces and hands. Despite having the shoulders of their flak jackets for padding, machine gunners and others often used the towels to cushion their load. When issued C rations, most threw away all but what they knew they would eat to help lighten their load. I wore my .45, ammo pouch, first aid kit, K-bar knife, compass, and 3 canteens on my belt. Most of the officers and some of the men wore shoulder harnesses and packs obtained from the Special Forces or the ARVN. They were lighter, more comfortable, water proof, and held more gear than those we were issued. I carried a map inside of a plastic pouch, and a notebook, pen, grease pencil, a card with radio frequencies, flash light, poncho liner, extra socks, C rations, heat tabs, and as little else as possible. During the rainy season, I carried an inflatable air mattress, dubbed by the troops as "rubber ladies." I always slept with my .45 beside my head.

On 26 August, intelligence reported that the VC were going to attack MCB-9, the Seabees supporting the Marines, and I was directed to send the 3rd Platoon to help defend their compound. Lt. Jones reported that the Seabees issued his platoon new boots (as some of his men were using duct tape to hold theirs together), new utilities, 782-gear, and an armorer went over their weapons and bore sighted their machine guns. They also received 3 hot meals a day. In return, Jones and his men helped the Seabees build better positions, clear fields of fire, and held classes on crew served weapons. I started rotating platoons to the Seabee base and they were treated the same way. Our battalion supply could not keep us uniformed and shod. They acted as if we were on maneuvers at Camp Pendleton!

We were supposed to be issued jungle hats and boots, but that had not occurred. 1stSgt. Smith and I went to the Medical Battalion one day to visit our sick and wounded. On our return, we stopped at the Air Wing mess for lunch. Everyone there was wearing the new jungle utilities and jungle boots! We could not believe it!

That morning at 0900, my company relieved Company B on the Main Line of Resistance and started conducted security patrols about 1700. About 1915, the 1st Platoon reported receiving about 15 rounds of small arms fire. One of our three tanks from Company B, 3rd Tank Battalion returned fire. There were no Marine casualties.

LCpl Mike Olsen,
Fire Team Leader A-1-9, E-2-9, F-2-9

LCpl "Chin" Malin

L-R: LCpl Malin, Cpl. Judge & SSgt. Evans
VC flag captured on Harvest Moon

81 mortars firing a mission in a village near Da Nang

17 August, Below Marble Mountain:

"My first night and day out here in the desert turned out to be one of combat. Just as I finished checking the lines at 1900 snipers opened up on us. The 1st Platoon returned the fire, as well as a tank, and it was soon all over. The 2nd Platoon got hit about the same time with sniper fire and it ceased also. All night there was firing around us. To top it off it poured rain all night. We were glad to see daylight and the rain stop.

That morning, I took a squad of men and 3 tanks and made a reconnaissance to the south about 5 miles. We ran into snipers and spotted quite a few VC and may have killed 4 from a tank round. We had a tanker wounded in the arm but his wounds weren't serious. We captured a VC's equipment, which included 2 grenades, a bandage, a flashlight, and a camouflage cover. We also found some documents in a village we searched.

It was a strange feeling of helplessness when you are fired at. I wasn't particularly afraid; actually wasn't afraid at all. What's frustrating is not being able to see who's firing at you. They're sneaky little devils! I fired at one VC with my grease gun but missed him. So did everyone else, so I didn't feel too bad. He was about 100 yards away running from us.

You feel sorry for the women and children, as they are more than dirt poor. There are no men of military age seen; only children, women, and old men. The husbands are all VC or VC controlled. The people seem to have nothing more than the shirts on their backs, a pig, a cow, some chickens or ducks, and a rice paddy."

The next night, one of my ambushes fired on 3 VC carrying BARs. They reported wounding one of the VC, but they all escaped in the darkness. LCpl. S. Hunter and PFCs D.G. Hoerauf and C.N. Pate were wounded that day.

When reporting enemy casualties, we could not claim a kill unless we found the body. As we often shot VC 100-200 yards away and saw them fall, we could not claim them without checking the body. This 'body count' rule led Marines to expose themselves unnecessarily to enemy fire and booby traps in order to prove the kill. This rule continued throughout the Vietnamese War.

One of many dead VC after a firefight

Typical house in a village

Bullet hole in 3.5 rocket launcher after a firefight

Trenches around villages

PFC Freece
A round went through his helmet & stuck in the liner

William Smallwood & Mike Olsen building position
near Marble Mountain, 1965
(photo courtesy of William Smallwood, Jr.)

On 29 August, we conducted our first real offensive operation against the VC as a unit. Lt. Carroll recalled, "Late in the afternoon, almost dark, you [Driver] returned from a recon, debarked from a tank, and hastily called key people together for a brief. I remember you were armed with a sub-machine gun, and the preparations for the night march were real fast. No 5 paragraph order, etc."

The plan was for Alpha Company (-) to make a night march of about 5 miles cross-country at about a 45 degree angle to the village of Ha Dong (4) near the beach below Marble Mountain. Delta Company would come down the beach in amphibious tractors about daylight, and we would link up and sweep the area back towards Marble Mountain. A platoon from Delta Company, 3rd Reconnaissance Battalion, led by Captain Pat Collins, would move on our left flank, and I was to detach a platoon about halfway to our objective to move between the company and the recon platoon. Strict radio silence was to be observed, and I don't believe the ARVN were briefed on this operation in order to maintain secrecy. We had tanks and amphibious tractors attached, so I left them with a small security force and radio men to send our normal situation reports to battalion, in case the VC were able to monitor our communications net. We had a section of 81s attached but we would be operating out of range for them and artillery, so I decided to take one gun along with us.

We departed our position at midnight, with recon following in trace. Jack Carroll acted as 'tail end Charlie,' keeping the company closed up and maintaining contact with recon. Recon broke off from our column at 0200. The area looked open on the maps we had, but it was actually made up of large sand dunes with tree lines around deep rice paddies that made the march extremely toilsome, especially the Marines carrying the 81 and ammunition. After about an hour (0300), we heard firing north of us from where recon was supposed to be. Because of radio silence, we could not learn what had happened. We continued to trudge along with the 81 crew becoming wearier and wearier. To keep them moving, I had to detail the platoon that was supposed to break off and have them aid the mortar men with their loads. This was a tough decision, but I had no choice if we were going to reach our objective by dawn. I was also concerned that the platoon might run into the recon patrol.

I had designated Lt. Laqueur to maintain our bearings by compass readings to keep us on course. He did an outstanding job as we slogged through the deep sand en route to our objective. The night was moonless, but the stars were the brightest and closest I had ever seen. This aided our visibility, especially with the sandy soil. During the trek, we spotted a light on a rise of ground on our left flank. It seemed to be following us. I was about to direct an M-79 round to be fired at the light when Laqueur suggested we should send a fire team to investigate. I did, and they found an old lady in a small temple praying to her ancestors. The light was from candles flickering through the windows of the grave.

We soon passed through a village, probably one of the Sa Viem Dong's, with huts built off the ground on either side of the trail. The people inside were talking, smoke was coming out of the huts, and candles were burning inside. I'm sure they heard us pass through because of the noise of the men carrying the 81, but no one came outside to investigate. They probably heard the sounds of the VC passing through at night many times.

By first light we reached our objective, Ha Dong (4), a village built on high ground surrounded by tree lines. All was quiet and not a sound was heard. My assault platoon, led by Lt. Jones, passed through a tree line, across an intermittent stream, and entered the village. The rest of the company was deployed to provide covering fire, if needed. Jones' men first surrounded the village, so no one could escape, and then started searching the huts. Our attack was a complete surprise, although no VC troops were found. We killed 3 VC; one a tax collector who tried to hide in a tunnel. We recovered his pistol, belt, and the tax rolls for the area. We also rounded up 8 suspects of military age.

Carroll remembered, "At first light, I was busy with map and compass trying to determine our exact location. A helicopter flew over and I popped a red smoke grenade to attract their attention, and they gave us our exact coordinates. We moved all day, had a few fire fights and some sniping."

We regrouped and started northward to link up with Delta Company. With the hot morning sun bearing down on us, the 81 crew were really struggling to keep up. I worried about them going down from heat exhaustion, so I communicated with Delta Company to have some amphibious tractors meet us. We were able to load the 81 team on them.

A tank joined us as we continued to move towards China Beach. The two companies moved on line with each other, but I had one platoon guarding our left flank, as there was a bayou like area with dense tree lines on the other side. I never heard from the recon platoon.

We made good progress towards our final objective despite the deep sand and torrid heat. About 1400, as we started to climb a high sand dune, we received mortar and automatic weapons fire from the tree line across the bayou. A mortar round landed about 10 yards to my left rear (they were probably aiming at all the radio antennas near me). As I whirled around at the sound of the explosion, I saw LCpl. Reuben Cantu get hit. I yelled for a Corpsman. I could see the tank with its turret and gun turned towards the area across the bayou where the enemy was shooting from, but I couldn't make radio contact with them to open fire. The only person I could get radio contact with was SSgt. Morton, who was near the end of the company, but not near the tank. Meanwhile, the sand was flying up around my boots, which I didn't pay any attention to at the time. Later, I realized there was a sniper in a large palm tree on our right flank who was shooting at us. The firing from across the bayou ended abruptly, and we continued on our way. During the whole operation, only five men were wounded; none serious. We killed 6 more VC and wounded 9.

In about another hour, we reached an area near China Beach, at the French fort, where Lt. Colonel Ludwig, Captain Shubert, and a Time magazine reporter were waiting. I could only give the Colonel a cursory briefing of events because of the noise of the tanks and amphibious tractors passing by. This was the only time I ever saw him in the field.

We loaded the company on the amphibious tractors and returned to our position on the Main Line of Resistance. Delta Company suffered no casualties but rounded up 12 VC suspects.

30 August, Below Marble Mountain:

"Everyone from the regimental commander on down said we did a good job. I thought so too! We made a 10-mile hike into VC territory Saturday night. It was a long, hot march with everyone loaded down with weapons and ammunition. The troops were magnificent! We started walking at midnight on the 28th and didn't stop until noon on the 29th."

That night of the 29th, the VC came looking for revenge. About 0300, some of the enemy crept up near our nighttime positions and threw grenades into our foxholes. Cpl. Terry J. Neumeier of Kewaunee, Wisconsin, a Machine Gunner, was mortally wounded, and Cpl. Dresch, his Machine Gun Team Leader, was also hit. Fortunately, 2 other CHICOM grenades and a rifle grenade failed to explode. On top of that, one of our slightly wounded men [LCpl. J.W. Brooks] from the day before came down with an attack of appendicitis and all three were evacuated by helicopter. With no sleep for about 36 hours, it was difficult to keep the men alert. LCpl. D.G. Chaney and PFCs R.B. Wade and G.E. Zeitz were the other slightly wounded men.

On patrol later that morning, the 2nd Platoon extracted some revenge on the enemy. They were fired on by a VC unit and returned fire immediately. A search of the area found blood pools, a cartridge belt, 2 CHICOM grenades, and 3 magazines loaded with 9 mm ammunition, all heavily stained with blood.

31 August, Below Marble Mountain:

"Had a rather quiet night last night for a change. Everything happened this morning. The 2nd Platoon was fired on by snipers [and returned fire]. No Marines were hurt. They searched the area and found a cartridge belt, ammunition, 2 grenades all covered with blood, so we at least wounded one. They captured 4 more VC [suspects] in the area. The 1st Platoon was fired on by snipers at noon, but couldn't find them. A tank infantry patrol was fired on by VC this morning. They think they killed 2. It's only 1400 so you can see we've been busy!

I've planned an operation for the company for tomorrow morning and I hope battalion will approve it. We should get some more VC. Just got the word another patrol apprehended 2 more VC suspects, one of which is wounded."

Starting in September 1965, the battalion was involved in two operations. Operation Golden Fleece was conducted to protect the rice harvest in the Hoa Van District of Quang Nam Province. Operation County Fair had Marines surround various villages in the province while the ARVN and Vietnamese Secret Police would search the huts and interrogate the villagers. In addition, each rifle company was required to conduct one combat patrol in our TAOR, employ one ambush and listening post each night, and employee one scout/sniper team each day. The rules of engagement had been changed for some time. We could now operate our weapons with the safety off, which was only common sense.

The company moved to a position on a large sand dune with no cover. It was in the middle of a large intermittent streambed with excellent fields of fire. The nearest tree line was about 50-75 yards away. We were not allowed to erect barbed wire defenses in the field, as we were to remain completely mobile. We were not allowed to have sandbags, either. It was difficult in the extreme to dig foxholes, as the sand continually fell into the hole. The troops improvised them with C ration and ammo boxes. Sleeping holes were dug behind their positions, and poncho liners were used to provide some protection from the boiling sun. The 81 mm section was dug in near the CP, as we were a bit crowded on the dune. We also had several tanks attached. Re-supply was by amphibious tractors every few days. When a helicopter landed, everyone held on to their belongings for dear life, as the sand storm that was created blew everything away.

The local villagers came and stared at us the day we arrived. They were all in black pajamas with straw hats. The women all chewed beetle nut, a form of narcotic, which turned their teeth and gums red. Our Vietnamese interpreter warned them to stay away from our position.

I decided to stop carrying the grease gun and usually carried my radioman's M-14. I came to the conclusion that if it got hot enough that I had to do the shooting there would be plenty of weapons around for me to use!

The 1st Section of the 81 mm mortar platoon was attached to A Company. They were led by SSgt. L.G. Garner, an experienced mortar man and a fine leader. Sgt. J.C. Sturges was my 81 Forward Observer, and an excellent one.

1 September proved to be a busy day for Alpha Company. At 0035, while on ambush, the 2nd Platoon received 10 rounds of sniper fire. They did not return fire and remained in their ambush site. Our artillery observer received a request for fire from the 2nd Platoon commander at 0115, where a reported 30-40 VC were believed located. The fire mission resulted in secondary explosions in the target area. The next morning the site was checked and large traces of blood were found.

2 September, Below Marble Mountain:

"Last night was something else. There was firing all over the area all night long. Flares were going off too. I don't think I slept more than 30 minutes at any one time. The Second Platoon received 10 rounds of sniper fire at 0300 this morning. No one was hurt. Someone threw a grenade at a hole in our lines and the concussion knocked a man down but didn't hurt him."

A 3rd Platoon patrol that morning at 0730 received about 15 rounds of sniper fire. LCpl. R. Carson was wounded. The patrol deployed and returned fire and received about another 9 rounds before the enemy fled. One VC suspect was detained when the area was searched.

Later in the day I added, "I've got two operations going on now involving all three platoons plus tanks and LVTs. No casualties so far. By the way, a Life Magazine photographer took my picture after the operation the other day. He took one of the whole company, also. Hope they make the magazine."

At 0100 on 3 September, the Company CP and the 1st Platoon received 30-40 rounds of small arms fire and returned fire. They believed they killed 2 VC. 81's fired illumination rounds. The tanks fired three 90 mm canister rounds into the suspected area and the VC fire ceased. At 0200 our scout/sniper team fired on a VC and he was seen to fall.

3 September, Below Marble Mountain:

"The 1st Sgt. came out last night and got a taste of how things are going. He and I went on a patrol with the 1st Platoon this morning. We didn't find much. A lot of trenches and punji traps, but no VC."

It was hard to keep 1st Sgt. Smith out of the field! We learned from him that Cpl. Dresch, LCpl. Brooks, and PFC Cantu had been medically evacuated to Okinawa.

That evening, an ambush from the 2nd Platoon fired on an estimated 11 VC. One was killed and 4 captured. Some of the prisoners were wounded. One CHICOM grenade, 5 VC ID cards, and other equipment were taken at the ambush site. The captured VC were sent to ITT for interrogation.

I continued in my letter, *"Heard through the grape vine that the Colonel and Capt. Shubert were really pleased with what the company has been doing. I certainly am. We had one man wounded slightly in the leg yesterday and captured another VC. Got word yesterday I'm not being transferred until the 7th."*

We learned that day that SSgt. H.R. George of Company D had stepped on a landmine and was wounded. George was a former Olympic Greco-Roman wrestler and a fine Marine.

The next day our scout/sniper team, deployed nearby, received 8 rounds of enemy fire. They returned fire and the enemy fled.

While on ambush that night at 2100, the 3rd Platoon received 10 rounds of sniper fire. They returned fire and the enemy fire ceased. I wrote, *"This morning an ARVN Ranger Battalion came through and is sweeping the same area we did last week. It appears they're doing it for Richard Nixon, who is here now. One of our patrols killed 1 VC, wounded 3, one of whom got away and we captured 4 more the other night. [My men had snatched them off the trail, something we trained for on Okinawa]. They were sent to the rear but some of the men may have beat them up, so there will be an investigation."*

My statement read, *"We had a combat patrol in the vicinity of Khai Tay (2). Upon arriving in the area they set up an ambush. About 2030 they snatched 1 VCS [VC suspect] off the trail. A little later 2 VCS were apprehended. Still later another VCS was apprehended. The patrol leader asked for instructions after capturing the first VCS and was told to bind & gag him and continue the mission. Each VCS was identified by the ARVN with the patrol as being VC. The patrol leader indicated upon debriefing that the VC had to be forced to the ground to be tied. The patrol returned about 2300. The prisoners were turned over the Company Gunnery Sergeant [SSgt. Morton] who in turn told the 3rd Platoon Sgt. to provide security for them during the night. An Ammo hole was cleaned out and the VC were placed in it. Some force had to be used to put several in, and they fell, one on the other. They were later checked to see that their bonds were tight and again several of them had to be pushed back into the hole. The next morning, the VC suspects were evacuated by helicopter."*

Lt. Carroll conducted an investigation, but I don't believe the men were punished, other than the tongue lashing from Morton.

"We are having a new bridge put in here and the villagers are happy. Their rice crop is due in a week, so they're hoping they won't have to pay off the VC. We'll be guarding them during the harvest also. The VC blew the bridge here in 1963 and really did a job on the road—trenches or holes every 20 yards for miles. All culverts are blown also."

Things heated up on 6 September. I led the company on a search and destroy mission of the villages of Tra Kee (2) and Tra Kee (3). We jumped off at 0500 that morning and swept through the two villages. They covered about 2 grid squares. At 1500, we arrested 15 VC suspects with the loss of four Marine wounded, LCpl. G W. Lane being the only one not returning to duty immediately. We returned to our old position at 1855.

During this operation, the CP group was following the point platoon down a trail, which was completely covered with bamboo, so it was invisible from the air. Because our Marines were taller than the Vietnamese, they had to bend over to get down the trail. Somehow, they all missed a CHICOM grenade booby trapped above their heads, with a cord leading off the trail. I spotted it and had the engineers blow it in place.

We reached a small village and found a woman with a small child in a hut. While our ARVN interpreter questioned her, a sniper fired at us and the round ricocheted off the floor and struck the child in the groin. My corpsmen attended to her wound, but she needed immediate medical attention. I had a quandary, as we were not allowed to call in medical evacuation helicopters for civilians. I called her in as a VC suspect, and the choppers came and took the woman and her child to Charlie Med. I never heard anything more about it. I just hope the child survived.

7 September, Below Marble Mountain:

"Had quite a day yesterday. We left here at 0500 with 5 tanks, 2 Ontos, and 6 LVTs, and moved south into VC territory. We were under fire almost the entire day. It ended in a complete success. We killed 8, wounded 21, and captured 53. We had 4 wounded, none serious. This getting shot at is getting old. One man was hit within 20 feet of me. I think we killed close to 100 but we have to count the bodies to get credit for them.

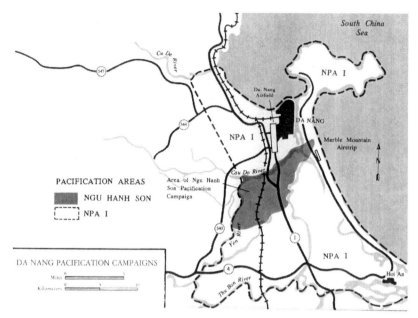

Da Nang Pacification Campaign Map

The bridge was finished yesterday. The villagers were very happy over it. We're protecting them now as they harvest their rice. Our People-to-People program."

On 8 September, the company was on another sweep with Company D. We jumped off again at 0600, this time supported by 5 tanks, 5 LVTs, and 2 Ontos. We moved into an area near Tra Khe (1) and started our search and clear operation. The 2nd Platoon encountered a booby trapped fence line at 0720, but they used one of the grappling hooks we had been issued, and the CHICOM grenades were destroyed with no casualties. We later found a land mine and had the attached engineers blow it in place. As we moved between the villages, one of the LVTs slid off the road into a rice paddy and 40-50 civilians came out protesting about it. Another LVT pulled it back on the trail and we continued. At 1000, we had the engineers destroy a 32 foot-long tunnel that was found. About 1100, the 1st Platoon received small arms and automatic weapons fire from a building. The platoon returned fire and two squads assaulted the position, while the third squad gave covering fire. LCpl. E.W. Lacey was wounded in the arm during the attack. One civilian was hit during the assault. I ordered a tank to their support but the mission was accomplished before it could fire. The VC fled the area and we returned to our position by dark.

8 September, Below Marble Mountain:

"[Captain] Dick Kerr drove up in his jeep yesterday. He had come out to see the bridge [he was an engineer officer] and we were equally surprised to see each other. He got here 24 August.

By the way, A Newsweek photographer took my picture during the operation in which we killed & captured all the VC. Look for it. Colonel [John E.] Gorman, the regimental CO, was out the other day and said my company was doing a real good job."

We were at it again on 9 September. While covering the rice harvest, a patrol from the 1st Platoon received sniper fire from all sides. They returned fire while a tank and two rifle squads rushed to reinforce them. One Popular Forces soldier operating with them was killed, and three Marines were wounded. One dead VC was found. The helicopters called in for the medevac were fired on but successfully evacuated LCpl. J.A. Marcus and PFCs L.P. Contreras and D.R. Noon.

We joined with 2 platoons of Company C and continued our search and destroy mission. Starting about 1600 we fought a running battle with an estimated VC battalion of 90-120 men. Intelligence later reported it was a Main Force VC battalion, their best. By 1610, we had found a large quantity of rice in a village. An hour later we came under heavy small arms, automatic, and mortar fire. We returned fire, and used our 60 mm mortar for the first time. I had my FOs call in fire missions and 81s were landing on target immediately. Despite our artillery and mortar fire, the VC fought on stubbornly. We continued to receive mortar and 57 mm recoilless rifle fire. We poured fire into the VC position for over 30 minutes, including 121 rounds from the 105s, and still they resisted. We could not evacuate our dead and wounded by helicopter until 1747. LCpl. James William Mahler, of Marshfield, Mass., lay dead, but we could not evacuate his body because he had been hit with a white phosphorus round and his clothing was still burning, and we couldn't put it out. The bodies of PFCs D.G. Chaney and J.E. Schmidt and the wounded, including Cpl. J.P. Boonstra, LCpl.s E.G. Kish and C.R. Cooper, PFCs M.L. Bakke, T.W. Busby, and R.B. Jordan, Jr., and AM1 D.O. Barnes, were flown out. Cooper, a Texan, was 10 feet from me when he was blown into the air by a mortar round. I whirled around and saw daylight between his tibia and his calf muscle. I shouted for a corpsman and continued on. Five other Marines were wounded and evacuated, but they were either from Company C or attached units. We also received an emergency re-supply of ammunition.

Lt. Carroll, who ran the medevacs, stated that Mahler had been shot between the eyes. "Mahler's body and parts of his clothing were burning. I tried putting him on the helo that night but couldn't. I had quite an argument with the crew chief of the CH-34. I later evacuated him on the back of a tank to the battalion CP the next day. I remember taking his wallet, dog tags, etc. and putting them in the pockets of my utilities. The next day, I included these effects as we further medevaced him. Subsequently, until I shit canned those utilities many months later, I could still smell LCpl. Mahler's remains. It never went away despite many washings—even laundry moms in the ville couldn't get the smell out."

Almost as soon as helicopters and supporting gun ships were out of sight, the VC were sniping at us again. We continued in pursuit of the enemy until 1910, when we were ordered to return to our position. By the time we had broken contact with them, we had suffered two more Marines wounded and evacuated by helicopter. These Marines must have been from Delta Company, as I did not find their names among our casualties. Amphibious tractors arrived to pick us up and we needed the lift, as it had been a bloody and tiresome day for Alpha, Charlie, and Delta companies. It was still 2300 before we finally reached our position. The next day, we were able to send the remains of Mahler to Charlie Med.

I reported on 23 September, "*About 1630, 9 September 1965, my company was making an attack on a Vietnamese village believed to contain a VC hardcore battalion reinforced by a company. At this time A Company received a heavy volume of automatic weapons, MG, 60, 81, 120 mm mortar and 57 mm recoilless rifle fire from across a wide rice paddy area on the right flank. First Lieutenant John B. Creel, Jr., and the [artillery] FO team went immediately into action to spot the VC positions. Cpl. Thomas E. Czzowitz exposed himself to the enemy MG fire to spot two MG's firing at us across the paddies on our right flank. He was immediately shot through the throat upon reporting their position. Lt. Creel and his radioman, Cpl. William F. Elder, rushed to Czzowitz's aid and were wounded themselves. They succeeded in moving Czzowitz to a defilade position and turned him over to a corpsman. Lt. Creel and Cpl. Elder instantly returned to their duties and, despite their wounds, coolly and calmly called in fire missions on the VC positions. Cpl. Elder was later evacuated by helicopter. Lt. Creel continued to call in fire missions until relieved by another FO team some three hours later.*" Cpl.s J.D. Carlous and R.C. Hempel, my radio operators, witnessed their acts. Creel received a Silver Star for his actions. Czzowitz of Butler, PA died from his wounds.

The 3rd Marine Division 'Triad' reported on October 1, "According to the village chief who reported the location of the VC battalion last week, the VC's mission was to get the rice from the area. Their attempt was foiled by Marines of the 1st Battalion, 9th Marines and its supporting units—for it was nearly dusk and the villagers still reaped their 'Golden Fleece.'"

10 September, Below Marble Mountain:

"*We had a lot of action yesterday. Had a squad size patrol with a tank out and they came under intense sniper fire and suffered 3 wounded and a Vietnamese soldier killed. None of the wounds were serious.*

About noon we received word that a VC Battalion and a separate company were in the area south of us. I was given 4 tanks, 4 Ontos, and 2 platoons of C Co. The VC were harvesting the rice, etc., early. We moved about 2 miles along a river and all of a sudden all hell broke loose. We were hit with 81, 60, and 120 mm mortars, 57 recoilless rifle fire, machine-gun, and small arms fire from across the paddies on the other side of the river. We had one hell of a fight. D Co. [Captain M. J. Harris of Kyogle, Australia, a member of the New South Wales Light Infantry, and an exchange officer] came around behind them [Khai Tay (3)] & they withdrew. We suffered 3 killed & 11 wounded. I don't know how many of them we killed but it was more of them than us. We know of 8 or 10 we killed. [Intelligence later reported we killed or wounded about 100 VC.]

Got to close and go visit the wounded. A sniper was after me and the radioman, but his aim was bad, thank goodness!"

On 11 September, we were back in action with Company D. Lt. Ray G. Snyder, an Annapolis graduate, serving in Company D, was wounded while trying to open a gate with a Poplar Forces squad leader. Both should have known better than try to open a gate in VC controlled territory. Another Marine in Delta was wounded by the blast. I ran to the site and called in the medevac helicopters. During the day we passed by the area where Mahler was hit. I picked up his helmet liner, which had melted to the size of a small pancake. We had continued to wear the steel pots.

Back at our position, at 0030 on 12 September, a listening post reported 10 people moving to and fro about 100 meters away. I sent a patrol and they spotted movement in a village south of our position. I had our 81s fire 13 rounds at the village, and we received 5 rounds of mortar fire in return, killing a Marine in the mortar section and wounding seven more. The men from Company A who were hit were Cpl. W.E. Hendrickson, LCpl.s R.L. Jost and J.R. Smith, and PFC P.S. Carlon. The other wounded were from C Company.

As we moved out on another search and clear operation that morning, a tank operating with the 3rd Platoon activated a booby trap when it ran over a barbed wire fence. This occurred at 0921 in the morning. LCpl. J.R. Price and one Poplar Force soldier were slightly wounded. We continued the operation and I did not have them medevaced until 1355. Price was treated and returned to duty the same day. At 1500, the 3rd Platoon captured 3 young males whom the Poplar Forces identified as VC. We returned to our old position and the VC didn't bother us during the night.

13 September, Below Marble Mountain:

"From our fight with a VC Battalion the villagers said we killed 'many, many VC.' There are a lot of fresh graves in the area. Lt. Robbins from Co. C got wounded on a patrol yesterday. He may lose 3 toes."

That day we were off on another sweep and destroy mission. We linked up with Company D and crossed the line of departure at 0908. This move took us north through several hamlets where the rice was being harvested. Our two companies rounded up 723 civilians, of whom the Village Chief found one VC and 33 suspected VC. We continued north until we reached the vicinity of Tam Kee (1). I sent out a patrol at dusk, and they observed VC firing at aircraft taking off from the Da Nang airbase. They also saw a woman carrying food in the direction of the VC. Suddenly they received small arms fire from three directions and heard 8 mortar rounds fired. They all returned safely. During the afternoon move, we apprehended another 27 VC suspects. The Village Chief only released 2 of these men. The rest were sent to ITT for interrogation. We also had engineers blow up a 32 foot long tunnel we discovered.

We continued to operate in the area the next day, apprehending a VC at 1700 that afternoon. He was believed to be a deserter from the ARVN. Our Poplar Forces troops believed the VC were using the nearby leprosarium as a refuge. The Marines were helping supply medicines and food to this hospital. We believed the VC were stealing these supplies and also having some of their wounded treated there.

I wrote home that night, *"It was really hot and humid today, and D Company had heat casualties. We have yet to have any!"*

The night of 14-15 September, we got our first taste of the monsoon season, as it poured all night and into the next day.

At 0950 on 15 September, one of my patrols received 20 rounds of small arms fire. They returned fire and assaulted the position. One VC suspect was captured and sent to ITT for interrogation. My men also picked up a VC ID card and some expended cartridges.

That afternoon, Company B relieved us at 1930. We had been in constant contact with the enemy for 31 days, living on a sand dune much of the time. During this period my men had not had a hot meal or a shower. 1st Sgt.

Smith had scrounged up some onions and apples and sent them to us, but basically we had lived on C rations the whole time. I was directed to bring back all the rations, ammunition, and other supplies we had accumulated, including the 81 mm ammunition. The amphibious tractors carried us to a bridge about one half mile from the battalion CP, arriving near dusk. No trucks arrived to haul this gear to the battalion CP. 1stSgt. Smith met us with our jeep and trailer. We commenced shuttling the jeep and trailer back and forth, and no help was received from the battalion. SSgt. Garner was able to get a jeep and trailer to move the 81 mm ammunition. The troops, of course, hiked in. The 1st Sergeant and I were the last two Marines from the company to enter the CP. It was 2015. I was as mad as I have ever been in my life. I confronted the S-4 as to why no trucks had been sent to help us move the supplies and ammunition he had directed for us to bring back. His excuse was that it was too dangerous to send the trucks out there when it was getting dark. I came as close to hitting another officer in my career, when he made that statement. I minced few words in explaining that my 1st Sgt. and driver had been out there alone waiting for us, and I believed they were worth a hell of a lot more than a truck! The delay in moving to the CP had also cost my Marines a hot meal and a shower, as both had been closed down, and besides, the cooks were watching a movie! I nearly exploded when I confronted the XO on these two issues. To add insult to injury, one of my platoons had to man the battalion perimeter that night! I was absolutely livid! None of my officers or men had ever been on the perimeter, and by that point it was pitch black outside. I told the platoon leaders the situation, ordered the men issued C rations, and sent one platoon to man the defenses. With only candles to light the tents, the rest of the company unfolded cots and made the best of their situation. At least they were off the sand dune!

The next day my Marines finally got a hot meal, shower, and were able to put on clean utilities for the first time in a month! The company was trucked to China Beach for the afternoon. The troops went unarmed, and only the officers and staff NCOs carried side arms. I felt completely vulnerable on the trip back and forth without my men having their weapons. China Beach consisted of a large mess hall type building with a kitchen at one end and a bar at the other. Picnic benches were provided inside and out. A few of the troops tried to surf on their air mattresses, but it was too rough. The surf was up and the water was dirty. Steaks were grilled to order with all the trimmings. The troops were allowed 2 beers and all the soda they could drink. We were back in time to occupy our defensive positions for the night. It was our first real break from duty.

On 16 September, one of the LVTs supporting Company B at our old position hit a land mine and burned. Despite the sandy terrain and large areas the LVTs could operate in, I knew it was just a matter of time before the VC figured out where the choke points were and mined them. One Marine was trapped inside and burned to death and four others were wounded.

17 September was my last day in command of Company A. One of my patrols was fired on about noon. They returned fire and assaulted the position. They found blood trails and followed them for a while before returning. I knew I had done an excellent job as CO of Alpha Company, but my fitness report failed to show it. I had been lied to again. My tirade over the treatment of my men cost me fitness report-wise, but I knew I had done the right thing for them.

I summed up the last three weeks to my brother: *"We lost a total of 4 KIA and 20 WIA from the company, plus 2 KIA and 21 WIA from attachments, tanks, ARVN, etc. It's a strange feeling being shot at, and I'm certainly no stranger after those 31 days!"*

I reported to the 2nd Battalion, 9th Marines, along with SSgt. Morton and others. The company I had trained at Camp Pendleton, Okinawa, and in Vietnam was torn to pieces by administrators in the rear. The transfers were because the trans-placement system was being broken up. The movement between units was meant to break up rotation dates so that one battalion would not lose everyone at once. This was great on paper, but it broke up the continuity of highly trained units, such as my company and others in my battalion, which had undergone amphibious raid training and could be used for that type mission. In retrospect, I probably should have requested mast with General Walt and reminded him of his promises to our company and what the 'mix master' was doing. I believe the 3rd Marine Division would have been better served to have one raid school trained company in each battalion or regiment for special missions that might arise.

In addition, when we lost a man to illness or a minor wound, he never returned to the company unless he insisted. Thus, we lost trained men and had to train their green replacements. This policy was changed later in the war. My main wish was that there was some real leadership in my new battalion.

Chapter Eleven

H&S Company,
September-December 1965
Commanding Officer, Company E,
2nd Battalion, 9th Marines

"My kids were so darn good it was unbelievable."
Captain Jack Maxwell

17 September, 2/9 CP:

"*Finally in 2/9 and CO of H&S Co. I've got a lot of work to do as they are moving back to the airfield next week. Lt. Jones and his platoon were transferred also.*"

18 September, 2/9 CP:

"*Had a busy day today. Went out to meet the Colonel. His name is [William F.] Donahue, [Jr.] and seems like a real fine man. Major McLernan is the XO, and he seems the same. He has been selected for Lt. Colonel. The battalion is moving back to the airfield, and I'm having to do a lot of supervising and coordinating to get the CP and the company moved. It's nice in a way to be back here eating hot chow and being able to take a shower, but I miss the company a lot already. Lt. [R.G.] Snyder [D/1/9] was wounded today. He was shot through the neck and chest but they think he will be all right.*

The monsoon season seems about on us. It poured last night and has rained off & on all day today."

19-20 September, 2/9 CP:

"*Spent a busy day running back and forth to the airfield concerning our move. The rains really came today. The bottom fell out most of the morning and afternoon, finally slacking off this evening. The roads are really bad now; can't imagine what they will be like if this continues.*"

21 September, 2/9 CP:

"*Today is moving day and confusion reigns. The XO isn't satisfied unless he in on the movement of every tent, but it's going well despite that. It's a real battle here tonight. The mosquitoes are determined I don't write you. I've killed 6 already and they keep coming.*

It poured rain again today, and water is standing everywhere. There's no breeze tonight either. I sprayed, but I think it bothered me more than them!"

23 September, 2/9 CP, in a letter to my brother:

"I could use some canned nuts and stationary. Beer and soft drinks are in short supply, but the beer situation is improving. Razor blades, shaving cream, etc. are also in short supply. The PXs are terrible—the shelves stay bare."

24 September, 2/9 CP:

"Keith Christensen and I have become good friends. He's the S-4, a senior Captain up for Major. We both waited all day on a bulldozer to fill in holes and level off an area for a mess hall. It came, got stuck twice, so we gave up and went to the Special Forces club and drank beer. Today was just a bad day! All the battalion is due back tomorrow and I hate for the CO to see this place."

25 September, 2/9 CP:

"Have been busy with the move and we almost moved again! Only 2 truckloads before we stopped. Someone higher up changed their mind. They're starting to build us strong back tents and a mess hall so we'll soon be out of the mud. Had my first hot shower since I've been here last night. It was great and had another tonight. We're eating C rations now because the mess facilities were so poor. Hot chow starts tomorrow night (we hope)."

26 September, 2/9 CP:

"Spent a busy day trying to get movies set up for the troops. Got the screen and projector but the communications section didn't get the wiring and the special services didn't get any film, so no movie!

We should have one tomorrow night. Got hot chow tonight for the first time. Swiss steak. It was tough but good. Better than C rations, anyway."

27 September, 2/9 CP:

"Jim McDavid has the company [A/1/9] now. We had a movie scheduled for tonight but never got to see it. First we couldn't get a film until 8 o'clock, then the power went off for 30 minutes, and then the projector wouldn't work. What a time!"

On 28 September, I had a man badly burned with gasoline. I went to C&C (Collection and Clearing) to visit him and take him his gear. I wrote home, "*You really know a war is on when you go out there. Helicopters brought 2 wounded in from 1/9 while I was there.*"

1 October, 2/9 CP:

"*Sitting here writing and watching firing going on in the distance. Tracers are going everywhere and flares are going off. It's coming from Hill 327, so 1/1 is having a little activity. There's a new order on transfers now that includes 1/1. We lose a third of the battalion between now and the 22nd rather than stretching it out to next year. What a mountain of paper work it has created!*

The weather has really gotten hot again. The heavy rains are due any day now. It's cooler, and instead of dust we have mud and more mosquitoes, so it comes out about even."

2 October, 2/9 CP:

"*Another long, hot, busy day. The officers and SNCOs are having a party tomorrow followed by a football game. Should be a lot of fun.*

Lt. Colonel Tunnell of 3/9 (CO) lost his foot and lower leg yesterday. He's the second Battalion CO who's become a casualty. Lt. Colonel Muir of 3/3 was killed by a mine, also.

1/9 is doing a good job. They're killing a lot of VC and getting bodies and weapons. And here I sit on the airbase! I'd rather be out there taking my chances than sitting back here doing paper work."

3 October, 2/9 CP:

"*We had our beer party and football game today. The party was a success and the game ended in a 6-6 tie. I played defense for the officers. We're going to have a playoff next Sunday.*"

4 October, 2/9 CP:

"*Lt. [Walter N.] Levy, who was at Zelm's wedding, lost a leg the other day and 1/1 has had one Lt. killed and another wounded. [Levy was the Lt. who was KIA. For more on his life and death see Caputo's 'Rumor of War,' pp. 208-213.] 3/9 had a big fight last night and had some 30 killed & wounded. Don't know the exact figures.*"

5 October, 2/9 CP:

"General Walt talked to all the officers this afternoon and was impressive as always. He's concerned about the airfield defense and, of course, that's our job. He talked about the fight the other day [3/9]. Final totals were 12 killed and 28 wounded. He even explained the tactical errors made by the platoon commander."

6 October, 2/9 CP:

"After all the rain last night, today dawned bright, clear, and hot. Guess the monsoon is not quite on us.

The Colonel had a 2 hour and fifteen minute meeting today. The kind I hate where things are gone over and over until you're bored to death."

7 October, 2/9 CP:

"Today was another real scorcher. Not a cloud in the sky and no breeze to speak of. Tomorrow is another big day for transfers. We lose 22 men to 3/3. [Captains] Cliff Rushing and [Clyde D.] 'Dickie' Dean are going. 3/3 is supposed to move up here in a few days. I lose my XO, Lt. Jim Fagan, on the 22nd and the 1stSgt.on the 15th, so you can see how things are changing around."

8 October, 2/9 CP:

"The Colonel just called and congratulated us on a real fine mount out drill. We had a platoon mustered, loaded on trucks and down to the company in 12 minutes. General Krulak is going to have breakfast with us Sunday morning at 0630. I'm really hustling to get the place looking good for him."

10 October, 2/9 CP:

"General's Krulak and Walt were here promptly at 0630 for breakfast. I ate with General Walt. Everything went real well and Lt. Colonel Donahue was well pleased. Krulak was very pleasant."

11 October, 2/9 CP:

"We had what seemed like the start of the monsoon last night and this morning. It poured for 12 straight hours before letting up. It's still dark and overcast but the rain has ceased for now. I slept well as it was cool and windy, not many mosquitoes. My 97 cent

raincoat from Okinawa is coming in handy. The regular Marine Corps raincoat is too heavy. It's a light plastic one that sheds rain rather well.

I've got a new company gunnery sergeant, and he's an improvement over the bum I had. He just came in from ITR at Camp Lejeune."

12 October, 2/9 CP:

"I guess the monsoon is here as it's been pouring off and on for 3 days now. Everything is quite a mess but at least it's cool!"

13 October, 2/9 CP:

"Just got back from a CO's meeting. We're going to have an inspection soon also we'll be going back out to the front lines. Don't know when or where. We've been having good chow here. Hope it keeps up!

I went to the PX today and got a haircut. The place was loaded with chow, beer, and soft drinks. Looks like they've got a good supply for a while.

Everything is in constant flux here as we're moving around the area. The troops are all moving into 'strong back' tents with wooden floors and screened sides, all up off the ground. I feel like a juggler moving them around. We should be through moving and building in time for someone else to move in!"

14 October, 2/9 CP:

"Our fifth day of rain but it finally stopped for a while this afternoon. It poured so much this morning that we had to move the mess hall! Heard that Captain Harris, the Australian officer [CO, Co. D] 1/9, was wounded yesterday, not too seriously, but enough to send him home. He's quite a guy!"

16 October, 2/9 CP:

"Keith Christiansen and I went to the Special Forces club tonight and had a few beers. It was really relaxing. The first time I've been anywhere since coming to 2/9.

The monsoon is in full force now and everything is flooded, including my sleeping area! Lt. Fagan just got back from Bangkok, Thailand. He had a ball and fell in love with an airline stewardess!"

17 October, 2/9 CP:

"*Today has been another one of monsoon weather, constant rain, and dark, cloudy skies. Tonight for chow we had steak and ice cream. It's the first steak in over a month, and was cooked to order and plenty of onions!*"

19 October, 2/9 CP:

"*The monsoon continues. Rains a while, sun comes out, rains some more. All the roads are terrible and nearly impassable. We've got most of the leaks in the roof fixed. We're in some old tin buildings built by the French and they're all about to fall down. The rats are nice and big, too.*"

20 October, 2/9 CP:

"*The monsoon continues, but today wasn't too bad. Only rained about half the day. We've finally gotten jungle boots! It's about time, too. They should be a big help in this weather.*"

22 October, 2/9 CP:

"*It's still raining and we're still moving and working! I got a new XO. Mike Reagan. He's from Texas and a nice guy. Four men in A Co. [1/9] have been wounded this week. None seriously I hope.*"

23 October, 2/9 CP:

"*No rain last night or today yet! The dark clouds are rolling in, though. We've still got a mud hole here. I washed clothes as they had been piling up. We opened an enlisted club today. We have tables, chairs, bar (beer only), and a record player. We've ordered a jukebox, too. They had a boxing smoker with prizes, etc.*

Tomorrow most everyone will move into strong backed tents. We've started on a [new] mess hall, too. We'll get it all set up for someone else to move into!"

24 October, 2/9 CP:

"*Today was moving day and the weather couldn't have been better. It was a bright, shiny day, although it rained last night. Nearly everyone has moved but me! I'm moving in the morning and it will probably be pouring.*"

The move went smoothly the next day.

25 October, 2/9 CP:

"There are only four Captains in our tent so we have plenty of room. We're hoping the two doctors and the chaplain don't move in! Can you imagine, only 2 days without rain and we've got dust blowing everywhere. I have been busy with busy work the last couple of days. We're building an Officer and SNCO club, and I am involved in that. We got an icebox and some tables and chains today. The wiring is in and we could open tonight."

27 October, 2/9 CP:

"I spent most of the day working on the Officers-SNCO club. We got beer and soda, but now the icebox isn't working. What next!

I had a court martial today. Lt. Jacoway was the defense counsel and did a good job. The weather remains hot and dry and the dust is really getting bad. Read a report today on the fight that my company had on 9 September, and we killed 117 VC! This was verified by reports from villagers and secret agents, etc. Makes me feel a lot better about those men who were killed and wounded."

28 October, 2/9 CP:

"Was awakened on my birthday with the news that the VC had hit the helicopter field over near Marble Mountain in the 1/9 area. 47 planes gone up in smoke! They hit Chu Lai too. Lt. [W.T.] Mills from 1/9 had his eardrums burst when his jeep hit a mine. He's back to duty today. Had a few beers to celebrate; other than that, a usual day in Vietnam."

29 October, 2/9 CP:

"Another long, hot dusty day in Vietnam. Dusty particularly. You can hardly see it is so thick and its gets on everything. We've finished moving the mess hall and have the bar about finished. Still no icebox, so the bar doesn't do us much good. Some of the officers and staff played volleyball the last two nights. Getting to be a lot of fun!"

31 October, 2/9 CP:

"Read in the Navy Times today that George Welsh got a Bronze Star for his actions in June and July. He really did a good job. One of his staff sergeants got one too. Jack Maxwell's Company got hit hard the other night [Hill 22]. Guess he's all right, as his name wasn't on the casualty list.

We had a lot of fun playing volleyball again last night. Beat the Lt.s three out of four."

1 November, 2/9 CP:

"Another long, hot day in Vietnam. Had a meeting with the CO this afternoon. That helped break up the day, anyway. Played volleyball again tonight. It helps pass the time away too.

I heard 1st Sgt. Smith got wounded and evacuated. Only a fractured finger, but I don't know how bad it was. [I later learned the he and Captain Maxwell had stood back to back in the CP bunker shooting the VC trying to enter with their .45s]. Cpl. [K.P.] Woods was shot through the leg. He was in my company too. They're both with Jack Maxwell in A/1/1. Jack's name was on the radio last night and they quoted him on the way the VC attacked. They killed 57 VC."

Caputo reported the company suffered 22 Marines KIA and 50 WIA out of about 80 men present. The company had been attacked by a VC Main Force battalion, using sappers to penetrate the perimeter.

A newspaper account quoted Maxwell: "I woke up to a rocking [rocket] explosion and made it fast to the bunker,' said Captain Jack Maxwell of Fort Collins, Colo. Maxwell said he found empty shell casings from 50-60 recoilless rifle shells. 'The Viet Cong had a lot of guts to come up here,' he said.

U.S. Marines, using pistols and fighting hand-to-hand from their tents, beat off a 'human wave' assault by the Viet Cong. One Marine squad was badly mauled. Two of its 14 men were killed and the rest wounded. A 13-year old boy was among the Viet Cong dead. Marines said he had been selling soft drinks to Americans in the area and they found drawings of key installations on his body.

'We dropped a lot of Viet Cong with pistols,' said Sgt. Harry Dowdy of Salisbury, Md. 'They came right up to our holes. We fired at a range of 10 yards.'

The assault, by an estimated 100 Viet Cong from a force of 400 was the second against the Marines in the Da Nang area since Thursday, when a Viet Cong suicide squad infiltrated the Marble Mountain air facility and destroyed and damaged 38 helicopters. The attack on the company of Marines was made by both hardcore Viet Cong and youngsters recruited hours earlier at a village and forced to join in the attack."

Corporal Richard A. Cesar (Corydon, Iowa) and Lance Corporal Richard D. Sharp were two of the men from my original company who were KIA on the 30th.

Cpt. John A. Maxwell presented the Bronze Star Medal

2 November, 2/9 CP:

"1/9 had a little action last night as the VC were after the helicopters again."

4 November, 2/9 CP:

"Had a good rain last night that settled the dust for a while at least. Played volleyball again last night. The new battalion XO [Major D. D. Finne] was even out with us. We won as usual! Last night was a quiet one around the perimeter too."

5 November, 2/9 CP:

"Spent most of the morning on a helicopter recon. It was raining, but I enjoyed it anyway. We're planning a big ceremony for the Marine Corps Birthday on the 10th. Naturally, I'm involved. Be glad when it is over with."

6 November, 2/9 CP:

"Had another good rain last night. It cooled things off for a while but today has become hot and sticky. I made another recon down to 3/9 today with Keith Christiansen. It was an enjoyable trip even with the heat."

7 November, 2/9 CP:

"A nice rainy day in Vietnam. Actually this morning wasn't too bad but it's been pouring this afternoon. Had a busy day today. Worked most of the morning on applications for commissions on all of our staff NCOs. Major Finne was around this afternoon and we had a long talk on H&S Co. He seems pleased about most everything.

Had a meeting with the CO a little later and got some more details squared away. General [Jonas M.] Platt walked in to break that up. He's a very impressive looking general."

8 November, 2/9 CP:

"The monsoon is here! It appears like it anyway, as it's been really coming down the last 24 hours. We played volleyball in the mud last night but it was still a lot of fun! The new XO is right much of a jock and he plays every night with us.

I saw a white female today! She was riding in a jeep with a raincoat on! A Red Cross girl no less! It's quite a topic of conversation to see one around here."

9 November, 2/9 CP:

"I saw Bill Zelm today and had a long talk with him. He said Linda will graduate in January. He also told me that 3 of the men killed when Jack's [Maxwell] company [A-1-1] got hit, were from A-1-9 and had been transferred there only a few days before."

10 November, 2/9 CP:

"The ceremony is over and the Marine Corps is 190 year old! They had some real good chow tonight! They awarded 30 Purple Hearts at the ceremony. None of the big wigs who were invited showed but several Vietnamese officials came.

We had free beer tonight and everyone was feeling good by four o'clock. I quit then and ate. If the VC come tonight, I want to be alert!

Tonight's volleyball game was a riot with everyone full of beer! Enjoyed it though."

12 November, 2/9 CP:

"The monsoon is over and the dust is back with us. We never have a happy medium. Still playing volleyball each night. We're getting too many players now and it isn't much fun. There is nothing much going on here. The VC have been quiet for a while now."

This period of hot, miserable days and quiet nights continued for several days.

15 November, 2/9 CP:

"Keith Christiansen made Major last night. He bought beer for everyone at the club. Heard Jim Shubert and Gary Hintz made it yesterday. We had our usual volleyball game last night and it was a good one."

16 November, 2/9 CP:

"Jim McDavid, who took over my company in 1/9 when I left, got relieved by General Walt yesterday. He had talked too much to reporters about some things he didn't like. Russ Lloyd was transferred over there to take the company. It is hardly the job for a passed over Captain. McDavid is now our S-4. Major Christensen is our S-3 replacing Lloyd. McDavid didn't think too much of Lt. Col. Ludwig either. We had two lieutenants to make Captain yesterday, so we've got more free beer.

We had some more good volleyball last night. I was on the winning team, as usual."

17 November, 2/9 CP:

"Went down to visit 3/9 today and saw Bob Weir. He's the S-4 down there now. Heard Lt. Jones was wounded in the face with grenade fragments, but nothing serious. He wasn't evacuated and was back to duty the next day. He's in 2/3, and they're boarding ships and heading for Okinawa, so he'll get a rest."

The next day I sent home a more detailed account of A/1/1's action on 30 October. Maxwell was quoted, "We got a bloody nose, but we're still here and they aren't. My kids were so darn good, it was unbelievable. They held their position beautifully." A/1/1 had been in Vietnam for two months and in their present position at La Chau, about 7 miles south of Da Nang, for 6 weeks. "When the first wave hit, our kids pulled into a tight perimeter around the command post. The sky was filled with all kinds of fire, but the VC never penetrated our tightened perimeter." 27 rifles, a sub-machine gun, and more than 150 grenades were captured. General Walt visited the company after the battle.

"The general seemed pleased with our performance," Maxwell said. "He got right down and talked with several of our men, asking them all what happened. His appearance there did wonders for our guys."

Maxwell was awarded a Bronze Star for his actions. However, word got around that Walt was not totally pleased with his company's performance. In fairness, to put a rifle company in such a position for six weeks and not provide them with barbed wire or enough sandbags and other protective measures to properly defend it was only asking for trouble.

We underestimated the ability of the VC Main Force units to plan, train for, and carryout such actions. In a year or so, a Marine position held for more than a few days would look like a fortress.

20 November, 2/9 CP:

"Lt. Jacoway has gone to Japan to have his knee operated on. He has a torn cartilage. He won't be back is my guess. Heard that 1st Sgt. Smith lost two fingers, the last ones on one of his hands. He's back in the states now."

22 November, 2/9 CP:

"The weather has been unbelievable the past three days. It has poured rain continuously. The tents are so soaked that they're starting to leak at the seams. I had to get up and move the last two nights due to the wind blowing the rain in or the tent leaking. The forecast is for 3-5 days more bad weather."

23 November, 2/9 CP:

"A plane crashed into one of the positions on the airfield, but only one of the Marines in the bunker was hurt. The plane was completely destroyed."

25 November, 2/9 CP:

"A lovely Thanksgiving Day! It's been pouring rain for the past 24 hours with no sign of letting up. It's business as usual here though; every day is a working day. The chow was good as usual on a holiday. We had turkey and all the trimmings.

We're getting all kinds of Christmas cards from people in the states wishing us well. It sure makes you feel good to realize people are thinking of you and care enough to send Christmas cards."

26 November, 2/9 CP:

"Forgot to tell you we had champagne with our Thanksgiving dinner. The mess sergeant bought it out of his own pocket. We had another long rainy day. It's almost cold with the wind blowing so hard. The average rainfall for the Da Nang area is only 84 inches a year!"

28 November, 2/9 CP:

"We had a football game today between the Officers and the SNCOs. It was suppose to have been played on Thanksgiving Day but was rained out. It should have been today! It rained until time for the game to start but stopped for the game. We won on a touchdown from Lt. [E.S.] Roane to me. [Roane was promoted to Captain and later commanded Company H.] The final score was 6-2. SSgt. Morton played on the other team. The Colonel and the Sgt. Major called the game and did a good job. It was a lot of fun."

1 December, 2/9 CP:

"We start moving tomorrow. I dread it in a way but at least it will keep be busy for next couple of weeks.

Things are still quiet here. Nothing much going on in any of the Marine areas. The rain finally stopped today but the sky looks as if it were going to start any time."

2 December, 2/9 CP:

"I washed a big load of clothes today as the sun was out for a few hours. Tomorrow we are moving so everything is clean to start with."

3 December, 2/9 CP:

"We've moved! Actually we're still in the process but almost through. Busy, busy, busy! An artillery battery is located near by and they make up for all the airplane noise we miss. We're re-supplying [the rifle companies] by helicopter so we're still getting some aviation noise. The Colonel seems pleased with the move. He's great to work for."

Our battalion relieved 3/9 on 3 December. The battalion CP was moved across the Song Cau Do River and up the old railroad bed about a mile.

5 December, 2/9 CP:

"Things started hopping today. We had a Sergeant from this company wounded. He was attached to Hotel Company.

Dick Kerr was by last night. He has B Company, 7th Engineer Battalion now and they're making a road survey of the area. He had 2 men killed today out here. They stepped on a mine."

6 December, 2/9 CP:

"Time is going faster out here. I stay busy with security and building up the area. We have blackout so everything has to be done during daylight. Dick Kerr was by today. His men were looking for the man who was blown off a bridge yesterday and disappeared into the river. They didn't have any luck."

Things remained quiet at the 2/9 CP until 9 December.

Promotion Day, December 1965
L-R: Driver, Sgt. Washington, Sgt. Booth,
Sgt. Major Potts & Sgt. Fields

9 December, 2/9 CP:

"One of our positions had 3 rounds fired at it. No one was hurt, but I sent some men out to see if they could find the sniper but no luck.

The mail and packages are really rolling in now. We received quite a few from schools and organizations. We've gotten cookies from the Coatesville, Penn. high school students and razors, blades, and shaving cream from the Schick Co. We're getting hundreds of Christmas cards from people all over the U.S., especially school children and teenagers. The troops love the ones from the teenage girls! It really makes the troops feel appreciated, and nearly all of the cards have been answered by them."

10 December, 2/9 CP:

"Today was another rainy one. The Colonel asked to tour the lines with me and it poured rain the whole time. Things were quiet last night except that artillery fired all night long. They're only a couple of hundred yards away."

13 December, 2/9 CP:

"Hugh O'Brien was in the area today. He came in the tent, shook my hand, and wished me a Merry Christmas. He had his '6-gun' on and practiced his fast draw for the troops."

Cpl. Jerry Judge greeted by actor Hugh O'Brien after patrol with E/2/9

14 December, 2/9 CP:

"We had a little action last night. One of our positions was fired on by the VC. We returned fire but don't believe we hit anyone. We didn't have any casualties. Needless to say, no one got much sleep last night. 1/9 had an active night too. Don't know what happened over there.

We had a tent burn down last night, which added to the excitement. One man was badly burned on his feet."

15 December, 2/9 CP:

"We had some more shots fired at our positions tonight. Nothing else has happened yet! Actually it's quiet tonight in comparison to some others we've had."

16 December, 2/9 CP:

"The VC are active again tonight. Just keeping us awake, I hope. It's pouring rain, as it has all day, so I know the troops are miserable. Today was a busy one, with a lot of administrative matters and work on the defensive perimeter."

17 December, 2/9 CP:

"Pat [Patrick M.] De Martino was by today and briefed us on the action south of here. He's the CO of L Co., 3/3. They had quite a few casualties but killed and captured a lot of VC, food, weapons, etc. We had 3 companies there but very few casualties. They're coming back tomorrow.

Tonight is miserable; there's a driving rain that's been going on for two days, going harder than ever outside and it's so dark you can't see your hand in front of your face. It's cold too, when you get wet and all the wind. I know the troops are miserable."

18 December, 2/9 CP:

"We wounded 2 VC last night, or so the villagers said. Three came through the village and 2 came back dragging the third, and one of those two was shot through the arm. The companies got back from Operation Harvest Moon. The troops were really beat but happy over capturing so much gear and weapons. Saw Bill Zelm and he is o.k."

Metras, Zelm's radio operator, related, "We were on that operation about two weeks. I got jungle rot on my feet from the constant rain, and wading through flooded rice paddies. Our platoon was following some VC one day and we were told to turn back, as we were almost in Cambodia.

We found a lot of enemy bunkers with rifles and ammunition. We were supposed to get a rifle each as war mementos, but never did. One of our men was shot in the neck."

Echo Co. on the move during Operation Harvest Moon

Echo Co. Harvest Moon

Unidentified, Mecuri & Florian: Operation Harvest Moon

Cpl. George Graves with machine gun on Operation Harvest Moon

Chapter Twelve

After Action Report,
December 1965
Excerpts from Captain William A. Coti, CO of E/2/9, on *Operation Harvest Moon*

"As a result of the defeat of the Vietnamese forces at Hiep Duc, the 1st Viet Cong Regiment, reinforced by elements of the North Vietnamese 30th Division and the 195th Anti-Air Battalion, was in an excellent position to enter the Que Son Valley and threaten the South Vietnamese outposts at Que Son and Viet An. To counter this threat, General Westmoreland ordered General Walt to hold two battalions on a 12-hour alert so that they could deploy rapidly. General Walt, concerned about the enemy's growing control of the Que Son Valley, met with General Thi (Warlord of the northern portion of Vietnam) on 4 December 1965 to discuss the mounting threat. Both commanders concurred on the need to launch a sizeable attack against the Viet Cong before they were able to establish a firm base of operations. The result was Operation Harvest Moon/Lien Ket 18."

5 December 1965:

Task Force Delta was activated.

TASK FORCE DELTA:

3rd Bn, 3rd Marines (3/3): Lt. Col. Joshua W. Dorsey, III
Lima Co., 3/3: Capt. Patrick M. DeMartino
Echo Co., 2/9: Capt. William A. Coti
1st Platoon: Lt. William E. Zelm
2nd Platoon: Lt. Roland J. Von Dorp
3rd Platoon: SSgt. John P. Kasparian
Hotel Co., 2/9: Capt. Paul L. Gormley
Golf Co, 2/4: Unknown
2nd Bn., 7th Marines (2/7)
2nd Bn., 1st Marines (2/1)
529 ARVN Ranger Co.
11th & 12th Marines (Artillery)
9th ARVN Regiment
11th ARVN Ranger Bn.

Special Intelligence Unit (ARVN) from Saigon attached to E/2/9.

Operation Harvest Moon 1965
L-R: 1st Sgt. Stephenson, Cpt. Codi & Radio Operators

9 December 1965:

E/2/9 departed 2/9 CP by truck to 3/3 (Hill 55). Lt. Colonel Dorsey of 3/3 advised Captain Coti that his men were not wearing flak jackets on the operation. Coti left if up to the individual Marines in Echo Company to wear them or not. They were then loaded on trucks and moved to an LZ at Than Binh.

1330: E/2/9 helilifted into LZ (GS 1430) for an assault on Hill 43 (GS 124321). Landed 1 ½ miles from Hill 43 and conducted a forced march in order to assault the hill before dark.

1500: L/3/3 was to assault Hill 43 while E/2/9 was to seize a hamlet on the right flank and support them by fire. G/2/9 remained in reserve. L/3/3 launched its attack before E/2/9 was in place, and the battalion came under intense enemy fire from four locations. The VC/NVA were firing automatic weapons, including twelve 7 mm machine guns.

"L Company ran into a force of 200 VC defending Hill 43. Fighting raged into the early evening throughout the area. Hill 43 was taken and contact was made with 40 South Vietnamese soldiers from the 1st Battalion, 5th ARVN regiment. 75 VC were killed, 11 Marines were killed and 17 wounded, including Captain DeMartino."

Unknown to Captain Coti at the time, SSgt. Kasparian, leading the 3rd Platoon, had tied in with the right flank of L/3/3 and had moved forward under intense fire to help capture Hill 43. Kasparian was hit in the back by a small piece of shrapnel, which he did not report. "The platoon acted admirably as they fired and maneuvered to the objective," Coti noted.

Meanwhile, the 1st Platoon, under heavy enemy weapons and mortar fire, assaulted the hamlet but was initially forced back. Lt. Zelm, after firing WP mortar rounds and LAWs into the village, setting it afire, took the objective and set up a perimeter defense around it. Coti and his CP group had accompanied the 1st Platoon.

"It was a miserable, wet, and hungry night on Hill 43," Coti reported. "The 3rd platoon was out of rations and water, however, when the choppers came in to evacuate the wounded, they dropped off several cases of C rations.

"My 2nd Platoon, along with them HQ and heavy weapons, were pinned down by intensive enemy fire somewhere in the rear. It was dark before we secured the hamlet and set up a perimeter defense at the edge of the tree line. I gave LtCol. Dorsey a status report. He told me to advance to Hill 43 to reinforce L Company. I told him that I had 5 seriously wounded Marines that could not be moved without jeopardizing their lives (per our corpsmen), 7 Marines missing from one of the helicopters back at the LZ area, 3 Marines missing from the 1st Platoon during the assault on the hamlet, and I had no radio contact with my 2nd Platoon. Dorsey said that he would call for a medevac helicopter to take my wounded so I could take my company to Hill 43. The whole hamlet was on fire, which provided enough light, so I sent a patrol back to it to search for the missing Marines—none were found."

2200: "Radio contact was established with my 2nd Platoon and CP somewhere in the rear. I gave the Platoon Leader my coordinates, and told him when they reached our perimeter, we could guide them in."

2300: 2nd Platoon and my company CP arrived at our position. 1st Sgt. Paul Stephenson had been wounded in the leg.

Pvt. Paul Stephenson, Camp Elliot, 1942

Sgt. Major Stephenson with wife Edna
Camp Lejeune 1965

2400: "Lt.Col. Dorsey called for an emergency helicopter to lift out my wounded Marines. His request was denied. He said helicopters would not come until daylight, as the LZ was too 'hostile' to attempt a night landing. I checked with my senior Corpsman and he told me that two, maybe more, of the wounded would not survive the night if they were not taken to the hospital."

10 December 1965:

0145: Dorsey called and said when he passed this information to the helicopter squadron, "they immediately got volunteers to make a hostile night landing to evacuate the wounded."

0200: With the LZ lit with flares, the helicopters landed and the wounded evacuated.

> lstSgt. Stephenson
> Sgt. Robert Lewis
> LCpl. Gene Hager [He had been in my company in A/1/9]
> LCpl. Darrell Elliott
> LCpl. Gerald Letendre [He had been in my company in A/1/9]
> PFC Richard E. "Dick" Spurlock
> PFC Kenneth R. Fisher

[PFC K.P. Florian was WIA with shrapnel all over his body, treated in the field, and returned to duty]

0300: Dorsey said to wait until daybreak and then move to Hill 43.

0600: "At daybreak I moved my company to Hill 43 and joined L/3/3 and my 3rd Platoon." The 3 missing Marines were found near the hamlet (they had gotten separated in the dark moving to assault the hamlet and waited for daylight to move out) and the 7 Marines missing from the LZ arrived.

"The battalion moved west to Hill 63, arriving at 1700. We set up defensive positions for the night."

11 December 1965:

3/3 commenced patrolling the area north of Hill 407 searching for the enemy.

0800: Echo Company patrolled an area 1800 meters to the west of Hill 407 and found a fortified complex on a hill, with four entrances leading to tunnels. The complex was still under construction and was too large to be destroyed. Lt.Col. Dorsey said to continue searching for the enemy and the complex would be destroyed later. We captured 15 VC and an assortment of VC documents, 40 metal punji stakes, 300 wooden punji stakes, and over 350 anti-helicopter stakes. We destroyed the stakes and returned to base at 1430.

12 December 1965:

3/3 helilifted to LZ with E/2/9 landing first and receiving intensive fire from a pagoda and the surrounding area. 3 VC were killed around the pagoda. One of the VC KIAs was a woman carrying a pack full of documents. One VC carrying a Russian rifle was captured. The VC had placed a group of children on the ground floor of the pagoda and held them there when they opened fire on my company. None of the children were killed but several were wounded and treated by our corpsmen. Bob Brown and Manuel Rodriguez were wounded and PFC David T. Walker, a non-battle casualty, were medevaced. Brown died from his wounds at 3rd Medical Bn. the next day.

2200: Lt.Col. Dorsey briefed his Company Commanders. Intelligence had placed 2 VC/NVA Battalions in the Phouc Ha Valley. 2/1 was to deploy south of the valley and 2/7 north of the valley. L/3/3 and G/2/4 were to move at 0800 the next day along two ridges covering the northern entrances to the valley and seize hills 100 and 180. Following a pre-dawn B-52 strike in the valley Echo Company was to enter the valley, locate and destroy the NVA Logistical Support Area for I Corps, and utilizing the Special ARVN Intelligence Unit, estimate the damage caused by the B-52s, and interrogate captured VC/NVA concerning the psychological effects of the bombing.

When General Thi was informed of the B-52 strikes in the valley, the VC found out and alerted their forces to leave before it occurred. This would account for the light resistance we met when we went into the valley. The CO of G/2/4 was sending one of his platoons on the high ground just above the valley floor for security.

13 December 1965:

Pre-dawn USAF B-52s struck the Phouc Ha Valley. General Jonas Platt called Lt.Col. Dorsey and had him move the battalion 1,000 meters to the north so they could strike again. Following the second strike, the battalion moved out.

Echo Company entered the valley and found first a hospital and VC documents listing the names of the doctors and nurses. 9 VC were captured, interrogated by the ARVN Intelligence Unit and evacuated.

1200: A sewing machine and 5 reams of dark blue/gray cloth were found in a hut and destroyed. We continued up the valley—rice paddies and dense jungle terrain. Throughout the area all battalions were having trouble due to the weather. The monsoon rains flooded the rice paddies, and made it tough going in the jungle-covered hills.

The VC/NVA Logistics Supply Area we found was well camouflaged on the hill sides in the dense growths of trees and brush. The area contained numerous storage bins (10 x 10 and 10 feet high) with straw roofs and tin sides. The bins were full of supplies—blue, gray and, black cloth, buttons, sewing thread, hospital material, bandages, stainless steel pots and lids, bundles of wood binding material, cans of kerosene, batteries, flashlights, salt, sugar, rice, bicycles and tires & tubes for them, medical boxes containing implements, malaria pills, dysentery pills, and others, and a doctor's diary. Also 20,000 pills of penicillin, chlorine tablets, rolls of brown plastic material, pick heads, 100 lb. sacks of soup and tea, new winter jungle uniforms, and 15 money receipts. One tall hut, 15 x 15 x 4' contained salt. Another, 10 x 10 x 4' was full of blank paper, books, pads, lined paper, pens, and typewriter ribbons.

The supplies in these caches were in excellent condition. The B-52 bombings did not cause any damage to the storage bins/huts. Several caches were located in marshy areas, which absorbed the impact of the bombs without any damage.

The company took up defensive positions for the night and sent out ambushes throughout the area. Very cold and wet—no VC contact during the night.

14 December 1965:

0730: "Continued searching the valley. Left my Company HQ in the VC supply area with the 2nd Platoon to provide security. Sent the 3rd Platoon to search the side of a hill to the southwest. I took the 1st Platoon and patrolled the area to the end of the valley and then to the northeast along the side of a hill. We captured 2 VC females, one who was the wife of the VC security leader for the valley. The other was the wife of the local guerilla leader. We found in their possessions papers outlining the road nets being built from the valley to Que Son District Headquarters, and 3 pouches of other documents found in a cave. Papers in one of the pouches explained the National Liberation Front in South Vietnam. Some of the papers were in Chinese. General Platt arrived by helicopter to pick them up. He had his pilot take me on a 15-minute reconnaissance around the Harvest Moon area in his helicopter."

During the day the 2nd Platoon found an arms cache containing 3 automatic rifles, 35 Russian AK-44 rifles, 3 M1 rifles, 10 60 mortar rounds, 1 MK-1, 1 PR-6 radio, 2 PR-10 radios, 3 TA-312s, 7 Czech rifles, 2 Chinese light machine guns, 1 BAR, 57 Chinese hand grenades, 10 rifle flares, 6 AP mines, 7 fuses for mines, 100 magazines, and thousands of rounds of small arms ammunition.

3rd Platoon found a storage hut full of paper and cloth, which they destroyed.

1st Platoon found sewing machines and 50 reams of blue and gray cloth which they destroyed.

3 civilians were picked up, a man and two women. The man claimed to be a hamlet police chief in a valley about 30 kilometers from here. They all claimed to have been kidnapped by the VC. They were turned over to the ARVN Intelligence Unit.

This intelligence unit interviewed the civilians found in the area and learned they had hidden in caves or hid in the mountains during the bombing. Hundreds of dead people were found in the caves when he returned, who were probably the evacuees from the VC hospital that was found by the Marines.

The company took up defensive positions for the night.

15 December 1965:

The patrolling continued.

1000: A cache was found containing four 81 mm mortar rounds, twenty-one 60 mm mortar rounds, and five AP mines.

Another patrol turned up 2 bins, 12 x 7 x 4' full of rice, 4 empty storage bins, 400 lbs. bandages, 500 blue and gray uniforms, 30 short sleeve shirts and short trousers, 70 rolls of cloth, 3,000 needles and pins, 100 reams of paper, 50 bundles of medical gauze, 200 rice sacks, 2,500 lbs. of rice, 10 lbs. plaster of Paris, and 20 rolls of plastic material. All of this was destroyed.

1800: The patrols returned and went into defensive positions for the night.

16 December 1965:

0800: Continued patrolling the valley.

1100: "I notified Lt.Col. Dorsey that the VC/NVA were being driven into the valley by 2/1 sweeping northeast, and I should set my company in at the end of the valley in blocking positions. We killed 16 VC during this movement."

1530: One patrol reported with a briefcase full of documents, 1 pistol holster, 4 M-1 rounds, 1 canteen, and a pair of sunglasses. They destroyed 2 tons of rice and 24 cubic feet of tea.

During the day we had to evacuate for emersion foot problems Cpl. Michale Laux, LCpl.s Gerald Letendre and George Morris, and PFCs David D. Sourwine, Richard B. Wade and Alvin L. Williams.

We set up defensive positions for the night.

17 December 1965:

"We completed the helilift of 60 tons of VC supplies, ammunition and weapons out of the valley.

We again set up defensive positions for the night."

18 December 1965:

"The battalion commenced moving back to the LZ to be evacuated. G/2/4 in the lead, followed by H&S 3/3, L/3/3 with Echo Company as rear guard. My company was taken under fire from VC across an open rice paddy. I sent the 1st Platoon across the river to take the VC under fire from the high ground. The VC were now attacking my right flank and they were seen moving towards a pagoda. G/2/4 could not find a river crossing to the proposed LZ because of high water, so an alternate LZ was selected and the evacuation started. Due to the late hour we arrived at the alternate LZ, the evacuation could not be completed before dark. Lt.Col. Dorsey evacuated L/3/3, H&S 3/3 and the ARVN Intelligence Unit and kept G/2/4 and my company and the 3/3 CP behind. Dorsey stated that intelligence had warned him that 2 VC battalions were heading our way. We set up defensive positions but had no VC attack, but it was a very cold and stormy night. Dorsey later learned that the VC had headed for the original LZ and did not know about the alternate one."

19 December 1965:

0800: "Helicopter lift commenced. Echo Company was the last to leave. We took 17 refugees along. The refugees said that the VC kept them from leaving the area but now that the VC were gone, they wanted to leave. From the helicopter, we observed a mass exodus of people heading for the South Vietnamese District Headquarters."

1600: "We returned to 2nd Battalion, 9th Marines headquarters. My whole company came down with 'hook worm' caused by immersion foot. The worms entered the body through sores on the feet. Treatment lasted 2 days (50% of the company at a time)."

Coti later added, "On 18 December, the 2nd Battalion, 7th Marines, on the last leg of its patrol, encountered the 80th VC Battalion in strength. Earlier that day 54 Marines from 2/7 had been evacuated suffering from immersion foot. G/2/7 led the battalion, followed by F/2/7, H&S Co. 2/7, and H/2/9. As the column entered the village of Ky Phu, the VC let the lead company pass through the village before taking them under fire. Lt. Col. [Leon N.] Utter, CO of 2/7, thought G Company was just under fire by snipers so he sent them to clear the area south of his position and ordered F Company forward. As F Company entered the village mortar rounds dropped on H&S, still in the open paddies. Two VC companies tried to enter the gap between F and H&S and envelop the battalion command group.

F Company attacked the VC, supported by helicopters and artillery. The VC broke and ran. H/2/9 remained in contact with the enemy, as a VC company struck both flanks and the rear. Both the Company Commander and his radio operator were mortally wounded and died.

The next day, all three battalions, 3/1, 2/7 and 3/3 completed their movement out of the operations area. Harvest Moon accounted for 407 enemy killed, unknown number of wounded, 33 captured, 13 crew-served weapons seized and 95 individual weapons seized. Marine casualties were 45 killed and 218 wounded. South Vietnamese casualties (most of which occurred during the first two days of the operation) 90 killed, 141 wounded and 91 missing."

General Walt & LCpl Mercuri: Operation Harvest Moon

19 December, 2/9 CP:

"Captain Paul [L.] Gormley [of Dracut, Ma.] was killed yesterday. [A mortar shell killed he and his radioman, LCpl. Robert J. Wilkins of St. Charles, Mo.] He was the CO of Hotel Company. He was the CO of H&S Company before me. [Captain] Lou Sullivan, the S-2, flew down to take over the company. They're still on Harvest Moon. He had a wife and one little girl. I've got to inventory his gear tomorrow. A sad job."

20 December, 2/9 CP:

"We had our usual sniper fire tonight. No one was hurt."

22 December, 2/9 CP:

"Packages are still pouring in. Today we received a package from the state of New Jersey. Everyone got razor blades, a ballpoint pen, writing paper (this is a sheet), nail clippers, comb, finger nail file and cigarettes. It was real nice of them.

Had a court martial that lasted all afternoon. Gave me a headache! Today was hectic to say the least. Tonight is too! We're having to use everyone to man the perimeter and no one wants to let anyone go."

Captain Coti of Echo Company reported PFC Spurlock was wounded again.

23 December, 2/9 CP:

"The rains have stopped so it has started getting hot again. It's good to get things dried out though.

Michigan really went all out with their gifts, everything from foot powder to vitamin pills! The stationary I'm sending to you! Don't think it appropriate for Marines! It's appreciated anyway.

Met Major Angelo for the first time since Basic School. He remembered me. He's the S-3 of 9th Marines.

The Vietnamese laundryman gave me a plaque for Christmas. He has invited me to his house for New Years. I doubt if I'll be able to make it."

24 December, 2/9 CP:

"All is quiet now and we hope it will be with the truce. Nevertheless we have every position manned and ready, just in case. For the average trooper it means they don't have to go on patrol tomorrow.

There's a little Christmas cheer flowing around here but I'm not in the mood, plus I don't trust the VC. I hardly ever drink a beer. I'm sitting here eating Macadamia nuts and drinking coffee, nuts courtesy of my sweet wife. No mail today. Packages comprised most of the mail. There must be a ton of cards and letter mail coming to the Battalion.

General's Walt and [Lowell E.] English were out today. Didn't see either of them, though."

December 25, 2/9 CP:

"A lovely Christmas day! Pouring rain as usual. It started an hour after I wrote you last night. I slept good when it started, though.

We had an excellent meal and everyone got a mug with '2/9' and 'Vietnam' on it.

The barber brought out his little boy and everyone gave him candy, chewing gum, etc. He was really cute, all dressed up and with shoes on, too.

The ceasefire must have worked, as I heard very little firing last night. Hope it continues!"

PFC William Ware had joined the 3rd Platoon as a Rifleman on 22 December. A member of his Fire Team had received a 'care package' from home and it contained packs of Lipton's onion soup mix. They heated it up in a helmet and that was their Christmas meal.

Christmas Day 1965
Cpl. Antal in front on right
Ware with cigarette, Nieto in t-shirt

26 December, 2/9 CP:

"Everyone is still eating Christmas goodies, as packages are still pouring in. Had a busy day today and tomorrow will be even busier as we have a big operation starting."

27 December 1965:

Captain Coti reported that while Echo Company was participating in Operation Golden Dagger LCpl. David A. Kovac, of Morgantown, West Virginia, was killed in action. PFCs Larry W. Lukeman and Raymond J. Nieto were wounded.

L-R: Nieto, Anderson, Mercuri & Hancock, E/2/9 Fire Team, 1965

Echo Company had been operating out of Thung Luong hamlet, called
Christmas Island by the Marines, and had managed to protect a South
Vietnamese Civil Affairs Team from Saigon since 1 November 1965. Captain
Coti recalled, "The Team Leader, Tan Huy, told me the day before we left
the island (26 December) that the village elders had told him the VC were
going to kill all of them as soon as the Marines left the island. I called 2/9
and explained the situation and requested that we take the Civil Affairs
Team off the island when we leave, drop them on the mainland and pick
them up again when we returned. The S-3 checked with Lt. Col. Donahue
and permission was denied. The next morning as we were boarding the
amtracs, the entire Civil Affairs Team approached our position—they were
terrified and again pleaded to be taken off the island until we returned. I
called 2/9 again and asked permission to remove them until our return and
permission was again denied. Their worst nightmare came true.

"I told a 3rd Marine Division reporter, who was with us at the time, 'On
1 November 1965, eight men, one girl, and one boy came to Trung Luong
hamlet. This pacification team came to help the people live a better life. They
taught the people to be proud of themselves and their country. They taught
school to the children. In less than two months, they had accomplished so

much good that the VC communists, in their sinister manner, planned to destroy them.'

"On the night of 27 December 1965, at 1915 when the pacification team was completely helpless [they were unarmed], the Viet Cong, in their cowardly fashion, from hidden positions ambushed them. While the team was walking away from a meeting near the pagoda the VC killed the first one, Nguyen Tan Huy, a 17-year-old boy and the younger brother of the pacification team leader. Next they killed Nguyen Van Hieu, age 31, who you all will remember his smiling face. He left a widow and children in Saigon. Next they shot and killed Doan Kim Bang, through the chest, several times. They killed the girl and the rest of the pacification team. They were not soldiers. They were only trained to do good which the communists, showing their true nature, have always deplored.

"When we got back to 'Christmas Island' on 28 December, the pacification team's house was deserted. The team leader appeared later and told us what happened. When he heard the shooting he ran into the jungle and hid waiting for our return. None of the team members were armed except him, and he had a pistol. A Buddhist funeral was held the next day for the nine members who were killed. I represented E Company at the funeral."

28 December, 2/9 CP:

"We just had a little excitement. About a dozen VC opened fire on the perimeter. We returned fire and for about 15 minutes we had a nice firefight going on. A lot of ammunition was fired but no casualties on our side and probably none on the VC side. Kept everyone alert and they'll probably stay that way tonight.

We had a big operation today and a lot of people were still eating chow when everything happened. We had 3 WIAs and 1 KIA. They killed 3 VC captured a dozen or so."

29 December, 2/9 CP:

"Went to 1/9 today and saw Jim Shubert, George Welsh and Joe Marada. B Co. killed 40 VC yesterday. They had a few casualties too.

Tonight is quiet. Hope it stays that way! Last night's excitement was enough for a while.

Got to see the Bob Hope show today! It poured rain and the show was 2 and a half hours late starting. We actually only saw about half the show. It was after dark when it was over. Took a few movies of all the cast, especially Carol Baker and Diana Batts! Whow! General's [Air Marshal Nguyen Cao] Ky and Walt and Senator Symington were there and I got pictures of them, too."

30 December, 2/9 CP:

"It's been almost cold today with the wind and rain. All is quiet and that is what counts! I'm sure it will be quiet tonight, unless the VC start something."

31 December, 2/9 CP:

"All is quiet here now. There was some firing about 2000, but only the artillery is firing now. They are going to fire a '66' with flares at midnight. It's cold here tonight even with the rain stopped. It was cold all day today even with the sun out. Doesn't seem like the same place with the 120 degree temperatures."

Chapter Thirteen

Da Nang TAOR,
January-Febraury 1966
Commanding Officer, Company E,
2nd Battalion, 9th Marines
Operations Rough Rider and Double Eagle II
"The battalion got a well done from General Pratt."

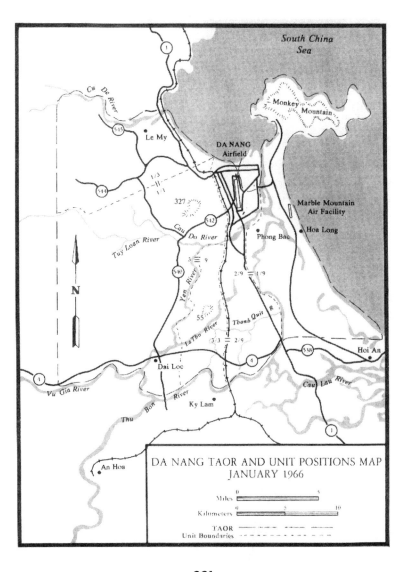

DA NANG TAOR AND UNIT POSITIONS MAP
JANUARY 1966

The New Year came in with a bang!

1 January, 2/9 CP:

"*Last night we had our own fireworks. The mortars fired some flares and then the troops started shooting—got me in Dutch with the Colonel. Guess he'll get over it. I don't know which unit started it, but as far as you could see every Marine outfit was firing pop up flares and tracers. It was beautiful to see, but hell on security!*"

There was supposed to be a shortage of pop up flares. I think the troops had hoarded them for New Year's Eve!

4 January, 2/9 CP:

"*Today was a nice one but it's started raining now. January is another rainy, cool month here. I like it better than the hot weather, though.*

The battalion got back [from an operation] tonight. Didn't have a single casualty but they didn't find any VC either.

Just got in from touring the lines and all is quiet. Last night was quiet too. Hope it stays that way!"

5 January, 2/9 CP:

"*Heard that Bob Sweeney drowned down at Chu Lai. He was walking along the beach with his relief showing him around and walked out on some rocks. A big wave knocked him off and he drowned. He had extended over here and had just made Major. We had another quiet night last night.*"

6 January, 2/9 CP:

"*Just finished checking the lines. All is quiet and there's a good moon out. Should be a quiet night.*"

8 January, 2/9 CP:

"*I had a man get badly burned today. He was using a flamethrower to burn brush and the hose burst. He wasn't in too bad shape. Burned both arms and his face [Sgt. Marvin H. Davis, the Flame Thrower Section Leader, showed great presence of mind in going to his assistance immediately, smothering the flames with wet blankets]. [Captain] Dick Pegler apparently cracked up and got evacuated back to the states. He had a bad fever and was in the hospital a few days; got well, and then cracked up! He had the artillery battery across the road from us."*

9 January, 2/9 CP:

"Everything was quiet last night. 1/9 had a little action yesterday. They had 3 men killed in an ambush."

10 January, 2/9 CP:

"I've got a court martial at 3/3 tomorrow; don't know how I get so lucky. I'm also working on an investigation and Lt. Reagan got transferred today, so I've really got my hands full."

11 January, 2/9 CP:

"Just finished making the rounds and everything is fairly quiet. 1/9 and 3/3 have a lot of flares up so there may be some action going on."

Members of my company who had transferred from A/1/9 learned of the death of one of our comrades who stayed behind. PFC David John Bystedt was killed by enemy fire. Bystedt was from Portland, Oregon.

12 January, 2/9 CP:

"Had a quiet night last night. Tonight we've got some VC outside the perimeter. No firing as yet, but we're staying alert. I learned today that the Colonel had put me in for the Naval Commendation Medal for the job I had done with H&S Company."

On 13 January, Captain Coti wrote, "During the night a vehicle traveling Hoi An to Da Nang carrying three Army Rangers was ambushed in the middle of my tactical area of operations [Highway 1]. In the jeep was an Army Captain carrying top secret documents, a Master Sergeant, and an Australian Warrant Officer. Shortly thereafter an Army Ranger Captain, advisor, arrived at my CP with a South Vietnamese Ranger unit. He told me of the ambush and the need to get to the ambush site and recover the top secret documents. I was concerned for the three men in the jeep and knew that time was of the essence if they were still alive. I called for my reaction squad and got ready to move out to the ambush site. I called the 2/9 CP and told them of my plans to accompany the Rangers, and was told not to move out until daylight. I stressed again that the 3 men may be alive and need medical attention. Again permission was denied. The Ranger Captain was on my case about the need to move immediately to recover the documents. I was in agreement, but not for the documents but the lives of the three soldiers. Remembering what had happened at Christmas Island a few weeks before, I called 2/9 again and said I was not waiting any longer and was taking my reaction squad and the Ranger unit to the ambush site. I was ordered by Lt.Col. Donahue to stay where I was. About 15 minutes later, I was told by Lt.Col. Donahue that the Rangers could go, but neither myself nor any of my Marines could go. (I did not know that 9th Marines Regiment was monitoring all the Battalions' communications nets and 2/9 was told by Regiment to go to the ambush site immediately).

"On 15 January, Major Finne, XO of 2/9, came to my CP and said he was to bring me back to 2/9 CP. Capt. Driver, C.O. of H&S Co., 2/9 was taking over the E Company and I was taking over his position. Major Finne asked me what I had said to Lt.Col. Donahue because he had never seen him so 'pissed.' I shrugged his question off and went back to the 2/9 CP with him. I was never told what happened to the three Army Rangers and I thought they all died.

"Thirty years later, at my first 2/9 reunion, I met my Echo Company Marines that were manning the ambush site on 13-14 January 1966, when the VC ambushed the jeep. They said they did not see the ambush but heard a lot of shooting and after awhile it became quiet again. About an hour later the Army Ranger Captain, carrying a briefcase with the top secret documents, ran into LCpl. Xavier Rodriguez's ambush position. The Master Sergeant, wounded, also ran into one of our ambush positions. At daylight, the Marines from the ambush positions found the body of the Australian Warrant Officer near the vehicle. All through the years I thought the 3 Rangers died and that I had not done enough to try to save them."

15 January, 2/9 CP:

"I had been asking Colonel Donahue to finish my tour with a rifle company, and I got my wish.

"The Colonel called me in last night and sent me on down here [to E/2/9]. He was dissatisfied with the job Captain [William A.] Coti was doing. I'm sure I can do better. Lt. Zelm is my XO and almost half of the troops were in A-1-9. Almost like a reunion! One of my squads killed a VC last night. It's a good way to start off."

16 January, 2/9 CP:

"The VC fired about 20 rounds at us last night but no one was hit. We found a grenade where they had been this morning. Tonight has been quiet so far."

17 January, Near Bo Mung:

"We had a little excitement today. My company got ambushed while moving on trucks along a main highway [Rt. 1]. We were going south to be a blocking force for 'Operation Big Lodge.' Two of the truck drivers panicked and jumped out of their trucks before they stopped them and we had five injured, one seriously, when the trucks ran together. The VC set off an explosion in the road [culvert] and then opened fire on us with a MG and other weapons from the right side of the road. We got sniper fire from the left side also, but stopped that with return fire. We overcame them with little or no trouble and captured 18 VC suspects. We only received a little sniper fire the rest of the day. SSgt. Lutz, commanding the Weapons Platoon, had the 60 mm mortars firing on the VC in seconds. Sgt.s John H. Payne and Vernon G. White, Jr. were WIA but returned to duty that afternoon. Sgt. Frank M. Tejeda, Jr. was wounded in the leg, and Cpl. James R. Ruiz, LCpl.s Peter E. Higgins and J.L. Lewis, PFC Danny C. Shultz, and Pvt. Gary A. Chaffee, also received minor wounds."

I believe that our movement was tipped off to the VC because we had to clear this operation down Highway 1 with the ARVN. The trucks also remained at the 2/9 CP rather than returning to Da Nang. The local VC who conducted the ambush were probably hoping to hit an ARVN unit, not a reinforced Marine Rifle Company! They had planted some six or eight 105 rounds in the culvert, but only one exploded. They lay gleaming in a row on the bottom of the stream. The culvert itself was destroyed, but fortunately none of the trucks ran into it. They blew it between the third truck—the one the CP group and I were riding on—and the fourth, so we just passed over when it blew. My troops had been trained to disembark over the sides of the trucks, so none of them were hurt. The attached personnel jumped out the backs of the vehicles. One engineer had his chest crushed between two trucks and died later. The truck driver jumped out of his truck and left it rolling towards the next one. We received some small arms fire from east of the road, but it was quickly silenced by our return fire. There was automatic weapons fire from west of the road; our machine gunners quieted it quickly. I left Lt. Zelm and a squad behind to handle the medical evacuation and guard the trucks while I led the rest of the company in pursuit of the VC.

We ran into an area where the VC had been planting nail mines, a board with metal spikes nailed through and buried just under the leaves and soil, for Marines to step or fall on. They were still in the process of digging the holes for them when we arrived. The VC dropped some 75-80 of them along the trail and fled. I picked up one as a souvenir and still have it.

I had not been in combat for some time, and this was my first ambush. I had difficulty finding my voice at first, but I gave the orders and my Marines moved out in pursuit with great alacrity. We continued to operate in the area along Highway 1 near Bo Mung.

Our company position was just west of Highway 1 and just east of the Thu Bon River. We inherited a large underground bunker from the previous occupants, and above ground positions surrounding the bunker. We were on a finger on a rise of ground which overlooked a large area covered with rice paddies and numerous tree lines and villages to our front (south). One platoon was stationed at a river block on the bank of the stream a few hundred yards southeast of our CP. I had my 60 mm mortar dug in near the CP. The troops improved their positions by digging foxholes and sandbagging them. We were only allowed to have one strand of barbed wire, which was used more to keep the cattle and civilians out than as a barrier. During the day, we manned a checkpoint on the highway with the ARVN Popular Forces. We placed barbed wire barricades across the road at night. Listening posts were put out after dark; one near the river and one forward of our position. I sent patrols out each day, varying the time so as not to set a pattern. They never returned by the same route they went out on. The PFs normally accompanied our patrols and proved very useful in finding booby traps and identifying the VC among the civilians. I had at least one reinforced squad ambush out each night. We also ran patrols at night. We wanted to deny the VC freedom of movement at night, which they had previously enjoyed.

18 January, On Highway 1:

"Today has been fairly quiet. One of our patrols got shot at and we shot back but no one was hit on either side. Last night was quiet, too."

I added to my brother, "I've got a rifle company again. Lucky me! Ha! Sure is a lot of hard work but I really enjoy it."

PFC Dennis Becton had just joined the company from Marine Barracks, Norfolk, Virginia. He was serving in the 1st Platoon, which was manning the river block position. They had a 106 mm recoilless rifle attached.

Becton related, "We almost lost the 106 mm off a boat in the canal leading to our position on the river bank. We saved it and set it up in the blocking position. I was a rifleman in Cpl. [Gilberto] Garcia's squad."

19 January, On Highway 1:

"Last night was quiet. Today we had a patrol fired on by snipers, but the only damage was one man getting a bullet hole in his trousers; in the leg, of course. Tonight we have an AP correspondent flying in to go on an ambush patrol.

I'm invited to a Vietnamese New Years party tomorrow at Mien Bong. Colonel Donahue and Capt. [Robert C.] Lawrence are also invited. They call it Tet, and it lasts three days. It starts on the 21st, actually. That day they visit their parents and cousins. The 22nd they mourn for their ancestors and get drunk. The 23rd their parents and cousins visit them. [This information came from our Vietnamese interpreter, who had attended college in California].

We finished painting the pagoda today. Should make the Buddhists happy. We're thinking of doing a nearby school next." [The recipe for the paint was four pounds of crushed seashells, add water, stir in Vietnamese dye and some paste and apply. The shrine was near Bo Mung.]

Metras recalled, "I remember we got a liberty while we were here. Our squad got aboard trucks and went to our company headquarters at the 2/9 CP. We had to change into our khaki uniforms, turn in our rifles, and go into Da Nang. A six-hour liberty call. We enjoyed it. Only General Walt cancelled all liberty in Da Nang after that."

21 January, Highway 1:

"One of our patrols had a grenade thrown at them last night and they fired at the VC but there were no casualties on either side. The correspondent never showed up last night. I was glad because they're a lot of trouble.

Just got back from celebrating Tet with the Vietnamese. It was real interesting. Col. Donahue didn't come but Col. Gorman, the Regimental CO, was there and three company commanders and army advisors. I sat beside the Vietnamese CO's wife. She spoke French but no English. We couldn't communicate too well, but we made ourselves understood. She served all the Marine Captains & Col. Gorman. The food was good, better than a Hawaiian luau. They had roast pork, skewered beef, rice cake, peanuts, lettuce, mint, a roll like bon tons, noodles, onions and their famous fish sauce—which is much like garlic. I ate with chopsticks and did quite well, if I do say so. They had whiskey, soft drinks, and rice wine. I had a little whiskey and an orange drink, but none of that wine! It looked too potent!

Enclosed are a Tet New Years card I got, plus the invitation to the Tet celebration with the 51st ARVN regiment."

The unit diary shows Sgt. David R. Burgess, age 23, of Kew Garden, N.Y., was KIA at 1115 that day. Cpl. William G. Smallwood, Jr. remembered the event. "We got a new Sgt. in our platoon. Bright red hair, a Canadian and one of the first 2 year E-5s I had seen. I was carrying the radio for him on patrol when a sniper got him right through the throat. He was highly respected by the troops."

Echo Co. taking a break, February 1966

Cpl. William Smallwood, Jr., on patrol
February 1966

1st Platoon, 1965-66
L-R: Cummings, 3 unidentified, Cpl. Sasser, LCpl. Letendre, LCpl. Copeland,
LCpl. Smallwood & LCpl. Laux (center back row w/ arms up)

Lt. David Garner, 1965-66

23 January, Highway 1:

"We had a day long patrol yesterday and they had 2 men killed, both were Sergeants and married. We killed 2 VC, captured 1, and 4 suspects. One man stepped on a punji stake also but didn't know it until today." [Pvt. Richard L. Nordyke].

Lt. David Garner, my Artillery FO, had volunteered to go on the patrol led by 2nd Lt. Wayne Loughery. "As we were crossing a wide open rice paddy from east to west, we took heavy fire from An Tu (1) to the north of us. With two squads already in the flooded paddies (the lead squad was about to clear the paddies), the CP group, with all its antennas, entered the paddy. Firing commenced when we were all in the water. I knew immediately that someone behind me had been hit. I was followed by my radioman PFC Larry Miller. Right behind Miller was Sgt. Peter Martinez, the 81 mm mortar FO who was mortally hit and dead before he hit the water. The round entered his left side immediately above the lower part of the armpit opening of his Flak jacket. I called in an artillery fire mission but probably to no avail except they ceased firing.

"Coincidentally, on the same day, my fellow Notre Dame classmate and Artillery Forward Observer, Jim Eagan, became MIA on a recon patrol. Peter Martinez's name immediately follows Jim's on the Wall. Since I could have been just as easily been killed as Sgt. Martinez [of Arkansas City, Kansas], I often think how ironic it would have been that Jim's and my name could have easily been listed together on the Wall. "

My letter continued, "Major Angelo is now our S-3. Major Christiansen got transferred to Division and a Major from Division got transferred to Regt. Big shuffle.

We had all kinds of reporters out here the last two days. ISO from 3rd Marine Division and AP reporters and photographers went on patrol yesterday. Bob Asprey was the AP man. Today NBC's Dean Brelis and a photographer went out with a patrol about 15 minutes ago. Hope they don't run into anything large. We can't stand many more casualties as we had 2 men to almost crack up yesterday, and both had to be sent back to Battalion. We're losing more by illness and injuries than by the VC. Bill Zelm was sick for 5 days with a virus. He's o.k. now.

I just heard that the 1st Marine Division is landing at Chu Lai. It's been rumored for some time."

24 January, Highway 1:

"Things have been rather quiet the last two days. Only a little sniper fire, but torrents of rain! No sign of let up and everything is soaked. We've got a big patrol out now looking for trouble. They'll probably find it!"

I attended a long meeting at Battalion that evening. By the time PFC Kerin "K.P." Florian, my driver, and I left the Battalion compound and headed up the road towards its junction with Rt. 1, it was getting dark. By the time we made the inverted v-shaped turn down Rt. 1, it was almost completely dark and the VC started firing at us from the nearby hamlets. Florian was driving with just the blackout lights on, and I had him floor it, as the bullets flew around us. The green tracer rounds were flying by. I had his M-14 across my lap, but didn't use it. We made it safely back to the Company position on Route 1.

Echo Co. patrol taking a break, 1966

25 January, Highway 1:

"Well the VC hit Da Nang Airfield with mortars again. There were only a few casualties. Naturally everything is bustling and I'm sending troops everywhere. The river block got hit by heavy sniper fire last night, but suffered no casualties."

SSgt. John P. Kasparian recalled that the shots came from a brick kiln on the other side of the river from the river block. He had the attached 106 recoilless rifle team fire one round at the top of the kiln. They hit it and they received no more sniper fire. The Frenchman who ran the kiln protested to Kasparian and wanted reparations for the damage. Kasparian, who spoke French, told the Frenchman he would fire again if shot at from the kiln, and he wasn't getting any compensation. There was no more enemy fire from the kiln. The Frenchman was probably paying off the VC to leave his kiln operation alone.

I continued, "*Yesterday was really a nightmare. We had a platoon under sniper fire and were firing a 60 mm mortar and one round landed short killing an engineer attached to us. Last night at dusk, we had a man shoot himself through the foot. Then still later, an ambush killed a corpsman [HN2 John M. Myers of Gross Point Woods, Michigan] who had strayed away from their position, didn't answer the challenges, hid when they illuminated the area, and tried to crawl away, so one of our men shot him. He was asleep when last seen. Doesn't make sense but he was wrong in all three cases.*"

Metras was the radioman for the platoon that night, and he couldn't understand Myers' actions either, but thought he might have been walking in his sleep. HM2 Rodger Mangus recalled trying to get Myers transferred back to the Battalion Aid Station, as he was not cut out to be in the field with the Marines.

Doc Mangus & a Vietnamese woman,
Spring 1966

LCpl. Bob Pringer

Doc Mangus

Cpl. Robert H. Pringer was out in front of his position cutting some sugar cane to add to his squad's rations. He and PFC Joe Brazil were cooking supper in front of their hole when the VC opened up. "All Hell broke loose. I slid down into the trench and Brazil was really giving them hell with his M-14 on automatic. I had left my rifle near the edge of the hole and had to belly craw out to get it. I emptied my first magazine at them and got down in the hole to reload. Green tracers came by right where my head had been. I finished off a couple of more magazines, but my head never got above the parapet. I was so shook up I pissed my pants. This went on for a good half hour. Brazil was solid as a rock, didn't even flinch, just gave that wry smile and kept firing."

26 January, Highway 1:

"Last night was a quiet one for a change. Not even any sniper fire. We have a patrol out now that just got fired on. No casualties as of yet."

27 January, Highway 1:

"Things were quiet last night and I hope they stay that way. It's stopped raining now and the weather is actually comfortable for a change."

28 January, Highway 1:

"Today has been miserable. Poured rain in buckets and it's still coming down."

29 January, Highway 1:

"Last night was quiet, cold, and rainy. Tonight is quiet for now; cold but no rain. We're expecting a little VC activity tonight. Most of the battalion has moved out on a big operation [Double Eagle I] and we're on a 6 hour standby."

31 January, Highway 1:

"Last night was quiet, but yesterday morning F Company was attacked by the VC and had 4 killed and 5 wounded. I sent a platoon to help and ended up killing 20 VC and wounding 15 more. We captured a Russian machinegun, 10 packs, 40 grenades, and 1,000 rounds of ammunition. As our platoon got back last night, one man, Cpl. Smallwood, jumped off the truck tore his ring finger off. His wedding ring hooked on something. We evacuated him and his finger by helicopter but they were unable to sew it back on. [I never wore my wedding ring in Vietnam.] General [Keith B.] McCutheon, CG of the 1st Marine Air Wing, Colonel Gorman, CO of 9th Marines and Lt. Col. Dorsey, CO of 3/3, stopped by in a helicopter today. The General asked a few questions and then left. I got a message a few minutes ago that the same 2 Colonels and an Army visitor (General, most likely), will be in tomorrow morning. No rest for the weary!

We have an operation with the ARVN early tomorrow morning. I hope it will be successful and we get some VC."

Smallwood, who had recently taken over as a squad leader in the 3rd platoon, recalled, "I had some inner sense something was going to happen that day. When I got back to the Company area, I was relieved. I had some warm beers in my hooch that I wanted to get to quick, so instead of going out the back of the truck, I went over the side, catching my wedding ring on a bolt or something. I remember going on to my hooch not remembering anything. Someone was yelling 'someone lost a finger.' I looked down and saw shreds of whatever where my finger was. I was medevaced after a shot of morphine with the rest of my finger on ice. They amputated the remainder of my finger and said something about a purple heart (which I declined because of my own stupidity), and I was sent to the Naval Hospital at Great Lakes. I always felt bad about leaving my buddies. I remember you [Col. Driver], Lt. Zelm, and SSgt. Elswick were excellent leaders, and I would have gone anywhere with you all."

1 February, Highway 1:

"Last night was quiet again. Our operation planned for this morning was cancelled but we're running it tomorrow morning.

One of our patrols riding on LVTs was fired on from the riverbank today. We killed 1 VC and wounded another. They were fired on in the same area tonight and fired back but we couldn't observe the results. Captain [Jerry D.] Lindauer [F/2/7] was wounded in the arm and evacuated.

Hotel Company killed 3 VC last night and captured a sub machine gun and 11 grenades."

The unit diary showed 4 officers and 164 men present for duty in my company.

I recommend LCpl. Steven Schaefer for a Bronze Star for his actions in the LVT ambush. He received the Naval Commendation Medal on 14 May 1966.

2 February, Highway 1:

"Another 24 hour nightmare! Last night one of our squads was ambushed and we had troopers searching the area until 0200 this morning. We had one man wounded in the leg [PFC David H. Bruneau]. The VC fired a .50 caliber machine gun at the medical evacuation helicopters. They had at least 2 machine guns in the ambush also.

Lt. Zelm took about half the company out at 0400 and moved about 2 miles south and set up while ARVN troops moved up from the south and east. At first light the ARVN swept the area and we killed 2 VC and captured a carbine. They had a lot of sniper fire and we [battalion] committed two more units. We ended up with 3 more VC KIA, 1 WIA, and 2 suspects captured. Zelm did a real good job. We had one man wounded in the chest and wrist. He wasn't hurt too bad, as he walked himself to get on the helicopter. He was scheduled to go home next week [PFC Francisco R. Soriano, Jr.]."

LCpl. Steven A. Schaefer, Bruneau's Fire Team Leader, recalled that he had been hit in the leg by the initial burst of VC automatic weapons fire. "I realized that Bruneau was about 50 meters from the VC position and couldn't last much longer without help, so I ran across the road to where he was." Schaefer carried him across the road to a ditch and then went back and recovered his rifle. He used the rifle for a splint when he bandaged Bruneau's leg. He was evacuated on an Ontos. Schaefer received a Naval Commendation Medal for his bravery.

"[Captain Patrick M.] Pat DeMartino stepped on a land mine today and had an arm torn up pretty bad. Severed an artery and he lost a lot of blood but he'll be o.k. A man that was with him is in serious condition.

An ARVN battalion has more or less moved in with us. The Army advisors are good people so we get along fine."

3 February, Highway 1:

"Last night and today have been real quiet. Hope it continues! General Krulak is here and may visit us tomorrow. I sure hope not."

4 February, Highway 1:

"The second platoon was sent to secure a downed helicopter until it could be lifted out. They found that the pilots had left all their maps, call signs, etc., in the chopper and secured them. They only received one round of sniper fire when they reached the downed bird."

5 February, Highway 1:

"We killed 2 more VC yesterday. No casualties on our side.

General Krulak didn't stop here after all. He visited the ARVN units here but not us.

Colonel Dorsey, CO of 3/3, who we're under [operational control] temporarily, visited us today. He was quite happy with what we've been doing.

It's started raining again and our patrols and ambushes have been miserable. We're not exactly comfortable here but we manage to stay dry.

The other two companies on 'Double Eagle' had their first casualties yesterday. They've gotten quite a few VC too. They were the companies lifted by helicopters into the mountains. We're still on a 6-hour alert to go down there and help them out."

These alerts were called the Sparrow Hawk technique, where a unit from a squad to a full company or more could rapidly reinforce Marines who needed assistance. The alert time was often one hour or shorter.

6 February, Highway 1:

I wrote my brother, "Things have been going well the last couple of weeks. We killed 5 VC, wounded 1, and apprehended 2 suspects on an operation with ARVN PFs and RFs. They killed 4 and captured 18 suspects. We have been averaging better than one a day for quite a while. Got 2 yesterday, but none so far today. We had the 2 sergeants killed during the TET season that made TV and Time and Newsweek. We've had 2 more WIAs, but that's all."

7 February, Highway 1:

"The last two days have been quiet but busy ones. Tomorrow the whole company is going down on an operation of our own and clearing the VC out of a village we're always getting fired at from. It's supposed to be full of tunnels, caves, etc. Should be a full day's work.

It's rained the last two days but the sun finally came out this afternoon and with a cool breeze it's most pleasant. I took a bath out of my wash pan and it really felt good. Had to put the same dirty clothes back on, but clean clothes won't do any good tomorrow!

We have two dog teams with us for tomorrow. They're huge German shepherds. I'd hate to be the VC with them after me!

Just got word that the operation is delayed 24 hours due to the ARVN having other commitments.

Major [A.G.] Comer was out today. He's the XO of 3/3."

9 February, Highway 1:

"We had another busy day yesterday. We ended up with 1 man killed, PFC Leslie C. Crouch [age 21, of East Bangor, Pa.]. We got 5 VC for sure and probably a dozen more from artillery, machine guns, etc. I have a patrol out in the same area now but nothing has happened yet.

Got a new Lt. in yesterday by the name of [Gerald P.] Hornick. He seems fairly good and is senior to Zelm so he'll probably be my XO."

I recommended Corporal Larry D. Crayne for the Bronze Star for exposing himself to enemy fire to rescue the mortally wounded Crouch. He received the Navy Commendation Medal. Crayne was an outstanding machine gunner team leader and brave as they come.

10 February, Highway 1:

"Things have been fairly quiet. Our patrol ran into some snipers and chased them for a while, killing 2 of them and capturing some documents and the enclosed picture of Ho Chi Min. Our river patrol on LVTs had a firefight with the VC, but no one was hit on either side. Today a patrol [and attached engineers] blew 32 tunnels and 3 bunkers and didn't have a shot fired at them."

I sent Lt. Hornick on one of these patrols as an observer. I wanted him to get used to being under fire and also to learn the terrain and what the patrol members were going through.

Metras recalled several of his platoon's actions during this period. "We were on an ambush about 1 or 2 in the morning and looked out across the field and a sweep was being done by what we thought were the ARVN, but they were VC. We called in and found out there were no ARVN operating in the area. We got out of there but ran into them by a shrine. I think they thought we were their men until we fired on them." In another incident, "We were on a platoon patrol along the river when they opened up on us. The 81 Mortar Radio Operator behind me was shot. We had our whip antennas up. The PC 10's antennas were about 15 feet tall. They liked to shoot at the radio operators." In the third action he related, "On a squad patrol we encountered the VC and started following them. We broke off contact after about half an hour. We continued on our patrol and were crossing some open ground between check points B and C, they opened up on us from three different directions. The only cover we had was a foot deep trench about a foot wide. We were pinned down there for about 2 hours when the rest of the company and a couple of Ontos arrived and got us out."

Lt. Hornick & a Vietnamese child

Marine from 2/9 pulls nails from his boot
after stepping on a Punji trap

11 February, Highway 1:

"We got two more VC today. Had 2 patrols out and both got fired on. Last night was quiet. Hope tonight is! Enclosed is an invitation to a going away party of Major Jopling, the Army advisor to the 51st ARVN Regiment here.

We have a big operation going tomorrow morning. Should get some more VC."

12 February, Highway 1:

"Our operation today is still going on. We had 2 wounded, neither seriously, and one is already back to duty [PFC Richard L. Solomon was the Marine wounded and returned to duty. The unit diary lists Cpl. David G. Stein and LCpl. s Richard L. Shuda and Henry Soliz as the other WIAs]. I don't know of how many VC we got but we know of two. Should have gotten a lot more, as we called artillery and mortar fire all day. Colonel [Edwin H.] Simmons is taking over 9th Marines Tuesday, relieving Colonel Gorman."

Major General McCutcheon, Commanding General,
1st Marine Aircraft Wing & Deputy Commander, III MAF,
congratulates Col. Edwin Simmons upon Simmons'
assumption of command of the 9th Marines.

Cpl. Antal & the 2nd Platoon coming in from a patrol, 1966

Shuda explained his wound. "I was shot in the shoulder by a small caliber round, probably by a carbine. The bullet entered my shoulder, glanced off my collarbone, and exited out my back. It didn't break my collar bone."

As we were advancing into a village, I had the artillery FO, Lt. Garner, fire a spotting round to get our exact coordinates. The round hit nearby and set a hut on fire. An old lady came screaming out of the hut. I had some Marines get water from her well and put the fire out. She thanked me profusely.

The village complex was full of trench lines and bunkers. I jumped into one trench line and a dead VC was staring up at me with no face. I asked Kasparian about it, and he said that the VC could not go to heaven without being identified.

An article in the <u>Stars & Stripes</u> stated, "LCpl. Jerry L. Wieczorkowski (Cincinnati, Ohio) limped in off patrol. He wasn't looking for a corpsman—he was looking for a cobbler. His boot heel was shot off while on a patrol with [the 1st Platoon,] 'E' Co., 9th Marine Regiment.

He and the other members of his fire team, LCpl. Dennis Becton, (Washington, N.J.), Corporal Curtis Watson, (St. Louis, Mo.), and PFC Charles R. Laberdee (Toledo, Ohio), were point men for their platoon when they we were fired on by Viet Cong snipers near the village of Phong Luc (1), seven miles south of Da Nang.

LCpl. Dennis Becton
1966

'The Viet Cong ran into the village when we returned fire,' the 20-year old Marine remarked. 'So, we started chasing them.'

'I was running full speed,' LCpl. Wieczorkowski related, 'and bullets were kicking up dust all around us. Suddenly my left leg went numb and I turned a complete loop in the air. For a second I thought my whole leg had been blown off.'

PFC Laberdee, the closest man to Wieczorkowski, ran over and helped him to his feet, still 25 yards from the safety of the village.

'Upon reaching safety, I looked for a wound, but couldn't find one. It wasn't until I started walking that I noticed the heel of my boot was missing. I was so stunned by the impact of what had happened; I sat down on the ground for several minutes and laughed.'"

14 February, Highway 1:

"*Another busy 24 hours. We've increased the number of our patrols and I've been kept running. We're also sending out joint patrols with the ARVN. They're real good troops. The ones we're working with are Rangers.*

Last night one of our ambushes killed 2 VC, wounded another who escaped and picked up a VC suspect on the way back. Everyone was happy over this.

We haven't had much news from the rest of the battalion on Double Eagle except for a few casualties.

Going to a party for an Army advisor to the ARVN who is leaving tomorrow. Lt. Zelm and I are invited."

15 February, Highway 1:

"*I had a busy day yesterday. One of our patrols ran into some snipers but we didn't have any casualties and neither did they.*

Went to a going away party and ate some more Vietnamese food. I've been running to the head since 0500! It was good, though. They gave him a Russian rifle to take home. I made a helicopter trip with him and his relief to the ARVN positions all over the area.

Today is payday so everyone is running around. We have a patrol out now but no VC contact. Last night was quiet, too.

I had an interesting conversation with a Vietnamese colonel who had just interviewed 5 VC defectors. They are very discouraged fighting the Marines. The 5 turned in 3 Russian rifles and a bunch of grenades.

I answered Mr. Becker's letter today [High School Principal, Flint, Michigan] and hope he'll get soap, etc., over here for the Vietnamese children. We're giving them medical treatment and soap to bathe with, but our supply is limited."

16 February, Highway 1:

"The battalion got back last night and really looked beat. A lot of people had lost weight. Colonel Donahue had a meeting this morning. They did a lot of hiking, saw a lot of the county side, but only a few VC. We got twice as many right here!"

During the day, one of my patrols found 10 newly dug fighting holes and 4 tunnels. The engineers blew up the tunnels. That evening we had to evacuate a Marine for appendicitis.

17 February, Highway 1:

"An eventful day. First they told us we're moving out tomorrow. Then Colonel Donahue and Colonel Simmons, the new CO of 9th Marines, came out and inspected our positions. They seemed pleased.

Tonight about dark the VC fired on our LVT patrol on the river. We ended up with 5 wounded, VC casualties unknown. We called in mortar fire on them and 3/9 sent two platoons in to check out the area [on the 3/9 side of the river]."

The unit diary lists only LCpl. Joe N. Parker and Pvt.s Clifford Berry and Andrew Lindsey, III, wounded on that date. My records show LCpl. H.M. Smith and PFC J.H. Dederich wounded during the month, so they were probably the other two.

The VC had fired a 57 mm recoilless rifle round at the LVT and 600 rounds of small arms fire at my patrol.

Lt. Garner called in counter battery fire on the VC mortar positions, with secondary explosions. 40 rounds of 81 mm and 36 rounds of artillery were fired at them. Lt. Frank Cox, the Artillery FO for Fox Company, reported the local villagers carried away 20 VC bodies. K/3/9 swept the area the next day and found discharged and damaged ammunition canisters and what was believed to be pieces of mortar tubes. My company swept the west bank of the Song Vinh Diem, without finding anything.

18 February, 2/9 CP:

"I'm going to sleep in a bunk tonight without worrying about a patrol, ambush, etc. Sure is going to feel good! Can't say where I'm going, but the operation is called 'Rough Rider' so you may read about it. We're leaving in the morning." [Rough Rider was the term used by the Marines for convoy escort.]

LCpl. John R. Templeton was on guard duty in the battalion area that day. "I saw a Marine cross over some concertina wire out of the corner of my eye," he stated. "Then I heard an explosion and turned around to see the Marine 'stand up' on two stumps and try to walk out. He had gone into one of our minefields to police up a tin can, which he had tossed in there, both his legs were blown off." Templeton blamed the NCO who made the Marine go after the can.

LCpl. Schramm recalled that his 2nd Platoon was set up at the Song Vinh Diem River while the rest of the company was located near Rt. 1. "Trucks brought in a platoon from Golf Company to relieve us and we loaded on the trucks and went back to the battalion to prepare for the operation.

Cpl. Mike Schramm

Captain Driver called a meeting of the platoon commanders, platoon sergeants, and squad leaders. Cpl. [Eugene] Osaw, my Squad Leader, had gone to the PX near Da Nang, so I went to the meeting for the 3rd Squad. The skipper filled us in on where we were going and that our job was to look for VC activity in the area. He pointed out that there was an NVA Battalion to the east of our landing zone and 2 VC companies to the north. Once he finished he asked if there were any questions. Nobody spoke up, so I did. I asked why we didn't go in after one of the known units so we could get the first shot off for a change. Captain Driver said, 'I'll give you the same answer I got when I asked the same question at Battalion: because those

244

are our orders.' He sounded as frustrated as I was." The unit diary shows 4 officers and 156 men present for duty.

19 February, Operation Rough Rider and Double Eagle II:

During our motor march to Tam Ky, my company was in the lead trucks. We received some small arms fire from west of Route 1, which we returned without stopping. The VC stopped firing. We arrived at the Tam Ky airstrip at 1145. Lt. Frank Cox, the FO for F/2/9 recalled, "Our two companies with the 2/9 Command Group departed at 0630 to Tam Ky. Echo Company was helilifted into Landing Zone Drake, Fox Company into Landing Zone Mallard."

"The next morning we were trucked to a small hill where the helicopters picked us up," Schramm noted. "The hill was nothing but bare ground and rock, the heat was stifling, and when the helicopters came in, the dust was so thick you could barely breathe. The flight to the landing zone was about 40 minutes. As we started to descend, the word came over the radio that the LZ was hot. We started off loading while the helicopter was 2 or 3 feet from the ground. When I hit the ground, I thought my legs would collapse from the weight we were carrying. Heavy fire was coming from two sides. We headed for the closest rice paddy dike and began to return fire. After the H-34s got out of the way the Huey gun ships came in and tore up both tree lines the gooks were firing from. A few seconds later, the word came we were in the wrong LZ. I looked around and there were only a handful of us on the ground. Within a short time, the H-34's were back in to pick us up. It only took about 5 minutes to get to the right LZ, but it was even hotter than the first one. Three rounds hit the helicopter; one of them ripped through the middle of the floor and out through the top. Everyone was shook up, but no one was hit. When we landed at the second LZ, we raced for cover and returned fire. It seemed like we were getting hit from all directions. The brush around the LZ was so thick you couldn't see anything, and we just fired at sound. Once the last helicopter was gone, the VC ceased fire and disappeared."

The men injured from jumping and or being pushed from the helicopters by overzealous crew chiefs were Pvt. Richard L. Nordyke, PFCs David S. Brannon, Robert B. Hillstrom, and Joe Rodriguez, Jr., LCpl.s Guy R. Murphy, Harlan M. Smith, and Henry Solitz, and Sgt. Ralph W. Wertz. We lost the equivalent of a squad from our company because the helicopters didn't set down to let our men out. Many others were hurt, but refused to be evacuated and hobbled along through the operation. This also delayed our movement out to the LZ until they could be medically evacuated. [I learned later that this was a new squadron and still green about putting troops on the ground.]

We landed in LZ Drake at 1220. Once we sent the casualties out, we moved northward toward the village of Ngoc Nha (1) and started receiving small arms fire. Two platoons laid down covering fire while one platoon assaulted the VC positions. We picked up 9 VC suspects and 1 confirmed VC during our search of the village. Later, we continued northward to the village of Long Son (8). We received some sniper fire and returned fire, and the VC fled. We set in near the village for the night and sent out several patrols and ambushes.

"The area was all hills," Schramm continued, "with only a few rice paddies. The weather was extremely hot with incredibly high humidity. Fortunately, there were numerous villages with good wells for water. This was going to be more like an oversize patrol, rather than the sweeps we had done in the past. Once we made contact then it would change."

The 2/9 Command Chronology stated, "The terrain was difficult to travel as Co. F [and Co. E] moved up on the high ground, the growth was extremely thick and movement was restricted to trails. The steep terrain also restricted communications. The hillsides and the river bottoms are too rough and the vegetation too thick for effective travel. Rivers were deep, fast and hazardous."

Lt. Fred Cox, the Artillery FO with Fox Company, recalled, "It was impossible to set out flank security and move at any speed other than a crawl."

20 February, Operation Double Eagle II:

We moved out at 0630 to clear the high ground and discovered 6,000 pounds of rice and captured 6 VC suspects. The rice was hidden in old, half cement buildings with no roofs. The rice was in plastic and covered with palm branches. When Fox Company arrived they took charge of the rice and we continued northward at 1145. Fox Company spent the rest of the day and part of the next filling rice bags and loading them onto helicopters. About 4,000 pounds were removed and the rest was destroyed. Later in the operation, they found a similar size rice cache.

We had not moved far before we started receiving small arms fire. Once again, two platoons lay down a base of fire while the other one assaulted the VC positions. We killed 2 VC—both clad in blue shirts and black trousers—and captured 2 more VC suspects. At 1320 some VC were spotted in the open and Lt. Garner called in a fire mission resulting in 1 VC killed.

We moved into very hilly country. During our movement two new men, FNGs is what the seasoned troopers called them, were wounded by picking up a C ration can with an M-26 grenade in it. This slowed us down until they could be evacuated. We picked up 4 more VC suspects later in the day.

We continued northward and found an extensive cave complex capable of holding a VC battalion. We picked up another VC suspect in the area. Before we halted for the night we had picked up 8 more VC suspects.

"We moved the rest of the day with no contact," Schramm noted. "We could feel the VC presence, but they never showed themselves. That evening we took position on one of the highest hills in the area. Fox Company was on the hill next to ours. While we were setting in, helicopters came with our re-supply. We had started with only one day's rations. As the helicopters started to descend the VC opened such a high volume of fire the helicopters couldn't land. They tried twice more with the same results. It was decided to re-supply us the next morning."

"The helicopters tried to re-supply us in the morning but were driven off by heavy ground fire from the VC," Schramm noted. "The second day went the same. We went almost 2 miles and through at least that many villages without a shot being fired, but as soon as the helicopters tried to re-supply us, the VC would open up on them. Charlie knew what he was doing. We now had gone the whole day without food."

21 February, Operation Double Eagle II:

"The third day went exactly the same," Schramm continued. "No action at all, all day. But as soon as we called in the helicopters to re-supply us the VC would drive them off with heavy fire. By now we were really hungry. [LCpl. Leonardo] Cruz and I made the mistake of starting a conversation about Mom's cooking. It almost drove us over the edge. All we could do is think about food."

We shoved off towards Hill 110 at 0830 that morning. In an hour, we had found another large cave and tunnel complex, which we had the engineers destroy. By 1900, we were set in our defensive perimeter and patrols and ambushes were sent out.

"We moved up on the hills we were going to use that night while they decided how they were going to pull this off," Schramm related. "As we came up on top, we could see the hill F Company was on. Their point had just hit the crest. Suddenly, there was a huge explosion. The only thing left was this guy's helmet, which went about 30 or 40 feet in the air. 'HOLY SHIT!' I thought. We just stood there watching with our mouths hanging open. We moved into position and the word came to open up on the whole area once the choppers got close and to keep firing until they were back out of range. The helicopters never landed. They got close and pushed the supplies out of the hatch. Sort of a helicopter version of an air-drop. They passed out the rations, but only one per man. We all felt we could eat at least three—until we started. Our stomachs had shrunk so much we could hardly eat one."

LCpl. Gabriel C. Coronado, Jr., a Machine Gunner, was wounded in the back by a grenade fragment on this date but was not evacuated.

Operation Double Eagle II
L-R: Florian, Mercuri, name unknown

22 February, Operation Double Eagle II:

The company moved out at 0730 that morning, this time in a northwesterly direction. We had not moved far before we started receiving heavy small arms fire, which we returned.

"This morning they decided to get on the move for a while before trying to bring in more supplies, so we formed up and headed down the hill," Schramm related. "2nd Platoon went first, then the 3rd, and 1st brought up the rear. The hill was covered with heavy brush down to the base. We then reached a flat field about 75 yards square. At the far end was a wet rice paddy about 20 yards deep, then a tree line. To our right was a huge rice paddy that went a good 200 yards to the next village. To our left was a wooded area.

"We got on line and started across. It didn't seem like anything other than another blistering hot, boring day, until we got about half way across the field. The VC were dug in the tree line to our front and 25 or 30 weapons opened on us. We dropped to the deck. There was no cover anywhere. The ground was as flat as a pancake. The cry for corpsmen went up and down the line. Six men were hit at this point. I remember thinking this is where I am going to die. The VC were only 30 or 40 yards away. They could hardly miss. There was a hut in the middle of the field about 30 yards from me. I could tell someone was firing from it. The M-79 man was lying next to me. I yelled to him to put one on the roof. When he fired a rag opened up like a parachute and the round only went a few yards and headed into the ground. We buried our faces in the dirt and waited for the blast. Nothing happened. It didn't travel far enough to arm. He had put his cleaning rag in the barrel after using it the night before. Rounds were hitting all around us now. I directed my men to pour everything we had into the tree line to our front, to gain fire superiority. The M-79 man reloaded and fired again and this time it went 10 yards over the roof and landed harmlessly in the paddy. Finally on the third try he hit the roof and the firing stopped from there.

"Word came down the line that the 1st Platoon had moved down through the wooded area to our left and was going to sweep through. We shifted our fire and they cleaned house. Within a few minutes it was over. To everyone's surprise the initial six men wounded were the only ones hit. This is something I still have a hard time believing. One of the men hit was a Machine Gun Squad Leader. He was hit five times before he hit the ground. He survived as far as I know. The men in the 1st Platoon said when they swept through most of the gooks never saw them coming. Some of them still had their breakfast rations sitting on the edge of their positions. Apparently they had been set in there all night waiting for us to come down off the hill.

"Word came that Fox Company was pinned down and needed help. The 3rd Platoon was left to finish evacuating the wounded and the rest of the company went to help F Troop. We pushed through a wooded area and around the base of the hill. We then moved along an embankment until we reached the flank of F Company. The 2nd Platoon had the point and my fire team was tail-end-Charlie. As soon as we made contact with the VC, mortar rounds started coming in. At first we though the gooks had M-79s the fire was so accurate. The next thing I knew the rest of the platoon was heading backwards towards us on the run. Sergeant [Clarence] Robinson was leading the pack yelling 'Don't run, you can't outrun them,' but he was leading them on. We sat there against the embankment for a few minutes trying to figure out what was going on. Then we realized the whole platoon had gone by and we were sitting there by ourselves.

"By the time we caught up with them, they had gone back down the embankment almost 50 yards before Captain Driver stopped them. When we got there he was reaming them out good. A Huey gunship overhead radioed that Fox Company was able to move and the VC had pulled back to a wooded area right in front of us. Driver got us on line and we started sweeping through. Within a minute or two, we hit the VC. They apparently weren't ready for us, as their fire was sporadic and undirected. The word came down the line to pick up the pace. The helicopter pilot radioed us that the VC were right in front of us. The brush was so thick we could hardly get a glimpse of them. We were all running now, firing from the hip, yelling and screaming like wild men. Every time we came to a clearing they were waiting for us, trying to slow us down, but we were too fired up at that point. The chase continued for almost a mile before they gave us the slip. I remember it being like an incredible high. The adrenalin was pumping like water—then it was over as quickly as it had started."

Corporal Robert H. Pringer recalled, "We caught some hard core VC in uniform in a rice paddy, and we went hollering, yelling, and charging after them. They had about a 300 yard head start and we never did catch up with them."

Schramm continued, "We set up a perimeter long enough to evacuate casualties and bring in supplies, mostly ammo, and then began to move again. Now things went back to the way they were for the past 3 days, no action and no sign of Charlie. After a while we stopped in one of the villages to fill canteens. While waiting my turn, I went to the edge of the village to look around. The village was nestled in the side of a hill, and you could see the whole area from there. It looked like a post card. The hills were a rich green color and the sky was blue as it could be. It was hard to believe a war was going on in such a beautiful place. By mid-afternoon, we had a radio message stating that the artillery battery next to the battalion CP back at Duong Son had been hit hard the night before, so we were being pulled out of the operation to go back and clear that area."

Bill Coti commented on this debacle, "I reorganized the defense of 2/9 incorporating E/2/12 into our perimeter defense. When completed, I visited the CO of the battery and laid out our defensive perimeter to him. I tried to incorporate his battery, contiguous to 2/9's perimeter, into 2/9's defense. When he told me that he could take care of himself and did not need 2/9's help, I explained that I needed to incorporate his battery into our 'sector of fire' and 'final protective fires' to adequately cover enemy avenues of approach to both his battery and our CP. He again told me he did not need 2/9's help. I reported his remarks to Lt.Col. Donahue who said, 'if that was his decision, let him live with it.'

"When checking 2/9's perimeter defensive positions, the Vietnamese children, who came to the perimeter late each afternoon to talk to the Marines manning the perimeter, would leave small pieces of branches aiming at our positions. I had everyone dig alternative positions and directed them every night to wait until several hours after dark and then change to their alternate positions.

"In the middle of the night, the VC launched a major attack. Major Finne and I were in his CP when the attack occurred. I left Major Finne, telling him I was going to the perimeter, and he told me to be careful and I left. The 2/9 Marines had switched to their alternate positions. No VC were able to penetrate our lines—their rockets landed on our unmanned positions. The battery was not so lucky. The VC totally destroyed all the artillery pieces and threw 'satchel charges' into all of the tents where Marines were sleeping. It was a total disaster—the VC attack commenced when an RPG round was fired at one of the artillery battery's 'fixed' positions, totally destroying the bunker, killing one Marine and wounding another."

The attack on E/2/12 had taken place on 21 February. At 0129, the 20 minute attack began when the battery received forty 60 mm and six 81 mm rounds fired from Le Son (1). "At least 5 VC sappers (and probably more) armed with charges and Russian sub-machine guns penetrated the perimeter at the position of Gun #3," read the after action report. "Gun #1 was absent, sent a few days earlier to FLSG for maintenance, so they placed a 15 pound charge against Gun #1's ammo bunker which caused minor damage. A similar charge was placed under the carriage of Gun #2 and the wheels, right equalizer, and the axle were damaged. A report says Gun #2 will be repaired and back on line by 22 or 23 February. The VC dragged at least three casualties away. One Marine was KIA and 7 were WIA."

Schramm noted, "While we were waiting to be lifted out, the scuttlebutt came around that the units that hit us today were the two VC companies Captain Driver had pointed out on the map before we left. I knew we were incredibly lucky again. This was the second time in two months we had been caught in a big ambush and came out with minimal casualties. The company had been in Vietnam 8 months and the 2nd Platoon still had not had a KIA. The eerie part was, we knew it was going to happen sometime. While I was thinking about this, a thought crossed my mind that made me laugh. It was that damn rag flying out of the M-79 man's barrel earlier. I would have given anything for a picture of the looks on our faces."

We returned to the Tam Ky airstrip at 1630 and were lifted back to the 2/9 CP by 1740. My company was assigned as mobile reserve company for the regiment. I sent one platoon to Le Son (1).

22 February, 2/9 CP:

"Back after a four day operation. It was fairly successful, as we got about 65 VC suspects and killed 3. We had 3 men wounded. It was a rugged 4 days and I'm glad it's over. [Cpl. Harry R. Williams, a machine gun squad leader, was shot in the stomach about 10 feet from me. The unit diary shows LCpl.s Robert T. Johnston and Robert L. Stokes, and PFC William S. Egerland wounded. The other casualties cited by Schramm must had been treated and returned to duty or were attached personnel.]

We're starting out anew now so my writing will be spotty. As soon as we got back last night we had to send people out on ambushes. Today we made a sweep and tomorrow we're preparing for another operation."

My friend, Captain Donald D. Brooks, had recently taken command of Company D, 1st Battalion, 7th Marine Regiment. On the night of February 21st the VC attempted to overrun his company in Binh Giang Village in Bihn Song District. Don lead a skillful defense of his position and successfully beat off the enemy force with only eight Marines being wounded. His men killed at least 20 of the attackers and wounded twice that many. Don was awarded a Bronze Star for his heroism.

L-R: Cpt. Brooks, Lt. Col. Kelly, Gen. Hendersen
Operation Piranha

Ha Dong Bridge & Engineer Bridge, 1966

Tanks stuck in the river, 1966

Echo Co. positions near
Ha Dong Bridge, 1966

Ha Dong Bridge position, 1966

Defensive position, Ha Dong Bridge, 1966

Stream crossing
February 1966

23 February, Ha Dong:

We moved out that afternoon at 1630 and moved to the crossing at Ha Dong Bridge [an aluminum foot bridge built by the engineers]. That night we sent out patrols and ambushes, with no contact. Every time we crossed this bridge we were fired on.

24 February, Ha Dong:

The company crossed the bridge at 0800. My lead elements were fired on at 0930 and we returned fire and added 14 rounds of 81 mm Willy Peter for good measure. The firing stopped and we moved on. We entered La Tho Bac (1) and searched the area with negative results. At 1600 we were ordered back across the river. We were also relieved of the mission as the mobile reserve company. I left one platoon to cover the bridge and set up at the old French bunker overlooking the river and bridge. I received an order to move my CP to another location at 1730. I requested that the order be cancelled because by the time we moved to the new position, we would have to make a night crossing of a very deep river. The order was cancelled. That night at 2015 one of my listening posts north of the CP reported VC activity. I put the company on 100% alert. At 2030 we received six 60 mm mortar rounds and about 600 rounds of small arms fire, which we returned. I had a squad search the area, but the VC had fled.

25 February, Ha Dong:

We crossed the river again that morning at 0700. As soon as we crossed the stream we started receiving small arms fire from a sizeable VC force in trench lines near La Tho Bac (3). We continued to engage the VC and I called in Sparrow Hawk, a platoon from Fox Company, to act as a blocking force. We finished the day with 11 VC KIAs confirmed and 9 more possibly KIA. My company pursued the VC through La Tho Bac (3), Dien Thien (1) and Dien Thien (2), before halting for the night at 2130. The area was covered with freshly dug punji foot traps, sniper holes, trench lines and tunnels. We picked up 1 VC WIA and 3 suspects. One of the suspects told us the VC had buried 10 dead near his village.

26 February, Ha Dong & 2/9 CP:

We were ordered back across the river at 0935 and returned to the battalion CP at 1050.

"Just in from another operation. We moved down south of the river and set up in a village and ran patrols and ambushes out of there. The first night the VC hit us about 2000 but we didn't have any casualties. We got four of them. The next morning we moved out before daylight and ran into a VC company and fought a running battle with them all morning. Fox Company and two other platoons were helilifted in and we ended getting about 30 VC. They left us alone last night and we came back in this morning. I'm worn out from the constant go, go, go! We had five wounded. [SSgt. Elwood Mc Michael, Sgt. Thomas F. Burke, Cpl. Robert H. Pringer, of Tulsa, Oklahoma, and LCpl. Gabriel C. Coronado, Jr., are listed on the unit diary]. *SSgt. Mc Michael and I were lying side by side behind a rise of ground when he was shot in the arm. The wound wasn't serious and he returned to duty in a few days."*

I related to my brother, *"We had a couple of big fights with the VC, killed 4 one night and 5 the next day, including a platoon leader. Other units working with us got 11 more and air got quite a few too. The villagers told us the next day we killed 36.*

Everyone is really pleased with the performance of the company. Major Angelo was real pleased. The battalion got a well done from General Platt [for Operation Double Eagle II].

I've just had a shower and shave and relaxing for a change. Need a cold beer and it's almost time for them! All the officers and staff are going down to the club.

While we were in the village we lived in the huts with the villagers and I learned quite a bit by doing so. We even had them fix us some meals. Our ARVN interpreter [Sgt. Han] did all this and it was something to watch. We gave them some 'C' rations when we left. He had the children taking baths when we pulled out. The people here are so poor it's unbelievable. They almost live from hand to mouth and only the two rice crops a year and all the other plants that grow naturally here such as bananas, mangoes, bread fruit, taro, etc. They raise a lot of tobacco here too. Sugarcane also—the VC snipers hide in it."

Sgt. Han, Vietnamese Interpreter

Pringer stated, "I had been lying in a depression firing my M-14 when all hell broke loose. Then all of a sudden I got up and ran over 20 yards to a hut and squatted down facing my old position (to this day I don't know why). I had no more than got down when a mortar round landed just were I had been. I remember covering up and looking down at my boots. I felt and saw smoke as a piece of shrapnel went in my boot and into my right foot. I hollered, "Corpsman! Corpsman! I'm hit! I'm hit!" I don't know where he came from, but he was there damn quick! As I got on the medevac helicopter, I held out my hand with a wad of MPCs at the guys and told them, 'thanks a lot for the money and see you stateside!'" He won a couple of thousand dollars playing poker with the troops after payday.

Pringer was sent to the hospital ship *U.S.S. Repose*. He too returned to duty with the company. He was informed by a Chaplain on the ship that he was going to the states, and shipped all his clothing home. When the plane landed at Da Nang, he was told he was returning to his unit. He was so mad that he didn't wait for transportation and walked about 5 miles back to the company in his khakis, unarmed. When he reported, the Company Gunnery Sergeant thought he was in the states and all his records had been sent there. He received new clothing and equipment. Pringer stated, "I was really Gung Ho anyway."

My troops got little or no rest. They were assigned to guard bridges and to Sparrow Hawk. My company became the mobile reserve for the 9th Marines.

29 February, 2/9 CP:

PFCs David Lawton and Richard W. 'Rick' Bauer joined the company and were assigned to the 1st Platoon. Pvt. Hector Ronald 'Ron' Hoyos joined the same day and was assigned to Weapons Platoon in a Machine Gun Team. Lawton, a Canadian, one of two in the company, recalled, "My first night with the company I was sleeping in the Company Supply tent. I was in the shower all soaped up, when Bang, Bang, Bang, three shots, and I'm down on the wooden skids with soap in my eyes groveling for my rifle leaning against the sand bags. Two other Marines in the shower looked at me with disdain. One said 'he shoots seven-eight rounds every night and he hasn't hit anyone yet, FNG.' I got up and got the soap off of me and slinked away. They were right; he fired several rounds at the CP every night and never hit anything.

The next morning, my Squad and Fire Team Leaders came and got me. I don't remember my squad leader's name, but he was a blond headed guy. Cpl. Ray Avila was my Fire Team Leader. I got a Company Commander named Driver and the name kind of scared me."

1 March, 2/9 CP:

"The weather is getting hot again. It must have been 90 degrees today with no breeze. We're going back out again on the 3rd."

Major General Landsdale, USAF, and 6 Senators visited the area, but my company was not involved. My company numbered 4 officers and 130 men for duty. The battalion T/O strength was at 87%. I provided one platoon for Rough Rider security (convoy escort) and had one squad in Duong Son (3) to guard gear left behind by Golf Company.

One of my platoons received 7 rounds of small arms fire. They returned fire with 60 rounds of small arms, 4 rounds from 81 mm, 15 rounds from 105s, and 6 rounds from 155s. Working with Golf Company the next day, they searched the area and found 1 dead VC and 2 huts destroyed.

2 March, 2/9 CP:

"Today has been another long, hot one. The platoons are all committed but not the whole company.

Some of my old people from A/1/9 start leaving tomorrow, SSgt. Morton for one. They're spreading our leaving over March and April."

One of my ambushes was fired on at 2030. They returned fire and then withdrew to Vien Tay. At 2210, another squad-sized ambush received 20 rounds of small arms fire. They returned fire and then changed their position.

3 March, 2/9 CP:

"Fox Company isn't back yet and we aren't going anywhere until they return.

We're getting some of our casualties back from the last two operations. One came in yesterday and three today. We had four men killed today in the battalion, but none wounded, which is unusual.

I checked our total the other day and we had 1 killed, 17 wounded, and 9 injured other than battle, during February. None this month and I hope it will stay that way.

I got a Chinese rifle [AK-47] to bring home today. It's in good shape and will make a good souvenir. It's missing the bayonet. It was captured by the company on 'Harvest Moon.'"

One of my patrols set off a booby trap at 1400 on this date, wounding 3 Marines. None required evacuation. They searched the area and found two more booby traps and destroyed them.

5 March, 2/9 CP:

"Today was a real scorcher, 106 degrees in the tent, and it must have been 120 degrees outside. It's cooled off some tonight. I've got the company spread out over different areas now, guarding bridges, villages, etc."

6 March, 2/9 CP:

"Today was almost unbearable! It was 116 degrees in the tent and must have been 130 degrees outside. Had a couple of cold beers and stripped down. It helped some.

Lt. Jacoway wrote the 1st Sgt. a letter today. He's on Okinawa and may be sent down here with 3/4."

My First Sergeant, Paul Stephenson, was an outstanding Marine. He had gone to the field on operation 'Harvest Moon' and was wounded in the leg. When he returned to duty, it was all I could do the keep him in the rear; making sure the company administration and reports were taken care of, replacements and returning men were armed, equipped and sent to the field, our re-supply was what we needed, mail was sent to us, the sick and wounded were visited in the hospital and got their gear, and a myriad of other details. He and others like him were the backbone of the Corps.

7-8 March, Duong Son (2) Operation County Fair & 2/9 CP:

"Had a busy day yesterday. We surrounded a nearby village night before last [0445] and then searched it yesterday. Moved all the civilians to one area and went through the village step by step (the ARVN that is). They killed 4, captured 3, and two weapons [1 K-44 rifle and a German Luger pistol]. Last night we stayed there and killed one more and got his weapon also. We also captured the packs of two that got away through the rice paddies. I was up all night so I'm pooped! The Colonel was pleased with last night when I was in charge but relieved Bill Zelm over the actions of his platoon. He went to regiment today. I hated to see him go and pleaded with Colonel Donahue not to do it, but he was mad, had made a decision, and would not relent.

Fox Company got back this afternoon so we'll be going out forward soon. Lt Fagan, who was my XO in H&S Co., had 2 toes blown off and his legs cut up from a booby trap.

The weather is still hot but it's overcast this afternoon. We could use a good rain to settle all the dust."

The Colonel did not understand that this was what everyone called a 'Dog & Pony Show.' My men had been out for two days and nights around the village, the ARVN were in the village in plain view, and most of my men were resting in the hot sun. Not a shot had been fired all day and only a few men were keeping watch. There was no better combat leader in Vietnam than Bill Zelm.

SSgt. Kasparian captured a Viet Cong flag and a woven image of Ho Chi Minh from the District Chief in Duong Son (2).

The flag was red with a gold hammer and sickle sewn on one side. He gave them to me. [I returned them to him at the 2/9 reunion in 2006.]

9 March, 2/9 CP:

"Most of the battalion is going on an operation tomorrow. I only have a platoon involved. [In Duong Song (2), 2,500 meters south of the Cau Do River and east of the old railroad bed.]

We had a bad incident tonight. Several men were drinking at a store outside the gate, including 2 of mine. One of my men went crazy and shot the H&S Co. gunnery sergeant in the groin. He threw grenades at several jeeps, but luckily no one else was hurt. Someone finally got his weapon away from him. He cussed the Colonel out, so we've got him under guard now. He has been good in combat but was a tough hood on the outside and doesn't care what happens to himself. That's obvious!"

He was a full-blooded Indian with no tolerance for alcohol. His fire team members were told not to let him get any liquor, but they failed to keep an eye on him. In the field, he walked point for the company and was able to smell the VC. He saved us from several ambushes.

10 March, 2/9 CP:

"The operation apparently went well today. My platoon just got back [They provided security for the Battalion Command Group forward, and the detention center. Another platoon was guarding the Battalion CP rear. My last platoon was guarding three bridges on the MSR and manning the Mien Dong checkpoint with the Vietnamese National Police]. Today has been a lot cooler and we're getting a slight shower now. The cooler weather feels good!"

11 March, 2/9 CP:

"This will be my last letter for a while as we're going back out forward tomorrow.

I had to cancel my R&R [to Hong Kong] again until the 18th due to this operation. I'll get out sometime!

I understand there has been a coup in Saigon. I don't know what it means but I hope it doesn't set us back, as things seem to be improving all the time. F Company is on 15 minute alert to go into Da Nang as riot control troops. Sure hope this doesn't happen. We need 100% effort by both U.S. and Vietnamese troops to defeat the VC.

Today was a quiet, cool one. I went down to Ha Dong where the rest of the battalion is operating, and they were still blowing tunnels, caves, etc. They killed 3 VC, captured 7 suspects and 1 rifle.

I also visited the local ARVN headquarters to coordinate my activities with them. Dick McHenry was there and he just extended for 6 months and is the new liaison officer with the ARVN."

I was now providing a reinforced squad to a pacification team operating in Duong Son (3). The platoon helping to secure the rear CP and was also a reserve force for the battalion.

12 March, 2/9 CP:

"We're still standing by and don't know when we will move out. Jack Maxwell was out yesterday and we got to talk a while. He's working in Division G-2.

My gunnery sergeant is leaving today on emergency leave so I'm really getting short of officers & staff NCOs. I'm losing 2 more staff this month."

13 March, 2/9 CP:

"We are still standing by to stand by. Hotel Company killed 3 VC last night and captured a sub machine gun and 11 grenades."

15-16 March, Ha Dong area:

On 151100, we requested a re-supply by helicopter. At 1420 that day, we blew up a large tunnel. We continued our search and destroy mission the next day and captured a VC suspect and blew up another tunnel. I sent a platoon to the southeast along the west bank of the Su Vinh Dien River.

17 March, 2/9 CP:

"Just got in after a 4 day operation. It was uneventful as far as VC contact was concerned. Some long walks in hot weather but other than that it wasn't bad at all.

Just talked with Colonel Donahue and Major Angelo and they approved my going to Hong Kong tomorrow! I need a little R&R. Hope I will be able to find all the things for you and your Mother."

Dressed in starched khakis and tie, my company driver took me to Da Nang to catch the airliner to Hong Kong the next morning. The airliner was air-conditioned and I nearly froze after being in the extreme heat of Vietnam for so long. The stewardesses were nice and they served us a great meal.

On arrival in Hong Kong, I took a taxi to the Hilton hotel and checked in. After a shower, I took a nap and woke up with what appeared to be a case of the hives! I was one big blister! The hotel doctor said I was allergic to the starch in the khakis. He gave me a shot and I was better the next day, so I started my shopping tour, including several tailor shops. I met an Australian Warrant Officer, also on R&R, and he took me to a couple of great pubs for some good beer.

That night, I went out to eat at an American style steakhouse where I met a Doctor from California and his wife and daughter. They were on a Pacific cruise and were also staying in the Hilton. The Doctor and his family asked me to join them and refused to let me pay for anything. The next few days we visited the sights in Hong Kong together.

The U.S. cruiser *St. Paul* was in port over the weekend, and I contacted the ship and Captain Tom Stump, the CO of the Marine detachment, and we got together for dinner. We had served together in 1/4 in Hawaii.

Schramm remembered, "We had just come in from a 4 day patrol between two of our outposts. Nothing much had happened. We had a few sniper rounds and that was about it. I was coming back from chow when members of my squad told me that 'Hanoi Hannah' had just announced that Company E, 2nd Battalion, 9th Marines, Captain Driver, had been [or was going to be] wiped out to the last man by a superior VC unit. We must have been giving them fits. All the other units she talked about, it was always 'we inflicted heavy casualties.' That was the only time anyone ever heard her say they had wiped a unit out to the last man. Damn near happened for real about a week later."

PFC Stephen Clemons recalled, "Someone had a cheap transistor radio and heard that Hanoi Hannah announced that Captain Driver and his entire Echo Company were wiped out. I remember several of the more senior guys going over to your position to congratulate you on your coming back to life." Ware remembered hearing this broadcast also.

One of the company clerks told PFC Becton that he could get a billet as the Security & Classified Material Clerk for the Battalion because he had a top-secret clearance. He applied for and got the job.

L-R: Gen. Greene, Gen. Walt (background),
Capt. Carl Reckewell, unidentified &Lt. Col. Donahue

18 March, 2/9 CP:

"I'll be rejoining the company in the field tomorrow so there will be a dry spell of letters. We've had one man wounded since I've been gone. Hope we stay so fortunate!

Got to close now and get unpacked and packed—and some sleep. I've got a million things to do to get caught up."

PFC Buster B. Martin was medically evacuated from the field on this date with a temperature of 104 degrees. The corpsmen believed he had malaria, but it turned out to be a virus.

HM2 Eddie Gallegos recalled, "I carried a .45 and sometimes an M-14. I carried a Unit 1 bag (medical kit) and several smoke grenades with different colors. Because of the heat, I wore a soft cover and no Flak jacket. I also carried two 60 mm mortar rounds and one or two bandoliers or belts of 100 rounds for an M-60."

HM 2 Mike Harmon reported to 2/9 and was assigned to the 3rd Platoon of Echo Company. He replaced HM 2 Hamilton.

While I was on R&R, the 3rd Platoon on the river block off Highway 1 and received sniper fire, wounding PFC Ramon J. Neito. He was shot through the heart and the corpsman could not get a pulse. The medics on the medevac helicopter were able to revive him, and the doctors at C&C found that the bullet passed through his heart but missed everything vital. Ware, who was in his Fire Team, helped load Nieto on the helicopter. "The next day we had an unauthorized Zippo party in the village he was shot from," he recalled.

19 March, 2/9 CP:

Fox Company had a big fight on this date killing 30 VC (confirmed). Villagers reported the VC carried off 200 more. One of my platoons was in support and killed 3 more.

23 March, 2/9 CP:

"Just got back from Hong Kong this afternoon. It was really great to get away for a while. Just what the doctor ordered! I think you will be happy with my purchases!

While I was away, Fox Company had a lot of casualties from mortars and Echo has been in the field ever since I left. Major Angelo said I left at the right time."

Company F Captain, Carl A. Reckewell, kicked off 2/9's participation in what was to become OPERATION KINGS, a search and destroy mission, with the ultimate intent to occupy the area from the La Tho-Thanh Quit Line to the Ky Lam, clearing the VC from Route 4. On 18 March, Company F ran into the VC on the northern bank of the La Tho just east of the old railroad line. The company was mortared and then repulsed three ground attacks. 10 enemy dead were found.

Colonel Simmons directed Lt. Colonel Donahue to lead the operation. The Battalion CP was moved temporarily to Hill 55 from Duong Son (2) for better command and control purposes. Hill 55 overlooked much of the area of operations. My company, Company E, was committed on the 18th and, along with 2 companies from 3/9, swept the area from La Tho River south to the Ky Lam and from the railroad bed east to the Suoi Co Ca River. On 23 March, Colonel Donahoe turned OPERATION KINGS over to Lt. Col. Dorsey of 3/3. Company E came under operational control of 3/3. M/3/3 remained in the field with my company.

Battalion CP Dong Son II after Operation Harvest Moon, 1965
L-R: McManicle, Nieto, Ray, Antal, Carbajol, Gibbs & Slemp
Front Row: Skelton & Cox

24 March, 2/9 CP:

"Waiting for the helicopters to take us out to the company, so thought I would write a quick letter. It's really hot here, 110 degrees right now. It's so dry we're having dust storms when the wind blows.

The company has been out 5 days now and it looks as if we'll be out two or three more.

I bought our interpreter a small TV set in Hong Kong, which the company is going to give him. He's a good man and a hard worker. He doesn't believe much the [VC] suspects say and can usually tell if they are lying."

Chapter Fourteen

Da Nang TAOR,
March 1966
Operation Kings

"The company performed magnificently."

Lt. David Garner

"These men showed valor and expertise way beyond their years. They were only 20 years of age or younger."

Cpl. Michael Schramm

Cpl. Michael Schramm, who photographed and recorded almost all the company's movements, recalled, "March 20, 1966 we were out sweeping the area south of our Battalion outpost at Duong Son (2), after Fox Company had been severely attacked while on patrol on March 18th. The XO was in charge, because Capt. Driver was on R&R. The company was at an all time low manpower wise. Between men being rotated back home and casualties, we were down to about 110 men. [The Table of Organization called for a rifle company to have over 200 men]. We should have been called Echo platoon."

The company had relieved Company F in Duong Son (3) on the 18th. In addition, they relieved them on the 3 bridges we were guarding and provided a reinforced squad for Sparrow Hawk, and maintained one platoon as battalion reserve.

Schramm continued, "An operation called KINGS was due to start at the end of the month, but after these attacks, it was started now. They helilifted us to Hill 55, on the north side of the La Tho River. This was 3/3's Outpost [CP]. Here we waited to be lifted to an area on the south side of the river. When the guys in 3/3 found out that's where we were going, they told us to watch our ass. They said that area was crawling with VC and even some NVA units."

20 March, Operation Kings:

"Since it was late in the afternoon," Schramm recalled, "we were hoping they would wait until morning to send us in, but at 1600 the word came to saddle up. The flight only took about ten minutes, and we were dropped

267

in the middle of a dry rice paddy about 5 miles west of Hill 55. We drew some small arms fire when we came in, but nothing to write home about [20 rounds]. It took about an hour to get everyone out there and on the ground, so the XO decided we would dig in right there for the night. It was flat ground with the closest tree line 75 yards away. It would be tough for Charlie to sneak in on us, but we were so obvious he could mortar the shit out of us."

The company captured 2 VC suspects and received small arms fire from both sides of the river from 8-10 VC. At 1810, they had another firefight and killed one VC, capturing his weapon and ID card. The man's wife was detained as a VC. Echo Company had 1 WIA during the day, but he was treated and returned to duty.

"Things stayed quiet until just after midnight," Schramm continued, "then there was a whistle of an incoming round. Everyone dove into their holes and it hit about 50 yards outside the perimeter. Then it was dead quiet. We could faintly hear voices on the radios at the CP trying to find out if the round was one of ours. It wasn't. We waited for all hell to break loose—but that was it."

PFC Joseph F. Jennings, a rifleman, was on his first real operation. He was burdened with a 3.5 inch rocket round strapped on the back of his pack, because of the lack of men in the rockets section to carry them. His other new-guy mistake was carrying only two canteens. "I figured that if two canteens was what the Marine Corps had issued me, then that was all I'd need," he recalled. "I soon learned that the hot sun in the dried rice paddies could suck the moisture out of my body faster than I could drink water to replace it. The only reasonably safe drinking water was in the cisterns and wells in the villages we passed through, and even these had to be heavily dosed with iodine tablets to avoid a monumental case of diarrhea. That day I drank thirteen 1-quart canteens of water and would have more if I had gotten it.

"The VC must have enjoyed watching us suffer in the heat because they did everything they could to compound our misery. They would hide a couple of snipers near each village, and they would open fire just when we were fully exposed in the middle of a rice paddy. They never hit anybody, but we would have to assault the tree line, which meant having to run 200 or 300 meters in the blast furnace heat. Almost every time we did this, one or two Marines would collapse from the heat and dehydration. If the corpsman couldn't lower body temperatures and bring them around, they [would have to be medically evacuated]."

21 March, Operation Kings:

The re-supply helicopters were fired on at 0745. An AO on station and a patrol was sent to check out the area with negative results. By 1115 the company had destroyed 8 tunnels and a cave.

Metras, now the Company Radio Operator, recalled that the re-supply helicopters dropped off 'goodie bags' for each man. "They contained cigarettes, candy, toothpaste, razors, and razor blades, etc."

22 March, Operation Kings:

The company continued on its search and destroy mission. At 1505, they received small arms fire from a village and assaulted the position, killing 2 VC. During the rest of the day they destroyed several bunkers and tunnels. The company had 2 officers and 158 men listed as present for duty on this date, but only about 110 on the operation.

23 March, Operation Kings:

Lt. Hornick had the company on the move early that morning and picked up a VC suspect by 0750. They were busy destroying tunnels and bunkers and picked up another VC suspect by noon. An hour later, a patrol found 2 pair of khaki trousers, a Marine utility jacket, and a cap. One Marine was wounded in the arm early that morning, but he got bandaged up and returned to duty. The attached ARVN troops were pulled off the operation at 1245 that day. About the same time, a patrol killed 2 VC and discovered a VC minefield.

PFC Lawton recalled standing watch with the 'Mutt & Jeff' Machine Gun Team on several occasions during this operation. This team consisted of a very tall and a very short Marine. LCpl. Albert L. 'Rod' Beckers, who stood six feet, six inches tall, was the gunner.

"Charlie loved it when we had a casualty," Jennings said, "because it normally meant that the whole company had to stop to set up security for the medevac bird, and those choppers made great targets when they landed to pick up the wounded. The arrival of the medevac usually precipitated a lively fire fight, with the VC shooting at the birds during their approach to the landing zone (LZ) and maybe dropping in a few mortar rounds for good measure.

"That day [24 March] had been the worst. It was the hottest day so far, and the VC kept us constantly moving from one little firefight to another. After 3 days of this, we were worn out and the numbers of heat casualties started to climb. At about 1500, the executive officer decided it was time to get everybody in the shade and off their feet before he lost the whole company. The nearest village was Cam Van [2], about a kilometer away, and that's where we headed. I had been handling the heat pretty well up to this point, but a couple of hundred yards before we reached the village I started to get cold chills. Now, when the temperature is 110 degrees and you're standing in the hot sun having chills, your body is telling you something is going wrong. I made it into the shade of the nearest trees before I collapsed. My buddies poured water on me and made me drink as much as I could swallow. After about a half hour's rest and a couple of canteens of water, I was able to stand up and rejoin the squad, but I was dead on my feet."

Lawton recalled that he and his fire team had been out on listening post the previous night with Corporal Avila and PFCs Tom King and Douglas Stewart. "I was the new guy, so I got to carry the PRC 6 radio in addition to my rifle. Around midnight the VC started beating on cans and moving in front of the LP. They started beating on cans on three sides of the perimeter. Avila had briefed us that if anything happened, they would shoot and I would take off toward our lines yelling over the radio 'LP coming in.' After he was sure we were located, Avila gave the order to shoot and I took off for the platoon lines yelling 'LP coming in!' Luckily there were no trigger-happy rookies in our platoon or I would have been shot. In retrospect, the VC were just playing a head game with us. They just wanted to let us know that they knew where we were."

"The next morning [24 March], we started moving east, sweeping the villages along the river," Schramm continued. "We could tell they were watching us. Don't ask me how, but we could all feel it. It was incredibly hot and no breeze. On the move like this, it wasn't unusual to go through 12 to 15 canteens of water a day. We would refill our canteens from wells in the villages. We lost several men from the heat and had to evacuate them. The village we were in was called Cam Van. We were exhausted so the XO decided to stay there for the night."

Lt. Garner recalled that we were located "near the Song Al Nghia river, which ran west to east and was between us and Hill 55, which our artillery was positioned to support the operation."

At 1500 that day, the ARVN reported to 2/9 that a VC Company with 125 men and 25 Chinese Advisors were at Dai An. The Chinese were wearing khaki uniforms. Neither Lt. Hornick nor I ever got the word on this.

Lawton continued, "The 24th started with a long movement. I was as hot as I had ever felt. The sun pounded down on my helmet and reflected up underneath off the hard gray rice paddies. I had all my gear and ammunition for the M-60. All during that long day it was like living in a boiler. Periodically, there was a helicopter gun ship overhead and gunfire way left or way right, but we weren't involved. A low flying helicopter dropped a red smoke grenade near the river. Avila, Stewart, and I went down the embankment to check. It was a cave or tunnel entrance but so small no one could get in it, so we threw in some grenades. The reason I remember this is because that night I was wishing I had those grenades back in the worst way! Finally, we stopped at some village. My canteens were empty and had been for a while. I was on the edge of never-never land [passing out]. I just waded into the river and sat down and drank river water. I think the gods of disease took pity on this FNG. I should have gotten typhoid fever or dysentery or something, but nothing happened. Someone pulled me out of the river."

Avila, who had been meritoriously promoted to Corporal, stated, "I walked into some mud along side the river and started to sink. I remember thinking about the old movies that showed people being swallowed up by quick sand. I don't know why but when I find myself in danger, I always get really calm. I thought to myself, 'if someone doesn't get me out of here I am going to drown in this mud.' No one realized I was in trouble at first and they kept moving forward, so I yelled out that I needed help. Two or three guys came back. By the time they got there, I was up to mid thigh in the mud and still sinking. They could not walk in the mud to help me. They rigged up a rifle and sling and pulled me out."

Corporal George M. Graves, a machine gunner, recalled, "Several of us went down to the river and washed our clothes and ourselves to cool off in the late afternoon."

PFC Stephen Clemons, who had just turned 18, was the Assistant Gunner for PFC Dennis C. "Dan" Kumaus. Despite being called "Private Numb Nuts," in Machine Gun School, he graduated as Honor Man in his class. Some nights he studied for the written exam, the other nights he practiced detail stripping the gun and re-assembling it blindfolded. "There were a few times we fought like teenagers over who was going to carry the M-60," he recalled. "Before night, we had been through some skirmishes and the M-60 showed signs of carbon build-up," he continued, "so after we established a fighting position, we moved back up on the bluff behind us and found a flat space on the ground. We laid out a poncho just after dark and we broke the M-60 down into its main groups. Then we detailed stripped each group and scrubbed, oiled, and wiped every last pin and spring that could be disassembled away from an armory. I was confident we could do this successfully. Nevertheless, it did occur to me if I lost a pin or spring or forgot where it fit, Kumaus might just beat me to death.

"Our position was in an awkward place. If we had dug in on top of the bluff, we would not have been able to cover our flanks. If we set up at the base of the bluff, we were too far forward and without any cover. Halfway down the bluff was a large clump of bushes. We dug in behind them so we would have some cover.

"A four man Fire Team from the 2nd Platoon was sent out in front of our position as a Listening Post. On the way out, the team leader [Cpl. James R. Ruiz] stopped at our position and asked Kumaus not to open up with the machine gun until they made it back into the perimeter. Dan agreed, and I knew he would honor this promise. To our front was a field and then a farm fence, bushes, and trees. We could not see past the fence line."

LCpl. John Templeton, a Fire Team Leader in the 2nd Platoon, remembered that his position was in the last foxhole facing to the west, just above the river. He and a Marine from Mexico found a position that had been dug previously, and it included a grenade sump. PFCs Mike Malone and George Morris were in the next hole, but facing the river.

LCpl John Templeton

"It was still light, so our squad was to go on a patrol and check the area around Cam Van," Schramm related. "I was glad, because this meant we wouldn't have to go out that night [on ambush]. We went out on the east side of the village and made a half circle around to the west side, checking the villages around Cam Van. About two thirds of the way around, we noticed the women and kids seemed uneasy. Then, one of the women came up frantically saying something about Da Nang. We couldn't understand what she was asking, but knew she was in hysteria. I told [Cpl.] Osaw [Squad Leader] we should take her back with us. He said no, because he was afraid the rest of the women would follow, and the XO would have a shit fit if we came in with all those people. I could tell there was something wrong, and these people knew what it was, but Osaw wouldn't give in. He said he would let them know about it when we got in.

"By the time we got in, it was dark. Choppers had brought out supplies and Capt. Driver, plus 6 new replacements. The word was 2 of the new replacements were brothers and they both wanted to be in the same platoon. Driver said 'no,' and one went to weapons and one went to first platoon."

I rejoined the company in the field that afternoon on the re-supply helicopter. I found my men in a state of near exhaustion from the day's efforts due to the excessive heat. Two men were medically evacuated for heat exhaustion by the helicopter. The company was located in a small village, Cam Van (2), near the river. A female with a baby had been found in one of the huts and she was crying her head off. I made the decision to turn her loose, and I'm sure she went straight to the local VC and told them our position. I was dissatisfied with the company's perimeter, so just at dark I moved the men back about 75 yards to the northern edge of the village and closer to the river. We set up in a 360-degree oblong defense with the northern end at the river, which had a sheer bank impossible for even the VC to scale.

Lawton remembered that several men where medevaced for heat stroke/exhaustion, including PFC Ron Hoyos, a machine gunner. PFC Dorie Lear, a friend of Hoyos, said he had eaten some bad ham and eggs [C rations], and with the heat and lack of water, had become very sick.

Pfc. Dorie Lear

LCpl Letendre with a Vietnamese child

Pfc. Joe Brazil

"Osaw went to fill the CO in on the patrol while the rest of us moved into our positions on the line," Schramm remembered. "2nd Platoon was set up on the west side and my team was placed at the north end, close to the river. Since the ground was pretty soft, it didn't take us long to dig the positions. Then, while [LCpl. Thomas] Phillips covered us, [PFC Wilfred E.] Brazil and I went out in front to set up trip flares. Our position covered a landing site at the river. On the other side of the landing was a tree line. It was about 15 yards thick and ran along the bank. This restricted our view of the water to only the landing. Inside the tree line, there was a swampy area that went from the trees to a dike 50 yards to the left of our position and out to another tree line about 60 yards to our front.

"When Osaw got back, he set himself with [Cpl. Robert H.] Pringer, with the M-79, on a knoll just above us and over close to the bank so they could watch our blind spot on the river side of the tree line. He also let us know Driver had moved the CP after dark to a position about 40 yards from the original one."

"We set up for the night," related Avila. "King and I dug our fighting hole in front of a hut. We were kind of stuck out on a corner. There was a rice paddy to the front and right of us, with a drop off of about 3 feet. To our right and rear, another squad stretched towards the river."

Lawton recalled, "We were assigned a squad area and told to dig in. Later, I was told to stand watch covering the machine gun position, as they were going out with the night ambush under Sgt. [Gilberto] Garcia. People were moved around and I ended up with one of the 3.5 Rocket Launcher Teams in a 3 man position behind a small berm looking out over a cane field to a distant tree line."

Cpl. John R. 'Dick' Sasser, another Fire Team Leader in the 1st Platoon, recalled, "We had a two man LP directly in front of my Fire Team's foxholes. PFC Laberdee was in the hole on my left, Laux was on my right, then Letendre, Copeland, and then the Machine Gun Team. When Laberdee first came to our squad, he was older than the rest of us and had a bad attitude. He only had 2 magazines for his M-14 and about 10 grenades. I asked him how far he could throw a grenade. Then I asked him how far he could shoot. He got the message and carried 10 magazines and fewer grenades.

"We had dug a 'pull back hole' about 20-30 feet directly behind my position. Around 2100, someone in the platoon on my left shot and killed a VC [actually 2] trying to get in our lines. I went to look at him and he had flashlights [to signal with]. About 2300, I heard a loud crack. One of the LP Marines came in to tell me about the noise. It was reported to Captain Driver and he sent the LP back out. The Marine was scared. I remember talking to Laux and I'll never forget what he said: 'Jesus Christ came from outer space.' An hour later and he was dead."

"The next few hours were spent improving positions and resting," Schramm noted. "At 2200, an ambush was sent out from the 1st Platoon and each platoon sent out a listing post. I took the first watch at our position and Brazil and Phillips got some sleep."

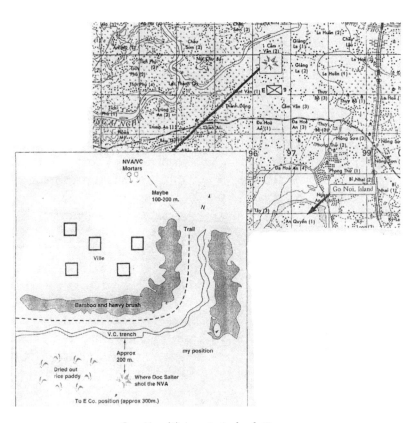

Cam Van (2) Area & Ambush Site

E/2/9 position night of 24-25 March, 1966   ➜

Da Nang TAOR, March 1966

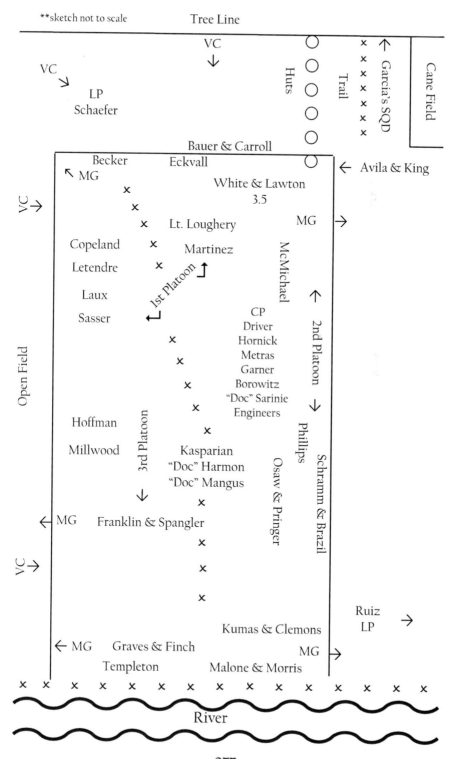

**sketch not to scale

Tree Line

VC ↓

VC ↓

LP
Schaefer

Huts

Trail

Garcia's SQD

Cane Field

Bauer & Carroll

Becker
↖ MG
Eckvall

Avila & King ←

White & Lawton
3.5

VC →

Lt. Loughery

MG →

Copeland
Martinez

McMichael

Letendre

1st Platoon ↰

Laux

Sasser
↵

CP
Driver
Hornick
Metras
Garner
Borowitz
"Doc" Sarinie
Engineers

2nd Platoon ↓

Open Field

Hoffman

3rd Platoon

Millwood

Phillips

Kasparian
"Doc" Harmon
"Doc" Mangus

Osaw & Pringer

Schramm & Brazil

↓

MG ←

Franklin & Spangler

VC →

Ruiz
LP
→

Kumas & Clemons

MG ←
Graves & Finch

MG →

Templeton
Malone & Morris

River

Jennings continued, "Things got worse when Sgt. Garcia, our squad leader, passed the word that we had the ambush patrol that night. Next, we learned that we had been assigned to ambush a trail junction almost 1,500 meters away. Sgt. Garcia tried to talk the lieutenant into assigning us a shorter patrol. The lieutenant said the orders had come down from battalion, and we didn't have any choice. I guess 1,500 meters looks a lot different on a map in a sandbagged command bunker back at Hill 55 than it did to us the growing darkness and ominous desolation of Cam Van. Knowing that we were all nervous about this patrol, one of our platoon corpsmen volunteered to go out with us. He was a good, solid man, and we all trusted him.

"Sgt. Garcia didn't waste much time giving orders. We had been patrolling together for the last three days and knew what to do. He would put us in our ambush position when, and if, we got to the ambush site. All too soon we had completed our radio checks and were passing through the fighting holes on the company perimeter heading almost due north [south] into the darkness.

"It was very dark. There was no moon and the clouds moved in to obscure the stars. It was too dark to maintain any sort of normal interval between individuals. Half the time we were holding on to the man ahead because we were so afraid of getting separated and being out there alone. I was walking just behind Doc in about the middle of the column. Doc was a trained medical technician and dedicated to saving lives, but he was neither a pacifist nor a fool. In addition to the .45 caliber pistol, he also had a 12-gage riot gun loaded with buckshot.

"Except for Doc, we were all carrying M-14 rifles; mine was one of two in the squad that had a selector switch, allowing it to be fired either single shot or full automatic. We each had 4 or 5 grenades, about 200 rounds of ammunition, a bayonet, and 2 or more canteens. Four Marines were carrying Claymore mines to be used at the ambush site, and one man had the squad's PRC-10 radio. We were about 200 meters outside the company perimeter when a strange, helmeted figure ghosted out of the blackness and started talking to Doc in Vietnamese! A few days later, we learned that our visitor was one of many North Vietnamese Army (NVA) replacements serving with the main force VC battalion that had surrounded Echo Company shortly after sundown. He had evidently mistaken us for one of his squads and was probably trying to find out why we were heading in the wrong direction. He may have realized his error for a moment when Doc stuck the shotgun muzzle into his chest and pulled the trigger. The blast of the 12-gage shattered the quiet and was the start of an almost continuous din that would not end until just before dawn.

"When Doc shot the NVA soldier, our immediate reaction was to flatten ourselves to the ground. The excited chatter of Vietnamese voices on all sides convinced us that we needed to be someplace else. Garcia took control and got us started moving toward a small hamlet, which we had passed through that afternoon and which should have been about 200 meters in front of us. Fortunately, the VC were even more confused than we were. We managed to half-crawl, half-run almost 100 meters before anyone started shooting at us. The VC knew we were somewhere near by, but they couldn't see in the dark any better than we could. None of their shots came close.

"I had been scrambling through the dust-dry paddies when I suddenly fell over Doc, who had stopped short in front of me. In a second there was a disorganized pile of gasping, struggling bodies as the rest of the squad ran into us. Doc told me that the man in front of him had lost contact with the rest of the squad and had stopped to try to figure out where they had gone. Just then we heard the THUNK, THUNK, THUNK of mortar rounds being fired from the vicinity of the company perimeter. A few seconds later we heard the same sound from our front, and we knew there were no friendly troops in that direction. So there we were, disorganized and separated in the middle of no-man's land with an all-out fight about to erupt all around us.

"Before we could decide what to do, the illumination rounds from the company's mortars turned the night into day and left us fully exposed in the open rice paddy. This left us no choice but to find some cover—fast. Fortunately, the illumination also showed us the hamlet we had been heading toward and we started moving in that direction. I moved as quickly as I could in a high crawl on my knees and elbows. I was so intent on searching for the other members of the squad that I literally crawled into a camouflaged trench line that stretched along the edge of the hamlet. One second I was crawling through the dust of the paddy, an instant later I was falling. My fall ended abruptly on top of a live body in the bottom of the trench. I was sure I had just fallen into the midst of a VC unit awaiting its attack order. I had just started to claw and kick my way back out of the trench when a stream of very American profanity reassured me that I had found the rest of the squad. Shortly, Doc and the others tumbled down from the flare-lit paddy, and after some initial confusion and a near knife fight, we settled in to catch our breath and collect our nerves.

"Sgt. Garcia took a quick head count, and we found that, miraculously, we were all present and accounted for. All around us the sounds of a major fight were building to a deafening roar. To our rear, back at the company perimeter, it sounded like every Marine with a weapon was firing as fast as he could squeeze the trigger. The rifle and machine gun fire from our lines was punctuated by the explosion of grenades and Claymore mines. Mortars and artillery were starting to fall on preplanned targets. Tracers from friendly fire zipped close by over our heads.

"Garcia started setting us up in a defensive position. Our trench ran along the edge of the hamlet for 20 meters or so and then turned sharply in the direction from which we could hear the VC mortars being fired. As soon as Garcia had us in position, he got on the radio. I could hear him telling the company commander our situation and describing his best guess where the VC mortars were located. After a little while, I could tell that he had changed frequencies and was talking on an artillery fire control net. Within a few minutes, the first spotting rounds started landing near our positions. I was amazed how calm Garcia's voice was. He sounded like he was on a training exercise at Camp Pendleton. He slowly worked the artillery in until rounds were falling 75 to 100 meters from our trench. Once he had the fire adjusted as close as he dared, he told them to fire for effect. In less than a minute, we were surrounded by explosions." PFC Omar Hadsell, who was in the squad, also recalled how cool Garcia was under the poncho with a flashlight and a map, calling in and adjusting the artillery fire.

"After what seemed like an eternity, the fire around us started to slacken," Jennings continued. "Evidently the VC mortars had completed their mission or had been silenced by Garcia's artillery request and the Marines back at the company perimeter had defeated the VC assault. Sporadic fire continued and occasionally built to a heavy exchange, but it seemed that the main fight was over.

"We heard the sound of Vietnamese voices from just in front of our position. There was a narrow trail running along the top of the trench, and it was apparent that a number of VC were walking towards us down the trail. Garcia crawled up next to me so he could look down the trail. He had the detonator for a Claymore mine in his hand. The Claymore was set up just a few yards forward of us—close enough that if we had to use it, we'd be hit by the back blast. It was too dark to actually see anything, but the VC had no idea we were so close because they were talking in normal voices and we could hear them clearly. They were moving slowly down the trail toward us. Suddenly they turned around, and we weren't going to start a firefight in the middle of a battalion of VC. That was when I pissed myself.

"We stayed there in the trench for the rest of the night. Occasionally, an artillery round would land nearby or there was a burst of fire from back at the company perimeter, but it seemed almost peaceful compared to what we had been through. I think I must have fallen asleep for a while because

I don't remember hearing the medevac choppers coming in to take out our seriously wounded."

Schramm recorded, "A few minutes before midnight, the word came around to go on 100% alert. It didn't seem like much was going on, so I decided to wait before waking these guys for a false alarm. Then the word came to fix bayonets. I remember thinking, 'Christ! Fix Bayonets! What the hell is going on!' I reached over to wake Brazil. Just as I grabbed his arm, the first mortar round hit. We dove for our holes as the rounds started exploding everywhere. Within seconds, I realized my hole was not deep enough, but my entrenching tool was on the ground 5 feet behind me. I yelled to Brazil I was going after it and scrambled out. 60 and 81 mortars were hitting everywhere. I got back and started digging between my legs to deepen my hole. This was the heaviest attack we had ever been under. An 81 round went off about 6 or 8 feet behind our positions and it lifted me right out of the hole. As I shot back in I looked at Brazil and his eyes were as big as saucers. He couldn't believe what he had just seen."

The men dug in behind paddy dikes on the left and right flanks. They had open rice paddies and sugar cane fields to their front. The center [1st] platoon, facing south, had to occupy a line that had a few huts in it, but it also had paddy dikes and a tree line to help conceal their positions. I moved the CP to a bunker built underground just outside the village. It had a half moon shaped mound of dirt around it with a thatched roof. The underground bunker had bamboo steps leading down inside with benches or beds of bamboo built down both sides. It saved a lot of lives in the CP group. The official report shows our position as 3,500 meters west of the railroad bed and 1,000 meters north of Route 4.

I sent the nightly ambush down the trail south of us and sent out 4 listening-posts at 2000. Machine guns were set up with the best fields of fire possible. Claymore mines and trip flares were set up in front of each platoon. The Artillery Observer, Lt. Garner, registered the artillery just before dark. He plotted time on target areas around our position, including "danger close" (within 50 yards). Our 60 mm mortar was set up near the CP. They only had about 20 rounds, including illumination. Private Kerin P. Florian, (don't let the rank fool you. He had been in country for about 9 months and was as brave a Marine as ever put on the uniform. He often acted as point man for the company, platoon, and/or squad. When he had a few beers in him he wanted to fight, and his escapades caused him to be reduced from Lance Corporal. When we were in the rear, I used him as my jeep driver so the 1st Sergeant and I could keep an eye on him. He was also a trained sniper) my Scout/Sniper, organized the men in the CP group into a defensive perimeter around the CP.

At 0030, two 60 mm mortar rounds landed inside the perimeter. I put the company on 100% alert. Metras, my Company Radio Operator, recalled, "The CP group was in a hut close to the 1st Platoon's lines. The 1st Platoon had the southern part of the perimeter, the 3rd Platoon along the river and to the east and the 2nd Platoon covered the west. I was sleeping outside of the door of the hut where my radio was. Suddenly, I was awakened by the mortar shells landing all around us. I started to the door of the hut where my radio was, when a mortar round went off behind me, knocking me through it. I got to my radio. I was the Company Tactical Net Operator, and I had contact with the three platoons, the ambush patrol and 5 [sic] listening posts. A corpsman took care of my wounded leg while I relayed information to Captain Driver. 3rd Platoon was reporting VC coming across the river. From what I heard, the VC were throwing mortar rounds at us by hand. I was receiving mortar and artillery coordinates from the ambush patrol, 1st Platoon and a listing post from the 2nd Platoon. I was passing this information to the Artillery FO and 81 mm Mortar FO."

PFC Ward A. Hoffman, Jr. was a rifleman in the 1st Fire Team, Second Squad, 3rd Platoon. "I think [LCpl. Harold D.] Millwood had taken over the position of fire team leader since [LCpl. Raymon J.] Nieto had been wounded several days before," Hoffman recalled. "The 2nd Squad was assigned a section of the perimeter facing a dried rice paddy which gave us an open field [of fire] with the only object being a single grave about 200 meters from our position. During the early evening we set our positions in front of a tree line and dug our sleeping holes. When it became dark we moved our fire team defensive position forward about 20 meters to a mound. When it was my turn to stand watch, I moved to the mound and sat on top of it. That night there was no moon and it was very dark. You could not see 20 feet in front of you and everything seemed quiet and peaceful. Off in the distance there was a village and during my watch I saw what looked like a flash of light but I could not tell what it was and never heard anything to indicate what it may have been.

"Since it was so dark and you could not see anything in front of you, you learned not to look at one spot too long but to keep your eyes moving. It suddenly appeared that there was something moving in front of me. I looked away and then looked back to where I saw the movement. At this time I could see there were 2 objects moving toward my position. The objects were about 15 feet in front of me but they did not see me or know that our position was there. I popped a flare and fired on these 2 objects with my M-14, firing a complete magazine. Then I called for the machine gun team to move forward and waited for any more movement from the front. My squad leader came up and asked what the firing was about and

I told him. We moved forward to check and found 2 Viet Cong bodies and we pulled them into our perimeter and they were taken to the CP."

They brought the bodies, weapons, packs and IDs to the CP. Their belts, vests and packs held grenades and satchel charges. Hoffman received the Bronze Star Medal for his actions.

At 0040, the 3rd Platoon's listening post came in and reported bolts clicking, talking and a lot of movement. The rest of the 3rd Platoon was instructed to use grenades if the VC approached them, to keep from giving away their positions. The machine gunners were cautioned not to open fire until the VC assaulted. The listening post was sent back out at 0100. By now movement could be heard even by the CP group, indicating there was a large number of VC creeping towards our lines. I passed the word to 'FIX BAYONETS,' the first and only time I ever gave that order. I was afraid that the men would not be able to reload fast enough if the VC attacked in overwhelming numbers. I had our 60 mm mortar crew fire some illumination rounds, but we were unable to see the enemy.

Cpl. Sasser recalled, "We were on 50% alert. I had an M-14 with an automatic selector, Claymore mines and hand grenades, 12 flares and a LAW in my position. A new replacement was with me in my hole. He asked me, 'what if a mortar round lands in our hole'? I told him, 'you won't have to worry about anything if that happens.'

'At 0100, I heard some noise to my 11o'clock to my 1 o'clock. I passed the word for 100% alert. For the only time in my life I passed the word to 'FIX BAYONETS.' I believe it was 0120 when all hell broke loose. I fired a flare and that was when I saw the VC at my 5 o'clock and knew they had gotten through the lines to the left of the machine gun position and to the right of Laux's position. I yelled to Sgt. Martinez, who was to my rear under a tree, that the VC were in the perimeter. The flare that I shot up blinded me for a few seconds. I fired the Claymore and let loose with my M-14. Some VC were yelling 'You die Marine,' and I remember calling them 'Mother Fuckers' or something like that."

Lt. Garner recalled "For some reason, I got up and started walking towards the LP that was located on the river bank just north of the CP. I was walking along a high berm, with the 81s [one 60 mm] to my left when the enemy mortar rounds started falling in the vicinity of the CP and small arms fire was coming our way. It wasn't long before all hell broke loose around the company perimeter." PFC Larry Miller, his radioman was with him.

About 0115, we suddenly heard the 'thump, thump' of mortar rounds being fired and the CP group took cover in the bunker. Metras lay behind the earthen mound while I stood on the top step of the bunker and called in the supporting fires. He was hit in the leg by a mortar fragment, but continued to operate the radio throughout the action. Metras remained with me, without further medical treatment, until the operation was over 3 days later, and received the Naval Commendation Medal for his valor.

My XO, Gerry Hornick, recalled, "I spent most of the time down in the bomb shelter coordinating the fire support."

Garner stated, "I immediately began calling in fires, with the first mission being received at 0135. My first targets were the suspected mortar locations—my first mission was called in southwest of our company position. The enemy troop movements were initially coming from that direction as well, so I called in additional missions in that area. Within the first 30 minutes of the attack, I had called 6 different missions switching from the suspected mortar positions to enemy troop movements. Within the first half hour, over 200 rounds of HE rounds had been fired consisting of 105 mm and 107 mm mortar (howtar) rounds and then 155 mm artillery. Battlefield illumination was provided by 100 rounds fired by the Howtar battery. That illumination was later augmented by a flare ship, but artillery provided immediate response."

Templeton remembered that one of the first mortar rounds to land hit in his hole and went into the grenade sump before detonating. "It blew the Mexican Marine completely out of the hole and knocked him unconscious." Templeton didn't receive a scratch.

At the same time, we received heavy machine gun and automatic weapons fire. Bullets screamed over our positions for about 30 minutes. The VC immediately tried to infiltrate our lines. My men turned them back with grenades and well aimed fire.

The listening post in front of the 1st Platoon was hit by a shower of grenades at about the same time as the platoon. One Marine was killed, one seriously wounded, one badly wounded, and one slightly wounded. The slightly wounded Marine [PFC Laberdee] continued to fire his rifle and throw grenades at the enemy despite the loss of his glasses. He carried the wounded and dead Marines to the rear and then returned to recover their weapons. Seven dead VC were found in front of their position. Laberdee was awarded a Bronze Star for his actions. Florian recalled that Laberdee found that the VC had turned two of the platoon's Claymores around towards them. He faced them the right way and booby trapped them with grenades.

In front of the 3rd Platoon, the listening post, a fire team led by LCpl. Steven A. Schaefer, came under heavy fire and grenade attack when the assault started. Schaefer, wounded in the head, ordered the other men to withdraw, while he covered them. He spotted the VC setting up a machine gun to fire on the company. He personally killed the 3 VC and knocked out the machine gun. The three bodies were still there the next morning. Schaefer was awarded his second Naval Commendation Medal for his exploits.

"When they attacked we started shooting and yelling," Avila remembered. "We yelled, 'Come on you mother fuckers, we'll kill all of you.' We could see them, especially when the flares went up. I always thought they were trying to cut us in half so they could attack us from behind. During the fighting, one of them jumped up from the dry rice paddy and threw a grenade. I tried to shoot him, but all I got was a click, so I reloaded. We got down and there was an explosion. We got up and then there was another explosion and that was when we got hit. We got really pissed off and started yelling even more. Somehow we held them off. I remember asking God to help me kill them.

"The fight was still going on when King was shot in the head [through the temple]. We were shoulder to shoulder in the midst of the fight. I heard the impact and he started to scream in pain. I still remember the sound. Then he lost consciousness. His blood filled our fighting hole."

Lawton remembered that King was only wearing a helmet liner with just the camouflage cover over it, and not the steel pot he should have had on over it.

They mortared us with an estimated 100 rounds. They followed this up with a company size assault on our positions. They nearly wiped out one squad in the 1st Platoon, inflicting eight casualties on the eleven men. Their attack has concentrated on the area where the CP had been located earlier in the afternoon. The squad members reported the VC shouting, "CP, CP," and appeared to be confused when they couldn't find it.

"I started yelling for Laux, Letendre, Copeland, and the M-60 gun crew with no response," Sasser continued. "I yelled to my right for Rich Carroll and he answered. I told everyone to stay put and that I was going to the CP for help. When I got there, I talked with Captain Driver. I told him about not getting an answer from my fire team members and the machine gunners, and I need more men. I recall the two engineers said they would go, and the three man 60 mm crew. SSgt. Kasparian was placed in charge. I had them drop their packs and placed them on line. We left the CP on line and ran to the trail through the village. I yelled out to everyone that we were coming in. We ran into the lines just a few yards from the machine gun position. We set up a 360-degree defense. One man from our listing post came in, and I sent him to the CP to get his wound taken care of. I told everyone to wait there while I went to check on my men. The first man I saw was Copeland; he had a very bad head wound and was dead. The next

Marine I saw was Letendre. He was in a sitting position, like reading a book or taking a nap. His helmet was over his head and face. When I moved his helmet, he had no face, only parts of his ears and forehead, but I knew it was him. By now I was getting emotionally fucked up. Next came Laux; he was on one knee over someone [a VC] who was dead. I looked him over but he had no wounds of any kind. He must have died from a concussion grenade. I went to the M-60 hole. One man was on his back in bad shape, so I turned him on his side. I tried to move another man, but when I tried to move him he cried out in pain. The M-60 hole must have taken a direct mortar hit on it, and there were a lot of Chicom grenades steaming in the dirt. I went back to the CP to get medical help for the wounded. Then I started de-linking the ammo off the M-60 barrel that was welded to the barrel by the heat." LCpl. Bert L. Beckers, PFC Eugene Franklin, and Pvt. Howard E. Luff, Jr., were the wounded machine gun team members.

SSgt. Kasparian & Cpl. Carbahol, Spring 1966

Lt. Garner had the artillery fire preplanned barrages using variable time fuses. This caused them to explode in the air above the exposed VC, which decimated their ranks. Gardner called in illumination rounds from the Howtar (4.2 mm mortars) Battery, Whiskey 3/12, and Echo Battery, 2nd Battalion, 12th Marines, on Hill 55, using 105s fired the 'danger close' rounds that proved so destructive on the VC. Lima Battery, 4th Battalion, 12th Marines, used their 155s to cover avenues of approach and retreat. The VC still kept coming, but our riflemen and machine gunners continued to mow them down. Later a Marine plane dropped flares for us the rest of the night [0200-0500].

"*Artillery fired 1,058 rounds and 81s [Howtars] 256 more,*" I stated in a letter to my brother.

Garner added, "As we received reports in the CP from the platoons, I would call in fires based upon their comments that were relayed to me by the CO. Periodically, I would venture out from the CP with my radio operator to monitor the effectiveness of the fires, as we had several missions being fired simultaneously by the various batteries. I would adjust the fires based both upon my observations and those being radioed to the CP. Lt. Loughery's platoon was bearing the brunt of the action, so much of the fires were directed in support of his platoon."

HM3's Harmon and Roger Mangus were assigned to the 3rd Platoon. "When the mortars started, Mangus and I dove into the hole SSgt. Kasparian was in," Harmon recalled. "We dove head first into the hole, forcing Kasparian up and out. I can still hear him screaming at us to quit pushing him out."

Lawton noted, "About midnight it all started—mortars—shouts of the LP coming in. I saw three distinct trails of sparks going up in the air, and I was sure it was mortars coming in. I fired and the 3.5 rocket team fired into the cane field where we sensed or felt we saw movement. We continued to fire our weapons and throw grenades. We couldn't hear from all of the noise of mortars, machine guns, rifles, and grenades going off. I saw some shadows at a distance on my right and they threw CHICOM grenades, which let off sparks. We kept firing. It seemed like it went on forever."

Corporal Graves remembered, "The VC put about 40-50 mortar rounds in the air before the first one hit the ground, and they lit us up like there was no tomorrow. My hole was about 10 meters from the riverbank; I felt the VC knew exactly were I was. I could feel the rounds hitting the parapet of my foxhole, and I could hear the VC shouting in the dark, and hear their whistles. My rubber lady was shot to pieces; that is how close the rounds were. I could not get my head up for what seemed like an eternity, so we threw grenades until we had no more. A mortar round exploded in a bamboo tree over our heads and showered our heads with shrapnel and branches. I think the tree saved us from being killed. I don't know how many rounds I fired."

PFC Dorie Lear, a Rifleman in the 1st Platoon, remembered hearing the "Whistles and shouting by the VC just before the mortars started coming in. The mortar rounds were extremely accurate, landing in the three or four foxholes on the line, including the machine gun team, which was to my right. One round also landed in the Platoon Sergeant's hole, mortally wounding him." During a lull in the action, Lear went to check on his condition. Sergeant Eckvall told him not to try to move him. "Be careful, I've got my guts in my hands." Lear went back to the fight. "The VC were behind a small pagoda or grave in my front and in the bamboo to my right," Lear continued. "I fired all my ammunition and threw all of my grenades to keep them back. I killed one between my hole and the machine gun to my right. I killed another behind the pagoda and one who charged directly in front of me. Those are the ones I am sure of. At one point I was staring down the barrel of an AK-47. Fortunately, it misfired, and that's why I am alive today. The fighting seemed to go on for hours."

Clemons recalled, "When the attack started, the Listening Post was on the far side of what we later learned was a VC automatic weapons squad. The VC spotted our position and began hammering us with fire, but Kumaus would not return fire on the machine gun until the Listening Post made it back into the perimeter. The bushes we thought would hide us were shredded and all over us. We had our eyes just above the parapet of our foxhole, waiting and watching for the four men to return.

"Each time I thought the VC were about to overwhelm us with fire they would have to turn about to return fire on the Listening Post. The four men were firing and maneuvering aggressively to get back in. They were keeping us from being shot to hell by a VC machine gun.

"I don't remember whether the artillery and flares started coming in before or after the Listening Post made it back to us, but I remember seeing the first man break out of the brush running at no-feet-on-the-ground speed across the field. We counted them one after the other. When the last man broke into the field, Kumaus opened with a stream of fire at a course parallel to the man's path coming in. As the last Marine entered our perimeter, he widened our fire across the whole of our gun's sector.

"During the fighting, a man [Pvt. Florian] worked around the perimeter passing the word for everyone to stay in their fighting holes, as a number of VC were believed to have penetrated the 1st Platoon lines and were in our midst. We were to stay in our holes and shoot anyone moving behind us. It seemed to me that moving from hole to hole to pass that word was a damned dangerous business."

Templeton found himself in the hole with Mike Malone, who was screaming that the VC were crossing the river, and firing magazine after magazine at them. Templeton found himself loading magazines into his and Malone's M-14s while Malone fired away at the VC in the river.

Schramm continued, "The barrage continued for almost half an hour. By now, artillery on Hill 55 had flares up and were pounding the villages around the south side of the perimeter. Then heavy rifle and automatic fire started, most of which seemed to be directed at the south side of the village where the 1st Platoon was. As I looked up, tracers were passing inches above my hole. This was turning into a nightmare. Then we could hear someone yelling, 'They're coming in,' and the whole south [west] side of the perimeter opened fire. The noise was deafening. The M-60 on that side of the line was firing almost nonstop. We were sure they would be coming up the draw from the river and were watching for any movement. Now someone was yelling, 'gook in the perimeter!' I thought, 'my God, we're being overrun.' SSgt. McMichael, the 2nd Platoon Sergeant [Leader], was armed with a shotgun. When one of the gooks got inside the perimeter started yelling for the CP in bad English, McMichael yelled, 'over here.' When the gook came to the tree line with a lighted satchel charge, McMichael fired. The blast from the shotgun set off the satchel charge and the gook was vaporized.

"It was now obvious that Charlie had staked in most of our positions before dark. One of the 3.5 rocket team in his foxhole counted 16 mortar holes within ten yards of them. Somehow, none of them were hurt."

"Soon the company came under attack with the main VC force attacking to our right through a sugar cane field that was very close to the 1st Platoon positions," Hoffman related. "We received fire from the single grave to our front and returned fire. The VC never attacked our platoon's positions."

"At one point, it appeared that the VC Main Force unit had broken through the perimeter and the CP was in jeopardy of being attacked," Garner recalled. "Things got tense."

I used the CP group to defend the command post. All except those actually manning radios were in a 360-degree perimeter. We had only M-14s and .45 pistols, but that was all we needed if they got to us. I sent Florian to warn the men on the line of the possible enemy penetration. He completely disregarded the enemy mortar, automatic weapons, and small arms fire as he made his way around the perimeter. During his round, he made sure that all avenues of approach were still covered.

Lt. Borowitz stated, "With the 1st Platoon nearly decimated from repeated frontal assaults, Captain Driver spoke with the 1st Platoon commander, reinforced him, and prepared the CP for an assault."

When Cpl. Sasser told me of his situation, I pulled a squad from the 3rd Platoon, manning the area facing the river, and sent them to reinforce the 1st Platoon. All of the men left in the 1st Platoon, including the wounded, continued to fire their weapons and throw grenades.

PFC Ware and his fire team were dug in facing the river. PFC Robert L. "Snake" Zinkham, his Fire Team Leader, and PFCs Gerald P. Hook and Joseph D. Lorme were with him. They were pulled out to help fill the void in the lines. "I tripped over a dead VC and fell beside him, face to face. I'll never forget that," Ware recalled.

Pfc. Robert L. Zinkham

Pfc. Bill Ware with a Vietnamese family

When large numbers of VC appeared before the 1st Platoon, the three Claymores were set off, causing a large number of enemy casualties. This also created a dust cloud, which the VC used as concealment to recover their dead and wounded. It was also allowed the VC to conduct another assault on the 1st Platoon's positions unseen. Several more Marines were killed and wounded and one rifle damaged. The VC got into the edge of the perimeter near a burning hut, where 4 Marines were dead, 5 wounded and the machine gun knocked out. Cpl. Avila, wounded in the shoulder and back, and having fired all his ammunition and thrown all his grenades, jumped from his hole, yelled, cursed and brandished his rifle and bayonet at them, caused 10 VC to flee. Cpl. Avila was awarded a Bronze Star for his actions. 28 dead VC were found in front of the 1st Platoon's position the next morning.

Avila remembered, "There was a lull in the fighting, and some Marines [Listening Post] yelled 'don't shoot,' and tried to get back into the perimeter. As they crossed the rice paddies, the VC started shooting at them. I shot at the VC. When the fighting was over, they asked me why I was shooting at them. I said I didn't, I was shooting at the VC trying to shoot them. They talked about playing catch with the hand grenades the VC threw at them."

Lawton mentioned, "During a lull, the FO [Garner] and Lt. Loughery showed up. We told them about the mortars beyond the tree line. A few minutes later, that part of the world just began to explode. It was a lot bigger than mortars or 105s. More artillery exploded around our position, but at a distance."

When Florian returned to the CP and reported all the casualties in the 1st Platoon, he volunteered to lead litter bearers to rescue the wounded under enemy fire.

In front of the 2nd Platoon, their listening post fired on numerous VC around some nearby huts. They believed they knocked out a .30 caliber machine gun, as it quit firing. Seven VC bodies were found there the next day.

Machine gunner Bill Spangler recalled, "George M. Graves was the Machine Gun Team Leader on my left facing the river. The machine gun team to their left but facing east was Dan Kumaus and Steve Clemons. The listening post in front of them became engaged with the VC and expended all their ammo and yelled that they were coming in. They all made it in safely and hooked up with Kumaus and Clemons, and the gunners gave them some of their linked ammo to reload their magazines.

"Water buffaloes were driven in front of the VC assault line and sappers coming from the east. The M-79s were used to bring them down because the M-60s were sort of busy. I remember fearing them. While patrolling in a village one day, I walked by one in a bamboo enclosure. It did not like the smell of Americans. It was really steamed. I remember taking my weapon off safety. Kumaus's birthday was the 26th, and he didn't know if he would live to see it."

Garner related, "Seems like the VC were using a herd of water buffalo to our east as cover during the attack. Again, the illumination did a good job of providing targets for our Marines."

Ware stated, "A black Machine Gunner [Pvt. Herbert Franklin] opened fire on the water buffalo and mowed them down. He fired so many rounds that the barrel of the machine gun turned red and was smoking."

"I had dysentery for a while and was some twenty feet behind my foxhole when everything hit the fan," Spangler continued. "I remember the explosions and rounds being fired at us from the east. Franklin was my gunner. PFC Frank Finch was in the hole with me and we threw all our grenades before we could get our heads up. We could hear the thumps as the incoming rounds hit our parapet, as the VC were not more than 20-30 yards from us and they knew exactly where we were. Word came down the line for one man to face inboard because some of the enemy may have gotten inside our lines. A mortar round hit a tree above our hole and showered us with shrapnel and branches, and my rubber lady was shot to pieces. We would fire from our position but dirt from the exploding ordnance clogged the chamber of the machine gun. We had expended most of the one hundred rounds in the belt when it jammed. I then grabbed for more ammunition, which was on a pack board and contained 400 rounds. To my horror, I could not locate it. I had positioned it just above ground right behind our foxhole. I fired all my M-14 rounds and threw all my grenades. Some of the shrapnel

sounded larger than 81s and 60s when they landed. I discovered in the morning why I couldn't locate my ammunition. My pack board had taken a direct hit. There were small links of machine gun ammunition hung in the branches of the tree above us, similar to Christmas tree decorations."

Pfc. Finch & Cpl. Graves, Spring 1966

292

The VC assault faltered and then dissipated in the face of our accurate small arms, automatic weapons, artillery, and mortar fire. The circling Marine flare plane kept our area illuminated during the night.

"After the attack broke off, I was taken from my fire team and moved to the 1st Platoon's position," Hoffman continued. "I helped move the KIAs and took a position and started digging the fighting holes deeper."

"The shooting in the 2nd Platoon's sector slowed and ended while the 1st Platoon was still fighting," related Clemons.

Other than light harassment fire, the attack was completely terminated by 0230. Artillery and mortar fire plus illumination were used until daylight to prevent the VC from recovering their dead, wounded, weapons, and equipment. An observation plane flew over at first light to check the area for VC activity.

"The majority of the action was over by approximately 0300, though I continued to call in missions at 0345, 0400, and 0430," related Garner. "It appears my last fire mission was fired at 0445 as suspected VC in the trees. As the main attack dissipated, I attempted to cover their egress routes with use of VT fuzes and white phosphorous rounds."

'Doc' Harmon noted, "I remember being told there were about a hundred 81 mm fins and two-three hundred 60 mm fins counted the next morning. The VC made a banzai charge using whistles and loud commands, and there were tracers flying all over the area. I made a house call during a lull in the fighting and was told I ran through a wall of tracers. The Marine had a nickel size chunk taken out of the muscle in the back of his neck and was bloody. I patched him up. Later the Chief Corpsman had me out checking over a bunch of the 1st Platoon and getting them ready for medevac. I was one scared HM, shadows moving and intermediate rifle fire from both sides. After things settled down, I dug a hole and sat at the bottom and shook while the artillery shot illumination rounds the rest of the night."

'Doc' Mangus recalled, "I used everything in my medical kit that night."

Medical evacuation helicopters were immediately called in and arrived about 0300. 1st Lt. Ronald R. Borowicz, my Forward Air Controller, and his Sergeant moved out into the rice paddies in front of the 3rd Platoon's position and stood in the open with strobe lights to guide the birds in. It was a tense moment, but the VC didn't fire on them or the helicopters. Both received the Naval Commendation Medal for their bravery. My fifteen most seriously wounded were evacuated. Sergeant Richard A. Eckvall [of Englewood, Colorado], who had just joined the company as the Platoon Sergeant of the 1st Platoon, died a few hours later at 3rd Medical Battalion. The chief corpsman, 'Doc' Dominic Sarinine, and I checked his wounds before he left and knew it didn't look good. He was moaning and had that death pallor look about him.

Doc Harmon recalled helping to load the wounded. "Several had fractures and others had soft tissue wounds. I found out later that I had missed a through and through on one Marine and he died. That still haunts me to this day. One of the corpsmen on the medevac helicopter tapped me on my helmet and it was 'Woodie,' who I had gone through most of my training with." It was pitch black and the corpsmen were working with flashlights.

Florian worked tirelessly to load the wounded on the helicopters, and later helped bring in the walking wounded and the dead, as well as their weapons and equipment. He was awarded a Bronze Star for his actions during the night.

"I helped guide the medevac choppers into the open area immediately to the east of the CP," recalled Garner. "It was a long night in which minutes slipped by like hours."

"I remember lots of flares and in the early morning setting my rifle sling like on the rifle range and shooting and killing anything that moved," Sasser related.

"The company performed magnificently," Garner stated. "The next morning, we mourned the dead who were transported out of the area as we mounted up to continue the operation."

My dead Marines were Cpl. Michael D. "Squirrel" Laux, of Appleton, Wisconsin; LCpl.s William E. Copeland, II, age 19, of Eskridge, Kansas and Gerald A. Letendre, age 23, of East Longmeadow, Massachusetts; PFCs Thomas K. King, age 19, of Commerce, Texas, Clyde D. McDonald, III, of Santa Ana, California, and Samuel M. Ramirez of Artesia, New Mexico. I was particularly moved by the loss of Laux, Copeland, and Letendre, as they had been under my command most of the time since December 1964 and were all going home in a few days. LCpl. Charles N. Rudd of Aberdeen, Maryland, age 22, died of his wounds the next day. He was married.

2nd Lt. Wayne F. Loughrey, the 1st Platoon Leader, was wounded in the arm, but continued to command his men during the night. Armed with only his .45, he fought off the VC trying to penetrate his position. I nominated him for a Navy Cross for his gallant leadership that night. He received a Silver Star. His Platoon Guide, Sgt. Clifton E. Harrison, was also hit. Sgt. Jose R. Martinez, Cpl.s Kenneth M. Antal and Richard M. Carroll, PFCs Fred L. Kane II, John H. Medlin, Michael J. Schroeder, Jerry W. Stevens and Douglas Stewart [of South River, N.J.], and Pvt. Paul W. Lockman were the other wounded men not already mentioned.

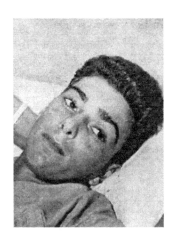

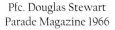
Pfc. Douglas Stewart
Parade Magazine 1966

Metras continued, "We called in the medical evacuation helicopters for the wounded. There was a lot of information being passed on to everyone in the CP, and vise versa. I was receiving casualty reports from the platoons and giving them to Captain Driver and the Battalion Tactical Net Operator to relay back to 2/9. Things settled down about 4 or 5 in the morning. After regrouping the company, Captain Driver had the platoons sweep the areas in front of their positions. I believe we had 16 wounded that we had to evacuate and about 8 killed. We were low on supplies and couldn't get them. I believe at first the battalion said we would be picked up by amphibious tractors and moved up river, but that didn't happen."

Lawton rejoined his fire team at first light. "Avila and Stewart were wounded and Tom King was dead," he recalled. "The only thing I could do was go to the LZ when the choppers came in and load King's body. Now I understood why the old guys did not want to be friends with the FNGs."

Avila stated, "When the fight was over, I checked on the Marines to my right and left. That's when I found Sgt. Eckvoll and that coward Sgt. White. It was still dark when the helicopters came in for the wounded. Someone told me to come on and get on the choppers that were here for the wounded. I said 'I'm not going.' I knew we were short of personnel and we didn't know if the VC were coming back."

"I remember someone asking me if they could help carry my guys and I said no," Sasser continued. "I carried them myself. Copeland was a big guy and it was tough. I was sitting next to my guys wrapped in ponchos and some officer wanted to look under Letendre's poncho. I said 'Sir, he has no face.' He said 'o.k. son, I'm sorry,' and moved on. I remember piling up the dead VC. We checked out in front of our positions 30 yards or so and found CHICOM grenades and a body of a VC, who must have had a satchel charge around him because all that was left was his rib cage. We found a shallow grave of a Chinese [dressed in khakis] who had been hit in the face by an M-60 round. Lt. Loughery had a wound on his upper arm. He told me not to say anything about it, but I believe I told a corpsman. Rich Carroll came by; he had been shot in the arm."

Lt. Borowicz continued, "Captain Driver stood out that night as an inspiration to all those who witnessed his dedicated leadership. Totally disregarding his own personal safety, he calmly and coolly directed his company through one of the major small unit victories of the war in Vietnam. Through 4 solid hours of exposure to enemy fire, this man exuded responsibility to his men and an aggressive spirit, which resulted in a resounding victory. I am proud to have been there and thankful to this day that Captain Driver was in command of Echo Company, 2/9."

Before daylight, I ordered the company on 100% alert. The VC were known to launch attacks then, hoping to find a unit relaxed. At daylight, I ordered the platoons forward about 50 yards to count the VC dead and to gather up the weapons and gear. The platoons started reporting large numbers of VC bodies, weapons, grenades, packs, etc.

The enemy soldiers were so blown apart it was unbelievable. Parts were even in the trees. Heads, arms, legs, brains, intestines, blood trails, and bandages lay everywhere. We settled on 43 VC KIAs (body count). The troopers brought in 1 BAR, 4 K-50 sub machine guns, 5 AK-47 rifles, 1 .03 Springfield rifle, 1 M-1 rifle, 1 M-1 carbine, 5,000 plus rounds of ammunition, 100 grenades, numerous magazines, BAR belts, cartridge belts, packs, gas masks, and sixteen 60 mm mortar rounds. Another 100 grenades, including M-26s, and most of the mortar rounds were destroyed. Based on the blood pools, trails of blood, and drag marks, we were later given credit for 20 more VC KIA. The S-2 of 3/3 also had 20 more probable KIA, plus the 4 found by Sergeant Garcia's squad.

Captured weapons

Two days later, the District Chief of Dai Loc District stated that his agents reported the VC carried more than 100 casualties from the area on the night of 24-25 March. 3/3 added another 60 probable KIAs to our record, making a total of 147.

"We were all given orders to stay in our positions," Schramm reported. "They thought the VC would launch a second attack if they saw us let our guard down. About 0700, Tom Austin and two others appeared out of the tree line that skirted the river, which surprised us. Stunned, I asked where they came from. There was a trail right through the middle of the trees. Since we got back after dark the night before, we never saw it. Tom told me what they had been through that night. They were the 2nd Platoon's listening post. They got out to their position about 100 yards in front of us. When the attack started, they realized they were cut off and decided to make a stand there. About halfway through the attack, they could hear VC moving down a trail that intersected with the one they were set up on. Cpl. Ruiz, his fire team leader, moved them down to the intersection, about 30 yards, and set up an ambush. However, Ruiz forgot to set up a signal to open fire. He thought the automatic rifleman would start it, and the AR man thought he would. Finally, Ruiz fired when the gooks were less than 10 feet way from them. They all emptied a magazine into the 8 VC and then waited. One VC was still alive and threw a grenade. It landed behind them and detonated. Ruiz was hit in the back of the head by a small piece of shrapnel, giving him a slight concussion. The fire team emptied another magazine into the pile of bodies. Then they pulled back to their original position. They were now down to one magazine each. They could hear someone shouting orders from a hut about 30 yards away through the tree lines to their front. They were sure he had to be a commander, so Ruiz told them to empty their last magazine into the hut and then they would get back to the lines. They said they heard a moan from the hut after they fired, so they were pretty sure they got him. They then took off for our lines. They got to the edge of a rice paddy and took off on a run screaming at the top of their lungs they were coming in, and we heard them. After they got in, they realized how lucky they had been that night. The men on the line said there were two gooks lying along a dike firing at our lines. The four Marines ran right between them coming in. The Marines never saw them. Austin was the last one through, and when he tried to hurdle the dike, he tripped and fell. The Marines on the line were horrified because he fell right in front of one of the gook's rifle barrel. Tom got up and finished his run in. Fortunately, the gook was changing magazines. Tom never saw him. He said he was too scared to see anything."

Dan Kumaus recalled the Fire Team running and screaming toward them. "The only problem was that they weren't alone. I had to try and pick the little bastards off their backs without gunning down my own people. It worked but Ruiz went down but got back up, and my heart skipped a beat on that one and I was swearing a blue streak. The gooks that were still standing backed off. I think they were confused because they thought Ruiz's listening post was our lines and when I hit them [with machine gun fire] they did not know what was going on. Ruiz showed me the hole in his helmet and the crease on his head where I think my round went through when I tried to pick a little mother fucker off his back."

"I asked Austin where he had just come from," Schramm went on. "He said the CO wanted them to find the bodies of the VC they ambushed and they did, bringing in 3 weapons, plus grenades, etc. They decided to see where the VC where going. The trail they were on led to a tree line along the river, and that brought them to our position. I remember getting very cold and shaky. The opening was less than 10 yards from our positions. To this day I don't think we could have reacted fast enough to have stopped them. It was obvious that Charlie had staked in most of our positions before dark. Of the two brothers that came in on the supply run earlier that evening, the one in Weapons Platoon was at the back of the perimeter and came through unscathed. The one assigned to the 1st Platoon was now lying covered with a poncho. He didn't even make it 6 hours."

Templeton remembered talking with Austin, who had sprayed the VC behind the paddy dike with his M-14 before dashing toward friendly lines. Templeton shared his remaining ammunition with Austin.

Clemons recalled, "The next morning, we found corpses with weapons just beyond the fence from which the VC were firing on our machine gun position. Only then could we appreciate what the Listening Post went through to fight their way through them and then dash across the field to us."

Jennings continued, "At first light we slowly crept out of the trench and retraced our steps back to the rest of the company. The rice paddies were littered with bodies and pieces of bodies. Echo Company was credited with killing 150 VC that night." [Sgt. Garcia reported his squad killed 4 VC and captured 2 weapons. They found 17 empty 81 mm mortar canisters on their way in.]

"When we got back to the company area, it was as though we had entered some strange slow-motion world. Everyone moved as though they were walking in thick syrup. As we talked about our friends who were killed or wounded, the conversations would often end in mid sentence, and we'd end up just staring off into the distance as if the act of speaking required more effort than we could muster. After 3 days of exhaustion and fear and the shock of a brutal battle, we had been reduced to the level of zombies. This was the state I was in when I started eating my breakfast amid the carnage that morning, cold C-Ration turkey loaf."

Jennings related that morning, "Although it is not yet 9 o'clock, the sun has been up long enough to push the temperature close to 90 degrees. About 10 feet away is the body of a Viet Cong soldier (VC or Charlie) who had been killed during the night. He is lying on his back with arms outstretched and is starting to bloat from the heat. It's been several hours since this particular VC was killed, and he is starting to smell bad, but his odor is lost in the pervading stench given off by scores of his comrades lying in similar attitudes nearby. The VC lying around him were not the first dead men this young Marine [age 19] has seen, but they are surely the most grotesque. One man's abdomen and chest are empty, scooped clean by a large mortar or artillery fragment. Another man has a face but no head. He'd been shot between the eyes at point blank range with a .45 caliber pistol. One body was distributed in roughly even parts to the four corners of a rice paddy square—his head rests in the center. There are no dead Marines here. They are back at the company command post wrapped in ponchos, waiting for a helicopter that will start them on their last journey home."

Lawton related, "We formed up to make a sweep of the area. I was 21, and had never seen a dead body. One VC was right at the edge of Rick Bauer's hole. Not twenty feet from there was a leg complete with a hip, and what looked like a rib cage split open. One of the squad said he fired a burst from his automatic M-14 and the guy blew up. We counted bodies. I think the count was 55. I heard that [Sgt. Albert E. Shults] the Supply Sergeant killed two. We did not investigate the cane field, so I don't know if we hit anyone."

"I was detailed to drag the gooks to a big pile," recalled Spangler. "We burned them later. There were signs of drag marks and blood trails to suggest the VC dead and wounded were moved before day break."

Ware remembered, "It looked like we had killed about 200 of them, from what I saw. We found one still alive with a grappling hook in his shoulder with a rope attached. They had tried to drag him off. He was still alive. One of the men shot him."

Kumaus recalled that Spangler had "a bleached spaced out look and seemed to be out of it and just going through the motions. I think the close shave had an impact on him as it did all of us but in different ways. I was the gunner that night and [Stephen] Clemons was the a-gunner.

"The next morning, we found an 81 mm mortar round about 2 feet from our foxhole stuck in the mud of the rice paddy. Luck was with us that night, and that is an understatement."

I had the platoon leaders redistribute weapons, ammunition, and grenades. When this occurred, Sasser found out a squad leader, Sgt. White, had not fired a round all night and was irate. Cpl. Ray Avila confirmed White's cowardliness. White claimed to have been helping the wounded, but the man he claimed to have helped was killed instantly. Some reorganization had to take place, especially in the 1st Platoon.

I was on the radio with 3/3 immediately after dawn requesting emergency re-supply of ammunition, food, and water. I also had the walking wounded, the dead, our damaged weapons, the captured ones, and 8 large rice drying mats filled with all the captured ammunition, grenades, packs, ID cards, etc. I got a 'Wait, out' from the other end and waited, and waited, and waited. Meanwhile, Metras was giving the casualties by name, rank, and serial number to 2/9. They had to repeat it twice, which seemed to take forever. The wounded sat lined up, lying on the ground, with their wounds bandaged and their medical tags on their collars, waiting to be lifted out. They had that 1,000 yard-stare, from their hollow eyes, as they waited patiently for the birds to arrive. I felt their eyes following me, but they knew I was doing everything possible to get them to the hospital. I was so busy, I'm not sure I ate or drank anything that morning. All I could see was the boots of the dead Marines, wrapped in their ponchos.

About 1100, I received a message from 3/3 telling me to 'Move out.' I asked for a repeat of the message, and got the same reply. I don't know who was on the other end but they got an earful from me. I repeated that it was next to impossible for me to move, as I would not abandon my dead, and they and the wounded would have to be carried or helped along. I was out of 60 mm rounds and low on all other ammunition. I had our damaged weapons, the captured ones, plus all the weapons and gear from our dead and wounded, and all the captured stuff. I refused to obey an order for the first and only time in my Marine Corps career. I got another 'Wait, out.' I was furious at the idea that someone thought we should continue our mission without any consideration for our situation. Finally, about 1200, I was told the helicopters were on their way. They arrived about 1230 and dropped off our supplies, 6 replacements and some ARVN interpreters, and took out everything. Huey gun ships covered them. It looked like half a squadron came to our relief as they continued to land, off load, load, and depart for quite a while. Someone on Hill 55, and or perhaps Regimental or Division Headquarters, had finally gotten the word on our true dilemma.

PFC Buster B. Martin returned to the field on one of the re-supply helicopters. "There were dead VC all over the place," he recalled.

Pfc. Buster Martin

Avila, who could no longer move his left arm (wounded in the back and shoulder), decided he should be medevaced. "I thought I was a liability, so I let someone know. The wounded left on the helicopter which took us to Charlie Med [in Da Nang]."

In my after action report, I wrote, "All of the dead Viet Cong were young males in their twenties. They were dressed in black jackets and dark blue or black shorts. Each had a cord around their wrists and ankles. [So they could be grabbed with hooks if they became a casualty.] All had pink ID cards in their wallets or packs. They were members of A-21, A-22, and A-23 companies of the R-20 or Doc Lap Battalion. Their packs contained food and extra ammunition (as many as 250 rounds, not counting what was in their cartridge belts). Browning Automatic Riflemen had 15 magazines or more. All had numerous grenades of various types. (The first two VC killed had a total of 25 grenades and satchel charges on them). All web gear was in good condition and the ammunition was new. Some wore helmets.

"Commands were given orally without regard to noise discipline. Communications wire was laid within 100 meters of our perimeter and led back to the mortar positions. The mortar positions were located only 200-400 meters from us, the 60 mm being much closer than the 81 mms. The mortars were distributed as follows; 2 60s to the east, 2 81s to the south and 1 60 to the west. Cane stalks were used as aiming stakes. [A patrol from E-2-12 confirmed these locations and reported, 'artillery craters were prominent throughout the area.' The artillery had fired until 0500 the morning of the 25th.]

"The Viet Cong appeared confused when they did not find the command post where they believed it to be and withdrew. They made no attempt to take prisoners, weapons, or to attack positions on their flanks that were firing at them. As many as 200 VC were seen at one time in front of the 1st Platoon, but the VC never took advantage of their superiority in numbers to overwhelm our positions. They were more intent on getting their dead and wounded out. At times, it seemed more VC were doing this than attacking my Marines. As soon as a VC was shot, he was immediately dragged away."

"The assault was confined to this one area although fire was received from 360 degrees. The assault upon the listening post and 1st Platoon commenced with extremely accurate mortar fire, followed by a shower of grenades. This resulted in almost half the casualties we suffered. The M-60 machine gun in this sector took a direct hit, knocking the gun out of action and wounding the crew."

The 9th Marine Regimental Command Chronology made the following observation on the fight: "The preliminary contacts, sequence of attacks, scheme of maneuver, large-scale employment of mortars, use of a diverting force [pinning down M/3/3 by fire], speed, and ferocity of attack once battle was joined and the very evident seeking out of the specific key targets and objectives during the attack, all indicate that this was a well-planned, deliberately executed, and hard fought action conducted by seasoned, well-trained Main Force Viet Cong troops."

PFC Gabriel Coronado returned to Da Nang from R&R in Tokyo that day. "When I got off the plane and walked towards the hangers to get my gear, I saw all these guys lying on stretchers on the ground. One guy called my name, so I headed over to see who it was. There was a whole bunch of men from my platoon, my squad, and my gun team, all lying there on stretchers. I said, 'What the hell is going on?' They started telling me that we almost got overrun the night before, and who got zapped. I wished the men well and headed back into the field where I went back to running my M-60 until I got hit again in La Tho Bac (3) [14 May 1966.]"

Cpl. Gabe Coronado

Schramm continued, "Now, the word came that the machine gun squad leader died on the medevac on the way out. The fatigue was already starting to hit us. Most of us had been with little or no sleep over the last 24 hours. We were sure they would pull us out and replace us with a fresh unit. After all, that's what they did with Fox Company. This was not the case. Word was, the brass thought if Charlie saw us pull out, even with the heavy losses they took, they would claim a victory. Instead, they sent another company [2] to help us track them down, and ARVN interpreters."

As we started to move out, I glanced back at the bunker I was in the night before. There was an 81 mm mortar round hung in the bamboo roof, just about where my head would have been the night before. It would have surely killed Metras and me. I had the engineers blow it in place.

We had only moved about 500 yards when Lt. Borowitz spotted an orange toothbrush sticking out of the ground. I halted the company and sent the engineers to check it out. They dug up an ammunition box full of 60 mortar rounds, grenades, ammunition and other equipment. I had the engineers blow it in place.

"It was stifling hot again," Schramm added. "Within 2 hours, we had captured 4 wounded VC trying to escape. The ARVN questioned them and found out the unit that hit us was 2 reinforced companies, over 350 men. The assault force consisted of 2 full platoons. The wounded VC said that one company was annihilated and the other was in disastrous shape and

303

on the run. Right after that word came from the other company [M/3/3 Captain George Griggs, a Princeton graduate, who I had served with in 1/4 in Hawaii] had found a mass grave with over 100 bodies in it. This picked our spirits up, but the lift didn't last long, the word came that two [1] more of the wounded died.

"We soon arrived at the ARVN outpost that had been mortared so badly several nights earlier. It was set up on a small knoll, with cleared ground for 300 yards around. We held up while Captain Driver went inside and talked to the commander."

I had the company in a diamond formation as we moved so that if we got hit, we had firepower in every direction. As we approached to outpost, the company moved into a large area of paddies and open fields. for the first time in Vietnam, I saw most of my company on the move with the men properly spaced, each one bend over in a half crouch like a boxer approaching his opponent, weapons at the ready; the machine gunners, unit leaders and corpsmen following in trace; all in their proper places. Their small numbers made it easier for me to see this sight.

"After half an hour, it was decided there was a good chance what was left of the unit we were chasing was in a village to the east of the outpost," Schramm went on. "The ARVN commander warned Driver to be careful, as the village was thick with booby traps.

"The village was pie shaped, so we started sweeping it with 2nd and 3rd Platoons, and what was left of the 1st Platoon would skirt along the south side and fill in as the village widened. The ARVN were right, we found 5 booby traps before we got to the first tree line. We were exhausted by now and weren't functioning well. Watching where we were stepping and out in front for gooks was almost too much.

"For an hour or so we moved one step at a time. By now, more than a dozen booby traps had been found, but no VC. At this point we were about three-fourths of the way through. Driver called a halt on a trail that went the width of the village, to get us back on line again. By now we were stretched pretty thin. My team was on the south edge of the village. There was a gate at the end of the trail that led out into the paddies, and it was closed. Brazil and Phillips started heading towards it, so I yelled at them to stay clear of it. Right then McMichael called me, letting me know 1st Platoon was sending some men to help fill in the line."

PFC Jennings noted, "We got a call to move to our left, and inside the village. It was surrounded by a bamboo fence and there was a trail going though a closed gate that led into it. Garcia was walking point for the squad and he headed toward the gate. Several of us yelled at him not to use the gate since it was sure to be booby trapped, but I guess he was so tired and hot that he either didn't care or wasn't thinking straight. He kicked down the gate, took one step, and hit the mine—a 60 mm mortar round. He was engulfed in the explosion and the guys behind him were all hit hard by shrapnel. I think there were four or five guys between me and Garcia, and they were all wounded. Neither I nor the two or three guys behind me were hit. 'Doc' Ward was right in front of me and he took a piece of shrapnel in the head, just below his helmet. He was spun around and knocked to the ground, but before I could react, he was back up and with blood streaming down his face, moving towards Garcia. [Cpl. Alex M. Kulikowich, Jr. and PFC William T. Caldwell were the other wounded Marines, along with Doc Ward.]

"Before I could turn around, there was an explosion that knocked me down," Schramm related. "Screams of pain broke the air, and through the smoke I could see two bodies on the ground. I got to my feet yelling for a corpsman, thinking it was Brazil and Phillips. 'Doc' Ward was already on the way and passed me. As I got closer I could see one of the men setting with his hands back behind him, holding himself up. His legs were gone from the middle of the thighs to the middle of his shins. His boots were lying there in front of him with the stumps sticking out. As Ward approached he kicked one boot out of the way, into the grass on the side of the trail. That sight almost made me loose it. I kept thinking, 'my God, that was his leg.' Then I realized they weren't my men – It was Garcia. I guess I went into shock at this point. I just stood there looking at this horrible scene. The man behind Garcia had one leg off, and there were three more men down behind them. Blood was everywhere and there was a large piece of flesh hanging on the gate. Suddenly there was a voice screaming at me for help that brought me out of it. It was Ward. I stooped down, but didn't know where to start. Garcia had blood pouring out of him from everywhere. He kept asking me if his legs were gone. I laid him back and then two more corpsmen came, so I stepped back out of the way. As I looked up, I saw Brazil and Phillips, they had gone into a hut just off from the gate."

"'Doc' Ward immediately got tourniquets on what was left of Garcia's legs and then started working on the other guys," recalled Jennings.

"By now 8 or 10 more people had come down through there, including the CO and XO and their radiomen, calling for medical evacuation helicopters," Schramm related.

When I heard the explosion, I knew what had happened. I ran down the trail towards the gate, and saw the bloody mess. While the corpsmen did their work, I called in a priority emergency medical evacuation. I recall 'Doc' Ward, with blood all over him, attending to the other wounded. I put him in for a Bronze Star for his heroic actions. We also received some

10 rounds of small arms fire from the village. We returned fire and I sent a platoon to assault the enemy. They returned with 5 VC suspects.

'Doc' Harmon remembered, "'Doc' Mangus stayed back with the platoon and I rushed to the scene. By the time I got there, there was only one casualty who had not been treated. The Marine had MSW [multiple shrapnel wounds] and the other corpsmen were working on him. All the other wounded were ready for medevac."

"Suddenly one of the engineers yelled, 'Don't anybody move,'" related Schramm. "I thought 'my God, what now?' There, in the middle of the path we had all just come down, was a Bouncing Betty mine. Miraculously, somehow we had all missed it."

The reason I, and the rest of my men, had missed it is was the VC had left a wooden stake beside the mine, and when we reached it, wearing packs and radios, we had to step off the paddy dike to get around it.

Lt. Garner was one of the lucky ones. "In retracing my steps on the trail to the casualties, I had run over a Bouncing Betty that was protruding from the ground, "he recalled.

"I remember being very shaky at this point," Schramm continued. "Too much was happening in too short a time. The corpsmen kept working on the wounded and the rest of us started checking the ground for more mines. There were none. By now, the medical evacuation helicopters had arrived but were afraid to land. They said the area was too hot. Driver got on the radio and used language I had never heard him use before. They decided to have us open fire 180 degrees to our front until the choppers got in and back out, which we did."

Harmon recalled that one of the engineers stopped him on the way back and "showed me my heel print about two inches from the nose of a mortar round buried in the trail. Now that shook me. I do remember Captain Driver chewing us out on the fact that the gate should have been opened by line and grapnel."

"After the evacuation we continued the sweep for another 75 yards," Schramm noted. "Then Driver called it off and we were ordered back to the ARVN compound. Things remained quiet until we started across the open area to the compound. We were exiting the village from the southwest corner. 1st Platoon went, then 3rd. 2nd was to pick up the rear. Just before 1st Platoon reached the outpost, we started taking fire from the northwest corner of the village [at 1530]. By the time we were in the cleared area, the fire had become heavy. McMichael told me to set up a base of fire covering the unit until they got to the compound. We found a spot and opened fire. Within a few minutes, most of the company was to the compound and we were down there by ourselves. I thought McMichael would let us know when to pull out, and he thought I would do it on my own. Then I heard him yell. He gave us the double time signal and yelled they were trying to cut us off. We leaped-frogged back to within 30 yards of the gate to the compound and I gave the word to go for it. Rounds were whistling past us and hitting the ground around us. We got to the gate and dove through the opening. None of us got a scratch."

We received about 70 rounds of small arms fire from the village. We fired 200 rounds from our rifles and machine guns, 9 M-79 rounds, 5 LAWs, and seven 60 mm mortar rounds, and I sent a platoon to assault the enemy. My Marines pursued them until losing them in a cane field. We killed one VC, wounded one, and picked up 8 VC suspects, with no ID cards in the village. None of my men were hurt.

"Word came down that we were to stay in the compound that night and the choppers would pick us up in the morning, so we dug in again," related Schramm. "That night, the three of us were sitting around our position talking about what all had gone on the night before and that day. I just could not figure why a man as experienced as Garcia was would try to pull open a closed gate. Especially during the day, and in a village we had already found a dozen booby traps in. We figured it had to be fatigue. By now, most of us had had little or no sleep in over 36 hours. We set up watches early that night and got some much needed rest."

I moved the company outside the compound near a road that ran to it. There were a number of cement buildings along side the road, used as open-air markets during the day. I put the company in a 360-degree defense, using the ditch along the road, the buildings, and tree lines for cover and concealment. I knew everyone was totally exhausted, so I warned the platoon leaders to check their men often and have the listening posts report in every 15 minutes. There was no problem getting the men to dig deep foxholes. The night passed peacefully.

Metras remembered that the villagers "gave us rice and bananas."

"That night I never slept," related Sasser. "I was moving my ammo and grenades around, always at the ready."

"Morning came [26 March] and the word was changed again," Schramm related. "The area was still too hot for the choppers to come in, so we were ordered to head back to the river."

My company and M/3/3 were both re-supplied by amphibious tractors early that morning. By about 0900, we both moved out on our search and destroy mission to the southwest. At 1100, my engineers blew up a large tunnel. An hour later we found a booby trap consisting of two CHICOM grenades and a trip wire. The engineers blew it up.

At 1330, one of my men tripped a booby trap, wounding himself and 3 others. None required evacuation. We were fired on at about 1630, so we returned fire and assaulted the position. The VC escaped into the tree lines.

After we halted for the night, we observed 20 VC moving nearby at 1925. I had Lt. Garner call in a fire mission of 33 105 rounds on them. Four of the VC were seen to fall. They were across a large stream so the area could not be searched.

9th Marines committed two more companies to Operation Kings that day. Following artillery and fixed-wing preparation of the landing zone, Company I, 3/3, Captain William F. Lee, was helilifted into an area just north of the Ky Lam River at 0730. They were about 3,700 meters southwest of my company. Two hours later, Company K, 3/3, under Captain Lyndell M. Orsborn landed 1,500 meters north of Company L. Both companies advanced to the northeast towards route 4. About 1400, Company I ran into heavy resistance near Phu Tay (3) and called in artillery and fixed-wing air support to help defeat the VC. Both companies were heavily engaged again on March 27th.

"When morning came [27 March], so did new word," related Schramm. "Now we were too far west, so they were afraid the amphibious tractors would get ambushed before they could reach us. We were to move 2 more miles east for the pick up."

While the company was moving, we received about 30 rounds of small arms fire at 1120. Because of the location of friendly units, we did not return fire.

"This time it actually happened," an elated Schramm recalled. "While we were loading on the amphibious tractors, one of the crewmen asked McMichael where the rest of us were. 'We were suppose to pick up a full company.' McMichael said, 'You are, and this is it.' The guy got a stunned look on his face and blurted out 'Oh my God.' A T/O Marine rifle company with attachments should be around 225 men. There were only 78 of us left to pick up. Total losses were 8 dead and 23 wounded in less than 24 hours, but Charlie lost close to 300 dead alone. We had done well, but the pain would never go away. These men showed valor and expertise way beyond their years. They were all only Corporals and below and 20 years of age or younger."

Going on an operation

When the amphibious tractors arrived I loaded the men aboard, placing a squad on the top of each one for protection. I had the CP group on top of the 3rd one. These vehicles were only armed with one M-60 machinegun, and I wasn't sure their fire could reach the top of the banks. The banks were 50-75 feet high, and hung out over the river. I could just see the VC firing or lobbing grenades down on us. The ride to Hill 55 went smoothly. We debarked and moved up towards the 3/3 CP. We were met by Colonel Dorsey, Major Dean, his S-3, and some of the rest of his staff, and a host of Marines from their battalion. Dorsey shook my hand and thanked me for a job well done. He also told me I would receive a medal for my actions. We boarded the waiting trucks and motored back to the 2/9 CP.

"We had a formation, Captain Driver was too overwhelmed with emotion to talk to us, so the Company Gunny [SSgt. Kasparian] took over and dismissed the Company," Sasser recalled. "I went to the Chapel right away [and prayed]. Then I went to the 1st Sergeant and complained about Sgt. [Vernon B.] White never firing a round all night [24-25 March]. He said he was helping a wounded Marine but that couldn't have been true because the Marine had too many wounds to be helped. He was already dead."

Schramm recalled that as they headed for the company area they passed by Hotel Company. "They were getting ready to go out. Some smart ass remarked 'I guess we're going out to finish what you guys couldn't,' and a fight broke out immediately, but was quickly contained. These guys would get their night in the barrel soon enough. Before getting some sleep, I wrote a letter home. We left in such a hurry I never got a chance to let them know we were going and I knew they would be worried. We had been gone over ten days and with everything that happened, it was a tough letter to write."

27 March, 2/9 CP:

"Got in about 3 hours ago from the operation—it was quite an experience to say the least. A VC battalion attacked us the first night I was out and we had 8 killed and 18 wounded. We had a bitter three-hour fight and artillery and mortars fired over a thousand rounds in support of us. We counted 43 bodies the next morning, 11 weapons, 200 grenades, 5,000 rounds of ammunition and seventeen 60 mm mortar rounds. They hit us with nearly 100 mortar rounds and heavy automatic and small arms fire. We were told by the villagers that the VC carried off 100 more bodies. [The villagers were forced to help carry them off.] We had a lot of heroes that night and I'm putting in quite a few people for medals."

Ware recalls hearing another broadcast from Hanoi Hannah stating that Echo Company, 2nd Battalion, 9th Marines had been wiped out. It was more like Echo Company wiped out a VC Main Force Battalion.

28 March, 2/9 CP:

"I feel a little more like writing tonight, as I'm not quite so tired. We joined a new Lt. last night, fresh from Quantico, Lieutenant [Robert S.] Fredericks, a graduate of the Naval Academy.

Lt. Loughery was evacuated to the states yesterday. The Stars & Stripes screwed up the story of our fight something awful, but I'm sending it to you anyway.

I've spent all day writing statements for awards for my men. I think we'll have 25 get them."

Schramm recalled, "The next morning they called a company formation. General Walt himself came down to congratulate us on the job we had done. This was always something that impressed me about this man. He always found time to give his men a pat on the back when they deserved it."

Cpl. Sasser and some of the other members of his platoon went to visit Sgt. Garcia in the hospital in Da Nang. "He was asleep and the nurse said that they had only told him he had lost one leg," Sasser recalled. "They were going to tell him about the loss of the other leg later. He had a wooden table across his lower part of his body and he was lying on his back. I figure he could not see that both legs were gone. I never heard from him."

One platoon was sent to secure the 3 bridges on the MSR, one platoon was responsible for the security of the pacification teams in Duong Son (3), and a reinforced squad assumed the Sparrow Hawk role again. I also provided a fire team to the Mien Dong traffic control point. With what I had left, I was to send out patrols and ambushes around Duong Son (2) and (3).

"Scuttlebutt had it that the Battalion Surgeon turned in a report for the third month in a row that the men were suffering from 'combat fatigue' and should be pulled from the field for a rest—and for the third month in a row nobody paid any attention," Schramm stated. "Over the next few days, we caught up on rest while waiting for replacements. I had to send Phillips to the 1st Platoon, so it was just Brazil and I in the fire team.

"One night, while a few of us were sitting around talking, somehow we got on the subject of things we missed. Things we hadn't seen or done since we'd been in this God forsaken place.

"A straight cigarette. One that wasn't bent up or wet from being in your flak jacket, or stuffed in your helmet. Being able to smoke a cigarette at night without worrying about getting your brains shot out. Eating off of a real plate instead of eating out of a can or mess kit. Being able to take a hot shower everyday and put clean clothes on and not be sweat soaked ten minutes later. One that received a cheer from everyone was 8 hours sleep. We had been going on 5 to 6 hours a night for so long—just the thought made everyone drift off to fantasy land for a few seconds. These were things we used to take for granted, and now we were talking about them as if they were luxuries."

29 March, 2/9 CP:

"Another sultry, dusty day in Vietnam. I've spent the day writing letters to the parents of the men who were killed. Fortunately, only one was married.

Lt. Hornick is taking over the company when I leave. He's done a good job as XO and as CO while I was on R&R. Two Marine reporters interviewed me today for a story. At least this one will be the truth.

I got a bayonet for the rifle I'm bringing home. I took it off one we captured the other day."

I reported 3 officers and 154 men on the rolls with 1 officer and 23 listed as non-effectives. They were absent wounded, sick, on leave, R&R, etc. We had received a few replacements.

30 March, 2/9 CP:

"Today was another scorcher! I'll be glad to get out of the heat and dust for a change. The story of our fight is being used by the Associated Press, so look for some stories. I was interviewed again last night."

"A few days after our return, I extended my tour in Vietnam and was assigned to 1st Sgt. Stephenson to become an 0141 [Administrative Clerk]," reported Metras. "I did this for a couple of weeks until the 1st Sgt. sent me to see the Battalion Sergeant Major. I and a man from Company F were interviewed to become the Battalion Commander's driver. Both of us had extended and were company radio operators. The man from Fox Company got the job, but I was sent to regiment. I was interviewed by the Regimental Sergeant Major and got the job as the Regimental XO's driver. I was later assigned as Colonel Simmons [Regimental CO] bodyguard. I was at 9th Marines from May 1966 through January 1967."

31 March, 2/9 CP:

"Good news! I'm leaving on the 2nd for Okinawa! I leave the battalion tomorrow to process out. I was surprised in a way, as the Colonel told Major Angelo he couldn't leave before the 15th. It was just in time, as the company is going back out on the 3rd.
I'll fly out Saturday morning and should fly out of Okinawa the 4th or 5th. That will put me in the states on the 5th or 6th and home the same day or the 7th. I'll probably call you as soon as I get plane reservations to Detroit or Flint."

Second Battalion, 9th Marines reported the loss of 15 KIAs, 3 DOWs, 109 WIAs, and 33 non-battle casualties for the month of March. The battalion was at 87% of T/O strength.

On 2 April, Florian drove me to Da Nang and I started processing out of the 3rd Marine Division.

That morning before I left, we had a change of command ceremony. I turned the company guidon over to Gerry Hornick. Gerry still has the guidon. I spoke to the company and thanked them for their bravery and sacrifice and wished them well. It was an emotional farewell for me.

My return home was relatively uneventful. Everything went according to plan and I flew to El Toro via Alaska by military aircraft. One of the clerks helping to process the Marines coming home at El Toro was Corporal Robert A. Workman, who had been wounded and evacuated in 1965. He had been in my original company in December 1964. Workman had been on unauthorized absence when I took over the company. He was apprehended and returned. The reason he had gone over the hill was because of his girlfriend, that he didn't want to leave. One of the Navy psychologist's from the Naval Hospital at Camp Pendleton came to me and recommended Workman's discharge for antisocial behavior. I listened to the learned doctor's analysis and told him there was nothing wrong with Workman mentally, he was just a teenager who thought he was in love and didn't want to leave his girlfriend. I made the same decision in another young Marine's case, and for the same reason. That private was recently married. Both men were marched aboard ship under guard and served their sentences in the ship's brig on the way to Okinawa. Afterwards, they both did well in training and in combat in Vietnam. Corporal Workman thanked me for not having him discharged, and he had reenlisted in the Corps.

When I arrived in Flint, I was met by my wife, children, and her family. I was amazed at how much my daughter Diana had grown! She was a babe in arms when I left and was now a walking, talking little girl. My son Jett had grown a foot and was quite the little man. Both greeted me as if I had never been gone.

During my leave, I visited the local high schools and talked to the students about my experiences in Vietnam, and how and why I believed the war was being fought. I thanked the Flint students and principal for the soap and other items they had sent, and told them how they were being used. The young male teachers seemed to be embarrassed, as none of them had ever been in the military and had no desire to go to Vietnam.

We soon left Flint and went to northern Virginia to look for a new home for the family. We stayed with Richard Huckaby and his wife Jan and son Steven. Richard was one of my OCS and TBS classmates and carpool buddies. My tour at Headquarters, Marine Corps, would be at least three years, so we ended up buying a house in Springfield, Virginia.

When I reported to Headquarters, Marine Corps, at Henderson Hall, I was disappointed to find that I had been assigned as Assistant Head/Operations Officer, Family Housing Management Branch in the Supply Department. I felt my services could have been better put to use in something pertaining to the war, but I accepted my fate and went to work to learn all about military family housing.

Chapter Fifteen

The War Continues,
April-June 1966
Echo Company, 2nd Battalion, 9th Marines

"By April 3rd the new men arrived," noted Schramm. "I got an 18-year-old private named [Donald L.] 'Donny' Bullard. He, as well as the rest, were right out of boot camp. They were given a couple more weeks of training at Camp Pendleton, a week's training once they got here, and that was it. These guys were really green."

On 4-6 April, Echo Company conducted a 'Rough Rider' convoy escort to Phu Bai without incident. Schramm recalled the operation lasted five days.

Lt. Garner noted that the "Rough Rider" to Hue/Phu Bai was his last operation with Echo Company. "It was a beautiful drive along the coast; nothing ever replicated crossing Hai Van Pass and heading north. It was amazing how beautiful Vietnam was. Upon returning to Da Nang, I was transferred to Headquarters Battery, 12th Marines on 12 April. I had great experiences with the command group of Echo Company, especially my relationships with Bill Coti and Bob Driver. I thought we made a good team, and I put rounds where and when they wanted them. As an old artilleryman, my heart will always be with Echo Company 2/9. I fired the last Marine artillery round from my battery in May 1971, but that pales in comparison to those rounds I called in that night in March 1966, and the reactions I received then (and still receive) from our Echo Marine grunts."

The day after the company returned, Lt. Hornick sent for Schramm. Cpl. Osaw had brought him the news. "What's going on?" Schramm asked.

Osaw replied, "I don't know, it's something about a patrol tonight."

"Oh shit, why me?" Schramm exclaimed.

Osaw got his usual sarcastic look and stated, "Hell, I don't know. You can ask him when you see him."

Schramm went to the CP, and there was a new Lieutenant with Hornick. "Corporal Schramm, this is Lieutenant [James W.] Murphy [a West Point graduate]. You know how we give new men a week's orientation?"

"Yes Sir."

"Well, we have some that have done everything except a night patrol. That is why I want you to take them out tonight. There are five of them, so pick five of your best men and put one with each new guy, and Lt. Murphy will be with you. You'll leave at 2200 out the north gate, skirt along Duong Son (2) to the east end of the village and set up an ambush. You should be there by 2400. If nothing happens by 0200 start back in around the south side. Make sure you radio in when you get to our perimeter, because you'll have to go across our lines getting in the gate. If Charlie does walk into the ambush, take them out and back by the fastest route. These new guys will spook easy, so make sure your men keep them in tow. Any questions?"

"No Sir."

"O.K., Lieutenant you can go. Corporal Schramm stay here a minute.'

The Lt. left the tent.

"Corporal, the reason I asked for you is because you have been here the longest and have the experience. You know and I know this area is fairly secure, but I want you to play this up tonight. If these men get the idea this is just a game, they'll never last once they get assigned to a unit. I want you to scare the hell out of them."

Schramm laughed. "Yes sir, that's no problem."

"One other thing, I don't really think this is going to be a problem, Lt. Murphy is a good man, but I want you to understand—you are the patrol leader. What you say goes. The Lt. is only along as an observer."

Schramm remembered, "As I left the CP, Lt. Murphy was waiting for me. 'Can I see you for a minute Corporal?'

"'Yes Sir.'

"'First of all—can I ask how old you are?'

"I was pretty sure I knew where this was going. 'I'm 21 sir.'

"He looked truly surprised. 'Jesus, no offence, but you don't look it.'

"'No offence taken Lieutenant, but you're sure as hell not the first one that's told me that.'

"'How long have you been here?'

"'Nine months, sir.'

"'Shit, I've only been here nine days and I already hate this place.'

"'God, Lieutenant, don't start thinking that way already, you've got too far to go.'

"'I can't help it. I hate this place. As for tonight, I assume everyone will be camouflaged and their faces blackened?'

"I had to do some quick thinking to get around this one. 'Lieutenant, there are only two ways in or out of this compound. Charlie has someone sitting there watching each one. We don't go out or come in without him knowing it. Stuffing branches in our shirts isn't going to change that. As far as the grease paint on our faces, these guys are lucky if they get a shower every three or four days. In short, we haven't done any of this shit since we landed.'

"He thought a second and then answered 'I know this is your patrol, and I'm new at this—I'll concede the foliage, but I really think the blackened faces are important. They can use charcoal or mud instead of grease paint.'

"'O. K. lieutenant, no weeds, but dirty faces. I'll meet you and the rest of them here at 2130.'

"I went back to the platoon area and rounded up the men I wanted. Brazil, [Thomas L.] 'Uncle Henry' Austin, [David J.] Brown, and Templeton. I briefed them on the patrol and what Lt. Hornick wanted. 'Austin, I want you on the point and I want everyone playing this thing up—any questions? Okay, we'll fall out here at 2115.'

"I headed over to the radio shack to pick up the radio and get our signals set with [Dwight J.] Lawson. Then back to the tent to get myself ready.

"At 2115, I pulled everyone outside and checked them over. This was routine, since these guys had done this many times before. By 2130, we were at the CP. Lt. Murphy and the other 5 men were there waiting. I introduced everyone and checked out the new people, making sure they had everything tied down. After pairing them up with my men, I broke out the map and showed them the route we would be following and where the ambush was to set up.

"'If someone walks into the ambush site, I'll give the signal to open fire. Don't fire until then. Fire a full magazine, reload, and wait for my signal. If there is any movement, we will fire again. Brazil, you and your man will be the search team. I'll let you know when and if you go out. That will depend on what we hit. Any questions?'

"One of the new men spoke up, 'Do you always go out this far?' This received a few muffled laughs from the old guys.

"'This is a short one. Once you get with a unit, you'll be going out 1200 to 1500 yards or more. So pay attention now. If we get hit out there, stick close to your partner and do what he tells you. These guys have been here a long time and know what they are doing. We'll do fine if nobody panics.'

"We moved out the north gate. From there, Austin lead us inside the tree line at Duong Son (2) heading east. There was a half moon, so visibility was good. After an hour, the column headed back out towards the trail on the outside of the village. Suddenly, the signal came back to stop and get down. I had placed Lt. Murphy and myself in the center so we could watch everything. Now the signal came that Austin wanted me up front. My heart began to pound a little faster. I told Murphy to stay put and I headed up front. Austin was crouched near a bend in the trail about 10 yards ahead of the patrol. I got up behind him and whispered, 'What the hell is going on?'

"He looked back with a grin on his face. 'Nothing—you said you wanted us to play it up.'

"'You asshole, you scared the shit out of me.' We sat there for a minute, then decided I'd go back and pass the word he'd seen movement on the other side of the paddies, so everyone keep alert.

"By 2400, we reached the ambush site. I picked a spot 20 yards off the trail with good cover. This was going to be the real test. These guys had to lie in one spot without moving for the next two hours and not fall asleep. I hated being on these ambushes; it always seemed we had a much better chance of Charlie ambushing us.

"The time dragged by, and finally at 0145 I figured we'd been there long enough. I moved down the line letting everyone know we were going to move out. To my surprise, every one of the new men was asleep, including Murphy. I expected to find some of them, but I sure as hell didn't expect to find all of them. I would deal with this when I got back.

"We moved on around the south side to the edge of the compound. I held the patrol up while I radioed Lawson that we were coming in. After trying for 5 minutes, either the radioman was asleep or his radio wasn't working. The only thing left to do was fire a green flare. I didn't really want to do this. The gooks could see it as well as our men. Besides, if someone on the line was sleeping and missed the flare, we would be in trouble anyhow. I tried the radio a few more times, then passed the word I was going to use a flare.

"Two green fireballs shot 150 to 200 feet in the air like a Roman candle. Murphy, who had stayed at end of the column on the return, came scampering up to find out what was going on. I explained what had happened and added 'I passed the word down. Didn't you get it?' He didn't—one more thing we were going to talk about when we got back.

"I started Austin out telling him to stick close to the wire [concertina wire around the compound] and move quickly, then I spaced the rest of the men about ten yards apart. We had about 300 yards to go to reach the gate. The ground was flat with no cover if firing started. I could see the positions stretched out, about 40 yards on the other side of the wire. Did they know we were there? Did they know we were Marines? Damn, where was that gate? I started working my way up front. I knew they would want me to approach the gate to identify the patrol and give a count. Then came that familiar sound that told me we had made it. 'HALT.'

"We moved though the gate and back to the company area. I pulled my men out, sending them back to the platoon area. 'You guys did a good job, go back and get some sack time.' Brazil spoke up 'Are you going to get their ass about falling asleep?' then Austin, 'Yeah, and passing the word?' 'Both; now go get some sleep.' I turned and went back to the new men.

"'Before you leave, I've got a few things to say. First, you had better get it in your heads that this is for real. This isn't a Goddamn field problem at Camp Pendleton. Those little bastards out there have one goal, and that's to kill your ass. Every one of you fell asleep out there last night. If you have any ideas about making it through this next year, that better be the last time it happens. If you end up in my Goddamn unit and fall asleep, you'll have more than just the gooks to worry about. The second thing is about passing the word when it comes to you. I sent the word down I was sending up the flare and it only got about halfway back. Somebody dropped the ball. Like I said, you better start getting it into your heads that this is for real—any questions?' They all stood there like scolded children. 'O.K., that's all, go hit the sack.'

"The whole time Murphy stood off to one side listening. After they left, he came over and said, 'You weren't really scared at all out there, were you?'

"I must have looked a little surprised. 'I don't know what made you think that, sir, but I was as scared out there as you were.'

"'You sure as hell didn't look it,' he replied.

"Without knowing it, he had just told me I was doing something I never thought I was capable of—not looking as scared outside as I was inside. 'Lieutenant, I've had a knot in my stomach ever since the day we landed—I guess after a while, it just stops showing. Besides, you can never let your men know how scared you are. If they think you are scared, you'll have a panic on your hands and you'll lose them.'

"He just stood there for a minute staring at me. 'You did damn good out there tonight Corporal. I hope I see you around here again,' he replied.

"'I'll be around for a while Lieutenant,' I responded and went to my tent and hit the sack."

Lt. Jim Murphy, 1966

Schramm continued, "That same week some shocking news came. Pat Doyle, who had been transferred during the 'Mix Master' had been killed. Pat was the first man from the original squad to be killed in action. I thought of the times we had gone on liberty together. It was hard to believe he was dead."

The battalion command group and companies E & H were helilifted to Da Nang to provide security and supervision for the evacuation of U.S. civilian and military personnel to the Pam Am facility, due to the political unrest in the city.

Schramm recalled, "Riots started in Da Nang. They were protesting the way the government was running the war. After two days, the Company was sent in to help put it down. It was April 9th, Holy Saturday. However, somehow, none of us felt very religious. Fortunately, as soon as we landed, the demonstrators scattered and the thing came to an abrupt end. By 1400, they lifted us back out to the battalion CP. [The CP group and Hotel Company remained on duty in Da Nang until April 11th]."

"General Thi, the Vietnamese Warlord, took his hoard of troops and on toward Da Nang up Route 1," Coti stated. I got a call from Lt.Col. Donahue that General Thi was marching on Da Nang and not to let him pass our position, and that he would get back to me ASAP. General Thi was at the head of his column, riding in a jeep followed by tanks, armored vehicles, and troops as far as one could see. I blocked the road with my jeep and had enough Marines on the road to let him know that he could not get around us. Our interpreter told me that General Thi said that we were to move out of the way. I told the interpreter to tell General Thi that we were not moving out of the way and he was to turn around. General Thi then moved his tanks up to the head of his column, lowered the guns, aiming straight at us, and said to move or he would blow us out of the way. I sent for several 3.5 rocket launcher teams and told them to take up positions on the flanks of the tanks, and to fire if the tanks fired at us, but first to take out the General and his jeep. I then called Lt.Col. Donahue and told him that General Thi was about to fire on our position and that we were ready to counter any threat against us. He said to tell General Thi that he would get his answer shortly from higher headquarters. This message was relayed to General Thi. A few minutes later, a squadron of fighters came in straight at General Thi and his column and made a low pass at them. Shortly thereafter, General Thi turned his hoard around and went back into the mountains."

"We had no more gotten our gear off when word came telling us to saddle up, we were going out again," Schramm related. "This time, we were sent to the west of Highway 1 near our outpost stationed there. There was a lot of grumbling going on. It seemed as if we were the only company in the battalion that was doing anything. Before we left, SSgt. Robinson brought in ten new men. Two of them I recognized from the ambush patrol I had taken out. One of them nudged the guy next to him and said, 'I hope I don't get put with that son-of-a-bitch,' looking over at me. Before I could react to the remark, Jerry Brown, a Lance Corporal who had joined the platoon back in December, before 'Harvest Moon,' stepped in and stated 'You should be so lucky, asshole; he's one of the best NCOs in the company.' I don't know why he jumped in like that, or where his statement came from, but it made me feel pretty good. I made a mental note to thank him later. Two hours later we were moving out.

"The company was supposed to patrol the area, basically looking for trouble. We were on the move the rest of the day, then stopped set up a perimeter for the night.

"The next morning, we started out again. Around noon, we stopped in a small village to eat chow. We set up just inside the tree line around the village. There was another village about 40 yards away, with open rice paddies in between. I took off my helmet and started to eat chow when a shot rang out and the bullet buzzed by my ear. On went my helmet and we dove into the tree line to return fire. It only lasted a couple of minutes and we went back to eating again.

I took my helmet off and started opening one of the cans when another shot came by narrowly missing me. I thought, 'Shit, what the hell is this asshole picking on me for?' This time, the firefight got a little more intense. I spotted one gook firing from a hut directly across from us and nailed his butt right through the clay wall. His body dropped across the doorway. Bullard looked over and exclaimed, 'Nice shot!' When we looked back, his body was already gone. 'Shit fire, there's another one in there!' I exclaimed. The three of us emptied a magazine, firing into the hut, tearing it all to hell, but we had no idea if we hit anyone inside. The firing stopped again, so we went back to finish eating.

"As I started to take my helmet off, Robinson yelled at me, 'Schramm, leave that Goddamn helmet on. What the hell do you think they were shooting at! Your red hair stands out like a beacon around here.' The worst of it was he might have been right, because there wasn't anymore shooting after that."

Templeton and Stein were taking a dump in a rice paddy during a 'take five' that day. "Stein looked at me and said 'The team that shits together, sticks together,'" recalled Templeton, as both were suffering from diarrhea.

"The next two days were pretty quiet, with only a few brief encounters," Schramm related. "The last night we set up in a village just east of Highway 1. We were going back in the next day, and Lt. Hornick decided to only send listening posts out and no patrols.

"By 2230, we had our watches on the line set up. Bullard took the first while Brazil and I got some sleep. An explosion jarred us awake, then screams of pain. One of the men on the listening post had hit a booby trap. Word came down that a fire team with a corpsman was going out. Five minutes later, one of them crawled back in, yelling for a poncho. He was right in front of one of our positions and about ten yards to our left. There were two new guys in the hole. We could hear them muttering, but neither threw out a poncho. The man yelled again 'throw me a poncho—we need it to bring him in.' Still nothing, so I grabbed mine and whipped it out to him. The man crawled back out into the darkness.

"Brazil looked at me and said, 'What the hell's with those assholes?' I replied, 'I don't know, but one of these times it's going to be one of them lying out there.'

"The word came down that the man hit was [William E.] Rogers. Brazil slammed his fist into the ground and exclaimed, 'Shit!' LCpl. Ed Rogers was another one that had been in the platoon since Camp Pendleton. I had a terrible feeling inside and replied, 'I was just talking with him two hours ago. I wonder how bad he is?'

"Almost as soon as they got him in, a helicopter landed taking him out. I have a lot of respect for medical evacuation pilots. Even on a night as dark as this, somehow they would find us when we needed them.

"A short while later, more word came. Rogers' leg was torn up badly. Doc figured he would loose it. He wasn't even supposed to be out there. The men going on listening post were fairly new, so Rogers volunteered to go out with them. I couldn't sleep after that, so I told Bullard to crap out and I'd take his watch.

"The next morning, we headed in and by noon we were back to Battalion. Two hours later, we were going out again. This time to the 'black bridge' [destroyed railroad bridge], stay there over night, then relieve Golf Company at the Song La Tho River outpost. The company would be there for two months. Before leaving the Battalion, we picked up some more new men, including a platoon commander. This time I was glad, as it was Lt. Murphy. For some reason I liked this guy, as he was down to earth."

On 16 April, I heard from SSgt. Nguyen-Ngoc-An, my ARVN interpreter with Echo Company. An, a native of Saigon, had attended college in California before entering the Vietnamese army. He wrote: "Today, I'm very happy to write this letter to you. We just came back from a 5-day sweep in the area of LA-THO-BAC village, in which we've hit VC, pretty hard so far, but this time we didn't have any action, just had some sniper fire at night. [LCpl. Curtis M. Hunter was wounded on this operation.] This morning Echo Company moved to the HA-DONG Bridge to take the Golf [Company's] place. As you know, after your leaving Vietnam, the demonstration situation in Da Nang became very hard, therefore no Marine[s] have been allowed to go out of the CP, and now the people have been striking in town until today. Alternately, I don't forget to thank you very much for the TV set for me. I'm going home on leave in 10 more days. I wish you and your family would have a good time in the States, and don't forget to send my regards to your family. I hope I'll see you back in Vietnam next time."

Two days later, I heard from 1st Sergeant Stephenson. He wrote, "I wanted to let you know that the two packages from the school in Flint have arrived and are being used in the People-to-People program. The selection of items was excellent also. Company E relieved Golf Company at Ha Dong on 16 April and is getting a break as the positions are already set in and the troops have the river for some swimming. Cpl. [William H.] Johnson [Ann Arbor, Michigan], 1st Platoon, was killed by a sniper, and a new man wounded at Bich Nam (1). LCpl. Rogers, 2nd Platoon, was wounded badly by a booby trap and was sent to CONUS. Hotel Company got hit the other morning near Highway 14. They had 6 KIAs and 15-20 WIAs. Lt. [Anthony J.] Battista [Dunsmore, Pa.] was KIA. The VC got a direct hit on an 81 mm mortar position with a 57 recoilless rifle. Golf Company is standing by for a 21-day operation now. We have C/1/4 and G/2/4 here with 2/9 now."

Clemons recalled, "Gerry Hornick was fairly new to us. He was tasked with collecting all the unauthorized side arms. We were promised that if we had any and turned them in, they would be stored by the armorers and people in the rear would make sure that they were waiting for us when it was time to go home. Sure! So some gunny or staff sergeant said to keep them out of sight until the new CO got broken in.

"We were out somewhere near La Tho Bac (3) and the CO and a couple of others were out behind a low paddy dike and out of bullets and working guns. The radioman asked if anyone could help them out. Bill Spanger had a S&W .38 Special service revolver with a four inch black leather gun belt; the kind that goes to police officers (his brother was a police officer). Spangler crawled out into the paddy and slung the pistol to Gerry Hornick & Co. He returned it several days later cleaned, oiled, and with a fresh supply of ammunition. He told Spangler, 'I never saw this weapon and thank you very much.'" The troops had no problem obtaining ammunition for their .38s. The pilots in the Air Wing carried them, so there was a plentiful supply.

Hornick didn't remember the incident but recalled, "That might explain why I later bought a 9 mm Walther P-38 from Jim Murphy. It was one of the few personal items that slipped through the system and was returned to me in the San Diego hospital. I later gave it to one of my Basic School 2nd Lt.s who was on his way to RVN. He said I would get it back when he returned. I never got it back.

"I experimented with carrying several additional weapons; M-1 carbine, shotgun, Thompson .45, French submachine gun, and others. They all 'got in the way' and set a bad example. Officers and staff NCOs were only allowed to carry a .45 at that time. I found the Winchester 12 Gauge riot gun was the best and most reliable for the close-in work, but boy those 12g. 3", double 00, brass shells were heavy. The shotgun was very reliable in extreme conditions and easy to clean and maintain. I remember that some of the Corpsmen carried them.

"During a brief period the rifle companies were allocated Model 70 Winchesters, 30-06 with Unertal scopes and match ammo, because the Corps didn't have any 'official' snipers at that time. We had a LCpl. in our Company who carried two sniper rifles, one for him and one for me, as a backup. He and I would 'practice' on VC who would harass us from time to time."

"We got to the bridge by 1500 [16 April]," Schramm continued, "and since there was a unit manning the position already we didn't have much to do the rest of the day, so most of us went down to the river and took a swim. Back home, none of us would have gone into water this dirty, but here nobody gave a shit—it was wet.

"The next morning, we moved to the outpost. This area was set up differently than the battalion CP or the outpost on Highway 1. The main section was on the north side of the river and was completely covered with sand. There were three tents, one for each platoon to store their gear in, and a mess tent set up 50 yards outside the main perimeter to the west. The bridge across the river had been blown so the engineers constructed a pontoon footbridge to the other side of the river. The south side was much smaller and was considered the hot side. Bunkers were built from the river on the east side in a semi circle over to the river on the west side. Triple concertina wire was strung in front of the bunkers. The positions were so close that there was only 20 yards between the wire and the bunkers. Outside the perimeter rice paddies stretched out to the nearby villages. However, on both sides, heavy brush came up to within a few yards of the wire. Claymore mines were set up just inside the wire about 10 yards apart.

"On the north side, the main perimeter had a trench around it, again running from the river in a half circle around back to the river. There were underground bunkers inside the area for the company and platoon CPs. They also had two tanks dug in, one on each side of the river. The sand, which had been trucked in, covered an area 200 yards square. Two strands of triple concertina set ten yards apart stretched around the area, including our tents. On this side, along with the claymores, there were 55-gallon oil drums filled with Napalm buried with explosive charges underneath. These were spaced about twenty yards apart. If Charlie tried to take this outpost, he would pay severely for it.

"The company was set up with one platoon on each side of the river, and the third would go out patrolling for two days, so after four days in we would go out for two days. We got the south perimeter first and I was glad, as it would give us some time to get a feel for things.

"I received a letter from my dad that day explaining that my letters home were upsetting my mother, and to tone them down, and send him a separate one at work, if I needed to get more off my chest.

"1st Platoon left that afternoon for their two-day patrol. Twenty minutes later we heard an explosion. They hit a booby trap, four men hit, one killed. The next day, they lost two more men to booby traps. They came in that night after midnight, and the 3rd Platoon went out the next morning. We moved to the bunkers on the north side. The 3rd Platoon hit booby traps and had casualties every day they were out."

From a radio message Hornick recalled, "Four more of my men just got it from a Bouncing Betty. One killed and three wounded. The kid that was killed was a new man [PFC Martin Robinson, acting as a radio operator]. This was his first patrol. You learn the basic things fast," he continued, having been wounded himself by a mine himself a few days before. "You look for the trip wires or a scuffed-up place on the trail that might mean a mine underneath. You keep thirty yards between men so that one mine cannot kill more than one. After that, it's a developed instinct about where a mine might be, not something you can explain or teach. This kid today never got a chance to learn."

Clemons recalled that the patrol on 17 April was lead by a new NCO, Cpl. Robert M. Banks. Robinson was his radioman. 'Doc' Harmon was among the wounded but "still walking long enough to try to save PFC Robinson." The 40 mm grenadier was wounded in the hand, as was Clemons. Banks was also hit. "The radio was damaged too badly to function, so two of us jogged back to the patrol base [Ha Dong bridge] to get help. As we returned to the village, completely out of breath, a helicopter was arriving and took several of the wounded out. Corporal Banks and I walked back with those who were left of the patrol. There was a ¾ ton ambulance waiting for Banks and me. A Navy Corpsman drove us to Charlie Med for outdoor backyard shrapnel removal. When the Corpsman drove us back to Ha Dong afterwards, he was pissed off because he did not want to drive anywhere near our area. He was right, too." PFC James A. "Arkansas" Rogers was one of the badly wounded. HM3 Mike Harmon stated he was evacuated to the hospital ship U.S.S. Repose along with the other seriously wounded.

An Echo Company ambush engaged an estimated 10 VC on the night of 17-18 April and suffered one Marine wounded.

"Now it was 2nd Platoon's turn," noted Schramm. "We went out and headed west to the first village. My insides were turning upside down. I hated mines and booby traps more than anything. At least with Charlie you could fight back, but once those things hit it was over, and they could be anywhere.

Inside the village, we rounded up several suspected VC and had to wait while a fire team took them back to the outpost and return. Then we moved through two more villages and ended up with half a dozen more suspects. We knew that most of them were not VC, since they already had two or three suspect tags on them, but it was necessary to take them in anyhow. My fire team took the second group in. We were out far enough now that it took a good hour getting in and back.

As we reached the platoon, we heard a shotgun fire on the far side of the hamlet. It was Robinson. He was talking to one of the fire teams when they spotted a gook crawling away from them. Robinson wheeled around and the gook tried to run just as Robinson fired. The blast caught the gook in the lower back and rear end. It's pretty incredible what 00 buckshot will do at close range.

"By now, it was mid-afternoon and the word came around we were to set up a perimeter. Since it was hotter than Hell, it was a great idea. We wouldn't be moving around and the trees gave us some shade.

"Within half an hour, Lt. Murphy came around and explained his plan for the night. 'I want everyone to dig in like we are going to stay here for the night. Then, after dark, each squad is going in a different direction setting up an ambush. Osaw, I want your squad to go the area just below the railroad bed [about 75 yards away] and set up facing the village. Hopefully Charlie will come in tonight, thinking we are here. When he comes out on this side, you'll be waiting.'

"The idea sounded pretty sound, since they had already been probing us. He showed us where the other squads would be setting up. He was going with the 1st Squad and Robinson would be with us.

The rest of the day was spent making it look like we were digging in. After dark, we slipped out to our ambush site. Osaw, Robinson, and the second and third fire teams set up on a line parallel to the village ten yards east of a trail running along there. My team was rear security. We were to set up along the top edge of the railroad bed, but once there, we found a bamboo fence running along the base as far as we could see in either direction. I sent Brazil and Bullard 50 yards in either direction scouting for an opening, but it was too thick, and this wasn't the kind of stuff you forced your way through, as they were usually booby trapped. We were twenty yards behind the squad, but it might as well have been a mile. There was no moon, and heavy cloud cover, so visibility was five yards at best.

Two hours went by, then, from the far side of the railroad bed, we heard a sound that was becoming too familiar, a mortar firing. Within a few minutes the round landed to the northeast. Bullard whispered 'Who's firing and at what?' Brazil and I already knew it was Charlie, and from the direction, the target had to be the Highway 1 outpost. Another round went off, and Brazil grabbed my arm. 'It sounds like they're only 50 to 60 yards away.' I was trying to place what was over there. Past the railroad bed was a 75 yard-wide dry rice paddy, then a village. 'They must have come out of La Tho Bac to get clearance from the trees. It sounds like they are set up in the paddy.'"

While Brazil hunted for an opening in the bamboo fence, Schramm sent Bullard to tell Osaw what was going on. Once he got him oriented, he sent Bullard on his mission. Bullard went through the ambush site without finding them and returned. Meanwhile, Brazil and Schramm had been trying to force an opening through the bamboo fence without success. The VC were mortaring away at the outpost. When a flare went off, Schramm was able to point out the squad to Bullard, who had walked right through them all the way to the tree line by the trail. The VC suddenly stopped firing. By the time Schramm reached Osaw he was hot, as the ambushers had all gone to sleep, and Bullard had walked right through them. None of the men would admit to going to sleep, but they had. Robinson explained to Schramm that he would take care of the men who had fallen asleep later.

"When morning came, we joined up with the others and continued our patrol," related Schramm. "The rest of the day was pretty quiet and by dark we were back in the outpost.

"The next morning, we took over the south side positions again, and 1st Platoon, instead of going on patrol, received orders to act as a blocking force for an ARVN sweep in a village to the southeast.

"As I sat eating chow, I realized it was the 21st of April and I had completely missed my birthday. Suddenly, my thoughts were broken by an incredible explosion. We could hear agonizing screams. A radio message came for help. 1st Platoon hit a big booby trap and had mass casualties. A squad from 3rd Platoon went out with every corpsman in the company. It seemed that no matter what was going on, 1st Platoon always got the worst of it. They still were not recovered from 'Operation Kings' [24-25 March]. Now scoop was coming fast and furious. Five men for sure lost both legs, multiple others with arms, hands, and fingers taken off. Once the squad and the corpsmen got there, new reports came—so many men down they didn't know where to start. It took almost an hour getting them medical attention and evacuated. Those that were left standing came back to the outpost. There weren't enough left to continue the mission. Out of 35 men in the platoon, 27 were evacuated as casualties.

"The only good thing about this whole mess was, somehow, at least at this point, they were all still alive. Those that went out said they had never seen so much blood and gore. It was a booby trapped 105 mm round. The man hitting it was blown 15 feet in the air. My buddy from weapons platoon, Gabe Coronado, ended up with the Silver Star for his incredible actions during the whole thing. They said he helped patch up so many guys they lost count."

Lear was with the 1st Platoon when they hit the booby trap. The Platoon Commander, Lt. Fredericks, had been advised not to go into that tree line, as the Vietnamese civilians even avoided it. Fredericks had told SSgt. Kasparian that he didn't need his advice, nor would he listen to his platoon sergeant and squad leaders who had been in that area before. The fire team that entered the tree line first all died.

Also on 21 April, a patrol detonated an M-26 grenade booby trap and had one man wounded. The next day, a patrol engaged 4 VC and exchanged fire. One Marine was wounded in this action. That night, another Echo Company ambush struck a booby trap while moving into position, resulting in 3 Marines being wounded.

Schramm said, "By the 23rd, we were manning the north side of river. Two more days and we'd be going out again. 1st Squad went on a perimeter patrol about 1000 hours. We were cleaning our weapons and writing letters. Fifteen new men came out to help fill in what was left of the 1st Platoon.

"Suddenly another explosion from in the same village. It seems now, every time it happens everyone's guts are tied in knots. This time it was 1st Squad. As the first messages came in they seemed to be in a panic. Lt. Murphy got on the radio and tried to calm them down. They apparently were going through a tree line when the fourth man through stepped on a 'Bouncing Betty.' It got him plus the man in front and behind. Medevacs were called in, but [Martin R.] Robinson [of Verona, Pa. age 20], the man who hit it, died before they arrived. The platoon had suffered its first KIA. This poor guy had only been there a little over a month. It put the whole platoon in a real downer. He was only 18. We were beginning to wonder what this was all about. We didn't seem to be accomplishing anything, but getting ourselves shot up or blown to hell, while the people back home were condemning us for being there." Doc Hamilton was again among the wounded, and was sent to the *U.S.S. Repose*. He didn't return until August 1966.

"The next morning, Lt. Murphy asked Lt. Fredericks from 1st Platoon to hold a prayer service," Schramm noted. "He was a deacon in his church back home. After that, some of the men took up a collection and asked me to ask my dad to send flowers to Robinson's parents with a card from the platoon. It was one of the toughest letters I had to write. God, I wanted to get out of there.

"The 25th and 26th, we were out again. Nothing much happened on this one. Osaw moved Bullard out of my team and replaced him with [PFC Willie Lee] Parks. After that, I figured things couldn't get worse. As far as I was concerned he was the biggest shit bird in the platoon. All he ever did was brag about how tough he was, but every time the shit hit the fan, we'd have to go find him.

"After we got back, it was 1st Platoon's turn again. This time I think they were glad to be going out. On the morning of their second day, skirting the edge of a cane field, two gooks walked out right into them. One was killed immediately and the second captured. They reported that both had all kinds of booby trap equipment on them. Lt. Hornick sent word to bring him in—alive. I was on the gate when they brought him through—or I should say dragged him through. They apparently worked him over the whole way back. 'He doesn't look like he's had a very good day,' I said. One of them looked at me with a grin 'the CO said he wanted him alive—but he didn't say how alive.'

"The next few days went by too fast and we were heading out again. Most of the first day was pretty quiet until late afternoon. We were heading south, and as we entered an open area between two villages they were waiting. A big firefight broke out. My fire team was in the rear as 'tail end Charlie.' We couldn't do anything but watch the rear and keep our butts down. Brazil was getting antsy, 'Come on, let's get up there, we're missing it all.'

'Settle down man, we're supposed to be covering the rear,' I replied. The firing was at fever pitch at this point. Now I was getting antsy. SSgt. Robinson was just in front of me. 'SSgt. Robinson, can we move up on the line, there's nothing happening back here.' Robinson got a smile on his face as said 'O.K., go ahead, I'll cover the back.' As we started crawling up, the rounds were flying just inches above us. I thought to myself, 'What the hell are you doing?' I yelled to Brazil, who had taken the lead, 'You are going to get my ass killed yet—I'm getting too short for this shit.' I heard him laugh but he never looked back. It took a couple of minutes to work our way up front, and we had no more than gotten there and the gooks broke contact. We moved across the opening into a village and set up a perimeter. A medical evacuation helicopter was called in to take out the three wounded Marines.

"We set up in an old bombed out hut. It was set out a little farther than the rest of our positions, but it gave us excellent cover and visibility. 'Joe, take Parks with you and get the canteens filled,' I stated. 'They say there is a well in the village. I'll watch things here.' As they left I hollered to Brazil, 'Watch your asses in there.'

"As I stood watch out front, it seemed so quiet and peaceful. It was hard to realize a few minutes ago we were in the middle of a firefight. Something caught my attention out of the corner of my eye. It was Lt. Murphy coming to check out our position. He came into the hut and looked around. 'Where the hell are your men, Corporal?'

"'I sent them after water, Sir.'

"'You are out here by yourself?

"'Well, there are positions on both sides of me Sir.'

"'Doesn't this bother you?'

"'No, Sir.'

"He shook his head with a puzzled look on his face, then changed the subject. 'You're getting real short aren't you?'

"'Yes Sir—at the longest, I should have only one more 2 day patrol to go on.'

"Then he spoke with a serious look on his face, 'You know, if this wasn't such a God forsaken place, I'd try talking you into extending.'

"I took that as a compliment and answered, 'Thank you Sir, but it is and I won't.'

"He laughed, paused for a few seconds and stated, 'Could I ask you to do me a favor?'

"That sounded like a loaded question coming from an officer, and I replied, 'If I can, Sir.'

"He proceeded to ask me to visit his girlfriend if I got stationed in the Washington, D.C. area. I had an older brother living there, so I agreed.

"About this time, Brazil and Parks got back. He talked to them a few minutes and then left. I told Brazil what had happened. He was almost as surprised as I was. 'He's a pretty cool guy isn't he?' I agreed; that was exactly what he was, a pretty cool guy.

"Within an hour we started moving again, this time heading east, continuing until just before dark. We then set in for the night. The hours went by slowly, but without incident. Charlie must have had enough for one day.

"After chow, word came that Osaw was going in to go on R&R. Our squad was taking Osaw in. We were about 1,000 yards, so it took a while to get back to the outpost. Osaw gave me his map and compass and off he went for five days in Bangkok.

"Before the squad moved out, I moved Brazil up to fire team leader. This didn't go over too well with Parks, as he was a month senior, but he'd have to get over it. I figured he had enough trouble taking care of himself, much less a fire team.

"The platoon had moved to a new position in a village, and it took us a good hour to get there. The village had one main area and a smaller area on the west side, where we were going to set up. Lt. Murphy liked to work at night, so we spent the rest of the day making it look like we were digging in to stay. At 1600, Murphy came over to show me were we were going that night. We walked to the far western edge of the village, staying in the tree line. Just past the trees was a large dry rice paddy that went west to the railroad bed 500 yards away. There was a brush filled field 50 yards southwest of us that went west for another 30 yards, then turned into a tree line and a village, again stretching to the railroad bed. A trail came out of the village, skirted the field ten feet in from the paddy for about 30 yards, then turned south. We were to set up an ambush along the area by the paddy. I was to leave two men here at the edge of this village as rear security. I didn't like the layout of this ambush, and told him, 'Lieutenant, there's a ¾ moon tonight and no cover along the edge of the paddy. We'll be lying out in plain sight.'

"He didn't even hesitate before answering, 'If your men lay still, they'll be fine. If you hit something in the ambush, radio second squad after it's secure and head for their location,' pointing to the map. 'If nothing happens, head in to the outpost at 0400.'

"'Yes Sir,' I replied, and he headed back to the other area.

"I called the fire teams' leaders together and briefed them. After going over the plan, I received the same reaction from them as Murphy got from me. PFC [Curtis H.] Hunter spoke up, 'I don't like the looks of this one. Charlie's going to spot us long before we spot him.'

"PFC [William] Kruger added, 'If the gooks come through this village, what's rear security supposed to do, run across 50 yards of open paddy to let us know?'

"Hunter stated, 'Schramm, you are getting too short for this shit.'

"I stepped in. 'Okay, I agree it's not the greatest spot, but that's what we've got, now go back and brief your men.' Hunter and Kruger left but Brazil waited. I knew he wanted to talk to me alone.

"'Joe, you didn't say anything,' I asked. 'What were you thinking?'

"'I don't know—with no cloud cover, we're going to be sitting ducks.'

"'I know, I've got to do some thinking,' I answered, and he left.

"At 1900, I passed the word to saddle up. We moved over to the edge of the tree line. Kruger and Hunter came up. Kruger spoke first. 'We've got an idea. There's a big crater in the top of the railroad bed about 100 yards north of the village.'

"'Yeah,' I replied.

"'Well, if nothing happened in the ambush, we were supposed to head over there and into the outpost aren't we?'

"'Yeah.'

"Now it was Hunter's turn. 'Look at it out there—with the moon, it's almost daylight. Why can't we just head for the railroad bed now and set up in the crater. There's open paddies on either side and the village is a hundred yards away. Up there, we can watch the whole area.

"I stood there thinking for a few seconds, when Kruger jumped in again. 'Come on man, you are too short for this crap.'

"'Yeah, and you are just doing this to protect my young ass, right?'

"They both laughed 'NO—we're trying to protect all our asses.'

"I looked at Brazil, who hadn't said a word, as usual. He shrugged his shoulders and said, 'It sounds like a good plan to me.'

"I thought a few seconds and then told them, 'Okay, but we've got 500 yards of open ground to cross getting over there. We will move slow, low, and quiet. If we get hit along the way, or once we get there—we're in deep shit. Nobody will know we're there, and nobody's close enough to help, anyhow. Brazil you take the lead. Put Parks on point. Stick close to the edge of the paddy, but down in it. I'll be behind you, then Kruger's team. Hunter, you pick up the rear. Keep it spread out—okay, let's go.'

"Hunter was right, I felt like everyone in the area could see us. We moved through a small graveyard. Brazil and I were keeping a close eye on Parks. He had only run point a couple of other times. As he passed between two mounds, we both saw it at the same time—a bamboo branch stretched between them—he hit it before we could even react. We dropped to the ground, the rest of the squad followed suit, but nothing happened. Parks turned around, and bewildered, he brought his rifle up thinking we had seen something. I scrambled up to him. 'Jesus Christ Parks, didn't you see that branch?'

"'Yeah, so what?'

"I was straining to keep my voice to a whisper, 'You are lucky your ass is still in one piece. By all rights, that should have been booby trapped and you walked right through it.'

"I could see by the look on his face he realized what he had done. 'Oh my God, oh my God, you've got to get somebody else up here. I don't know what the hell I'm doing.'

"'Settle down, man, just watch where the hell you are walking.' We started on again. It took almost an hour and a half to get to the crater. Once we got there, the first thing we did was check for booby traps. Then I set everyone in. It was going to be a long night.

"Just after midnight, heavy firing erupted in the area south of us. Within a few minutes, flares lit up the sky.

"Kruger whispered, 'Somebody is in the middle of it.'

"I checked the map and replied, 'It's got to be the ARVN outpost over there.' The firing raged for almost an hour, then began to taper off. The ARVN held their position since they continued to send flares up. Twenty minutes later [Cpl. Steven] Lambert nudged me and pointed in the direction we had come from. I looked over the edge of the crater. In the dim light we could make out the figures of 7 or 8 VC as they headed out of the tree line, right down the trail and through the ambush site we were supposed to be in. I rolled over on my back and thought, 'Son of a bitch—SON OF A BITCH.'

"Brazil crawled over, 'What's wrong?'

"With a disgusted tone in my voice I whispered, '7 or 8 gooks just walked through our ambush site back there.'

"He looked, but they were gone. 'Are you sure?' he asked.

"Kruger spoke up, 'It sure looked like it.'

"Over the next two hours, things settled down, and by 0330 we headed in. After entering the outpost, we moved across to the north side and found a place to crap out and fell asleep.

"Just after the sun came up Robinson kicked my boot. I woke up and realized I was already sweating in the heat. 'Schramm, get your men down to chow, and then go to the CP. The Lieutenant wants to see you.'

"After taking a few minutes to rouse my men and send them to chow, I headed on to the CP. I felt that Murphy had found out we skated on the ambush, and if that was it, I was in deep shit.

"As I approached the bunker, Robinson and Murphy both came out. My palms began to sweat. Murphy looked up at me and said, 'Have you been expecting a birthday cake?'

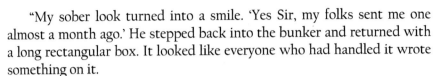

"My sober look turned into a smile. 'Yes Sir, my folks sent me one almost a month ago.' He stepped back into the bunker and returned with a long rectangular box. It looked like everyone who had handled it wrote something on it.

"Then came the usual questions: 'How old are you?' 'When was your birthday?' 'You sure as hell don't look that old.' 'Are you shaving yet?' I, off course, was getting use to this shit now.

"As I turned to leave with my cake, Murphy stopped me again. 'Hold on,' he said, 'I have one more present for you.'

"I expected him to reach back in the bunker for another package, but instead he got a big smile on his face. 'Pack your gear, Corporal, you are going home!' A shockwave went through my system like I had never felt before. I guess I just stood there with my mouth hanging open, and he and Robinson laughed. 'Did you hear me Corporal, pack your gear, you are going home!'

"My insides were ready to explode, 'Oh my God! This is for real?'

"'It's for real, you and [Cpl. David G.] Stein.'

"From there on, what happened was a blur. Murphy filled me in on what to do to check out. Then I shook their hands and headed for the platoon tent. As I entered, Brazil was waiting. 'What's up?'

"'I'm going home, man, I'm getting out of this Goddamn place.'

"I could tell by the looks on their faces they were glad and envious at the same time. I passed out my 782 gear to guys that needed it. They only required me to keep my helmet, rifle, and one magazine for the trip back to battalion.

"The platoon moved over to the south side of the outpost taking over the positions for the next two days. I told Brazil to get the squad over, and I would be there in a few minutes. It was only a half hour before I left. 'What the hell are you coming over there for? Pack your gear and get the hell out of here,' he replied. 'I've got something for you before I leave. I'll bring it over in a few minutes.'

"After packing everything and moving it out to the staging area, I grabbed the cake box and headed across the pontoon bridge. Crouching low and moving fast, I wasn't going to give Charlie a last chance at me before I left. When I reached the squad I opened the box. We stood there staring—the cake was perfect, none of icing out of place. Bullard broke the silence. 'Christ, it's in one piece, what the hell did they do, hand carry the thing over here?'

"I took Brazil's K-bar and began to cut it. 'This is for you guys, since I'm leaving. I'll cut it, then my ass is out of here.' Even though I couldn't wait to get out of there, leaving them was one of the toughest things I ever had to do. We had become like brothers, and I knew once I left, I would probably never see any of them again.

"They sent a man out to pick us up in a [mechanical] mule. Stein and I told the driver to put the pedal to the metal and don't stop until you get us to battalion. It was a two-mile run through Indian country and we only had one magazine each. The driver laughed and said, 'No sweat, I make this run every day –USUALLY nothing happens.'

"We spent one day at the battalion turning in our gear and checking out. They had the rifle we captured on 'Harvest Moon' for me, and the paperwork to get it home. We spent a day at the Da Nang airstrip filling out debarkation papers to go home. On May 4th, we loaded on a C-130 and it took off. All the way out, until we were over the ocean, I was waiting for something to happen, someone saying, 'it ain't over yet pal,' but it was. In the 10 months I was there, we had cleared 57 villages and participated in 6 major operations. Of the original 15 men that remained with Echo Company after the 'mix-master' transfer during October and November, only LCpl. John Templeton and SSgt. Clarence Robinson and myself would leave without wearing a Purple Heart.

"We spent 3 days on Okinawa under quarantine to make sure we weren't bringing and diseases back with us. The first night there, I spent an hour in the hot shower washing. It was the first time in a year that I felt clean.

"They flew us to El Toro Marine Air Station in California. After a short 'Welcome Home' ceremony, we headed for town to a bus station that had telephones. As I placed the call home, I felt like a kid calling his first date. My mother answered the telephone. 'Mom, it's Mike—I'm home.' It was Sunday, May 8, 1966—Mothers Day."

Clemons wrote that the company visited a South Vietnamese fort that was later abandoned when the soldiers went to participate in the political standoff in Da Nang. "We were out of C-Rations and they sold us some cooked rice from bags marked with the Hands Across the Sea logo. The CO and the Gunny put up 50 MPC scrip for the rice, but tried to hide the fact so we would not get pissed off at our valiant allies."

Lt. Hornick wrote on 2 May, "The Company you heard about being hit was Hotel. The ARVN abandoned a fort on Hwy. 14, leaving 13 tons of munitions [and 4 105 howitzers.] Hotel had the job of stopping the VC from getting their hands on it. They didn't make it. Hotel had 7 KIA and 37 WIAs. Hotel only got 12 VC KIA, but figures on a lot more. Golf Company went down to reinforce them and ran into Bouncing Bettys that the VC recovered from the fort. Lt. Sutton and 12 others were hit. Lt. Sutton will be blind for the rest of his life. They hope to save most of his face.

"As you have probably guessed, VC activity has really stepped up in my TAOR (Ha Dong Bridge). We've had 39 casualties in the last two weeks— 5 KIA and two more fighting for their lives. Killed were PFCs [Martin R.] Robinson [of Verona, Pa.], [David] Stevens, Jr. [age 20, of Philadelphia, Pa.], [Edward R.] Luff [age 23, of Pittsburg, Pa.], Sgt. [Walter L.] Pumpelly [a Mexican national, age 24 and married], and [Joseph A. Cruz [age 20, of Merico, Guam.] [PFCs Ralph] Basiliere [Haverhill, Mass.] and [Sherwin C.] Schoppe[age 20] are the critical ones." Schoppe, of San Antonio, Texas, was hit by a Bouncing Betty tripped by another man, and died from his wounds on May 27th. Basilere died later also. Lear, who visited him in the hospital, said his face and upper torso were all torn up. He told Lear, "I'm not going home like this." His wife had just had a baby. He later pulled all the tubes out of his body and died.

"Lt. Fredericks was badly wounded when his platoon took 20 casualties from an enormous booby trap. As you can imagine we're really short handed (107 fighters) with no promise of replacements." Fredericks was warned not to go through the "No Name Village," Bich Nam (1) as we called it, because we had always been fired on from there and found booby traps there. Instead of taking a route around the village he chose to go through it with the above results.

On 29 April, the 1st Platoon under Lt. Fredericks was en route to reinforce Company H's CP, which had only tanks, Ontos, and 81 mm mortars defending it. The platoon entered Bich Nam (1) from east to west with two squads up and one back. As they moved through the eastern edge of the village, someone tripped an 81 mm mortar round booby trap placed 4 feet off the ground. The explosion was so great that men were hit 100 meters away from the blast. Steel pellets had been placed inside the round to create more casualties. 20 Marines were hit in the initial blast, 1 was KIA immediately, and 4 others died soon after, and they were among 7 critically wounded medevacs. Of the total of 15 wounded, only 4 did not require evacuation. The rest of the battalion only lost 2 killed and 17 wounded during April.

PFC Ed Gorman, a Machine Gunner, recalled, "My team consisted of Jenkins and McRossin, and I had just moved away from them a little when the booby trap was tripped. They both had shrapnel wounds and I was lucky and only got knocked down to the ground by the concussion."

Lear, who was two men back from entering the tree line, was not hurt. The survivors were incensed at Lt. Fredericks for causing the casualties by not listening to the experienced NCOs. While he was crying over losing his platoon, one Machine Gunner pulled his .45 and was going to kill Fredericks if Lear had not stopped him. The same Marine was so angry at the VC that when a bunker was found with people inside who would not come out, he threw a grenade it, killing them all. They turned out to be civilians. He had to live with that rash decision.

"I remember trying to figure out what the hell happened," noted Kumaus, "and I talked to all the guys who walked through the tree line. They all said they followed the guy in front of them and stepped over the tree line while the rookie stepped on it. One of my new replacements had pieces of the rookie all over his Flak jacket, and I had to knock them off and get him to set up the machine gun while we prepared for the medevac."

During the period 1-3 May, Echo Company was under operational control of 1/9 for 'COUNTY FAIR' operations in Le Son (1) and Thai Cam (1) complexes.

On May 2 a patrol from Company E had one Marine wounded by a booby trap.

A patrol from Echo found a marked minefield in La Tho Bac (3) on May 7. It was near the center of the village and marked with white flags, mine signs and stars. The VC had also dug what appeared to be an anti-tank ditch in the same area.

HM3 Henry Lopez had joined Hotel Company in April 1966. He has seen little or no action. "Echo Company was short of corpsman and I was reassigned on April 14th. I was assigned to the 3rd Platoon commanded by SSgt. Kasparian. Echo moved out at night into Lau Tho Bac (1). It was very scary for me when we received sniper fire that first night. We lost a Marine to a mine from 1st Platoon the next night. [9 May: 1 Marine KIA and 3 WIA.] We swept Lau Tho Bac (1), (2), and (3) and were under constant sniper fire. 2nd Platoon got into a firefight and killed a couple of Viet Cong. I never knew I could be so scared and I shook all over.

"I went on an overnight ambush the 3rd night with Cpl. Carbajal's squad. We heard a constant barrage of gunfire and explosions for most of the night. We learned that Hotel Company had been hit very hard that night.

"Upon returning, Echo Company took over the Ha Dong Bridge position from Golf Company. Hill 55 was visible 3 or 4 miles to the west of us. We rotated platoons on constant 3-day sweeps across the river bridgehead. We had constant small arms fights and ran into a lot of booby traps. On our first platoon sweep, I went on a patrol with Cpl. Carbajal's squad and we were ambushed. I pulled a Marine named Roberts back who was shot in his left wrist and spleen. SSgt. Kasparian brought up the rest of the platoon and pulled us back after Roberts was med-evacuated.

"I quickly bonded with the Marines of the 3rd Platoon. Most of them were veterans of four to six months in Echo Company. One day, one of the

Marines called me 'Lupe' instead of 'Lopez' and so my nickname of 'Doc Lupe' was born. The Marines of the 3rd Platoon would sing to the song 'Hang on Sloopy' when it came on the radio, and loudly sing it to me as, 'Hang on Lupe, Lupe hang on,' and joke with me about it. It made me feel proud to be a part of them.

"We lost several Marines to mines during our three-day platoon sweeps. PFC Jacob H. Fowner [Albuquerque, N.M.] was killed. PFCs Dennis Gundling, Joseph Murphy, and Gerald P. Hook were wounded on these sweeps. Several men in the 1st and 2nd Platoons were also killed and wounded during the last week of April and the first week of May."

PFC Robert Slatterly joined Echo Company on 6 May, and was assigned as a rifleman in the 2nd Platoon. He later moved up to radio operator when Cpl. Graves was WIA.

Pfc. Robert J. Slatterly E/2/9 Radioman, 1966

"On May 7," Lopez went on, "we were told the company was going out on a 'County Fair' operation late that night. My mind automatically had visions of a getaway with food and fun, until I was told that it was an operation where the Marines surrounded and sealed off a village while the ARVN troops went into the village during the day and dug out all the hidden Viet Cong. We were told that every Marine patrol that had gone into this village had been hit. The village was to our west across a long line of rice paddies."

The advance guard of the 3rd Platoon was attempting to establish contact with D/1/9 at 0520 that morning, when, as they approached a gate, they were fired on and hit with 5 or 6 grenades.

Lopez continued, "We moved out late on the night of May 7, with 3rd Platoon in the lead. I was fourth in the point squad. About halfway to the village, my fellow corpsman, 'Doc' Roger Mangus, who had been with the 3rd Platoon for 7 or 8 months, came up the line and said he would take point squad and for me to drop back with the 3rd Squad because it might get hairy in the village. I know that he was concerned for me, as I had only been in Vietnam a month and had less experience. At the time, I did not understand the change, but it was a change I eventually came to understand. I believe he wanted me out of harm's way as long as possible to gain experience slowly. I moved down the line and passed SSgt. Kasparian and his radioman PFC Timothy Ray [age 19 of Dayton, Ohio]. Ray was a short, stocky guy with big Clark Kent glasses on and he looked like Radar on the TV show 'MASH.' He always had a big smile and looked like he was about 15 years old. I used to look at him and think to myself, 'what are you doing here?' I remember him guarding the Stars and Stripes newspapers to make sure SSgt. Kasparian always got them first.

"We moved in single file as we approached the village and commenced to move along its edge to tie in with D/1/9, which was moving in from the opposite direction. It was pitch black and we moved slowly. There was a sudden volley of gunfire and explosions and the cry of 'corpsman!' came up and down the line. I moved up quickly. I heard a lot of screams and could hear SSgt. Kasparian hysterically screaming over and over for Ray to bring the radio.

"There was fire coming from the village and explosions were going off around us. The point squad and the CP group were caught in an ambush. Marines were returning fire and Cpl. Carbajal was yelling to his grenadier, PFC [John W.] Medlin, to fire into the village. I crawled until I came across Cpl. Robert Staump. He was lying on his stomach and as I felt his body, his legs were bloody. As I bandaged both his legs and applied tourniquets, he looked back at me, and he moaned saying, 'I'm hurt Doc.' I told him to hang on, that I would be back, as I heard another Marine saying, 'help me.' I moved to my left and came across a Marine named Guiterrez. He was wounded in both arms, hands, and legs. I bandaged him up quickly and told him I would be back, as I heard 'Doc' Mangus crying for help. I moved and found him lying on his back. He had shrapnel to the head, face, arms, and legs. He kept saying 'I'm hurt bro,' as I bandaged him up [Mangus lost an eye]. I then moved back and found another Marine, PFC [Glen M.] Carter, wounded in the arm. I could still hear Kasparian screaming for Ray and the radio. There was still firing coming from the village as I moved on my stomach looking for other wounded Marines. I came across Ray lying dead on his back, with the radio still strapped to him. I still remember his image because an illumination round went off to my far right. Ray was looking up with his eyes and mouth open and he still had his glasses on. The explosion that killed him caused his glasses to crack like a spider web, but not break. As I looked at Ray, it was as though time suddenly moved in slow motion as the illumination slowly faded. It was as though I was watching a movie, and it was a very strange feeling. I moved away from Ray and yelled to Kasparian that Ray was dead. Kasparian started yelling for someone to bring up another radio.

"By this time, the firing and explosions had stopped. More Marines were moving up and consolidating our position and set up a perimeter. The other company corpsmen moved up and started helping with the wounded. I went back to 'Doc' Mangus and sat next to him. I was in total shock about what had just happened. Lying there, Mangus looked up at me and said, 'Bro, it looks like you're feeling hurt for me.'

"I half sobbed and said, 'You're leaving me here alone.'

"Even in his wounded state he said, 'You'll do well bro. I taught you good.' Mangus and I had become very close. He had been my mentor for the first month and I was feeling his loss and feeling alone. I knew that if Mangus had not made the switch earlier that night, it would have been me lying there instead of him. I then moved to Kasparian and had not been aware that he had received shrapnel wounds and the close explosions had affected his hearing. As I treated him, he was very shaken and wanted to know who was down and was very concerned for his Marines.

"The shock of the sudden ambush and the loss of my Marine friends had left me very shaken but there was no time to mourn. Little did I realize that more of the same awaited Echo Company in the coming weeks and months.

"The med-evacuation helicopters came in around dawn to evacuate our casualties. A Marine with the 3.5 rocket section, LCpl. [William R.] Reilly started taking pictures and Kasparian flipped out and started screaming at him to stop. Lt. Hornick calmed him down. Kasparian refused to be evacuated and remained with the 3rd Platoon during the 3-4 day operation. A little deaf, but he hung in there with us."

Pfc. Reilly & Cpl. Carbahal with captured VC flag, Spring 1966

The after action report stated that 20 hand grenades were thrown and 5 or 6 M79 rounds we fired against the hidden VC. PFC Ray was the only Marine KIA, but 9 Marines and corpsmen were wounded. Only 1 VC body was found. McMillan recalled that LCpl. Edgar J. Cardoza suffered a broken jaw, broken leg, and lost several fingers.

In the fighting that day, Cpl. Graves, acting as the Company Radioman, recalled, "We were just approaching a tree line across from a rice paddy and were in a small group. PFC Timothy Ray, 3rd Platoon Radioman, was kneeling down as we discussed our approach to the village. A hidden VC threw a grenade that killed Ray and wounded the 3rd Platoon Commander, SSgt. Kasparian."

Templeton believed Ray bent over to grab the grenade when it went off.

"I was hit that morning also," Graves continued, "'Doc' Crittenden took care of me. Corporal [Robert M.] 'Bob' Staump was hit in the arm and both legs, losing a leg."

On 10 May, Templeton was talking with Tom Austin, of West Carrollton, Ohio, about being short timers. This was their last patrol, and they were going home together. Austin told him, "I'm not going home." Templeton, who knew that Austin was married and had a child, couldn't understand his reaction. Templeton tried to reassure him he would make it, but Austin was insistent; he wasn't going to make it home.

While on patrol that day, the squad received small arms fire from a village across the rice paddies. There was a small village on an island near where the fire was coming from and they went to clear it out. When they neared the village they found it surrounded by a trench line. They decided to use the trench to go around the village and meet on the other side. When they were about halfway around, Austin, who was walking point, moved a bamboo pole to get through the trench. By doing so, he set off a large booby trap. The explosion blew Austin's arms and legs off, and took the head off of PFC Leroy W. Williams of Indianapolis, Indiana. Mike Malone was behind Williams, but he didn't receive a scratch. When the medevac choppers arrived, Malone carried Austin's torso and Williams' head and put them on the helicopter. Austin was still breathing, but he died the next day. Malone almost cracked up over the incident. Pvt. James McMillan found one of Austin's feet the next day and buried it.

Machine Gunner Dan Kumaus related, "After 3/25/66, a lot of platoon leaders wanted me to be on their patrols. Superstition was rampant, and I guess they thought I was lucky. I know they asked me to go on a lot of patrols with my gun, and I always did. I remember a couple of journalists that came out to go on a patrol. One was from *Newsweek* and the other was from *Time* magazine. One was a fat asshole wearing tan Hemingway type pants with pockets down the side of the pants and jacket. He was sweating like a pig and it was only about 10 in the morning. We were all use to it. They had a lot of cameras and were yucking it up. I took a 'big' exception to their attitude and told the officer that was briefing us that they had to carry weapons in case we were attacked. I even remember suggesting they carry some gun ammo. They stopped laughing when we made them carry a side arm, some ammo, and a cartridge belt. They thought it was going to be fun to go out on a patrol with Marines and go back and tell their buddies what heroes they were. Sort of pissed me off, so I made a big deal out of it. We were scheduled to cross the same area that a booby trap had taken out one of our guys the day before and these idiots did not understand that it was dangerous. The squad leader got even with me. I can't remember who it was, but he told the idiots to get behind me and stay with me if anything happened. I knew if they got in my way they were history, and I told them so. They were no longer laughing and they stayed out of my way."

Ware recalled the photographers asking them to pose as if they were under fire. He and the rest of the Marines told them to "Go to Hell."

Echo Company reported 2 officers and 125 for duty at the end of the month. 1 officer and 28 were listed as non-effectives (the sick and wounded).

3rd Platoon, June 1966
Standing (rear): Bob Hilstrom, Dan Manson, "Doc" Greg Salter,
unidentified, Larry Jordan, Norris Edwards, John Frostraom & Curtis Watson
Kneeling: Ed Gorman, unidentified, Ron Hoyus, Don Grob,
Wieczorkowski, unidentified, Gabe Coronado
Sitting: Dorie Lear, James Smallwood & unidentified

LCpl. Herbert Thrasher, back row, 3rd from left, 1966

Pfc. Henry Solis, 1966

Stocks, Phillips, Brazil, Solis & Coronado

Hatcher

Fireteam, L-R: unknown, Millwood, Zinkham & Ware

An undated roster of the 3rd Platoon gives an idea of the heavy casualties the company and platoons suffered during this period:

Platoon Commander	SSgt. John P. Kasparian WIA (head) 8 May 1966
Sergeant	Sgt. Thomas F. Burke WIA February 1966
Platoon Guide	Sgt. Paul Washington WIA
Radioman	PFC Glen M. Carter WIA (arm) 8 May 1966
Messenger	PFC Timothy Ray [Dayton, Ohio] KIA 8 May 1966
Corpsman	HN2. Michael Harmon WIA
Corpsman	HN2. Roger Mangus WIA (lost an eye) 8 May 1966
1st Squad	
Squad Leader	Cpl. Kenneth M. Antal WIA 25 March 1966
Grenadier	PFC John W. Medlin WIA 25 March 1966
1st Fire Team Leader	Cpl. Charles Carbajal WIA
Automatic Rifleman	PFC Samuel D. Ramirez KIA 25 March 1966
Rifleman	PFC Ernest A. Mills WIA
Rifleman	PFC Clyde D. H. McDonald KIA 25 March 1966
2nd Fire Team Leader	PFC James L. Cox - Went Crazy

Cox received a General Court Martial for shooting the Battalion Sergeant Major in the groin. Ware recalled that they were guarding a bridge and some of the men were "Drinking Tiger Piss in a shack beside the road near the bridge. Cox saw a Vietnamese man across the room smoking

346

hash-hash or opium in a pipe and went over and asked him for a smoke. It made him crazy."

Automatic Rifleman	PFC Jimmy Lee Daniel - Absent a lot with foot problems
Rifleman	PFC Allen R. Bezek
Rifleman	PFC Louis J. Seprodi - Absent a lot with foot problems
3rd Fire Team Leader	PFC Joseph D. Lorme shot himself in the foot
Automatic Rifleman	PFC Douglas Stevens - Went Crazy
Rifleman	PFC Fred L. Kane WIA 25 March 1966
2ND Squad	
2nd Squad Leader	Cpl. Robert M. Staump WIA (lost a leg and in other leg and arm) 8 May 1966
Grenadier	Pvt. Dennis Gundling WIA April 1966
1st Fire Team Leader	PFC Ramon J. Nieto WIA 17 March 1966.
Automatic Rifleman	PFC Harold Millwood WIA
Rifleman	PFC Anthony Leggington WIA
Rifleman	PFC Ward A. Hoffman
2nd Fire Team Leader	PFC Joseph Murphy WIA 14 May 1966
Automatic Rifleman	PFC Jacob H. Fowner KIA April 1966.
Rifleman	PFC Donald M. Paul WIA
Rifleman	PFC Dennis Brotherton
3rd Fire Team Leader	PFC Jimmy K. Slimp
Automatic Rifleman	Pvt. Alvin L. Williams
Rifleman	PFC Dale L. Vouch
Rifleman	None Assigned
3rd Squad	[Casualties in 3rd Squad are incomplete]
3rd Squad Leader	Cpl. Donald L. Hoops
Grenadier	PFC Buster B. Martin WIA 14 May 1966
1st Fire Team Leader	LCpl. Larry V. Brown
Automatic Rifleman	PFC David J. White
Rifleman PFC	Jerry D. Hatcher KIA
Rifleman	PFC Leonard Lawless

2nd Fire Team Leader	PFC Robert L. Zinkham WIA April-May 1966
Automatic Rifleman	PFC William S. Ware WIA May 1966
Rifleman	PFC Gerald P. Hook WIA April 1966
Rifleman	PFC Herbert Franklin
3rd Fire Team Leader	None Assigned
Automatic Rifleman	None Assigned
Rifleman	None Assigned
Rifleman	None Assigned

Doc Lopez continued his memoir, "After Echo Company returned to the bridgehead, the 3rd Platoon went back out on its 3-day sweep without Kasparian, whose hearing had gotten considerably worse. When we got back we learned that he had been med-evacuated out."

On the night of 11 May, a squad ambush was fired on and had one Marine WIA.

Hornick wrote again on 25 May, "The casualty situation has calmed down for the past couple of weeks. On the 14th the 1st Platoon was ambushed by 200-250 VC in Lau Tho Bac (3). There were 200-300 more VC on the other side of the river. Anyway, we lost 5 KIAs and 15 WIAs. The 1st Platoon alone killed 30 and wounded a possible 40. The rest of the company didn't arrive (along with our Sparrow Hawk) until after the shooting was nearly over. Hotel's mobile platoons came to our aid and got 42 KIAs (body count, too) and possibly 50-75 WIAs without any casualties."

The after action report indicated the platoon had walked into a "V" shaped ambush "with the apparent intent of allowing the Marines to enter the 'V' prior to opening fire. Due to the excellent dispersion by the point squad, the ambush was forced to commence fire prematurely, and was unable to fix the entire platoon in the killing zone. Simultaneously, approximately 40 VC were seen by FOs in the vicinity moving west in an attempt to bring the Marines under fire from the [flank]. The platoon returned fire on the ambush with a heavy volume of small arms fire resulting in 10 VC KIA (body count). The VC withdrew from their ambush site in an apparent state of confusion.

"Shortly after the initial contact, Sparrow Hawk [a reinforced rifle squad] and a rifle platoon from Co. H were dispatched to cut off the VC withdrawal across the Song La Tho. The platoon from Company E kept pursuing the VC to the south as the other units tried to cut off their withdrawal. The VC were finally pursued 1,000 meters south of the Song La Tho [River] by the platoon from Company H. A total of 37 VC bodies were found after the firefight."

Graves stated, "They brought in some huge tracked vehicles equipped with what looked like snow removal blades. Lt. Hornick took issue with the Battalion Commander about the merits of dozing over an entire village. I think they had offensive positions connected by trenches. They bladed over those positions completely."

PFC Buster B. Martin was wounded in the right hand by a mortar fragment. He was treated in the field and returned to duty.

Coronado stated, "I got hit by a grenade fragment in the lower back. I was in the same hole as Ron Hoyos, and we were down to only a couple of rounds for our .45s when the action ended."

Gorman stated that Cpl. John M. Frostom, a Machine Gun Squad Leader, was hit that day.

Clemons recalled, "Jimmy McMillan, Dan Kumaus, and I were scouting for a position [for our Machine Gun]. We had just emerged from a canebrake when automatic weapons fire swept our front. I was between the two of them. Dan got bullets in both knees and Jimmy in one. Lt. Murphy was very forceful on the radio to get a Medevac as quickly as possible to minimize the permanent damage to their legs."

McMillan stated, "One of the bullets came through Kumaus's leg and into my knee. Another round hit me below the knee."

PFC James McMillian at Ammo Bunker, 1966

Lawton remembered, "We had a new Platoon Commander, Lt. Clarey. Ski [Wieczorkoski] was now my Squad Leader. We set up in some no name village near La Tho Bac (3). We ate chow, and then it was my turn to walk point (Marines, non-grunts, and FNGs were amazed at how spread out the platoon would be). We lived in a land of mines, booby traps, and snipers. Up close and personal was not an option. Not like in the movies where everyone wants to be on the screen. The last thing Lt. Clarey said to me was, 'Go find us some,' or something like that. We moved across the rice paddies and entered Lau Tho Bac (3). I was about 50 yards past this little fence when the world exploded. My rifle stopped firing after the first or second round. I cocked it again and nothing happened. Then Cpl. Watson was beside me. There was an explosion and Watson went down. One of the 'Docs' came up to work on Watson, and I dropped down behind a large bush. There, amid all these explosions and machine gun fire, came a gook around the corner of a hut. He had this excited look upon his face. Amid all this chaos he was tiptoeing! Then he was shot."

Lear stated he was almost across the rice paddy when the VC opened fire. He believes that LCpl. James F. Smallwood saw the VC when he reached a gate into the village and opened fire on them, thus keeping about half the platoon outside the kill zone of the ambush. Ron Hoyos, with his Machine Gun Team, were behind a paddy dike to give covering fire in case the platoon was ambushed. Their fire kept the VC from encircling the Marines caught in the ambush. For some reason, the platoon Radioman was with the Machine gunners and called for help.

HN Eddie 'Doc' Gallegos detailed his experiences of being hit the same day. "On May 15, 1966, I was a 19-year-old Corpsman with Echo 2/9 when we were ambushed near Lau Tho Bac (3). My recollection begins with an early dawn briefing by Sgt. Ocuna. We had to cross open areas two men at a time. When the 'L' shaped ambush hit, about half the platoon were in the tree line ahead on the other side of the paddy and I was crossing the paddy with another Marine. The enemy had many automatic rifles and machine guns. There was machine gun, rifle fire, and explosions all around. Marines were returning fire. I don't remember what happened to the guy next to me, but the Marines in the tree line several yards ahead were screaming, 'Corpsman up,' so I went. I was hit twice before I got to the tree line and hit a third time when I reached it. In the tree line, there were several Marines firing from behind a small berm. There were several of the enemy closing in on us from both our right and our front. Lance Corporal Craig Horton was hit in the calf of his leg real bad, so I worked on him and gave him morphine. PFC [Joseph] Murphy yelled and held up his arm at me, which was bleeding. I was facing him and working on him when he pushed me aside and shot two of the enemy just behind my back. I then crawled to Corporal [Curtis Lee] Watson [of Richmond Heights, Mo.] who showed me his thumb, which was falling off his hand. He panicked and put his head over the berm. I grabbed his collar to pull him down. It was too late. He was hit in the head. He died. I looked up and saw three VC coming at us. I grabbed an M-14 lying nearby and emptied the magazine at the enemy. I think a communist grenade was thrown by one of the enemy and it landed next to me and exploded.

"I could not hear. I could not breathe. I could not feel my right leg. I could not see for the blood in my eyes. I was later treated for multiple shrapnel wounds in the head, chest, right arm, both legs, liver, stomach, right buttock, lungs, and broken ribs. Corpsman Greg Salter tried to treat me, but the firefight was still fierce and he had many other Marines to attend to. He went to them first. After going in and out of consciousness, and after a long time lying in the dirt with Watson and Horton, I was eventually rescued by three Marines. One of them said to me, 'Goddamn Doc, you're all fucked up!' I said, 'Yep!' They carried me to a hut and placed me on the dirt floor. A skinny Marine with blonde hair and two missing upper front teeth [Dorie Lear] stood at the open door with his M-14 pointed out. Sgt. Ocuna was lying on the floor. His body was smoking and grease was dripping from his burning body onto the floor. The gap-toothed Marine [Lear] said a Willy Peter grenade on Ocuna's web belt had detonated. After what seemed like an eternity, medevac helicopters arrived. I spent almost a year in Balboa Naval Hospital." [Lear says that Watson was shot inside the hut, when looking for the VC out of a window, after he had dragged Gallegos and Watson inside.]

Lawton stated, "I heard Ski calling me from a house in the yard I was in. I got to the house. It was made of cement and had a tile roof. The weirdest thing was I now had a rifle that worked! I knew it was not mine because it had a selector switch. Ski has an M-79 and [PFC Philip] 'Pappy' Thompson was in the house shooting out the window. PFC Murphy came in and was in the back. Doc Gallegos had patched him up. They must have been shooting M-79s or RPGs at us, because several hit the roof but did not penetrate. Then one came through and a fragment hit Ski in the chest. I remembered from Doc Salter's class on sucking chest wounds and put my battle dressing over his wound with a piece of plastic. Thompson had his pack and canteen shot through.

"We were running low on ammunition and it felt like we had been there for hours. I kept Ski on his wounded side and fired at the gooks in gray-green uniforms with brush tied on their backs. One stumbled and was grabbed by two others and they make it to the tree line on the other side of the yard. I fired several M-79 rounds into the base of the tree line and they disappeared. I moved to the front door and fired at some moving bushes. Pappy and I were almost out of ammunition. I had my last magazine in my rifle. I fired the M-79 out the front door and then I could no longer cock it. Ski has his .45 and Thompson was down to his last magazine.

"I realized on one of my moves to the side door that it was Doc Gallegos lying in the side yard. Pappy yelled that he could see Sgt. Ocuna and that he was on fire. Suddenly, the cavalry arrived. A Huey gun ship seemed to hover over top of the house with its machine guns firing long bursts. Then Doc Salter was there asking me to help open the back of Ski's jacket to see if he was hit through and though. He wasn't. Then one of the helicopters that just dropped off some of the Sparrow Hawk reinforcements lifted off, got some altitude, and began to spin in the air and goes down behind the tree line by the river.

"After all the wounded and dead were found, Pappy and I found the flank Fire Team. They were all dead except Smallwood, who was wounded and had been lying bareheaded in the sun. He was helilifted out but died later in the day. We formed up and went down to the river to check on the helicopter. They had been evacuated, so we headed back to the downed railroad bridge." The Marines recovered maps, radios, and helmets from the downed helicopter.

Templeton recalled, "The helicopter was entangled in the trees with crew members hanging lifeless from it." He showed his platoon sergeant, SSgt. Clarence Robinson, the site. Ware remembered the helicopter spiraling down.

Lear remembers Hoyos telling him that the helicopters reported the VC in company strength massing across the railroad berm, about three rice paddies away, and they should 'get the hell out of there!' The platoon fell back, reorganized, and then swept back through the village, finding only a couple of dead VC.

Ware was wounded by grenade fragments in the face and leg. "I picked small pieces of metal out of my face for years," he recalled. He refused evacuation.

Three of the Marines killed that day were LCpl. Smallwood [age 23] of Lanham, Md., PFCs John S. Davis of San Antonio, Texas, and Bobby Joe Jacobs of Henderson, Texas. Cpl. Gabriel C. Coronado, Jr. received a bullet wound in the lower back and shrapnel in the face. LCpl. Edgar J. Cardoza was hit in the leg and lost several fingers.

Kumaus was medevaced to Da Nang with the other casualties. "Some General gave me a Purple Heart while I was being put under with morphine so they could operate on my legs, and I vaguely recollect that I said I forgot to duck to the General. He laughed and sort of shook his head. If I was going to put thoughts in his head, he was thinking, 'Marines are crazy.'"

"They had canister-firing tanks with them to account for the majority of the kills," Hornick wrote. "An estimated 100 KIAs or WIAs were taken out by fixed-wing and Huey's south of the river. 1/9 on Hill 55 have killed almost 250 VC in the past two weeks. All of this took place north of Hill 55 and close to 2/9's CP. As you can tell, the VC have really stepped up their activities because of the recent political disturbances and rainy weather.

"The replacement situation becomes worse each week. I don't know when it will end. I do have 2 more Lts. Bob Fredericks was evacuated to Japan (then probably CONUS). SSgt. Kasparian was med-evacuated to Okinawa last week with busted eardrums caused by a VC grenade. [Kasparian had a piece of shrapnel enter his ear, which was later located by X rays at the Bethesda Naval Hospital, where he was treated for over a year]. The Battalion moved down to its new CP located at Phong Luc (2) yesterday. That place is really up for grabs. 3/1 was permanently given to 9th Marines (Operational Control) and they moved into our old CP. Mission—guarding bridges, pacification, etc. As a deserving consequence, 2/9 had no tents to move to the new CP and a flap resulted. They finally moved in on the ground. I haven't seen it yet, but I understand it requires a mite [Mighty Mite jeep type vehicle] to get to the mess hall. It is suppose to be enormous. The perimeter has fake bunkers and all because of the huge area covered."

A patrol from Echo Company hit a Bouncing Betty booby trap on 26 May and suffered two Marines wounded. Pringer recalled, "The 1st Platoon was hit hard that night at Dong Son (1). The VC came out of tunnels inside their perimeter. It was about 0300, and by the time we got there, the VC had fled. We set up an LZ and evacuated the wounded. It was a bloody mess.

"At first light, we took off after the VC. Second Platoon had the point and 2nd Squad was the point unit. I was now a Squad Leader, and most of the men in my squad were FNGs. I briefed them to stay off the trails, as the VC booby trapped them. I also told them to maintain an interval of at least 10 yards, so that if someone hit a mine or booby trap it wouldn't take out the whole squad. I decided to walk point, as I didn't trust any of the new men. We had moved about a mile and were moving through a jungle area when I heard and felt the explosion. When I looked back, one of the FNGs had hit a Bouncing Betty mine on the trail, where he wasn't suppose to be. I took a piece of shrapnel in the elbow joint. My Platoon Commander wanted me to continue on the patrol, but when he heard the metal scraping when I flexed my arm, he told me to get on the medevac chopper." Pringer had the shrapnel removed in Da Nang, and his arm placed in a cast. He ended up in the Naval Hospital in Memphis, Tennessee, where he was later promoted to Sergeant.

Doc Greg Salter treated Cpl. Wieczorski for "a classic sucking chest wound. I placed a sheet of plastic over the wound and helped load him on the medevac helicopter. I didn't know if he survived or not. Two years later, at the 2nd Infantry Training Regiment at Camp Pendleton, I was at a firing range and one of the instructors was Cpl. Ski. We had a quick and emotional reunion."

Graves remembered, "LCpl. Dennis R. Reilly [age 20, of Brooklyn, New York] and PFC Gordon E. Gullett [of Brownsville, Texas], were killed in Lau Tho Bac (3) that night. I was close to both of those guys. Reilly was hit by a mortar round and Gullett was shot. Both died instantly. I remember a guy named Osborn going outside the perimeter looking for gooks."

Pfc. Gullett, 1966

On 28 May, PFC Michael W. Mulick of Poway, California was killed in action.

Echo Company's strength at the end of May was 4 officers and 141 enlisted on the rolls. Twenty-five of the enlisted men were absent wounded; more than twice as many as the other rifle companies.

"The Battalion is losing 11 officers, plus numerous SNCOs, in June," Hornick continued. "There is no sign of replacements. The Colonel is supposed to leave in 6 days, and they don't know who will replace him."

Jimmy McMillian recalled that he and Steve Clemons were on a working party sent to Da Nang to pick up a pallet of C rations. After the forklift operator loaded the C rations, McMillian told him to load a pallet of jungle boots, and the Marine did it! When they got back to the bridge, almost the whole company was issued new jungle boots! An inquiry was made if anyone knew anything about a pallet of jungle boots, and of course, no one knew a thing!

Lawton found out that his lost rifle woes were not over. Lt. Brown, a new officer in the company, told him he was investigating it.

In June, he learned that his parents in Canada had received an IOU letter stating that he had been killed and that Lawton still owed them $22.00. The letter was from a men's store in Jacksonville, N.C., and a debt he had already paid. Lawton had a receipt for it. His father had just taken a job with the Canadian Embassy in Rome, Italy. They had moved out of their house and were staying in a hotel before flying to Rome. His parents contacted the Canadian Red Cross, but flew on to Italy. There, they contacted the Naval Attaché in the American Embassy. They finally found out their son was o.k.

Meanwhile, the CID was at Echo Company questioning Lawton about the bad debt, the false report of his death, and the lost rifle. "I finally convinced them I was in the field, did not have access to a typewriter, was not trying to fake my death, and the charges against me were finally dropped."

Fox Company found a minefield on 11 June while participating in Operation Liberty. It was located in a grassy area just south of the footbridge across the La Tho River. It was 100 x 40 meters and contained M-16-A1 mines, M-26 grenades, and dud artillery and mortar rounds. Two shaped charges were also found. The battalion reported, "Two M-16-A1 mines were detonated by Marines and an additional 8 exploded as a result of a grass fire that started in the area. 25 USMC casualties occurred, all from the initial two mines. An artillery destruction mission was fired in the area the following day and an estimated 7 secondary explosions occurred." Echo Company was also involved in the operation.

PFC Ralph V. Renauld, Jr., of Worchester, Massachusetts, was killed in action on 15 June.

On 17-18 June, Echo Company served as a blocking force for the 2nd ARVN Battalion, without any contact. All of the rifle companies in 2/9 eventually participated in the operation.

Operation Liberty continued through 30 June, with only Hotel Company being seriously engaged. Echo Company had to battle the usual mines, booby traps and the heat. On 27 June a large quantity of medical supplies were found and on 29 June, fifty-seven 60 mm mortar rounds were discovered.

PFC Buster Martin recalled a 'County Fair' operation near Da Nang. "At daybreak, the ARVN went in and for about an hour there was lots of gunfire inside the village. Before long here came a load of U.S. & ARVN brass, led by General Walt himself. There was a U.S. Army two-star, about three ARVN generals, plus many colonels and the like. There were reporters and cameramen, too. Some Marine colonel selected six of us to act as security when they went in the village. The ARVN had done quite a job. In one part of the village there were nine dead VC laid out in a row. There were a few more nearby. After about an hour, all of the brass departed and the Civil Affairs folks moved in. We went back to our area later that afternoon."

Sergeant An, our Vietnamese interpreter, wrote Lt. Hornick on 4 June 1966:

"Today I have been in the Hospital 9 days already! You probably know I lost my left leg, which was cut off about 1½ inches below my knee. I felt very sad when I knew I lost one leg in my life, but I realized that my mind was still good, so I think I can do well what I want in the future, because I lose my leg but I don't lose my mind.

"Lt. Belden [Thomas M. Beldon, the S-2] has come here two times to visit me and brought one letter from Colonel, our Battalion Commander, sent to me. This letter made me very happy and satisfied during the time of my staying in 2/9 Battalion. I'm supposed to be sent to Saigon to fix another leg some time next week. I hope I will get along [with] my new leg.

"I'm very sorry I won't go back to work together with you. I shall miss my many good friends. I like them. I like to stay close with them to fight VC. I don't care to move out with them to anywhere, but for the time being I care about the booby traps for them. I suggest that in order to avoid the booby traps a little bit, Marines had better not to move on the same trails, and walking the same ways every day.

"Finally, I would like to send my regards to you and all your officers and men in the Echo Company.

P.S. Because my hand is still pain[ful], so I write you a very bad letter. Would you help the old laundry [man] for me and keep them having the service at your company as long as possible.

Cincerely [sic] yours,
Nguyen Ngoc An
INTERPRETER"

Clemons recalled the company operating south of Rt. 14. "We went over a bamboo bridge that must have been shot up and patched up a lot. I was nervous about the bridge because I was not very good at balancing all my gear and stepping lightly with my size 13 boots and the M-60 Machine Gun on delicate bamboo bridges.

"There were some old dud Bouncing Bettys in the earthen abutment of the bridge. About five or six Marines must have started across before I realized that I was standing on something—pins to a Bouncing Betty! I took off my gear and set it all down very carefully within arms reach. I put the machine gun down gingerly, knowing we could more readily afford to lose one gunner than to lose the gun. Then several flak jackets were passed to me. I jumped off the bridge and dove for the dirt. It did not go off. Then I crawled around feeling for more and counted seven mines at the approach to the bridge. Of course, I was appointed to take all who followed past the Bouncing Bettys! 'We are going to walk through seven Bouncing Bettys. Put your hand on my shoulder and follow in my steps until I say that we are clear,' I told each man. But I did not want to be Tail End Charlie across the damn bridge. So when the point man from the next platoon came up, I showed him—on hands and knees—where the mines were and appointed him to take over my duty. I saddled up quickly, took the M-60 by the handle and scooted to catch up with Second Platoon across the bridge.

"Looking back on it, someone else should have taken the gun across while I was serving as mine field guide. But it was a dark and dangerous place and there was no time to discuss the details—we just had to wing it as so often we did.

"Later, we came to some villages with nearly impenetrable tall hedges lining the trails. They were obviously fortifications, but I had no idea whose. After we settled into a perimeter, I saw a map with the symbol for the Cao Dai on a temple close to our company position. The Cao Dai were often exceptionally resistant to the Viet Cong—but not always. The great hedges in the village were expected of the Cao Dai. I persuaded the Platoon Commander into bringing a radioman and going with me to see the priests. We paid our respects as best we could and got a better reception than was normal in the villages.

On the way out, I was pointing out elements of Cao Dai temple architecture to the Platoon Commander. His reply was, 'We are fifteen hundred meters from where we are supposed to be with no good excuse because you wanted to be a tourist. Next time, come by yourself.' Or words to that effect."

I next heard from Gerry Hornick on 27 August. "I was wounded again, this time a little more seriously. It occurred on Operation Liberty down on the 'big river' south of Hwy. 14 [2 July 1966]. We were mortared pretty hard, but I was the only one seriously wounded. I caught some shrapnel in the left leg and arm. The one in my arm cut the nerve to my hand, preventing any sensitivity or control. I was evacuated to San Diego Naval Hospital. I've been here about a month with things improving every day. The doctors say it will be about 2 or 3 more months before my release. I've run into a lot of my old troopers here, most of who came after you left. Some of them are in pretty bad shape, but have outstanding morale."

Hornick ended up in the Bethesda, Maryland Naval Hospital until he was medically retired on 31 December 1968. Kasparian returned to duty and was commissioned a Second Lieutenant. He served another tour in Vietnam.

John Kasparian being promoted to 2nd Lt.

Florian was also wounded for the second time on 2 July. A mortar round landed in his hole, blew him out, knocked him unconscious, and put shrapnel in his leg. When he came to, he almost shot a Marine who was moving to his front in the darkness. He refused evacuation.

Lt. Garner wrote from Ft. Still, Oklahoma, upon receiving his Bronze Star, "The best time I had in RVN were the months I spent with you and Echo Company, for as far as I am concerned, that was the combined arms team working at its best."

PFC Robert Slatterly had joined Echo Company and the 2nd Platoon on 6 May 1966. He served as an automatic rifleman and fire team leader until becoming the platoon radio operator for Lt. Jim Murphy. Bob was wounded in the hand in August 1966. He continued to serve as a radio operator for the 2nd Platoon when 2/9 moved to the DMZ. He was made the Company Radioman when Graves made Sergeant. Echo Company, under Captain Reynolds, served at Phu Bai, Hue, Dong Ha, the Rock Pile, Camp Carroll, Con Thien, Cam Lo, and Khesanh before the siege. After Lt. Murphy was wounded, the platoon was led by SSgt. Spencer Olsen, and Captain Terrill had command of the company.

Slatterly recalled, "The 3rd Platoon was ambushed on Hill 861 on 16 March 1967. I was with Captain Terrill's command group that relieved SSgt. Olsen's platoon and evacuated the WIA and KIAs. I spent a tense night with Lt. Young on a listening post atop Hill 861. He called in artillery most of the night to keep the retiring NVA from policing up our abandoned weapons and 782 gear.

"After accomplishing the evacuations, we patrolled through the ambush site on the western side of the hill and maneuvered across the ridgelines of both Hills 881 South and 881 North. The NVA were there, but didn't try to hit us until it was too late. We were well away from the hill on a night march when they came after us. It was rather hairy since we could hear the NVA on our radio frequency and their voices upon the ridgeline. So we set the bamboo on fire behind us as we left."

PFC Herbert E. Thrasher described the action in which he was wounded on the night of 16 November 1966 for his hometown newspaper. "I was leaning against a tree while my bubbies were dozing waiting for the word whether they would move on or stay put for the night. At 2200, my thoughts were interrupted by voices, as several figures were making their way down the trail towards me. I thought it might be the guys bringing the orders, but as they came near I heard them speaking Vietnamese. There were four of them dressed in black pajamas, carrying weapons. [Later he learned they were armed with Russian made AK-47s]. They were about 15 yards away when I rolled over and fired my M-79 grenade launcher at them, killing two and the others ran away. A fragment from the M-79, fired at such close range, hit me in the head just below the helmet line. I was bandaged by a Corpsman and walked to the Company CP. I was still stunned and hadn't felt any pain. My right hand was also injured. In about 10 minutes, my head started hurting and the Corpsman gave me some pills to ease the pain, which helped some, but I couldn't sleep the rest of the night. The Corpsman thought my wound was not too serious.

"It was raining and foggy the next morning, but a medevac helicopter finally got in and took me to a Dispensary Unit in Da Nang. They took X-rays and found a piece of metal inside my skull. I was rushed to emergency surgery where they removed it." Thrasher was later sent to the Clark Air Force Base Hospital in the Philippines, and then to Hawaii. He received a Bronze Star for his actions that night.

Lawton recalled that when the company was up north, they were sent before dawn one morning to set up a road block on Highway 1. While they were setting in, an Army truck came down the road towards their position, even before it had been swept for mines. An Army sergeant was driving the truck and Pvt. Florian, complete with an Army jacket with sergeant stripes on it, was with him. They had been on a "spree" in Hue! Florian, an outstanding field Marine, always got in trouble when not in the bush, so they tried to keep him there. On his next to last day in Vietnam, the Regimental Executive Officer's helicopter flew in and picked him up. Florian's outfit when he boarded the helicopter consisted of a Vietnamese black pajama jacket and tiger striped trousers! He was kept under guard until he boarded the plane to come home the next day.

Chapter Sixteen

HQMC,
1966-1969

My tour in Family Housing at HQMC proved to be interesting. I had to learn about how the Marine Corps was funded by DOD for family housing, and at most Marine bases, the Navy provided the staff and civilians to operate and maintain them. The Marine Corps has always lagged behind the other services in providing housing for its personnel. Many Marine officers still felt that 'if the Marine Corps wanted you to have a wife, they would have issued you one.' Officers were provided for much better than the enlisted personnel. Camp Lejeune provides a good example. They were still housing young Marines and their families in aluminum trailers placed there during the Korean War. They were just shells with no air conditioning. One of the projects I worked on was getting rid of such housing, which counted against Marine Corps assets. We were successful.

I sat on many committees as the Marine Corps representative with Navy Captains, and Air Force and Army Generals and Colonels. These committees made recommendations to DOD on improvements and funding for family housing. I briefed Pentagon officials on the Marine Corps problems and helped us gain new family housing units and upgrade the existing units with additional funding; some with Marine Corps funds and some with Blue Dollars (Navy). With the Vietnam War going full blast, many stateside posts and stations of all the services had family housing that was not being used. A program was established forcing the other services to provide their housing units to Marines stationed in the area, or their dependents, if the Marine was overseas. The idea was to keep these housing units filled, rather than paying servicemen or their families to live on the local economy.

I served on a Marine Inspector General Team that inspected all Marine installations on both the east and west coasts. I inspected the family housing units on occupancy rates, down time between move outs and move ins, the quality and quantity of furniture furnished, and how well the housing was maintained. The most striking results came from an inspection of the Cherry Point Marine Corps Air Station. A Marine Warrant Officer, who was the Family Housing Officer for the base, had warned me that the Navy and civilian personnel involved in the maintenance, upkeep, and movement of furniture were running 6-10 weeks behind. I found this to be true. Marines and their families were sleeping on bare mattresses because the bedroom furniture had not been delivered. Units were sitting empty because repairs, painting, etc., had not been done. Meanwhile, Marines and their families were forced to live on the economy.

I pulled no punches when I briefed General Marion Carl, the base commander. When all of the inspecting officers finished their briefs, General Carl thanked us for doing such a thorough job and commented, 'I can't believe the family housing situation!' or words to that effect. It was his only comment.

The Marine Family Housing Officer called me about 10 days later. He was elated! He was given several flat bed trucks and work crews who picked up, delivered, and redistributed furniture throughout the base. The wait for furniture was now less than a week. Family housing repair, painting, and maintenance had top priority, and units were being turned over rapidly. The wait for housing had dropped to only a week or so from several months, and the Navy Captain in charge had been called on the carpet by General Carl. I felt my trip had really made a difference!

James H. Warnock, OSD (I&L) Coordinator for Housing Referral Services in the Department of Defense, wrote the following to my Commanding Officer:

"Subject: Participation of Captain Robert J. Driver, Jr., USMC, in Housing Referral Visits, March 17-30, 1968.

"At the request of the Office of the Secretary of Defense, Captain Driver was assigned by the Marine Corps to participate, as a Marine Corps member, in OSD Housing Referral Team visits. Captain Driver was assigned to Team No. 1, of which I was chairman.

"Team No. 1 visited 16 individual Housing Referral Offices and held five major area meetings on the West Coast, attended by top management personnel from 70 installations; 575,000 military personnel are assigned to installations represented at these area meetings of which an estimated 125,431 are married and live off base.

"At a number of the area meetings, Captain Driver made a formal viewgraph presentation and held a separate meeting with Marine Corps representatives to discuss and solve problems specifically involving Marine Corps administration of Housing Referral. In addition, he was the Marine Corps representative to observe the operations and progress of individual Referral Offices.

"We wish to thank you for Captain Driver's participation. He had a very thorough knowledge of the subject matter and performed outstandingly in making presentations to the senior representatives of installations. His conduct of the Marine Corps meetings was done most authoritatively, smoothly, and effectively. He demonstrated outstanding perceptiveness in anticipating questions and the replies were indicative of his very incisive mind and analytical ability. His participation in visits to installations was extremely effective. All in all, Captain Driver did an outstanding job and made substantial contributions toward the success of the visits and in getting the Housing Referral program started including the drafting and coordination of the various official memoranda and instructions issued by OSD."

The working hours for this job were great, and I was able to coach my son in Little League Baseball. I had very successful teams, and my last one, before heading back to Vietnam, won the championship.

I played basketball at lunchtime with a number of officers, up to and including generals. The games were great fun and a good conditioner. One of the players was Captain Rex Robinson who worked in the Personnel Department. From him, I learned of a billet opening up in the Enlisted Assignment Section. I was interviewed by the Major in charge, and he agreed to request me as a replacement, if I could arrange a split tour. My request was approved, and I was reassigned to be the Assistant Head of the Enlisted Assignment Section of Combat MOS's 02, 03, 08, 18, 35, Drill Instructor, NROTC duty, and other special assignments. The hours were much longer, but I thoroughly enjoyed the work and believed I was contributing more to the war effort.

On 23 February 1968, I learned with great sorrow of the death of Gunnery Sergeant Paul E. Robitaille of South Attleboro, Massachusetts, my platoon sergeant in C/1/4, who was killed by a mortar round on that date. He was an outstanding Marine and a great leader of men.

I was promoted to the rank of Major in 1969 and finally received my Bronze Star award for the night of 24-25 March 1966.

I received a letter from Gunnery Sergeant Morton just before I departed HQMC. He retired in July 1968, and moved to Harligan, Texas as part of the staff of the Marine Corps Military Academy. Morton also served as the head football coach and went 9-1 in his first year.

"I was real glad to see you made the Major's list. See you're on your way back to WesPac. Need a good Gunnery Sergeant? I enjoyed serving with you and always think about our tour in Vietnam. Would have served with you again. Take care, Skipper, and drop me a note if you find time."

Morton coached successfully at the Marine Corps Military Academy for a number of years. When he died, one of his sons took over as head coach.

I left my family in Springfield, Virginia when I headed back to Vietnam. I flew to the west coast and reported to Staging Battalion at Camp Pendleton. The training I received there was a refresher course on the VC/NVA tactics, mines, and booby traps, etc., and re-qualification with the M-16 and .45 pistol. The M-16 was new to me, so I took special interest in becoming efficient with it. I visited with several friends who were stationed in the area.

Chapter Seventeen

Okinawa,
1969

29 August, Camp Hansen, Okinawa:

"I'm finally on Okinawa and will be flying south at 0700 tomorrow morning. The trip over was something else. We were suppose to leave Camp Pendleton at 1900 and sat around until 2200. Got to El Toro about 2330 and sat around there until after 0100 before we took off. The trip was rather uneventful, although I couldn't sleep. We stopped in Hawaii for 45 minutes to refuel, but it was 0330 in the morning so I didn't call the Cartwrights. We stopped again at Wake Island to refuel, also. At any rate, 16 hours after we took off we finally arrived at Kadena AFB, Okinawa. [Before our arrival on Okinawa, the senior Marine officer on board stood up and read out our duty assignments. Some of the officers stood up and cheered at their good fortune when they learned they were staying on Okinawa. I could not believe that some infantry officers did not want a combat assignment! I was pleased to learn I was going to the 1st Marine Division at Da Nang.]

They took us immediately to Camp Hansen where we were processed and I got booked out on a flight to Da Nang on the 30th. We arrived here at 0900 local time. After processing, chow, and a couple of beers, we all decided to take a nap' 6 hours later I awoke, only because I had to go to the bathroom! That's how exhausted we all were. At the officers' mess after chow, they had a floorshow, which was excellent and we came back and went back to bed at midnight.

Today has been spent getting our laundry done, briefings, turning in gear we're not taking to Vietnam, packing, etc. I'm all ready to go except for a little packing and picking up my nametags, required in Vietnam, at the PX. John Buckley, my roommate and constant companion since Staging Battalion at Camp Pendleton, and I are flying out together. We get picked up at 0315 for the 0700 flight. John is going to the 3rd Marine Division.

I ran into Tom Rich the first day I was here. He's on the staff of the 9th Marine Amphibious Brigade here on Okinawa. He said Col. John Keith is the G-4 of the 9th MAB.

I called Kent Shockey and he is out of the hospital and back as CO of E Company, 2nd Battalion, 9th Marines; my old company! He had the same company in Vietnam. All of the 9th Marines are on Okinawa, at Camp Schwab."

31 August, Da Nang:

"Well, I'm back in Vietnam again, but still don't know what I'm going to be doing. It's Saturday night here and General [Ormond R.] Simpson won't make a decision on my assignment until Monday. The suspense is killing me! I can hardly believe Da Nang. It has really grown, especially the airfield.

Well, I am beat from lack of sleep and the heat here so I had better close. I have briefings all day tomorrow."

What I noticed when we drove through Dog Patch, on the road to the Division CP, was the large number of servicemen with long hair, beads around their neck, and large wooden poles called 'knocking sticks.' They were all over the sides of the road. I wondered what so many men, mostly black, were doing there in the middle of the morning.

I was glad to see that the metal towers, the old French bunkers, and the mine fields were gone from around the Air Base.

1 September, Da Nang:

"Another hot day at the Division CP. The sweat has just poured out of me all day long. Of course I'm still wearing starched utilities with my jacket tucked in, so this doesn't help much. I can't draw the jungle utilities until I am assigned. 'Rock' Davidson, who I played basketball with at HQMC, is here and has promised to get me a set of jungle utilities until I get to my unit.

There's much speculation as to my assignment based on the vacancies opening up, but where I will go is a well kept secret. As the saying goes here, field grade assignments are a better-kept secret than any operational plans. General Simpson has a thing about wanting to tell an officer personally what his assignment will be. I'll sure be glad when tomorrow morning comes!

Denver Dale, who was in 3/4 in Hawaii, got me a bunk in his hut and it sure beats the transit officer's quarters. They have 4 officers to a hut. They have beds, mattresses, pillows, sheets, wall lockers, chairs, etc. Most have bought small iceboxes, fans, lamps, etc., so they really live well. Maid service also, which includes doing their laundry. The chow is good and a lot of the working spaces are air-conditioned."

Chapter Eighteen

An Hoa,
September 1969-January 1970
S-3, 2nd Battalion, 5th Marines
"The troops are magnificent, as usual."

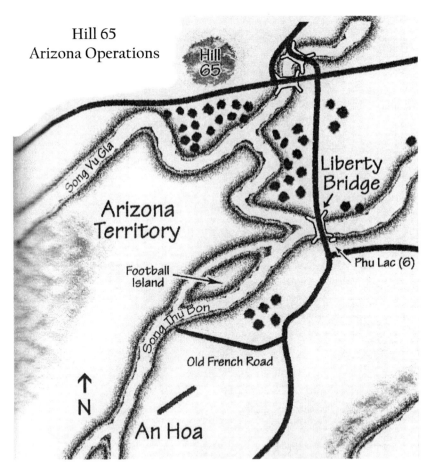

Map of 2/5 TAOR

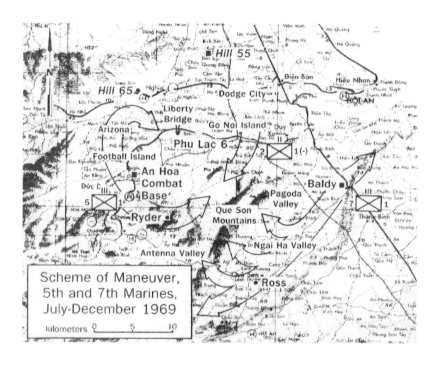

Scheme of Maneuver,
5th and 7th Marines,
July-December 1969
kilometers 0   5   10

2 September, Hill 65:

"Well, I finally got assigned! I saw General Simpson at 0930 yesterday morning and 30 minutes later I was on a helicopter with him on my way to the 5th Marines CP at An Hoa. An Hoa is an industrial complex under construction about 20 miles south of Da Nang. They have an airstrip there and it's a large combat base.

I waited around the 5th Marine CP until 1600 and finally saw Colonel [Noble L.] Beck. I was assigned as the S-3 (Operations Officer) of the 2nd Battalion, 5th Marines. Thirty minutes later, I had drawn my gear and was on my way to Hill 65, where most of the battalion is located. Hill 65 is about 18 miles southeast of Da Nang. Lt. Colonel James E. Bowen is the CO. I have been busy ever since getting snapped in by Major A.L. 'Abe' Vallese, who is leaving tomorrow for Quantico."

The 2nd Battalion's mission was to conduct company size patrols and participation in the district pacification program, north of the Song Vu Gia River, within the villages surrounding Hill 65. We were also required to provide rice denial to the VC/NVA. Golf Company, Captain H.R. Finlayson, was under operational control of Headquarters Company, 1st Marine Division in the defense of the Da Nang area until 25 September. Fox Company, Captain Ken R. Furr, was in the northern Arizona providing a blocking force for 3/5. Hotel Company, Captain Robert F. Poolaw, was conducting night and day movements in a search and clear mission on Charlie Ridge. Echo Company, Captain J.L. McClung, was providing CP security and conducting local operations around Hill 65. In our People-to-People Program, we were supporting a school with 700 students in Lee My village.

Bob Driver, 1969

3 September, Hill 65:

"It has poured rain for the last 2 days, as we're catching part of a typhoon. Living is good here, although we're somewhat isolated. Re-supply is by truck convoy every 2 days. We're in huts off the ground and with electricity. The chow is good, actually better than I ate at Regiment yesterday.

Jerry Ledin, who I believe you met once at HQMC, is the S-3 of 5th Marines. [Martin J.] 'Jerry' Dahlquist is the S-3 of 3/5.

The battalion has been on the go a lot. They have been on a big operation in the mountains and have had 106 cases of malaria since the 1st of August. Most of them aren't hospitalized too long."

4 September, Hill 65:

"The rain stopped last night and I've have had a hot but pleasant day today. Across the river from our position is an area called 'The Arizona.' It's an unfriendly area, and only VC live over there. It's also a free fire zone. You would be amazed at the amount of air and artillery we pour into the area both night and day. Our snipers killed 4 VC yesterday and 2 already today.

The war hasn't really progressed too far since my last tour. We're still fighting in many of the same areas.

I took a helicopter ride out to the Thuong Duc Special Forces Camp west of our position along with Lt. Colonel Bowen, Colonel Beck, and Jerry Ledin. I met the Dai Loc district chief today and his Army advisor. We're doing a lot of combined operations with the South Vietnamese units to help pacify the area.

I've got so many projects going on I can hardly keep up with them all. I'm going back to An Hoa tomorrow to read all the orders, etc. Major Vallese left today. Lucky stiff!

Lt. Colonel Bowen I knew at the Basic School. He's a real hard charger and we get along well."

5 September, Hill 65:

"Went on an all morning helicopter ride yesterday and ended up on top of a mountain at the Non Son Special Forces Camp. Real interesting place!

In the afternoon, we rode out to visit one of the company's positions. All of the houses have been destroyed and destroyed vehicles line the road. It looks as if quite a fight went on to clear the area. The villagers are now moving back in and rebuilding their homes. We met with the village chief and the Army advisor about protecting the rice harvest and the VC problem.

We're waiting this morning to catch a helicopter to An Hoa for a briefing on an upcoming operation."

6 September, Hill 65:

"Another long day over here. It was quite a night we had last night. Da Nang and almost every position around us came under attack. We only had a few mortar rounds fired at us. Spent most of the night in the CP bunker. Major Bob [Robert E.] Loehe, the

XO, has his family in Springfield. He has 29 days to go. My Assistant S-3, 1st Lt. [H.W.] Brookshire is from North Wilkesboro, North Carolina, and played football at Wake Forest.

The Vietnamese Rangers started an operation in front of us today [in the Arizona]. Nice to sit back and let them fight the war and watch from our vantage point [a tower built for the snipers to use]! We can see for miles in all directions from here.
Fox Company was attacked last night [40 rounds of 60 mm mortar fire] and 8 Marines were wounded [Only 2 required evacuation. They found 2 dead VC the next morning]. An amphibious tractor hit a [50 lb. box] mine and 21 Marines were wounded."

A platoon from Fox Company was returning from a mine sweep. Fox reported 15 WIAs, with 9 requiring evacuation. Hotel and Echo companies were both attacked during the night but suffered no casualties.

7 September, Hill 65:

"Sitting here fighting the bugs away to write this letter. Today is the first slack day I've had since joining the battalion. Last night was real quiet, as it poured rain from dark to dawn.

Fox Company had 3 men wounded from a booby trap and they found another artillery [155] round booby trapped today. They captured [500 lbs. rice and] 300 lbs. of corn. The ARVN Rangers had another good day, killing 14 VC and capturing 4 weapons. Echo Company bought 2 rocket rounds from children.

We had a USO show today. The 'Imperial Flowers.' They were quite good, and the troopers loved them. A 4 piece combo and 3 girls, including a stripper. The men danced with each other to all the latest hits, and after a few beers, it really got wild! A company had just come out of the field and had no chance to bathe, shave, or change clothes. They stomped around the mess hall in their filthy, ragged attire and boots, bearded, long hair, with their heads thrown back, yelling and laughing to 'Proud Mary' and the likes. The Vietnamese watching were funnier than the show. They don't see many of our women and are fascinated by them, especially their size."

8 September, Hill 65:

"Quite a day today. Last night Fox Co. [Captain Ken R. Furr, a former captain of the University of North Carolina wrestling team], had a listening post attacked with 2 killed and 3 wounded. [LCpl. David Michael Hartogh and PFC Larry Kenneth Robillard both died of wounds.] They found 2 VC dead, blood trails and captured 2 rifles [AK 47s]."

One of the dead VC was a local village chief. Fox Company was ordered to another area about 2,000 meters away. Learning that this area was in an ARVN impact area, I ordered the company back to a village they has just passed through. About 1730, LCpl. George Garcia was sitting in his fighting hole waiting for the word to move out when an NVA officer came down a trail and almost stepped on him. Garcia spun around and shot him and he fell partly in his hole.

I continued, *"Tonight already Fox Company has killed another VC and captured a weapon [AK-50 rifle].*

Five Marines and a corpsman received medals today. Captain Bob Poolaw, a full-blooded Indian, received a Bronze Star. Lt. Colonel Bowen presented the awards although Colonel Beck was supposed to. We sat here and watched the Vietnamese Rangers fight a full-scale battle today. Quite a change to have a ringside seat and be in the middle of it! The ARVN were in armored personnel carriers, and the VC could be seen swarming around them, but getting out of their way when they advanced.

Spent the morning riding around meeting some of the adjacent unit leaders. Met the S-3 of 3/1. They are at Dai Loc and occupy a large French bunker. Also met the District Chief of Dai Loc, his Army advisor and the area intelligence officer.

General [William B.] Rosson, the commander of I Corps, is flying in tomorrow for a short visit. More dog & pony shows! There is a lot of firing going on tonight all over the area and it's lit up like daylight!"

9 September, Hill 65:

"The war goes on. Last night, we had 1 Marine killed and four wounded. [Company F lost LCpl. Donnie Joe Clough KIA, LCpl. Byron 'Bud' Canada, PFC 'Tennessee' Randall, and a dog handler from Division was wounded. Randall was a platoon radio operator who was hit in the eye by a grenade fragment. He remained at his post until the medevacs arrived before turning over the radio to someone else and boarding the helicopter. He lost his vision in that eye.] Killed 1 VC, captured 3 NVA and 3 weapons. Fox Company captured 3 enemy, 2 young males, and 1 young female. The weapons were 2 AK-47s and an M-16 rifle. Two of our companies were engaged. Only a few minutes ago, one of our patrols was engaged [Echo Company]. Going to be another long night! Just heard that no one was hurt.

It poured rain most of the day. I think the monsoon is about to set in. General's Rosson, Simpson and [George S.] Bowman flew in for a visit today. We stood in the mud and rain for 45 minutes waiting for them. All were very pleasant."

10 September, Hill 65:

"We had a quiet night last night and a quiet day today. Fox Company came back by helicopter from the Arizona territory and Hotel Company went out west of our position.

It's hot and sticky here tonight after a day of the same. We only have cold-water showers, but it sure feels good!

I had to interrupt my letter to get a helicopter to evacuate a Marine with malaria for the third time. Also one of our ambushes was fired on from across the river."

11 September, Hill 65:

"Another busy, hot day. No battle casualties, though. We shot a few VC across the river, but other than that all was quiet. [Snipers killed 2 VC/NVA]. It appears we're going to be on this hill for quite a period of time. I'm tired of it already and Lt. Col. Bowen doesn't have anything to do so he gets involved in everyone else's business, which doesn't help. I'm also playing Battalion Executive Officer out here as Major Loehe stays at An Hoa."

12 September, Hill 65:

"This is a sad occasion to write home. Jerry Dahlquist had his right leg blown off below the knee yesterday by a booby trap. He had some other minor wounds. I'm going to try to make it to Da Nang tomorrow to see him.

The Lt. Colonel's list came out. Lt. Col. Bowen was not reselected, so this counts as a pass over. John Buckley, who I came over with, made it, as did Bob Loehe and two other officers in the regiment.

We killed 1 of 5 VC trying to cross the river near our position a few minutes ago. Wish we could have gotten them all. It was really hot here today, 97 degrees with 70% humidity."

13 September, Hill 65:

"I went to see Jerry Dahlquist today. He's in good spirits and I was able to talk to him for about 30 minutes. He's being flown out tomorrow, but he's not sure where. He may go to Guam or all the way to Philadelphia. General Simpson pinned a Bronze Star and Purple Heart on him.

There's a lot of action going on tonight. One of our ambushes fired on a group of 15 VC/NVA crossing the river and killed 4. One of our snipers killed one earlier in the day. Some Vietnamese troops are going across the river tomorrow. That should prove interesting!

I got fired on today on my way to Da Nang. We passed a truck, which was stopped to fix a flat tire and they ended up with 7 bullet holes in the vehicle."

I always carried the driver's M-16 locked and loaded when I traveled by vehicle, and kept my eyes pealed for any sign of the enemy.

14 September, Hill 65:

"I am happy with my assignment as far as being the Battalion S-3; however, I am far from happy with Lt. Col. Bowen. Since his pass over, he has no trust and confidence in his officers and men. I've already been threatened with relief if I do anything wrong! I hope they move him somewhere else soon! Or me! Everyone on the staff and the company commanders are upset with his attitude. Lt. Brookshire's uncle is a Marine Colonel, and he said Bowen had a reputation for not backing up his men. Bob Loehe came out today. He's the cool head who keeps the battalion tied together.

Generals [Charles S.] Robertson and [William G.] Johnson flew in today with Colonel Beck on a surprise visit. Stayed a few minutes and flew off to harass someone else."

15 September, Hill 65:

"The war goes slowly on. Took a helicopter ride today and the gunners fired on some VC. We killed 4 across the river last night and one tonight [A platoon from Company E providing security for Company F was crossing the river. We suffered one Marine KIA and one WIA]. We [Company E] also captured a North Vietnamese Master Sergeant tonight. He was skinny, sickly looking and had sores all over him. He came down out of the mountains looking for rice and he had a pack full when we caught him. The villagers around here are harvesting their rice now.

The Colonel was gone to a meeting today and everything was quiet and peaceful."

Part of our mission was rice denial and destruction operations, working with the ARVN and district forces. A sniper, firing from the tower on Hill 65, killed another VC.

16 September, Hill 65:

"I went to Hill 37 to coordinate with the S-3 of 3/1 today, and also to Liberty Bridge to see 3/5's positions and CP setup. They live in a dust bowl, due to all the convoys coming and going from An Hoa.

One of our companies killed 2 VC and captured 3 today [Company H]. We had one Marine receive a minor wound. We killed one across the river from here today, also.

It's started to rain. Just hope it isn't the start of the monsoon, which is due any time.

We're putting in a new CP bunker and I've managed to keep busy supervising that and also acting as the XO in the field.

We're losing almost all our officers in the next month or so, and we're really hurting in a lot of areas.

Just had some firing in the village down below us, interrupting my letter. The artillery battery here had some movement in front of their positions also. Just enough to get everybody out in the rain!"

17 September, Hill 65:

"Another hot, dusty day! Went to Dai Loc District Headquarters today and visited with Major Warren, the District Advisor.

The Colonel is going to visit Golf Company tomorrow. They are up guarding the Division CP.

Some Vietnamese came in today with a young girl sick with TB. They had carried her 70 miles from up in the mountains! The doctor said she would be o.k. We have a good doctor [Lt. D.S. Whitney] and chaplain [Lt. H.J. Hultbey], both brand new."

18 September, Hill 65:

"Just heard about the new troop withdrawals. Everyone knew they would take out the rest of the 3rd Marine Division first. They'll probably go to Okinawa.

We had a real monsoon type downpour last night and this morning. It's still drizzling now. No power tonight, so I'm writing by candlelight.

The Colonel has been gone all morning, so things have been quiet. He's calmed down a little from last week, but he's still sour grapes on everything and everyone."

19 September, Hill 65:

"We had two floods today, or I did, anyway. The monsoon seems to have started. We still don't have any power, so I'm writing by candlelight again. All our food and medical supplies are spoiling.

Last night was quiet. The Vietnamese Rangers are back in the Arizona and we could see VC running all over the place. There's been a lot of firing tonight, so they must be busy! Went to An Hoa with the convoy today. Two big trucks ran off the road and almost overturned as it was wet, miserable, and very muddy!"

20 September, Hill 65:

"The ARVN Rangers are engaged in a battle across the river tonight and my desk and pen are bouncing all over the place. I've seen more VC through binoculars in the last

2 days than I've ever seen before. They are all evading and watching the Rangers & they know we aren't allowed to shoot across the river. Smart, aren't they!

It stopped raining and the sun came out today but it's pouring again now. The river is way up and overflowing its banks. Fox Company took a long walk in the rain up in the mountains but didn't find anything. We haven't had any contact with the VC for three days now. Too quiet!"

21 September, Hill 65:

"Another long, hot, humid quiet Sunday. It was 97 degrees today. I was busy with paper work so that helped some. Nothing much going on except rumor spreading—always the fashion over here."

22 September, Hill 65:

"Another day like yesterday, 97 degrees again, but there is a slight breeze blowing. The Colonel has gone to An Hoa, so I'm in charge. We're having inspections of the rear elements of the battalion.

The Vietnamese are busy harvesting their rice crop. I can sit here and watch them out of the side of my hut. Last night was a quiet as far as the VC were concerned. However, the artillery fired all night long and kept me awake!"

23 September, Hill 65:

"Another quiet night last night. We had a North Vietnamese to surrender this morning. Wish they all would! Another hot day in Vietnam! I went to Dai Loc District Headquarters this morning. I had a pleasant trip. Anything to get off the hill!

I just found out that it's official on the 12-month tour! That means I'll be coming home in August instead of September!

The Colonel is going to spend the night in An Hoa tonight. Things should be especially quiet tonight!"

Later, I continued, "He changed his mind and we went out to visit Hotel Company. A long, hot ride and walk. I got a copy of those awards I put Captain Borowitz and four others in for [in 1966!]. They were forwarded to FMF Pac by the Commander in Chief, U.S. Pacific Fleet."

24 September, Hill 65:

"Jerry Ledin, the 5th Marines S-3, was evacuated for a possible heart attack today. Colonel Beck came out and presented some awards to the troops today. An hour later General [Charles S.] Robertson flew in. VIP day! Lt. Colonel Orr was with General Robertson today. He's the new Division plans officer.

Went to Dai Loc District Headquarters and to visit 3/1 today. The Vietnamese are going to send a convoy through tomorrow to the Special Forces Camp at Thong Duc. We have to protect them while they are passing through our area. Roland Monnette, who was in the Brigade in Hawaii, is the new S-3 of 3/5 replacing Jerry Dahlquist."

25 September, Hill 65:

"Writing by candlelight again. The generator went out right at dark. It was really hot here today, in the high 90s. Last night was noisy, but we didn't have any contact. Eight Marines were wounded down near Dai Loc.

The convoy got through to Thuong Duc Special Forces Camp. We did a lot of roadwork to get them through. We're going on a one-day operation tomorrow. I'll be on Hill 52 tomorrow night."

1st Lt. Robert F. Conti relieved Captain McClung as CO of Company E.

26 September, Hill 65:

"Will get a chance to write after all. The amphibious tractors have been delayed."

27 September, Hill 65:

"Spent the last 6 hours wading in water up to my chest as the Colonel walked us most of the way back from Hill 52. It was quite an ordeal. We evacuated 2 men for heat exhaustion. I think the Colonel learned a good lesson."

He had insisted on running a CPX in a war zone! In others words, an exercise of the CP group for no reason except he didn't believe the radio operators were in shape! The CP group moved out with just the security of the S-2 scouts and an infantry platoon. As soon as we started up the road westward, the VC started sniping at us. We climbed up the side of Hill 52 through a dense jungle before reaching an area covered with large boulders. The men had to cut their way through the bamboo and vines. It was about 100 degrees, no shade on top, and we ended up having to have two men evacuated for heat exhaustion. They were not our radio operators! I don't know how regiment let him get away with it.

On our way when we first started out, we reached a village close to the right side of the road with a stream that had been dammed up to form a large pond. The village was full of people, including adult males of military age. They stopped what they were doing and just stared at us. A woman with a young child was washing clothes on the edge of the pond, when all of a sudden the child waded in over its head and she started screaming. I saw what had happened and shouted, 'Give me a swimmer, quick!' to the S-2. One of his scouts was almost beside me and as we ran, he stripping off his gear as we moved. He jumped into the pond and swam out and rescued the child from drowning. We gave the child artificial respiration, and soon he spit up some water and started crying. The woman could not thank us enough. None of the villagers made any move to help the child. They just stood and stared at us.

About a week later, one of our ARVN interpreters came to me and said the woman wanted the Marine from S-2 and I to come to her house so she could give us a gift. I thought about if for a while and finally agreed to go. I took the S-2 and his scouts, the ARVN interpreter, and a radioman and hiked the mile or so westward to the village. When we reach her hut, there was smoke coming out as someone was cooking. We could hear noises coming from within, as if a party was going on. The ARVN interpreter told me that he, the S-2 scout, and I were the only ones who could enter. The S-2 set his men up along the road as we crossed a footbridge to enter the hut. The woman and her child met us just inside the doorway. I glanced towards the rear of the hut and there sat 6 or 8 male Vietnamese of military age, all dressed in black pajamas, around a table. They were eating, drinking, and smoking some kind of pot. I thought for sure that they were VC. Her husband was among the group. They stopped their party and just stared at us. There was a tense moment between us as we looked each other over. The S-2 scout had left his M-16 with the S-2, and the ARVN interpreter was unarmed. All I had was my .45 in my holster. The woman had the child hand each of us a bag of rice candy she had made, and thanked us again for saving her child's life, through the interpreter. We left immediately. The ARVN interpreter would not say if the men were VC or not, because he wasn't sure. I think he was intimidated. We had a walk in the sun back to Hill 65. Not a shot was fired at us. Normally, when a Marine patrol left Hill 65, the VC would start firing at them. It was as if they knew what our mission was and that it wasn't a hostile one.

I continued, "*Last night was quiet on Hill 52 but the mosquitoes ate us up. They had beer and coke iced down for us when we got back. I was a little dehydrated but not really tired. Hotel Company climbed Charlie Ridge starting at 0300 this morning and killed 5 VC and captured a lot of munitions and rice. No Marine casualties. A good day's work.*"

28 September, Hill 65:

"*Another long, hot day in Vietnam. Last night was a quiet one. The elections are going on today with no incidents so far. We killed 1 VC today up near the mountains.*

We're going to have a party tonight for the officers and SNCOs going home. All those troops scheduled to leave during October-November are leaving with the 3rd Marines, and we're getting their troops who have 6 months or more to go."

29 September, Hill 65:

"*Another long, hot day. A storm is coming up and I believe it will be pouring shortly. Last night was a quiet one. I've been busy planning future operations with Colonel Bowen. Busy, busy, busy!*

Lt. Brookshire is now the CO of H&S Co. 1st Lt. [Samuel G.] Easterbrook is my assistant S-3. Got to close now and write an order."

30 September, Hill 65:

"*Another hot, humid day. Last night was quiet, as usual. Can't believe the VC are so quiet. Guess they're waiting for all the Marines to pull out! Ha!*

We're going for a helicopter ride in a few minutes to look over the area we're going to be operating in, in the next few days."

The battalion submitted 37 awards and received 8, which were presented during September.

1 October, Hill 65:

"*We had another quiet night last night. It started raining this morning and it is still going strong.*

Fox Company is going to wade the river into the Arizona at 0500 in the morning, so we're worried about the river being up.

Joe Alexander was out to see me yesterday. He's the S-3 of 3rd Amphibious Tractor Battalion."

1st Lt. T.R. Woolens took command of Golf Company on this date.

2 October, Hill 65:

"*We didn't send Fox Company across the river as it was up and visibility was about 100 yards. It has poured rain for the last 24 hours and this has slowed everything down.*

The VC must not like the rain either, as it has been very quiet. [Major J.W.] 'Denny' Lanigan is the new XO. Bob Loehe leaves the 1st of November."

Company G was on 'Stack Arms' at China Beach 2-4 October.

3 October, Hill 65:

"Quiet last night here, but Da Nang got hit with rockets. I went to Dai Loc and to visit 3/1 on Hill 37 today. Their areas have been quiet also. It is really boring with nothing going on and the rain pouring down."

4 October, Hill 65:

"I believe the monsoon has set in, as it's pouring rain and has for the past 3 days.

The Colonel went to An Hoa today by helicopter. They got a .50 caliber round through it, too! They were flying low because of visibility. We had another VC surrender today. Also found a booby trap beside the road between here and Dai Loc. Glad the Engineers found it!"

5 October, Hill 65:

"It's raining tonight like it's the end of the world. It's the 5th straight day and it's only stopped for about an hour or so the whole 5 days. [I recall having to sleep in a sleeping bag with a sweat suit and socks on and my field jacket over me, it was so cold! Our blood was thin from the near 100 degree temperatures we had been experiencing.]

It must be too wet for the VC, too, as nothing is going on. We did have a villager shot by the VC for refusing to give them rice.

Denny Lanigan is coming out for a visit tomorrow. I'm going to An Hoa Tuesday to prepare for an inspection that's coming up. I'll be back and forth between now and the 10th, when the inspection is scheduled. I heard that Jerry Dahlquist was taken to Guam, where they amputated more of his leg above the knee. I also heard that his arms are in danger, although he had full use of them when I saw him.

Denver Dale is the new XO of 3/5. I know he is happy to be out of Division Headquarters."

Hotel Company was on 'Stack Arms' at China Beach 5-8 October.

6 October, Hill 65:

"The 6th day of pouring rain. All the roads are closed and only the Amphibious Tractors are able to move now. Liberty Bridge is under 3-4 feet of water and will be closed *for at least a week. All our companies have moved to high ground. The river here must be a half mile wide in places. Hotel Company is going through R&R at China Beach and I don't know when they'll get back. I'm sure they don't mine! Heard that Phu Bai had 21 inches of rain in 24 hours. Believe we came close!"*

7 October, Hill 65:

"Another night of pouring rain. It has slacked off some but everything is still flooded. Three trucks had to be abandoned on the road between here and Dai Loc due to high water. I haven't had a bath in 5 days due to the water truck turning over and now the road is out. I'm going to splurge tonight if I have to stand out in the rain!

I'm going to An Hoa by helicopter if it ever comes! I've got to get the paperwork in the rear ready for inspection by Division."

8 October, An Hoa:

"It's still pouring rain here. An Hoa is a mud hole and we don't have any power. I still haven't had a real shower. I washed some in the rain last night, as I've been too busy to take one during shower hours and they've changed them both days I've been here.

The helicopter I came in on got shot at, but they missed. A Marine had just been wounded in it just before I got on. There were 4 Marines from 3/5 wounded by a booby trap near here tonight.

Two men from 3/5 drowned yesterday when the tower they were in at Liberty Bridge was toppled by high water. They still haven't found one body.

Everything is quiet on Hill 65. We still have a truck under water."

Fox Company was on 'Stack Arms' at China Beach 8-11 October.

9 October, An Hoa:

"Our 9th straight day of rain. It really poured about noon with a lot of wind. The prediction for the next 48 hours is—you guessed it—more rain!

They finally got our truck out of the river at Hill 65. It was underwater for 3 days. [It was full of fresh vegetables and fruit, which were ruined.]

Everything was quiet here last night. We didn't have any electrical power, as the generator is down, so we worked by candle and lantern light.

Seven officers and staff NCOs are coming from Division to inspect us tomorrow. We have half a sea hut, which is very small, for all of us to get into. Should be fun! I know some of the inspecting party. I'll be going back to Hill 65 after the inspection tomorrow. The chow is much better than here. The battalion hasn't had any action since I have been gone. It's almost too quiet.

I finally got a shower tonight. The water was cold but it sure felt good to be clean for a change! They're re-supplying An Hoa by plane now. Eight came in today, even though the weather was terrible. Denny Lanigan came back from Hill 65 today and we went to the 5th Marines club tonight."

10 October, An Hoa:

"The inspection party didn't make it because their helicopter broke down. They're coming in the morning. Denny Lanigan went back to Hill 65 to mind the store as the Colonel wants to go to Da Nang tomorrow.

Last night was quiet as usual. Guess the VC don't like the rain and mud either.

We're rotating the companies on R&R for 3 days at China Beach. All the steak, hamburgers, and hotdogs they can eat, and all the beer and soda they can drink. They sleep in beds with clean sheets, too, and no patrols, ambushes, etc. to go on.

Guess I'll go over to the 5th Marines club tonight with Lt. Brookshire."

11 October, 1969: Taken by MSgt. Haynes, S-3 Chief

11 October, An Hoa:

"'Sunshine Airlines,' as we call Marine Aviation, didn't fly much today, so the inspection has been put off until tomorrow.

Denny Lanigan came back from Hill 65 and we went to the 5th Marines club. Jerry Ledin and Colonel Beck were there and we had a good time playing liar's dice. I met Greg Lee, a VMI grad, Class of 1961, tonight. He remembers Bill [my brother].

Another quiet night, but rainy—it rained most of the day and tonight. Hope the inspection party can get here tomorrow. We've had 24 inches of rain here so far this month and Phu Bai has had 51!"

Hotel Company was on 'Stack Arms' at China Beach 11-14 October.

12 October, An Hoa:

"As you probably guessed, it poured rain yesterday and the inspection team didn't make it. If they don't come today, we're going to ask for a cancellation. I'm going back to Hill 65 this afternoon as soon as the inspection is over. I'll be glad to get out of here, despite the showers. We still don't have any power here.

Lt. Colonel Bowen came in on a helicopter just now."

13 October, Hill 65:

"I'm glad to be back on Hill 65 even though Lt. Colonel Bowen had a million things for me to do when I got back.

The inspection fell through again, even though the sun was out most of the day. I ended up waiting 3 hours for a helicopter to bring me back up here.

I've had a shower and some clean clothes to put on! Really great! I haven't had a hot shower since I left the Division CP, but am quite use to taking cold ones now. We moved into our new bunker here and it is so much better than before."

14 October, Hill 65:

"We had plenty of sunshine today, with just a sprinkle of rain. General Robertson and Colonel Beck were in today for a visit. No helicopters for anything else, but plenty for the brass to ride around in! We were supposed to make a trip to Thuong Duc Special Forces Camp, and naturally we couldn't go—no helicopters. We're going to try to make it again tomorrow.

One of the companies [Golf] found a bunch of rice, sardines, noodles, etc. today. It's the first thing that's happened in our area in a while. A hamlet chief said a PF was captured and the VC took rice from his hamlet last night.

Echo Company had a man drown yesterday when they were on R&R at China Beach. Denny Lanigan came out today. He's going back by helicopter tonight."

15 October, Hill 65:

"I went to the Dai Loc District Headquarters today. Nothing new there."

1st Lt. W.H. Taylor took command of Hotel Company.

16 October, Hill 65:

"The VC are coming down out of the mountains and we have had 3 contacts in the last 24 hours. No casualties on either side. We captured 2 NVA helmets. We did kill 3 with artillery fire across the river today. Last night was quiet as usual. The weather has turned hot and humid, in the mid 90s the last 2 days.

The Colonel has gone to An Hoa for an awards ceremony this afternoon. One of our SNCOs is getting a Silver Star. Lt. Easterbrook, my Assistant S-3, is getting a Bronze Star.

The engineers are working on the roads—upgrading them so we won't have to use helicopters for re-supply.

Oh! Yes! Yesterday we finally got to fly up to Thuong Duc and the Non Song Special Forces Camp. They're always glad to see us."

These flights took us by a huge mountain jutting out of the valley floor, and it looked like the conning tower of a submarine. The north and south slopes were sheer rock cliffs. The east and west slopes are more gradual and are covered with thick vegetation. The top appears to be almost flat, but has heavy vegetation on it. The rumor was that the VC Da Nang Command Post was located in caves in the sides of this mountain. We never flew too close, but I can never recall any planes being fired on from that area. The terrain around the mountain looked extremely rugged, with a thick canopy of trees, and no trails and signs of habitation were visible. It was in the ARVN TAOR, but I don't believe anyone ever ventured into that area.

17 October, Hill 65:

"Another nice hot day. It looks like rain tonight. The power is off so I'm writing by candlelight.

The VC are still active. We sprang 2 ambushes last night but don't think we got any.

I took a long helicopter ride today. Flew in a Huey which is like riding in a car, it is so smooth."

18 October, Hill 65:

"Another long, hot day. It's in the upper 90s. They're pulling the Vietnamese Rangers out of the Arizona and helilifting them to Hill 65 where they'll be taking trucks to Da Nang. They've been over there a month. 1/5 went in to replace them. 3/1 has a big operation going south of Hill 55.

Fox Company finally had success today. They killed 3 VC and captured a rifle [AK-47] and 5 packs, documents, etc. The squad that got them had been up in the mountains for 2 days with only 1 meal! They just missed getting 2 more, earlier this morning, but they got away.

I went to Dai Loc to see the District Chief, but no interpreters were available so I'm going back this afternoon."

19 October, Hill 65:

"The temperature was in the 100s today and tonight is not much better. We had a busy day today. Two companies changed positions and we re-supplied all 4 companies. One of our snipers killed a VC today across the river. We also found several mines and booby traps. Company G had a VC Chieu Hoi today [Surrendered or turned himself in]."

Battlelines recorded Sgt. Albert N. Wright, Jr. dying on this date [of wounds received 18 October].

20 October, Hill 65:

"Last night was quiet as usual. I rode out to Hill 52 to visit Golf Company today. They've been having a lot of activity. Captured some packs and documents today and got sniped at by the VC. [They found a harboring site large enough for 50 men]. No casualties. We killed 4 from here today [106s firing beehive rounds]. Today was another hot one. We picked up a heat casualty from Golf Company and brought him back here. 97 degrees was the prediction but it hit 100 degrees easy. I think we're going to have a real storm tonight."

21 October, Hill 65:

"Another long, hot day today. The dust is starting to get bad now.

The Colonel went to Da Nang and I'm in charge when he is away, so when he's gone something always happens. The Vietnamese who work on the hill got into it over who was suppose to work where. Some Vietnamese policemen from Da Nang were out here and trying to intimidate them.

Golf Company continued to be harassed by sniper fire and booby traps. No casualties as of yet. We're sending 2 companies up into the mountains tonight to try and clear them out. Everything was quiet here last night.

Nixon and his announcements! I just hope he knows what he's doing, as I'm not sure the Vietnamese Army is ready to take over this war. Like everyone else over here, I'd rather be home, but I'll be damn if I want Jett [my son] to fight over here 10 years from now because we didn't finish the job!

I just chased a mouse around the hut. Missed him with my helmet!"

22 October, Hill 65:

"Our two companies [Golf & Hotel] up on Charlie Ridge killed 2 VC, captured 2 weapons [M-1 carbines], some grenades, documents, etc. We had one heat casualty. Found a bunker complex complete with mess hall!

A recon insert is in trouble tonight. They got ambushed and 3 are known dead, 1 wounded, and 4 missing. We have a company standing by to go in and get them out. They'll probably go in at first light in the morning.

Last night was quiet, but tonight they're trying to get across the river. We've been shooting at them since dark. Generals [Herman] Nickerson and Simpson were out to visit us today. A big dog & pony show."

23 October, Hill 65:

"Another long, hot day. The Vietnamese say it should be pouring rain. The VC were quiet again last night.

We killed a few today with air, artillery, and 106 mm recoilless rifle fire trying to cross the river.

Echo Company is going across the river at 0600 in the morning on a search and clear operation. Golf Company is going on a search and clear operation in the mountains tomorrow. Should be a busy day!

I went to Dai Loc District Headquarters this morning over an incident yesterday. We separated the two companies. The Colonel and the District Chief went out and talked to both companies."

A Marine company and an ARVN company were co-located on a hill. Some of the Vietnamese soldiers stole articles from some Marines who were on patrol.

24 October, Hill 65:

"I had a real busy day today. It took Echo Company most of the morning to get across the river, as the Vietnamese were late getting there with the boats. This afternoon they failed to show up at all, but we managed to get a couple of boats ourselves and started back across. About dusk the VC opened up on them. Luckily we had no casualties. We finally got all of them back across at 2200 tonight, after another firefight with the VC. The company left at 0400 this morning so they must really be pooped. They captured 4 VC suspects.

Golf Company's operation netted nothing. Hotel Company sprang an ambush tonight but only found some blood trails. They had one man receive a minor wound.

Colonel Beck and Jerry Ledin were out for a visit today, also Denny Lanigan.

Had a real scare yesterday. The Flamethrower Section was burning brush on the side of the hill and they set off a mine in the minefield near my hut. Neither of them was hurt and neither was I, but a lot of rocks, etc., hit the side of my hut!"

25 October, Hill 65:

"Another long, hot day. I was busy all morning but took it easy this afternoon. I'm going out to visit two companies tomorrow and won't be back until the 28th. It was the Colonel's bright idea. He thinks he's still at Camp Pendleton."

26 October, Hill 65:

"A real scorcher today. It feels hotter than it is because the humidity is so high. General Robertson and Colonel Beck are coming in to disrupt our Sunday tomorrow, as usual. We're having an awards ceremony and I've got to brief them on what's been going on. I'll probably leave for Hotel Company about 1700."

28 October, Hill 65:

"Got back about noon today. It poured rain both days I was out, as usual. I enjoyed being out with the companies but I got sniped at and didn't appreciate that at all."

Echo Company found 60 lbs. of rice, packs, and an NVA helmet. Hotel Company found 3 caves and captured a .38 revolver, a M-26 grenade, 3 NVA packs, 2 hammocks, and an NVA helmet.

29 October, Hill 65:

"Celebrated my birthday a day late tonight. Lt Easterbrook and the enlisted men who work for me bought me a 5th of Canadian Club and gave me an original card. Everyone came by and had a drink tonight.

It poured rain again today. I had to go to Dai Loc and coordinate with the District Chief, as we're going on an operation in the Arizona territory tomorrow morning. This may be my last letter for a while as we may be gone for up to 10 days. Denny Lanigan is out here now to run things while the Colonel and I are gone."

We moved Golf and Hotel companies into blocking positions near the east end of the Arizona, with Regional Force Company 369, along the Song Thu Bon River. Two companies from 1st Battalion, 5th Marines established blocking positions from My Hoa (3) to Phu Long (1) in the northern Arizona. India Company 3/5 landed by LVTs on Football Island and joined with Company E of our battalion. All the companies began platoon size patrols searching for bunkers, food caches, dud rounds, and booby traps. After 10 days of successful operations, 2/5 was withdrawn from the area. We killed 17 VC/NVA and captured 11, along with 900 lbs. of rice. The other units killed 10 VC/NVA during the operation.

While we were in the Arizona, Company H had a jeep with 4 Marines in it ambushed between An Hoa and Liberty Bridge. Willie J. Kelly, the company driver, was killed, and Mark D. Oliver and the other two Marines were wounded. The VC took the mailbags from the jeep.

Driver's birthday card from the S-3 Shop

30 October, Northern Arizona:

Company E found a cache of 400 lbs. of rice. They were later lifted back to Hill 65. Our CP group, S-2 scouts, killed 8 and captured VC/NVA in a 'stay behind ambush.' Golf and Hotel companies found two 250 lb. bombs, one 155 and one 105 rounds, which they destroyed. We had no Marine casualties during the day.

31 October, Northern Arizona:

Hotel Company arrested 28 VC suspects in the morning and in the afternoon brought in 23 women and children and captured 1,800 lbs. of rice, 850 lbs. corn, 10 lbs. beans, 50 lbs. of oats, and 30 lbs. of tobacco. Still later, they captured a VC, an M-1 carbine, and an SKS rifle. Before dark they had killed another VC and captured 3, plus a 9 mm pistol. Golf Company killed 2 VC and captured an M-16 early in the day. Later they killed 5 more and captured another that they had wounded. They also picked up 2 weapons, an AK-47 and an AK-50, plus grenades, ammunition, etc. The CP group had been busy, taking 2 prisoners and blowing up dud bombs and artillery shells.

The battalion processed 37 awards during the month including a Legion of Merit, 5 Bronze Stars, 3 Naval Commendation Medals and 27 Naval Achievement Medals.

1 November, Northern Arizona:

Hotel Company found a major river crossing point, 2 rubber boats, and numerous caves the VC/NVA hide in. In the caves, they found 250 lbs. of rice, clothing, and equipment. They had one man wounded during the day and wounded and captured a North Vietnamese soldier. Golf Company located 500 lbs. of rice and captured 3 VC suspects. While in their night position they were hit with grenades, wounding 3 Marines.

2 November, Northern Arizona:

Hotel Company captured 2 VC and later destroyed 3 submerged boats. Golf Company killed 2 NVA and later in the day wounded and captured a VC. The Battalion CP blew up two CHICOM booby traps and during helicopter re-supply had a Marine wounded in the left shoulder by a sniper round.

3 November, Northern Arizona:

Golf Company was engaged with a VC force in the morning, suffering one Marine wounded. Later they blew up a dud 500 lb. bomb. Hotel Company captured 100 lbs. of corn, 50 lbs. of rice, batteries, blasting caps, and ammunition. Still later, they killed a VC and captured 2 more, carrying first aid packs and other equipment. Echo Company located and blew up another dud 500 lb. bomb. The Battalion CP found 2 dead NVA, with weapons, packs, and CHICOM grenades.

4 November, Northern Arizona:

Our 81 mm Mortar Platoon fired on a group of VC, killing one. Hotel Company blew up three bunkers. Golf Company destroyed 7 bunkers and, with the help of the Vietnamese National Police, captured 4 VC suspects.

5 November, Northern Arizona:

Echo Company was mortared during the day and returned fire. There were no Marine casualties. During a search of the suspected mortar site, they found an NVA helmet and pack. Golf Company was fired on and later captured 2 VC and destroyed the bunker they were hiding in. Fox Company killed one VC during the day.

6 November, Northern Arizona:

"I have been on this operation since the 30th and haven't had a chance to write until now. We've killed and captured a lot of VC/NVA and weapons, over 4,000 pounds of rice and 2,000 pounds of corn, and other foods. We've sent in about 80 VC suspects and captured 10. The CP group captured 2 NVA."

We were on the move, and the S-2 scouts spotted them trying to hide near a river. The Marines waded in with guns blazing, but didn't hit them because they hid under the water. They waded in and pulled them out. The two were unarmed and ragged looking. They had packs, which were almost empty. They told our interpreter they had come down out of the mountains looking for food.

The 'Sea Tiger' reported, "The command post of the 2nd Bn., 5th Marines was moving to a new position in the 'Arizona Territory,' 23 miles southwest of Da Nang, when they spotted four Viet Cong soldiers running through the high elephant grass; a brief firefight commenced [all by the Marines] and the enemy soldiers attempted to flee across a near-by river.

"'By the time we got to the river bank, two of them had already made it across but they had discarded their packs in the water,' commented 1st Lt. Dennis M. Storm, (Wooddale, Ill.), the battalion intelligence officer.

"'One of the enemy soldiers was lying motionless in the water and I took it for granted that he was dead. I waded out to recover the body but when I got about 5 feet from it, he jumped up with a frightened expression,' continued Storm. 'It startled me at first, but I grabbed him by the back of the neck and led him to shore.'

"At the same time, Cpl. Jose Anzaldus, (Refugio, Texas), an S-2 scout, had waded out to recover the discarded packs from the two enemy soldiers who had made it across the river. Halfway across, he spotted another VC hiding in the brush along the riverbank. Anzaldus, who speaks the Vietnamese language, had an easy time of talking the VC out of the water. Along with the two enemy prisoners, the Leathernecks also captured several Chinese Communist grenades, documents, and an assortment of other gear."

I continued, *"We're scheduled to be lifted out on the 8th so we're looking forward to that. It's poured rain most of the time and we've lost a lot of Marines with emersion (sic) foot. We've only had 2 wounded, and neither was serious. We're operating in rice paddies from foot to chest deep with water. I'd give anything for a bath and change of clothes right now! I shaved this morning for the first time. The Sergeant Major said I had more hair on my face than on my head!"*

Golf Company found and destroyed 16 bunkers during the day.

7 November, Northern Arizona:

Golf Company had another good day. They killed one VC and captured his 9 mm. pistol and Chinese pack. They also captured 5 VC suspects and destroyed 6 bunkers. Echo Company had an excellent day, killing 4 NVA and capturing 1 M-1 carbine, 3 NVA packs, and an NVA helmet.

8 November, Hill 65:

"We got helilifted out of our mud hole this afternoon, and yes, it rained as usual. The last couple of days were fairly quiet. We killed 1 VC, captured another and 2 weapons. We [Fox Company] blew up a grenade factory we found. On the other side of the river, Echo Company killed 4 and captured 1 weapon up on Charlie Ridge. They had one man slightly wounded.

I've had a steak, a bath, and a couple of beers and feel like a new man! I was so dirty it was unbelievable. Denny Lanigan stayed in my hut and made a lot of improvements. He's at An Hoa now."

Fox Company had a very busy day before they found the grenade factory. They had gathered in 4 VC suspects and an SKS rifle. They spent the rest of the day blowing bunkers and tunnels in the same area. Golf Company was busy doing the same thing. Our Artillery Observer in the tower on Hill 65 called in a fire mission on 13 VC harvesting rice and killed 9 of them.

9 November, Hill 65:

"Another long rainy day, but I was dry for a change. I flew out to visit 1/5's CP in the southern Arizona today. Looks like more of the same. We're scheduled to go back in for 30 days on the 16th.

General Robertson is coming out tomorrow to cut the cake for the Marine Corps birthday. Colonel Beck is coming also. We have a USO show scheduled afterwards and then T-bone steaks. Major Warren, the District Advisor, and the District Chief are coming also.

Hotel Company found a 20-bed hospital in the mountains today, also some ammunition, rice, documents and C rations. The hospital site included 30 caves with double racks. They also took an NVA flag and 3 banners, canteens, and medical supplies. They blew up the hospital and all the caves. Our Artillery Observer was busy again today, killing 4 VC near a bunker in the Arizona.

No power tonight so I writing by candlelight. It just burned out so I'm finishing by flashlight."

10 November, Hill 65:

"Happy Marine Corps Birthday! It was that on Hill 65 today. The booze and beer flowed. The 'Imperial Flowers' were back. Not as good as the first time. The General showed up but the cake didn't get here in time, so the ceremony didn't come off as planned but I think it was good. The [1st Marine Division] band came in and played during the ceremony. I spent the day running around getting things set up as the Colonel went to An Hoa for the ceremony there.

Last night and today were exceptionally quiet. Hope it keeps up! I was a little worried that some of the troops had too much to drink. I had a few beers and that's all."

11 November, Hill 65:

"We had a real tragedy tonight. A friendly mortar round landed on one of our [Hotel Company] platoon's position on Charlie Ridge, killing 4 Marines and wounding 2 others. It's a rainy, soupy night and the helicopters can't get in up there to get them out. Hopefully we'll be able to get them out in the morning. [The Marines killed were Robert C. Barr, John D. Harrington, James A. Jackson and Roger A. Steele].

Echo Company killed 2 VC this morning, but it sure doesn't make up for us killing 4 of our own.

The weather is getting cooler all the time, almost cold at night and early morning. I rather enjoy it, but I feel for those troopers lying out there in the cold rain. The Canadian Club came from the SNCO club in Da Nang. MSgt. Haynes, my Operations Chief, got it for me."

Later in the day, 2 VC Chieu Hois turned themselves in to them.

12 November, Hill 65:

"Another long, busy day. The sun was out for a change, so that helped. They finally got the wounded off the mountain about 0130 this morning. The weather broke some so the medical evacuation helicopters could get in. They found 1 dead VC up there today.

Three of our officers got the Bronze Star, one a Silver Star, and one a Navy-Marine Corps medal today in An Hoa. The Colonel was gone all day and that helped. I got an operation order written and a lot of legwork accomplished with him gone. We're moving everything to An Hoa that isn't going to the Arizona with us."

1st Lt. D.J. Andrea took command of Golf Company. Hotel Company blew up a dud 500 lb. bomb and captured some ammunition, packs, and other equipment during the day.

13 November, Hill 65:

"We had visitors from regiment today to fill us in on the southern Arizona. I'm staying busy getting ready for that operation."

Echo Company found 2 cave complexes during the day with beds in them and found 4 packs and other gear. They blew up the caves.

I wrote my brother that evening, "We were on an operation (unnamed) in the Arizona for 10 days and we killed and captured quite number of VC/NVA. Captured 6,000 pounds of rice and corn with some weapons."

14 November, Hill 65:

"Well, we're almost ready to go back in the Arizona, for at least a month this time. I'm not looking forward to it, but I'm reconciled to the fact. MSgt. Haynes, who is in the rear at An Hoa, wants a transfer because he is being promoted. Lt. Easterbrook and one man are on R&R, and one man has an abscessed tooth. That leaves me with three others, and one of them has to stay in An Hoa with the MSgt!

If you noticed how slanted my writing is it's because I'm writing on my knee. I've sent everything but my rack to An Hoa."

Delta Battery, 1/11, fired on 2 VC across the river and killed them both.

15 November, Hill 65:

"Our move has been postponed until the 17th, and possibly longer, as the VC/NVA are supposed to start their big offensive for the winter any day now. I don't think it will amount to much, but you never can tell!"

Delta Battery was busy again during the day. They fired on and killed 2 VC during the morning. In the afternoon, their Forward Observer in the tower fired on a group of 15-20 and killed 11. Later they fired on 6 more and killed 5. Before dark, they had fired on another group, killing one. Fox Battery, 1/11, also got into the act, firing on a group of 15-20 VC, killing 2. Hotel Company had 3 men wounded from a CHICOM grenade booby trap. Only one required medical evacuation.

16 November, Hill 65:

"The big operation starts tomorrow, so you won't be hearing from me for a while. They keep changing the word, but I guess it's really starting tomorrow. Major Bob Crabtree, S-3 of 1/5, had a heart attack today and was medevaced."

The operation had our CP group and two [Fox and Golf] companies being lifted in during the normal re-supply missions in the afternoon, joining 1/5 and 3/5. We conducted a night movement to the Northeast Arizona. The three battalions drove the enemy forces of the Q83 Battalion onto Football Island. The 1st Battalion killed 18 VC/NVA trying to escape and captured a large amount of rice.

17 November, Arizona Territory:

Delta battery fired on 12 VC in a rice field, killing 4. Echo Company picked up a VC suspect carrying medical supplies and food. Golf Company apprehended another carrying a bag of rice.

18 November, Arizona Territory:

The Battalion CP located an ammunition and food cache of eight 60 mm rounds, 2 CHICOM grenades, and two M-26 grenades. We blew up all the munitions and gave the rice and medical supplies to the ARVN. Fox Company had a busy day, killing 1 VC, capturing a rice cache of 325 lbs., and 100 lbs. of corn, but suffered one Marine wounded from a CHICOM booby trap. They were the blocking force for Golf Company and A/1/5. Golf found a small rice and ammunition cache and blew it up. Echo Company found a small rice cache and 5 flare containers. A/1/5, which was attached to 2/5, found a 2,200 lb. rice cache. As they continued their mission, they captured 1 VC armed with 2 M-26 grenades. They also took 4 detainees and an NVA pack filled with rice. The captured rice was flown to An Hoa. Delta Battery continued their good work, killing 3 VC in two separate fire missions.

19 November, Arizona Territory:

Fox, Golf and Alpha 1/5 swept Football Island. Fox had a busy day. They picked up 6 VC suspects and blew a dud 250 lb. bomb. Earlier, they hit a booby trapped CHICOM grenade, having one Marine and one Navy Corpsman wounded. Golf was engaged several times during the day, having 9 Marines wounded but only 1 requiring evacuation. They also found and destroyed another 250 lb. bomb. Hotel Company killed one VC hiding in a cave. Our Battalion CP located and destroyed 100 rounds of AK-47 ammunition at one site and uniforms and other clothing and equipment at another. Delta Battery fired on 6 VC and killed 3 during the day.

20 November, Arizona Territory:

Echo Company [operating off of Hill 52] started the day capturing 2 VC in a cave. Later, they killed 1 and captured 4, who were carrying medical supplies and rice. Fox Company captured 2 VC suspects in the morning and in the afternoon engaged 20 VC/NVA, killing 2, taking 2 prisoners, and captured packs, rice, and other equipment. An aerial observer, flying in their support, killed 2 of 4 VC he spotted. A/1/5 killed 2 VC and captured a bag of rice and some NVA equipment. Our Battalion CP group discovered a cache of 150 lbs. of rice. Delta Battery continued in our support, firing 2 missions on 2 small and 1 large group of VC, killing a total of 26. Echo and Hotel were busy in their areas. Echo captured 2 VC hiding in a cave and killed another during the day. They also found the bodies of 2 killed by an aerial observer that day. Hotel engaged a force of 10 VC/NVA, killing 2, and capturing 2 AK-47s, packs, ammunition, food, etc. The 117th Regional Force Company, operating with us, engaged some 20-25 VC and killed 8.

21 November, Arizona Territory:

"This is the first time in four days we have stopped long enough for me to write. We helilifted in on the 17th and made a night march in a driving rainstorm that lasted from 0700 until 0200 the next morning. We killed a couple of VC the next morning and captured about 4,000 pounds of rice. The next day, we took another long hike and ran into some VC and had 1 Marine killed and 10 wounded. Only 2 of the wounded were serious enough to be evacuated. Yesterday, we made a big sweep and killed 14 VC and captured 10. The companies are off again, but the CP group is sitting still for a change. The weather hasn't been too hot, but we've been doing a lot of wading through rice paddies. Lt. Easterbrook just got back from R&R in Australia. He had a ball! One of our companies is in contact so I'd better close for now."

Golf Company commenced a search and destroy mission along the Thu Bon River while Fox and Alpha blocked for them. Golf caught some VC trying to cross the river that morning and killed 3. Later they captured 2 VC suspects. Late that afternoon they engaged another VC unit and had one Marine wounded and evacuated. Alpha Company killed 2 VC in each of 2 engagements, capturing CHICOM grenades and other equipment. Fox Company killed 1 VC, and captured his grenades and equipment. Echo continued their good work near Hill 52, killing 4 VC, and capturing grenades, packs and magazines loaded with AK-47 rounds. The CP group was not idle, capturing 100 lbs. of rice and 50 lbs. of tobacco.

22 November, Arizona Territory:

During the day, we switched positions with 1/5 and A/1/5 reverted back to them.

An Hoa

23 November, The Hotdog, Arizona Territory:

"We've finally got settled in one place long enough to write. We received re-supply from An Hoa last night. We haven't had much contact with the VC/NVA the last few days. We killed 8 and captured 4 on the 21st and found 3 dead ones yesterday and one surrendered [to Golf Company] today. Today, 10 civilians reported to us and wanted to refugee out of the Arizona to the Duc Duc refugee camp. I don't blame them, as the bombs and artillery that are used in here don't discriminate between VC and civilians. We've only had 3 minor wounded in the last five days. Hope that keeps up! It poured rain last night and I managed to get soaked. Slept for a while, though."

During our movement, we knew the VC were following us. After a break for chow, we moved on, as usual, but left a stay behind ambush, consisting of the S-2 scouts, who killed and captured 6 VC. Golf Company found 10 VC/NVA bodies, probably killed by air or artillery.

The Hotdog is a hill shaped like its name, which had been used numerous times by both the Marine and ARVN. It looked like a big sand pile, with no vegetation on it. Old fighting holes had been partially filled in with sand bags, etc. sticking out of all of them. It was difficult for the troops to dig in without digging into an old hole. The VC often booby trapped the abandoned fighting positions. The previous occupants usually left their trash in the holes also. In watching one of the air strikes, we were all standing up cheering, and of course the pilots waved their wings at us as they flew over. One of the bombs went off and I heard something hit the ground at my feet. I reached down and picked up a piece of shrapnel and dropped it quickly, as it burned my fingers! That's how close they were dropping the bombs and napalm. The napalm took out whole tree lines, which is what we wanted, as this is where the VC dug their spider holes and bunkers.

Our position on the Hotdog overlooked large rice paddies where the civilians had their seedbeds and were planting their rice. One of our missions was to prevent them from doing that. They usually wore white pajamas and had on straw hats, so they were easy to identify. When we saw them heading to the paddies with their hoes over their shoulders, we would fire a warning round of white phosphorous to let them know we didn't want them in their rice paddies, and they would leave. We never shot at them to hit them, just to warn them.

24 November, The Hotdog:

Echo Company was engaged twice during the day, losing one Marine wounded slightly in the morning and one KIA from a CHICOM booby trap. There were 2 wounded during the second firefight. Fox Company killed 2 VC and Hotel Company engaged 4 VC and wounded and captured one of them. They later blew up another 500 lb. bomb.

25 November, The Hotdog:

"It has been a long 2 days since I have had a chance to write. I haven't really been that busy but it has poured rain the last 3 days and nothing has been flying to re-supply us. We had good luck 2 nights ago when we killed 6 VC. Yesterday, we had some terrible luck. 1st. Lt. [Robert F.] Conti, the CO of Echo Co., was killed by a booby trap and 2 others wounded. He was a real fine young officer and newly married. [1st Lt. J.H. Steihl took command of Echo Company.]

The sky has cleared a little today so maybe we'll get re-supplied. They're supposed to fly in hot chow tomorrow for Thanksgiving."

26 November, The Hotdog:

"We finally got re-supplied late yesterday. I have my usual run-ins with the Colonel. He's so wishy-washy I can't stand it at times. I stay away from him as much as possible. He interferes with my job and doesn't always know what he is doing. Three more months with him and then a change of scenery! Can't wait! I'm about ready for one of those paper-pushing jobs with hot showers, clean sheets, a PX, a club, etc. Nothing much happened yesterday. We had 4 wounded [in Golf Company], all scratches.

We had a memorial service today for Bob Conti. Almost 200 men attended. The Catholic chaplain (ours) [Lt Hultbey] did a fine job."

Echo Company had a good day operating from Hill 52. They hit an M-26 booby trap and had one Marine slightly wounded, but they later killed 2 VC and captured 2 packs, 31 lbs. of rice, salt, and other items. Before dark, they arrested 1 VC suspect. During the night, Fox and Hotel companies moved to Football Island and assumed blocking positions for Lima 3/5.

27 November, The Hotdog:

Echo Company got off to bad start today, when a returning ambush squad was hit by a M-26 grenade from the company perimeter, killing one Marine and wounding another. During the rest of the day, they killed one

VC, captured a VC and a suspect, and had one to surrender. The VC that Chieu Hoied brought in 2 SKS rifles. Golf Company killed 2 VC and picked up a suspect during the day. Hotel Company was engaged three times with a large group of VC, killing 4 and capturing 8 suspects, 2 pistols, a .45, and a 9 mm. During the fighting, they suffered 6 men wounded.

28 November, The Hotdog:

"We had a busy Thanksgiving Day. Three of our companies closed in on an island called Football Island, because of its shape, and killed 6 VC/NVA, captured 19, including at least one officer, and 3 pistols. We killed one other in this area, and another 15 refugees came in requesting to be flown out of here. On the 26th we killed several and captured 2 rifles but had 2 Marines killed and 3 wounded. We had 5 Marines wounded yesterday.

They flew in hot chow for all the troops, which was great. Most important was all the mail that came in!

It's pouring rain today, so probably no re-supply or mail. At least it's not 100 degrees!

I'm determined to take a bath today, rain and cold regardless. 12 days is about all I can stand! I have shaved and washed a couple of times, but that's all!"

Fox Company had a bad day. They engaged 3 VC and killed one of them. Later, they hit a booby trapped 155 round, losing 1 Marine KIA [LCpl. Robert Lee Spence], and 7 wounded. The Battalion CP was fired on, wounding one Marine.

29 November, The Hotdog:

"Another day of pouring rain just like yesterday. Naturally, we had no re-supply so no mail came in or went out.

We had another tragedy yesterday. A platoon for F Company hit a 155 mm artillery shell that the VC had rigged as a booby trap. One Marine was killed and 7 wounded. We had a probe of our lines last night and had one Marine slightly wounded in the knee. We managed to kill 1 NVA yesterday and captured 2 rifles and a couple of mortar rounds. We had 2 more to surrender and 1 refugee who had been a prisoner of the VC.

I had my radio, shaving gear, clean clothes, etc., brought out here, and it's great. I got out in the pouring down rain and scrubbed myself down yesterday and it felt great!"

Hotel Company had a good day. In one engagement, they killed 1 VC and captured 2. Later, they killed another, capturing his AK-50 and 4 M-26s. An Aerial Observer operating with Hotel Company killed 2 VC trying to escape.

30 November, The Hotdog:

"Yesterday was another rainy one. We killed a couple more VC and captured 1 weapon. Today, we've killed 4 more and captured 3 weapons.

We had another tragedy this morning. Echo Company was burning trash in an old foxhole and set off a booby trap, wounding 6 men, none too seriously. Colonel Beck and a Chaplain are coming out today.

Since I've started this letter, we've captured 3 VC, 1 surrendered, picked up 2 detainees [suspects], and captured 1700 pounds of rice and corn."

Fox and Golf companies blocked to the north and L/3/5 blocked to the south. Hotel Company conducted a search and destroy operation on Football Island.

Fox Company was engaged early with 7 VC and found blood trails. Later, they ambushed 12 VC carrying a mortar tube. They killed 4 and captured one. After the fight, they picked up 1 M-16, 1 AK-47, and 1 AK-50, ammunition, grenades, a U.S. medical bag, a Marine's personal diary, and documents. Continuing with their mission, they found 1,000 lbs. of rice and 700 lbs. of corn on a riverbank. Later, they were hit with small arms fire, wounding one Marine. Hotel Company found a cache of medical supplies in a hut and picked up two VC, one of which was wounded. Echo Company, operating from Hill 65, hit an M-26 booby trap and had a man wounded and later in the day, another Marine was wounded by small arms fire. The totals for the day were 6 VC/NVA KIA and 23 prisoners. From the prisoners, 8 were identified as NVA and 7 as VC, including 2 officers.

The enemy prisoners captured during the month were from the Q83 Battalion, 575th and 577th Artillery regiments, 141st Infantry regiment, C-28 Medical School, and 69th Battalion.

The battalion submitted 52 recommendations for awards during the month, including 5 Naval Commendation Medals and 47 Naval Achievement Medals.

The illnesses reported were 9 cases of malaria, 20 cases of VD, 245 cases of dermatitis, 25 gastritis, 68 orthopedic, 6 with ear problems, and 65 with immersion foot problems.

During this period, we tried to put more emphasis on thoroughness of searches rather than worrying about patrols or companies reaching checkpoints or keeping timetables, and it paid off.

1 December, The Hotdog:

Fox Company picked up one VC suspect during the day. Golf Company killed 1 VC, and in his pack found C rations and rice. Hotel Company killed 1 VC, an officer, according to his ID card. They also recovered his .45 pistol and other documents. They grabbed 2 VC suspects later in the day. Echo Company had a North Vietnamese soldier to surrender to them with his AK-47 rifle and CHICOM grenades. Later in the day, a North Vietnamese corpsman surrendered to them, with his pack full of medical supplies.

2 December, The Hotdog:

"We changed positions yesterday, so I didn't get a chance to write. We moved the CP about a mile west but still on the Hotdog. After we got set in, we found a 500-pound bomb in the middle of the position! EOD came out today and disarmed it. Rumors are that we will be here until the 15th and then move to An Hoa. We killed 3, captured 1, 4 surrendered, and 61 refugees came in yesterday."

The day before, the village chief had come to me about not shooting at his villagers planting rice. He was taller than most Vietnamese and was probably about 50 years old. His hair and whiskers were gray, and he wore white pajamas and a straw hat. He looked like a leader. Through the interpreter, I explained that we could not let them plant the rice, as we knew the VC and NVA were taking it. We only fired on them to make them leave the rice paddies. He heard me out and asked about moving the entire village to a refugee settlement. I agreed, and told him we would provide helicopters to move the people and animals out of the Arizona.

The next morning at dawn they came, all in white pajamas, carrying their few possessions and babies, chickens in crates, and rice mats while the young boys rode their water buffalo or drove the pigs, etc., towards the hill. The helicopters showed up with Vietnamese troops to help with the loading. It was the greatest moment I had in Vietnam, watching these people boarded the helicopters and fly away to safety. I'll never forget the sight of the water buffalo and other animals hanging by straps under the helicopters as they lifted off. However, it didn't end here. Over the next few days, some of the men from that village came back with Vietnamese troops. They pointed out where they had hidden their rice crops, which were in huge ceramic jars wrapped in black plastic and buried in the middle of flooded rice paddies. More refugees continued to come to us each morning, having seen that we did what we said we would do. I'm sure word came back to them that they were safe, for the moment, in the refugee camps. I'm prouder of this than anything I did in Vietnam.

3 December, The Hotdog:

"Today, we've killed 6 and captured 2, plus 500 pounds of rice and 1 rifle already, and it's not half over yet. Yesterday was the first day with no rain since we have been out here, so we picked a good one to move, as it took all day. Today it's raining, naturally."

Fox Company captured a wounded VC along with his AK-47, 3 M-26s, and documents in his pack. Golf Company killed one NVA and found his pack with rice, canned fish, and other items. Hotel Company brought in 9 refugees and 500 lbs. of rice. These women and children were sent to the Duc Duc refugee camp. They also captured a wounded VC. Echo Company was extremely busy near Hill 65. They killed 5 VC/NVA is five separate engagements, but they also hit a 60 mm booby trap. This wounded 3 Marines.

3 December, The Hotdog:

"We've had 5 VC to surrender this morning and 52 refugees [and five children], so we're starting the day right. [I was beginning to feel like the Pied Piper!] Another Lieutenant was wounded yesterday. That's 1 killed and 2 wounded in 10 days. One of the VC led a patrol to one of our 3.5 rocket launchers. He got paid for it."

Echo Company had another busy day, killing 4 VC/NVA in four different firefights and finding another dead one from the previous day. In one of the NVA packs was a diary, Russian battle dressings, a U.S. canteen, clothing, etc. They also evacuated 11 refugees to Duc Duc. Golf Company killed 1 VC and found his pack with papers and medical supplies. Not to be outdone, Hotel Company sent in 40 refugees to go to Duc Duc. They also destroyed 5 boats during the day. The S-2 bought 360 rounds of ammunition and an M-26 grenade from children, paying them 400 dollars in Vietnamese currency.

4 December, The Hotdog:

"We've been fairly busy. We killed 5 VC yesterday, 8 surrendered, and 153 refugees. Today, we killed 6 and had 5 refugees. We also found 1,000 pounds of tar and 1,150 pounds of rice. No casualties on our side. The sun was out again today, and it sure felt good. I've been sleeping in my rain suit to keep warm.

The Vietnamese are coming here to relieve us and we're moving back to the northern Arizona. One's as bad as the other except the northern area has more open rice paddies and more civilians. It's dryer in this area. Hill 65 was hit with six 60 mm mortar rounds last night. I don't know if they had any casualties or not." [There were none.]

Fox Company with a CIT team and a Chieu Hoi found the rice and tar. Company G killed 2 NVA, capturing an A-K 47, NVA packs, food and clothing. Hotel Company found 1,000 lbs. of rice and picked up a VC suspect. Later they blew up an 8 inch artillery dud and some shotguns shells that were booby trapped.

5 December, The Hotdog:

"We had a good day today. 5 VC kills, 1 rifle, 5,000 pounds of rice, 2 VC surrendered, and 20 refugees.

The Colonel went to An Hoa for a meeting and was gone most of the day and will be gone most of tomorrow, as General [Henry W.] Buse will be in An Hoa.

The 51st ARVN Regiment and an artillery battalion are coming in here tomorrow and we've moving back to the east—a long walk! No casualties again today—thank goodness, as we've had enough for a while."

During the night, Golf Company sprang an ambush killing one NVA, and recovered his documents and some CHICOM grenades. Later they killed 3 VC, and found 3 CHICOM grenades, 1 M-26, 2 M-16 magazines, cartridge belts, C rations, and rice. A CIT team joined them with a Chieu Hoi and he located 9,000 lbs. of rice. They found another 1,800 lbs. that had gotten wet, so they destroyed it. Hotel Company fired on 3 VC and found a heavy blood trail. Later they found 2,500 lbs. of rice. All of the rice and refugees were sent to An Hoa. Fox Company hit an M-26 booby trap and had 2 Marines wounded. They found a 105 round booby trap and blew it up.

6 December, The Hotdog:

The Battalion CP remained busy, sending 30 refugees to Duc Duc and a wounded VC to An Hoa. As we moved to Hill 10, we blew up one 105 and one 155 rounds that were booby trapped. A Fox Company ambush fired on 2 VC and recovered the rice they were carrying. Later, they ran into 3 different booby traps, blowing up a 105 round. The other 2 were made up of a Claymore mine and C-4 buried in the ground. They hit another C-4 booby trap and suffered 9 wounded Marines. Golf Company killed 4 VC and captured 1 M-26 and 4 CHICOM grenades. Hotel Company killed 1 VC and captured 1 with a flashlight and documents.

7 December, Hill 10, Arizona Territory:

"Spent most of yesterday walking and, naturally, the sun was out in full force and it got up into the 90s. We received re-supply yesterday, but no mail.

After we got our shelters up, Lt. Easterbrook and I went down to a nearby well and took a bath. The water was ice cold. but it felt great! I just finished shaving and put on clean utilities and I feel like a new man. The Colonel is going to Da Nang today so things will be quiet, I hope!

Last night the VC hit Liberty Bridge—don't know what the outcome was, but they fired all night long. We killed 1 VC, captured 2, and flew 21 refugees out yesterday. We ended up with 12,000 pounds of rice day before yesterday. Fox Company was setting up on a nearby hill yesterday and found 3 booby traps, but tripped another one and 9 Marines were wounded, only 3 seriously enough to be evacuated.

We're now destroying all the rice seedling beds in the area. That's quite a task, but the 'Huskies,' tracked vehicles which can move across the rice paddies, are being used to destroy them. That's not my way to fight a war, but it's the only way to keep them from growing rice for the VC.

I'm losing my Operations Chief, who has been handling all the paperwork in the rear for me, to Regiment, as he made E-9. I'm getting a new E-8 to replace him."

A dog handler and his dog were wounded by a booby trap while operating with Echo Company. Fox Company, using the Huskies, destroyed 30 seedling beds during the day. In the afternoon, they engaged 6 VC and found heavy blood trails and a set of USMC utilities. Golf Company, with the help of the Huskies, destroyed 20 seedling beds and 2 booby traps they found. That evening, they engaged a VC force and suffered 2 Marines wounded. When they searched the area, they picked up a few CHICOM grenades the enemy had dropped. Hotel Company sent off two groups of refugees, totaling 31, to Duc Duc. They engaged a small VC force, having 1 Marine slightly wounded. Later, they found a trap door in the ground containing medical supplies. The VC had booby trapped it, so the engineers blew it up.

8 December, Hill 10, Arizona Territory:

"Had an exciting night last night. We had an emergency medical evacuation and the helicopter crashed and burned. Pilot error as far as we could determine. The pilots and crew got bloody noses and one may have a broken jaw, but that's all. Very lucky! Another

medical evacuation helicopter came in and took out our Marine and the pilots and crew. We had to leave a platoon to guard the downed helicopter the next day until a flying crane came in and removed it."

I was watching as it came in to land. The pilot tried to make a one wheel touch down, just long enough to get the wounded Marine aboard. The helicopter suddenly flipped over on its left side and down the hill. I notified 5th Marines as soon as it happened.

"We were probed by the VC last night. Nothing really happened, but we heard them beating sticks, etc.

Golf Company got hit with small arms, grenades, satchel charges, and rocket grenades. They had 4 wounded, 3 seriously. We killed 1, wounded 4, captured 3, and destroyed a lot of seedbeds yesterday.

It's raining this morning, but we had a CBS cameraman come out and take some pictures. They're doing a feature on the Arizona territory. You might see me in the news one night."

Fox Company found a grenade factory that day and blew it up. They also destroyed 26 seedling beds using the Huskies.

9 December, Hill 10, Arizona Territory:

Fox Company started the day with a Marine wounded by an M-26 booby trap. Using the Huskies, they destroyed 15 seedling beds. During the day, they sent off 106 refugees to Dai Loc District Headquarters. They also found an ammunition box with 500 AK-47 rounds in it, which they blew up. Hotel Company was engaged throughout the day. In their first encounter with 6 or 8 VC, the enemy got away, but they picked up an M-26 grenade. Next, they found 5 VC/NVA in a spider hole, who surrendered. They recovered 5 AK-47s, 3 CHICOM, and 7 M-26 grenades, plus magazines, rice, and equipment. Later, they killed 3 VC, capturing their rice supply, ARVN rations, clothing, and equipment. In another spider hole, they killed 2 VC and found 21 lbs. of rice. Nearby, they killed a VC and captured his medical gear. Their luck ended there, as they struck an M-26 booby trap, which wounded 2 Marines.

10 December, Hill 10, Arizona Territory:

"I've really been busy the last 2 days and didn't get a chance to write yesterday. I flew to Dai Loc and then to An Hoa, and by the time I got back, re-supply had gone and it

was too late to write a letter. I managed to get a haircut and a hot meal in An Hoa before coming back out.

We had a good day yesterday. Killed 6 VC, captured 5, and 5 weapons. We sent out 106 refugees. Not much going on today."

That was a bit of an understatement. Fox Company and the CP group engaged 7 VC and killed 2. During the day, 2 VC Chieu Hois turned themselves in, and 7 refugees were sent to Duc Duc. Fox later found 25 bunkers, which they blew up. Just before dark, they killed 1 NVA and captured his AK-47 and medical gear. Golf had one Marine wounded by a sniper round. Hotel was busy again, killing 1 VC and capturing his documents. Later, they killed 2 more hiding in a spider hole and recovered 2 AK-47s and documents. One Marine was wounded in this action. Hotel took another 5 VC as prisoners and recovered documents on them.

11 December, Hill 10, Arizona Territory:

"Another long rainy, muddy day and night. We had good success yesterday. Killed 6 VC, captured 8, 5 weapons. 2 VC surrendered, and we sent out 34 refugees. Colonel Beck has sent notes to the Colonel complimenting 2 individual companies on their feats.

One of my NCOs had to be evacuated for malaria. His third time, and he makes the third NCO who works for me to be evacuated with it.

I'm flying to Liberty Bridge in about an hour for a liaison visit with the S-3 of 3/5. They are scheduled to relieve us, and we them. I had just as soon stay here as go there. It's a mud hole or a dust bowl and the area is heavily mined and booby trapped. Everyone leaves you alone out here, and we've really been successful. The mines and booby traps aren't nearly so numerous."

Fox Company killed one VC that morning and recovered a CHICOM grenade and documents from the body. They later picked up a VC suspect and killed one more. During the day, they destroyed 6 seedling beds. As they were moving to their night position, they struck an M-26 booby trap, suffering 1 Marine killed and 3 wounded. Golf Company reported destroying 628 seedling beds and picked up 1 VC suspect. Hotel Company continued their success, killing 2 NVA is a short engagement. They destroyed 29 seedling beds during the day. They killed 2 more VC before the day was over. The Battalion CP sent 6 more refugees to Duc Duc.

12 December, Hill 10, Arizona Territory:

"We had another good day yesterday. 5 kills, 6 captured and 7 refugees. Unfortunately Fox Company hit a booby trap and had 1 Marine killed and 3 wounded."

During the day Fox destroyed 62 seedling beds and found a dead VC with his ID card. Golf destroyed 10 seedling beds and killed 1 VC. Hotel destroyed 25 potato patches, killed 4 VC, wounded and captured 1, and arrested one suspect. They found packs, grenades, food and clothing on the dead VC.

The Arizona, 1969, F/2/5
Cpt. Furr briefing Lt. Col. Bowen & Major Driver.
Lt. Tom Williams seated on the left. Lt. Willis next to Cpt. Furr.
Bernie (Furr's radioman) standing behind him.
photo courtesy of Cpt. Ken Furr

13 December, Hill 10, Arizona Territory:

"Yesterday was one of those long rainy ones. Colonel Beck, Denny Lanigan, and Tom Barton, the acting Regimental S-3, visited us today. Not much news but a lot of praise for what we've been doing.

We killed 6, captured 2, and had 7 refugees yesterday. We have 4 VC kills, 2 prisoners, and captured a pistol so far today. 3 Marines wounded, but none seriously enough to be evacuated.

We're making a big ritual out of our meals trying to come up with something different. Last night, we had some dehydrated steaks, which with dehydrated onions, garlic salt, Worcestershire sauce, meat sauce, salt and pepper, were really good. Today, I had some dehydrated beef hash, which was also good. Anything beats C rations!"

Fox Company destroyed 10 seedling beds before one of the Huskies hit an M-26 booby trap. The 2 wounded Marines did not require evacuation. That afternoon, the company suffered 2 Marines and 1 Navy Corpsman wounded by a 60 mm booby trap. Golf Company killed 1 VC and later in the day had a Marine wounded by an M-26 booby trap. Hotel was extremely busy, killing 2 VC and capturing 2, one of which was wounded. They found another tree line full of spider/sniper holes. In the first one, they recovered a .45 pistol, compass, maps, supplies, and other documents. One Marine was slightly wounded. In the next hole, they killed 2 VC and captured 2 AK-47s, but had another Marine wounded. In the third hole, they found documents and medical supplies. Meanwhile, the Huskies destroyed 28 vegetable gardens. Before the day was over they had killed another VC, taken a suspect, and recovered a pack, rice and medical gear.

14 December, Hill 10, Arizona Territory:

The CP sent 10 refugees to An Hoa. Fox Company killed 2 VC and arrested 2 female suspects. Later in the day, they had an engagement. Four Marines were lost and Navy corpsman was wounded. While searching the area, 9 more Marines were wounded by a 60 mm booby trap. Golf Company found 6,000 lbs. of rice, destroyed 20 seed beds, and captured 1 VC. Hotel Company killed 1 VC and captured his two grenades.

15 December, Hill 10, Arizona Territory:

"Another long rainy day. We've killed 4 VC today and 2 prisoners so far. Fox Company had 2 seriously wounded a few minutes ago. Now 3.

I took a helicopter ride this morning, and we're really tearing up the rice seedbeds. Most of them are torn up now. Hope to finish the job before we leave! Golf Company just found 10,000 [4,000] pounds of rice! That's quite a haul."

In addition to the rice cache found in jars, Golf sent off 40 refugees to Duc Duc, captured some grenades, medical gear and other equipment, and destroyed 8 bunkers. A patrol from Echo Company tripped an M-26 booby trap, wounding 1 Marine. Fox Company had a busy day, killing 4 VC in three separate actions, capturing an AK-47, grenades, medical gear, clothing, and equipment. They also sent off 4 children to Duc Duc. Hotel Company killed 1 VC and captured 51 lbs. of rice and 2 lbs. of corn.

16 December, Hill 10, Arizona Territory:

"Two busy days. Yesterday we killed 5, captured 2, 1 rifle and 400 pounds of rice. We flew out 100 refugees too. So far today, 9 kills, 9 prisoners, and 1 rifle captured. One of the prisoners is a NVA officer."

16 December 1969 is known as 'Fox's Big Day.' In their first engagement with 5 VC, they killed 1 and captured his AK-47. Later, they killed 8 and took 25 prisoners, all VC or NVA, including an officer, his 9 mm pistol, and documents. As they continued across Football Island, they killed 12 more VC/NVA and captured 3, including one they had wounded. They had 6 Marines wounded in this last action. Golf Company started the morning by killing 1 VC and captured some packs with rice and clothing. Later, they killed 4 VC, capturing medical gear and documents. In the afternoon, they killed one more. Hotel Company, operating in a heavily booby trapped area, destroyed several of them, plus a 500 lb. bomb. In several firefights in the afternoon, they killed 2 VC and captured their packs and 10 lbs. of rice. One Marine received a minor wound in these skirmishes. Later in the day, they hit several booby traps, resulting in 4 men being wounded. A CIT team brought a Chieu Hoi in, and he located 500 lbs. of rice. We also sent out 20 more refugees with the rice.

Marine from 2/5 searches a bomb crater in the
"Arizona Territory"

Arizona fighting; 2/5 Marine
firing M79 grenade launcher

H/2/5 Marines patrol Go Noi Island

An Hoa

NVA prisoner taken during an
ambush on Go Noi Island, 1969

Fox's Big Day: 16 December, 1969

17 December, Hill 10, Arizona Territory:

"We had the greatest day in the history of 2/5 yesterday. We ended up with 28 kills, 33 prisoners and 7 weapons [AK-47s]. Regiment could not say enough good things about us. It's been pouring rain all day, as usual, but we hope to get re-supplied today—if it goes."

Fox Company accounted for most of the enemy casualties. Cpl. Hank Berkowitz, a reporter for the 'Sea Tiger,' wrote two articles on that day's actions. "PFC Lewis E. Grover, (Riverside, Calif.), a radioman with Co. H, 2nd Battalion, 5th Marines, was with a squad searching the dense brush in the Arizona Territory, looking for spider holes and trap doors.

"The foliage was so thick that it hampered movement of the Marines carrying rifles. Grover left his rifle with the rear security, but took his entrenching tool and joined with two riflemen who would provide security while he searched.

"Scouting the heavily vegetated area, the riflemen discovered what appeared to be air holes, so they stopped to check them out. Grover continued moving his search forward.

"'I came around the corner of a clump of brush, and there was an NVA staring at me. Just his head and shoulders were sticking out of a trap door,' exclaimed Grover. 'All I could do is threaten him with the E-tool, but he disappeared back into his hole.'

"Grover's squad leader, LCpl. Elijah Rameriz, (Detroit, Michigan) related what happened next. 'We heard some noise, but it was coming from so far away that we didn't think it could be any of our men. We counted heads anyway and found that Grover was missing, so we started looking. When we found him, he was screaming bloody murder and swinging his E-tool in the air. It was hard to believe, but we decided to try talking the enemy out of the hole. After about five minutes, he came out,' explained Rameriz, 'followed by four others! I looked over at Grover and he was starting to turn white. I went down to investigate the hole and discovered an underground bunker big enough for a platoon of enemy soldiers. Digging around the hard-packed floor, I came up with five AK-47 assault rifles that they had hurriedly buried, some chi-com grenades and lots of ammo.'

"'The shock really didn't hit me until I saw all those weapons,' Grover said, 'And then I started imagining what could have happened if they had wanted to fight.'"

Berkowitz wrote later, "Twenty NVA and VC soldiers were killed and 29 captured in a two-hour firefight after the Leathernecks of Company F, 2nd Battalion, 5th Marines, trapped them on a peninsula in the Song Vu Gia River.

'Sweeping along the southern back of the river 5 miles northwest of the An Hoa Combat Base, the 1st Platoon spotted an enemy soldier hiding in dense grass on a small peninsula. SSgt. Edward B. Fryer, (Jacksonville, N.C.), 1st Platoon commander, described the action that followed. 'The point man opened up on the enemy, but he ran farther into the peninsula. I sent a squad after him, and they came under heavy automatic weapons fire and a grenade attack. We couldn't see any of the action because of the high river grass, but I sent in another squad to reinforce them. Captain Furr sent another platoon around the far end of the peninsula to block any escape, and as soon as they were in position, we started sweeping through,' he explained.

"Leathernecks swept through the thick grass, [wading up to their chins and holding hands so the VC/NVA couldn't be missed] capturing some enemy soldiers who had hidden in the dense brush, and pulling others from the water where they had hidden. Ten of them tried to escape by rushing the blocking force that had swept around to the end of the peninsula. They were pushed back. Three others tried to swim the river and, when they didn't halt after the Marines called for them to surrender, they were killed by small arms fire. Finally, after 20 of them had been killed, what was left of the enemy platoon surrendered.

"'After the battle was over,' explained Fryer, 'we started checking the prisoners out. We found one NVA engineer, who said he was there to set up booby traps; and my boys just glared at him, thinking about the buddies they had lost, probably to the same booby traps this man had set. We found a couple of officers among the prisoners with their notebooks and documents still intact.'

"The Leathernecks also captured one 9 mm pistol, one AK-47 assault rifle, more than 20 packs loaded with food, medical supplies, clothing and documents and more than 40 chi-com hand grenades. LCpl. Mike Farrell reported that within moments of starting the sweep of the small island, 'Marines were almost tripping over the little NVA troops, some cowering in a pre-natal position, others sitting on their heels, Vietnamese style, and others crawling away seeking cover. Those that resisted we killed, particularly the ten that tried to run through the blocking force. One female nurse and two others tried to swim across the Son Vu Gia [River]. All three were shot and killed. At the edge of the island, standing on the riverbank with a smirk on his face, was a NVA warrant officer with pistol in hand. The Marines approached him cautiously. He had no intentions of allowing his weapon to be confiscated and, with a bit of bravado, threw it into the water. With the same smirk on his face and his brave act of defiance completed, he turned to a nearby Marine, who was ready to apprehend him, and winked. Big mistake? Must have been, because the Marine shot him, and he fell in the water and floated away. All the POWs were NVA, except 5 VC. There were seven women in the mix.

"'What really made the men angry was that we only captured a few of their weapons because they were throwing them in the river before being taken prisoner,' Captain Furr stated. 'The rain-swollen river was too deep and swift to risk sending men in after them, so we called in for reconnaissance scuba divers to come out the next day.' The scuba drivers recovered over 20 weapons.

"'I can't understand why their commander had them in such a ridiculous position with no avenues of escape, but it was a sweet victory for my Marines. All together we accounted for 49 NVA and VC and only three of my men received minor wounds from grenade fragments. We had been humping for three days through rain-soaked rice paddies and the men were looking for action, but we never expected to find this much,' he concluded."

Fox Company was busy destroying 17 seedling beds during the day. Hotel Company killed 1 VC and found his documents. The CP sent 16 more refugees to Duc Duc.

18 December, Hill 10, Arizona Territory:

"Only one helicopter got in today before the weather closed in. I'm enclosing a picture of me and Lt. Easterbrook that one of the radio operators took a couple of weeks ago. Naturally, the sun wasn't out! The mud is getting deeper and deeper here."

The Arizona,
December 1969, 2/5
Major Driver &
Lt. Easterbrook (standing),
GySgt. Warner, SSgt. Carter
& Sgt. Cooper (seated)

Bad weather or not, we continued operations on and around Football Island. Fox Company had a couple of men slightly wounded during the day and picked up a VC suspect. Golf Company killed 3 VC and recovered packs, a diary, and medical gear. Hotel Company killed one and took his pack and personal gear. The CP group was busy destroying seedling beds, capturing 500 lbs. of rice, and sending 10 refugees to Duc Duc. We also bought 25 M-79 rounds from some children, paying them 400 Vietnamese dollars.

19 December, Hill 10, Arizona Territory:

"Another miserable day in the Arizona. We did get re-supplied today. Yesterday, we killed 5 VC and captured 1. Today we killed 11 and captured 7. Denny Lanigan is going to be the Regimental S-4 and Major [Barry S.] Collasard is going to be the XO.

We are losing more people from emersion (sic) foot than from the VC. We haven't seen the sun in two weeks. Just rain and fog. The troops are magnificent as usual!"

The CP destroyed 6 seedling beds with the help of the Huskies. Fox Company captured a VC suspect. Hotel Company killed 7 VC, captured 1, and destroyed 2 separate bunker complexes.

20 December, Hill 10, Arizona Territory:

"We had hot chow (beef) and sunshine today. Both were great!"

Today we began a 3-day operation with the 51st ARVN regiment. 2/5 (-) and part of the 51st blocked while one ARVN battalion swept Football Island north to south. The ARVN later reported killing 49 VC/NVA with the help of gun-ships. Only 1 ARVN was killed.

We sent off another 10 refugees to Duc Duc and destroyed 4 more seedling beds. Fox Company sent out an additional 13 refugees. Hotel Company found an 82 mm round and destroyed it, 7 seedling beds, and 2 vegetable gardens.

21 December, Hill 10, Arizona Territory:

The ARVN were doing the fighting so we had an extremely quiet day. We sent off another 7 refugees to Duc Duc.

22 December, Hill 10, Arizona Territory:

"Colonel Bowen and I just got back from visiting the 51st ARVN Regiment. They have put us both in for the Vietnamese Cross of Gallantry, for what we don't know, but Colonel Beck told us not to ask any questions! [I never got this award.] General [Edwin B.] Wheeler, the new Division Commander, is going to visit us today. We cleaned up the area the best we could. Everything has been quiet for the last 3 days as we are blocking for the ARVN. They've been getting quite a few VC.

We are now scheduled to be lifted out tomorrow, but I'll believe it when I see it!"

Echo Company had one Marine wounded by an M-26 booby trap. Fox Company destroyed 7 seedling beds and Hotel Company 6. Hotel also found and destroyed 730 rounds of .44 caliber ammunition.

Change of Command: Major Gen. Simpson (right)
to Major Gen. Edwin B. Wheeler (left)

Summer 1969: Sniper tower on the
west side of An Hoa combat base

23 December, An Hoa:

2/5 (-) was helilifted to An Hoa commencing at 1000 and we were given a 24-hour stand down. Hot food, cold showers, clean utilities, cold beer or soda, and not having to spend the night on ambush, patrol, listening post, or just standing watch was a real break for the troops.

24 December, An Hoa:

We took over control of the eastern portion of the 5th Marines TAOR from 1/5. We got Echo Company back and had Lima/3/5 attached. Echo was assigned to the defense of Liberty Bridge. Fox Company was assigned to security along Liberty Road from the bridge to An Hoa. Lima was assigned to security along Liberty Road north of the bridge, and kept one platoon operating on Football Island. Golf and Hotel companies were to conduct local operations until after the Christmas truce, and then go on long-range operations. 1st Lt. Terrence W. 'Terry' Murray, a former football star at the Naval Academy, took command of Company F.

25 December, An Hoa:

"Merry Christmas to everyone there! Better a Happy New Year by the time you get this.

We came out of the Arizona on the 23rd, and I've just now found time to sit down and write. I've been busy getting things squared away here and getting the companies back into the bush. We have the defense of Liberty Bridge, Liberty Road, and the area around An Hoa.

Last night we had a tragedy, in that the Marines on the bridge are required to throw grenades into the water to keep the VC sappers away. One exploded prematurely resulting in 2 dead Marines and 2 wounded.

I have been able to get a bath, haircut, clean clothes, and several rides on helicopters and briefings. Barry Collosard is the new battalion XO. I knew Barry at HQMC.

I've enclosed some Christmas cards, handmade by Vietnamese school children. They are really good artists.

Our battalion can send only 34 men to the Bob Hope Show in Da Nang. So out of 1,200 men, that few will get to go. It looks like we'll be in An Hoa until after the first of the year.

Colonel Bowen is putting me and three company commanders in for Bronze Stars. [I never got this award, either.] Today is supposed to be quiet, but I've got a busy schedule tomorrow. I'll be visiting 2 new District Headquarters and spend the night at Liberty Bridge."

A group of children approached one of Fox's positions. One child tripped a 60 mm booby trap, resulting in 5 Marines being wounded and 2 children killed and 1 wounded.

26 December, An Hoa:

A patrol from Lima Company spotted a boat floating towards Liberty Bridge. They fired M-79s at the boat and one landed in it, causing a large secondary explosion, resulting in 3 Marines being wounded. Lima also found and destroyed a booby trapped 155 mm round.

27 December, An Hoa:

Echo Company destroyed 40 seedling beds near Liberty Bridge. Two helicopters flying out of the Liberty Bridge area were hit by ground fire and had to remain there overnight until repairs could be made. Hotel Company blew up a booby trapped 500 lb. bomb and an M-26 in a C ration can. They bought an M-26 grenade, a 105 WP round, and a 105 HE round from children, paying them 2,800 Vietnamese dollars. During the night, they wounded one of their own men returning from an ambush to the perimeter with a grenade.

I wrote my brother, *"We had a very successful operation in the Arizona – 184 enemy killed, 105 POWs, 26 weapons, plus 24,000 pounds of rice. That's the best any battalion had done in there ever! We came in on the 23d but the rifle companies went right back out on operations. It's the monsoon season and really muddy."*

28 December, An Hoa:

"Could hardly hear you on the phone hook-up today, but it was sure good to hear your voice. Wish we had had a better connection. It's really been pouring rain here the last 3 days. I feel sorry for the troops in the bush."

Echo Company engaged 15 VC/NVA and searched the area with negative results. During a helicopter insertion, they were fired on and evacuated the LZ. Fox Company had a shootout with some 15 VC/NVA and killed 2, capturing a lot of medical supplies. They later captured 2 more, with their packs and contents. Fox also captured 500 lbs. of rice, which was sent to An Hoa. Hotel Company located 6 bunkers, built with reinforced concrete, and blew them up.

29 December, An Hoa:

"I'm staying busy with Liberty Bridge, as it is our responsibility and everyone is concerned over it. Overly concerned! I'm flying out to visit 2 of the companies tomorrow."

Echo Company spotted 6 bodies floating by Liberty Bridge. When they fired on them, an M-26 booby trap exploded, wounding 3 Marines. Fox Company bought a 105 round, a 60 mm round, C-4, and two M-79 rounds from children for 500 Vietnamese dollars. Hotel Company bought one 155 round, one 8 inch round, one 105 round, six M-26s and one hundred rounds of linked 7.62 ammunition from children. One of their patrols hit a 60 mm booby trap, wounding 2 Marines. Lima struck one too, having 1 Marine wounded.

30 December, An Hoa:

"There is not much going on here, just working on the bridge and getting a lot of paper work done. The sun was out today for a change."

The S-2 spent a busy day buying ordnance from children: one 155 round, one 105 round, one 81 mm, three 60 mm, six TNT charges, five M-79 rounds, eight M-26s, one hundred rounds of M-16, twenty rounds of .50 caliber linked, and one AK-50 rifle. They were paid 11,400 Vietnamese dollars.

Echo Company found another dead VC near the bridge. Fox Company had an accidental discharge from an M-60, wounding a Marine. Hotel Company started the day with a self-inflicted wound by one man. They found 5 booby traps, blew up a 250 lb. bomb, a 105 round, a 20 mm round, and an M-26. One booby trap found them, wounding 3 Marines.

31 December, An Hoa:

Echo Company destroyed 5 seedling beds and found 700 lbs. of rice, which was sent to An Hoa. Fox Company destroyed 2 booby traps, including a 105 round. Hotel Company also found two, a 60 mm and a Bouncing Betty mine. Lima Company arrested 2 VC suspects. An aerial observer spotted another body on a sand bar in the river.

The battalion recommended 49 Marines and Navy Corpsmen for awards during the month. Five were recommended for Bronze Stars, 6 for Navy and Marine Corps Medals, 11 for the Naval Commendation Medal, and 27 for the Naval Achievement Medal.

The medical report for the month showed the type of terrain and weather conditions we had been operating in. We had 398 men treated for foot problems, 10 for malaria, 9 for VD, 54 for dermatitis, 71 for gastritis, 90 for orthopedic, and 42 for other problems.

1 January 1970, An Hoa:

"Had a very quiet New Years. Colonel Bowen and I went to the 5th Marines club and had a couple of drinks. Colonel Beck and Jerry Ledin were there, among others. Colonel Bowen got the word yesterday that he's going to Saigon for duty on the 15th. Lt. Colonel [Frederick D.] Leder is going to be the new CO of 2/5. Jerry Ledin is going to Division and John Sheridan is going to be the new Regimental S-3. He's the XO of 1/5. Roland Monnette is going to be the new Regimental S-2. He's now the S-3 of 3/5. I'm hoping to get the XO job in 1/5. Major David Townsend is coming in and is senior to me, so he may get it. I'll be the oldest major in terms of having one job after Jerry Ledin leaves. I don't know what is in store for me but Colonel Bowen is going to recommend I become the XO of 1/5. All this takes place in late January or early February. It looks like the battalion will be here until mid-February.

The sun has been out for 2 straight days and the mud is starting to dry up. We played volleyball against the SNCOs today and beat them 6 straight games!

I'm busy now on the change of command order as well as running 5 companies. We lose L/3/5 tomorrow. The Communications Section invited me to a cookout today, hamburgers and beer. Had a good time."

Echo Company found a booby trapped 105 round on the morning road sweep and children brought them a dud 155 round. They also nabbed a VC suspect. Hotel Company located and destroyed a 60 mm booby trap. The S-2 was busy buying ordnance from children. They brought in one 105 round, one 60 mm, four M-26s, two CS grenades, three CHICOM grenades, four M-79 rounds, and one hundred rounds 7.62 ammunition. They were paid 4,300 Vietnamese dollars.

2 January, An Hoa:

"Colonel Bowen said he told Colonel Beck some time ago that I didn't want to move up on the regimental staff, so I guess that saved me—in one way. It may have been taken to indicate I didn't want to work for Colonel Beck, which is not the case at all. I understand that Major Townsend is going to 1/5 as the XO.

Colonel Bowen wrote a letter of continuity to the next CO on me, and it was a good one to say the least. He's calmed down some—up until today when we had an engineer killed and one seriously wounded blowing up munitions. He was looking for someone to hang to save his rear end. That's the reason I can't stand him. When the pressure is on, he won't back you up! He's worried about being re-selected for permanent Lt. Colonel and he would ruin anyone below him to pass the buck."

The engineers dropped an M-79 round, which blew up. Echo Company bought some blasting caps and other gear from children during the day.

3 January, An Hoa:

"We've got a big operation going tomorrow with the ARVN. You won't hear from me for 4-5 days, but don't worry about it. Colonel Beck is going to III MAF about 10 February. I don't know who is getting the Regiment."

The Battalion CP and Echo and Fox companies were going to Goi Noi Island. The 51st ARVN regiment and K/3/5 would block to the east.

4 January, Hill 119:

Fox Company ran into a daisy chain booby trap of 60 mm rounds and had 1 Marine KIA and 13 WIA. Then they ran into some VC and suffered another man wounded. Golf Company had a bad day also. A patrol hit an M-26 booby trap and 3 Marines were wounded. Later a vehicle hit a 40 lb. box mine, resulting in 3 more WIA. Hotel Company reported the VC attempted to lob a 250 lb. bomb into their position, but it exploded prematurely. They bought some ordnance from children, including a dud 105 round.

5 January, Hill 119:

This was Hotel Company's day, but not a good one. They hit an M-26 booby trap and had 2 Marines wounded. Later, they killed 2 VC and captured 1. Still later, they were engaged with a large force of VC/NVA and had 2 more men wounded.

6 January, Hill 119:

Echo Company lost 1 Marine wounded by an M-26 booby trap. K/3/5 tripped a booby trapped 105 round and had 3 men wounded.

7 January, Hill 119:

Golf Company reported a dump truck from Company D, 7th Engineers struck a 40 lb. box mine, resulting in 1 Marine KIA and 6 WIA. Hotel Company had a Marine wounded in a firefight that afternoon.

8 January, An Hoa:

"I've spent the last 5 days on an operation near Goi Noi Island. Three companies and one command group were on the island. I sat on Hill 119 with recon until this morning, and then I directed the move back. Quite a hike, but nothing but one booby trap encountered [a grenade in a C ration can]. The rain came down the whole operation and we didn't accomplish anything except take casualties from mines and booby traps. We waded a chest deep stream to get back today. Colonel Bowen is going to III MAF now instead of Saigon. Someone must have done some politicking."

I remember on our hike back that the water was really cold coming out of the mountains. It was up to our necks. The move was to Liberty Road. I was shaking from the cold until I managed to heat up a cup of coffee. Trucks finally arrived and took us back to An Hoa.

During the move, we came through an area just vacated by one of our companies. We picked up three grenades they had dropped. I chewed out the company commander, who later became a General Officer in the

Marine Corps. I witnessed a duel between a couple of VC armed with rifles and an aerial observer. The AO spotted the VC moving near a hut in a small clearing below our moving column. He honed in on them firing rockets. They dodged behind trees and fired their rifles at the plane. This duel went on for about 5 minutes, with the VC dodging from tree to tree and the AO circling about, then diving to fire his rockets. I stood in awe at the bravery displayed by both sides, and if I had been armed with a rifle, I could have killed one of the VC, as he was only about 500 yards away.

We could not get re-supplied during this operation because Marine helicopters don't normally fly when the ceiling is 1,000 yards or less. The next day, we were socked in again, but the Army helicopters re-supplied us. Their warrant officers pilots flew in with a ceiling of about 500 yards. They came in at near tree top level. They were a brave bunch of helicopter pilots.

Echo Company had two engagements during the day. They killed 2 VC and captured 1, along with a .45 cal. pistol and a lot of money. Later, they killed another VC and captured one. Hotel Company had a dud 105 round turned in by children. K/3/5 found and destroyed an 81 mm booby trap but struck an M-26, resulting in 1 Marine WIA. An LVT fired a line charge near Liberty Bridge and set off two 81 mm booby traps. The area was searched and one 105 round, one 60 mm, and one M-26 booby traps were found and destroyed.

9 January, An Hoa:

"Another busy, rainy day. I had to go to Dai Loc to make liaison with the District Chief about clearing the sides of the roads of bamboo and brush. I spent most of the day up there. I had lunch with Bob Warren, the Army advisor. Tom Barton, from 5th Marines, went along. He's going to be the S-3 of 3/5. I saw a change of command at 3/1 today. The pressure is on for us to have a good one. Colonel Beck is leaving the 10th of February and he's on everyone's back.

Going out to Liberty Bridge tomorrow. That's a real pain until the outpost is finished and the VC stop blowing up vehicles!"

Golf Company found two 60 mm rounds, one 81 mm round, and one 40 lb. box mine during the day.

10 January, An Hoa:

"I've come down with dysentery. I've had it worse, but it's bad enough. Should be over it in a few days.

Colonel Bowen is going to Saigon after all. He's real happy. Lt. Colonel Leder is taking command. I've been busy working on the change of command ceremony.

Things have been fairly quiet the last few days. We're still killing a few of them and they're still blowing us up with booby traps."

Echo Company had a firefight with some VC and had one Marine wounded. Hotel Company hit a 105 round booby trap and had one Marine wounded. They blew up another one. Children brought them one LAW, two 60 mm rounds, and one CHICOM grenade. 7th Engineers found and blew up a 100 lb. box mine.

11 January, An Hoa:

"Still busier than a one armed paper hanger. I'll sure be glad to get the change of command over with.

The Commandant of the Marine Corps [Leonard F. Chapman, Jr.] was in An Hoa today. I didn't bother to go down. No one else did except Colonel Bowen, who had no choice.

My dysentery isn't much better. I'm so weak I can hardly walk around and I've still got the runs. I'm taking the medicine religiously."

Echo Company had a short round from their own 60 mm mortar resulting in 3 Marines being wounded. Fox Company had children bring them ten TNT charges, two M-26s, and one 60 mm round. They were paid 500 Vietnamese dollars. The S-2 bought sixteen 60 mm, twenty six M-79s, two Claymores, four trip flares, and three M-26s. Hotel Company hit a booby trapped Coke can, but only one Marine received a slight wound. Later, they engaged an estimated 30 VC, killing 6 and capturing 3. Still later, they killed 2 more.

12 January, An Hoa:

Fox Company bought an M-26 and an M-16 magazine with 18 rounds from local children. Golf Company hit an M-26 booby trap, resulting in 3 Marines being wounded. Hotel Company hit another and lost 2 men WIA. Golf Company got a new commanding officer, 1st Lt. W.T. Collins.

13 January, An Hoa:

Echo Company found 60 lbs. of rice. Fox Company blew up a bunker they found. Hotel Company hit a booby trap losing 4 Marines WIA. Later children turned in one 105 round, one 20 mm round, one Claymore complete with fuse, and one CHICOM grenade. They were paid 2,400 Vietnamese dollars.

14 January, An Hoa:

Echo Company found and destroyed 2 bunkers containing eight 60 mm rounds, 270 rounds of M-16 and 80 rounds of AK-47 ammunition. Fox Company destroyed a canoe and bought 2 105 rounds, two M-79 rounds, and 3 boxes of documents. The children were paid 1,000 Vietnamese dollars and given C rations. Golf Company hit an M-26 booby trap having 2 Marines wounded. The S-2 was busy buying thirty-two 60 mm rounds, one M-79 round, and one M-26 grenade.

15 January, An Hoa:

Echo Company found a large bunker and blew it up. Hotel Company purchased twenty eight blasting caps, one 105 round, one 20 mm round, two corfram, two 60 mm rounds, and five M-79 rounds.

16 January, An Hoa:

Golf Company struck a 155 round booby trap, having 1 Marine KIA. They later hit an M-26 booby trap, and had a man slightly wounded.

17 January, An Hoa:

Fox Company hit an M-26 booby trap resulting in 3 Marines being wounded. They later located a 250 lb. bomb and some bunkers, which they blew up.

I stopped writing to my wife because I was going to meet her in Hawaii for R&R on the 18th. The change of command went fine while I was away. I departed Da Nang on the 17th and met my wife at the Hilton Hotel in Honolulu the next day. We had a great time together, but I had a relapse of dysentery and had to get some medicine from the Navy Clinic. We toured the island and renewed memories of our three years there.

18 January, An Hoa:

Fox Company was engaged during the day and had one Marine slightly wounded. Golf Company hit another booby trap and had 2 Marines wounded. The Popular Forces Platoon at Phu Loc received two 60 mm rounds during the night.

19 January, An Hoa:

Echo Company conducted a cordon and search of La Nam (1) south of Le Bac Island. L/3/5 blocked along South Liberty Road. Echo found and destroyed a 105 round booby trap. Fox Company found and blew up a bunker during the day. A child turned in a C-4 booby trap to Golf Company. Later on one of their patrols struck a daisy chain booby trap of 3 M-26s and suffered 3 Marines wounded.

20 January, An Hoa:

Fox Company discovered another bunker and destroyed it and an M-79 booby trap. Golf Company purchased an 8-inch round from some children and paid them 500 Vietnamese dollars. A patrol from Hotel Company hit an M-26 booby trap and had 1 Marine wounded.

21 January, An Hoa:

Echo's attached sniper team struck an M-26 booby trap in a C ration can and both were wounded. Golf Company found and destroyed an M-26 booby trap. Hotel Company bought 2 M-26s from children and paid them 400 Vietnamese dollars. The Duc Duc refugee camp reported that four refugees had been identified as VC. Yesterday, an S-2 Scout and a Kit Carson Scout (VC turncoat) went to visit a girl in Phu Lac (6) with 2 Popular Forces troops. The 4 engaged a large VC force, killing 2 and capturing an AK-47. The PFs decided to return to their unit, and the S-2 Scout gave one of the PFs his .45 to give to Golf Company. The two scouts then headed east at about 1340 that day. They were declared MIA at 0430.

22 January, An Hoa:

Fox Company found a bunker with 20 lbs. of rice and clothing in it and then blew it up. Later they fired on 3 VC, who escaped, but a pack, an AK-47 magazine and two grenades were captured. Hotel Company found a flak jacket with a bullet hole in it and a pair of boots with EWM marked in side. They were believed to have belonged to the missing Marine Scout. Hotel Company also found 4 wounded civilians who had been injured by artillery fire. They later reported some VC with bullhorns near Phu Loc (6) broadcasting to the villagers. They called in an artillery fire mission and the broadcasting ceased. The S-2 Scouts and ARVN operating out of Phu Loc (6) were fired on by a VC force.

23 January, An Hoa:

Fox Company captured a VC suspect and later engaged some VC and found 1 RPG round, bunkers, and documents. The bunkers and the round were destroyed. Golf Company purchased a dud 8-inch shell and paid the children 800 Vietnamese dollars. Later, they blew up an M-26 booby trap. S-2 scouts operating with Hotel were told by a Vietnamese woman that she saw the captured S-2 Scout and Kit Carson Scout tied up and moving with a party of VC towards the Arizona. She described the Marine as being Caucasian and 6'1" tall. They were being taken to the mountains. [This was the last reported sighting of these two men. Cpl. Jose Anzaldua survived the trek to a POW camp in Laos, the ordeal of the camp, the march up the Ho Chi Min Trail to Hanoi, and the prison camp there. His Vietnamese language skills helped him and the other POWs know what was going on and what was being said by the guards. He was exchanged in 1973 and stayed in the Marine Corps, retiring as a Major.]

Hotel Company conducted a Med Cap for 135 people in a village. The Regional Forces and Popular Forces at Phu Loc (6) were fired on by a large VC force during the day. The VC killed the village chief and the village policeman. The PFs captured a 16 year-old VC who participated in the attack the next day. 1st Lt. J.D. Andrea took command of Echo Company.

24 January, An Hoa:

Echo Company found 2 minefields 10 x 15 that were marked. Later, they tripped a booby trapped 105 round, resulting in one Marine being wounded. Fox Company spent the morning destroying a bunker complex with the help of engineers. Later they engaged a small force of VC and had one Marine slightly wounded. They picked up a VC suspect. Golf Company purchased an M-26 and an NVA belt from a young boy and paid him with 4 cans of C rations. Later one of their patrols hit an M-26 booby trap and one Marine was wounded. That evening the 106 Platoon, positioned at Liberty Bridge, was fired on.

25 January, An Hoa:

"I slept almost all the way to Guam and part of the way to Da Nang. I checked on my orders and found I'm going to Division G-2 on the 30th. [Major D.R.] 'Don' Hanson from Division G-3 is taking my place and came down today.

The CP is out at Liberty Bridge for the night, the Colonel, Lt. Easterbrook and Major Hanson. They'll be in early in the morning. Things have been fairly quiet since I've been gone. Lt. Easterbrook has done an outstanding job."

Fox Company found and destroyed 2 booby trapped grenades during the day. Golf Company struck a booby trapped 105 round and lost 2 men wounded. Later they destroyed a 175 mm round which the VC had been trying to move with parachute cord. They also had a homemade Bangalore torpedo turned in by children and paid them 100 Vietnamese dollars. Hotel Company was on Operation 'Dry Well' and reported 2 secondary explosions from an air strike.

26 January, An Hoa:

"I have been real busy today. Acting as the XO and S-3. My Bronze Star was turned down. Regiment said it would be a part of an end of tour award. Same old b.s.!

Lt. Colonel Leder is 180 degrees different from Lt. Colonel Bowen. He really knows what is going on and keeps up with everything and keeps us on our toes. I think I would have enjoyed working longer for him as the S-3."

27 January, An Hoa:

"I'm staying busy with fitness reports and other paper work on the people working for me.

Tonight we have a report that the VC plan to attack Liberty Bridge, so everything and everyone is all excited. I personally don't think they will." They didn't.

Echo Company killed 1 VC and captured his pack and equipment. Later, they picked up a VC suspect. Golf Company found and destroyed a 105 round booby trapped. They spent the rest of the morning blowing up bunkers and picked up 2 VC suspects. In the afternoon, they struck a 60 mm booby trap and had 2 Marines wounded. A man from Hotel Company was injured when engineers destroyed some ordnance. He failed to take cover when 'fire in the hole' was shouted. Later, they engaged a VC force and killed 3. An aerial observer flying in support of them killed 2 more VC/ NVA with his rockets.

28 January, An Hoa:

"I took Major Hanson on a helicopter view of the 5th Marines TAOR. Tomorrow I'm turning over all my gear to him and checking out."

The VC/NVA gave me an early send off, firing five 60 mm rounds into the CP. Echo Company had a good day, killing an NVA and capturing his field glasses, 2 AK-47 magazines, a U.S. cartridge belt, NVA uniforms, and other personal gear. Later they fired on and captured a VC and his SKS rifle, ammunition, U.S. canteen, pliers and food. Golf Company arrested a VC suspect, while Hotel Company captured three 81 mm canisters filled with ammonia nitrate to be used as booby traps. 7th Engineers tripped an M-26 grenade booby trap and had one Marine wounded.

29 January, An Hoa:

"All packed and ready to go! Just had my last cold shower in An Hoa (I hope)! One of my men is going to drive me up to Division in the morning. Everything has been fairly quiet despite the Tet threat. We killed 6 in last 2 days, captured 4 and 3 weapons.

Major Hanson is a Reservist, and came back in to 'find out what was going on in Vietnam.' He's a real nice guy. I like Lt. Col. Leder more and more each day.

As I probably told you, I'm acting as XO and enjoying it. Wish I could stay in the job."

Echo Company killed 2 VC and found heavy blood trails, which they followed and found an AK-47, maps, and other equipment. Golf Company had a Marine wounded by an M-26 booby trap. Hotel Company received an incoming 60 mm round that killed 2 Marines and wounded another. The Combined Unit Pacification Platoon [CUPP] found and blew up one M-26 booby trap but tripped another, losing 1 Marine wounded. This unit was under operational control of 2/5.

30 January, An Hoa:

Echo Company started the day by engaging 6 VC and saw the enemy carry off one of their number. They blew up a bunker they had found 50 lbs. of rice in. In the afternoon they fired on 3 VC and saw 1 fall in the river. They found his body the next morning and recovered a 9 mm pistol.

31 January, An Hoa:

The battalion CP received 5 M-79 rounds from another Marine unit, but no casualties. Echo Company engaged 2 VC. They killed one and captured the other, along with a Russian 7.62 pistol.

The battalion processed and submitted 59 awards during the month. There were 15 for Bronze Stars, 30 for Naval Achievement Medals, 12 for Naval Commendation Medals, and 2 for Navy & Marine Corps Medals. 25 awards were received, 11 were presented, and 14 forwarded.

The medical report for the month was a typical one for the rainy season. The battalion suffered 5 cases of malaria, 23 cases of VD, 5 for rabies, 145 with dermatitis, 63 with gastritis, 82 orthopedic problems, 11 with ear problems, 16 with eye problems, 183 with cellulitis, and 235 with other ailments, most related to immersion foot.

Chapter Nineteen

Da Nang,
February-June 1970
Officer in Charge, Da Nang Barrier,
S-2, 1st Marine Division

31 January, Da Nang:

"I got to Division Headquarters last night after a long dusty ride from An Hoa. It sure is nice to sleep between clean sheets and in a bed with a mattress. Had a nice hot shower, too!

My new job is Ground Surveillance Officer in G-2. It's one of the best jobs in the Division for a Major. Colonel [Edward A.] Wilcox seems like a real fine man to work for. My job consists of installing seismic sensor devices and controlling them, etc. Most of it is classified, so I can't write about it. Captain Whalen, who was a Lt. in 2/9 my last tour, is my assistant. He's a good officer. The other officer, Lt. Prins, and all the enlisted men seem to be real good. My working hours are going to be bad. About 0730-1630 and then 1800-2300, or there about!"

1 February, Dan Nang:

"I think I'm going to like this job. Everyone leaves you alone and you work your own hours and go where you want to. Of course, I've got to keep the 2 officers and 22 enlisted men busy. I'm almost totally ignorant of the seismic program, but I'm going to do my best to make it a success. [Most of these officers and men were school trained on sensors and were extremely valuable in getting and keeping me up to speed on them.]

I attended the General's briefing this morning, had a 2 hour class on what equipment we have, etc., and then an hour briefing on G-2 matters."

2 February, Da Nang:

"A beautiful day today; about 70 degrees. I took a helicopter ride for about 30 minutes looking at areas where we want to implant sensors. Enjoyed it as we flew over parts of Da Nang at tree top level.

I'm staying busy, as I've got so much to learn. The working hours are going to be long but that makes the time pass faster. I still don't have a permanent billeting area, as all the spaces are taken. I'm supposed to get one this week.

Everyone is uptight over Tet. They hit Liberty Bridge with mortars two nights ago and a refugee village near by. Also, An Hoa took 9 rockets yesterday afternoon."

3 February, Da Nang:

"I've really stayed quite busy today. Tomorrow looks to be the same way. I'm starting to understand a little better what all is involved and I'm getting things better organized.

It's been beautiful again today, but it sure gets cold at night! I slept under 2 blankets last night.

The VC were quiet last night but I look for a change tonight. Colonel Wilcox is going to take over the 1st Marines on the 10th, so I won't be working for him long."

4 February, Da Nang:

"The more I find out about my job, the less I like it! There are so many problems, and we're at the mercy of what the units do and report. The rest of the problems I can't discuss but I'm a little discouraged. Maybe I can move up when Col. Wilcox leaves, but they'll probably assign another Colonel, though.

The VC were unusually quiet again yesterday and so far today. Hope it stays that way!"

The problems with seismic devices are that they react to all movement, enemy or friendly, artillery, airplanes, vehicles, animals, or anything that could set them off. It took a well-trained operator to determine if the movement was the enemy. Sensors and batteries fail and have to be replaced or repaired. Cables are cut by friend and foe alike, and they have to be repaired or replaced. There was always the problem of providing security for my men to work on the devices and the possibility of the VC booby trapping them. This program was the offshoot of McNamara's 'Da Nang Barrier,' which had proven to be a failure. With the withdrawal of the Marine ground forces from the area, it was hoped that this system would help detect enemy movement. [For a complete run down on the Da Nang Barrier see "U.S. Marines in Vietnam: Vietnamization and Redeployment, 1970-1971," pp. 256-262.]

5 February, Da Nang:

"I went on top of Hill 327, which over looks Da Nang today on a recon. The area has really changed since 1965."

6 February, Da Nang:

"The Vietnamese who work here are all off celebrating Tet. So far it has been very quiet, almost too quiet. Today was cloudy with a little rain but quite comfortable otherwise."

7 February, Da Nang:

"I worked late tonight and almost didn't get a letter written. Preparing a brief for the Colonel tomorrow so he can brief the General on Monday. We spend half our time briefing VIPs.

It was another quiet night. It rained again today."

8 February, Da Nang:

"I'm working late, as I have to brief the General on sensors tomorrow morning. I've had two rehearsals today. I did much better on the second one.

I still don't have a permanent billet. Hope to get one this week, as several officers are leaving."

9 February, Da Nang:

"Really had a busy day today. Briefed the General at 0730 this morning. Lt. Colonel [Charles M.] Mosher, the acting G-2, said I did real well.

We had visitors all day yesterday, including 2 Lt. Colonels from the Defense Communication Planning Group in Washington. In the afternoon, I went to III MAF Headquarters on the other side of Da Nang. It's quite nice, much better than the Division CP. Last night, we worked until 2300. The G-2, FMFPAC is coming on the 11th and I am the escort officer as well as having to brief him.

I'm going to Udorn, Thailand on the 12th to see what the Air Force is doing with sensors over there. I'll be back on the 14th. It should be an interesting trip."

10 February, Da Nang:

"Today was another busy and rainy one. I hope to relax a little tonight and take in a movie.

Major Jim Masters and I have to brief the General on the 12th—just before I leave for Thailand. Hope it goes o.k."

11 February, Da Nang:

"The briefing of Colonel [Jerry J.] Mitchell, the G-2, FMFPAC went o.k. It was really a busy day, though. He left about 1530 and I got a call that they had a place for me to move into, so I took off and did that the rest of the afternoon. It's the first time I've ever unpacked everything since I have been back in Vietnam. Scrounged up a fan for the hot weather, too. We have a sink and mirror in the hut, an icebox, and plenty of fans, so living is good. Lt. Colonel Graves, Major Kinney, and Lt. Commander Drake are my hut mates. They are all Supply officers but very nice.

We brief the General tomorrow morning. I need some guidance from the top, so maybe I'll get it. I leave for Thailand at 1400 tomorrow.

We got to eat in the General's mess today. Saw Colonel [John H.] Keith and Colonel Beck. Colonel Beck is going to be the new Chief of Staff of the Division, a grooming job for General! I met several captains who came to 1/4 in Hawaii just before I left. Pat Burns and Roger Staley were two of them. Pat was Kent Shockey's roommate in college."

12 February, Da Nang:

"Our briefing of General Wheeler this morning proved fruitful, as we got the guidance we needed. I'll end up with close to 100 men.

My trip to Thailand is delayed until tomorrow. Don Johnson, who was is Basic School at Quantico with me, and is in the 1st Marine Air Wing G-2 section, is going with me so I'll be seeing him and know someone on the trip."

15 February, Da Nang:

"My trip to Thailand was very interesting but I can't tell you what I saw! I did get into town and got to see some temples, complete with Buddhist monks. I was able to see Laos across the river. It was hot and dusty there. It hasn't rained since October! The Thai's are a handsome people, much taller and bulkier that the other Asians I've seen. A lot of the women are pretty and have good figures. Naturally, I noticed that!"

We were briefed on the sensors being dropped by air along the Ho Chi Minh Trail and the roads and trails leading into South Vietnam. Some of the sensors were seismic and others were audio. They were dropped into the triple canopy with the idea their small parachutes would catch in the branches of the trees, and the operators in Thailand could monitor movement and sounds. Some were dropped out of range of the base in Thailand but were monitored by planes flying over the area. They had actually heard NVA troops talking, trucks and tanks moving, etc. They had carried out air strikes on these targets with excellent results. The batteries in these sensors were only good for 30 days, so this was a continuing process. The NVA had captured some of these and had troops out looking to spot them in the jungle canopy. Sometimes they would run one truck back and forth to throw us off.

16 February, Da Nang:

"I have to brief General Wheeler every Tuesday now. I should be a professional briefer by the time I'm through! Also, I have to brief General [William F.] Doehler tomorrow. It's going to be a busy day! He is suppose to be real tough to brief and has a million questions to ask. I'll be burning the midnight oil tonight!"

17 February, Da Nang:

"Sure glad the briefings are over! The regular briefing of General Wheeler and his staff went fine. I spent 2 hours with General Doehler, and he really put me through the wringer! It wasn't nearly as bad as I thought it would be!

I've had the runs again ever since I got back from R&R, so I finally went to the doctor this afternoon. They're going to give me a complete checkup after taking blood and feces samples. I've been miserable for some time but don't like to complain.

Dick Kerr is here now. He's the Division Engineering Officer."

18 February, Da Nang:

"I'm still busy getting ready for briefings, etc. We've reorganized our section into a platoon and we've had to explain it in detail to everyone but God! I'm a little tired of all the paperwork—and no results but more of the same!"

19 February, Da Nang:

"The sun came out today and it was a beautiful day if any are in Vietnam.

I went to the doctor, and he can't figure out what is wrong with me. I'm not anemic and have no parasites in me. They think it is a virus and it will go away. I'm still running except when I take the pills.

The maid finally washed my sheets today after 3 weeks. They were getting ripe!

I'm losing Captain Whalen tomorrow. He's going on R&R to Hawaii and then to 5th Marines.

There's a Lt. Barber here who served with me at Camp Lejeune in 1954-55. He was a cook in the battalion, stayed in, made Gunnery Sergeant, Warrant Officer, and now 2nd Lt.! The war has been quiet although the ARVN killed 255 and captured about 50 VC south of here."

20 February, Da Nang:

"I'm staying busy with a bunch more briefings coming up, but I'm not doing quite so much night work. Today was another beautiful one, although it is starting to get hot. The VC are remaining fairly quiet around Da Nang."

21 February, Da Nang:

"The weather is getting warmer every day. It was almost hot today. I'm still not feeling 100% but some better. The pills I'm taking stopped me up.

Lt. Colonel Leder stopped in today. He sent my letter of continuity up which I got a copy of today."

22 February, Da Nang:

"I had my briefing for the Colonel today prior to briefing General Wheeler tomorrow. Be glad when that is over! The following day I have my usual briefing of both Generals and theirs staffs. Busy few days!"

23 February, Da Nang:

"The briefing for General Wheeler didn't go today, so I'm faced with two briefings tomorrow.

I saw Pete O'Brien the other night. He was a company commander for about 10 weeks and is now the S-4 of 2nd Battalion, 7th Marines."

24 February, Da Nang:

"The briefing went fine this morning. I'm briefing General Wheeler privately tomorrow morning. I'm sure getting tired of it!

The officers in the hut had a cookout tonight. Filets! I only ate 3! That was all they had except wine. I didn't drink any of that because of my intestinal problems."

25 February, Da Nang:

"My briefing of General Wheeler went off fine. No real problems. He complimented me on a good job and bought all of my recommendations. The Chief of Staff, Colonel [Charles E.] Walker, and Colonel Beck, who is going to be the new Chief of Staff, said I did a good job. General Doehler was present too. I'm just relieved it is over!"

26 February, Da Nang:

"Another busy day today, and a hot one, too. I went out after work this afternoon and played basketball for about 30 minutes. Really pooped me out! That's the first real running I've done since I've been over here. Bob Walsh, who I played basketball with at HQMC, played with us. He just came back from emergency leave. He's on his first tour because of his wife's health problems."

27 February, Da Nang:

"Another busy day trying to get this new platoon formed with 80 men, 5 vehicles, and all kinds of communications gear. Pete LeFevre is the new S-3 of 3/1 replacing Ron Garten, who I know. Ron doesn't know his new assignment yet."

28 February, Da Nang:

"Another busy, hot day today. Captain Whalen came back from R&R. He's going to 5th Marines tomorrow. Tom Rich is going to be in G-3 next week. He's the XO of 2/26 now."

1 March, Da Nang:

"I was busy as usual with the Sunday brief of Lt. Colonel Mosher. I seem to spend all my time preparing for briefings, giving them, or making charts, graphs, or something of that nature. The sensor program seems to be the General's pet project.

Captain Rex Robinson called and came over to see me. We went to chow and then to the club. Jerry Ledin was there, so we took Rex back into Da Nang to the I Corps BOQ. Rex is an advisor to the 2nd ARVN Division and really likes it. Ran into Ed Butchart in the I Corps BOQ. It's a plush place and is completely air-conditioned. Ed is with the Combat Information Bureau and escorts the press around. Kent Shockey is in country again. He's a Combined Action Company Commander somewhere in this area."

2 March, Da Nang:

"The weather is really getting hot now. I'm sitting here sweating now while writing this. Ed Butchart was over today and we talked over old times while in 1/4 in Hawaii."

3 March, Da Nang:

"Colonel [Ernest R.] 'Len' Reed reported in the other day and will be CO of 11th Marines. He was the Provost Marshal at Kaneohe when we were there.

The briefing of the Division staff went well."

4 March, Da Nang:

"I briefed the General and his staff today and everyone said I did real well. I'm scheduled to go to Saigon for a conference on the 11th. Lt. Prins will have to brief the General and is he scared!"

5 March, Da Nang:

"Today was nice, not too hot. I was over at Wing Headquarters to see Don Johnson today. I see him or call him nearly everyday on business.
I haven't been working out lately; too busy. Need to get started, though."

6 March, Da Nang:

"Elements of the 1st Marine Division are going to Camp Pendleton, but no word yet on the infantry regiments and Division Headquarters."

8 March, Da Nang:

"I called Don Brooks today in Saigon to tell him I was coming down, but he was out."

9 March, Da Nang:

"Another busy day today. Don Brooks called back and he's going to meet me at the airport in Saigon. He wanted a refrigerator, so I've gotten him one. Hope I can get it on the plane tomorrow. I'm flying down at noon, and back on the morning of the 12th."

12 March, Da Nang:

"Got back from Saigon about 1700 today. It was really hot down there. I didn't get to see any of the city, just Tan Sa Nhut Air Base. Don was there with a car a few minutes after I arrived.
Don looks good and likes his job. MACV Headquarters beats the Pentagon. It's completely air conditioned and furnished well. Don got me a room in the BOQ he stays in outside the base. It's really a hotel. They live 2 to a room. They aren't plush, but it beats anything I've lived in over here!
Don left for R&R this afternoon. He was excited as usual, you know Don! All the Vietnamese waitresses called him 'Dee-Dee,' which in Vietnamese means 'go away.' He keeps them stirred up since he's picked up some of their language.

I saw Lt. Colonel Bowen and Bill Rowley. Bill just arrived from the 26th Marines and had pneumonia as soon as he checked in. Colonel Bowen could only talk about awards—his!"

13 March, Da Nang:

"Another busy, hot day. Must have been close to 100 degrees.

I checked on Lt. Colonel Bowen's and my Vietnamese awards today. They haven't come back from the Vietnamese yet. Lt. Colonel Bowen got a Bronze Star end of tour award. He wanted to trade it in for a letter of continuity so he could get a Legion of Merit!

Everything is still quiet around here. Hope it stays that way until I leave!"

14 March, Da Nang:

"I've been too busy to even see a movie since I've gotten back from Saigon. Everything seems to happen at once! All our additional men and vehicles aren't in yet, but everyone thinks we can still do the job and more!"

15 March, Da Nang:

"I haven't been out of the office today except to eat brunch, as we began operations and we're having growing pains. I have 99 enlisted men now. Kent Shockey called tonight. He's on his way home. He's been a Combined Action Company Commander up at Phu Bai, which is just south of Hue."

We started implanting addition seismic devices in the Da Nang Barrier or McNamara's Line. One of the problems was that most of the men were grunts who didn't know how to install the sensors properly. This forced me to use all my trained personnel in the field supervising, leaving no one in the rear to keep them supplied and fed.

16 March, Da Nang:

"I have really been busy today but I didn't have to brief the General. Get to do that tomorrow!

I worked until 2130 tonight before going to the club. Inexperience on everyone's part, including my own! Now I have a new title: Officer in Charge of the Da Nang Barrier. That's all I need to get an ulcer or go out of my mind! Guess I'll make it somehow!

Kent Shockey made it out tonight. He, Tom Rich, and I had a couple of drinks together. The 26th Marines left officially today. They had a big ceremony."

17 March, Da Nang:

"*Another busy day today and I've got to brief the General tomorrow, so it's back to work as soon as I finish this letter. The war is still fairly quiet. Nothing much going on.*"

19 March, Da Nang:

"*I briefed the General for an hour and 15 minutes today. Everyone said I did real well, so I'm satisfied! Sure glad it's over!*"

20 March, Da Nang:

"*Another busy day. My Lt.s aren't much help. I have to redo everything they write. No attention to detail! The war is very quiet now in this area. I believe the VC are waiting for us to pull out!*"

I received another Lt. from a grunt outfit, who was almost worthless. When I sent him out to supervise the sensor installation, he called me every night, reporting movement. I told him he had the equivalent of a rifle platoon out there and to calm down. All of his men had seen combat in the infantry, so they knew what to do. He still called me every night.

21 March, Da Nang:

"*Colonel [Clarence W.] 'Clancy' Boyd took over as G-2 today. He seems real nice, and I believe he'll be easy to work for and to talk to.*"

22 March, Da Nang:

"*Colonel Keith stopped by today to invite me to his change of command tomorrow. He's taking over Headquarters Battalion.*"

23 March, Da Nang:

"*I went to Colonel Keith's change of command today. Quite a turn out. The Officers club served chow that was out of this world! Steak, lobster, chicken, ham, fresh bread, rice, potatoes, and peas all served in silver service with wine and drinks before and after.*
I'm still working day and night but take a couple of hours off for a drink and a movie/floor show when I can."

24 March, Da Nang:

"Jim Baier came by to see me today. He's in 5th Communications Battalion. He's on a 6 month extension!"

25 March, Da Nang:

"I've been staying busy, working night and day, but the time sure flies when you are on the go!"

26 March, Da Nang:

"I stayed extremely busy today and will be working late tonight.
I've been feeling a lot better lately, despite a bad head cold. I've finally gotten over the runs but really have to watch what I eat."

27 March, Da Nang:

"I had to brief the CO and staff of 1st Marines today. It took an hour and a half! Colonel Wilcox had a lot of questions but was easy to brief. I've got the 5th Marines and 7th Marines to go!
The weather has been great the last week; sunny days and cool nights. It will really be getting hot soon, though!"

28 March, Da Nang:

"I'm still busy as can be! Helps make the time fly! I'll be going to a conference in Saigon 15-17 April."

29 March, Da Nang:

"Colonel Len Reed invited several of us to the 11th Marines club for drinks, steaks, and a floor show. I really enjoyed it. Met Burl Stonum, who I knew from HQMC. Colonel Reed thinks the world of Don and Rickey Brooks. Came back from that and worked another 3 hours, so I'm pooped!"

30 March, Da Nang:

"Another busy, hot day. I think a heat wave is about to hit here. Going down to 7th Marines tomorrow to give a presentation."

31 March, Da Nang:

"Don Brooks called. He just got back from R&R. He said he would pick me up at the airport when I go down for the conference on the 14th."

1 April, Da Nang:

"Was awakened with a jolt this morning, as we took 3 rockets at 0600. Many an early reveille!

The VC/NVA launched their expected spring offensive last night. No one was hurt here and no damage. Da Nang and other areas were hit and some casualties occurred, mostly civilians. One of our companies captured 3 un-launched rockets this afternoon.

I'm going to 7th Marines in the morning to brief on sensors. That will consume the whole day Friday. I'll brief 5th Marines and 3/5 on Hill 65 Saturday. Sunday we brief the Colonel, so it's going to be a busy week!"

2 April, Da Nang:

"Started for 7th Marines today and only got as far as An Hoa. The helicopter had a broken fuel line. Spent the rest of the day trying to get down there, but finally gave up at 1530 and came back. A wasted day!

We had rockets again last night, and An Hoa had some this morning just before I arrived. Things have livened up over here! I've got to go to An Hoa again tomorrow to give the presentation to them. Hope I make it!

I'm all broken out with an allergy. I'd just started feeling like a human being again after over a month of stomach trouble and the runs, plus a bad head cold. What next? I shouldn't complain, as time is passing rapidly."

3 April, Da Nang:

"Went to 5th Marines and briefed them today. The troops in the S-3 of 2/5 gave me a large color photo of the whole gang. It was a real pleasant surprise."

4 April, Da Nang:

"Went to Hill 65 today and briefed the CO and staff. It hasn't changed much!"

5 April, Da Nang:

Colonel Keith stopped by while I was working last night and said you and his wife had talked. I told you about the large colored picture the men in the S-3 at 2/5 gave me. It's real nice.

Rex Robinson called today and said he was coming over and would spend the night. He's an hour and a half late, so I don't know if he's coming or not. The weather has cooled a little in the last few days, but the humidity is still high."

6 April, Da Nang:

"Rex never showed up last night and didn't call, and I don't know what happened."

7 April, Da Nang:

"Today was hot and sticky, and we're on water hours now. Can't even brush my teeth! I was really busy all day and didn't leave until 1730. I've got to go back later, but I'm going to relax for a while and take in a movie. Tomorrow is going to be equally bad. I have to brief an Army General and 3 other Army officers in two separate briefings in the morning and attend a meeting at XXIV Corps in the afternoon."

8 April, Da Nang:

"Another busy day today. Briefed 3 officers from Saigon this morning and then had a meeting at XXIV Corps from 1330-1900! Came back, ate, watched a movie, then back to work. I'm still at work but wanted to answer your letter. Should be in bed by 0100."

9 April, Da Nang:

"Had another busy, hot day today. Going to take time out for chow, a drink, and a movie. Then back to work!"

10 April, Da Nang:

"Spent another busy day and have to go back to work tonight."

11 April, Da Nang:

"Today I went with General Doehler to visit 4 of our readout sites. I took the mail to the troops and they were really happy to see me! That took all morning and I didn't get out from behind the desk all afternoon! I'm going back after the movie tonight for a 'few'

more hours! I'm trying to get everything squared away before I go to Saigon on the 15th. I have another briefing tomorrow. I'm becoming a professional briefer!"

12 April, Da Nang:

"Don Brooks called today and said I could stay with him while I'm in Saigon next week. I saw Bob Wolfenden this week. He's the advisor to the 1st ARVN Division on sensors. I'm scheduled to go up there on the 20th.

Had another busy, hot day. It's cooled off some tonight. I've got to get a haircut, some chow, and watch a movie. Then back to work as usual!

13 April, Da Nang:

"Rex Robinson came by today and is spending the night."

14 April, Da Nang:

"Visited Jim Baier today. He showed me a newspaper write up on himself that Ed Butchart did when he and his wife adopted a Vietnamese girl. It was quite a good article. He's on an extension over here, now has 19 months in country.

All set for my trip to Saigon. Don Johnson from the 1st Marine Air Wing is going, along with Bob Wolfenden."

17 April, Saigon:

"Made it down here all right and Don met me at the airport. The conference ended today and I'm going back in the morning. It's hot here, and they've had some rockets and terrorist activities going on.

I finally got downtown and saw the President's Palace, etc. It's just one big, noisy, dirty city.

I saw Lt. Colonel Bowen today. He didn't have much to say. "

18 April, Da Nang:

"I got back o.k. Don Brooks took me to catch the plane. When I got back, I found out I was being considered for another assignment! Saigon! I would be replacing Ron Drost, who I may have mentioned in one of my letters. His job is in the Operation Centers in MACV Headquarters as the XXIV Corps representative. I would brief on all actions in the XXIV Corps area (1st Marine Division, 1st & 2nd ARVN Divisions, 101st Airborne Division) and several other units! I'm going to talk to Colonel Boyd about it. It might not be a bad deal career wise.

General Wheeler broke a leg in a helicopter crash today. He'll be in a walking cast for 2 weeks, but a replacement is already coming in from Washington to replace him. Colonel Wilcox, CO of 1st Marines, had 9 stitches in his scalp, Colonel [Floyd H.] Waldrop, the G-3, had his shoulder dislocated. The pilot suffered a broken back and other lesser injuries."

19 April, Da Nang:

"It was another long, hot day today. I'm going to Hue by helicopter tomorrow. Will spend the night with Bob Wolfenden and come back the next day. Should be an interesting trip, as Hue is supposed to be a beautiful city."

21 April, Da Nang:

"I really enjoyed the trip to Hue. Bob Wolfenden met me at the airport. I got to tour the walled city of Hue where the Marines had the big battles in 1968.

No word on how the President's speech is going to affect us as of yet. I suspect we will know soon."

22 April, Da Nang:

"A real hot sticky day today."

23 April, Da Nang:

"Today was another hot one and I was the escort officer for an Army Colonel from Ft. Belvoir all morning. Got to eat in the General's mess today. It's a lot nicer than ours!"

24 April, Da Nang:

"The weather is hot and sticky although it rained a little this morning.

The floorshow last night was really good – an old Australian broad about 60 who has been entertaining troops since WWII. She was a riot. The Vietnamese waitresses said, 'mama-san a dirty old man!'"

25 April, Da Nang:

"I was so successful scrounging gear today that nothing could bother me! I got a ditch-digger from the Seabees, 2 pieces of heavy equipment from the 7th Engineer Battalion, and 15,000 feet of cable from 5th Communications Battalion! General Wheeler leaves tomorrow. He's going to HQMC."

26 April, Da Nang:

*"Today was cloudy with a little rain but it is good sleeping weather tonight.
The papers now say no withdrawals from the 1st Marine Division until August. I guess that's it."*

27 April, Da Nang:

"It poured rain last night and I didn't think it would ever stop! It had this morning. General Wheeler left today and General [Charles F.] Widdecke came in to relieve him. More briefings!"

28 April, Da Nang:

"Went to 1/1 today and saw Dave Marks. Things are going well and I'm staying busy."

29 April, Da Nang:

"I had another busy day today. Lt. Prins was sick today, running at both ends. He's my assistant. It was really hot here today, but I got a lot accomplished."

30 April, Da Nang:

*"Had another busy day. Bob Wolfenden came down from Hue today and is spending the night.
The VC launched a series of attacks by fire last night and tonight. We haven't been hit, but the night is early!"*

1 May, Da Nang:

"I'm planning on going to Australia tomorrow—if there is space available on the plane! Hope to tour the country as much as I can. Ironically, I had to brief 3 Australian officers today!"

2 May, Da Nang:

"I have to be at the R&R center at 1600, and naturally the flight doesn't leave until 1900. Eleven hours to Sydney! Hope it is worth going there. I plan to get Jett a boomerang and Diana a Koala bear—surprises for you! Bob Wolfenden gave me some good ideas!"

3 May, Sydney:

"Thirteen hours after leaving Da Nang we arrived in Sydney. We had to stop in Darwin, Australia for customs. They really search your luggage! Looking for dope!

It's the fall season here and cold when you're not in the sun. The climate is much like San Francisco's. It's a beautiful city, even the older sections, built in the 1800s, are fairly well kept up. It's a seaport and seafood abounds. Haven't seen the beaches, but they're all public and well taken care of. It's the cleanest place I've ever seen—with a population of about 3 million. It looks much like the USA, except they drive on the wrong side of the road! The steering wheel is on the wrong side too.

We got in about 1000 this morning and Bill Taylor, one of the company commanders in 2/5, and I signed up to go to a rugby football game. We almost froze! It was enjoyable but hard to understand. We were invited to one of the sports clubs. It's a combination YMCA-YWCA and Las Vegas casino. They have huge rooms filled with slot machines and bars. They serve excellent food at a reasonable price. I had a T-bone steak, which was delicious! The rest of the building is a big auditorium for movies and floor shows, a swimming pool, gym, sauna, and game rooms—unbelievable!

Most of the downtown parks are dedicated to athletic fields for both girls and boys. Everyone participates in sports, young and old, boys and girls, and they look it, too.

I'm watching the Queen of England's departure on TV. A lot of U.S. TV shows are on."

10 May, Da Nang:

"They went through a high threat period here while I was gone. Took a few rockets, etc., but nothing much. I didn't get the job in Saigon, but I'm not disappointed.

I had a real nice time in Sydney. I contacted a friend of a friend and business associate, and he showed me a lot of the city, introduced me to the best families in Sydney, and had me out to his house for dinner. The Australians, once you get to know them, are really friendly. I actually went out to lunch with him twice and ended up at a wine distributor's drinking champagne—free! We had quite a time! I met the boss's son who will race in the Americas Cup off Newport, R.I. in August. I also met the owners of the Kentucky Fried Chicken chain in Australia, the owner of one of the largest hotels, etc., etc. The food, clothing, TV, radio, music, you name it, is from the U.S.

It's really hot and humid here now, 96 degrees and 85 % humidity yesterday. Most of the work I had mapped out got done, but naturally some of it didn't. Last night and most of today was spent getting things going again."

11 May, Da Nang:

"It must have been 100 degrees today. We had a shower about 1600 that cooled things off."

13 May, Da Nang:

"Bob Wolfenden was down from Hue yesterday and spent the night.

The weather here is really hot, 102 degrees yesterday and almost as hot today. We're having a shower now, which is cooling things off.

I sent a thank you note to the family in Australia who were so nice to me, and ordered a plaque for the wine company that entertained me so often.

1st Lt. Allen reported in today to replace Lt. Prins who is going to Force Recon Company next week. I think I will enjoy having him work for me."

16 May, Da Nang:

"The officers in the hut had a steak cookout tonight and then adjourned to the club for the floor show. For a change it was a good one!

We've had a couple of good showers the last two days which has helped to keep things cooled off and it's pouring now.

I went to visit several of my read out positions today to promote some personnel. Good to get out and around."

17 May, Da Nang:

"Had a busy day today; a lot going on. Lt. Allen is going on R&R, so I'll have everything to myself starting Friday. Lt. Prins leaves Tuesday."

19 May, Da Nang:

"Rex Robinson was up again yesterday and today to see me. He leaves in July and still doesn't have orders.

We went to see Colonel [Wilber F.] Semlick[G-4, III MAF]. He's doing fine. Lost a lot of weight and is going home in two weeks. I saw SSgt. Zombro, also. He's going back to HQMC for duty. [Zombro had worked for me at HQMC]. I have been staying busy with lots of visitors from Saigon and other places."

20 May, Da Nang:

"We're still having showers, which is helping to keep things cooled off.
I'm still staying busy but not nearly as busy as I was previously. Things have slowed down and my NCOs are doing a real good job."

21 May, Da Nang:

"I'm still enjoying the new pictures you sent. The Vietnamese woman who cleans our hut says Diana and Jett look 'same-same' as me. She wanted a picture of Diana, so I gave her one. She has 5 children of her own!"

22 May, Da Nang:

"Lt. Allen left on R&R today, so I've got the whole shebang for a week. He's going to be real good, though."

23 May, Da Nang:

"Went to Hoa An today by helicopter. Saw Jim McCarty who was at HQMC. He leaves in about three weeks.
The weather is getting hot again. The war remains cool. The airfield and Da Nang did take some rockets the other night. There have been 3 tigers killed around here lately and a black panther seen."

24 May, Da Nang:

"Gave a briefing today for the first time in a while. Everyone is being transferred around due to the shortage of majors. Jim Masters, who I work for, is going to 5th Marines as the S-3 in June. Don't know whether I'll move again or not.
Going to go out now and shoot some basketball before the movie."

25 May, Dan Nang:

"The weather is real hot here now, but we're getting a breeze in the evening that helps cool things off.
I'm working on a briefing for the General sometime this week. It has to be 15 minutes long.
Played basketball for a while tonight. I'm getting a fair tan."

26 May, Da Nang:

"The Colonel gave the brief to the General! It's a new policy, which I don't mind at all! Didn't cool off until late this afternoon, so I didn't play basketball today."

27 May, Da Nang:

"It was 99 degrees yesterday and as hot today. We had a shower that cooled things off today.
Saw Dale Dorman today. He's the S-3 of 2/1. He has been here since last September and wants to stay there until he leaves."

28 May, Da Nang:

"Don Brooks called and he is coming up tomorrow and will spend the night."

30 May, Da Nang:

"Don spent the night and we had a floor show, so it was quite an enjoyable evening. He slept in the hut across the way. I took him to the airport, but he's not sure he will get out, as he's a standby passenger.
The weather is still real hot. I haven't played basketball because it doesn't cool off until late."

31 May, Da Nang:

"I have to brief General McCutcheon Tuesday. Should be fun! The war is still quiet. Just hope it stays that way!"

1 June, Da Nang:

"[Lt. Colonel Joseph J.] Louder is taking over 1st Motor Transport Battalion tomorrow. I haven't seen him but I'm sure he is happy.
Don Hanson, who relieved me as S-3 of 2/5, came by today. He's going on R&R to Hawaii. Roland Monette came back from his second R&R there! Actually, it was a 7-day leave, but I'm envious of him!
Don Evens, the S-3 of 3/7 stopped by today also. He was at HQMC."

2 June, Da Nang:

"The briefing of General McCutcheon went fine. Colonel Boyd was well pleased. The General flew the helicopter we traveled in. He's quite a pilot!"

General McCutcheon wanted to see the areas in which the sensors had been placed, so we flew at low altitudes over the whole Da Nang Barrier.

3 June, Da Nang:

"Today was another hot one. I'm planning to shoot some baskets as soon as the sun goes down.

I heard today that a lot of majors are getting message type orders over here who were not on the slate to come. HQMC was so sure we would be pulled out! Everyone else thought so, too! I understand the Vietnamese don't want the Marines to leave. Da Nang has never been penetrated like Saigon, Hue, and now Dalat."

4 June, Da Nang:

"The President's announcement didn't come as too big a surprise. Everyone thinks some Marines will be involved in the 50,000 troops to be withdrawn."

5 June, Da Nang:

"It's a hot, sticky night, but a storm is coming in the distance."

6 June, Da Nang:

"Another hot day today. I rode out to Hill 10 to visit our readout post and over to the 1st Marine Air Wing. Don Johnson leaves in 4 weeks. He's going to Beaufort now instead of HQMC."

7 June, Da Nang:

"Today was another scorcher, but the area I work in is partly air conditioned so it isn't too bad.

Colonel Keith has his orders and he's going to Marine Barracks, Subic Bay in the Philippines as the CO."

9 June, Da Nang:

"It was 100 degrees here today."

10 June, Da Nang:

"Today was long and hot, but one more closer to going home!"

12 June, Da Nang:

"I played basketball the last 2 nights until dark. It hasn't been too hot today, but we're having a shower now."

13 June, Da Nang:

"We're having a heavy rain tonight. It came up about 1500 and isn't an electrical storm, so it may last for a while. It's nice and cool tonight."

14 June, Da Nang:

"It poured rain all day today and is still coming down. Got to get back to work!"

15 June, Da Nang:

"We had another rainy day today. My troops couldn't get more work done in the field. It sure makes for nice sleeping weather, though!"

16 June, Da Nang:

"The rain stopped today and is real nice out—about 95 degrees! We're getting ready to play basketball anyway. General [Edwin H.] Simmons reported in today to be the new Assistant Division Commander."

17 June, Da Nang:

"Had a busy day today. Briefed General Simmons for about 30 minutes. He was fairly easy to brief.
Played basketball again tonight. Really pooped!"

18 June, Da Nang:

"I have a briefing tomorrow for a Colonel from Saigon. Today was fairly busy and hot. I went over to the 1st Marine Air Wing and saw Don Johnson. He has about 2 weeks left!

Colonel Boyd got his orders to HQMC today. He leaves 24 July. Don't know who is going to be the new G-2 but hope it's going to be Lt. Colonel Mosher.

Saw Bob Gadwell today. He was at HQMC and is now in the Division Engineers office. His rotation tour date is 2 days before mine but we're betting on coming home on the same plane like we did last time!"

19 June, Da Nang:

"The briefings went well today. I'm always glad when they are over with."

20 June, Da Nang:

"Had a Sergeant wounded today. Just a piece of metal in his arm, and he'll be out of the hospital in a couple of days. I visited him today and found out he was from Norfolk, Virginia, and went to VMI for 2 years and has been in the Marines for 3 years! He's a good Marine.

Rex Robinson just called and he's coming over tonight to spend the night. He has orders to I&I, Salt Lake City and leaves in July."

21 June, Da Nang:

"We just had a tremendous downpour that flooded the hut. It's stopped now, and Commander Rameriz, U.S. Navy, is swabbing the deck! We're all laughing at him since he has 28 years in the Navy!

We had a party at China Beach this afternoon. Gunnery Sergeant Johnson is leaving next week and I gave him a plaque on behalf of the personnel who work for me. He's an outstanding SNCO."

China Beach 22 June 1970
Sensor Platoon
Major Bob Driver & GySgt. Gus R. Johnson

22 June, Da Nang:

"Went out to 1st Marines today just to get out of the CP. I'm going with the Colonel to visit 5th Marines and 7th Marines tomorrow.

It was cloudy with occasional showers today, which made the day most pleasant. Played basketball again tonight and really enjoyed it. We have a good group of players."

23 June, Da Nang:

"My orders to Quantico came in today. I can't leave before the 20th and not later than the 25th of August.

There's a good chance I'll be transferred to 1/7 to be the XO. The Colonel is against it, but we're so short of field grade officers I'm almost sure to go. The CO, XO, and S-3 all leave in July.

Lt. Colonel Graves leaves Friday. He's a really nice guy. He's 'willing' me his lawn chair—since I use it all the time anyway! It's been pouring rain today, but it sure makes for nice sleeping weather."

24 June, Da Nang:

"Spent most of the afternoon at An Hoa visiting the District Advisors. Spent about 30 minutes briefing and 4 hours of gabbing and waiting for the helicopters.
No more word on going to 7th Marines. Standing by to stand by!"

25 June, Da Nang:

"Got the word today that I'm definitely going to 7th Marines, but I don't know to what billet or which battalion! John Sheridan, who was sent down yesterday, is now the XO of 1/7. Colonel [Edmund G.] Derning, the CO of 7th Marines, told Lt. Colonel Mosher that I will be S-3 of 2/7. Captain Barnett, the S-2 of 7th Marines, told me Lt. Colonel [Kenneth L.] Robinson was asking about me because I was going to be his XO. He has 3/7. Guess I'll know for sure on the 28th when I get down there!

The Secretary of the Navy is coming tomorrow and we're involved, so I had a rehearsal this afternoon.

I went over to the 1st Marine Air Wing and saw Don Johnson today. I played basketball with Bill Bonds, who is going to Quantico, also. We're having a real thunderstorm now and the rain is pouring down! Really cooled off!

I'm leaving my gear, or most of it, here at Division and have Will Kinney look after it for me. No one is coming in now, so my billet will probably stay empty.

Gunnery Sergeant Johnson, my Operations Chief, left today for home. He's an outstanding Marine. Sure hated to see him go. Captain Telford is going to be my replacement. No experience, but a fine officer. I worked with him in the 5th Marines."

26 June, Da Nang:

"Spent the day snapping in my relief, Captain Telford. Played basketball tonight. Was I lousy!"

28 June, Da Nang:

"Getting ready to go to Landing Zone Baldy to report to 7th Marines."

I relieved Major E.L. Evans on this date, according to the Battalion Command Chronology for June. Major T.G. McFarland was the Battalion XO.

29 June, LZ Baldy:

"Drove down here yesterday afternoon. Met Colonel Derning and he has me staying here until the 1st and then I will go down to 2/7 as the S-3. They are at Landing Zone Ross. I'm being briefed the two days here. Spent today doing just that.

Played volleyball with the Regimental staff today. Had a lot of fun. The Colonel usually plays.

It is hotter here than in Da Nang. It poured rain last night, which made it bearable. LZ Ross is supposed to be hotter. Saw Pete O'Brien today. He's the S-4 of 2/7."

Chapter Twenty

Operation Pickens Forest,
July-September 1970
S-3, 2nd Battalion, 7th Marines

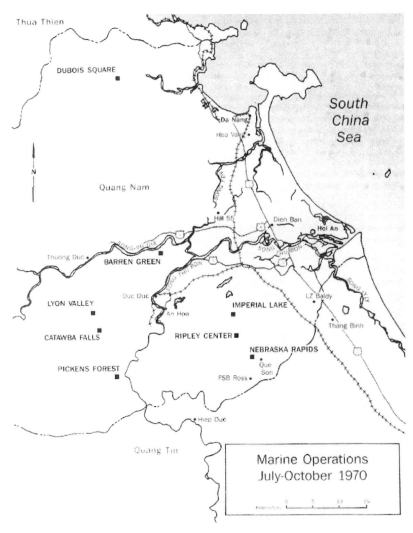

Map of Marine Operations, July-October 1970

1 July, LZ Ross:

"Starting a new month in a new job. My last full month in country! LZ Ross is located about 20 miles south of Da Nang in the Que Son Valley. It is really a Fire Support Base. Lt. Colonel [Vincent A.] Albers is the CO. I had met him before at Division when he was the G-5 (Civil Affairs). I believe I'll enjoy working for him.

I was really on the go yesterday. They cut short my stay at LZ Baldy and I came down to LZ Ross long enough to drop my gear, get back on the helicopter, and went to a briefing for an operation that started today! Got back at 1900 last night and slept in the CP bunker all night. I was not very comfortable.

We [Golf Company] killed 5 and brought out 34 refugees with no casualties on our part."

During the period 1-4 July, the Battalion defended FSB Ross, FSB Ryder, and OP Lion. Two rifle companies [Echo Company under Captain C.H. Mulherin and Fox Company under 1st. Lt. A.C. Florence] continued pacification efforts, while the other two provided security for FSB Ryder [Hotel Company under 1st. Lt. C.A. Edwards] and OP Lion [Golf Company under 1st Lt. J.M. Egan]. I did not have an Assistant S-3.

One of the unwritten reasons Lt. Col. Albers and I were assigned to 2/7 was recent fraggings that had taken place. Black militants, part of McNamara's 100,000, were responsible. McNamara's 100,000 forced the military to take mentally and morally unqualified youths into the service. The idea was for the military to educate and train them while a war was going on! Another of McNamara's follies! Many came from street gangs that plagued our inner cities. The Army took the lion's share, but the Marines were forced to take a large number and were also forced to graduate them from recruit training. Because of their lack of education and trainability, they ended up in the infantry, motor transport, and supply billets. Once assigned to Vietnam, they reverted to their gang attitudes and became a serious problem in the rear areas. They refused to go the field, malingered, failed to obey lawful orders, intimidated other blacks, NCOs, and Staff NCOs. Drug and alcohol use was rampant. Fights and assaults took place nightly. General Widdecke received authority to administratively discharge them. Some 78 were pending discharge in 2/7 when we reported. The problem seldom extended to the rifle companies in the field. They were too busy depending on each other to stay alive. The problem was getting them to the field and away from their ringleaders.

2 July, LZ Ross:

"Another long, hot day. Colonel Albers and I went with Colonel Derning to visit the Non Son and Thuong Duc Special Forces camps and that took all morning. It must reach 100 degrees every day here and it is really humid. I've given up wearing underwear again! Nice, huh?

Colonel Albers said his wife had met you. He's a Civil War buff of sorts, too!

We killed 3 VC today but lost 4 wounded including a Lieutenant [Echo Company tripped a M-26 booby trap]. *We sent out 92 refugees."*

3 July, LZ Ross:

Golf Company killed 4 VC/NVA today. The 1st Platoon of Echo Company hit a daisy chain booby trap of M-26 grenades, resulting in 2 Marines wounded.

4 July, LZ Ross:

"We're moving to LZ Baldy tomorrow. I'm sure staying busy and the time is passing fast. We killed 2 more VC last night, but had 2 Marines wounded by a booby trap."

Fox Company was operating in Antenna Valley 4-8 July, with SCAMP personnel, finding and replacing batteries in sensors.

5 July, LZ Baldy:

The battalion conducted a relief in place of 3/7. Echo Company was placed under operational control of 1st Marines until 14 July. Hotel Company was moved into the Que Son Mountains. Golf Company moved to LZ Baldy and operated in the adjacent flatlands and foothills around the base.

6 July, LZ Baldy:

"Made the move from Ross to Baldy yesterday and are fairly well settled in. I'll sure be glad when I start receiving my mail!

We had another real downpour last night and the power went off and is still off. All we could do is use candles and sweat! General Widdecke is coming to visit one of our companies tomorrow."

Fox Company had a good day, killing 1 VC and bringing in 8 Chieu Hois, including a village chief.

7 July, LZ Baldy:

"Another long, hot day. We had our usual rain shower this afternoon.
Have really had a busy day today. We had 8 VC surrender and all their families came in with them. We hauled out 60 people in all.
Colonel Derning made a surprise visit today. He's easy to talk to. He and the General visited Hotel Company today, the one that had all the VC surrender."

Hotel Company had two engagements during the day, accounting for 1 VC KIA in the first one. In the second, they were sweeping through the enemy's position and lost 2 WIAs to a booby trap.

9 July, LZ Baldy:

"Two busy, hot days, but nothing to write home about. The war is quiet, at least in our area.
Went on a helicopter recon this morning. It took 2 hours. We visited the Non Son Special Forces Camp again. The jungle is beautiful from the air. It looks so peaceful!
I keep flying over areas I walked and fought through and all the houses, people, and fields are gone!"

10 July, LZ Baldy:

"Another hot one today. It hasn't been below 96 degrees yet. I'm going with the Colonel to the field today by helicopter to visit Echo Company. The war is still quiet. We found a rice cache yesterday, about 700 pounds."

The 1st Platoon of Hotel Company received a grenade while setting in a night defensive position, wounding one Marine.

12 July, LZ Baldy:

"It is over 100 degrees today. Generals Widdecke and Simmons were down to be briefed on an upcoming operation yesterday."

Lt. Col. Albers and I attended this meeting, along with most of the Division, Wing, and Regimental staffs, battalion and helicopter squadron COs, etc. Intelligence indicated that the NVA 4th Front Headquarters,

38th NVA, 1st VC Regiments, and the 490th Sapper Battalions, comprising about 1,500 combat troops, were operating in our TAOR. The Division staff presented a plan to launch a helicopter assault into the heart of the enemy's forces. This operation would involve most of the ground and air units left in Vietnam. The NVA were known to have 12.7 mm machine guns near the proposed landing zones. 2/7 was to lead the attack. Lt. Col. Albers and I, with the CP group, would land with the second wave. Two other infantry battalions would land on our flanks. After the Division briefing officers finished their presentations, including anticipated losses of men and helicopters, you could have heard a pin drop. It was the most somber meeting I have ever attended. The commanding officers were to report their recommendations to the Division commander the next day. Lt. Col. Albers and I left the meeting in disbelief. For the first time in my two years in Vietnam, I was afraid. I believe he was too, based on our conversation on our way back to the battalion. Our companies were under strength as it was, engaged in combat almost every day, and to be landed in that situation was asking almost too much from them. Fortunately, the helicopter squadron commanders blinked first, telling the Division they could not support this proposed operation with the assets they had. That operation was called off and 'Operations Pickens Forest' became the modified version. Fox Company, with the help of a sniper team, killed 3 VC during the day.

I continued, "*I got my orders today. I'll leave the battalion on the 18th of August and fly to Okinawa on the 20th. I have to be in the states by the 25th, so that is about when you can expect me.*"

13 July, LZ Baldy:

"*It's a particularly hot day today—over 100 degrees. It was a successful one for the battalion. Fox Company killed 3 last night, and 2 more today. Golf Company killed 2 and captured 1. Hotel Company killed 1, captured 5, 4 weapons, and a radio, and have some more penned up in a cave. They're going in after them in the morning. Hotel had 4 wounded, none seriously, when they went in the cave after them today. The 2 VC left inside are supposed to be wounded but they have a weapon.*

General McCutcheon visited one of our companies today. Pete O'Brien is really doing a good job as our S-4."

461

14 July, LZ Baldy:

"Another busy hot day. Hotel Company spent the day getting a total of 20 VC out of the cave and killed a total of 8. [A Kit Carson Scout talked them out.] Fox Company killed one more, and Golf Company killed one and wounded and captured another. General Widdecke flew out and promoted 4 men in Hotel Company on the spot.

Seven of the VC killed by Hotel in a night-long siege, some of them by Marines who crawled into the cave and shot them at short range with their .45s. Among those surrendering was the VC leader of the village."

Hotel Company searched the cave and found one AK-47, one AK-50, one M-16 and one PRC-25 radio. The prisoners were almost the entire VC cadre of Phu Dien Hamlet.

I continued, *"I've got to start getting my shots for going home this month. Getting that short! It's too hot to think about shots!"*

15 July, LZ Baldy:

"Things have been quiet but hot here. We're starting a big operation tomorrow called 'Pickens Forest.' I'll be helilifting out in the morning, so the mail may get a little sporadic for a while. I don't know how long I'll be gone.

The Commandant of the Marine Corps [Leonard C. Chapman, Jr.] and General [William K.] Jones, CG, FMFPAC, are in the area now."

The block of terrain selected for Operation Pickens Forest was southwest of the Vietnamese Marines' area of operations. In the western part of the area, the Marines would encounter typical Vietnamese mountain terrain—a tangle of ridges cut up by steep-sided gullies and streambeds and overgrown with dense jungle, underbrush, and, in many places, bamboo. Near the Thu Bon River were a few Viet Cong controlled hamlets, where farmers grew rice and corn for the enemy. The area around the hamlets was surrounded by level paddy fields and farmland, interspersed with tree lines, palm and rubber tree groves, and stretches of elephant grass. The mission of the operation was to 'locate and destroy the NVA forces, supplies and installations in the highlands before they can interfere with pacification.'

Both the 1st and 2nd Battalions of the 7th Marines were committed to this operation. The morning of the 16th, Echo Company landed at FSB Starling, about 2 miles south of FSB Defiance, where the supporting artillery was moved to. Echo was under operational control of 1/7 until 22 July. Starling was on east side of the Thu Bon River and Defiance was on the west side. Later in the day, Companies F and G and the CP group landed on FSB Dart, along with four 4.2 inch mortars. For the next 10 days, Company E gradually worked its way southward, up the Thu Bon. Companies F and G pushed across county towards the river. These two companies moved through extremely rough and overgrown mountainous terrain and followed the major trails and streambeds, assuming this was where the enemy would be found. This proved to be correct, but it forced the Marines to follow predictable routes, which enabled the NVA units to avoid them. Hotel Company was under operational control of 3/7 until 27 July.

16 July, FSB Dart:

The 3rd Platoon of Fox Company found a harboring site large enough to accommodate 15-20 VC, which they destroyed.

18 July, FSB Dart:

"We are sitting on top of a high mountain about 30 miles from anywhere. Not much has been going on. Fox Company killed an NVA officer yesterday and got his pistol and some documents. They also found a base camp large enough for 150 men. [The 8 huts were well built with rock sides. There were bunkers and spider holes surrounding the camp. They destroyed the camp]. They had a shootout with 3 more NVA and wounded one, but they all got away.

Echo Company, which is under operational control of 1/7, captured 12 light machine guns, 300 SKS rifles and 70,000 rounds of small arms ammunition, and some other gear.

Hotel Company, which is back near LZ Baldy, killed 1 VC, captured four 82 mm mortar rounds and 14 new French bicycles.

It has been quiet and peaceful up here, and a lot cooler than LZ Baldy. Today is going to be a hot one. The General is coming out to visit us today. Each time a helicopter lands here, they create a dust storm that is unbelievable!

The nights have been real nice, except for the mortars firing all night long. No bugs though. We haven't gotten any mail up here yet, but we should get some today.

This day next month, I'll be leaving the battalion to go to Da Nang and catch 'The Freedom Bird,' as the troops call it!"

Fox Company, with the help of an AO, killed 2 VC and captured one AK-47.

Fire Support Base Dart, 18 July 1970, COC Bunker 2/7

20 July, FSB Dart:

"It has really been miserable two days since I wrote. It's been over 100 degrees and there is no shade. We just sit and bake. We're glad to see the sun go down!

General Simmons was out yesterday and the Colonel was gone, so I ended up showing him around the hill. He hasn't changed much since he was CO of 9th Marines. [Simmons was derisively known as 'the great police sergeant in the sky,' as he had a habit of dropping in on units and criticizing them for the general state of police of their area. I never had this problem with him, but we always made an effort to keep our area looking good.]

I went to a meeting at Regiment today—my first trip off the hill. It is almost as hot where they are!

We found another base camp today and captured a lot of ammunition. Golf Company had a man killed and 3 wounded by a command-detonated booby trap.

We're getting ready to have shower, which has really cooled things off considerably. I'm really getting cruddy, as we only have enough water to shave in and not enough to take a bath."

21 July, FSB Dart:

Fox Company found a dead NVA today. What was interesting was that he was wearing a flak jacket!

22 July, FSB Dart:

"Two more long, hot days have passed since I wrote last. I've been busy flying around the area and getting ready to move. We're going to another position tomorrow.

We captured 5 weapons and quite a bit of munitions the last two days and found one dead NVA. Otherwise it has been quiet.

When we visited Echo Company yesterday, the Colonel and all of us jumped into a stream and took a bath. It felt great! Would like to do it now, as it is over 100 degrees and rising.

Colonel Bowen wrote me from Saigon and sent a copy of a Meritorious Unit Citation 2/5 was put in for. He leaves for Camp Pendleton on 2 August. They've flown hot chow and beer in the last 2 days. It really helps, as it is too hot to cook C rations at noon."

Company E was reassigned back to the battalion that day. Delta/1/7 was placed under operational control of 2/7 until 29 July.

23 July, Hill 110:

Echo Company found a .30 caliber machine gun hidden in a hut. Golf Company discovered six 82 mm mortar rounds with Russian markings.

24 July, Hill 110:

"We moved to this hill yesterday and it is much better than the one we came from. This one is covered with tall grass. We traded the dirt for the mosquitoes, as we are right next to a large river.

We killed 2, captured 3 rifles, 6 grenades and 6 mortar rounds yesterday."

Fox Company discovered a large base camp and bunkers and destroyed them. The same day, helicopters started arriving at LZ Baldy packed with peasants who were sent to the fields to pick corn, escorted by Marines and provided with half-ton trailers to load the corn into. Before noon each day, the trailers would be filled and all would be helilifted back to LZ Baldy. The peasants were paid for their efforts. The Marines soon ran out of money to pay them, but they continued to harvest the corn for part of the crop. An estimated 42,000 pounds of corn was harvested during the season, and it could be seen lying out on the pavement of Rt. 1 to dry from the Ba Ren River to near LZ Baldy.

SSgt. J.W. Sedberry F/2/7 examines a primitive enemy explosive device

25 July, Hill 110:

Delta Company had 5 men wounded from two booby traps while moving into a night defensive position. Golf Company found a large base camp, complete with watchtowers, inside and outside it. The towers were platforms in trees.

26 July, Hill 110:

"We had another couple of long, hot days but we had a nice cooling shower last night.

Between the jungle rot, ringworms, and whiteheads from being dirty for 10 days, and the sun, I guess I'm doing o.k. I picked up a head cold to go along with the rest.

It looks as if we are going to be out here for a long time, so I'll probably be here until I rotate."

Golf Company had two brief firefights with small groups of VC during the day with no casualties on either side.

27 July, Hill 110:

"A quiet, hot day yesterday, but a busy night. Echo Company sprang an ambush on about 30, killing 5 NVA, capturing 2 weapons and 24 packs. We had four wounded."

Documents found indicated that these NVA were part of a naval sapper unit, which had started south from Hanoi in February.

I continued, *"D/1/7, attached to us, had 6 casualties during the day from booby traps. I took a bath last night and put on clean clothes. It really felt great."*

Company H was reassigned back to the battalion today. They began combing the hills north of FSB Defiance.

29 July, Hill 110:

"Another long, hot day. We've been successful in the last few days. Echo Company captured 139 rifles and about 1 ton of munitions the other day. They also ambushed about 30 VC, killing 5, capturing 3 weapons and 24 packs. We captured a VC and found 1,100 pounds of rice yesterday. D/1/7 found a VC hospital with 18 bodies and 1 ton of corn. You can see we have really been busy."

Echo Company was working with Vietnamese province officials and RF troops and was guided by a VC defector.

30 July, Hill 110:

"Another hot day starting. I'll be catching a helicopter in a few minutes to go back to Baldy. Then a jeep ride to Da Nang, get my other gear, I left behind there, then to shipping and receiving to ship it. After that I'll spend the night at Division with my old hut mates and return to Baldy tomorrow morning. Then back to Hill 110.
We uncovered another good size ammunition cache yesterday and captured 3 rifles. Hope to have another good day today."

31 July, Hill 110:

Hotel Company, assisted by an AO, killed 3 of 7 VC and captured an AK-47.

During the month, the battalion submitted recommendations for 1 Legion of Merit, 4 Bronze Stars, 13 Naval Commendation Medals, 49 Naval Achievement Medals and 46 Purple Hearts.

The battalion called in 188 artillery fire missions during the month, totaling over 3,000 rounds, and 433,500 pounds of ordnance were dropped in 36 close air support missions.

1 August, Hill 110:

"The trip to Da Nang was uneventful. Got my gear shipped o.k. 10 boxes. I've still got my clothes in a wall locker, plus some things I want to hand carry home.

I stopped in the G-2 and got my plaque from the new G-2, Colonel [Albert C.] Smith. Got to see everyone who was left, and most everyone I knew had gone. Saw the movie, drank 3 Cokes, and just relaxed. Enjoyed sleeping between clean sheets for a change! Got my shots yesterday before I came back and my arms are a little sore today.

Soon after I left on the 30th, Echo Company ran into 30 VC with machine guns. Echo Company was on both sides of a river and in boats and the VC positioned on the high ground on both sides of the river. The VC sank the boats, killing 2 Marines and wounding 6. One of the dead is missing. Hotel Company killed 2 VC yesterday and Charlie Company, 1/5, under our operational control, killed 1 [a sniper], captured 5 and 1 weapon. [They were the Pacifier (called Sparrow Hawk in the 3rd Marine Division) unit brought in to assist Company E and act as a blocking force to the south and west of the enemy ambush site]. Echo Company just picked up 2 more detainees this morning. Fox Company found one dead VC floating down the river last night."

Echo Company was working its way upstream in a southwesterly direction along both banks of the Thu Bon. They were about 4 miles south of Hill 110 at a point where the river flows through a narrow, deep gorge. About noon eight Marines were in two boats hunting for caves in the cliffs overhanging the river, while patrols moved along on either banks. About 50 VC/NVA using 4 machine guns opened fire on the men in the boats from concealed caves and bunkers along the river. The survivors from the boats managed to swim to safety as the river flowed away from the ambush. The Marines on the banks covered them with fire. An air strike managed to drop napalm to silence the VC and a medevac was able to get the wounded out.

I continued, "I should be leaving here on the 17th to check out of the battalion. Then I'll go to Da Nang on the 18th and fly out on the 19th or 20th to Okinawa. I'll probably have to spend at least 3 days there.

General Widdecke is coming out for a visit today with Colonel Derning. Colonel Derning is being replaced and goes home on the 5th."

Fox Company was pulled out of the operation and returned to LZ Baldy for a well deserved R&R. C/1/5 was pulled out of the operation the same day and returned to Da Nang as the Pacifier unit. Golf Company, coming off an R&R, replaced Fox in the field.

3 August, Hill 110:

"Another two long, hot, and wet days are gone. It's been real hot until late in the afternoon and then we have a storm. Last night it rained until about midnight.

We recovered the bodies of the two Marines killed the other day. We also captured 58 detainees, 1 rifle, 6,000 pounds of corn, and 3,000 pounds of rice. This morning, we've killed 5, and possibly one more, and captured 2 weapons and some packs.

General Simmons and Colonel Derning were out the other day, and General Widdecke and the Colonel are coming out today. I'm about to go on a helicopter recon of the area in a few minutes."

I wrote my brother, *"We're on operation Pickens Forest, probably the last Marine operation of the war. We have done real well—158 weapons captured and 41 VC/ NVA killed and tons of munitions, rice and corn captured."*

5 August, Hill 110:

"I haven't heard from you in 5 days. I heard a Flying Tigers Airline plane crashed on Okinawa with 16,000 pounds of mail on board.

Things have been fairly quiet. We killed 1 VC and had 1 to surrender yesterday.

Colonel [Robert H.] Piehl, the new Regimental Commander, was out to visit us yesterday. Lt. Colonel Albers is going in this morning to the change of command ceremony. I'm going to try and go to LZ Baldy tomorrow for a bath, haircut, and change of clothes.

The weather has been overcast most of the last few days and the heat hasn't been too bad. Today looks like more of the same."

Echo Company was pulled out of the operation today.

7 August, Hill 110:

"I made the trip to LZ Baldy yesterday and it really felt good to be clean again, but we had a tremendous rain storm about 1600 which soaked everything and everyone, plus nearly blew our tent off the hill. It was all we could do to hold up the poles and keep it from blowing away.

The Sergeant Major got transferred, so Colonel Albers asked me to move in with him and I'm taking him up on it! Our tent was full of holes anyway!

Things have been kind of quiet. We killed 3 VC yesterday and found a big base camp and about 5,000 pounds of rice, corn and tobacco.

I sold my portable radio. It was kind of beat up from rain, mud, dust, sun, and being drug around from place to place."

9 August, Hill 110:

"Very little has been going on here except violent thunder storms which have about blown and washed us away!

We found a small cache of mortar rounds and several rice and corn caches of 1,000 pounds each. The 100 Vietnamese corn pickers we've had working out here got scared off, since 2 of them were wounded by a booby trap yesterday.

The other day, we visited some Vietnamese Marine positions and whom did I run into—[Richard] 'Pat' Carlisle. He volunteered to come back over early. He just arrived in May.

Did I tell you Colonel Simlik was selected for Brigadier General? It was a real surprise to everyone. Colonel Beck wasn't selected which surprised a lot of people, including him, I'm sure!

We're getting ready to move again. Hope it will be my last one."

Hotel Company killed 3 VC during the day. Fox Company killed 2 VC and captured 91 CHICOM grenades and some medical equipment.

Company E and two 105s occupied FSB Hatchet today. FSB Hatchet was already occupied by a Vietnamese Marine artillery battery. It was a located on a high hill just east of the Cai River. The surrounding country is mountainous with the exception of some level ground and a few hamlets near the river. The NVA greeted Echo Company's arrival with a barrage of 5 122 mm rockets. One Marine was wounded.

10 August, Hill 110:

"Had a busy day yesterday. We ended up with 7 VC killed and quite a few documents captured.

For a change we didn't have a downpour last night. The weather continues to be hot and humid, 96 degrees yesterday.

We moved a company to Fire Support Base Hatchet about 16 miles west of here and they took no casualties, but the ARNV Marines had 1 killed and 1 wounded by rocket fire. [Two 105 and two 155 howitzers moved there also.]

Flew around and visited Fox and Golf companies yesterday. General Simmons is coming out here today with Colonel Piehl. We are hoping to fly out to FSB Hatchet and visit Echo Company.

I'm just counting the days and staying busy. I'm ready to go anytime, but no replacement. Colonel Albers is going to bring it up to the Regimental Commander today."

12 August, FSB Hatchet:

"We moved up here yesterday by helicopter. We spent all day yesterday digging in. The place is a real mess, as it has been used by the ARVN Marines and they left the hill a garbage dump! The new Division G-3, Colonel [Don H.] Blanchard was out yesterday and he concurred. Nothing else is going on, and we had a quiet night."

13 August, FSB Hatchet:

"The Colonel just left for the rear, so I won't get this letter out until re-supply this afternoon.

We had a real electrical storm, and it poured for over an hour. You should have seen 300 naked Marines standing out in the rain taking a bath! It was great though!

We had a fairly quiet day and night. Golf Company killed 1 VC and Hotel captured 1. We had a near miss last night and killed 3 of the attackers.

Lt. Colonel Albers has approved my going in on the 16th to fill out fitness reports, etc. We are still busy digging in and cleaning up this place.

We got some cold beer and soda yesterday. Boy, did it taste good! Hope the Colonel brings some more when he comes."

15 August, FSB Hatchet:

"Getting ready to spend my last day and night in the bush. It's been real quiet. We've had our usual rain showers each evening, which cools things off and allows everyone to take a bath.

We had General Widdecke out yesterday and also the Regimental XO, Colonel [Charles G.] Little. We've cleaned up a lot of the mess left behind by the ARVN Marines but we've still got a ways to go. I got the word yesterday my flight date is the 21st, so I'll be staying in country one more day. They have to get me to the states by the 25th!

We get re-supplied today so I hope to get some mail from you. Better get this in the mail as the helicopters are on the way!"

16 August, LZ Baldy:

"Caught a helicopter in from the field and immediately started checking out! Today is Sunday and they only serve 2 meals, so I'm about to starve! They cook steaks starting at 1500.

My replacement is [Major M.T.] 'Terry' Cooper, just out of the Amphibious Warfare School at Quantico.

I may get a chance to go to Bangkok for a day's shopping; over and back the same day.

The troops in G-2 are giving me a party at China Beach on the 18th, so I can't miss that. They've gotten a plaque for me too. Well, it's about time for me to take a shower and get some clean clothes on. I stink!"

Company G and part of an artillery battery moved back to LZ Baldy from LZ Ross, effectively ending 'Operation Pickens Forest.'

17 August, LZ Baldy:

"Terry Cooper is going to the bush today, as the Colonel is due in this morning on one of the re-supply birds.

I had 2 steaks, 4 beers and 2 cokes last night. I really celebrated, huh! I've got a lot more checking out to do and fitness reports to sign. Haven't packed a thing! Most of my gear is in Da Nang, so I'll have to repack up there anyway."

18 August, Da Nang:

"I said my goodbyes to the battalion today and came up to Division. The Colonel told me before I left that he had put me in for a Legion of Merit. How about that! It's my end of tour award, but not too many majors get them. I hope it doesn't get downgraded! [I got it.]

I'm flying to Udorn, Thailand at 0800 in the morning and will be back about 1730. Hope to get you some silk and some surprises!

It's poured rain the last few days but it has made for good sleeping weather! I've already been manifested for my flight. It leaves Da Nang at 1330 on the 21st. It's a two hour flight by commercial jet.

Most of the people I knew at Division Headquarters have all left.

Going to take a shower, get dressed, have a couple of cokes, and watch the movie."

19 August, Da Nang:

"Got to Udorn, Thailand and back in one day. It only took an hour and a half to get there. It was pouring rain, but one of the local jewelers had vehicles meet us and take us around, free of charge. I saw the most beautiful Buddhist temple. It's the rainy season, but I still got to see quite a bit of the place.

I ate Thai food for lunch: rice, shrimp, onions, and peppers (the hot kind). It was good. Washed it down with Thai beer! It's potent!

Saw Denny Lanigan tonight. 5th Marines have moved up here. He goes home in October."

23 August, Okinawa:

"Got here last night finally! I missed one flight, and another was cancelled. Now my brown suitcase is missing! [I had all the Thai silk, etc., in it.] What a mess! I'm scheduled to fly out on the 27th and will arrive at Norton Air Force Base, California at 1800 the same day.

Burl Stonum is with me and we just moved into the BOQ at Kadena Air Force Base. He's leaving the 27th also. I saw Lt. Colonel Don Austgen a few minutes ago. He's leaving tomorrow."

Chapter Twenty-One

Marine Corps Career After the War,
1970-1979
Quantico, Command & Staff College, and Marine
Corps Recruiting Station, New Orleans

The flight back to the 'real world' was uneventful. When we arrived at Norton AFB, we had to go though customs. They were searching for drugs. This held up our getting off the base until early afternoon. I had a flight scheduled out of LA International, and caught a bus for that terminal. We made a stop for lunch someplace along the way. I was in the head and the bus left without me. I tried to get the dispatcher for the bus line to have it return, as all my baggage was on it. The bus driver said he would drop my luggage at the proper airline. That was the last I ever saw of it! I checked with every airline when I got there, but no luggage. I boarded the plane to Dulles International Airport with just my handbag, with my shaving kit and the precious stones I had bought my wife. Everything could be replaced except the photographs and plaques given me by the troops.

During the trip, I sat on the back row with a stewardess who had a brother in the Marines, a Lt., who was in Vietnam. Upon arrival, I was met by my dear wife Edna and the two children! My daughter was now walking and talking, and my son had grown several inches. We visited some of our relatives in Virginia during my leave, and I did a lot of 'honey dos,' including painting our house.

When I reported in to Quantico, I was assigned to the Development Center as an Administrative Officer. I didn't relish the idea, but went to work for a Marine Aviator Colonel, who I truly enjoyed working for. Colonel Mitchell was the senior aviator in the Corps at that time, but he was much more than that. He was a thinker, a planner, and an organizer. The Marine Corps was starting to do more and more of its own research and development, being somewhat dissatisfied with merely taking what the other services had to offer. We wanted equipment and arms that worked for the Marine Corps amphibious and helicopter borne doctrines. There was a large influx of senior officers and staff NCOs to man the new billets and conduct the research. Civilian contracts came on board to work. Some civilian personnel were interviewed and hired to provide continuity for all the programs. Buildings were made available, but they lacked desks, chairs, filing cabinets, typewriters, telephone lines, partitions, and all the other items to make them functional. The Department of Defense was cutting back on their agencies in the Washington area, and I found a warehouse center filled with everything we needed, and some of it was brand new. I arranged for flatbed trucks, with my senior Marine on board, to visit this center and requisition everything we required. My clerks became working parties until we could get the furniture and equipment installed. We made rapid progress, and Colonel Mitchell was very pleased. I worked diligently to keep everyone supplied, equipped, and happy in the Research and Development Center. When I had free time, I volunteered to assist with certain projects I felt competent to work on. I worked out at the gym or ran each day at lunchtime. After I had been in this job about a year, I found out that the Base Personnel Officer billet was coming open. I talked with Colonel Mitchell and he agreed to let me go, if the Base provided a suitable replacement. I arranged for a WM 1st Lt. to be transferred into my billet, and I took over as the MCDEC Personnel Officer.

HQMC staffed the Development Center, Command and Staff College, Junior School (now Amphibious Warfare School), TBS, and T&T Regiment at 100%. Marine Corps Base Quantico was staffed at about 95%. This left little leeway in assigning personnel. During the summer months, TBS and T&T Regiment were staffed at 110% and qualified Drill Instructors were added to their staff from on base commands to handle the influx of PLC candidates, NROTC and Naval Academy cadets, and others requiring special instruction. HQMC ordered in Captains slated for the Junior School in September and extra Lieutenants to handle the increased workload.

Several special requirements were laid on the organizations at Quantico. One was the training of tank and amphibious vehicle crewmen by the Basic School. This became a problem when these new Marines were used as extra messmen and on working parties and were not being qualified in their MOS. HQMC wanted to order these men overseas, but could not unless they were qualified. The Basic School had agreed to train these personnel, but the COs had changed and somehow they were being treated as permanent personnel. HQMC threatened to stop sending these trainees to Quantico if we did not comply with the original agreement. After a series of meetings with the G-1 and myself, TBS started training these men properly. Short timers from Camp Lejeune were sent to provide the extra messmen and working parties needed during the summer.

With the cutback in personnel within the Marine Corps, a decision was made by the Commandant to do away with the Marine Corps Football Team. This team has given the Marine Corps valuable publicity and had aided recruiting, especially at the colleges the team played. It had grown to be a year round program involving dozens of officers and about 150 enlisted men. These officers and men, some with critical skills, were needed to fill billets in units all over the world and had been unavailable for assignment because of their football status. I worked out the details with the coaches, and HQMC was soon satisfied that we had reassigned the players back into their MOS.

My working hours were such that I could continue my previous efforts as a Little League Baseball Coach each summer. My son continued to play, and with the help of my assistants, we had championship teams. I always enjoyed coaching and teaching youngsters how to play the game.

In 1974, I was selected to attend the Command and Staff College. This proved to be mini-reunion of friends from OCS, TBS, 1st Marine Brigade, Vietnam, HQMC, and Quantico. My faculty advisor was an Army Major by the name of Jim Rogers, who became a good friend. I enjoyed the school and my classmates.

During early 1975, the Majors and Lt. Colonels monitors from HQMC came down and gave us our next assignments. Lt. Colonel William M. Cryan, who I had known as a Lt. at Camp Lejeune, gave me my next duty assignment: the Marine Corps Recruiting Station in New Orleans. I hoped to go back to the FMF and utilize all the training I had received, but it was not to be. I quickly learned that the 8th Marine Corps District, which was in New Orleans, and who I would be working for, was a very political billet. The District Director has some officers on his staff that he wanted to have the job, and each time I called the District Headquarters in New Orleans, I was told I was going to Dallas, Phoenix, Little Rock, etc. With graduation near, I had to ship my household goods somewhere, and I kept getting different information each time I called. Finally, I got fed up with this runaround and called Lt. Colonel Cryan. He assured me that I was going to Recruiting Station, New Orleans, and the District Director did not have the authority to change my orders without the approval of HQMC. I shipped my gear to New Orleans, despite repeated telephone calls from the District Headquarters telling me I might be going somewhere else.

When I reported to the District Headquarters, it was not exactly a warm welcome. The Colonel, who was the District Director and was nearing retirement, realized his plans had been foiled by HQMC and welcomed me aboard quite coolly. The Operations Officer, a Lt. Colonel, tried to take me under his wing. He gave me all kinds of advice on how to handle recruiters and quotas, and he wanted me to stop by each day after work. Dave Henderson, the Major I was relieving, apparently had fallen into that trap.

I tried to get my family situated as quickly as possible. We bought a house in the Algiers section of New Orleans, located on the west bank of the Mississippi River.

When I reported to the Recruiting Station, I quickly learned two important things. The District had taken my top recruiter in New Orleans and made him a traveling trainer for the District. The second thing I learned was that my recruiting station was required to over ship 7 men, so that the District could make quota. This meant that my recruiters had to recruit that many extra men to meet next month's shipping quota over their normal quota. I made a point to visit all my recruiting stations in Louisiana: Alexandria, Shreveport, Lake Charles, Monroe, Lafayette, Baton Rouge, and Slidell. I was impressed by some of the recruiters, but found most of them thinking they could talk me into reducing their monthly quotas, which was a myth I quickly dispelled. When in New Orleans, I started off visiting the Operations Officer on my way home each evening. Because we were running behind our quota for the next month, thanks in part to over shipping and losing my best recruiter, these meetings turned into a mini ass chewing, which I didn't appreciate. I finally decided that since the other recruiting officers didn't have to report each evening, I saw no reason why I should, and I stopped doing it. Life got better. They could call me on the telephone just like they did the rest!

It took a while, but I slowly got the Recruiting Station back on top within the District. We were generally meeting our quota, but still being required to over ship almost every month. My recruiters resented the fact that they were filling quotas for recruits that another recruiter in another RS had failed to enlist, but I tried to show them it was in the best interest of the District and the Marine Corps. Excellent recruiters were rewarded with excellent fitness reports, and those who I had to get rid of got unsatisfactory ones and were shipped off to other duty. I also realized that some of the recruiters were not cut out to be on recruiting duty, and tried to let them down softly. I utilized the meritorious promotion program to the utmost. I had one Sergeant report in, and in about two and a half years he had been promoted to Staff Sergeant and Gunnery Sergeant. He believed me, and he made the system work for him by being a top recruiter. All of his enlistees were high school graduates.

The Army was failing miserably in meeting their quotas and they had several major cheating scandals during my tour, and I warned my recruiters not to get involved with any underhand tactics.

When the recruiting substations were failing to meet quota, I often showed up unannounced at 0800 and worked with the recruiters during the day and that night. I assigned extended working hours and stayed in my office and checked with the NCO in charge during the evening. I sent the District recruiter to work with failing recruiters. I sent the Sergeant Major on announced and unannounced visits. I had the Officer Selection

Officers, who worked for me, stop in when making visits to nearby colleges and offer their assistance. It was never an easy task, and District never gave us a break.

The Marine Corps revamped its recruiting system, tying the Districts in with the Recruit Depots, and holding meetings on why recruits were not finishing boot camp and other problems. We came under the Recruit Depot at San Diego, California. The Systematic Recruiting Program was installed by HQMC, and while some of the recruiters rebelled, the system was a good one, and they learned to use it to their advantage. I made myself and my staff available for high school visitation days. I attended educational meetings of high school counselors and principals to insure they were getting the right message about the military, and especially the Marine Corps. I took about 100 counselors and principals on a weeklong visit to MCRD San Diego, Camp Pendleton, and El Toro. We recruited two 'Bayou State' platoons, young men from all over Louisiana, who went to boot camp together and came home together. We gave them a big send off in New Orleans, with the Lt. Governor and the Mayor present. They were all wearing tee shirts that read 'Bayou State Platoon' with the Marine Corps emblem in the center. They had been given these when they first enlisted to wear in their high schools. We fed them all the seafood they could eat at the Falstaff Brewery. They were all too young to drink the beer, but the recruiters got to enjoy that! When they returned from San Diego, they were met at the New Orleans airport by the Lt. Governor, the Mayor, and the 4th Marine Air Wing band, and of course their families and girlfriends. The Marine Reserve Officers in New Orleans arranged for all of the food and drink, tee shirts, and no Marine Corps funds were used.

Platoon Honor Man, Bayou State Platoon

Bayou State Platoon Platoon Recruited in Louisiana (before)

Bayou State Platoon (after)

General Kenneth Houghton, the Commanding General of the Recruit Depot at San Diego, visited the District and, of course, my Recruiting Station. After I had briefed him, I took him downstairs to the Armed Forces Examining Station and he met two young men who were being shipped to recruit training that day. One was black and one was white. Both were high school graduates and had enlisted for a specific program. The general questioned them thoroughly and was pleased with the answers he received from them. The Officer in charge of the Armed Forces Examining Station, an Army Lt. Colonel, met the general and told him he thought the Marine Corps recruits that he interviewed were better quality than those going into the other services. General Houghton loved that statement! We also visited several of the Recruiting substations in the New Orleans area. He liked what he saw and the answers he was given.

Gen. Houghton's visit to Recruiting Station New Orleans

The Commandant, General Louis H. Wilson, was very much concerned about recruiting, and he visited the 8th District and my Recruiting Station. He was impressed that we were enlisting 100% high school graduates and were meeting all our quotas. I found him easy to brief.

Somehow, I found time to coach my son's Junior League baseball team. We won the championship his last year. Our team scored the winning run in the last inning, and the umpires called the game. The opposing coach somehow got to the league officials and the umpires and had them change the results, making them the winners! Only in New Orleans! I never bothered to tell my players and I never returned the trophy.

I now found myself coaching my daughter's softball team! She wasn't very big, but she was quick, and we practiced in the back yard every evening until she became an excellent fielder, and I made her my shortstop. There was less pressure to win with the girls, but some of the parents didn't understand that all of the girls had to play three innings, according to the league rules, so their daughter might not get to play the whole game. Once I cleared that up with the parents, things went well, and the girls were very successful.

Recruiting went well, as we continued to make our quotas each month. I had to fire a few recruiters, but that was part of the program as far as I was concerned. I insisted that the recruiters stay in good physical condition, and had them run the physical fitness test each quarter. We would have an annual recruiting seminar in New Orleans, and during that time we would have all of the recruiters run the physical fitness test. Those who failed were retested by the Sergeant Major or one of my officers on their next visit to that substation.

I was promoted to Lieutenant Colonel during my third year on recruiting, and when the assignment slate came out, my next duty assignment was the 4th Marine Air Wing, located two floors up, in the same building! The Marine Reserves were having recruiting problems, and I knew my assignment was going to be the Recruiting Officer for the 4th Marine Air Wing. I decided to extend my tour as the Recruiting Officer for RS, New Orleans, where I was my own boss, rather than work for the general commanding the Marine Air Reserves.

Bob Driver gets promoted to Lt. Col., July 19, 1976

My Recruiting Station continued to be successful in meeting the monthly quotas. During my fourth year, the Lieutenant Colonel's slate had me going to the 3rd Marine Division on Okinawa. The Commandant, General Wilson, made all of the battalion commander assignments, and I was slated for a staff assignment. I was disappointed in not getting a command billet, and my wife did not want to stay in New Orleans with two teenagers, so I decided to retire. This occurred on 1 April 1979. I was awarded a second Legion of Merit for my five successful years on recruiting duty.

While on leave one summer, my wife and I had found an old three-story brick house in the village of Brownsburg, Virginia. I checked with the owner and found that he was nearing retirement and was moving to Florida, and his mother was living in the house by herself. He agreed to give me first chance at the house when the situation changed. About a year later, he called and said his mother had moved out of the house and was now living with one of her daughters, and the house was for sale. We reached an agreement, and I purchased it in 1978. I hired a contractor to do some needed restoration work and when I retired a year later, we moved to Brownsburg. I became a 'jack legged carpenter,' or better yet a laborer, with the work crew I had hired. We stayed with relatives for a few weeks before we could occupy part of the house. Work progressed slowly because of the death of one contractor and the disability of the next one. The work progressed to a point I felt confident to supervise the rest of the restoration. I kept the same workmen and hired subcontractors for the sheet rock and refinishing the wooden floors. The house dated from at least the 1830s and had wonderful woodwork and five fireplaces. We tried to put it back in original condition, but with new electrical wiring and plumbing. This kept me busy for several years, and I really lost touch with the Marine Corps.

When Colonel Tom Solack took over as the CO of the Navy-Marine ROTC unit at nearby Virginia Military Institute in Lexington, I started attending the Marine Corps Birthday Balls and some commissioning parties for new officers entering the Corps. When Tom left, I didn't know the new officers and sort of lost interest in attending these ceremonies.

I had always been interested in the American Civil War and I found out a publisher, Harold Howard in Lynchburg, was looking for writers for his Virginia Regimental Series. Harold was an ex-paratrooper, and we got along fine. I ended up doing eleven books for the Regimental Series and 'Lexington and Rockbridge County in the Civil War' for his Battles and Leaders Series. Writing these books, as well as several others, kept me busy over the years. We purchased several buildings in our village and restored them, and with a 21-acre farm and a lot of outbuildings, maintenance and repair became almost a full time job.

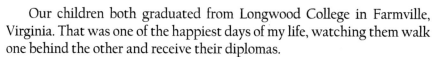

Our children both graduated from Longwood College in Farmville, Virginia. That was one of the happiest days of my life, watching them walk one behind the other and receive their diplomas.

I've forgotten how I found out about the 2/9 Network, but it put me back in touch with many of the Marines I served with over the years. I finally attended a reunion and met John Kasparian, Dave Garner, and many others I had served with in Vietnam. I did not want to go to the Wall. I avoided going there for many years, but I went with my comrades at my first reunion, and cried, as I knew I would, when I saw the names of those brave young Marines forever etched on that memorial. Everyone else was crying, so it didn't matter. I've been back several times, and I cry each time. Some of the names brought back faces I remembered, while others were in my company only a few days before being killed and I never really knew them.

The camaraderie that was shown by all was great to behold, as we discussed our tour or tours in Vietnam. We talked of the brave young Marines and Navy Corpsmen that fought and died with us. No one worried about rank; we were a band of brothers who had fought for our country and were damn proud of it! Bob Staump, who was a Corporal in my company and had lost one of his legs to a booby trap, had a wonderful memory of events, times, places, and names of the Marines and Navy Corpsmen who served in E/2/9. We wheel-chaired him to every event. While the Birthday Ceremony is always impressive and fun, perhaps the greatest thrill is attending the ceremony at the Marine Corps Memorial in Arlington. The Commandant is always there with a host of other notables, including Medal of Honor winners and politicians who served in the Corps. The Marine Corps Band, Drum and Bugle Corps, and the troops from Marine Barracks, 8th & I Street, bring back the old thrill of marching in a parade or ceremony and hearing the Marine Corps Hymn played. It is always a touching performance and brings back memories of Marines, past and present, and how much being a part of our beloved Corps means to all of us.

L-R: Sasser, Driver, Spangler & Clemons holding a captured
VC flag that was returned to Kasparian

L-R: Kasparian, Nieto, Driver & Schramm

2/9 Reunion, 2005
Cpl. Stump in wheelchair

2/9 Reunion 2005, L-R: Kasparian, Driver, Gen. Hagee & Nieto

2/9 Reunion 2005

Epilogue

At least two Marines I know have returned to Vietnam. Dave Garner made a tour of the country, and he sent me this:

"Throughout my first tour in Vietnam, I often marveled at the beauty of the countryside and its people, and hoped that I could return as a tourist. (That second tour didn't count as much of a vacation.)

"In August 1994, I met Julie at a symposium on Vietnam sponsored by the Smithsonian. We bonded quickly and one of the links was that her dad, a three-war Army veteran, had been a colonel in Vietnam while I was there on my first tour. Soon after meeting, I shared with her my desire to return to Vietnam—not for any deep psychological need, but out of a desire to share a beautiful country with the woman I loved.

"Our opportunity came in September 1999, when we journeyed to Vietnam as part of one of the Military Historical Tour trips. I chose this particular trip because we would spend most of our time in the Da Nang area.

"We visited Red Beach, the scene of 2/9's landing on 7 July 1965. It was a calm, peaceful day, much like that July morning. I saw the same old graves across the road on our drive into Da Nang; the graves adorned with swastika-like sculptures. I wondered in 1965 how the Nazis got there— only later did I learn that they were traditional Buddhist symbols.

"Of course we drove to the site of the 2/9's first encampment in the 9th Marines CP area (Khu Quan), overlooking the hamlet of Phong Bac and the Song Cau Do River. We could see for 30 kilometers over the flat ocean of rice paddies dotted with islands of bamboo and villages, all the way to the base of the Que Son Mountains in the hazy distance. The old French bunker still guards the old 9th Marines CP area; however, as on almost every piece of high ground that we visited, a monument to the victorious North Vietnamese Army sits where Fox 2/9 originally bivouacked.

"The city of Da Nang has grown in population, density, buildings, vehicles, bicycles, and highways—only the smell remains the same. The old road that ran east-west, north of the Song Cau Do was now a four lane divided 'highway.' The eastern bridge that carries traffic directly into Da Nang had been destroyed; I don't know whether during the war or from a monsoon flood. Thus, all traffic coming into Da Nang from the south on Route 1 drives into Da Nang along the diagonal road south of the river,

489

crossing at the old water point near Mien Dong (1), near the destroyed railroad bridge.

"The bridge has been rebuilt and the railroad runs from Hanoi to Saigon (Ho Chi Minh City to today's generation). Route 1 carries more traffic than before, with newer cars and faster motorcycles, but many of the same old multicolored busses of the past, still full of people hanging on with chickens and pigs on top.

"As part of the tour group, we visited Hills 65, 55, and Marble Mountain. On the hills were monuments to the victors. Along Route 1 were several cemeteries to fallen Vietnamese soldiers. We walked up Hill 55—you could tell that artillery had been there by the remnants of the old gun pits. But little else would indicate an old military presence, as was true throughout most of our visit. It was hard to tell we had been there.

"Apart from the tour, one day Julie and I hired a car and driver and drove to some of the sites already mentioned, but also spent a good part of the day walking along the old MSR, the then deserted railroad bed. In 1999, they were still building a road along the elevated railroad bed, which now carried the railroad. We actually saw trains using it! What a sight for sore eyes!

"Walking along the rail bed, the area looked much the same as it did on that July day in 1965, when I first crossed the river as part of a 3rd Recon Platoon led by the legendary Captain P.G. "Pat" Collins. However, instead of getting shot at from the neighboring 'friendly' villages, we received waves of greetings from those in the fields or walking by. Girls in their ao dais on bikes headed to school; boys in blue shorts and white shirts. It was harvest time and using methods centuries old, the Vietnamese were harvesting their rice. However, in some cases, there were a few mechanical threshing machines to help them, but very few.

"On the hardstands and along the roadways, the rice was laid out to dry. Life in the villages really hasn't changed much since we were there, except they have electricity, but no running water. Roadways in several of the villages are now paved. We walked past Duong Son (1) where 2/9 received its baptism of fire—three of my lieutenant classmates were wounded the first night. I could see the tree line where I lay crouched with Captain Cliff Rushing and Fox Company—jumping from one side of the berm to the other, depending upon where the fire was coming from.

"We continued to Duong Son (2), the site of the 2/9 CP for most of that first year. Along the way, we passed the Cam Ne and Yen Ne villages—it was nice to be silhouetted on the rail bed and not worried about being sniped at. In Duong Son (2) we were shown the hardstand that had been the base for 2/9's CP—now full of rice drying yellow. The children were as friendly as ever, with their perpetual smiles, and not begging for anything. Their parents were probably not even born yet when we were there; the older Vietnamese eyed us, knowing that I had probably been there before, though none of them volunteered that he or she had shot at us. The old mamasans and papasans had probably been youths when we were there, as you know how the Vietnamese age quickly. It's still a tough life.

"After 2/9 assumed airfield security at Da Nang, I remained in the area with 3/3. In late October 1965, the famed war correspondent, Dickey Chappele, was sitting around a small fire in Duong Son (2). At first, because of her small frame, I thought she was a Vietnamese interpreter. Talk about being surprised to meet an American female journalist in tiger stripe utilities! It seemed like we talked into the night—four days later she died while accompanying a Marine patrol south of Chu Lai—lots of memories.

"With the tour group, we walked through several of the operating areas along the Son Vu Gia that we had worked in 1965-66. We drove along Route 4 westward from Route 1, past the Liberty Bridge site (only pilings remaining), past Hill 65 to Thuong Duc. Along the way, we saw several Vietnamese flags; a yellow star centered on a red field. But truthfully, that was about the extent of our notice of the current government of Vietnam. Outside of the guidance to avoid military cantonment areas or taking pictures around those areas, the government's presence was benign—not like many of my travels to Eastern Europe, the Caucasus, or central Asia.

"We journeyed to the An Hoa Combat Base site. Nothing remains but the outlines of old gun pits and the runway, slightly grown over. We drove past Hill 22 and skirted the edge of the Arizona Territory, no longer a bastion of Main Force or North Vietnamese units, but still covered with hamlets full of people struggling to survive as they had for centuries. We walked south the river south of Hill 55—the areas we had operated in March 1966, before the Main Force attack against E/2/9 on the night of 24-25 March at Cam Van (2). It looked pretty much the same. We tramped along paddy dikes and walked through the villages, meeting old men and women, some of whom still spoke French! No one really stared—we were probably not the first old veterans who had returned there—but then again, for many, we might have been.

"We drove through the Que Sons, scene of Harvest Moon. We passed by Hill 510, the southernmost Marine firebase in 1971 (I had a composite battery there). I saw the side of the hill where LtCol. Bill Leftwich crashed while on a Recon extract mission in November 1970. We stopped at my old firebase site, LZ Ross (Again the stark war memorial, and once the scene of a 'reeducation camp'). I was able to identify the old battery position, though a hamlet now occupied what was once home to a 5th Marines battalion. We passed by LZ Baldy, now home to a Vietnamese Army unit, thus we couldn't get close. We visited Hoi An, an area close to where Echo Company and most of 2/9 conducted a relatively uneventful operation in early January 1966 (Double Eagle II).

"Two highlights I saved for last. In early April 1966, Echo Company participated in a Rough Rider re-supply convoy escort to Hue/Phu Bai. Again, it was uneventful militarily, and was just what the company needed after the night of 24-25 March. Lazing on the back of a deuce and a half we crossed Hai Van Pass—cresting the hill is one of the most beautiful sights in my experience—the spit of sand stretching north and the fishing village of Loc Hai. Seeing that sight again was one of the reasons I wanted to return to Vietnam. It hadn't changed! To the left was the still peaceful cove—why it still hadn't been developed eluded me! I think the company thoroughly enjoyed the ride. We didn't get shot at—and cold beer awaited our arrival at Phu Bai! All that remains at Phu Bai indicating our presence is a tattered runway.

"My personal highlight, on the day we hired the car, was driving along the water buffalo path to the village of Thon Thung Luong, in the area we spent Christmas 1965. I wanted to find the church where several Catholic members of Echo Company and I attended midnight Mass that long-ago Christmas Eve. We found the church and the grotto next to it replicating the Grotto of Lourdes, which reminded me that night of Notre Dame, where a similar grotto nestles on the campus. Amazingly, the church was in even better shape than it was in 1965! It had recently had a fresh coat of paint, the traditional ochre-yellow. The then-adjoining orphanage no longer existed (thank goodness), but the same priest who was there in 1965 was still there! He remembered the group of Marines who attended midnight Mass that Christmas!

"I went inside the church and recalled the smell of the candles, the women in their lovely ao dais—women on one side, men on the other, and the sound of Vietnamese voices singing their Christmas carols! Given the condition of the church, I would be hard pressed to say that religion was being squashed in modern Vietnam.

"For those who had been to Hue during Tet, you would not believe how the Imperial Palace has been restored. I can't say much about Saigon—and won't! We concluded our trip with a couple of days in Hong Kong—not exactly like my 1966 R&R. Lots of modern buildings, and Communist China hasn't screwed it up. The old Star ferry still runs!

"I'm glad we went! Julie was a good trooper, carrying her own weight and her own water! To walk through Vietnamese villages and not worry about tripping booby traps or Bouncing Betties; not sweating under a helmet, flak jacket, and 100 pounds of gear (but still sweating!); going to Marble Mountain and seeing a thriving stone cutting industry (on a small scale geared for tourists) in place of a sparsely populated area of scrub pine; going to a beach referred to as China Beach, but actually south of the original, and enjoying the soothing waters of the South China Sea—it brought back lots of memories. Memories of comrades left behind and memories especially of months of working with E/2/9—the highlight of my Marine Corps career! Semper Fi, my fellow warriors!"

John Kasparian visited Vietnam in 2004 with a Missionary Group involved in building schools in economically deprived and undeveloped areas of the county. When he toured the country, he wore a cap with the 2/9 logo 'Hell in a Helmet' with a Marine Corps emblem on it. John kept a diary of his travels through the Vietnamese cities and countryside.

"26 March 2004: The highlight of my trip, John (a friend) and I rented a van with driver and a guide named Thong who hung around Marines as a young boy during the war. He knew more about the U.S. Forces, the operations, and military slang in English than I did. We headed for Da Nang-Hoi An and my old operational areas. Four hour's ride through military history—former bases, battles, etc. At Da Nang, stopped at the exact spot where the first American troops (the 9th Marines) landed at Red Beach in 1965.

Visited Da Nang and headed for Hill 55, which my platoon took in 1965. Next, we went in search of my river block position across from Dodge City and near the Arizona territories. Thanks to the perseverance of our guide and my topographical remembrance of the area, after an hour or so of questioning old natives, and over the worst roads, dikes, and hiking through the countryside, we finally located the position of my river block. [John found the 106 mm position, although the sandbags had rotted away.] I was reminiscing about the old days when an old farmer and his son approached us. Our guide questioned him, 'During the war do you remember Marines here?'

"'Yes! The Marines occupied my farm area and set up a river block. I was one of the local commanders who attacked the Marines. All the people in the area were Viet Cong. Every time they moved we tried to hit them from the rear. We were very scared of the Marines. They were crazy. When we attacked many of our soldiers were killed. Artillery blew up our houses and our animals. After a while we stopped attacking them, as it wasn't worth it.' [John told me that he told him the VC hid in tunnels during the day and came out and fought the Marines and ARVN at night.]

"When he stopped talking, our guide pointed to me and told him that I was the Commander of the unit that was here. He instantly grabbed my arms, and hugs and handshakes followed. He said he was so happy to meet me. It was very emotional. Two enemies after 39 years, hugging, laughing, and taking pictures together—what a moment! I gave his son $20.00 to buy himself some new clothes. He couldn't stop thanking me."

John Kasparian & John Borman: River block position

John Kasparian & John Borman with the Captain of the local VC Unit & his son

What John didn't write in his diary in case it was taken from him was that the man's wife also remembered him and that he had made her house his CP. John had always shared his C rations with her. She was very shy but remembered him.

John questioned the former VC commander about the fighting. "Every time we attacked and our women and children were killed by the Marines, we displayed their bodies on Route 1 for propaganda purposes—for Jane Fonda, Senator McGovern, etc."

John asked, "Although you cannot talk about your government and its policies, can you tell me about your life and situation now?"

He answered, "Why did I fight for unification? After the war people from the North came down and took half of my farm. Hanoi is no good."

John's guide took them to see Marble Mountain, China Beach, which was now a resort, Da Nang, and back over the Hai Van Pass to Hue.

While in Hue, John visited the old walled city and 'The Citadel' which the 5th Marines recaptured during Tet 1968. The group flew to Hanoi from the old Phu Bai airfield.

"28 March 2004: We left for Dien Bien Phu. Drove by the North Vietnamese Army Headquarters, where General Giap sent thousands of recruits to South Vietnam to fight the war. This spot was the start of the Ho Chi Minh trail.

29 March 2004: We visited the Dien Bien Phu Museum. We met a North Vietnamese Army Commander [in charge of the Museum] who fought in the siege of Khe Sanh in the 1968 Tet offensive. We exchanged war stories and toured the battlefield areas together. Entered Colonel de Castries's bunker [off limits to tourists], and saw where he had committed suicide. He was the French commander at Dien Bien Phu."

Again, John did not write this in his diary because he did not want to get the old North Vietnamese army commander in trouble.

"He told me after noticing my 2/9 cover that the Marines were the best fighters in the world. I was honored. 'We surrounded them at Khe Sanh with thousands of North Vietnamese soldiers and shelled them day and night, but we couldn't make them surrender. On the contrary, they killed and wounded a lot of my men.'

"At this time, he lifted the army coat he was wearing above his chest and showed me his scars. 'I spent 7 years in a hospital. I was riddled by a Marine helicopter.' I showed him my scars and we both hugged—soldiers' mutual respect.

"I asked him about the political situation now. He said, 'Ho Chi Minh is dead and the old guard is dying; pretty soon Vietnam will be capitalist.' From what I could see, it already was."

Kasparian with NVA Colonel who commanded
& was wounded at Khe Saan

Awards

In the name of the Secretary of the Navy, the Commanding General, Fleet Marine Force, Pacific takes pleasure in presenting the NAVY COMMENDATION MEDAL to

CAPTAIN ROBERT JETT   DRIVER

UNITED STATES MARINE CORPS

for service as set forth in the following

CITATION:

"For meritorious service while serving as Commanding Officer, Headquarters and Service Company, Second Battalion, Ninth Marines from 18 September 1965 to 14 January 1966, and as Commanding Officer of Company E, Second Battalion, Ninth Marines from 15 January to 30 March 1966 in the Republic of Vietnam. In his initial billet, Captain DRIVER exhibited resourcefulness and keen professional skill in instituting a program to dismantle all above-ground bunkers and reestablish a better concealed, better protected perimeter defense for the Battalion Command Post. As Commanding Officer of Company E during Operation Double Eagle II, he displayed courageous leadership and aggressiveness which contributed to the successful rout and defeat of a numerically superior insurgent communist (Viet Cong) force and inflicted heavy casualties on them. By his initiative and devotion to duty, Captain DRIVER upheld the finest traditions of the United States Naval Service."

Captain DRIVER is authorized to wear the Combat "V".

FOR THE SECRETARY OF THE NAVY,

A. R. KIER
MAJOR GENERAL, U. S. MARINE CORPS
ACTING COMMANDING GENERAL

TEMPORARY CITATION

The President of the United States takes pleasure in presenting the BRONZE STAR MEDAL *to*

MAJOR ROBERT J. DRIVER, JR.

UNITED STATES MARINE CORPS

for service as set forth in the following

CITATION:

"For heroic achievement in connection with operations against the enemy in the Republic of Vietnam while serving as Commanding Officer of Company E, Second Battalion, Ninth Marines, Third Marine Division. On the night of 24 March 1966, Company E was occupying a defensive position south of DaNang when the Marines came under a heavy volume of mortar and automatic weapons fire from a Viet Cong battalion. Reacting immediately, Major Driver, then a Captain, skillfully directed supporting artillery and mortar fires on the attacking units. When his outer defenses were threatened with penetration, he expertly maneuvered personnel into those positions, denying the enemy access to the perimeter. With complete disregard for his own safety, Major Driver moved about the battle area encouraging his men and coordinating the medical evacuation of the casualties. Displaying outstanding tactical skill, he adeptly employed artillery fire on suspected enemy avenues of withdrawal, and as the hostile forces retreated in panic and confusion, these fires were instrumental in accounting for 43 Viet Cong killed with an additional 105 enemy dead subsequently found nearby. His initiative and resolute determination inspired all who observed him and contributed significantly to the accomplishment of his unit's mission. Major Driver's courage, extraordinary professionalism and steadfast devotion to duty in the face of great personal danger were in keeping with the highest traditions of the Marine Corps and of the United States Naval Service."

Major Driver is authorized to wear the Combat "V".

FOR THE PRESIDENT,

H. W. Buse jr.

H. W. BUSE, JR.
LIEUTENANT GENERAL, U. S. MARINE CORPS
COMMANDING GENERAL, FLEET MARINE FORCE, PACIFIC

The President of the United States takes pleasure in presenting the
LEGION OF MERIT to

MAJOR ROBERT J. DRIVER, JR.

UNITED STATES MARINE CORPS

for service as set forth in the following

CITATION:

"For exceptionally meritorious conduct in the performance of
outstanding service with the First Marine Division in connection with combat
operations against the enemy in the Republic of Vietnam from 31 August 1969 to
12 August 1970. Throughout this period, Major Driver performed his demanding
duties in an exemplary and highly professional manner. Initially assigned as
Operations Officer of the Second Battalion, Fifth Marines, he ably managed the
tactical deployment of the Battalion and developed schemes of maneuver which
significantly reduced the enemy's manpower and material assets. Working tirelessly,
he initiated effective training programs, implemented sound tactical reporting
procedures, and planned and supervised the execution of numerous combined
cordon and search operations and daily patrols and ambushes. During combat
operations, he repeatedly disregarded his own safety as he boldly moved to the most
forward areas to inspect defensive positions, coordinate supporting arms fires, and
ensure that tactical commanders received the latest intelligence estimates.
Reassigned as Ground Surveillance Officer with the G-2 Section, Headquarters, First
Marine Division on 31 January 1970, Major Driver exercised staff control over the
Division's sensor systems and, in less than six months, more than quadrupled the
number of skillfully placed sensor strings. In addition, he developed the concept and
assisted in structuring the Sensor Control and Management Platoon which served as
the controlling element for the tactical application of sensor equipment. Carefully
monitoring and analyzing sensor readings submitted by elements of the platoon
from strategically located readout sites, he compiled current intelligence reports
concerning enemy infiltrations and staging areas and plotted lucrative targets for
supporting arms fire missions. Assuming duties as Operations Officer of the Second
Battalion, Seventh Marines on 29 June 1970, Major Driver participated in Operation
Pickens Forest deep in the Trung Son Mountains and displayed a professionalism
and aggressiveness which greatly enhanced the fighting spirit of subordinate units.
His resolute determination and seemingly unlimited resourcefulness earned the
respect and admiration of all who served with him and contributed immeasurably to
the accomplishment of his unit's mission. By his professional acumen, extraordinary
initiative, and unwavering devotion to duty, Major Driver rendered distinguished
service to his country and thereby upheld the highest traditions of the Marine Corps
and of the United States Naval Service."

The Combat Distinguishing Device is authorized.

FOR THE PRESIDENT,

WILLIAM K. JONES
LIEUTENANT GENERAL, U. S. MARINE CORPS
COMMANDING GENERAL, FLEET MARINE FORCE, PACIFIC

THE SECRETARY OF THE NAVY
WASHINGTON

    The President of the United States takes pleasure in presenting the LEGION OF MERIT (Gold Star in lieu of the Second Award) to

LIEUTENANT COLONEL ROBERT J. DRIVER
UNITED STATES MARINE CORPS

for service as set forth in the following

CITATION:

    For exceptionally meritorious conduct in the performance of outstanding service as Commanding Officer, Marine Corps Recruiting Station, New Orleans, Louisiana from July 1974 through March 1979. During his tenure, Lieutenant Colonel Driver consistently demonstrated the highest degree of professional competence in the performance of his demanding duties. He personally organized and was the driving force behind the Annual Louisiana Bayou Platoon Project which became a state-wide patriotic tradition, and his exemplary conduct and generous contributions of time and talent to the civilian community further enhanced the Marine Corps image in the New Orleans area. Lieutenant Colonel Driver's unique ability to perceive and analyze the complexities of recruiter management in the All-Volunteer Force environment coupled with his mature judgment and administrative skill proved to be positive factors in Recruiting Station New Orleans placing at the top in District competition. Further, his sterling personal example and penchant for hard work resulted in a record 100.9 percent attainment of total force recruiting goals over a two year period. Lieutenant Colonel Driver's diligent efforts and dynamic leadership inspired all with whom he was associated and substantially advanced the effectiveness of the recruiting effort. By his complete professionalism, personal initiative, and total dedication to duty, Lieutenant Colonel Driver reflected great credit upon himself and upheld the highest traditions of the Marine Corps and the United States Naval Service.

For the President,

W. Rahum Cuntee J.

Secretary of the Navy

Contributors

AVILA, RAYMOND W. Ray enlisted in the Marine Corps at San Diego on 30 June 1964 at age 17. He was the Platoon, Series, and Regimental Honor Man of his platoon in boot camp and was meritoriously promoted to PFC. Ray served with A/1/9 and E/2/9 from December 1964 until wounded on 24 March 1966, and was promoted to Corporal and Fire Team Leader during that time. He received a Bronze Star for his actions on the night of 24-25 March 1966. Evacuated to the Philippines for his wound, he ended up in the Balboa Naval Hospital at San Diego, along with many of his comrades. When he left the Marines, he served as a Deputy Sheriff in San Diego County for 8 years. Ray became a DA Investigator and then Prosecutor from 1979-2002, with emphasis on gangs for the Juvenile Division of San Diego, California, until his retirement.

BECTON, DENNIS. He enlisted in Easton, Pennsylvania in December 1962. Following boot camp and ITR, he served in the 2nd Marine Division. When he arrived in Vietnam in October 1965, he was assigned to the 3rd Platoon of E/2/9 as a rifleman and served on Operations Harvest Moon and Double Eagle I. Dennis was discharged in November 1966 and worked as a cable splicer for New Jersey Bell, now Verizon, for 35 years. He is now retired in Sicklerville, N.J.

BROOKS, DONALD DEAN. Major USMC (Ret.) A native of Albuquerque, New Mexico, Don graduated from the U. of New Mexico in 1956. He was commissioned in the Marine Corps through the Platoon Leaders Class upon graduation. He served as a Lieutenant in Co. A, 1st Battalion, 1st Marines at Camp Pendleton. He later served in Co. M, 3rd Battalion, 9th Marines on Okinawa, Marine Barracks, Point Magu Missile Center, California, and as Adjutant of the Marine Corps Air Station in Hawaii. He then served at Camp Pendleton until joining 1st Battalion, 7th Marines and deploying to Vietnam in 1965. Don was the S-2 and CO of C/1/7. He was awarded a Bronze Star for his actions on 21 February 1966. Returning to Camp Pendleton, he served as the S-3 and S-1 of the 2nd Infantry Training Regiment, until ordered back to Vietnam in 1969. He served as an Intelligence Officer in J-2 COMASMACV in Saigon and was awarded his second Bronze Star for his actions. Don served at the 1st Infantry Training Regiment at Camp Lejeune and at FMFLANT at Norfolk until retiring in 1976. He received an MA from George Washington U. and served as an instructor in the Junior Naval ROTC in Williamsburg, Va. and Commerce City, Colo. Don later worked for the New York Life Ins. Co. until retiring. His son, 2nd Lt. Donald D. Brooks, Jr. USMC, was killed in a training accident at Pickle Meadows, Bridgeport, California in 1987. Don now lives on a lake in Alabama.

BROWN, DAVID B. Lt. Col. USMC (Ret.). Dave served in Charlie Company, 1st Battalion, 4th Marines, with me in the early 60s. He got out of the Marine Corps for a while but decided to come back in and made it a career. He is now a Realtor in Durham, N. C. and is the author of "Battlelines," a book on Fox Company, 2nd Battalion, 5th Marines in 1968-1969, which he commanded.

CARROLL, JOHN J. "JACK." Colonel, USMC(Ret.). Jack was born in the Bronx, New York and was commissioned in the Marine Corps through the PLC Program upon graduation from Iona College in 1962. He served in the 2nd Battalion, 1st Marines at Camp Pendleton as a Platoon and Company Commander. When the Battalion deployed to Okinawa in 1965, he was serving as the XO of India Company, 3rd Battalion, 3rd Marines. Jack spent a short tour with Vietnamese Marine Corps before landing at Chu Lia with his unit. He was transferred to A/1/9 as my XO and later commanded B/1/9. Carroll helped train officers at the Basic School at Quantico and attended the Amphibious Warfare School, before returning to Vietnam as the Senior Advisor to the 6th Battalion, Vietnamese Marine Corps in 1968-69. He served a tour at HQMC and as the Marine Officer Instructor at Ohio University before attending the U. S. Army Command & General Staff College. In 1977-8 he served as the XO of 2nd Battalion 4th Marines and S-3, 4th Marines. Following a tour of duty at Parris Island, S.C., he was assigned to the Naval War College, Newport, R.I. In 1981, he served as Instructor and Head of the Landing Force Operations of the Marine Corps Command & Staff College and later, when promoted to Colonel, Director of the Amphibious Warfare School. In 1986 he was assigned as G-3, 2nd Marine Division and the next year CO, 6th Marine Regiment and 28th MEU. He served at Marine Corps Base, Camp Lejeune in charge of Training & Operations and as Chief of Staff until his retirement in June 1990. Jack was awarded two Legions of Merit, two Bronze Stars with Combat V, and numerous Vietnamese and other awards. He taught high school history and geography and coached basketball at West Montgomery HS, N.C. until 1998, when he retired. His two brothers served as Marine officers in

Vietnam and his two sons are Lieutenant Colonels in the Marine Corps. He and his wife Sara live in Mt. Gilead, N.C.

CLEMONS, STEPHEN. Steve enlisted in the Marines at Austin, Texas in July 1965. Gunnery Sergeant Rodriguez, his recruiter, would only enlist him as a Reservist, and with a promise he would go back to school after his enlistment. He later met the then Lt. Rodriguez at the Da Nang airfield. Rodriguez remarked that he had been keeping up with Steve. Clemons served in E/2/9 until they moved up to the DMZ, when he was assigned to an I Corps Guard unit in Hue until returning to the states in the fall of 1967. He later served as a Weapons and Tactics Instructor at 1st ITR at Camp Lejeune. He made Sergeant a few months before his 20th birthday. Steve later served in 1st Battalion, 8th Marines as Chief Scout and Assistant Battalion Intelligence Sergeant. He was sent to the Defense Language Institute at Monterey, California to learn Vietnamese. Steve served as a Rifle Platoon Sergeant and Weapons Platoon Sergeant in 1/9 on Okinawa before leaving the Corps in 1970. He used his GI Bill to earn a degree in Economics from the University of Maryland while working in a factory. Steve has worked as a programmer, database mechanic, and customer support person as a contractor to government agencies in the D.C. area. He has worked tirelessly in support of the 2/9 Reunions in Arlington.

CORONADO, GABRIEL C., JR. Gabe enlisted at Port Huron, Michigan in 1963. He served as a Machine Gun Squad Leader in E/2/9 from April 1965-May 1966 and was wounded on Double Eagle II and at Latho Bac (3). He received a Bronze Star for his actions in May 1966. Following his Vietnam tour he served out his enlistment as a guard and chaser at the Great Lakes Naval Prison. He stayed in the Marine Corps Reserve and served as a Drill Instructor. Gabe used his GI Bill to earn a degree in Industrial Engineering from Wayne State University. He worked as a plant manager for TRW & El Dorado corporations. Gabe now works part-time at the local Home Depot and is head of the 2/9 Network.

FLORIAN, KERIN P. "K.P." enlisted in the Marines at Buffalo, New York in 1959. He served in the 2nd Marine Division at Camp Lejeune. While stationed there he attended Sniper School, and shot on the Rifle and Pistol Team. K.P. first went to Vietnam with 3rd Reconnaissance Battalion in 1964. He joined E/2/9 in 1965 and served in a rifle platoon and was wounded on Operation Harvest Moon in December. I used him as a sniper and my driver. He was wounded again on 2 July 1966 when a mortar round landed in his hole, blowing him out and knocking him unconscious.

He extended his tour and served with the company until January 1967. Following another tour in E/2/6 at Camp Lejeune and at Marine Barracks, Sasebo, Japan, he retrained in the disbursing field because "I was tired of sleeping in the mud." He rose to Gunnery Sergeant before his retirement. K.P. managed the Hobby Shop at Camp Lejeune for 17 years before retiring. He now spends his time playing golf.

GALLEGOS, EDDIE. 'Doc' Eddie Gallegos enlisted in the Navy at Albuquerque, New Mexico in December 1964. He attended the Hospital Corpsman 'A' School at San Diego with Greg Salter. While serving in Jacksonville, Florida he attended the Field Medical School at Camp Lejeune. When he arrived in 2/9 he was originally assigned to Hotel Company. His first day in the field with Hotel Company, "two Marines told me to 'Come Up' during a firefight, 'or the next firefight we get a new Doc.' I was later reassigned to Echo Company. The Marines were not friendly. I just went when the Marines said 'Corpsman Up.'" Following his wounding on 14 May 1966 for injuries to his brain, skull, both legs, right arm, intestines, chest, liver, lungs and buttocks, Eddie spent eight months in the Balboa Naval Hospital in San Diego. "During my time in Balboa I was on a neurology ward with mostly paralyzed and brain damaged Marines. It was sad to see their girlfriends or wives visit once or twice and later to divorce or abandon them. I was medically retired in January 1967." Eddie received his undergraduate and law degrees. "I practiced law for nearly 30 years in honor of the dead and my survival. I am unable to work now and I receive both VA and Social Security benefits. I am twice divorced and single the last ten years. I have two children and two grandchildren who are the love of my life. My soul never left Vietnam."

GARNER, DAVID P. Dave is a graduate of Notre Dame University. He was assigned to 2/9 on Okinawa in June 1965 as an Artillery Forward Observer. He landed with them over Red Beach near Da Nang in July 1965. Dave was originally attached to Fox Company, but accompanied Captain P.G. 'Pat' Collins on several patrols with Recon. Bn., and worked with the ARVN north of Da Nang. He served with E/2/9 on Operations Harvest Moon and War Bonnet with Captain Bill Coti and as my FO on Double Eagle II and Kings. He returned to Vietnam as a Captain in 1970 and commanded Whiskey Battery 2/11 at LZ Baldy and later D/2/11 at LZ Ross. Dave was there when the Americal Division relieved the Marines in place. "I've never seen so many Huey's at one time as they arrived in position." Lt. Colonel Ogden, who commanded 1/11, was the gunner and he was the assistant gunner when 1/11 fired its last round in Vietnam on 8

May 1971. Dave served as a Tactical Instructor at Ft. Sill, Oklahoma, MOI at Notre Dame, CO of 3/12 on Okinawa, two tours in Installation & Logistics Department at HQMC, and Logistic Directorate (S-4), The Joint Staff, until his retirement as a Colonel in September 1988. He also received his MBA from Harvard University. He has been a Project Leader for a variety of multinational logistic projects associated with NATO for the Logistics Management Institute in the Washington, D.C. area.

GORMAN, EDWARD P. Ed dropped out of college after a year and a half and enlisted in the Marines in the summer of 1965. He arrived in Vietnam and joined Echo Company on 1 April 1966 and was assigned as a Machine Gunner, although he had only trained as a Rifleman, and served with the 1st Platoon his entire tour. He served at Khe Sanh from 7 March 1967 as a Machine Gun Squad Leader until rotating back to the states 10 April 1967. Ed finished his tour at Marine Barracks, Moffett Field, California. He went back and finished college and taught in a middle school in Colorado until his retirement. Ed now lives in Oceanside, California and has a great view of the hills of Camp Pendleton, where he can hear the artillery firing at times. Ed has been a great contributor to the 2/9 reunions.

GRAVES, GEORGE M. George enlisted in New York City in September 1962 and served in the 2nd Marine Division. He joined E/2/9 in December 1965 as a Machine Gunner. George served on Operations Harvest Moon, Double Eagle I & II and Kings. Later he served as the Company Radio Operator. George was promoted to Sergeant, reenlisted, and attended Jungle Operations School in Panama and served at Parris Island. He worked for an engineering firm in New York City for 13 years rebuilding old bridges and in other places. George retired after 30 years and moved to Florida. He is now a FEMA Contractor for the State of Florida.

HARMON, MICHAEL. Mike enlisted in the Navy at Spokane, Washington in August 1964. He was a conscientious objector at the time. Mike attended General Service Medical School at San Diego and Field Medical School at Camp Pendleton. He joined E/2/9 as a Corpsman on 15 March 1966. He lives in retirement in Washington State.

HORNICK, GERALD P. Following his retirement from the Marine Corps Gerry had a successful business career, and now lives on a farm near Raleigh, North Carolina. He now works part-time as an investment banker.

JENNINGS, JOSEPH F. Joe enlisted in the Marine Corps at Washington, D. C. in August 1964. He served as a rifleman in E/2/9 until volunteering for the CAP (Combined Action Program) in June 1966 and served in the An Hoa and Da Nang areas for 18 months after extending his tour. Promoted to Sergeant, he was wounded at An Hoa during the 1968 Tet Offensive. Joe finished his enlistment in the 6th Marines at Camp Lejeune. He graduated from the University of Virginia with a degree in Applied Mathematics in 1972 and was commissioned in the Marine Corps through the Platoon Leaders Program. Joe served in Recon units as a platoon commander and as S-3 and XO of 1st Bn., 2nd Marines. He retired in 1988 as a Major. He did Operational Research Analyst work for several major corporations until retiring in 2004. Joe is now backcountry ski guide at Powder Mountain, Utah. His fine article on his experiences on Operation Kings was used extensively in this book.

JUDGE, GERALD D. Jerry enlisted in Detroit, Michigan in June 1963. Following boot camp and ITR, he was assigned to 3/1 as a rifleman. When the battalion arrived on Okinawa and became 1/9, he joined with Alpha Company during Jungle Warfare and Amphibious Raid School. Jerry had been promoted to Corporal and was a Squad Leader in the 3rd Platoon when he entered Vietnam. After transferring to E/2/9, he served on Operation Harvest Moon and Double Eagle I & II. During the 'mixmaster,' he was again transferred to F/2/9. Returning to the States in May 1966, he was assigned as a Marksmanship Instructor at Parris Island until discharged in June 1967. Jerry graduated from Central Michigan University in 1971 and served as a high school teacher, coach, and principal. He also earned his MA and PhD degrees during that time. He is now a professor at Grand Valley State University in Grand Rapids, Michigan. His son served in the Marine Corps and a daughter is a Captain in the Marine Corps Reserve.

KASPARIAN, JOHN P. "Kas" enlisted in the Marine Corps in January 1955. A career Marine, he attended Jungle Warfare, Escape & Evasion, Mountain Leadership, and Reconnaissance schools. He joined E/2/9 in October 1965, and served as the 3rd Platoon Commander most of his tour. Speaking French, he was sent to Interrogation School and spent his second tour with MACV 15, in Hoi An with the Phoenix Program, and was awarded the Army Commendation Medal and the Vietnamese Medal of Honor. Kas served at Recruiting Station, Hartford, Connecticut, and was commissioned a Second Lieutenant. He retired in 1976 as a Captain with 22 years service. After retiring, he taught French and Math in Junior and Senior High Schools. He is still active in the building trade and as a volunteer on

512

missionary projects, such as the one that took him back to Vietnam. His son John, a Marine Major, served in Iraq, and is now stationed at the Pentagon. He and his wife Sharon live in Springfield, Massachusetts.

KUMAUS, DENNIS C. "DAN." Dan came from a long line of warriors. His grandfather served in the German Army in WWI, coming from the same area of Bavaria as Adolph Hitler, and knew him. He enlisted in the Marines while a senior in high school in Michigan. Dan graduated on a Friday in June 1965, and was on his way to San Diego by Monday morning. He wanted to get the GI Bill so he could attend college. Dan joined Echo Company in 1966 as a Machine Gunner. His 'on the job training' was in combat. Shot through both legs in May 1966, he recovered in hospitals in the Philippines and Japan. Offered a job 'in the rear with the gear' when he returned to the company, he chose to rejoin his Machine Gunner buddies. "They thought I was nuts," he recalled. "I had deep fears of going back into combat because my belief of being invincible were shattered when I was wounded. I knew I was mortal and could be killed. I knew I had to face that fear or forever live in doubt, so I went back into combat and conquered that fear. In my entire tour I never saw a Marine back up or not do his job. I saw some break down and cry after fights were over because they lost a buddy, but I never saw a Marine falter under fire. I'm sure it happened because we are human, but I never saw it among the men I fought with. It is a proud and dangerous tradition to live up to, but we did and I am proud to have fought with those men." Dan was discharged in 1969 and graduated from Cal State Northridge and received his Master's degree from the University of Phoenix. He is an Accounting Supervisor in Los Angeles County and has served as an Assessor on the Board of Supervisors, City Council, and as Mayor of the town he lives in. His oldest daughter is married to a Marine who has served two tours in Iraq.

LAWTON, DAVID. David is a Canadian who enlisted in the Marines at Watertown, N.Y. on 19 August 1964. Following boot camp and ITR, he served in F/2/6 in the 2nd Marine Division before joining E/2/9 in February 1966. He served in the 1st Platoon where he rose from Rifleman to Fire Team Leader. David served on Operations Kings, New York, and Prairie I. He was wounded in the head and butt in July 1966. David reenlisted and served a tour on recruiting duty, and then returned to WESTPAC and served at Camp Geiger 1968-69. After leaving the Marine Corps, he worked for Pratt Whitney for over 27 years. He served in the Air Force Reserve from 1987-2001 and was active for the Gulf War. David is now retired in Mesa, Arizona.

LEAR, DORIE. Lear enlisted in the Corps in Richmond, Virginia in March 1963. He spent several years in 2nd Battalion, 2nd Marines at Camp Lejeune before joining Echo Company in Vietnam. He served a full tour with the company but was wounded near the DMZ by a mortar round that killed 2 other Marines in his squad. Following his discharge, he became a carpenter and contractor in the Washington, D.C. area. He is now an antique dealer and duck carver on the eastern shore of Maryland.

LOPEZ, HENRY D. 'Doc Lupe' enlisted in the Navy at Pomona, California in May 1963. He graduated from the Hospital Corpsman Class A School and the Field Medical School in March 1966. Doc served with E/2/9 until November 1966. He participated in Operations Macon, Liberty, Hastings, and Prairie III. He served a short time with 3rd Medical Battalion and finished his Vietnam tour with 1st Amtrac Battalion. He has been a painter for the Los Angles Department of Water and Power for 25 years.

MCMILLAN, JAMES. He ran away from home as a teenager and lived with an uncle until he graduated from high school. He joined the Marines in 1965, immediately after graduation. James joined Echo Company as a rifleman in early 1966. Wounded twice in the leg in May 1966 (one round above the knee and one below), he was sent to Balboa Naval Hospital in San Diego to recuperate. The ward he was in was full of his comrades from Echo Company. He and others stopped taking the pain killers they were given and instead drank whiskey in the lounge each day while watching TV. He and another wounded Marine were on crutches waiting to get on an elevator one day, when a Navy officer came rushing out of the elevator and knocking McMillan's companion to the deck. Without a word the officer walked on. McMillan grabbed him by the shoulder, spun him around, and hit him in the face. He was court-martialed and reduced to Private and fined two months pay by a Marine Lieutenant Colonel named Fisher. After the trial, Fisher explained that he had to punish him. He asked McMillan if he had really meant to hurt the Lieutenant. "Damn right, Colonel, when he didn't stop to help my buddy after knocking him down, I saw red, and hit him in the nose as hard as I could." The Colonel laughed and said "Good for you!" The same Doctor had botched the stitching of a wounded Marine after an operation, stating, "I don't have time for these people, I want to get back to civilian life." Another Surgeon redid the sutures to help remove part of the scaring. James lives in Mesa, Arizona.

MARTIN, BUSTER. Buster enlisted in the Marine Corps at Lubbock, Texas in June 1965 at age 17. He was a recent high school graduate from Lovington, New Mexico. He joined E/2/9 in January 1966 and served with the company until February 1967. Buster started out as a Grenadier in the 3rd Platoon and later served as a Fire Team Leader and Squad Leader. Following a short tour with the 2nd Marine Division, Buster volunteered to come back to Vietnam in September 1967 and served in G/2/9. He participated on Operations Lancaster and Kentucky in the DMZ before being wounded near Con Thien by an anti-personnel mine in the left leg, right foot, and right arm. His lower left leg was amputated at Clark AFB hospital in the Philippines. He was then sent to Oak Knoll Naval Hospital in Oakland, California for rehabilitation. Buster was medically retired in March 1968. He attended college in San Diego for a year and worked in construction throughout the Southwest. Buster lives in his hometown of Lovington, New Mexico, where he tends bar.

METRAS, CARL F. He enlisted in the Marine Corps in June 1962. After boot camp at San Diego and ITR at Camp Pendleton, he served in L/3/7, which became C/1/9 on Okinawa. Carl attended Cold Weather Training at Camp Fuji, Japan and Jungle Warfare at Subic Bay in the Philippines. Back at Camp Pendleton, he served in L/3/5 and attended Mountain Warfare & Cold Weather Training at Bridgeport, California. Carl extended his enlistment and served at Marine Barracks, Philadelphia 1964-65. Along with 20 other volunteers for Vietnam duty, he was flown to Okinawa, and two days later joined A/1/9 in Vietnam. His platoon was assigned to E/2/9 during the 'mixmaster,' and he participated in Operations Harvest Moon, Double Eagle I & II, and Kings. From May 1966 until January 1967, he served as the driver/body guard for the CO of 9th Marines. After reenlisting, Carl changed his MOS to administration and served in Quantico, Virginia, where he was promoted to Sergeant. From 1968-69, he served in Vietnam with 5th Communications Battalion. Returning to Quantico, he served as an Administrative Chief for several units until being ordered to the 1st Marine Air Wing and later to Cherry Point, N.C. He graduated from the Staff NCO Academy at Quantico in 1978 and was assigned to HQMC. He retired as a Master Sergeant in 1982. Carl worked as a warehouse manager for several major corporations and recently retired from the Commissary Agency at Camp Lejeune, N.C., where he still lives.

NIETO, RAMON. Ray recovered from the near fatal wound to his heart. He spent almost seven years in hospitals, endured numerous operations, and received "42 pints of Navy blood, so I am more of a sailor now than a Marine." He and his wife Mary live in Sacramento, California, and frequently attend the 2/9 reunions.

PRINGER, ROBERT H. Robert spent over 4 months in Naval hospitals, regaining the use of his arm. He recently retired as a Beer Salesman in Tulsa, Oklahoma.

SASSER, JOHN R. Dick enlisted in the Marines in April 1962. He was promoted to Private First Class upon graduation from San Diego. He attended the Field Radio Operators School at Camp Pendleton, where he passed the tests for Recon. Dick attended Jump School at Ft. Benning, Georgia, Scuba School at San Diego, and Crypto Classes at Camp Delmar. He was assigned to 1st Force Reconnaissance Battalion. He served with them on Formosa, Japan, and Hawaii, and was promoted to Corporal. Dick was reassigned the 3/1 in 1964. He deployed with the battalion, which became 1/9 on arrival in Okinawa. He graduated from NCO and Jungle Warfare schools before going to Vietnam with A/1/9. Dick served as a Fire Team Leader and Squad Leader and was among the men transferred to E/2/9. He served on Operations Harvest Moon, Double Eagle I & II, and Kings. Dick was awarded a Bronze Star for his actions on Harvest Moon and was promoted to Sergeant. He served as an Instructor at the 1st Infantry Training Regiment at Camp Pendleton until his discharge. Dick owns a ranch in Angels Camp, California. He erected a memorial on his ranch, complete with flagpole and the names of the Marines he served with in A/1/9 and E/2/9 who were killed in action during his tour in Vietnam.

Dick Sasser's memorial to the fallen heros of A/1/9 & E/2/9.
This memorial is on Sasser's ranch in Angels Camp, California.

Contributors

SCHRAMM, MICHAEL L. Mike enlisted in the Marine Corps in Toledo, Ohio in May 1963. Although trained as a Machine Gunner, he served as a Fire Team Leader in E/2/9 at Camp Pendleton before deployment to Vietnam in March 1965. He graduated from NCO School. Mike was on Operations Harvest Moon, Golden Fleece, War Bonnet, Double Eagle I & II, and Kings. He served in H/2/8 in the 2nd Marine Division, and participated in the Congressional Test of the M-16 rifle in Panama before being discharged. Mike is a trained jeweler and gemologist, and owns Schramm-Boder Jewelers in Chatham, Illinois.

SMALLWOOD, WILLIAM G., JR. Bill enlisted in Ft. Wayne, Indiana on 3 June 1963. After Boot Camp & ITR, he served as a rifleman in 3/1 until arrival on Okinawa, when the battalion was re-designated 1/9. He was promoted to Lance Corporal before deploying. Bill attended the Guerilla Warfare School and Amphibious Raid School with A/1/9 prior to going to Da Nang. He was promoted to Corporal and served as Lt. Zelm's radioman before being made a squad leader. His platoon was transferred to E/2/9. Following the loss of his finger, he was in the Great Lakes Naval Hospital until fit for duty. Bill became an Assistant Brig Warden at Parris Island and was promoted to Sergeant before being discharged in July 1967. He joined the Allen County Sheriff's Department in Fort Wayne as a police officer and retired 30 May 2006 as Chief Deputy.

SPANGLER, WILLIAM L. Bill enlisted in the Marine Corps in Ypsilanti, Michigan in July 1965. Following boot camp and ITR, he joined E/2/9 as a Machine Gunner in January 1966. He served with the Company until January 1967. When he left the Marines, Bill graduated from Eastern Michigan University with an undergraduate degree and an M.A. in Guidance and Counseling. He served as a Circuit Court Probation Officer for 13 years and as a Prison Manager for 15 years. Bill is semi-retired and now lives in Manchester, Michigan.

STEPHENSON, PAUL. SGT. MAJOR, USMC (Ret.). Paul enlisted in the Marine Corps in Cleveland, Ohio in July 1942 and served in WWII and in Korea. He married his wife, Edna, at Quantico in 1950. Their two daughters married Marines. Following his tour as 1st Sergeant of E/2/9, he returned to Vietnam in 1968-69 with HMM 364 'The Purple Foxes,' a CH-46 Squadron. He retired as a Sergeant Major and lives near Camp Pendleton. Paul is active in the 1st Marine Division Association and spends a lot of time visiting the wounded in the local military hospitals.

SLATTERLY, ROBERT. Bob enlisted in the Marines Corps in New York City on 22 November 1965 and joined E/2/9 on 6 May 1966. He served as an automatic rifleman, fire team leader, and radio operator for the 2nd Platoon. Bob was the radio operator for Lt. Jim Murphy under Captain Reynolds, Sgt. Spencer Olsen, and Lt. Humphrey under Captain Terrill. He was wounded in the hand in August 1966. Bob participated in Operations Hastings, Prairie I, II, and III, and in the battles around Khesanh before the siege. He left E/2/9 on 6 June 1967 and served in D/1/8 in the 2nd Marine Division. Bob served as a New York City police officer and detective for 20 years, and as a security advisor for Merrill Lynch for another 18 years. He received a 'Cop of the Month' award for rescuing four injured construction workers when a building collapsed. He received a phone call announcing the birth of his fourth child while en route to the accident site. His wife understood and was quite proud of his efforts in rescuing the injured men. Bob was on duty at the World Finance Center across the street from the World Trade Center on the morning of 11 September 2001. He got off duty at 0700 and passed by the World Trade Center at 0720 on his way home. By 1000, the building was gone. Bob and his wife Lynn live in Lynbrook, N.Y. and are regulars at the 2/9 reunions.

TEMPLETON, JOHN R. He enlisted in the Marine Corps in Oklahoma City, Oklahoma on his 18th birthday, 29 July 1963. John served in A/1/5 in 1964-65 before being transferred to E/2/9 in Vietnam in July 1965. He was one of the few men who participated in all the actions with the company, including Operations Harvest Moon, Starlight, Double Eagle I & II, and Kings without receiving a scratch. John finished his enlistment at Camp Lejeune in 1968. He is now a lay minister for a prison near Chandler, Arizona.

THRASHER, HERBERT E. Herbert enlisted in the Marine Corps from El Reno, Oklahoma and served in E/2/9 in 1966. He was wounded in the head by grenade fragments on the night of 16 November 1966. Herbert was also wounded in his arms, legs, and back. Being medically retired, Thrasher worked as an assistant plant manager for the El Reno Water Department. Eighteen months before his retirement, in October 2001, he had gone to work on the night shift and fell to his death because workmen had failed to replace a guardrail. His widow, Alice M. Thrasher, still resides in El Reno.

WARE, WILLIAM S. Bill enlisted in the Marines out of Mississippi in 1964. He and a buddy from Tennessee made up their minds that they were going to make it through boot camp by taking the attitude of "Fuck it," to everything the D.I.s could dish out, since thousands of others had made it through Parris Island. Bill continued that approach on his tour in Vietnam, and just put what was happening out of his mind. He was serving at Marine Barracks, Key West, Florida when the Vietnam War broke out, and he immediately volunteered for duty there. When he finished his tour in Vietnam, he returned to Marine Barracks, Key West until discharged. Bill used the GI Bill to attend a barber college. While talking about Vietnam with a retired Army Sergeant and fellow student one day, a young man said to him, "Oh, you are one of those baby killers." He never talked about Vietnam again except to the Marines he served with. He is still a barber in Pulaski, Mississippi and he and his wife raise horses.

Glossary

AFB: Air Force Base.

Actual: The commander of a company, platoon, etc.

Air burst: Explosive device designed to detonate above ground.

Air strike: Attack by fixed wing aircraft.

Agent Orange: Highly toxic defoliant sprayed on vegetation throughout Vietnam.

AK-47: The standard rifle used by the Viet Cong and North Vietnamese. Fired a 7.62 mm round.

AMBUSH: A covert attack method employed by Marines and the VC/NVA, by firing on an unawares enemy from seclusion, often employing booby traps or mines.

Amtrac: Amphibious armored tracked vehicle used to transport troops and supplies, armed with a .30-caliber machine gun.

AN HOA: The ancient French fortress that comprised the westernmost logistical base of the Marines. Located thirty miles south of Da Nang.

AO: Area of operations. Specific location for planned military operations.

AO: Aerial Observer.

APC: Armored personnel carried used by the Army and ARVN to transport troops and supplies. Armed with a .50 caliber machine gun.

ARC LIGHT: B-52 bomber strike.

ARTY: Artillery.

ARVN: Army of the Republic of Vietnam. A member of the Vietnamese Army.

AZIMUTH: Compass heading towards an objective or target.

BASE CAMP: Usually a large size headquarters.

BEAUCOUP or Boo Koo: French for 'many' and Marine slang meaning the same.

BIRD: Any aircraft.

BIRD DOG: A small fixed wing aircraft used mainly for observation.

BLOOD TRAIL: Spoor sign left by the removal of enemy dead or wounded.

BODY BAG: Plastic bags used to retrieve dead bodies from the battlefield.

BUSH: An infantry term for the field, jungle or the 'boonies' or 'boondocks.'

BUST CAPS: A Marine Corps term for firing weapons.

C-4: Plastic putty-textured explosive device carried by the engineers.

C RATIONS: Combat field rations issued to the troops.

C&C: Command and control. Also Collection and Clearing for medical evacuations.

CAMMO STICK: Two-colored camouflage applicator. Used for night operations.

CAP: To 'cap' an enemy is bust a primer cap when firing at Charlie. To kill an enemy.

CAPT.: Captain.

CAV: Air Cavalry or helicopter-borne infantry in the Army. Helicopter gun ships for the Marines.

C-MED or Charlie Med: Charlie Medical Unit at Da Nang. A surgical unit where casualties were evacuated too.

CHARLIE or CHARLES: American military slang for Viet Cong (military radio code Victor Charlie).

CHICOM: Chinese Communist. Usually referred to the grenades used by the VC/NVA.

CHIEU HOI: A voluntary surrendered VC or NVA soldier to be repatriated through a government program. Some joined the South Vietnamese military and a few became Kit Carson Scouts and worked with the Marines.

CHOPPER: Slang for a helicopter.

CHOPPER PAD: Helicopter landing pad.

CLAYMORE: Anti-personnel mine carried by the infantry.

CHOW: Slang for food or mealtime.

CLEARANCE: Permission to engage the enemy in a given area.

CLICK: Slang for kilometer.

CO: Commanding Officer.

COL.: Colonel.

CONCERTINA: Rolls of barbed wire used around fixed defensive positions.

CONTACT: Engaged with the enemy.

CP: Command Post.

Dai Loc: Province in the Arizona.

Da Nang: Port city and Marine base on the China Sea, thirty miles from An Hoa. Route 1 starts in Da Nang.

DECK: The floor or the ground. 'Hit the deck' is a command to get down, usually when under fire.

DEFILADE: A low spot on the ground and usually out of observation of the enemy.

DELAYED FUSE: Artillery projectiles and bombs that have delayed fuses that penetrate the ground before exploding.

DEMO: Demolitions that were used to destroy enemy bunkers and tunnels. The engineers who usually did this were called 'demo men.'

Di di mau: Vietnamese term for 'run away' or 'escape', slang adopted by the Marines.

DIKE: Raised earthen boundary of a rice paddy usually with a trail on the top. Usually referred to as a paddy dike.

DINK: Slang for Vietnamese or Viet Cong.

DIVISON: A military unit usually with three regiments and numerous other units. The 1st and 3rd Marine Divisions served in Vietnam. Div's was the slang for divisions.

DMZ: Demilitarized zone between North and South Vietnam.

Doc: Navy Corpsmen or Doctor.

Double Canopy: Jungle or forest with two layers of overhead vegetation.

DUC DUC: Vietnamese District Headquarters and a rich rice growing area north of An Hoa.

Dung lai: Vietnamese to halt or stop.

ENFILADE FIRE: Fire directed down the long axis of a combat formation.

ENVELOPE: A tactic where a unit encircles the enemy from the right or left flank while part of the unit lays down a base of fire to prevent the enemy from moving.

EVASION: Tactics used by the Viet Cong to avoid contact with Marines.

EOD: Explosive Ordnance Disposal. Trained personnel who disarm or defuse live ordnance.

F-4: The McDonnell Douglas F-4 Phantom twin engine fighter/bomber used by the Marines for close air support for infantry units.

FAC: Forward Air Control Team. A Marine pilot and radio operator attached to Marine infantry units to call in close air support and medical evacuations.

FIELD: Any area outside the main base where combat readiness is mandatory. Marine slang for training, as in 'going to the field.'

FIELD OF FIRE: The radius that a weapon can cover in an arc from port to starboard. Aiming stakes were used at night to keep the weapon covering its assigned area.

FINGER: A secondary ridge line running out from a primary ridge line, hill or mountain.

FIREBASE: Fire bases or fire support bases were established artillery support positions supporting the infantry. Always on hill tops for observation and increased range. PHU LOC 6 was the main fire base covering the Arizona, but artillery was also located on Hills 55 and 65 and An Hoa. As the Marine infantry pushed towards Laos, fire support bases were moved to commanding hill tops to support them.

FIREFIGHT: An engagement with the enemy by Marine units using small arms.

FIRE IN THE HOLE: Warning before demolitions were being set off. Also used when a mine or booby trap was detonated.

FIRE MISSION: An artillery or mortar mission in support of Marines in the field.

FIRE TEAM: The basic unit of the Marine rifle squad. Three fire teams made up the squad. They consisted of a fire team leader, a rifleman, an automatic rifleman (M-14 or M-16 with an automatic selector), and an assistant automatic rifleman.

FIX: The specific coordinates of a unit's position relative to a target.

FLAK JACKET: Fiberglass-paneled cloth jacket or vest worn by Marines as protection from shrapnel and small arms fire.

FLANK: The side of a unit, where it is weakest.

FMF: Fleet Marine Force.

FNG: Fucking New Guy. Term for newly assigned Marines or Corpsmen.

FO: Forward Observer, either artillery or mortars, attached to infantry units, who can call in fire missions and adjust it in support of them.

FORCE RECON: Reconnaissance units attached under operational control of the division.

FRAG: Fragmentation grenade. The U.S. M-26 was the standard fragmentation grenade used in Vietnam. The M-34 was a white phosphorus ('Willy Peter') grenade used for burning and signaling.

FRAGGING: The assassination of a military leader by his own troops. Usually by a grenade.

G-1: Administration unit at division or higher.

G-2: Intelligence unit at division or higher.

G-3: Operations unit at division or higher.

G-4: Logistics unit at division or higher.

G-5: Psychological unit at division or higher.

GARBLED: Radio communication that is indecipherable.

GO NOI ISLAND: A main force headquarters for the VC/NVA in the Arizona on the Song Thu Bon to the northeast of An Hoa.

GRAZING FIRE: Small arms fire that is low to the ground.

GRID SQUARE: Vertical and horizontal navigation markings on a map comprising one kilometer by one kilometer.

GROUND POUNDERS: Slang for Marine infantry. Grunts.

GRUNTS: Slang for Marine infantry.

GUNG HO: Marine term meaning doing things with spirit and enthusiasm.

GUNSHIP: A helicopter fitted with attack armament.

H-34: Sikorksy UH-34 helicopter. The work horse for the Marines, carrying troops, supplies, and doing medical evacuations.

HALOZONE: Water purifications tablets carried by each Marine. One or two were to be used to a canteen of water.

HAM and MOTHERFUCKERS: Ham and lima beans C-ration, hated by the troops.

HAMLET: Small village complex, some had branched out and were identified as (1), (2), etc.

HAWK: Very cold climate or high wind.

H & I: Harassment and interdiction fire by mortars and artillery. H & I fire was aimed at trail junctions, stream crossings, hill tops, etc., where the VC/NVA were suspected to be.

HE: High Explosive. Usually referred to artillery or mortar rounds.

HELIPAD: A hardened helicopter landing site.

HO CHI MINH TRAIL: An extensive road and trail network running from North Vietnam down through Laos and Cambodia into South Vietnam, which enabled the NVA to bring supplies and personnel to their units.

HONCHO: Village chief or Vietnamese leader.

HOOCH: Slang for living quarters and also Vietnamese huts.

HOT AREA or ZONE: Dangerous, enemy controlled landing zone.

HUG: To close with the enemy following closely to supporting fires.

HUMP: To walk a long distance on patrol or on an operation, usually loaded down with ammo and equipment.

HQ: Headquarters.

I CORPS: The northernmost of 4 U.S. military zones in South Vietnam, where the Marines served.

I&I: Instructor and Inspector. Usually term for active duty Marines assigned to a Marine Reserve unit.

ILLUMINATION: Artillery and mortar rounds to illuminate an area at night, using a phosphorus filament suspended by a parachute. Similar flares were dropped by airplanes.

IMMERSION FOOT: A foot condition caused by prolonged exposure to moisture. Characterized by sloughing off of skin, raw spots, and bleeding. Also know as trench foot.

INCENDIARY: A shell that burns on impact. White phosphorus rounds. Used as marking rounds to determine locations and targets.

INCOMING: Incoming fire from enemy mortars or artillery.

INDIAN TERRITORY: Hostile area controlled by the enemy.

INFILTRATION ROUTE: One of the network of roads and trails used by the North Vietnamese to enter South Vietnam.

K-BAR: A standard issue combat knife.

KC-130: Lockheed Hercules four engine cargo and or troop plane.

KIA: Killed in action.

KIT CARSON SCOUT: A VC/NVA soldier who deserted and served as a scout with the Marines.

KLICK or CLICK: A unit of distance equal to 1,000 linear meters. Commonly used gauge for estimating distances. One kilometer.

LAAW: Light Antitank Assault Weapon. Contained in collapsible, disposable fiberglass tubes. Rifle Squads usually carried several of these to use on enemy bunkers, etc. Basically replaced the 3.5 Rocket Launcher in the field.

LAND MINE: Various types were used by the VC/NVA in Vietnam. Homemade ones were made up with all types or ordnance, including dud bombs.

LST: Landing Ship Troops. Flat bottom Navy vessel developed during WWII and used to move Marines, their vehicles, including tanks to the objective.

LIBERTY BRIDGE: Spanned the Song Thu Bon River between Da Nang and An Hoi in the Arizona Territory. A fire support base was built at Phu Loc (6), near the crossing, and Marine infantry guarded the bridge day and night.

LIFER: A career Marine.

LMG: Light Machine Gun.

LP: Listening post. An outpost established outside the units perimeter with the mission of early detection of an approaching enemy. Two to four men manned these.

LT.: Lieutenant.

LT. COL.: Lieutenant Colonel.

LVT: Landing Vehicle Troops. An amphibious tractor used to land troops over the beach and to support them. Used as a troop and supply carrier in the sandy areas along the coastal plain of South Vietnam.

LZ: Helicopter Landing Zone. Usually large enough to handle more than one helicopter.

M-1: Standard issue rifle for Marines in most of WWII and Korea. .30 caliber. air-cooled, magazine fed, semiautomatic, shoulder weapon. Issued to the ARVN and captured by the VC.

M-l/M-2: .30 cal. Carbine. WWII weapon favored by the ARVN because of its light weight. M-2 version can fire automatic.

M-14: Standard issue rifle for Marine infantry during the early portion of the war. Fired 7.62 mm NATO round, interchangeable with the M-60 machine gun ammunition.

M-16: Standard issue rifle for Marine infantry from 1966 on.

M-26: Standard U.S. fragmentation hand grenade.

M-48: Medium tank used by the Marines in 1965-66.

M-60: 7.62 mm light machine gun. Usually carried with the bipod attached and a replacement barrel.

M-60: Main U.S. battle tank equipped with 90 mm main gun and .30 caliber machine guns.

M-72: Light Antitank Weapon (LAAW). A plastic tube extended to fire a shaped, charged rocket that would penetrate eleven inches of concrete or a heavy logged bunker. Replaced the 3.5 inch rocket launcher, although both were carried by Marines in 1965-66.

M-79: Single barreled grenade launcher that fired a 40 mm round carried by a Marine rifle squad.

MACV: Military Assistance Command Vietnam. Advisors from all services.

Mama-san/Momma-san: Mature Okinawan or Vietnamese woman; the oldest Vietnamese women.

Medevac: Medical evacuation, usually referring to helicopter evacuation from the battlefield.

III MAF: Third Marine Amphibious Force. The senior headquarters of Marine Operations in Vietnam's I Corps area.

MAIN FORCE: Well-trained and well-equipped full time Viet Cong units as opposed to local guerillas.

MAG: Marine Air Group.

MAJ: Major.

MG: Machine gun.

MIA: Missing in action.

Mike Mike: Radio call sign for artillery pieces defined by caliber in millimeters. Example: 105 Mike Mike refers to the 105 mm gun.

MORTARS: U.S. mortars were the 60 mm portable mortar and the 81 mm used in the field generally from a fixed position. 4.2 mm mortar "Four deuce." Vehicle towed and usually served in artillery units.

MOS: Military occupational specialty.

MP: Military Police.

NAPALM: Jellied gasoline dropped in canisters from aircraft.

NASAN: Vietnamese or Okinawan women who did the cleaning and laundry for Marines.

NCO: Non commissioned officer, Sergeant through Sergeant Major.

NET: Radio network.

Number one: Vietnamese slang for "the best."

Number ten: Vietnamese slang for "the worst."

NVA: North Vietnamese Army.

O-1 BIRD DOG: A light observation aircraft.

ONTOS: Marine tracked vehicle with six 106 mm recoilless rifles and a .50 caliber spotting rifle.

OP: Observation post.

Op: Short for operation.

OPCON: Operational control. Marine units from one battalion were often assigned to operational control of another battalion for an operation.

PADDY: A rectangular rice field bordered by dikes and footpaths.

PF: Popular Forces, South Vietnamese National Guard type local militia units.

PFC: Private First Class.

POINT: The forward most man in the formation of a combat patrol.

POINT DETONATING FUSES: Shells and bombs that exploded upon impact.

POLICE: To clean up an area.

PONCHO: Rain proof cloth.

PONCHO LINER: Nylon insert to the poncho used as a blanket.

POW: Prisoner of War.

PRC-25: "Prick twenty-five" or combat radio.

PROBE: To attack a defensive perimeter to locate weapons placement or find a weak point in the defenses.

PUNJI STAKES: Sharpened wooden or bamboo stakes placed in the bottom of a camouflaged hole to cause foot and or leg injuries.

PURPLE HEART: A U.S. medal awarded to military personnel who were wounded in combat.

PX: Post Exchange.

RACKS: Bomb racks were on airplanes. Marine slang for bed or bunk.

R&R: Rest and relaxation, a vacation away from the war.

RECOILLESS RIFLE: The 106 mm recoilless rifle were either ground or vehicle mounted with a .50 caliber spotting rifle. Fired perforated cased shells that blew the gases out the rear breach ports, reducing recoil.

RECON: Reconnaissance, usually a small patrol sent out to search for enemy activity. The Marine Corps had a RECON Battalion in each Marine Division and a Force RECON Company from FMFPAC for airborne or other special means of entry.

REGIMENT: Marine unit composed of three or more infantry battalions and a headquarters. Commanded by a Colonel.

REPEAT: Repeat a radio transmission.

RNV: Republic of Vietnam.

RO: Radio Operator. Any Marine carrying a radio.

ROTATE: To return to the States after a tour in Vietnam.

SADDLE UP: An informal order to grab your gear and prepare to move out.

SAPPER: VC or NVA commando, usually armed with explosives.

SATCHEL CHARGE: An explosive charge carried in a bag or satchel by sappers.

SCUTTLEBUTT: Rumors or unfounded facts passed between Marines.

SEARCH and DESTROY: Combat operations by infantry units to locate and annihilate enemy units.

SEVEN EIGHTY TWO (782) GEAR: Standard issue of equipment carried by each Marine. Helmet, packs, belts, canteens, etc.

SHIT BURNING: The sanitation of latrines by kerosene incineration of excrement.

SHORT ROUND: Shells that fall short of their targets. Also reference to short Marines.

SHORT TIMER: A Marine getting near his end of tour in Vietnam or enlistment.

SITREP: Situation report.

SKIRMISHERS: Marines who advance on line with distance between them.

SKS: A Communist bloc 7.62 mm standard issue automatic rifle.

SKY CRANE: Large double engine helicopter used for moving heavy equipment.

SLACK: Marine slang for any easy treatment by a Marine towards another. "Cut me some slack." This seldom happened.

SMOKE: A canister containing colored smoke used for marking ground positions for aircraft or other visual signaling purposes.

SNCO: Staff Sergeant through Sergeant Major.

SNUFFIE: A private or lowest ranking enlisted Marine.

SPIDER HOLE: A concealed one-man fighting position often used by the VC and NVA troops.

SPOOKY: AC-47 or AC-19 aircraft outfitted with Gatling guns and illumination flares used to support ground troops.

SPOTTER ROUND: A single artillery or mortar shell fired to mark a position or determine target coverage for the artillery forward observer.

Glossary

SSGT: Staff Sergeant.

SQUARE AWAY: Marine slang for making things orderly and neat, usually uniform and equipment, but sometimes to an individual to change his attitude, etc.

T&T: Training and Testing, usually refers to the unit at Quantico that trains officers, and tests weapons & equipment.

TAOR: Tactical Area of Responsibility.

THE WORLD: The United States or home.

TIGER PISS: Vietnamese beer.

T/O: Table of organization.

TOP or TOP SERGEANT: Slang for 1st Sergeant or senior enlisted man in a unit.

TOPO: Topographical map showing elevations of hills, valleys and contour lines.

TRAIL: A well used path linking villages or leading through the jungle.

UTILITIES: Green Marine combat uniform made of light-weight cotton.

VAPORIZE: To blow an enemy to pieces.

V C: Viet Cong.

VIETNAMIZATION: President Nixon's program to gradually turn over the war to the South Vietnamese.

VOLLEY FIRE: When a Marine unit fires a certain number of rounds on command.

WASTE: To kill without mercy.

WEB GEAR: Cloth belt and shoulder straps for packing equipment and ammunition.

WP or WILEY PETER: White phosphorous grenade, mortar or artillery round.

WIA: Wounded in action.

XO: Executive Officer, the second in command of a unit.
XRAY: Letter X in radio call signs.

ZAP: To shoot or hit with a bullet.

ZERO: To bring a rifle's sights into alignment at two hundred meters for accurate battle dope.

ZILCH: Nothing, no luck.

Bibliography

CORRESPONDENCE

Correspondence, Emails and Telephone Calls with former A/1/9, E/2/9 and 2nd Battalion, 5th Marines and attachments personnel, 2005-2009.

Copies of Award Recommendations submitted 1965-66.

Copies of rough Fitness Reports for officers, SNCO's and NCO's 1964-1966.

Letters from Robert J. Driver, Jr. to Edna Guyer Driver, 1952-1970.

Letter from 1stLt. David Garner 14 December 1966.

Letters from 1st Lt. Gerald L. Hornick 3 and 28 May, 29 August, and 12 October 1966.

Letter from GySgt. J. A. Morton, USMC (Ret.) 1969.

Letter from Sgt. Nguyen-Ngoc-An 16 April 1966.

Letter from Sgt. Nguyen-Ngoc-An to 1st Lt. Gerald L. Hornick 4 June 1966.

Letter from 1stSgt. Paul Stephenson 18 April 1966.

GENEALOGY

Payne, Barbara Ann, Compiler and Editor, The Samuel Thomas Driver Family, 1989.

Swope, Fred, Compiler, The Swope Family of Rockbridge County, Virginia, 1977.

OFFICIAL RECORDS

After Action Report, Company E, 2nd Battalion, 9th Marines, Captain Robert J. Driver, Jr. (enclosure in 2/9 command chronology, March 1966).

Command Chronologies, 1st Battalion, 9th Marines June-August 1965. Command Chronologies, 2nd Battalion, 9th Marines, August-December 1966.

Command Chronologies, 2nd Battalion, 9th Marines, January-July 1966.

Command Chronologies, 2nd Battalion, 5th Marines, September-December 1969.

Command Chronology, 2nd Battalion, 5th Marines, January 1970.

Command Chronologies, 2nd Battalion, 7th Marines, April-October 1970.

Command Chronology, 2nd Battalion, 12th Marines, March 1966.

Company Rosters, Company E, 2nd Battalion, 9th Marines, January-May 1966.

Unit Diaries, Company E, 2nd Battalion, 9th Marines January-April 1966. Undated Roster 2nd Platoon, Company E, 2nd Battalion, 9th Marines, circa May 1966.

UNOFFICIAL RECORDS

"OUR MEN ON THE WALL," ECHO COMPANY, 2nd BATTALION, 9th MARINES 1965-1969.

SECOND BATTALION, 9th MARINES 'NETWORK' Publications.

MEMOIR OF MY SERVICE IN VIETNAM, 1965-66, by Corporal Michael Schramm.

OPERATION HARVEST MOON: E COMPANY, 2nd BATTALION, 9th MARINES by Colonel William A. Coti.

Bibliography

MAGAZINES

MARINE CORPS GAZETTE, November 1996. "The Long Night." Major Joseph F. Jennings.

MARINE CORPS GAZETTE, February 1997. "A Company Commander Remembers." Lt. Col. Robert J. Driver, Jr.

SATURDAY EVENING POST, March 25, 1967. "Believe Me He Can Kill You." Richard Armstrong.

BOOKS

BARTLETT, Tom, Editor, *AMBASSADORS IN GREEN*, Leatherneck Association, Washington, D.C. 1971.

BROWN, David B. & Tiffany Brown Holmes. *BATTLELINES*, I Universe, Inc. New York, 2005.

BROWN, Ronald J. *A FEW GOOD MEN: THE STORY OF THE FIGHTING FIFTH MARINES*. Presidio Press, Inc. Novato, Ca., 2001.

CAPUTO, Philip. *A RUMOR OF WAR*. Ballantine Books, New York, 1977.

CULBERTSON, John J. *13 CENT KILLERS: THE FIFTH MARINES SNIPERS IN VIETNAM*. Ballantine Books, New York, 2003.

FIRST BATTALION, NINTH MARINES CRUISE BOOK, pp., Okinawa, Japan, 1966.

GRANT, Zalin. *SURVIVORS: VIETNAM P.O.W.S TELL THEIR STORIES*. Da Capo Press, New York, 1994.

KARNOW, Stanley. *VIETNAM: A HISTORY*, Viking Press, New York, 1983.

NARGELE, Dominik G. *FROM IMMIGRANT TO U.S. MARINE*, pp. 2004.

PARKER, William D. *A CONCISE HISTORY OF THE UNITED STATES MARINE CORPS 1775-1969*. Historical Division, Headquarters, U.S. Marine Corps, Washington, D.C., 1970.

SHULIMSON, Jack and Johnson, Charles M. *U.S. MARINES IN VIETNAM: THE LANDING AND THE BUILDUP,* 1965.

THE MARINES IN VIETNAM, 1954-73. An Anthology and Annotated Bibliography, 1973.

U.S. MARINES IN VIETNAM, 1969. Government Printing Office, Washington, D.C., 1969.

U.S. MARINES IN VIETNAM, 1970-71. Government Printing Office, Washington, D.C. 1971.

WARD, Joseph T. *DEAR MOM, A SNIPER'S VIETNAM.* Ivy Books, New York, 1991.